THE VEDIC EPIPHANY

Volume Two

THE VEDIC ACTION

THE VEDIC EPIPHANY

An exposition and celebration
of the Inaugural Dawn
in the Light of Sri Aurobindo

Volume Two

THE VEDIC ACTION

V. Madhusudan Reddy

Sri Aurobindo Study Circle
of Greater Chicago (U.S.A)

THE VEDIC EPIPHANY

Volume Two: The Vedic Action

First U.S.A. Edition: 21 February 1994

Published by Sri Aurobindo Study Circle of Greater Chicago,
318 Haddon Circle, Vernon Hills, Illinois 60061, U.S.A.

ISBN 81-85853-02-9

Printed at:
Sri Aurobindo Ashram Press
Pondicherry 605 002
Printed in India

At the Feet of my supreme Master

SRI AUROBINDO

AUTHOR'S NOTE

The present work is based on Sri Aurobindo's epoch-making exposition, *The Secret of the Veda*, which is the profoundest expression of his own luminous experience of the Vedic Truth and the Word. To retain the original deep vibration and the subtle import, translations of the Riks quoted herein have been provided, as far as it was possible, from Sri Aurobindo. They all bear an asterisk mark (*) in the text. The rest are free renderings by the author and not literal translations made with a view to bring out their esoteric sense and significance.

The Riks are mostly from the Rig-veda.

ACKNOWLEDGEMENT

It is difficult to acknowledge adequately the kind help given me by friends and well-wishers in Chicago, Los Angeles and Houston for the publication of this book. My loving gratitude goes out especially to Dr. Ravi R. Reddy, Shri Hanumanth Reddy, Shri Gnaneshwar J. Kaveti, Ashok R. Danda, Vikas, Vishwas B. Reddy, Dr. Lloyd W. Fellows, Dr. Hanumanth R. Dharam, Dr. Sanjiva Reddy (Iowa) and Dr. G. Radhakrishna.

PUBLISHER'S OBSERVATION

The third and last volume of this comprehensive work, *The Vedic Epiphany*, entitled *The Vedic Victory*, along with an exhaustive index is under preparation, and will be made available to our readers in due course.

Volume Two

THE VEDIC ACTION

CONTENTS

PART ONE

PART TWO

Part One

THE VEDIC GODS AND GODDESSES

I

AGNI

The Vedas are the apotheosis of a divine inspiration and revelation, a consummate expression of the experience of an infinite, eternal and impersonal Truth. Their authors are the hearers of the Truth, *kavayaḥ satyaśrutaḥ*. They are regarded as infallible and authoritative in spiritual knowledge, dependable and trustworthy in experience, and indisputable and irrefutable in higher truth. Certainly, they are not the work of any primitive sacrificial liturgy or myth haloed by tradition as it is made out to be by critical and prejudiced scholarship. The Vedas are massive records of self-knowledge and world-knowledge, of the luminous and deeper experiences of the single supreme Truth behind each individual as well as the universe around. They contain the spiritual and occult knowledge of the many worlds behind and beyond the physical world presented in a manner verifiable by every initiated seeker. This secret and sacred knowledge lies concealed behind familiar symbols and discoverable figuration. Their mystic wisdom flowing from higher planes of consciousness can be realised or appreciated only by those who are themselves mystically oriented,

Nivacanā kavaye kāvyāni.[1]

"Seer-wisdoms that utter their inner meaning to the seer."*

The Vedic experience belongs to the three higher planes of consciousness which are ordinarily not known to the human mind.

Indraṁ mitraṁ varuṇamagnimāhur
atho divyaḥ sa suparṇo garutmān,
ekaṁ sadviprā bahudhā vadanty
agniṁ yamaṁ mātariśvānamāhuḥ.[2]

It is "the best and most faultless form"[3] of Truth-expression.

Bṛhaspate prathamaṁ vāco agraṁ yatprairata
nāmadheyaṁ dadhānāḥ
yadesāṁ śreṣṭhaṁ yadaripramāsīt
preṇā tadeṣāṁ nihitaṁ guhāviḥ.[4]

Only the initiated have access to their secret meaning and significance. "Those who do not know the inner sense", says the Veda, "are as men who seeing see not, hearing hear not, only to one here and there the Word desiring him like a beautifully robed wife to a husband lays open her body. Others unable to drink steadily of the milk of the Word, the Vedic cow, move with it as with one that gives no milk, to him the Word is a tree without flowers or fruits."[5]

Uta tvaḥ paśyanna dadarśa vācam
uta tvaḥ śṛṇvanna śṛṇotyenām,
uto tvasmai tanvaṃvi sasre jāyéva
patya uśatī suvāsāḥ.[6]

There is a tradition that speaks of a three-tiered knowledge in the Veda, — "a sacrificial or ritualistic knowledge, a knowledge of the gods and finally a spiritual knowledge"[7], — it is the third one directly obtained by an inner vision that is the highest and truest. It is this secret truth that constitutes the bed-rock of Indian civilisation. Though the supreme Truth is the central object of the Vedic seeking, it also includes "a truth of things, a truth of the world and of the gods, a truth behind all we are and all that things are."[8] The Veda seeks to veil the Truth deliberately from the commoner — the uninitiated in an occult form of speech full of symbols and oblique figuration. For example, when it speaks of Agni as 'the luminous guardian of the Truth' and of Mitra, Varuna as 'born in the Truth' and 'making the Truth grow', evidently, it is referring to the inner Truth that is the source and support of all things.

Under some inexplicable inner pressure and occult obligation to protect the layman from the blinding dazzle and splendour of naked Truth, the seer masks its experience in symbolic expression, thus resorting to double meanings: the rays of the Sun of Truth and Light and Knowledge are described symbolically as cows, the horses of Indra as dripping with Light, Agni himself is invoked to flood the sacrificial offering 'with a mind pouring *ghṛta*', and so disclose the specific seats or centres of action of the many gods as well as the three higher heavens. "What the Rishi means", explains Sri Aurobindo, "is a 'mind pouring the light', a labour of the clarity of an enlightened or illumined mind; it is not a human priest or a sacrificial fire, but the inner Flame, the mystic seer-will, *kavikratu*, and that can certainly manifest by this process the Gods and the worlds and all planes of the being. The Rishis, it must be remembered, were seers as well as sages, they were men of vision who saw things in their meditation in images, often symbolic images which might precede or accompany an experience and put it in a concrete form, might predict or give an occult body to it: so it would be quite possible for him to see at once the inner experience and in image its symbolic happening, the flow of clarifying light and the priest god pouring this clarified butter on the inner self-offering which brought the experience."[9] The seers always see physical things as symbols of inner realities. The cow as such is the symbol of Light and the horse that of spiritual Power. "When the Rishi asks Agni for a 'horse-form cow-in-front gift' he is not asking really for a number of horses forming a body of the gift with some cows walking in front, he is asking for a great body of spiritual power led by the light or, as we may translate it, 'with the Ray-Cow walking in its front.'[10] The *mantra*s have therefore to be understood in an esoteric sense and not interpreted literally. When they speak of Agni himself as born to us, as the offspring of our sacrifice, it has to be understood in a figurative sense; they are referring to an inner birth — a birth into a higher plane of existence. "Agni himself is our son, the child of our works, the child who as the Universal Fire is the father of his fathers, and it is by setting the steps on things that have fair offspring that we create or discover a path to the higher world of Truth."[11] Agni is variously invoked as the seer-will, *kavikratu,* the will in the heart, *kratur hṛdi,* and the summoner and divine dispenser of delight, *hotāram ratna dhātamam.*

A deeper and psychological understanding of the Veda thus becomes necessary for a coherent account of the *mantra*s. It is also the case with the nature of Mysteries elsewhere. The Vedas provide the seed of this spiritual truth which in later times develops into the body of Vedanta. The quest for a greater Truth, a higher Light and an integral Immortality is the sole preoccupation of the Vedic Rishis. The way to their finding and the means to ascend into the world of Immortality and to live in it is the cherished goal.

The Rishis are seekers and seers of a single Truth, and use almost a common language to express it. While some employ a rich and profound symbolism, others use a simpler diction. As such some of the *suktas* are obscure and complex, while others are plain and almost modern in their language. Nonetheless they all reveal a unity of spiritual experience. "In the deep and mystic style of Dirghatamas Achutya as in the melodious lucidity of Medhatithi Kanwa", observes Sri Aurobindo, "in the puissant and energetic hymns of Vishwamitra as in Vasistha's even harmonies we have the same firm foundation of knowledge and the same scrupulous adherence to the sacred conventions of the Initiates."[12]

The Vedic Rishis speak of two worlds — the inferior world of falsehood and error and that of the Truth, the Right and the Vast. The latter is the world of *svar* — the world of the highest Truth and Light, the Great Heaven.

Kṛṣṇaṁ niyānaṁ harayaḥ suparṇa
apo vasānā divamutpatanti,
ta āvavṛtransadanādṛtasyādidghṛtena
pṛthivī vyudyate.[13]

Ā yātvindro diva ā pṛthivyā makṣu
samudrāduta vā purīṣāt,
svarṇarādavase no marutvān parāvato
vā sadanādṛtasya.[14]

The central teachings of the Vedic Rishis, as summarised by Sri Aurobindo are:

i) "We have to find our way to that, to get into touch with this Truth and Immortality, *sapanta ṛtam amṛtam*, to be born into the Truth, to grow in it, to ascend in spirit into the world of Truth and to live in it. To do so is to unite ourselves with the Godhead and to pass from mortality into immortality. This is the first and the central teaching of the Vedic mystics.

ii) "We have to find the path to this Great Heaven, the path of Truth, *ṛtasya panthāḥ*, or as it is sometimes called the way of the gods. This is the second mystic doctrine.

iii) "The third is that our life is a battle between the powers of Light and Truth, the Gods who are the Immortals and the powers of Darkness.... We have to call in the aid of the Gods to destroy the opposition of these powers of Darkness who conceal the Light from us or rob us of it, who obstruct the flowing of the streams of Truth, *ṛtasya dhārāḥ*, the streams of Heaven and obstruct in every way the soul's ascent. We have to invoke the Gods by the inner sacrifice, and by the Word call them into us ... to offer to them the gifts of the sacrifice and by that giving secure their gifts, so that by this process we may build the way of our ascent to the goal.

iv) "Finally, as the summit of the teaching of the Vedic mystics comes the secret of the one Reality, *ekaṁ sat*, or *tad ekam*, which became the central word of the Upanishads. The Gods, the powers of Light and Truth are powers and names of the One, each God is himself all the Gods or carries them in him: there is the one Truth, *tat satyam*, and one bliss to which we must rise."[15]

The sacrifice, *yajña*, so spoken of is a process, a pilgrimage and a combat with the forces of Inconscience and Ignorance and Falsehood. On this arduous, upward journey Agni is the friend and the path-finder. He is the inner Flame, the mystic Fire ever burning in the being of the seeker and leading him to Immortality.

In all the ten *Mandalas* of the Rig-veda Samhita we find the hymns arranged in a special way. The hymns addressed to Agni are collected first followed by those addressed to Indra. Then come the invocation to the rest of the gods. There is also seen a certain principle of thought-development in the arrangement of the hymns of the Rig-veda. The first *Mandala* contains the general thought of the Veda in its various elements. This thought gradually unfolds itself until the tenth *Mandala* which gives us the last and final developments of the Vedic thought. It is in this *Mandala* that the Rishis sing of the Hymn of Creation — the sacrifice of the Purusha. The first hymn of the Rig-veda, *Mandala* one, is addressed to Agni; this suggests the Vedic vision of the Truth.

Agni is variously envisioned and experienced by the Rishis as the Truth, as the guardian of the Truth, the illumination of the Truth and the seer-will governing its rich illumination. Agni in the Veda is both Force and Light — the "divine power that builds up the worlds, a power which acts always with a perfect knowledge... *jātavedas*, knower of all-births, *viśvāni vayunāni vidvān*... the immortal in mortals, the divine power in man, the energy of fulfilment through which they (the gods) do their work in him."[16] This work of the gods in man is symbolised by the sacrifice. Agni, thus, is the divine Will which is one with divine Wisdom and the effective power of the supramental Truth-Consciousness at work in the universe. He is the inward force of Light and Power; he is the *hotṛ*, the high-priest of the sacrifice, the supreme Power with divine powers. It is Agni again who creates the good for the giver. He is ever the right-going, *suvitam*, the good and the most auspicious. Eternally he shines out in the sacrifice and exercises a divine control in all states of consciousness. He always supports the Truth in man and protects him from Falsehood.

Adyā no deva savitaḥ prajāvatsāvīḥ saubhagam,
parā duḥsvapnyaṁ suva.

viśvāni deva savitarduritāni parā suva,
yadbhadraṁ tanna ā suva.[17]

The Truth, the Right, the Vast, *satyam ṛtam bṛhat* is Agni's own home that is the goal of the sacrifice. Agni is the great leader and helper in the journey to his own home of Truth-Consciousness.

Yajā no mitrāvaruṇā, yajā devāñ ṛtaṁ bṛhat
agne yakṣi svaṁ damam.[18]

"Sacrifice for us to Mitra and Varuna, Sacrifice to the gods, to the Truth, the Vast; O Agni, sacrifice to thy own home."*

He is born in the Truth-Consciousness and increases in it; he breaks down all limitation in the seeker and makes him wide and limitless.

Agni is described as the great devourer and enjoyer, the perfect purifier and transfigurator. He is the most important of the Vedic gods; he is the most universal of them all, the heat of all life as well as the essence of the being of all things. "He is equally the Will in Prana, the dynamic Life-energy, and in that energy performs the same functions.... he is also the Will in the mind and clarifies it by aspiration."[19] Entering the intellect he helps the seeker-sacrificer to activate his energies towards the Light and get closer to his home — the supramental Truth-Consciousness. He is the soul of the aspirant, the power of his upward thoughts as well as the head of the cosmic sacrifice. It is he who transfigures the intellect, opens up the transition from mind to supermind, and grants the inspired Word that effects the transition.

Agni increasingly becomes conscious in the seeker, who expresses it by the inspired Word and confirms its felt-presence on the altar-seat of the sacrifice. It is at the sacrifice that the first of all human activities are equitably distributed among the different cosmic Powers according to a divine decree. If this supreme law has to rule the world, the seeker has only to prepare himself and his fellow beings. And in this he is helped again by Agni. The inspired thought flows from the Truth-world helping the seeker to utter the illuminative Word which in turn brings about in him right realisation and right affirmation. Agni therefore is "both a light of knowledge and a flame of action".

Agni is the flaming aspiration and action of the Immortal in mortals. It is by him that the other gods work out the manifestation of the Supreme. The aim of the sacrifice is to accomplish this self-extension of the Divine, and it is Agni who possessed of the Truth always prepares and supports the intricate and multiple advance of the universe of manifestation. Concealed in the darkness of Nature, hidden in inconscient Matter, Agni the divine Will forces their movements to bend closer, to follow and to express the descending Truth. In the words of Sri Aurobindo, "In the last obscuration of Nature, in the lowest unintelligence of Matter, it is this Will that is a concealed knowledge and compels all ... darkened movements to obey, as if mechanically, the divine Law and adhere to the truth of their Nature. It is this which makes the tree grow according to its seed and each action bear its appropriate fruit. In the obscurity of man's ignorance, — less than material Nature's, yet greater, — it is this divine Will that governs and guides, knows the sense of his blindness and the goal of his aberration and out of the crooked workings of the Cosmic Falsehood in him evolves the progressive manifestation of the cosmic Truth. Alone of the brilliant Gods, he burns bright and has full vision in the darkness of Night no less than in the splendours of day. The other gods are *uṣarbudhaḥ*, wakers with the Dawn."[20] Agni, therefore is the omnipotent priest most predisposed for conducting the sacrifice with success.

Suffused with the law of the Truth, he always guides all activity both in Nature and in man towards the goal; he is behind all sacrifice both cosmic and individual. His presence becomes progressively visible and felt as the offering turns out to be more and more conscious.

Kathā dāśemāgnāye kāsmai
devajuṣṭocyate bhāmine gīḥ
yo martyeṣvamṛta ṛtāvā hotā
yajiṣṭha itkṛṇoti devān.[21]

How shall we offer (our oblations) to Agni? What Word (hymn of praise) for him is agreeable to the Gods? What invocation to the luminous Lord? For him who is the Immortal in mortals, possessed of the Truth, guide and performer of sacrifices, whilst present amongst humans manifests the gods?

(1)

The Birth of the Sacrificial God

According to Yaska there is a classification which speaks of three deities: Agni whose abode is the earth, Vayu whose place is in the air, and Surya who fills the sky. In the Rig-veda this number is increased to thirty-three of whom eleven are said to be on earth, eleven in mid-region and the rest in heaven. Agni is spoken of as the wise one who brings succour to all the thirty-three. Elsewhere the Veda mentions that 300, 3000 gods have worshipped Agni. Dyaus and Prithivi, Heaven and Earth are extolled as the great, wise and energetic parents who have made all creatures and as helping their offspring to become immortal. Agni is the most important of the Vedic deities with the single exception of Indra.

Agni, the sacrificial god, takes the first place in the Rig-veda immediately beside Indra; oftentimes he enjoys a decisive superiority over the latter because of his infinite wisdom and invincible will. He is the son of the gods, who becomes their father:

Pari prajātaḥ kratvā babhūtha bhuvo
devānāṁ pitā putraḥ san.[22]

Various are the myths about Agni's births, his forms of appearance and his places of residence. He is produced from *aranis*, the kindling-sticks, he is the Son of Waters, *apani napat*, and also born in the highest Heaven and brought down by Matarishvan. The seekers want to serve him in the earth, in the heavenly beings and in his highest abode, for he has his seats everywhere. The threefold nature of this Fire-god is often extolled by the Rishis; like-wise his heads and bodies, stations and splendours, births and functions are threefold.

Śataṁ cakṣāṇo akṣabhirdevo vaneṣu turvaṇiḥ,
sado dadhāna upareṣu sānuṣvagniḥ
pareṣu sānuṣu.[23]

He the vigorous and loud-sounding arrives swiftly at the altar when invoked by praise; he manifests himself a hundredfold by his flames. Agni, who has his abode in high heavens, comes quickly to the place of worship.

Vidhema te parame janmannagne
vidhema stomairavare sadhasthe,
yasmādyonerudārithā yaje taṁ pra tve
havīṁṣi juhure samiddhe.[24]

We adore thee, O Agni, in heavens, thy loftiest birthplace, and with hymns in the mid-region. We worship thee again here on earth with oblations when kindled and ablaze.

Imaṁ mahe vidathyāya śūṣaṁ śaśvat
kṛtva īḍyāya pra jabhruḥ,
śṛṇotu no damyebhiranīkaiḥ
śṛnotvagnirdivyairajasraḥ.[25]

They repeatedly praise the mighty Lord who manifests during the sacrifice. May he who is endowed with helpful near radiance hear us, may he who is vibrant with divine radiance care for us.

Whether earth-born or water-born, born of strength or heaven-born they worship him with the same devotion:

Yadagne divijā asyapsujā vā sahaskṛta,
taṁ tvā gīrbhirhavāmahe.[26]

We worship thee, O Agni, whether born in heavens or in the waters, educed by luminous force.

Elsewhere it is said that Agni was first born from the heavens, then from the gods and finally from the waters:

Trīṇi jānā pari bhūṣantyasya samudra
ekaṁ divyekamapsu,
pūrvāmanu pra diśaṁ parthivānāmṛtun
praśāsadvi dadhāvanuṣṭhu.[27]

They reflect and adore the three places of his birth — the heavens, the mid-air and the waters. For dividing the seasons for the good of the earthly creatures, he formed in regular succession, the quarters.

His lustre is found in the heaven and on the earth, in plants, in the waters and in the wide air:

Tvamagne dyubhistvamāśuśukṣaṇistvam
adbhyastvamaśmanaspari,
tvaṁ vanebhyastvamoṣadhībhyastvaṁ
nṛṇāṁ nṛpate jāyase śuciḥ.[28]

O Agni, sovereign Lord of men, ever ready to take birth for the sake of sacrifice, thy glory is manifested in firmament, in the forests and in the rocks all around.

Agne yatte divi varcaḥ pṛthivyāṁ yad
oṣadhīṣvapsvā yajatra,
yenāntarikṣamurvātatantha tveṣaḥ
sa bhānurarṇavo nṛcakṣāḥ.[29]

O adorable Agni, your splendour is visible in the heaven, on earth and in the plants and the waters. Your glory overspreads all with radiance and refulgence, overlooking men.

His earthly existence is derived from his heavenly existence. Agni, the Jatavedas, is the son of Truth and the father of the human race. He is Angirasa, the first-designated semi-divine ancestor of the later generations of priests. He is the destroyer of demons.

In the external sense Agni is one of the five subtle elements, *tanmātras* in *Sankhya Darshana* created out of causal matter. It is a primary elemental substance, a subtle condition of matter which is irresolvable into any further simpler state. Agni with four other such substances constitutes the numberless subtle forms in subtle matter; these underlie as basic principles of the formation of the material universe. Agni is one of the fundamental states known to the Vedic Rishis; it is "the formatory principle of intension represented to our senses in matter as heat, light and fire..."[30]

Agni, in general, is not to be construed as physical flame; it is the fire of Brahman, *brahmāgni*, the fire of sacrifice, the conscient energy within that constantly lends and supports inner evolution. In the material universe it is the vital energy and the powerful demiurge running through it as the nisus of its growth. In Yoga it is the fire of self-control and the fire of self-knowledge and the flame of self-surrender. Whereas at the psychic level it is the pure flame that burns deep in the recesses of the heart, and which from there slowly but steadily lights up all the parts and planes of the being. In the mind it creates a light of intuitive perception and clear discrimination, in the vital it kindles the flames of intuitive feeling and right emotion, and in the body an automatic right response to happenings in the physical.

When Agni is spoken of as being born out of the Waters, certainly it is not the lightning — a view so erroneously supported by most scholars and commentators. It is not even the sun that appears out of the waters at dawn and disappears behind it at night. In all the hymns the Rishis are invoking and extolling the merits of the secret Fire within who is also the one in the Heavens. When the Veda speaks of the three origins of Agni in 'Heaven', in the 'Waters' and within 'us', they are not referring to the three fires of the sacrificial place — the *Ahavanīya* in the east, the *Gārhapatya* and the *Dakṣiṇa*. The *Brahmanas* with their focus on the external — the ritual and the ceremony — considerably contribute to the confusion. Besides, the difference in terminology of the Rig-veda and the later period is another confounding factor. The hymns are deliberately clothed in subtle and symbolic language packed with manifold imagery. The mounting flames of Agni are compared with swift birds which fly upward from a tree, and with sturdy horses.

Yahvā iva pra vayāmujjihānāḥ pra
bhānavaḥ sisrate nākamaccha.[31]

The radiant flames of Agni rise up like lofty trees throwing their branches upward.

Adha bhramasta urviyā vi bhāti
yātayamāno adhi sānu pṛśneḥ.[32]

Your flames, O Agni, frequenting the earth's summits shine out everywhere and their swiftly moving flickers mounting high flare up furiously.

Viṣūco aśvānyuyuje vanejā ṛjītibhī
raśanābhirgribhītān.[33]

Born of the forest his flames, like fierce horses, speed out in all directions. He harnesses them with shining reins.

The flames are often imaged as Agni's tongues.

Adha jihvā pāpatīti pra vṛṣṇo
goṣuyudho nāśaniḥ sṛjānā
Śūrasyeva prasitiḥ kṣātiragner
durvarturbhīmo dayate vanāni.[34]

The flames of mighty Agni descend like the hurled thunderbolt of the

Lord of heaven. They have the power of destroying all physical forms; he, the irresistible and formidable consumes all.

At the time of his birth Agni is figuratively described as devouring both his parents, earth and heaven, for he the Fire-god is forging forward to the Truth:

Tadvāmṛtaṁ rodasī pra bravīmi
jāyamāno mātarā garbho atti.[35]

He awakens and strengthens the aspiration and supports the increase of cows and horses — powers of Light and Energy.

Vṛṣā hariḥ śucirā bhāti bhāsā
dhiyo hinvāna uśatīrajīgaḥ.[36]

He, the fire-divine, the lover of the Sun, sends forth his resplendent lustre; shining in his splendour he encourages sacrifices and arouses new aspirations.

Patiṁ kṛṣṭīnāṁ rathayaṁ rayīṇāṁ
vaiśvānaramuṣasāṁ ketumahnām.[37]

Thou art the Lord of men who givest riches, thou the banner and bringer of dawns and days.

Many are the manifestations of the divine Fire: he lives in the sun, in the moon, in the fire-place at home, in all forms of Nature and in all that shines and thrives:

Ye agnayo apsv'antarye vṛtre
ye puruṣe ye aśmasu,
ya āviveśoṣdhīryo vanaspatīṁstebhyo
agnibhyo hutamastvetat.[38]

He is the forest-fire that burns down the hide-out of the Adversary and runs amuck over the earth assailing the forces of inertia and darkness.

Ya ugra iva śaryahā tigmaśṛṅgo na vaṅsagaḥ,
agne puro rurojitha.[39]

O adorable Agni, like a fierce fighter, like a sharp-horned bull, thou art capable of breaking the citadel of the Enemy.

Tvadbhiyā viśa āyannasiknīrasamanā
jahatīrbhojanāni,
vaiśvānara pūrave śośucānaḥ puro
yadagne darayannadīdeḥ.[40]

Through your fear, O Fire, the many dark forces come under your control abandoning their evil possessions. May you shine upon all men and blaze and consume the strongholds of their enemies.

Agni, the fire-god is said to be born before the parents; he guards their birth:

Putro yatpūrvaḥ pitrorjaniṣṭa śamyaṁ
gaurjagāra yaddha pṛcchān.[41]

Heaven and Earth are his parents — the two mothers of Agni.

Ubhā pitarā mahayannajāyatāgnir
dyāvāpṛthivī bhūriretasā.[42]

Agni, the fire-divine, adoring his parents — Heaven and Earth, becomes manifest by his own supreme splendour.

The great Fire is firmly established between heaven and earth:

Mahānsadhasthe dhruva ā niṣatto'ntar
dyāvā māhine haryamāṇaḥ.[43]

Agni is frequently associated with the lotus, he being churned out of *puṣkara* by Atharvan.

Tvāmagne puṣkarādadhyatharvā niramanthata,
mūrdhno viśvasya vāghataḥ.[44]

O Agni, after much contemplation and penance, the determined seeker discovers you out from the lotus-leaf-like expanse which is the support and summit of the universe.

However, the lotus-leaf is considered in the Veda only as a symbol of the Waters out of which Agni, the Fire-god is born. Moreover Agni is perceived as self-born, *svayaṁbhu*, and self-perfected.

According to the Veda, the Fire-god has to be installed in the heart of the seeker, again and again, by himself. The Fire has to be produced constantly and strengthened in oneself, rather continuously renewed for his perpetual inner growth. Which means, the Fire has to be fanned uninterruptedly by the sacrificer.

Yuvoratriściketati narā sumnena cetasā.[45]

The thrice-liberated seeker celebrates your benevolence with adorable attitude.

The Rig-veda speaks of the three Fires. The sacrificers kindle the Fire on the threefold seat; therefore he is described as *triṣadhastha.*

a) *Ā vakṣi devāñ iha vipra yakṣi cośan*
hotarni ṣadā yoniṣu triṣu.[46]

Bringing Nature's bounties, O Seer, worship them, and devoutly aspiring for them remain seated in the three fields of thought, word and deed.

b) *Agne devāñ ihā vaha sādayā yoniṣu.*[47]

O thou radiant God, Agni, pray direct thy puissances through our mind, heart and intellect — the glorious triad.

c) *Yajñasya ketuṁ prathamaṁ purohitamagniṁ*
narāstriṣadhasthe samīdhire.[48]

Seekers absorbed in meditation first enkindle in the three realms — physical, vital and mental, the flame of thy adoration.

d) *Asmākamagne adhvaraṁ juṣasva sahasaḥ*
sūno triṣadhastha havyam.[49]

O Agni, source of our strength, omnipotent inhabitant of the three worlds,. pray accept our sacrificial offerings.

e) *Adabdhebhistava gopābhiriṣṭe'smākaṁ*
pāhi triṣadhastha sūrīn.[50]

O thou radiant God, present in the three worlds, pray protect us with your invincible powers.

He is also referred to as *tripastyā* — established in *Pṛthivī*, *antarikṣa* and *dyauḥ*.

Tamāganma tripastyaṁ mandhāturdasyuhantamam
agniṁ yajñeṣu pūrvyaṁ nabhantāmanyake same.[51]

His is a threefold habitation; he destroys the demonic forces for the good of the devotees. May our misfortunes come to an end by his courageous action.

Again and again the celestial Fire is mentioned as closely connected with the sacrificial Fire, one Agni both as the head of Heaven and as the navel of the earth. He is the Agni of the earth, the mid-region and of the sky. This threefold distribution the Veda calls *tretinī*.

a) *Tisro yahvasya samidhaḥ parijmano'gner*
apunannuśijo amṛtyavaḥ
tāsāmekāmadadhurmartye bhujamu lokam
u dve upa jāmimīyatuḥ.[52]

The immortal priests dedicated their offerings to the three Fires — Agni of the earth, of the atmosphere and of the sky.

b) *Stomena hi divi devāso agnimajījanañ*
chaktibhī rodasiprām,
tamū akṛṇvan tredhā bhuve kaṁ
sa oṣadhīḥ pacati viśvarūpāḥ.[53]

Agni fills heaven and earth by his will and vigour: Nature's plenitudes enkindle him in the sky and apportion his threefold functions in the three regions. He, verily, helps the plant kingdom to its golden ripening.

Agni dwells in the waters and in the woods, both in the animate and inanimate worlds.

a) *Mitraṁ na yaṁ śimyā goṣu gavyavaḥ*
svādhyo vidathe apsu jījanan.[54]

Heaven and earth are fully activated by the force of the divine Fire. Agni is like a friend and benefactor of men; he richly deserves our adoration.

b) *Avindannu darśatamapsvantar*
devāso agnimapasi svasṛṇam.[55]

Nature's forces find the Fire-divine both in the ethereal spaces of the cosmos and in the movements of waters.

c) *Apāṁ garbhaṁ darśatamoṣadhīnāṁ*
vanā jajāna subhagā virūpam.[56]

The sacred wood generates Fire who is splendorous in varied forms; he is present in the spaces of the universe and in the plants.

d) *Kāyamāno vanā tvaṁ yanmātṛrajagannapaḥ.*[57]

Through your love to dwell in the woods below, O Fire, You rise up to fill the skies above.

The Sama-veda speaks of Agni as dwelling deep in the woods as well as in the waters:

Tamoṣadhīrdadhire garbhamṛtviyaṁ
tamāpo agniṁ janayanta mātaraḥ,
tamitsamānaṁ vaninaśca virudho'ntar
vatīśca suvate ca viśvahā.[58]

Him, duly emerging, the plants have received as their life-germ; him the Waters have brought to life. So too, the trees bear him within them and increase him ever more.

The Rig-veda variously extols his omniscience and omnipotence.

1. *Pituścidūdharjanuṣā viveda*
vyasya dhārā asṛjadvi dhenāḥ,

guhā carantaṁ sakhibhiḥ śivebhir
divo yahvībhirna guhā babhūva.

2. *Pituśca garbhaṁ janituśca babhre*
pūrvīreko adhayatpīpyānāḥ,
vṛṣṇe sapantī śucaye sabandhū
ubhe asmai manuṣye ni pāhi.

3. *Urau mahāñ anibādhe vavardh*
āpo agniṁ yaśasaḥ saṁ hi pūrvīḥ,
ṛtasya yonāvaśayaddamūnā
jāmīnāmagnirapasi svasṛṇām.[59]

1. At his birth Agni, the Fire-divine, is conversant with the secret source of the luminous opulence of the Father and lets forth wide His words, and His waters in motion. By the help of his many companions (gods) and by the Mighty Ones of Heaven (rivers) he finds Him immanent and moving secretly in all existences; and yet he himself is not lost in their secrecy.

2. He bears the child of the Father (Heaven) and of him that generated him (Earth), one, he feeds upon many a swelling bosom in their increasing. In him both the powers in man (Earth and Heaven) have their common master and spouse. May thou, O Agni, ever preserve them both.

3. In the unbounded Vast, the great Agni increases; the many Waters victoriously nourish him. There in the source of the Truth he makes his home, enjoying the integral working of the undivided sisters.

He who is the child of the Waters is, to begin with, born as the Son of Force from the inner growth of the earth; he then is born in many progressive forms of consciousness even as the earth evolves and the humans are helped to journey toward the Truth. In the home of Agni, the Truth, the rivers no longer work separately as they do on the earth. The gods established in the pure mentality of man unite around Agni in his endeavour to uplift man to the shoreless infinite. The gods themselves are the radiances of the superconscient Truth who cleave to Agni and help him in his drawing of man upward to Immortality.

1. *Apāṁ garbhaṁ darśatamoṣadhīnāṁ*
vanā jajāna subhagā virūpam,
devāsaścinmanasā saṁ hi jagmuḥ
paniṣṭhaṁ jātaṁ tavasaṁ duvasyan.

2. *Bṛhanta idbhānavo bhārjīkam*
agniṁ sacanta vidyuto na śukrāḥ,
guheva vṛddhaṁ sadāsi sve antar
apāra ūrve amṛtaṁ duhānāḥ.[60]

1. The auspicious wood genders the birth of Agni, the graceful Fire-divine, he who is born ever anew in varied forms from the bliss supreme.The gods approach him reverently and worship the mighty Fire in all his new-births.

2. All the mighty luminaries accompany the self-shining Agni, the fire of the superconscient Truth. He then grows omnipotent in his abode of boundless bliss as they pour forth ambrosia into the infinite ocean.

(2)

The Awakening of Agni

The Rishi sings in praise of the awakening of Agni and its conscious action in man to usher in a new life of flaming aspiration. It is an expression of admiration and joyous adoration. It is intended to establish in the soul of the seeker the sevenfold delight of the divine Force and to assure its effectiveness in all the planes and parts of his being.

Agni, the universal force, awakens when the seeker accumulates all that power and richness of being on which the Force feeds itself. It wakes towards the dawning illumination, the ideal enlightening vision entering the soul that helps its ascent to the vastness and the immortality of the Truth. The awakening of the great godhead is, in fact, his great release out of the womb of Darkness, *māhan devastamaso niramochi.*

The awakening towards the coming dawn symbolises man's approaching enlightenment which he rises to receive. Once he is touched by the divine knowledge, the seeker begins to move heavenward; the forces of the Truth when released from their prison in the secrecy of our mortal nature, surge up openly and freely. This psychic phenomenon is described by the Rishi as "the wide uprush of divine being and consciousness, *yahvā iva pra vayām ujjihānāḥ.*"[61]

This awakening and release of Agni precipitates divine action in man. And in the dawn is seen the presence of the priest of the sacrifice ready to offer the oblation to the great gods and goddesses — "to each great god his portion, to Indra a pure and deified mentality, to Vayu a pure and divine vital joy and action, to the four great Vasus, Varuna, Mitra, Bhaga and Aryaman the greatnesses, felicities, enjoyments and strengths of perfected being, to the Ashwins the youth of the soul and its raptures and swiftnesses, to Daksha and Saraswati, Ila, Sarama and Mahi the activities... Agni has stood up in the dawning illumination high uplifted in the pure mentality, *ūrdhva*, with a perfected mind, *sumanāḥ*."[62] The great god Agni, in his rising, purifies the temperament and the intellectuality and makes them receptive to the descending Truth and the Rightness. The awakening of Agni brings about a total change in the whole external and internal being of man; it fulfils the innate impulse "which raises matter towards life, life towards mind, mind towards ideality and spirit, and thus consummating God's intention in the creature."[63]

With his release the Lord of Fire puts forth his powers for the uplifting of his adorers. He inspires him to constantly strain his mind upward through the heart and through the intellect to the Truth. It is through joyous and pure and perfect activity that the journey can be accomplished. Agni gives his host a foretaste of the Truth in all things that he undertakes. He puts forth his powers, *ganaḥ*, in a mass, who yet work individually, each contributing to the sum total of the enjoyment and promotion of vital energies and vital pleasures. Such enjoyment is necessarily supportive, of Agni's higher action in the host. However, this enjoyment is the pure and illumined enjoyment of uplifted nature, and certainly not of the unregenerate creature. When the divine force of Agni burns down the gross in us and purifies and illuminates our nature, our enjoyments and illuminations become pure and sublime, uplifting and transforming. It is under these helpful and auspicious conditions that Agni exercises his upraising action. At this stage he performs a delicate and important mission in respect of helping the intellectual mind to right and unerring discernment. The discriminative intellect, *dakṣiṇa*, is unerring in the ideality but not in the intellect and much less in the mind. Mind and intellect acquire perfect discernment only when Agni manifests both in the *prāṇa* and *manas*:

Yadīṁ gaṇasya raśanāmajigaḥ śucir
aṅkte śucibhirgobhiragniḥ,

āddakṣiṇā yujyate vājayantyuttānām
ūrdhvo adhayajjuhūbhiḥ.[64]

The fourth verse of the above *sukta* brings out clearly the relation of Agni and the purified mind. We often confuse the sense-mind, *manas*, with the idea-mind, *mahas*; they are not the same. The sense-mind is incapable of effecting the Truth-knowledge which is original, pure and unlimited. But when we rise into god-nature and pass on from mortal impurity to immortal purity, then all the planes and parts of our being work perfectly in the Truth and the gods, each performing its own specific role and function in accordance with a law of higher harmony and preserving its right relation with each one around it and in the hierarchy. To seek and to establish this right relation with each one in the cosmos, and to have a right state and always act rightly the sense-mind has to continuously strain towards Agni, the deputy of the divine Truth in us, as well as move into Surya. For, Surya is the god of pure idea-mind with its four attending powers of self-revelation, self-inspiration, self-intuition and self-discernment. With both Agni and Surya acting on the sense-mind, it becomes a passive and willing receptor of the impacts coming both from inside and outside and enables Agni to act fully and freely in the world and to possess and enjoy it for the Divine immanent in us:

Agnimacchā devayatāṁ manāṅsi
cakṣūṅṣīva sūrye saṁ caranti,
yadīṁ suvāte uṣasā virūpe śveto
vājī jāyate agre ahnām.[65]

Agni's birth, growth and manifestation are of paramount importance in the Vedic context. "Night and Dawn", observes Sri Aurobindo, "are the two unlike mothers who jointly give birth to Agni, Night, the *avyakta*, unmanifest state of knowledge and being, the power of Avidya, Dawn, the *vyakta*, manifest state of knowledge and being, the power of Vidya. They are the two dawns, the two agencies which prepare the manifestation of God in us, Night fostering Agni in secret on the activities of Avidya, the activities of unillumined mind, life and body by which the god in us grows out of matter towards spirit, out of earth up to heaven, Dawn manifesting him again, more and more, until he is ready here for his continuous, pure and perfect activity. When this point of our journey towards perfection is reached he is born, *śveto vājī*, in the van of the days."[66] Having born, he increases by the oblation of the adorers. Agni is Being, Itself manifested in substance; he therefore rapidly manifests as the fullness and wideness and rightness of Being in all its radiant purity and alongside as the wideness and purity and illumination of our own being. "Agni... manifests as the fullness, the infinity, the *bṛhat* of all this sevenfold substantial being that is the world we are, but white, the colour of illumined purity. He manifests... at this stage primarily as that mighty wideness, purity and illumination of our being which is the true basis of the complete and unassailable *siddhi* in the yoga, the only basis on which right knowledge, right thinking, right living, right enjoyment can be firmly, vastly and perpetually seated. He appears therefore in the van of the days, the great increasing states of illuminated force and being ... which are the eternal future of the mortal when he has attained immortality."[67]

Purity and perfect illumination of being, the Rishi emphasizes, form the complete basis of *siddhi* in the yoga. By its very radiant purity and wideness, Agni comes out victorious over the hostile forces, and by his victory helps the aspirant in his upward inner movement. By his purity and power he effectively transforms the movements of the lower nature into channels of immortal strength and joy of the divine nature. "Manifesting progressively that Ananda, he the force of God establishes and maintains in each house of our habitation, in each of our five bodies, in each of our seven levels of conscious existence, the seven essential forms of Ananda, the bliss of body, the bliss of life, the bliss of mind, the senses, the bliss of ideal illumination, the bliss of pure divine universal ecstasy, the bliss of cosmic Force, the bliss of cosmic being. For although we tend upwards immediately to the pure Idea, yet not that but Ananda is the goal of our journey; the manifestation in our lower members of the divine bliss reposing on the divine force and being is the law of our perfection. Agni, whether he raises us to live in pure mind or yet beyond to the high plateaus of the pure ideal existence, *adhı ṣṇuna bṛhata vartamānam*, establishes and supports as the divine force that divine bliss in its seven forms in whatever houses of our being, whatever worlds of our consciousness have been already possessed by our waking existence, life, body and mind, or life, body, mind and idea, *dame-dame dadhānaḥ*."[68]

Janiṣṭa hı jenyo agre ahnāṁ hito
hiteṣvaruṣo vaneṣu,
damedame sapta ratnā dadhāno'gnir
hotā ni ṣasādā yajīyān.[69]

Agni fulfils the sacrifice through human activity, for, it is in man that mind, life and body are blended to some extent; earth, the middle world and heaven co-exist in him which is ideally suited for the effective working of the divine Will-Force. In the mid-region the life-energies joyously fulfil themselves unrestricted by the constraints of material existence. Seated in the physical, and engrossed in the vitalised mental he brings into it the greater joys of the middle world. This action of Agni supports and enlarges even the physical and vital activities of man and their enjoyments. Agni is in constant possession of the Truth and the Light and releases them in all human activity on the ascending movement. His prime masculinity and forcefulness are supportive of every human effort at self-transcendence and in all forms from physical heat to the divine askesis in us and outside us which sustain the universe. He is everywhere from the inconscient microcosm to the vitally vibrant macrocosm.

Man is a self-conscious instrument of Nature. In him are interblended both mind and life and their interdependent existences. He therefore becomes the ideal *kṣetra* for Agni's action to connect earth-existence with divine-existence. Firmly entrenched in matter he works in the realised vitalised consciousness of the middle world, and hews and paves the way for the descent of the Truth-Consciousness. It is therefore that he is the supreme supporter of all upward-climbing human activity, steadily and diligently leading it to the Truth:

Agnirhotā nyasīdadyajīyānupasthe
mātuḥ surabhā u loke,
yuvā kaviḥ puruniṣṭha ṛtāvā dhartā
kṛṣṭīnāmuta madhya iddhaḥ.[70]

(3)

His All-inclusive Functions

"The Vedic deity Agni is the first of the Powers, the pristine and pre-eminent, that have issued from the vast and secret Godhead. By conscious force of the Godhead the worlds have been created and are governed from within by that hidden and inner Control; Agni is the form, the fire, the forceful heat and flaming will of this Divinity. As a flaming Force of knowledge he descends to build up the worlds and seated within them, a secret deity, initiates movement and action. This divine Conscious Force contains all the other godheads in itself as the nave of a wheel contains its spokes. All puissance of action, strength in the being, beauty of form, splendour of light and knowledge, glory

> and greatness are the manifestation of Agni. And when he is entirely delivered and fulfilled out of the envelope of the world's crookedness this deity of flame and force is revealed as the solar godhead of love and harmony and light, Mitra, who leads men towards the Truth."[71]

In the Vedic context, Agni is the facade of divine Force — a combine of burning heat and light which forms all things, devours and rebuilds all things. He is the flame of force imbued with intuitive intelligence, the seer-will in the universe and the indefatigable worker guided by the light of the superconscient Truth. He is the immortal in the mortal, the seer, the priest and the Truth. "His mission is to purify all that he works upon and to raise up the soul struggling in Nature from obscurity to the light, from the strife and the suffering to love and joy, from the heat and the labour to the peace and the bliss."[72] He awakes through the Day and through the Night and guards the law of the Truth of things in all obscuration and chaos. This flame of Truth-will ceaselessly burns and is visible even in the depths of the inconscient. He is the aspiring Force and Will kindled in the heart of all seekers, he is the flame on the altar and the priest of the sacrifice. He is the indispensable summoner who carries the oblations and brings down the gods and their felicities. He is the perfect purifier, the infallible will-force that conducts the onward march of the seeker soul. He is the friend of the pilgrim-soul, the leader of the marathon inner sacrifice, the great protector against the enemy-hordes. "Flaming upward to heaven to meet the divine Dawn, it rises through the vital or nervous mid-world and through our mental skies and enters at last the Paradise of Light, its own supreme home above where joyous for ever in the eternal Truth that is the foundation of the sempiternal Bliss the shining Immortals sit in their celestial sessions and drink the wine of the infinite beatitude."[73]

(i)

In the beginning Agni lies concealed in material Nature, works hidden in plants and trees, and is released into overt action in human beings. He emerges first as the vital Will, the ravaging appetite that feeds upon Nature's growths, the consuming passion that leaves in its wake a trail of painful waste. Agni purifies by destruction and thus prepares for the advent of a new and higher order. "Agni destroys and purifies. His very hunger and desire, infinite in its scope, prepares the establishment of a higher universal order. The smoke of his passion is overcome and this vital Will, this burning desire in the Life becomes the Steed that carries us up to the highest levels, — the white Steed that gallops in the front of the Dawns."[74] It is only later and at a different level that Agni appears as the Seer-Will and becomes the guardian of an ascending series of the illuminations of knowledge. In the end, after overcoming the enemies of Light and Truth, Agni emerges as the immortal conquerer, 'the seer, self-ruler and king over Nature'. The Veda portrays him in a series of impressive images. "He is the rapturous priest of the sacrifice, the God-Will intoxicated with its own delight, the young sage, the sleepless envoy, the ever-wakeful flame in the house, the master of our gated dwelling-place, the beloved guest, the lord in the creature, the seer of the flaming tresses, the divine child, the pure and virgin God, the invincible warrior, the leader on the path who marches in front of the human peoples, the immortal in mortals, the worker established in man by the gods, the unobstructed in knowledge, the infinite in being, the vast and flaming sun of the Truth, the sustainer of the sacrifice and discerner of its steps, the divine perception, the light, the vision, the firm foundation."[75] Agni is described by the Rishis as having many births; he is born of the Truth, the child of Heaven and Earth, of pure mental and physical consciousness and brought up by the Seven Mothers. Fostered by the cows he rapidly grows to divine greatness and fills all the planes with his flaming splendour. Together with Indra he slays the Dasyus, mediates between earth and heaven and devouring dynamism advances to the world of Truth and Light and Bliss:

1. *Abodhyagniḥ samidhā janānāṁ prati*
   dhenumivāyatīmuṣāsam,
   yahva iva pra vayāmujjihānāḥ pra
   bhānavaḥ sisrate nākamaccha.

2. *Abodhi hotā yajathāya devānūrdhvo*
   agniḥ sumanāḥ prātarasthāt
   samiddhasya ruśadadarśi pājo mahān
   devastamaso niramoci.

3. *Yadīṁ gaṇasya raśanāmajīgaḥ śucir*
   aṅkte śucibhirgobhiragniḥ
   addakṣiṇā yujyate vājayantyuttānām
   ūrdhvo adhayajjuhūbhiḥ.

4. *Agnimacchā devayatāṁ manāṅsi*
   cakṣūṅṣiva sūrye saṁ caranti,

yadīṁ suvāte uṣasā virūpe śveto
vājī jāyate agre ahnām.

5. *Janiṣṭa hi jenyo agre ahnāṃ*
hito hiteshvaruṣo vaneṣu
damedame sapta ratnā dadhāno'gnir
hotā ni ṣasādā yajīyān.

6. *Agnirhotā nyasīdadyajīyānupasthe*
mātuḥ surabhā u loke,
yuvā kaviḥ puruniṣṭha ṛtāvā dhartā
kṛṣṭīnāmūta madhya iddhaḥ.

7. *Pra ṇu tyaṁ vipramadhvareṣu sādhum*
agniṁ hotāramīḷate namobhiḥ,
ā yastatāna rodasī ṛtena nityaṁ
mṛjanti vājinaṁ ghṛtena.

8. *Mārjālyo mṛjyate sve damūnāḥ*
kavipraśasto atithiḥ śivo naḥ,
sahasraśṛṅgo vṛṣabhastadojā viśvāñ
agne sahasā prāsyanyān.

9. *Pra sadyo agne atyeṣyanyānāvir*
yasmai cārutamo babhūtha,
īḷenyo vapuṣyo vibhāvā priyo viśām
atithirmānuṣīṇām

10. *Tubhyaṁ bharanti kṣitayo yaviṣṭha*
balimagne antita ota dūrāt,
ā bhandiṣṭhasya sumatíṁ cikiddhi
bṛhatte agne mahi śarma bhadram.

11. *Ādya rathaṁ bhānumo bhānumantamagne*
tiṣṭha yajatebhiḥ samantam,
vidvānpathīnāmurv antarikṣameha
devānhaviradyāya vakṣi.

12. *Avocāma kavaye medhyāya vaco vandāru*
vṛṣabhāya vṛṣṇe,
gaviṣṭhiro namasā stomamagnau divīva
rukmamuruvyañcamaśret.[76]

1. "Strength is awake by kindling of the peoples and he fronts the Dawn that comes to him as the Cow that fosters; like mightinesses that rush upward to their expanding his lustres advancing mount towards the heavenly level.

2. "The Priest of our oblation has awakened for sacrifice to the gods; with right mentality in him Strength stands up exalted in our mornings; he is entirely kindled, red-flushing the mass of him is seen; a great godhead has been delivered out of the darkness.

3. "When he has uncoiled the long cord of his hosts, Strength shines pure by the pure herd of the radiances. For the goddess who discerns grows in plenitude and is yoked to her works; he exalted, she extended supine, he feeds on her with his flames of the offering.

4. "The minds of men who grow in the godhead move entirely towards the flame of Will even as all their seeings converge in the Sun that illumines. When two Dawns of opposite forms are delivered of him, he is born as the White Steed in front of the days.

5. "Yea, he is born victorious in the front of the days, a ruddy worker established in the established delights of things; upholding in house after house the seven ecstasies Strength has taken his seat as the Priest of the offering mighty for sacrifice.

6. "Strength has taken his seat as the Priest of the offering mighty for sacrifice in the lap of the Mother and in that rapturous other world, young and a seer, standing out in his multitudes, possessed of the Truth, the upholder of those that do the work; and also in between he is kindled.

7. "Men seek with their obeisances of submission this illumined Strength that achieves our perfection in the progressing sacrifices and is the priest of their oblation, because he shapes in the power of the Truth both firmaments of our being. Him they press into brightness by the clarity, the eternal steed of life's plenitude.

8. "Bright, he is rubbed bright, expressed by the seer, domiciled in his own home and our beneficient guest. The bull of the thousand horns,

because thou hast that force, O Strength, thou precedest in thy puissance all others.

9. "At once, O Strength, thou outstrippest all others, in whomsoever thou art manifested in all the glory of thy beauty, desirable, full of body, extended in light, the beloved guest of the human peoples.

10. "To thee, O Strength, O youngest vigour, all the worlds and their peoples bring from near and bring from afar their offering. Awake in a man's knowledge to that right-mindedness of his happiest state. A vastness, O Strength, is the great and blissful peace of thee.

11. "Mount today with the lords of the sacrifice, O luminous Will, thy luminous complete car! Thou who knowest the wide middle world in all its paths, bring hither the gods to eat of our oblation.

12. "To the Seer, to the Intelligence we have uttered today the word of our adoration, to the Bull that fertilises the herds; the Steadfast in the Light by his surrender rises in the flame of Will as in the heavens to a golden Affirmation manifesting a vastness."*

(ii)

The divine Flame-Force is limited in its workings in material Nature. It progressively manifests even as consciousness enlarges itself in the universe in its movement towards the Infinite. It is Agni that guards and guides the ascent, protects the higher illuminations in the seeker against the onslaughts of the Adversary and brings down the streams of the Truth and the Felicity and bestows the final liberation:

1. *Kumāraṁ mātā yuvatiḥ samubdhaṁ guhā*
bibharti na dadāti pitre,
anīkamasya na minajjanāsaḥ puraḥ
paśyanti nihitamaratau.

2. *Kametaṁ tvaṁ yuvate kumāraṁ peṣī*
bibharṣi mahiṣī jajāna,
pūrvīrhi garbhaḥ śarado vavardhāpaśyaṁ
jātaṁ yadasūta mātā.

3. *Hiraṇyadantaṁ śucivarṇamārātkṣetrād*
apaśyamāyudhā mimānam,
dadāno asmā amṛtaṁ vipṛkvatkiṁ mām
anindrāḥ kṛṇavannanukthāḥ.

4. *Kṣetrādapaśyaṁ sanutaścarantaṁ sumad*
yūthaṁ na puru śobhamānam,
na tā agṛbhrannajaniṣṭa hi ṣaḥ
paliknīridyuvatayo bhavanti.

5. *Ke me maryakaṁ vi yavanta gobhirna*
yeṣāṁ gopā araṇaścidāsa,
ya īṁ jagṛbhurava te sṛjantv
ājāti paśva upa naścikitvān.

6. *Vasāṁ rājānaṁ vasatiṁ janānāmarātayo*
ni dadhurmartyeṣu,
brahmāṇyatrerava taṁ sṛjantu
ninditāro nindyāso bhavantu.

7. *Śunaścicchepaṁ niditaṁ sahasrād*
yūpādamuñco aśamiṣṭa hi ṣaḥ,
evāsmadagne vi mumugdhi pāśānhotaś
cikitva iha tū niṣadya.

8. *Hṛṇīyamāno apa hi madaiyeḥ pra me*
devānāṁ vratapāuvāca,
indro vidvāñ anu hi tvā cacakṣa
tenāhamagne anuśiṣṭa āgām.

9. *Vi jyotiṣā bṛhatā bhātyagnirāvir*
viśvāni kṛṇute mahitvā,
prādevīrmāyāḥ sahate durevāḥ śiśīte
śṛṅge rakṣase vinikṣe.

10. *Uta svānāso diviṣ hantvagnes*
tigmāyudhā rakṣase hantavā u,
made cidasya pra rujanti bhāmā
na varante paribādho adevīḥ.

11. *Etaṁ te stomaṁ tuvijāta vipro rathaṁ*
na dhīraḥ svapā atakṣam,
yadīdagne prati tvaṁ deva haryāḥ
svarvatīrapa enā jayema.

12. *Tuvigrīvo vṛṣabho vāvṛdhāno'śatrv*
aryaḥ samajāti vedaḥ,
itīmamagnimamṛtā avocanbarhiṣmate manave
śarma yaṅsaddhaviṣmate manave śarma yaṅsat.[77]

1. The young Mother nurses the Boy in her innermost being and delivers him not to the Father; but when he is established in the front, men see his undiminishing, perpetuating splendour in the upward working of Nature.

2. O youthful Mother, who is this Boy whom you so lovingly nurse? You carry him in your being when you are condensed into form, and deliver him only when you regain your immensity. The unborn has grown in your womb through many autumns; I have seen him when you have brought him forth.

3. I have seen in the distance the golden-tusked bright-coloured luminous one, forging his weapons of force. I offer him the wine of immortality in me, stored in the three planes of my being; Why then should I be disturbed of those who have neither the Word nor the God-Mind.

4. I have seen the happy Flame shining through many forms of exquisite beauty. None could conceal his splendour, for he was triumphantly born; even those who were aged and time-worn among them, became young once again.

5. Who are those that disunite my might from the shining herds? Let those who have seized them restore them to me; for he, the master of conscious intellection, comes to us bringing the lost herds of Light.

6. The enemies of Light have confined the immortal King within the mortals. Let the soul-powers of the Seer set him free who is the sole refuge of all; let the incarcerators themselves be incarcerated.

7. O adorable Lord, even as you have liberated the most wise sage Shunahshepa bound to the thousandfold post of the sacrifice, so do you, O supreme priest of sacrifice taking your seat here firmly in us, emancipate us from our dark bondage.

8. O worshipful God pray do not grow angry and desert me. The upholder of the Law that governs the godheads has instructed me of your workings. Indra the resplendent Lord knowing the Truth realised your splendour. And taught by him his knowledge of you, O Flame, have I approached you.

9. The radiant Flame shines out with the vast light of the Truth, and with it makes all things manifest. With it he overcomes the many formations of undivine knowledge and those of falsehood. He sharpens his weapons to destroy the Rakshasa.

10. May your sharpened horn-like flames manifest in our skies to slay the Rakshasa. In his wild ecstasy, the angry lustres of the adorable Flame destroy all opposition. The undivine forces that impede us from all sides cannot hedge him in nor obstruct his movement.

11. Many are your forms of manifestation O Lord; as your devout worshipper, consummate in discernment, masterful in works have I composed this hymn for you as if it be your chariot. If it meets with your approval, O Strength, then by it, it would be possible to conquer the celestial waters that carry the Truth supreme.

12. May the many-necked Bull increase in us and bring back the wealth of the luminous cattle detained by the Adversary; indeed no one can destroy him. The immortal Powers have therefore asked of him to work out peace and happiness for the one who enlarges the seat of sacrifice, for the one who is filled with oblation.

(iii)

As Agni increases in men he brings into manifestation all the other godheads — Varuna, Mitra, Indra, Aryaman and others — for they are the various powers of one supreme Godhead of which he is the infinite Will-Force. Together they attain manifold perfection for the seeker; they share with the sacrificer the truth and power of their multiple existence and support him on his journey to Immortality. Agni is the self-marshalling strength in Nature; as the indweller of the host-seeker he helps him to overcome all obstacles and limitations common to mortal existence. He awakens his secret soul, fosters his aspiration, strengthens his sinews and impels him to the great pilgrimage. The divine Flame with the clarity and purity of his knowledge puts away evil and carries the sacrificer across the vast stretches of inner space to the kingdom of the Truth:

1. *Tvamagne varuṇo jāyase yattvaṁ mitro*
   bhavasi yatsamiddhaḥ,
   tve viśve sahasasputra devāstvamindro
   dāśuṣe martyāya.

2. *Tvamaryamā bhavasi yatkanīnāṁ nāma*
   svadhāvanguhyaṁ bibharṣi,
   añjanti mitram sudhitaṁ na gobhiryad
   dampatī samanasā kṛṇoṣi.

3. *Tava śriye maruto majaryanta rudra yat*
   te janima cāru citram,
   padaṁ yadviṣṇorupamaṁ nidhāyi tena
   pāsi guhyaṁ nāma gonām.

4. *Tava śriyā sudṛśo deva devāḥ purū*
   dadhānā amṛtaṁ sapanta,
   hotāramagniṁ manuṣo ni ṣedur
   daśasyanta uśijaḥ śaṅsamāyoḥ.

5. *Na tvaddhotā pūrvo agne yajīyān*
   na kāvyaiḥ paro asti svadhāvaḥ,
   viśaśca yasyā atithirbhavāsi
   sa yajñena vanavaddeva martān.

6. *Vayamagne vanuyāma tvotā vasūyovo*
   haviṣā budhyamānāḥ,
   vayaṁ samarye vidatheṣvahnāṁ vayaṁ
   rāyā sahasasputra martān.

7. *Yo na āgo abhyeno bharātyadhīd*
   aghamaghaśaṅse dadhāta,

jahī cikitvo abhiśastimetāmagne
yo no marcayati dvayena.

8. *Tvāmasyā vyuṣi deva pūrve dūtaṁ*
kṛṇvānā ayajanta havyaiḥ,
saṁsthe yadagna īyase rayīṇāṁ
devo martairvasubhiridhyamānaḥ.

9. *Ava spṛdhi pitaraṁ yodhi vidvānputro*
yaste sahasaḥ sūna ūhe,
kadā cikitvo abhi cakṣase no'gne
kadāṅ ṛtacidyātayāse.

10. *Bhūri nāma vandamāno dadhāti pitā*
vaso yadi tajjoṣayāse,
kuviddevasya sahasā cakānaḥ sumnam
agnirvanate vāvṛdhānaḥ.

11. *Tvamaṅga jaritāraṁ yaviṣṭha viśvāny*
agne duritāti parṣi,
stenā adṛśranripavo janāso'jñātaketā
vṛjinā abhūvan.

12. *Ime yāmāsastvadrigabhūvanvasave*
vā tadidāgo avāci,
nāhāyamagnirabhiśastaye no
na rīṣate vāvṛdhānaḥ parā dāt.[78]

1. O adorable Flame, you are Varuna of the infinite vastness when you are born; when you are fully revealed you become the all-embracing Mitra, the Lord of Love; in you, O source of Strength, are centred all the gods; you are the Master of the luminous Mind, Indra, for the mortal who with all devotion makes the offering.

2. O lord of self-organised Nature, you become the might of Aryaman — the aspiring power of the Truth — when you set out to help the 'unripe Radiances' (Virgins) to unite with the Truth. They anoint you with their love and light when you succeed in uniting the Lord (soul) and his Spouse (Nature) in their chamber (of the body).

3. For your exultation, O Powerful One, the Thought-Powers by their drive help you to become in your being that which is your shining best. With the establishment within of the supreme world of Light of Vishnu, you protect by it the illuminations of Knowledge supreme.

4. By your glory, O Lord of the Truth-Vision, all the gods of multiple existences enjoy immortality, and men get grounded in the strength that enables them to offer their oblation, and yearning, they apportion to the gods the offering of self-expression of their being.

5. You are the foremost priest of the oblation, mightiest and most venerable in the sacrifice; you are the wisest one, O adorable Flame, who possess the power of self-organisation of Nature. The one of whom you agree to be the guest, O God, surely attains immortality.

6. O adorable God, may we, the seekers of the substance, nourished and awakened by you, overcome all difficulties by the offering, and by the supreme felicity of Light surmount all mortality.

7. O conscious knower of all, inflict evil on him who seeks to bring sin and violation into our lives. Destroy him who torments us with double-dealing and pugnacious self-expression.

8. Since the beginning of this, our Night, the ancient seers made you their luminous Messenger, and through you performed their sacrifices. Verily, you are the shining godhead who is being kindled by mortal men within them, and you have always helped them to move in your ascent to the supreme world of Truth and Bliss.

9. Bring forth the Father (the luminous Mind) and in thy flaming Wisdom put away evil from him who is being borne in us as your radiant representative. We intensely await the hour when you, O Truth-Conscious seer, will have that vision for us, and actuate us on the great journey.

10. Verily, the Father (the luminous Mind) glorifies the supreme Truth when you help him to realise and cling to it. The seer-Will in us constantly yearns for bliss, and progressively wins it entirely by the force of the supreme Deity.

11. Most youthful and adorable Lord, you carry safely your worshippers beyond all stumblings and pitfalls; for they are helped to know their enemies, the hunters and the thieves hidden in their hearts. Only those whose perceptions are void of knowledge and bereft of right discernment fall into crooked ways.

12. All the movements on our journeying to the Truth have turned towards you, O Lord, and we have declared our shortcomings to the Dweller within. Confident we are that this seer-Will steadily growing in us shall not malign us, nor ever deliver us into the hands of our arch enemy.

(iv)

The Rishi is full of praise and thankfulness to Agni the divine Force that is in him as well as in all existences. He is described variously and cherished as the all-knowing Light and Force who knows the many successive births of the seeker-soul on its ascending planes of existence. He is the priest of the upward-spiralling sacrifice, the purifier and the power that brings inner felicities. He is the immortal fashioner who ever forms the soul anew to fulfil the need of its constant growth into Immortality. He annihilates the powers of Dasyus, enriches the soul with increasing illuminations and grants it complete control of the phenomenal world and its integral transcendence. He, the Son of Force and the conscious Knower and Enjoyer of the Truth, then finally facilitates the entry of the soul into the world of Immortality, *satyam ṛtam bṛhat.*

1. *Tvāmagne vasupatiṁ vasūnāmabhi pra*
mande adhvareṣu rājan,
tvayā vājaṁ vājayanto jayemābhi ṣyāma
pṛtsutīrmartyānām.

2. *Havyavāḷagnirajaraḥ pitā no vibhúr*
vibhāvā sudṛśīko asme,
sugārhapatyāḥ samisho didīhyasmadryāk
sam mimīhi ṣravāṅsi.

3. *Viśāṁ kaviṁ viśpatiṁ mānuṣiṇāṁ śuciṁ*
pāvakaṁ ghṛtapṛṣṭhamagnim,
ni hotāraṁ viśvavidaṁ dadhidhve sa
deveṣu vanate vāryaṇi.

4. *Juṣasvāgna iḷayā sajoṣā yatamāno*
raśmibhiḥ sūryasya,
juṣasva naḥ samidhaṁ jātaveda ā ca
devānhaviradyāya vakṣi.

5. *Juṣṭo damūnā atithirduroṇa imaṁ*
no yajñamupa yāhi vidvān,
viśvā agne abhiyujo vihatyā śatrūyatām
ā bharā bhojanāni.

6. *Vadhéna dasyuṁ pra hi cātayasva vayaḥ*
kṛṇvānastanve svāyai,
piparṣi yatsahasasputra devānso agne
pāhi nṛtama vāje asmān.

7. *Vayaṁ te agna ukthairvidhema vayaṁ*
havyaiḥ pāvaka bhadraśoce,
asme rayiṁ viśvavāraṁ saminvāsme
viśvāni draviṇāni dhehi.

8. *Asmākamagne adhvaraṁ juṣasva sahasaḥ*
sūno triṣadhastha havyam,
vayaṁ deveṣu sukṛtaḥ syāma śarmaṇā
nastrivarūthena pāhi.

9. *Visvāni no durgahā jātavedaḥ sindhuṁ*
na nāvā duritāti parṣi,
agne atrivannamasā gṛṇāno'smākaṁ
bodhyavitā tanūnām.

10. *Yastvā hṛdā kīriṇā manyamāno*
'martyaṁ martyo johavīmi,
jātavedo yaśo asmāsu dhehi prajābhir
agne amṛtatvamaśyām.

11. *Yasmai tvaṁ sukṛte jātaveda u lokam*
agne kṛṇavaḥ syonam,
aśvinaṁ sa putriṇaṁ vīravantaṁ
gomantaṁ rayiṁ naśate svasti.[79]

1. O mighty Lord, master of the fashioners of our being, I glorify you, and direct all my joys to you in the progress of my sacrifices. O luminous Magnate, grant that by increasing your plenitudes, may we win our wealth, and defeat the evil designs of the Adversary.

2. The mighty unaging God, the bearer of our oblations, is our adorable protector; he is all-pervading, resplendent and all-seeing. May he, the supreme Will immanent in us, kindle his powers of impulsion and act within us, entirely by his perfect Will and Wisdom.

3. He is the Seer-Will and Lord of all the struggling souls, he who is pure and the purifier. May he the omniscient God, priest of our oblations, win for us the choicest felicities in the godheads.

4. Growing into the Truth-vision and the Truth-Light, may you always guide us with love, O Strength Supreme. Pray accept our oblations, carry them to the many godheads, O all-knower and promoter of our successive soul-births in consciousness.

5. O adorable Lord, dwelling deep in our being, loved and worshipped by us all, pray come to our sacrifices with all your resplendence and knowledge. Slay and scatter all our enemies, and bring to us their possessions so very helpful in our onward march.

6. Drive away from our midst the vile Divider, and establish your presence within our being, O adorable God. By your Will working in us, verily, you carry the divine powers in us to their goal in the Truth; protect us in the plenitude of our spiritual enjoyment, O mighty One.

7. May we organise rightly for you our sacrifice by our hymns and oblations, O purifying Flame. May you bestow upon us all puissances; may you establish in us the truth of our felicities.

8. O mighty Will, source of all strength, who dwells in the three worlds of our existence (physical, vital and mental), keep close to our sacrifice and accept our oblation. May we become perfect in our sacrifice; protect us by your peace and joy and fullest satisfaction in the threefold world.

9. O knower of our soul-births, carry us safely over all difficult crossings, through all evil pitfalls as on a boat across the waters. O

adorable Lord, you who are aware of our total reverence, awake in us, and be the increaser of the truth of our embodied states the three sheaths of the soul.

10. Though mortal, I earnestly meditate on you, O immortal One, with a devout heart. O omniscient Will, may we be vouchsafed of victory; by the luminous consequences of our dedicated works, may we enjoy immortality.

11. O knower of our increasing soul-births, you create for him, who attains self-perfection through constant consciousness-expansion, the supreme world of bliss and supramental Truth; he thus reaches a felicitous world (of new soul-formations) filled with life's swiftnesses and herds of Light and horses of divine Energy.

(v)

The gods share their powers and graces with the worshippers. They are invoked by the seekers to arrive at the altar of their sacrifice to participate in their preparation for the pilgrimage. Their oblations are carried to the gods by Agni who summons them to descend and give the seeker their respective felicities in the continuous growth of the soul and its perfect perfection. The gods have different capacities and functions and are needed to collaborate with the sacrificer in his individual endeavour which is also cosmic in effect.

1. *Susamiddhāya śociṣe ghṛtaṁ tīvraṁ juhotana,*
   agnaye jātavedase.

2. *Narāśansaḥ suṣūdatīmaṁ yajñamadābhyaḥ,*
   kavirhi madhuhastyaḥ.

3. *Īḷito agna ā vahendraṁ citramiha priyam,*
   sukhai rathebhirūtaye.

4. *Ūrṇamradā vi prathasvābhya rkā anūṣata,*
   bhavā naḥ śubhra sātaye.

5. *Devīrdvāro vi śrayadhvaṁ suprāyaṇā na ūtaye,*
   prapra yajñaṁ pṛṇītana.

6. *Supratīke vayovṛdhā yahvī ṛtasya mātarā,*
doṣāmuṣāsamīmahe.

7. *Vātasya patmanniḷitā daivyā hotārā manuṣaḥ,*
imaṁ no yajñamā gatam.

8. *Iḷā sarasvatī mahī tisto devīrmayobhuvaḥ*
varhiḥ sīdantvasridhaḥ

9. *Śivastvaṣṭarihā gahi vibhuḥ poṣa uta tmanā,*
yajñeyajñe na udava.

10. *Yatra vettha vanaspate devānāṁ guhyā nāmāni,*
tatra havyāni gāmaya.

11. *Svāhāgnaye varuṇāya svāhendrāya marudbhyaḥ,*
svāhā devebhyo haviḥ.[80]

1. To the supreme Will that knows all our progressive soul-births, to the well-kindled, omnipresent Flame, let us all offer our perfectly clarified, poignant thoughts.

2. He is the one who manifests the powers of all the gods, he the untractable who increases the sacrifice; he is the wise one who brings the wine of Ananda.

3. O adorable Fire-divine, bring here to us the resplendent god, Indra (the God-Mind) in his happy chariots (manifold movement) for our protection and progress.

4. O resplendent Lord (Indra, the Divine Mind), increasingly move forward and draw towards you our hymns of awakening; may you ever shine bright in us that we may overcome all impediments on the way.

5. May the doors divine swing open before us, giving us easy access to the concealed heavens; may we be led by them farther and farther and farther making our sacrifice a success.

6. We always adore both Night and Day; we desire them as they are the mighty mothers of Light, who ceaselessly foster all that the Dawn brings out into our being and increases our consciousness.

7. O much worshipped ones, come to this our sacrifice on the paths of Prana; glory to you, O divine priests of our humanity (thirsting for Truth).

8. May Ila, goddess of the vision of knowledge, Saraswati of its rising inspiration and Mahi of its vastness, the threesome who are invincible and unassailable, take their respective seats at the sacrifice made ready for them. For they invariably give birth to the Bliss.

9. O magnificent and beneficent architect of the universe, come here to us all; fashioning all things you pervade them all, O Twashtri; you nourish them all, and increase them in sacrifice after sacrifice, O Lord and Maker of everything.

10. May you lead our offerings to the goal of supreme beatitude, O Master of delight, O you Knower of the secret strengths of all the gods.

11. Victory to the divine Will, victory to Varuna, Lord of infinite Wideness; victory to Indra the resplendent God-Mind as well as to the mighty Maruts, the luminous Thought-Powers (who give conscious expression to the vital energies). May all our oblations be turned into the Light and Force of the Divine concealed in us.

(vi)

The Vedic sacrifice symbolises the unending aspiration of man and his heroic effort at perpetual self-transcendence. Self-offering is the key to self-transcendence, and constant and increasing offering of one's all intensifies Agni, the divine Will, working within him. It is this divine Will that is the centre, seat and concourse of all life-energies in their increasing impulsion. The flames of Agni, increased by the sacrifice, burn down the barriers and effect the release of the imprisoned illuminations. Armed with divine knowledge, the Son of Strength then steadily moves forward carrying the seeker to that supreme goal.

1. *Agniṁ taṁ manye yo vasurastaṁ yaṁ*
   yanti dhenavaḥ,
astamarvanta āśavo'staṁ nityāso vājina iṣaṁ
   stotṛbhya ā bhara.

2. *So agniryo vasurgṛṇe saṁ yam*
   āyanti dhenavaḥ,
samarvanto raghudruvaḥ saṁ sujātāsaḥ
   sūraya iṣaṁ stotríbhya ā bhara.

3. *Agnirhi vājinaṁ viśe dadāti*
   viśvacarṣāṇiḥ,
agnī rāye svābhuvaṁ sa prīto yāti
   vāryamiṣaṁ stotṛbhya ā bhara.

4. *Ā te agna idhīmahi dyumantaṁ*
   devājaram,
yaddha syā te panīyasī samiddīdayati,
   dyavīṣaṁ stotṛbhya ā bhara.

5. *Ā te agna ṛcā haviḥ śukrasya*
   śociṣaspate,
suścañdra dasma viśpate havyavāṭ tubhyaṁ hūyata,
   iṣaṁ stotṛbhya ā bhara.

6. *Pro tye agnayo'gniṣu viśvam*
   puṣyanti vāryam,
te hinvire ta invire ta iṣaṇyanty
   ānuṣagiṣaṁ stotṛbhya ā bhara.

7. *Tava tye agne arcayo mahi vrādhanta*
   vājinaḥ,
ye patvabhiḥ śaphānāṁ vrajā bhuranta
   gonāmiṣaṁ stotṛbhya ā bhara.

8. *Navā no agna ā bhara stotṛbhyaḥ*
   sukṣitiriṣaḥ,
te syama ya ānṛcustvādūtāso
   damedama iṣaṁ stotṛbhya ā bhara.

9. *Ubhe suścandra sarpiṣo darvī*
śrīṇīṣa āsani,
uto na utpupūryā ukthesu śavasas
pata iṣaṁ stotṛbhya ā bhara.

10. *Evāñ agnimajuryamurgīrbhir*
yajñebhirānuṣak,
dadhadasme suvīryamuta tyad
āśvaśvyamiṣaṁ stotṛbhya ā bhara.[81]

1. I meditate on that mighty Lord who is the indweller of our being, to whom go our milch-cows and our war-horses (the powers of Knowledge and Force) as their natural habitation. To him go all our powers and puissances.
O Lord grant the power of journeying upward and onward to those who affirm and ever adore you.

2. He is the mighty Lord who dwells in our being; I express him in whom meet all our herds of light and hordes of energies, in whom all the wise ones converge to manifest in us the divine Knowledge-Force.
O Lord grant the power of journeying upward and onward to those who affirm and ever adore you.

3. Most adorable God, the universal striver, you are the bestower of the energies of joy luminous; you bring to the worshippers that which makes them receptive to the supreme felicity. May you, O Seer-Will, guide them to the desirable good.
O Lord grant the power of journeying upward and onward to those who affirm and ever adore you.

4. O adorable Lord, we kindle in us that brightest flame of yours, undiminishing and most effective, when it blazes high in our heavens.
O Lord grant the power of journeying upward and onward to those who affirm and ever adore you.

5. O adorable Lord, Master of the brightest flame, yours is the offering shaped by the transforming Word; you who are the bene-

volent carrier of our oblations, pray accept our worship, O accomplisher of works, perfect in joy supreme.

O Lord grant the power of journeying upward and onward to those who affirm and ever adore you.

6. Those are your brightest and most effective flames, O Seer-Will, which nourish and effectuate the other ones in the hearts of the strivers; your flames divine spread wide everywhere and speed forth in their impulsions, uninterrupted and unabated.

O Lord, grant the power of journeying upward and onward to those who affirm and ever adore you.

7. Those are your fiercest and most swift rays, O Seer-Will, energies of your felicity which steadily increase and fill the wideness, and strike open the caverns of the luminous kine.

O Lord, grant the power of journeying upward and onward to those who affirm and ever adore you.

8. Bring to those who establish within them your presence — renewed powers of impulsion, O Seer-Will, that advancing steadily find their dwelling place (in the superconscient plane). May we, O Lord, ever worship you alone for, we have you as our most luminous messenger.

O Lord, grant the power of journeying upward and onward to those who affirm and ever adore you.

9. May you ever fill our inspired utterances with your luminous and fiery presence, O Master of shining strength; may you freely accept our worship of you, even as you readily receive both ladles of perennial felicity (the wealth of human and divine delight).

O Lord, grant the power of journeying upward and onward to those who affirm and ever adore you.

10. We serve you steadily and constantly, O adorable Lord, by our illumined words and sacrifices. May you establish in us 'the hero-power of the battling soul', as well as the swiftest galloping force that can take us to the goal.

O Lord, grant the power of journeying upward and onward to those who affirm and ever adore you.

(vii)

Agni, the flame of divine Will-Force, mounts up steadily from the animal to the human through the plant-kingdom. He brings Light and Truth and Bliss and Immortality into the human being leading him to his own Home of the Infinite. He is the purifier of the animal being of man and the founder and consolidator of divine light in the awakened soul of the seeker. He is the creator of illumined perception in those who are enveloped in darkness. He is the builder of the universal in the individual, architect of the eternal in the temporal and the enjoyer of the two consciousnesses.

1. *Sakhāyaḥ saṁ vaḥ samyañcamiṣaṁ*
   stomaṁ cāgnaye,
varṣiṣṭhāya kṣitīnāmūrjo
   naptre sahasvate.

2. *Kutrā cidyasya samṛtau raṇvā*
   naro nṛṣadane,
arhantaścidyamindhate
   sañjanayanti jantavaḥ.

3. *Saṁ yadiṣo vanāmahe saṁ,*
   havyā mānuṣāṇām,
uta dyumnasya śavasa ṛtasya
   raśmimā dade.

4. *Sa smā kṛṇoti ketumā naktaṁ*
   ciddūra ā saté,
pāvako yadvanaspatīnpra smā
   minātyajaraḥ.

5. *Ava sma yasya veṣaṇe svedaṁ*
   pathiṣu juhvati,
abhīmaha svajenyaṁ bhūmā
   pṛṣṭheva ruruhuḥ.

6. *Yaṁ martyaḥ puruspṛhaṁ vidad*
   viśvasya dhāyase,
pra svādanaṁ pitūnāmastatātiṁ
   cidāyave.

7. *Sa hi ṣmā dhanvākṣitaṁ dātā*
na dātyā paśuḥ,
hiriśmaśruḥ śucidannṛbhur
anibhṛṣṭataviṣiḥ.

8. *Śuciḥ ṣma yasmā atrivatpra*
svadhitīva rīyate,
sushūrasūta mātā krāṇā yad
ānaśe bhagam.

9. *Ā yaste sarpirāsute'gne śam*
asti dhāyase,
aiṣu dyumnamuta śrava ā cittam
martyeṣu dhāḥ.

10. *Iti cinmanyumadhrijastvādātam*
ā paśuṁ dade,
ādagne apṛṇato'triḥ sāsahyād
dasyuniṣaḥ sāsahyānnṛn.[82]

1. O fellow-strivers, offer all that is best in you to the Fire-divine, the absolute force of supreme impulsion; utterly establish him within who is the master of Force, the son of infinite Energy, and who lavishes all his wealth on the dwellers in the world.

2. The seeker-soul finds its joyous fulfilment when it meets him, the shining God, in his dwelling (the supramental plane). Even the worthiest and wisest of seekers constantly and continuously kindle the flame of him, as also all the creatures ceaselessly strive to bring him to perfect birth.

3. Only when the seeker possesses perfectly and enjoys fully the secret strengths of impulsion, and offers his all as a sacrifice that he receives the Light, realises the Force and reaches the Truth.

4. Verily he bestows the light of right-seeing even on him who is lost in the darkness of the Night; for, he is the undecaying, invincible fighter, the supreme purifier who compresses the lords of the forest and brings about the growths of the earth, and produces the immortalising wine of delight.

5. Only when the seekers sweat hard in the sacrifice, and offer their all to him on their paths, that they ascend to him who sits self-victorious on the summit-planes of existence founded on the Truth, free and infinite.

6. The mortal seeker comes to know of him (through sacrifice) as the one who transforms all his human desires (and enjoyments) to be able to establish in him the divine all. He devours all that is material and mortal in us and builds the home of complete Beatitude for us.

7. Truly, he tears down the desert of material existence unwatered by the streams of the Truth, even as the Animal does with its food. He with his beard of golden light and shining teeth purifies us (and enforces the desired change).

8. Blessed indeed is the seeker for whom as for the Son of Force there is the continuous self-ordering progression of Nature as with an axe. His Mother, the World-Energy, brings him forth that he may lead us through the woods of material existence and bless us with the experience of divine bliss.

9. O adorable mighty God, may you press out on us the perennial puissance. When you come across some one who is founded in the peace and joy of accomplished labour (the strenuous work of sacrifice), in him pray establish the desired illumination, wisdom and the conscious soul.

10. O adorable Lord, may I who is a creature in the material existence receive your gift of emotional mind and the illumined mind. May you, O Son of Force and the Eater of things, destroy the Dividers (the powers of Darkness) who impede true progress; may you overcome those who attack the seekers with negative and harmful impulsions.

(viii)

Agni, the Flame of the Truth, represents the continuity of the battle for Light in Nature since the beginning of Time. He is the innate growth process of creation, the burning nisus in the universe itself. He is the puissant seer, the supremely desirable quest and the master of the house who fulfils the divine Will in all.

1. *Tvāmagna ṛtāyavaḥ samīdhire pratnaṁ*
pratnāsa ūtaye sahaskṛta,
puruścandraṁ yajataṁ viśvadhāyasaṁ
damūnasaṁ gṛhapatiṁ vareṇyam.

2. *Tvāmagne atithiṁ pūrvyaṁ viśaḥ*
śociṣkeśaṁ gṛhapatiṁ ni ṣedire,
bṛhatketuṁ pururūpaṁ dhanaspṛtaṁ
suśarmāṇaṁ svavasaṁ jaradviṣam.

3. *Tvāmagne mānuṣirīḷate viśo hotrāvidaṁ*
viviciṁ ratnadhātamam,
guhā santaṁ subhaga viśvadarśataṁ
tuviṣvaṇasaṁ suyajaṁ ghṛtaśriyam.

4. *Tvāmagne dharṇasiṃ viśvadhā vayam gīrbhir*
gṛṇanto namasopa sedima,
sa no juṣasva samidhāno aṅgiro devo
martasya yaśasā sudītibhiḥ.

5. *Tvāmagne pururūpo viśeviśe vayo*
dadhāsi pratnathā puruṣṭuta,
purūṇyannā sahasā vi rājasi tviṣiḥ
sā te titviṣaṇasva nādhṛṣe.

6. *Tvāmagne samidhānaṁ yaviṣṭhya devā*
dūtaṃ cakrire havyavāhanam,
urujrayasaṁ ghṛtayonimāhutaṁ tveṣaṁ
cakṣurdadhire codayanmati.

7. *Tvāmagne pradiva āhutaṁ ghṛtaiḥ sumnāyavaḥ*
suṣamidhā samīdhire,
sa vāvṛdhāna oṣadhibhirukṣito'bhi
jrayāṅsi pārthivā vi tiṣṭhase.[83]

1. O Seer-Will, you have by your strength created in us the flaming inspiration; the seekers of the Truth from the earliest times have enkindled you in their hearts that they might grow in their being. O adorable God in the sacrifice, supreme indweller and Master of the dwelling, well-founded in manifold delights, you have truly fostered all.

2. O Seer-Will, you are the supreme Indweller and the original Guest well-enshrined in our hearts. You are brilliant with your flowing locks of light and multi-formed and vast-visioned. In you the seekers take their foundation for the evulsion of their varied wealth, and for the perfect peace and truest being, and for the destruction of the Adversary.

3. O Seer-Will, men glorify you and seek you with their offering, who has perfect knowledge of the powers of the sacrifice and the process of oblation, and with right discrimination holds for the seekers utter delight. O you right Enjoyer, seated securely in our secret being, endowed with a universal vision, you pour out multitudinous voices and perform perfectly the sacrifice with purified and clarified thoughts.

4. O Seer-Will, you are the all-sustaining universal law of things; we approach you with adoration and submission, and express you in our hymns of praise. May you, O self-illumined puissant seer, approve and accept our oblation; rejoice by the splendour of the mortal's victorious attainment of right illuminings.

5. O Seer-Will, you, who take multiple forms according to the needs of men and establish for each worshipper his widest manifestation, illumine by your might the many things that are your food; none can rival your splendour when you so blaze up brightest in your strength supreme.

6. O Seer-Will, most vigorous and mighty, the gods without exception kindle you high and make you their effective messenger and the carrier of their oblations; wide and swift in workings, born of perfect and pure mind, you are the receiver of their offerings. The gods have set you in the seeker as a burning, ever vigilant, all-seeing eye that promotes illumined awareness.

7. O Seer-Will, seekers of bliss supreme kindle you in their hearts with earnestness and utter devotion, constantly fed by the clarities of the pure mind; so increasing, and spreading your heat all over the earth, you enter widely into the earth-life's upward movements.

(ix)

Agni, the divine Will, manifests increasingly with the working of the pure mental on the material consciousness. However, its involved action can be inferred from the stirrings of the nervous, emotional states of the human being. His presence becomes overtly cognisable at the psychological and spiritual levels when he is firmly set for liberation and spiritual conquest. His ascent to the Truth is the saga of heroic struggle, of effective mediation between men and the gods, of felicitous commutation between heaven and earth.

1. *Tvāmagne haviṣmanto devaṁ*
martāsa īḷate,
manye tvā jātavedasaṁ sa havyā
vakṣyānuṣak.

2. *Agnirhotā dāsvataḥ kṣayasya*
vṛktabarhiṣaḥ,
saṁ yajñāsaścaranti yaṁ saṁ
vājāsaḥ śravasyavaḥ.

3. *Uta sma yaṁ śiśuṁ yathā navaṁ*
janiṣṭāraṇī,
dhartāraṁ mānuṣīṇāṁ viśām
agniṁ svadhvaram.

4. *Uta sma durgṛbhīyase putro*
na hvāryāṇām,
purū yo dagdhāsi vānāgne
paśurna yavase.

5. *Adha sma yasyārcayaḥ samyak*
saṁyanti dhūminaḥ,
yadimaha trito divyupa dhmāteva
dhamati śiśīte dhmātarī yathā.

6. *Tavāhamagna ūtibhirmitrasya*
ca praśastibhiḥ,
dveṣoyuto na duritā turyāma
martyānām.

7. *Taṁ no agne abhī naro rayiṁ*
sahasva ā bhara,
sa kṣepayatsa poṣayadbhuvad
vājasya sātaya utaidhi pṛtsu no vṛdhe.[84]

1. Mortal men seek you and glorify you with oblations, O Seer-Will, on you I meditate who is cognisant of all soul-births; it is therefore that you bear our offerings to the goal without breach.

2. O Seer-Will, you are the high priest of our oblations, you liberally give us the boons and arrange the seat of sacrifice and attain to the Truth. In you, O adorable Lord, converge all our works of sacrifice, and congregate our plenitudes of Light and Bliss.

3. O Seer-Will, true it is that you are struck out of the two Aranis, like a new-born flame-child, you who are the mighty supporter of seekers. May you lead us all aright in the sacrifice.

4. It is indeed very hard to harness the Fire even as it is difficult to seize the crooked ones (the wriggling movements of our mortal existence), when it burns down the forests like an Animal that consumes its pastures.

5. O Fire-divine, your fiery rays blend entirely with their smoky passion, and finally the mental Purusha forges them 'like a smith in his smithy' and whets them all into one blazing weapon of sharpness.

6. O mighty Seer-Will, may we, through your own expandings by your manifestations of Mitra, escape the attacks of the enemies and pass through and beyond the many pitfalls and besieging discords.

7. O Seer-Will, bring to us that luminous plenitude; may we be pushed forward on our path, may we be nourished and increased that we may conquer the coveted wealth. O mighty one, accompany us in our struggles that we may overcome all difficulties and progress constantly.

(x)

The work of awakening the soul and its fulfilment is effectuated only when Agni acts by its threefold power of Light, Force and Delight. His flame-rays are overpowering and bear down the forces of resistance, and support the seeker to self-mastery and world-mastery. It is the continual affirmation of Agni in men that helps them to speed towards the supreme plenitude.

1. *Agna ojiṣṭhamā bhara dyumnam*
asmabhyamadhrigo,
pra no rāyā parīṇasā ratsi
vājāya panthām.

2. *Tvaṁ no agne adbhuta kratvā*
dakṣasya maṅhanā,
tve asurya māruhatkrāṇā
mitro na yajñiyaḥ.

3. *Tvaṁ no agna eṣāṁ gayaṁ*
puṣṭiṁ ca vardhaya,
ye stomebhiḥ pra sūrayo naro
maghānyānaśuḥ.

4. *Ye agne candra te giraḥ*
śumbhantyaśvarādhasaḥ,
śuṣmebhiḥ śuṣmiṇo naro divaścid
yeṣāṁ bṛhatsukīrtīrbodhati tmanā.

5. *Tava tye agne arcayo bhrājanto*
yanti dhṛṣṇuyā,
parijmāno na vidyutaḥ svāno
ratho na vājayuḥ.

6. *Nū no agna ūtaye sabādhasaś*
ca rātaye,
asmākāsaśca sūrayo viśvā
āśāstarīṣaṇi.

7. *Tvaṁ no agne aṅgiraḥ stuta*
stavāna ā bhara,
hotarvibhvāsahaṁ rayiṁ stotṛbhya
stavase ca na utaidhi pṛtsu no vṛdhe.[85]

1. O adorable Flame of limitless light, bring into our limited existence a ray of your powerful illumination; may you invest us with an all-encompassing felicity that we may leap forward on the path towards the supreme plenitude.

2. O marvellous Flame, O Supreme Lord, you invest us with the force of your illumined Will that grows into the power of discernment. It is in you that the Lord of Love and Harmony accomplishes the work of sacrifice, and helps us to climb to the divine mastery.

3. O mighty Flame, may you increase the attainment, and promote the progress of illumined souls that they may, by their affirmations of you, attain to the fullness of the Truth.

4. O blissful Lord, O mighty one, they enjoy the wealth of vitality who turn their luminous thoughts to you; they are the powerful souls with heroic attainments who on the summits of their pure mentality enjoy the immense Vastness. For them the luminous mind by its own perfect workings awakes to the Truth.

5. O mighty Lord, your flaming rays that blaze forth are like the lightnings flashing around in all directions; like a strident chariot they speed forward towards the supreme felicity.

6. O adorable Lord, may those who are needy and oppressed, equally progress and attain to the soul's plenitude; may the enlightened ones travel all the regions of the heavens of mental existence as well as go beyond.

7. O mighty Lord, O Soul of supreme felicity, when you are luminously established in us, and in your affirmation you bring to us the wealth of an all-pervading forcefulness that again makes us affirm your splendour. May you march with us and support us in our struggles that we may steadily progress.

(xi)

Agni is the ever vigilant, keenly observing and divining sacrificial Flame. His vision and will turn human passion into illumined consciousness. His concealed presence can be felt in all that the seeker-soul enjoys. He shines wide in the three worlds of mind, life and body, the vicar of the sacrifice. Undaunted and pure, born of heaven and earth, ecstatic and all-luminous, he increases with the clarity of mind.

1. *Janasya gopā ajaniṣṭa jāgṛviragniḥ*
sudakṣaḥ suvitāya navyase,
ghṛtapratiko bṛhatā divispṛśā dyumad
vi bhāti bharatebhyaḥ śuciḥ.

2. *Yajñasya ketuṁ prathamaṁ purohitamagniṁ*
narastriṣadhasthe samīdhire,
indreṇa devaiḥ sarathaṁ sa barhiṣi sīdan
ni hotā yajathāya sukratuḥ.

3. *Asammṛṣto jāyase mātroḥ śucirmandraḥ*
kavirudatiṣṭho vivasvataḥ,
ghṛtena tvāvardhayannagna āhuta dhūmas
te keturabhavaddivi śritaḥ.

4. *Agnirno yajñamupa vetu sādhuyāgniṁ*
naro vi bharante gṛhegṛhe,
agnirdūto abhavaddhavyavāhano'gniṁ
vṛṇānā vṛṇate kavikratum.

5. *Tubhyedamagne madhumattamaṁ vacastubhyaṁ*
manīṣā iyamastu śaṁ hṛde,
tvāṁ giraḥ sindhumivāvanīrmahīrā pṛṇanti
śavasā vardhayanti ca.

6. *Tvāmagne aṅgiraso guhā hitamanvavindañ*
chiśriyāṇaṁ vanevane,
sa jāyase mathyamānaḥ saho mahattvamāhuḥ
sahasasputramaṅgiraḥ.[86]

1. O adorable Flame, O supreme Protector, ever wakeful and perfect in discernment, you are constantly born for a new march to greater plenitude. You are full of clarities, pure and liberal in benefactions; shining wide you touch the summits.

2. The seekers, in the sacrifice, kindle the Flame in the triple world of mind, life and body for the vision, and to be their vicar. He, the adorable One, arrives in his shining chariot armed with 'the God-Mind and the divine Powers' and leads the sacrifice; he is the perfect Priest, the luminous Will-Power who successfully conducts our sacrifice.

3. O resplendent Seer-Will, essentially pure, born of the Aranis twain, you arise from the all-luminous sun. The worshippers have intensified you with their clarities, O adorable Flame; your passion-smoke of the vital gets transformed into lambent vision when it reaches the heavens of the Truth.

4. O adorable Flame, fulfiller of our seekings, may you come to our sacrifice. The strivers carry you and instal you in every plane of their being, for you are the right messenger and carrier of their oblation. The wise readily accept the Flame for it is their own seer-will.

5. O adorable Flame, to you this honeyed hymn is offered; for you are our luminous thoughts, to increase in you the peace and happiness pure. For truly the perfect clarities of consciousness intensify you even as the streams of the Truth from heavens increase the ocean of our existence.

6. O adorable Flame, the ancient fathers discovered you in the subconscient regions, hidden in all things; you are born by our intense sacrificial toil, and your immense glory manifested. Therefore, O Puissance they call you the prime Source of Strength.

(xii)

Agni, the Lord of the superconscient Truth, is invoked to accept the oblation of pure thought of the seeker and become Truth-conscient in him. For, the seeker can attain to the supreme status not by the force of his effort, nor by the law of the twofold truth of existence, but by the Truth itself. The powers of this great Seer-Will not only guard and conquer the forces of Falsehood but help the Truth-seeker in his upward march. In addition, Agni with his clear vision, creates in us the knowledge of the new expression of the Truth as opposed to the old that clings to the foundation of falsehood and resists progress.

1. *Prāgnaye bṛhate yajñiyāya ṛtasya*
vṛṣṇe asurāya manma,
ghṛtaṁ na yajña āsye supūtaṁ giram
bhare vṛṣabhāya pratīcīm.

2. *Ṛtaṁ cikitva ṛtamiccikiddhyṛtasya*
dhārā anu tṛndhi pūrviḥ,
nāhaṁ yātuṁ sahasā na dvayena ṛtaṁ
sapāmyaruṣasya vṛṣṇaḥ.

3. *Kayā no agna ṛtayannṛtena bhuvo*
navedā ucathasya navyaḥ,
vedā me deva ṛtupā ṛtūnāṁ nāhaṁ patiṁ
saniturasya rāyaḥ.

4. *Ke te agne ripave bandhanāsaḥ ke pāyavaḥ*
saniṣanta dyumantaḥ,
ke dhāsimagne anṛtasya pānti ka āsato
vacasaḥ santi gopāḥ.

5. *Sakhāyaste viṣuṇā agna ete śivāsaḥ*
santo aśivā abhūvan,
adhūrṣata svayamete vacobhirṛjūyate
vṛjināni bruvantaḥ.

6. *Yaste agne namasā yajñamiṭṭa ṛtaṁ*
sa pātyaruṣasya vṛṣṇaḥ,
tasya kṣayaḥ pṛthurā sādhuretu
prasarsrāṇasya nahuṣasya śeshaḥ.[87]

1. O Seer-Will, the mighty master of the sacrifice, to you I offer all my purified thoughts just as clarified butter is poured in the mouth of the flame. To you, O adorable Lord, great radiator of the Truth, I bring my luminous Word that fronts and offers itself to the Godhead.

2. O Seer-Will, the great seer of the Truth, see the Truth alone in me, and bring forth streams of the Truth from within me. Neither physical force, nor mental division and duality can help me on the path, much less can they lead me to the Truth. You alone are the luminous Labourer, the sustaining God.

3. O Seer-Will, by what effective luminous thought in us do you 'seeking the Truth by the Truth' grow to actuate us to become aware of the Word. O Lord of the plenitudes, guardian of the periods of the progress of our sacrifice, I know not him who knows all in me.

4. O Seer-Will, who are the vanquishers of the Enemy? Who are the guardians, the protectors, the seekers and conquerors of the shining wealth? Who, O adorable Lord are the friends of Falsehood, who the defenders of the false word?

5. O Seer-Will, those who abandoned you and gone astray are unhappy; they who were once kind and gracious have now turned malignant. They indeed do harm to themselves who speak ill of those who seek after righteousness.

6. O Seer-Will, he who performs assiduously your sacrifice, lives truly according to the Law of the luminous Labourer, the great Diffuser of abundance. May he attain the wide world of the Truth in which all is accomplished and perfected, as also everything in this phenomenal world.

(xiii)

It is Agni who enables man to win the spiritual wealth and attain to the Truth. He is central to his inner progress and holds all other gods within his being as the nave of a wheel contains the spokes. Having been affirmed by the Word, Agni becomes the priest of the sacrifice and brings for his devotees the divine substance.

1. *Arcantastvā havāmahe'rcantaḥ samidhīmahi,*
   agne arcanta ūtaye.

2. *Agneḥ stomaṁ manāmahe sidhramadya divispṛśaḥ,*
   devaṣya draviṇasyavaḥ.

3. *Agnirjuṣata no giro hotā yo mānuṣeṣvā,*
   sa yakṣaddaivyaṁ janam.

4. *Tvamagne saprathā asi juṣṭo hotā vareṇyaḥ,*
   tvayā yajñaṁ vi tanvate.

5. *Tvāmagne vājasātamaṁ viprā vardhanti suṣṭutam,*
sa no rāsva suvīryam.

6. *Agne nemirarāṅ̃ iva devāṅ̃stvam paribhurasi,*
ā rādhaścitramṛñjase.[88]

1. O adorable Lord, with hymns of praise we invoke you; with words of illumination we enkindle you, and invoking you we seek your support for our progress.

2. Aspiring to be illumined, O Seer-Will, we recite the hymn of all-effective affirmation of you; may you find for us our divine felicity; verily your radiance touches the heavenly dwelling.

3. O Seer-Will, the luminous priest in us all, may you accept our oblations; may you offer the sacrifice and bear our offerings to the enlightened ones.

4. O Seer-Will, widest and vastest of godheads, you are the most cherished and longed for priest of the offering. By you the seekers extend wide their sacred works of sacrifice.

5. O Seer-Will, the wise ones by establishing you within themselves rapidly increase, so that you may conquer for them the celestial plenitude. May you bestow upon them perfect vitality and total virility.

6. O Seer-Will, O adorable Lord, you encompass in your being all the gods, as the nave of a wheel contains all the spokes. May you bestow upon us the varied joy of those manifold riches.

(xiv)

Agni is described as the finder of the world of the Sun of Truth, as the destroyer of the forces of Falsehood and the one who constantly supports the seeker's movement towards the Truth. He always increases by the clarities of right thought of those who worship him; they increase him by their positive approach and praise.

1. *Agniṁ stomena bodhaya samidhāno amartyam,*
havyā deveṣu no dadhat.

2. *Tamadhvareṣvīḷate devaṁ martā amartyam,*
yajiṣṭhaṁ mānuṣe jane.

3. *Taṁ hi śaśvanta īḷate srucā devaṁ ghṛtaścutā,*
agniṁ havyāya voḷhave.

4. *Agnirjāto arocata ghnandasyūñjyotiṣā tamaḥ,*
avindad gā apaḥ svaḥ.

5. *Agnimīḷenyaṁ kaviṁ ghṛtapṛṣṭhaṁ saparyata,*
vetu me śṛṇavaddhavam.

6. *Agniṁ ghṛtena vāvṛdhuḥ stomebhirviśvacarṣaṇim,*
svādhībhirvacasyubhiḥ.[89]

1. May we awaken the Flame by the luminous Word that establishes him; may we intensify the immortal Fire that he can bear our oblations to the gods above.

2. Mortal men extol him in their sacrifice; he is the strongest, the immortal in the creatures, the divine and the most adorable and helpful in sacrifice.

3. Generations of worshippers, constantly lifted in aspiration, adore him with the ladle dripping with clarified butter, they glorify the Fire-divine that he may carry their oblations.

4. The Fire-divine, when born destroys the powers of Darkness; yes, he dissolves the Night with the Light. He restores the trooping Rays, the luminous movement of the Waters, and reveals the solar world of the Truth.

5. May we serve and seek the Fire-divine; he is the object of our worship, the source of all illuminations. May he respond to my invocation.

6. Men increase the Seer-Will by the offering of their illuminations; they intensify the Flame by their affirmative hymns of praise which are uniquely purifying of thought, and express the revealing Word.

(xv)

He is the Mighty One, the seer and the ordainer to whom the Rishi brings the offering of the victorious Word. Established in bliss, he upholds the Truth by which the seekers travel to the godheads unborn and are seated in the supreme heavens. Like an angry lion he breaks through the encircling armies of the opposers and confirms for the seeker many new births and builds in him the firm citadel of the superconscient, and by increasing his illumined knowledge delivers him into the vast world of immortality.

1. *Pra vedhase kavaye vedyāya giraṁ*
bhare yaśase pūrvyāya,
ghṛtaprasatto asuraḥ suśevo rāyo
dhartā dharuṇo vasvo agniḥ.

2. *Ṛtena ṛtaṃ dharuṇaṁ dhārayanta*
yajñasya śāke parame vyoman,
divo dharmandharuṇe seduṣo nṛñ
jātairajātāñ abhi ye nanakṣuḥ.

3. *Aṅhoyuvastanvastanvate vi vayo mahad*
duṣṭaram pūrvyāya,
sa saṁvato navajātastuturyātsiṅhaṁ na
kruddhamabhitaḥ pari ṣṭhuḥ.

4. *Māteva yadbharase paprathāno janañjanaṁ*
dhāyase cakṣase ca,
vayovayo jarase yaddadhānaḥ pari tmanā
viṣurūpo jigāsi.

5. *Vājo nu te śavasaspātvantamuruṁ doghaṁ*
dharuṇaṁ deva rāyaḥ,
padaṁ na tāyurguhā dadhāno mahó rāye
citayannatrimaspaḥ.[90]

1. He is the Seer and Director; he alone is the object of our knowledge and adoration. I bring to him the offering of the luminous Word, who is the most magnificent and triumphant, the mighty and the adorable ever marching forward to the illuminations; to him I offer my oblations who is blissful and Truthful.

2. It is by the Truth that the wise ones uphold the Truth that holds everything; they find it manifested in the sacrifice and in the heavens above. Even those, who progress by the birth and growth of the godheads within them and travel much beyond to heavenly heights, wherein are established in the Law still higher Powers, do so by the sole sustenance of the Truth.

3. They, who create pure and receptive and broad-based embodiments for the manifestation of progressive soul-formations which facilitate the vast birth of the Fire-divine, indeed, put away, all evil and crookedness and decision from their substance. The new-born Son of Force, the fiery Flame breaks through the hordes of the Adversary that darkly converge upon him; the Powers of Darkness surround and beset him like vile hunters who encircle an irate lion.

4. O adorable Fire-divine, even when you are pervading everywhere, you carry us in your loving arms like a fond mother, birth after birth, uplifting us to the wide vision and to the firm divine foundation. O universal Fire, you hold in you many manifestations and enjoy them all; also, you assume several forms and constantly grow through them.

5. O mighty godhead, may our plenitude be the vastest and the richest of your possessions that in its abundance upholds the bliss divine. O adorable Lord, we seek refuge in you who shapes and sustains the supreme abode towards which we all move; by awakening us to the truth of this knowledge you have rescued the petty enjoyer in us for the realisation of that supreme beatitude.

(xvi)

The Rishi becomes aware within him and in all men of the presence of the Divine Will that is the source and strength of all that seeks to manifest. It is Agni who brings light and knowledge and felicity to the seeker-sacrificer; in him is contained the power and the plenitude of all the gods.

1. *Bṛhadvayo hi bhānave'rcā devāyāgnaye,*
yam mitraṁ na praśastibhirmartāso
dadhire puraḥ.

2. *Sa hi dyubhirjanānāṁ hotā*
dakṣasya bāhvoḥ,
vi havyamagnirānuṣagbhago
na vāramṛṇvati.

3. *Asya stome maghonaḥ sakhye*
vṛddhaśociṣaḥ,
viśvā yasmintuviṣvaṇi sam
arye śuṣmamādadhuḥ.

4. *Adhā hyagna eṣāṁ suvīryasya*
maṅhanā,
tamidyahvaṁ na rodasī pari
śravo babhūvatuḥ.

5. *Nū na ehi vāryamagne*
gṛṇāna ā bhara,
ye vayaṁ ye ca sūrayaḥ svasti dhāmahe
sacotaidhi pṛtsu no vṛdhe.[91]

1. May we sing hymns of praise for a vaster and diviner manifestation of your light and might, O adorable Lord and friend of mortals; by our worship of you, may we set in front of our consciousness your Mitra-power (of love and harmony).

2. O Seer-Will, you are the priest of our oblations; by the clarities of conscious thoughts you carry forward our Godward work without interruption through the right stages of the march of sacrifice. And with your Bhaga-power you move to the enjoyment of the divine living.

3. O Force-divine, in your predication and in your fellowship when you grow purest and mightiest, you contain and sustain all the gods of varied plenitudes. O adorable one, in your voice are embodied all the other voices; on your mounting aspiration they depend for their strength and onward movement.

4. O Seer-Will, may all the godheads attain the fullness of their luminous force. As you move about among them, may the conscious-

ness of earth and heaven become full of the Truth-Knowledge bringing about their desired transfiguration.

5. O Seer-Will, may you luminously and constantly grow in us hymned by our inspired words, and bring to us our precious plenitude. May we, your worshippers, as well as the wise ones together attain that desirable state of beatitude; may you always move with us in our struggles that we may steadily grow.

(xvii)

In his marathon search for the ultimate good man arrives at a state beyond all intelligence in which he experiences the infinitude of soul and the ecstasy and felicity of the wideness of knowledge. He enjoys the full possession of his soul-force and soul-knowledge. Nonetheless, he needs a greater power to carry him further beyond to the divine source of all thought and action. Agni alone has the light, the mantric Word, the right actuation and the power of perfect effectuation. He has the all-embracing knowledge and the all-achieving authority and capacity; he is the secret godhead in all creatures who has to be expressed and manifested.

1. *Ā yajñairdeva martya itthā*
   tavyāṅsamūtaye,
agniṁ kṛte svadhvare pūrur
   īḷītāvase.

2. *Asya hi svayaśastara āsā*
   vidharmanmanyase,
taṁ nākaṁ citraśociṣaṁ mandraṁ
   paro manīṣayā.

3. *Asya vāsā u arciṣā ya āyukta*
   tujā girā,
divo na yasya retasā bṛhac
   chocantyarcayaḥ.

4. *Asya kratvā vicetaso dasmasya*
   vasu ratha ā,
adhā viśvāsu havyo'gnirvikṣu
   pra śasyate.

5. *Nū na iddhi vāryamāsā sacanta*
sūrayaḥ,
ūrjo napādabhiṣṭaye pāhi śagdhi
svastaya utaidhi pṛtsu no vṛdhe.[92]

1. The awakened mortal, for his enlightenment, invokes the radiant God who is mightier and righteous in works. May he of multiple soul, who has attained perfection in sacrifice, worship the resplendent Seer-Will for his steady increasing.

2. O seeker of pure illumination, you who have attained to the larger working of consciousness and power in your being by the strength of the Seer-Will, will be readied for greater attainment, and embody in the mind the celestial splendour of his richest flamings and the heavens of rapturous bliss beyond the reach of the mind.

3. Verily, by the strength and splendour of the Flame, the sacrificer has united himself with the forward-moving Force and the inspired Word, and growing vast flashes on high as though springing from the seed of heaven.

4. O Fire-divine, by the force of your fiery workings, the all-embracing knowledge and the all-conquering power, your chariot carries heavenly opulence. Verily, O adorable Lord, you are the godhead in all creatures who is sought to be expressed and whom they invoke and glorify.

5. O Son of Energy, may the luminous gods in us keep our consciousness firmly established in the Light and the Truth; protect us that we may fulfil our aspirations and attain our highest state of beatitude. May you always be with us in our struggles and effectuate our growth.

(xviii)

Agni is the Lord of the plenitudes. He is invoked to manifest his powers at every stage on the epic journey. After breaking through the shackles of the inconscient material existence when man arrives at the vital plane he is bestowed by Agni with the vibrant energies of life's play. And when the seeker now enters the third state, the mental, then once again Agni enriches him with the workings of the free and luminous mind capable of manifesting in him the first rays of the supramental Light. This state of realisation consequently leads to the manifestation of the intuitive mind. All along, Agni is the inspiration, Agni is the strength. He is the constant guide and the vigilant warrior. The pilgrim's journey is not complete with the attainment of an inspired and illumined consciousness; he has many more plateaus to ascend beyond the god-filled vitality and the intuitive mind. He has to enter the state of Truth-Knowledge itself which needs a vastest foundation of light and purity. And Agni, the dependable friend of the seeker, creates this condition with which he crowns all his realisations.

1. *Prātaragniḥ purupriyo viśa*
stavetātithiḥ,
viśvāni yo amartyo havyā
marteṣu raṇyati.

2. *Dvitāya mṛktavāhase svasya*
dakṣasya maṁhanā,
induṁ sa dhatta ānuṣakstotā
citte amartya.

3. *Taṁ vo dīrghāyuśociṣaṁ girā*
huve maghonām,
ariṣṭo yeṣāṁ ratho vy
aśvadāvannīyate.

4. *Citrā vā yeṣu dīdhitirāsann*
ukthā pānti ye,
stīrṇaṁ barhiḥ svarṇare śravāṅsi
dadhire pari.

5. *Ye me pañcāśataṁ daduraśvānāṁ*
sadhastuti,
dyumadagne mahi śravo bṛhatkṛdhi
maghonāṁnṛvadamṛta nṛṇām.[93]

1. May we affirm you, O Seer-Will, in the dawning of the higher knowledge. You are the shining guest of the creatures; you are the immortal in us mortals, O Flame of multiple delights, take joy in all our oblations.

2. O ascending Flame, you are the fullness of your own luminous mind for ascent to the plane of fulfilled Life-Force where you enjoy a purified, limitless and free intelligence. It is then O immortal Flame, that you hold in yourself streams of the wine of delight ever affirming you.

3. O pure Flame, verily, you are the plenitude of the far-extending existence beyond material and vital limitations for the godheads whose divine movements are fulfilled there unhindered by the Powers of Darkness and Death.

4. In a still higher realm of the soul's ascent, the godheads of supreme felicity are replete with the rich light of consciousness and hold our sublimest hymns in their mouth. It is here that the fullness of the soul and its inspirations and illuminations formed by the Truth is spread out as a seat of sacrifice.

5. O Flame-Immortal, may you bestow the vast and most luminous knowledge on those divine souls, the godheads of the varied plenitudes, who have given me fully the swiftest Life-forces with a perfect affirmation.

(xix)

Agni helps the seeker to penetrate one by one all the higher states of consciousness and existence leading to the vast world of the divine Light and Truth. The supramental is closed to the embodied soul; the physical and mental consciousness are closed, resistant and impervious to the Supramental Light. But by the persistent action of the divine Will, Agni, by the flaming onslaught of his omnipotent life-force he not only opens the vital-mental to the supramental, but welds the former with it, and harmonises them all in the wideness of the divine knowledge.

1. *Abhyavasthāḥ pra jāyante pra*
vavrervavriściketa,
upasthe māturvi caṣṭe.

2. *Juhure vi citayanto'nimiṣaṁ*
nṛmṇam pānti,
ā dṛḷhām puraṁ viviśuḥ.

3. *Ā śvaitreyasya jantavo dyumad*
vardhanta kṛṣṭayaḥ,
niṣkagrīvo bṛhaduktha enā
madhvā na vājayuḥ.

4. *Priyaṁ dugdhaṁ na kāmyamajāmi*
jāmyoḥ sacā,
gharmo na vājajaṭharo'dabdhaḥ
śaśvato dabhaḥ.

5. *Kriḷanno raśma ā bhuvaḥ saṁ*
bhasmanā vāyunā vevidānaḥ,
tā asya sandhṛṣajo na tigmāḥ susaṁśitā
vakṣyo vakṣaṇesthāḥ.[94]

1. Plane upon plane of consciousness is born, veil upon veil opens revealing ever-new realms of knowledge; in the bosom of the infinite Mother, the seeker-soul attains the all-embracing vision.

2. O immortal Flame, those who are awakened to your all-embracing knowledge invoke you incessantly and offer their oblations; they feed the sleepless Fire and enter the well-guarded city of the Truth, and stay unharmed and unhurt.

3. O Son of the white-shining Aditi, those who are earnest in worship and work hard at the sacrifice, increase your splendour and shining strength. You, O Golden Flame, are the Sun of the Truth, who has the vast Word with which, and drunk with the wine of divine delight, you seek the heavenly plenitudes for us.

4. O adorable Lord, you are the most desirable and delightful shining offspring of Aditi; you are the all-creating and self-sufficing Strength and Light far superior to and above all phenomenal planes of existence, yet dwell with the two companions (of the physical and mental). Verily, you are the luminosity of the Light and the foundations of all felicity, the eternal invincible Fire that conquers all obstacles.

5. O most luminous Ray, may you be born in us and grow there blending your Light with the shining Life-god. May your flames, O

Seer-Will, that bear our sacrifices be fierce and fiery and intensified and firmly founded in the supreme Bearer of all things.

(xx)

The goal of the aspirant is a state of spiritual felicity which ensures purity, perfection and unity and identity with the divine workings in the universe, a state in which falsehood and disunity have no room. This can be attained by increasing the divine Force in him, which will eventually and invariably result in the attainment of the Truth and the Bliss.

1. *Yamagne vājasātama tvaṁ cin*
manyase rayim,
taṁ no gīrbhiḥ śravāyyaṁ devatrā
panayā yujam.

2. *Ye agne nerayanti te vṛddhā*
ugrasya śavasaḥ,
apa dveṣo apa hvaro'nyavratasya
saścire.

3. *Hotāraṁ tvā vṛṇīmahe'gne*
dakṣasya sādhanam,
yajñeṣu pūrvyaṁ girā prayasvanto
havāmahe.

4. *Itthā yathā ta ūtaye sahasāvan*
divedive,
rāya ṛtāya sukrato gobhiḥ ṣyāma
sadhamādo vīraiḥ syāma sadhamādaḥ.[95]

1. O Seer-Will, O procurer of our plenitude, may the supreme felicity that is beyond the comprehension of the divisive mind, be increased by your works and strengthened by our illumined thoughts; may that felicity increasing in the gods promote our progress.

2. May those powers, who increase in their strength and wealth by you and yet do not help us on the path, invariably become victims of division and limitation, and cling to a crooked law other than yours.

3. O Seer-Will, we joyously accept you as the priest of our oblations and the promoter of discerning knowledge. We adore you, and offer you all our delights, and invoke you, O ancient and Supreme one, to our sacrifices.

4. O mighty Lord, O perfect power of works, may we steadily increase in our plenitudes that we attain to the Bliss and the Truth, and realise the rapture of the Rays of the pure knowledge and the felicity of the pure Force.

(XXI)

Agni, the divine Flame, is invoked by the Rishi to burn steadily and increasingly as the Divine's representative in man, and to lead him successfully to the seat of the supreme Truth, Perfection and Bliss.

1. *Manuṣvattvā ni dhīmahi manuṣvat*
   samidhīmahi,
agne manuṣvadaṅgiro devān
   devayate yaja.

2. *Tvaṁ hi mānuṣe jane'gne*
   suprīta idhyase,
srucastvā yantyānuṣak
   sujāta sarpirāsute.

3. *Tvāṁ viśve sajoṣaso devāso*
   dūtamakrata,
saparyantastvā kave yajñeṣu
   devamīḷate.

4. *Devaṁ vo devayajyayāgnimīḷīta*
   martyaḥ,
samiddhaḥ śukra dīdihyṛtasya yonim
   āsadaḥ sasasya yonimāsadaḥ.[96]

1. O adorable Flame, as men we instal you within us, as seekers we kindle you and offer sacrifices to the godheads that you may grow in us (and manifest your completeness, and we attain to the Truth).

2. O adorable Flame, you increase in the sacrificer when you are satisfied with his offerings; his invocations, like ladles filled with clarified butter, are constantly offered to you, O eternal seer and increaser of the plenitudes.

3. O adorable Seer, all the gods, of one accord, have confirmed you as their sole ambassador; they all worship you and serve you in their sacrifices as their resplendent Lord.

4. O Seer-Will, mortal men adore you as the Divine; they offer their sacrifices to the divine powers. O resplendent Lord, ever kindled, ever-increasing you shine out high in the heavens and enter the home of the Truth and the Bliss.

(xxii)

For the satisfactory, and perfect fulfilment of desires man needs purification, conscious vision and utter delight. And Agni is the godhead who holds in himself divine Light and Delight, Knowledge and the conquering Force. The seeker must therefore offer his all — physical, vital and mental — as food for the enjoyment of this godhead.

1. *Pra viśvasāmannatrivadarcā*
pāvakaṣociṣe,
yo adhvareṣvīḍyo hotā
mandratamo viśi.

2. *Nyagniṁ jātavedasaṁ dadhātā*
devamṛtvijam,
pra yajña etvānuṣagadyā
devavyacastamaḥ.

3. *Cikitvinmanasaṁ tvā devaṁ*
martāsa ūtaye,
vareṇyasya te'vasa iyānāso
amanmahi.

4. *Agne cikiddhyasya na idaṁ*
vacaḥ sahasya,
taṁ tvā suśipra dampate stomairvardhanty
atrayo gīrbhiḥ śumbhantyatrayaḥ.[97]

1. O adorable Lord, he who seeks your equal fulfilment in all things, invokes you as the supreme Enjoyer. O pure and purifying Flame, you are the object of our adoration in the progress of our struggles; may we always worship you, the flaming priest of our offering who provides happiness to all.

2. O Seer-Will, may we instal you within us who knows all our soul-births; you are the adorable sacrificer in all the seasons. O Fire-divine, may you move forward increasingly in the sacrifice, for it opens to us the whole epiphany of the cosmic Powers.

3. O adorable Lord, may we always enshrine you in our being, for you have the conscious mind and the supreme vision; we constantly invoke you on journey for our protection and for our progress. May we increase in the plenitude even as you grow in strength, the most appropriate to yearn for.

4. O Seer-Will, perennial source of strength, may we become aware of your Presence within us. This is our prayer to you, O supreme Enjoyer of things, master of our dwelling, may we steadily increase you by our affirmations, and by our praises embellish you and gladden you.

(xxiii)

On the road to the Truth — the world of Immortality, the armies of the Enemy of Light besiege the aspirant, and the forces of Darkness envelop him. It is only the powers of the divine Flame that can overpower and defeat them at all the successive levels of his ascent. Agni, the child of the Truth and the Son of strength, destroys the Adversary of the soul's progress, and makes available to the seeker all that he desires on all the planes for luminous enjoyment.

1. *Agne sahantamā bhara dyumnasya*
prāsahā rayim,
viśvā yaścarṣaṇīrabhyāsā
vājeṣu sāsahat.

2. *Tamagne pṛtanāṣahaṁ rayiṁ*
sahasva ā bhara,

tvaṁ hi satyo adbhuto dātā
vājasya gomataḥ.

3. *Viśve hi tvā sajoṣaso janāso*
vṛktabarhiṣaḥ,
hotāraṁ sadmasu priyaṁ vyanti
vāryā puru.

4. *Sa hi ṣmā viśvacarṣaṇirabhimāti*
saho dadhe,
agna eṣu kṣayeṣvā revannaḥ śukra
dīdihi dyumatpāvaka dīdihi.[98]

1. O Son of Force, bestow upon us that victory-yielding wealth of the Light, which in every area of our struggle will overcome the Adversary, and help us gain entry into the supreme fullnesses.

2. O mighty Flame, O Strength, grant us that felicity which shall vanquish the armies of the Enemy of our endeavour. Verily, O adorable Lord, you are the true and the transcendent, who gives us the supremely luminous felicity.

3. All men, with loving hearts and of one accord, have prepared the seat for you at the sacrifice; they enshrine you in all the cities of the soul, and instal you as the supreme priest of the works, and attain to their choicest felicities immanent in them.

4. O luminous Labourer, you are the one who strives in all our endeavours; you hold in yourself an all-conquering power. O radiant One, shine forth bright and full of joy in our dwelling places; O great Purifier, shine out in supreme resplendence.

(xxiv)

The Rishi filled with hope and certitude invokes Agni for continued protection from Evil and for the fullness of the divine knowledge and essentiality.

1-2. *Agne tvaṁ no antama uta trātā*
śivo bhavā varūthyaḥ,

vasuragnirvasuśravā acchā nakṣi
dyumattamaṁ rayiṁ dāḥ.

3-4. *Sa no bodhi śrudhī havamuruṣyā*
ṇo aghāyataḥ samasmāt,
taṁ tvā śociṣṭha dīdivaḥ sumnāya
nūnamīmahe sakhibhyaḥ.[99]

1-2. O Seer-Will, may you be our 'inmost inmate', our most intimate friend and protector, our gracious benefactor and supreme deliverer. O adorable Lord, you are the master of our being, the all-knower of our existence; remain always close to us, O divine dispenser of immortal food, bestow upon us 'the most luminous opulence' our substance can yield.

3-4. O ever-awake! Pray, listen to our prayers; may we be kept away from all those who seek to turn us to crookedness and wrong-doing. O most shining and the purest, we sincerely solicit your support for the happiness and peace of ourselves and all our friends.

(xxv)

Agni, the Seer-Will, is the embodiment of light and truth and the sumptuous bestower of the divine substance on the seeker. Himself born of the pure and luminous thought of the seers, he gives to us the divine truth and the power to fight the battle and to walk the journey to the desired goal. The movement is to the Superconscient, and the Seer-Will by its perfect working takes us beyond all limitation and darkness.

1. *Acchā vo agnimavase devaṁ*
gāsi sa no vasuḥ,
rāsatputra ṛshūṇāmṛtāvā
parṣati dviṣaḥ.

2. *Sa hi satyo yaṁ pūrve cid*
devāsaścidyamīdhire,
hotāraṁ mandrajihvamit
sudītibhirvibhāvasum.

3. *Sa no dhītī váriṣṭhayā śreṣṭhayā*
ca sumatyā,
agne rāyo didīhi naḥ suvṛktibhir
vareṇya.

4. *Agnirdeveṣu rājatyagnir*
marteṣvāviśan,
agnirno havyavāhano'gniṁ
dhībhiḥ saparyata.

5. *Agnistuviśravastamaṁ tuvibrahmāṇam*
uttamam,
atūrtaṁ śrāvayatpatiṁ putraṁ
dadāti dāśuṣe.

6. *Agnirdadāti satpatiṁ sāsāha*
yo yudhā nṛbhiḥ,
agniratyaṁ raghuṣyadaṁ
jetāramaparājitam.

7. *Yadvāhiṣṭhaṁ tadagnaye*
bṛhadarca vibhāvaso,
mahiṣīva tvadrayistvad
vajā udīrate.

8. *Tava dyumanto arcayo grāvevocyate*
bṛhat,
uto te tanyaturyathā svāno arta
tmanā divaḥ.

9. *Evañ agniṁ vasūyavaḥ sahasānaṁ*
vavandima,
sa no viśvā ati dviṣaḥ parṣan
nāveva sukratuḥ.[100]

1. O Seer-Will, may we constantly invoke you for our increasing; you are the lord of our substance, the benevolent granter of the bounties. You are born and nourished by the ardent devotion of the seekers, you are the upholder of the Truth and bear us beyond the reach of our destroyers.

2. The ancient seers kindled him in their being, and the gods too manifest his perfect splendour and the wide radiant substance. Verily, he is the high priest of our oblations who bears us to the world of bliss.

3. O adorable Flame, most worthy of our invocation by our luminous thinking and by our pure mind, may you with your surpassing will and wisdom give us the most desirable peace and bliss.

4. O adorable Seer-Will, you are the one that shines out in the gods above, as well as that which enters in all its splendour and glory into mortal men. You are the benevolent bearer of our oblations; may we ever seek and serve you in all our thoughts.

5. O Seer-Will, you in all your glory give yourself as a Son to the conscious sacrifice, who strengthened and emboldened by the many inspirations and illuminations of the seeker-soul grows into the highest, the invincible and the mightiest Master of things, and opens us to the Truth-Knowledge.

6. O Seer-Will, may you give yourself to us the Lord of all existences — the mighty and the most radiant form of yours, that helped by its heroic followers vanquishes the hordes of the Enemy. May you bestow us the swift-galloping war-horses who will carry us through the grim battle to the goal, 'ever conquering, never conquered'.

7. O adorable Lord, we offer to you that which is brightest and best in us. May you reveal to us the Vast, the substance of which is Light and Bliss. Your luminous opulence is as large as the vast Mother herself; it always takes us upward and Truthward.

8. O Fire-divine, most luminous and resplendent are your rays, and loud is your vast utterance like the joyous roar of clouds. And your cry of awakening rises up resounding like a thunder in the skies.

9. In search of our luminous soul-substance we glorify you, O adorable Will, the invincible Son of Force. May you, the perfect power of all workings, carry us beyond all our enemy-forces that seek to destroy us, like a boat over the waters.

(xxvi)

He is the high priest and the sacrificial flame, the luminous seer and the summoner of the gods, the carrier of the oblation and the conquerer of the hordes of the Enemy. He is the all-knower — knower of the manifold births of the soul on the journey — and the leader of the godward march to the supreme epiphany. He is the prime purifier, the bringer of perfect clarity and the increaser of the divine laws on all planes.

1. *Agne pāvaka rociṣā mandrayā deva jihvayā,*
ā devānvakṣi yakṣi ca.

2. *Taṁ tvā ghṛtasnavīmahe citrabhāno svardṛśam,*
devāñ ā vītaye vaha.

3. *Vītihotraṁ tvā kave dyumantaṁ samidhīmahi,*
agne bṛhantamadhvare.

4. *Agne viṣvebhirā gahi devebhirhavyadātaye,*
hotāraṁ tvā vṛṇīmahe.

5. *Yajamānāya ṣunvata agne suvīryaṁ vaha,*
devairā satsi barhiṣi.

6. *Samidhānaḥ sahasrajidagne dharmāṇi puṣyasi,*
devānāṁ dūta ukthyaḥ.

7. *Nyagniṁ jātavedasaṁ hotravāhaṁ yaviṣṭhyam,*
dadhātā devamṛtvijam.

8. *Pra yajña etvānuṣagadyā devavyacastamaḥ,*
stṛṇīta barhirāsade.

9. *Edaṁ maruto aśvinā mitraḥ sīdantu varuṇaḥ,*
devāsaḥ sarvayā viśā.[101]

1. O adorable Fire-divine, may you bring here to us, by your rapturous flames, the many godheads so that we would offer to them our sacrifice.

2. O Flame of clarities supreme, rich and bright and varied in radiance, we adore you for you have the vision of the supreme Truth. May you bring to us the godheads for their manifestations, for the journeying to the world of the Truth.

3. O Seer-Will, we worship you for the Light and the Vastness of radiance in the march of our sacrifice, and the carrying of the oblations on our journey.

4. O Seer-Will, come with all the godheads for accepting our offering; we accept you as the supreme priest of our sacrifice.

5. O Fire-divine bring pure and perfect vigour to him who readily offers you the libation of his delight. May you sit here with all the godheads in the sacrificial assembly and share the soul's fullnesses.

6. O adorable Flame, conqueror of manifold felicity, may you shine high and brilliant, and increase the Law; Verily you are the ambassador of the gods and have the divine Word.

7. May we enshrine in us the omniscient Flame who knows all the soul-births, the bearer of our oblations, the most vigorous and victorious and the supreme sacrificer on the many planes of the Truth.

8. O adorable Lord, may the sacrifice proceed forward uninterruptedly — the sacrifice that alone can bring about the luminous and effective manifestations of all the godheads. May we spread wide our hearts and our souls that they all may sit and participate in the sacrifice.

9. May all the life-powers, the Riders, the Lords of Love and of Vastness (the Maruts, the Ashwins, Mitra and Varuna) as well as all the godheads come and be seated here around the sacrifice and participate in its munificence.

(xxvii)

Traivrishna Tryaruna Trasadasyu is the one who by aspiration and askesis has attained the status of a demigod. He is the reflector and the receptor of the God-Mind that Indra symbolises, as well as the receiver in his vital being of the God-Will that Agni stands for. The Mind-Soul awakened to the Truth gives the Rishi the two vision-powers of direct truth discernment and intuition. While the Mind-Soul gives the seer mental intelligence and the power to possess and use it perfectly, the Life-Soul soaked in the divine Light saturated with the Truth gives him the multiple abundance native to the vital plane. It is the outpouring, as it were, of the wine of divine delight that raises the soul to supreme heights. The Rishi ardently prays that the Life-Soul may attain to the infinite truth-vision of the superconscient.

1. *Anasvantā satpatirmāmahe me gāvā*
cetiṣṭho asuro maghonaḥ,
traivṛṣṇo agne daśabhiḥ sahasrair
vaiśvānara tryaruṇaściketa.

2. *Yo me śatā ca viṁśatiṁ ca gonāṁ harī*
ca yuktā sudhurā dadāti,
vaiśvānara suṣṭuto vāvṛdhāno'gne
yaccha tryaruṇāya śarma.

3. *Evā te agne sumatiṃ cakāno naviṣṭhāya*
navamaṁ trasadasyuḥ,
yo me girastuvijātasya pūrvīryuktenābhi
tryaruṇo gṛṇāti.

4. *Yo ma iti pravocatyaśvamedhāya sūraye,*
dadadṛcā saniṁ yate dadanmedhāmṛtāyate.

5. *Yasya mā paruṣāḥ śatamuddharṣayanty*
ukṣaṇaḥ,
aśvamedhasya dānāḥ somā iva tryāśiraḥ.

6. *Indrāgnī śatadāvnyaśvamedhe suvīryam,*
kṣatraṁ dhārayataṁbṛhaddivi sūryam,
ivājaram.[102]

1. O Seer-Will, O mighty Flame, verily, you are supreme in vision, master of your being and lord of manifold riches. You have given me two cows of Light that pull your wagon. You are the Lord of the triple dawn, son of the triple Bull, Indra, the embodiment of complete

divine knowledge obtained as a series of illuminations of the human mentality in its entire plenitude.

2. O adorable Lord, bestower of countless and complete illuminations of divine knowledge, giver of two shining horses (the powers of direct truth-discernment and intuition) yoked to the shining chariot (the liberated pure mind). O Seer-Will, rightly established within us, may you, increasing, extend peace and bliss to our illumined mind.

3. Aspiring to have your Divine Mind it is given, and he new-manifests it, who then overcomes the hordes of the Adversary, he the lord of the triple dawn. Born on the higher plane, when I enter into numberless planes of consciousness, and from there rise up words expressive of their respective impulses, there he, the Mind-Soul, answers to these perfectly and satisfactorily.

4. O adorable Agni, may you who willingly give me everything, yourself give to the wise seer Ashwamedha (the Life-Soul, giver of Horse-sacrifice) by the word of illumination, the possession of supreme peace and bliss; may you grant the power of illumined intelligence to the seeker of the Truth.

5. A complete hundred Life-powers pouring out the wine of divine delight raise our souls to intoxicating heights. Equally ecstatic are the gifts of the sacrificer of the Horse with their threefold infusions into the mental, vital and physical.

6. May Indra and Agni (the God-Mind and the God-Will) uphold in the sacrificer of the Horse a perfect and vast energy (in the vital) even as they bestow infinite and immortal Light in heaven (in the mental).

(xxviii)

In a hymn of celebration, the Rishi praises Agni as the Flame of the divine Will who gives to the soul the mastery of Nature and its inexhaustible wealth. He is extolled as the shining guest who holds in himself the divine substance, as the illumined guide to the divine goal, and moving upward shares with him the highest illuminations and the vast enjoyment of bliss and immortality of divine and infinite existence, of the perfect union of Soul and Nature.

1. *Samiddho agnirdivi śocirasretpratyañṅ*
uṣasamurviyā vi bhāti,
eti prācī viśvavārā namobhirdevāñ īḷānā
haviṣā ghṛtācī.

2. *Samidhyamāno amṛtasya rājasi haviṣ*
kṛṇvantaṁ sacase svastaye,
viśvaṁ sa dhatte draviṇaṁ yaminvasy
ātithyamagne ni ca dhatta itpuraḥ.

3. *Agne śardha mahate saubhagāya tava*
dyumnānyuttamāni santu,
saṁ jāspatyaṁ suyamamā kṛṇuṣva
śatrūyatāmabhi tiṣṭhā mahāṅsi.

4. *Samiddhasya pramahaso'gne vande*
tava śriyam,
vṛṣabho dyumnavāñ asi sam
adhvareṣvidhyase.

5. *Samiddho agna āhuta devānyakṣi*
svadhvara,
tvaṁ hi havyavāḷasi.

6. *Ā juhotā duvasyatāgnim prayaty*
adhvare,
vṛṇīdhvaṁ havyavāhanam.[103]

1. Glory to you, O Seer-Will, you spread your mounting flames in the sky, when enkindled, and extend your lustre widely becoming the Dawn. Usha comes, widening on the horizon, pregnant with the plenitudes; radiant with the clarities, she seeks the gods with the offerings.

2. O adorable Lord, when you burn brightest, you become the King of Immortality, and separately bestow upon the sacrificer the supreme felicity of bliss. He whom you favour with your visitation acquires all the desired opulence, and sets you uppermost within him.

3. O adorable Lord, may your flaming might come into play for a vast beatitude, may you put forth your highest illumination and bring

about a perfect union between the Soul and Nature; may you vanquish the armies of the mighty Enemy.

4. O adorable Flame, I worship your supreme splendour and strength. You are the Bull of many illuminations, the mighty showerer of gifts; you increase constantly in the march of our sacrifices.

5. O worshipped Flame, perfect priest of the sacrifice and gracious receiver of our offerings; when high-kindled, bear our oblations to the godheads for, indeed, you are the most illumined bearer.

6. May we offer our oblations to the Seer-Will, and set him to its supreme workings even as our sacrifices move upward to reach the Truth. To him we offer our devotion and beseech him to be the bearer of our oblation.

(4)

Agni and the other Gods

The Veda

> "recognises an Unknowable, Timeless and Unnameable behind and above all things and not seizable by the studious pursuit of the mind. Impersonally, it is that, the One Existence; to the pursuit of our personality it reveals itself out of the secrecy of things as the God or Deva, — nameless though he has many names, immeasurable and beyond description though he holds in himself all descriptions of name and knowledge and all measures of form and substance, force and activity.
>
> "The Deva or Godhead is both the original cause and the final result. Divine Existent, builder of the worlds, lord and begetter of all things, Male and Female, Being and Consciousness, Father and Mother of the worlds and their inhabitants, he is also their Son and ours: for he is the Divine Child born into the Worlds who manifests himself in the growth of the creature. He is Rudra and Vishnu, Prajapati and Hiranyagarbha, Surya, Agni, Indra, Vayu, Soma, Brihaspati — Varuna and Mitra and Bhaga and Aryaman, all the gods. He is the wise, mighty and liberating Son born from our works and our sacrifice, the hero in our warfare and Seer of our knowledge, the White Steed in the front of our days who gallops towards the upper Ocean.

> "The soul of man soars as the Bird, the Hansa, past the shining firmaments of physical and mental consciousness, climbs as the traveller and fighter beyond earth of body and heaven of mind by the ascending path of the Truth to find this Godhead waiting for us, leaning down to us from the secrecy of the highest supreme where it is seated in the triple divine Principle and the source of the Beatitude. The Deva is indeed, whether attracting and exalted there or here helpful to us in the person of the greater Gods, always the Friend and Lover of man, the pastoral Master of the Herds who gives us the sweet milk and the clarified butter from the udder of the shining Cow of the infinitude. He is the source and outpourer of the ambrosial Wine of divine delight and we drink it drawn from the sevenfold waters of existence or pressed out from the luminous plant on the hill of being and uplifted by its raptures we become immortal."[104]

Our universe of manifestation is a complex system of worlds built by the Supreme. It is imaged as a series of trios — three earths and three heavens, a triple world below, a triple world above and a triple world between them. Man is aware of this world only; there is the superconscient above in which are many more worlds hidden from him in a luminous secrecy. Also, there are the worlds below, the subconscient and the inconscient, born of the Night, as the Veda puts it. Man owes his composition to the physical world, the vital and the mental worlds. Even as he constantly but secretly communicates with these, he can consciously commence and enter the solar and superconscient worlds above. The increasing soul has a golden destiny open before it. For the attainment of this destiny an ascending series of ordered states of consciousness from the mortal to the immortal condition is built by the gods in man's consciousness. They support his ascent by sharing with him their varied lights and felicities. This aspiration and the attending endeavour is the key to the Vedic vision and action. The Veda is the most authentic and earliest testament of yoga for reaching the goal.

The gods and the system of the worlds in the Veda have therefore to be understood symbolically. The three worlds are the three *vyahṛtis*, *Bhūḥ*, *Bhuvaḥ*, *Svaḥ* — the earth, the middle region and heaven, *pṛthivī*, *antarikṣa* and *dyauḥ*. A fourth *vyahṛti* signifies *Mahas*, the vaster world of Light above which is the triple highest world of *Jana*, *Tapas* and *Satya*. The Vedic gods are powers of the one supreme Godhead and represent his many puissances. "They manifest the cosmos", as Sri Aurobindo observes, "and are manifest in it. Children of Light, Sons of the Infinite, they recognise in the soul of man their brother and ally and desire to help and increase him by themselves increasing in him so as to possess his world with their light, strength and beauty. The Gods call man to a divine companionship and alliance; they attract and uplift him to their luminous fraternity, invite his aid and offer theirs against the Sons of Darkness and Division. Man in return calls the Gods to his sacrifice, offers to them his swiftnesses and his strengths, his clarities and his sweetnesses, — milk and butter of the shining Cow, distilled juices of the Plant of Joy, the Horse of the sacrifice, the cake and the wine, the grain for the God-Mind's radiant coursers. He receives them into his being and their gifts into his life, increases them by the hymn and the wine and forms perfectly, — as a smith forges iron, says the Veda, — their great and luminous godheads."[105]

The Vedic gods are cosmic manifestations of the Supreme with specific functions. They are known as *lokapālas*, protectors of the world, and *dikpālas* or defenders of the cardinal directions. They are usually enumerated as thirty three: eight Vasus, eleven Rudras, twelve Adityas, Indra and Prajapati. These gods are assigned to the three realms of the earth, the heavens and the mid-region, *pṛthivī, dyaus* and *antarikṣa*. The gods are the different aspects of the one supreme God — *ekam sad viprāḥ bahudhā vadanti*; they all are facets of the same Brahman. Gods, sons of Aditi the infinite Mother, are invariably described as bringing light to man, increasing him in inner strength and truth and felicity, and leading him unfalteringly to perfect bliss and peace. The legends associated with them and the descriptive terms expressing their functions indicate their distinctness. Whereas the *asuras*, those who oppose them, are all powers of division, limitation and negation. These are the 'Coverers, Tearers, Devourers, Confiners, Dualisers, Obstructors, Vritras, Panis, Atris, Rakshasas, Sambara, Vala, Namuchi' etc. These evil powers relentlessly work against the forces of truth and light and integrality and harmony. The gods, *devas*, ceaselessly work for the fostering of integral fullness and felicity in man, for his continual spiritual progress, for the increase of Truth-Consciousness and dependably support him in his struggle against the *asuras*, the hostile forces. They pour in the aspirant's consciousness the celestial waters, the streams of the Truth, *ṛtasya dhārāḥ*, and carry him across all obstacles to his home in the Truth-Consciousness, *satyam ṛtam bṛhat*. They themselves are untouched and unharmed by the attacks of the assailants, and zealously support and sustain the pilgrim in his journey to the great goal. Born of the infinite consciousness, Aditi, the gods by their increasing formation and activity in us which is so very necessary for our inner growth, lead us to Immortality. "The Vedic gods", observes Sri Aurobindo, "are a parable of human life emerging, mounting, lifting itself towards the Godhead."[106]

The Vedas repeat it again and again that the gods are the children of Light, forms and personalities and powers of the one Truth, who by their growth and workings in man raise him to the Truth which is their own home beyond all limitation and fear. Externally all the gods are powers of physical Nature, yet from an inner standpoint all have a psychic function and a psychological reference and accreditation for they are the various powers of the one infinite Truth. Each of these in himself is a complete and different cosmic expression of the Truth, and together they form the one Supreme Godhead. "These godheads", says Sri Aurobindo, "were at once masters of physical Nature and its principles and forms, their godheads and their bodies and inward divine powers with their corresponding states and energies born in our psychic being because they are the soul powers of the cosmos, the guardians of truth and immortality, the children of the Infinite, and each of them too is in his origin and his last reality the supreme Spirit putting in front one of his aspects."[107]

In the Sri Aurobindonian context, if the gods are regarded as so many powers of the one Reality, the Overmind can be construed as releasing numberless godheads into cosmic action, each vested with the power of creating its own unique world, and each capable of interrelating itself with the others. All the gods essentially are one Existence. "There are in the Veda different formulations of the nature of the Gods: it is said they are all one Existence to which the sages give different names; yet each God is worshipped as if he by himself is that Existence, one who is all the other Gods together or contains them in his being; and yet again each is a separate Deity acting sometimes in unison with companion deities, sometimes separately, sometimes even in apparent opposition to other Godheads of the same Existence."[108] The Vedic gods have, therefore, to be understood symbolically and in the inner sense. The Riks do not deify the forces of Nature; rather they speak of the Powers that preside over natural phenomena — the visible bodies in the physical universe. Surya, for example, is the *deva* who presides over the physical sun. But Surya is much more than the sun; the hymns addressed to Surya are esoteric, and answer to an inner truth and experience. The sun is spoken of as being always visible to the eye of the wise ones.

a) *Tadviṣṇoḥ paramaṁ padaṁ sadā paśyanti sūrayaḥ*
divīva cakṣurātatam.[109]

The true seekers always see the step, the transcendent abode of Vishnu like an eye spread out in heaven.

b) *Udvayaṁ tamasaspari jyotiṣ*
paśyanta uttaram,
devaṁ devatrā sūryamaganma
jyotiruttamam.[110]

Seeing the special light that springs up beyond Darkness we have arrived at the Sun, the supreme godhead, the loftiest of lights.

The Vedic gods are unmistakably different powers and personalities of the supreme Godhead. They have psychological and spiritual functions which accrue from their real and inner nature. The uninitiated and ordinary minds cannot understand this import of the Riks.

a) *Ejad dhruvaṁ patyate viśvamekaṁ carat*
patatri viṣnuṇaṁ vi jātam.[111]

All immobile and stationary ones — whether those who walk (on earth) or fly (in air) or various other beings — rest upon the Universal One.

b) *Ṛtena ṛtamapihitaṁ dhruvaṁ vāṁ sūryasya*
yatra vimucantyaśvān,
daśa śatā saha tasthustadekaṁ devānāṁ
śreṣṭhaṁ vapuṣāmapaśyam.[112]

"There is a truth covered by a Truth where they unyoke the horses of the Sun: the ten hundreds stood together, there was that One. I saw the greatest of the embodied gods."[*]

c) *Suparṇaṁ viprāḥ kavayo vacobhirekaṁ*
santaṁ bahudhā kalpayanti.[113]

The illumined seers by their words portray the bird of beautiful plumage, the One Existent, in many forms.

This deep perception of That One, who is the God of all other deities, has always been throughout in the Riks most covertly though. All the gods derive their sustenance and support from That One, *tad ekam*, and help the aspirant in his upward journey to the Supreme. The gods are all manifestations of the one Supreme Godhead manifested out of its own substance and consciousness. They have different functions in upholding the cosmic order and fulfilling the cosmic intention. The gods are invoked with a view to obtain the necessary support in the psychological and spiritual discipline of the seekers. As such they are not to be graded according to the number of Riks addressed to them. The seeker gets help of the gods in enlarging his inner existence, and in the measure he enlarges himself and becomes receptive, he enters progressively the province of their effective influence. This conscious self-giving is at the basis of Yajna which enables the sacrificer to earn the solicitude of the *devas* in the recovery of his native infinitude. Sacrifice is the supreme law by which the Supreme becomes all-existence and world-existence, and ever sustains it. It is also the Law — the power of true inner sacrifice — by which the seeker grows into the Supreme and manifests him increasingly in the phenomenal world.

Perpetual new creation and progressive rebirth are made possible by a constant interchange with the cosmic powers of the Infinite and the Supracosmic. This Infinite and the immeasurable is Aditi, described in the Veda as the ocean, *samudra*. It is from the upper ocean that streams of Light and Force, Joy and Truth, *ṛtasya dhārāḥ*, flow upon the earth. And by conscious aspiration and askesis, the seeker entering the inner ocean, *antaḥ samudra*, partakes of the strength and munificence of the cosmic personalities of Aditi. It is by inner sacrifice and constant self-giving that man attains access to the felicity of gods that successfully supports and leads him to the abode of the Truth and Immortality. He, thus proceeding upward from the inmost depths of his being reaches the realms of superconscient Truth — the world of *satyam ṛtam bṛhat*. By being born in the seeker, the gods increase their own being and import in him. It is this rebirth of the gods in man that helps mortal men to become immortal. This progression to the Truth is effected in many stages, *dhamani*. The first three are those of the earth, the mid-world and heaven; then there are the other four worlds — the vaster and luminous regions of inner existence at the summit of which is the world of Immortality and Bliss. But this heavenward journey is infested with the forces of the Adversary, the *asuras* which have to be overcome with the help of the gods. And the help is solicited by an inner Yajna, a conscious and perfect self-offering that is necessary for the participation of the gods in man's endeavour to reach the Truth. In this great conquest and victory every god has his own special contribution, and it is indispensable therefore that each one has his share of the sacrificial offering. It is through an equitable distribution of the gains of inner sacrifice among the gods that man helps the gods to effectively and luminously compose the body of the Supreme. Being sons of the Infinite, and being Its part and parcel, the gods thus become competent to support the sacrificer. The different colours, vehicles and weapons of the gods are symbolic of their nature as envisioned and experienced by the Rishis. "Indra has two green horses, Agni's ruddy, Aditya's tawny, Ashwins have two donkeys and Pushan goats; antelopes of Maruts, rosy rays of Ushas and Savitri's dusky horses along with the vehicle of Brihaspati called Vishwarupa are mentioned and Vayu's horses are called Niyuta."[114] The gods exercise a profound and powerful influence on the life of the aspirant consistent with their individual nature. Their help is tangible and concrete in the measure of the seeker's self-giving. The gods, who are themselves the distinct powers of the Supreme, recreate the Supreme in the seeker when he progressively succeeds in the increase of gods in him by perpetual inner sacrifice.

Agni, the god who is closer to the earth than the others, is the one easily accessible to the seeker. He represents the intuitive knowledge of the sacrifice in whom the sacrificer finds succour and strength, and the gods their joy of fulfilment. He is both the face and the mouth of the gods as he carries to them all the oblations of the sacrificer. He is the ambassador from above, as well as the leader from below who guides man in the sacrifice and calls upon the gods to be born in him. He too, is born again in the sacrificer and thereby helps him to move heavenward.

The Veda frequently speaks of the seven principles of cosmic consciousness and force, and uses the image of the seven rivers to signify them. Agni is the child of the seven Mothers and nourished and fostered by the seven sisters — the manifold cosmic energies. He is described as the seven-tongued god who accepts the offerings for the multiple needs of the seven planes of existence. According to the Vedic perception, for the fulfilment of the sacrifice and to grow into the supreme Godhead the seeker has to integrally manifest in his soul all these planes.

Though the Veda enumerates seven planes of existence, it deals mostly with the first three worlds and their gods. That is one of the reasons why more Mantras are devoted to Agni who presides over the earth; Indra receives most of the hymns as the lord of all the gods, whereas Surya, the lord of the solar world has a lesser number in praise of him. In the Veda, the earth represents the physical consciousness, and heaven the consciousness of the Pure Mind, whereas *antarikṣa* that of the force of Life.

Agni the immortal guest in the mortal, is the power of Divine Will and Wisdom;

Indra, the pure and luminous Mind, is the power that destroys all obscurity and ignorance;

Surya, the Lord of the Truth, the Creator of all things, is the resplendent power of the Infinite that governs and guides the evolving universe;

And Soma, the divine delight of all existence, the Lord of Bliss and Immortality is the power of infinite beatitude that transforms perfectly and totally and integrally.

"The Gods are immortals", observes T.V. Kapali Sastry, "because they live by the essential delight of all created existence. In man the immortalising juices (*rasa*) are hidden and when by *tapasyā*, discipline, and with the help of the higher Powers, chiefly beginning with Agni the Divine Child born to man, these are extracted and offered to the Gods they get the needed nourishment in him, 'they increase him by themselves increasing in him'. Again, there is Varuna the God of Vast Purity destructive of all crookedness and sin; Mitra, luminous Power of love harmonising all thoughts and feelings and acts and impulses. There are goddesses also; each god has his Female Energy and is mentioned occasionally and also hymned, such as Indrani, Varunani, Agnayi. Besides there are Devatas who are in their own right Female Powers of whom Aditi the Infinite is the foremost, the Mother of the Gods, Adityas; Mahi or Bharati, 'the vast word that brings us all things out of the Divine source', Ila 'the strong primal word of the Truth who gives us its active vision', 'Sarama, the Intuition' and a few other names with their functions are mentioned in the '*Doctrine of the Mystics*' (authored by Sri Aurobindo). The distinction between the Male and Female energies, it must be noted, lies in the fact that the former are 'activising souls' while the latter 'passively executive and methodising energies'."[115]

Among the gods, Agni gets the place of pride. He is eulogised as the creator, the sustainer and the all-pervading Supreme. Agni in the external sense and to the physical eye is the Lord of Fire, the sacrificial Flame. He is found in the tinders, *aranis*, and in the waters, in the plants and in the heat of the sun. Psychologically and spiritually he is the light and the force, *tapas* and *tejas*. He is the Light of the superconscient and the conscious

Force of the Truth. He is a material force, as well as a pranic force and a mental power. He is both a god of the earth and a god of Swar. "...he manifests himself as Surya; he is born in the Truth, a master of Truth, a guardian of Truth and Immortality, a getter and keeper of the shining herds, the eternal Youth, and he renews the youth of these mystic cattle. He is triply extended in the Infinite.... He is the horse of battle and the horse of swiftness and again he gives the white horse; he is the son and he creates for man the son. He is the warrior and he brings to man the heroes of his battle. He destroys by his flame the Dasyu and the Rakshasa; he is a Vritra-slayer."[116]

Agni, the one who is born first, born even before the gods, signifies strength, luminosity and movement. He is the priest who carries out the work of sacrifice and the principal summoner who brings all the other gods to the place of sacrifice. He is the bearer and founder of all felicity. He, the most adorable, bestows upon the sacrificer the strength and vigour necessary for the heroic inner journey as well as protects him on every side from all evil.

The Sama-veda speaks of Agni as one of three principal deities; he presides over the earth, and is the messenger between men and the gods. He is the material fire as well as the celestial one — the divine Will. He is omniscient and present everywhere; he is an embodiment of knowledge, an immortal preceptor and worthy of worship.

a) *Tvāmagne aṅgiraso guhā hitamanvavindaṁ cchi*
śriyāṇaṁ vane vane,
sa jāyase mathyamānaḥ saho mahatvāmāhuḥ
sahasasputramaṅgiraḥ.[117]

O thou omniscient One, present in each soul, concealed in the inmost recesses of the heart, the wise find thee everywhere. Thou art mighty, O Fosterer, always worthy of praise; thou art the embodiment of knowledge, the sages know thee as saviour of men from all sin.

b) *Pra so agne tavotibhiḥ suvīrābhistarati*
vājakarmabhiḥ, yasya tvañ
sakhyamāvitha.[118]

O Fire, he whom thou befriendest surmounts all hurdles aided by thy heroic armour and deeds of power.

The Yajur-veda describes Agni as the guardian and protector of the many forces of Nature. He carries to them the oblations offered to him.

a) *Upa tvā'agne haviṣmatīrghṛtā*
chīryantu haryata,
juṣasva samidho mama.[119]

O resplendent Fire, woodsticks wetted in *ghṛtam* reach thee along with our oblations. May thou approbate our offering to thee.

b) *Vrataṁ kṛṇutāgnirbrahmāgniryajño*
vanaspatiryajñiyaḥ,
dāivīṁ dhiyaṁ manāmahe sumṛḍī kāmabhiṣṭaye
varcodhāṁ yajñavāhasagvañ
sutīrthā no asadvaśe, ye devā
manojātā manoyujo dakṣakratavaste
no'vantu te naḥ pāntu tebhyaḥ svāhā.[120]

Declare that God is Agni, Sacrifice is Agni. He, the guardian of our spirit, is worthy of worship. For reaching the goal (of Immortality) we need the guidance of his radiant Intelligence that can unite us with the supreme Truth. May that Intelligence help us to cross the ocean of phenomenal existence and be always within our reach.

May the energies of the wise urge us on the path, may they protect us. We invoke them sincerely and truly.

c) *Agne tvagvañ su jāgṛhi vayagvañ su*
mandiṣīmahi,
rakṣā ṇo aprayucchan
prabudhe naḥ punaskṛdhi.[121]

O Agni, thou who art ever wakeful, always protect us who are sleeping in ignorance. Awaken us again and again to thy presence and lead us to the true Knowledge.

d) *Tadevāgnistadādityastadvāyustadu*
chandramāḥ, tádeva śukraṁ
tadbrahma tā āpaḥ sa prajāpatiḥ.[122]

He is Agni the resplendent god, He is Aditya who inundates all at the time of Pralaya; He is the all-powerful Vayu, He is the pleasureful Chandrama. He is the pure Sukra, He is Brahma and the all-pervading Apa as well as the great Prajapati the guardian of the universe.

e) *Sarve nimeṣā jajñire vidyutaḥ*
puruṣādadhi, nāinamūrdhvaṁ
na tiryañcaṁ na madhye
pari jagrabhat.[123]

All divisions of Time spring forth from him the resplendent, perfect god. No one can comprehend him either from below, or above, or in the middle.

f) *Nā tasya pratimā asti yasya*
nāma mahadyaśaḥ,
hiraṇyagarbha ityeṣa mā mā higvañsī
dityeṣā yasmanna jāta ityeṣaḥ.[124]

He is matchless in greatness and glory. He sustains in himself the Sun and all other luminous objects. May he always protect us; he the eternal is worthy of our worship.

g) *Eṣo ha devaḥ pradiśo'nu sarvāḥ pūrvo ha*
jātaḥ sa u garbhe antaḥ,
sa eva jātaḥ sa janiṣyamāṇaḥ
pratyañ janāstiṣṭhati sarvatomukhaḥ.[125]

O the wise one, this god is all-pervasive. He is the timeless one who was present in the previous cycle of existence, is present now and will be there in all the cycles to come. He exists eternally controlling everything, protecting everything.

h) *Enā vo agniṁ namasorjo napātamā huve,*
priyaṁ cetiṣṭhamaratigvañ
svadhvaraṁ viśvasya dūtamamṛtam.[126]

Agni is the world's supreme messenger; he moves everywhere in the world and puts life in it. Through the sacrifice he brings rain and produces food grains; he thus is the source of ripening the harvest. He is eternal in nature, eternally present in the material universe and in living beings and everywhere above.

There are several hymns where the gods are described as kindling the fire themselves. Agni holds a special position and is installed among them. He is the messenger, the leader of the sacrifice, the *hotṛ*, their eye, their body and spokesman. He is also ensconced among men by the gods.

a) *Kratvā dakṣasya taruṣo vidharmaṇi*
devāso agniṁ janayanta cittibhiḥ.[127]

The wise priests kindle the Flame in many forms by their surpassing strength and with their illumined thoughts.

b) *Vicarśaniragnirdevānāmabhavatpurohitaḥ*[128]

He is the foremost conductor of the great sacrifice placed in front of the gods.

c) *Trīṇi śatā trī sahasrāṇyagniṃ*
triṅśacca devā nava cāsaparyan,
aukṣanghṛtairastṛṇanbarhirasmā
ādiddhotāraṁ nyasādayanta.[129]

Three thousand three hundred thirty-nine wise ones (gods) worship Agni; they sprinkle him with clarified butter, spread for him the sacred grass and enshrine him upon it as their radiant priest.

d) *Ayamagniḥ pṛtanāśaṭ suvīro*
yena devāso asahanta dasyūn.[130]

May you produce smoke, the showerer of gifts; persist assiduously with Agni, for he is able to encounter the Adversary, and by him the very gods overcome their enemies.

It is Agni Vaishwanara whom the gods enkindle for the sacrifice.

a) *Mūrdhānaṁ divo aratiṁ pṛthivyāḥ*
vaiśvānaramṛta ā jātamagnim,

kaviṁ samrājamatithiṁ janānām
āsannā pātraṁ janayanta devāḥ.[131]

The gods have manifested Vaishwanara, Agni, as the symbol of heaven and the unceasing pervader of earth. He is born of *ṛta*, is the bearer of oblations.

b) *Nābhiṁ yajñānām sadanaṁ rayīṇām*
mahāmāhāvamabhi saṁ navanta,
vaiśvānaraṁ rathyamadhvarānāṁ yajñasya
ketuṁ janayanta devāḥ.[132]

The worshippers manifest him and glorify him who is the great receptacle of offerings. He is the conveyer of oblations, the ensign of all sacrifices, the universal Lord and the source of all felicities.

In the hymns of the Atris, Agni is variously invoked as the Intuition of the Sacrifice, the representative Priest strong in will to sacrifice, Lord of the brilliant plane, possessed of the Truth and creator of the Gods. He is the shining Guest the Sun of Force possessed of the felicity of Light.

a) *Sa no vibhāvā cakṣaṇirnā vastor*
agnirvandāru vedyaścano dhāt,
viśvāyuryo amṛto martyeṣūṣarbhud
bhūdatithirjātavedāḥ.[133]

May the adorable Lord, who like the seer of the Day is resplendent and known to all, grant us abundant joy. He is the life of all, the Immortal in mortal; he is the Waker in the Dawn, our shining Guest who knows all that exists.

b) *Yaste yajñena samidhaya ukthair*
arkebhiḥ sūno sahaso dadāśat,
sa martyeṣvamṛta pracetā rāyā
dyumnena śravasā vi bhāti.[134]

O Son of Force, immortal Lord, verily when a person serves you with the sacrifice and with luminous words and sacred chants, he becomes a mind of wisdom and possesses the wealth of inspiration and light.

Agni is repeatedly described as hidden in the secrecies of our inner being and diligently guarding the cherished footprints of the Cow of Vision.

a) *Paśvā na tāyuṁ guhā catantaṁ namo*
yujānaṁ namo vahantam,
sajoṣā dhīrāḥ padairanu gmann
upa tvā sīdanviśve yajatrāḥ.[135]

The wise worshippers discover you hiding like a thief with the Cow of Vision in the dark cavern. He, accepting their oblations, arrives here.

b) *Haste dadhāno nṛmṇā viśvānyame*
devāndhādguhā niṣīdan,
vidantīmatra naro dhiyandhā hridā
yattaṣṭānmantrāň asaṅsan.[136]

Holding in his hand the wide earth, he up-pillared the heaven with *mantras* of Truth. Guarding the cherished footprints of the Cow of Vision, he shuts himself in the deep secrecies of the heart. And when the sages find him in the secret Cave with deep devotion, to them he bestows the Word of supreme felicity.

Dwelling in the secret cave, all-knowing and all-powerful, he urges the seeker to some unknown goal above.

a) *Taṁ śaśvatīṣu mātṛṣu vana*
ā vītamaśritam,
citraṁ santaṁ guhā hitaṁ
suvedaṁ kūcidarthinam.[137]

He is worshipped, who is enshrined and widespread in the many Mothers, and in the forest, and hidden in the secret cave; he is endowed with all knowledge and moves to the unknown goal.

b) *Ā yasminasaptt raśmayastatā*
yajñasya netari,
maṇuṣvaddaivyamaṣṭamaṁ
potā viśvaṁ tadinvati.[138]

O adorable Lord of sacrifice in you are extended the seven rays. Whereas the divine eighth manifests itself in all of humanity as the protector and the priest of purification, and sets everything in motion.

Purifying in action, victorious without compare, Agni sees established within him the seven Rishis.

Sakhāyastvā vavṛmahe devaṁ martāsa ūtaye.[139]

O resplendent God, we choose you for our protection; you are the blessed one, force auspicious, victorious without compare.

The rivers in the Veda, according to Sri Aurobindo, symbolise the streams of consciousness — the sevenfold waters of Truth flowing down from the Supreme Being. They represent the seven cosmic principles or the seven planes of existence which become enriched in Agni. Having discovered Agni in the waters, the seven rivers increase by him; whereas he himself increases in the obstructed Vast. He makes his home in the Truth, and helps the seekers to attain Immortality. He is described by the Rishis as *adbhuta*, wonderful, as one who has an amazing, indomitable will, *adbhuta-kratu*, and as one who knows the Supreme and Wonderful.

a) *Na nūnamasti no śvaḥ kas*
tadveda yadadbhutam.[140]

It is neither now, nor is It tomorrow. Who knows that which is Supreme and Wonderful.

b) *Sadasaspatimadbhutaṁ priyaṁ*
indrasya kāmyam,
sanan medhāmayāsiṣam.[141]

I seek pure understanding from the presiding Lord, the adorable and desirable, the beautiful and the Wonderful who gives.

c) *Śuciḥ pavako adbhuto madhvā*
yajñam mimikṣati[142]

O adorable, radiant one, you are pure and purifying, divine and Wonderful; may you sprinkle the sacrifice with honey.

d) *Devo devānāmasi mitro adbhuto*
vasurvasūnāmasi cāruradhvare[143]

O illustrious God, you are the friend of the virtuous, the most Wonderful.

e) *Viśāṁ rājānamadbhutamadhyakṣaṁ dharmaṇāmimam,*
agnimīḷe sa u ṣravat.[144]

O sovereign of men, the Wonderful, may we worship you who presides over the cosmic laws; may you listen to our prayers.

Agni is the mighty god who brings rich felicity that overpowers the Enemy.

Tamagne pṛtanāṣahaṁ rayiṁ
sahasva ā bhara[145]

O mighty Flame, may you grant us the rich felicity that vanquishes the armies of the Adversary that embattle against us.

He plays an important role in the inner life of the Rishis. He brings the many gods to the doors of the sacrificial chamber in the heart of the awakened aspirant. The 'Apri Hymns' bring out the special nature and the significant function of Agni in the progressive manifestation in the seeker of the substance of the gods and his onward march. Apart from being the principle of heat and light in external Nature, Agni has a significant spiritual and psychological import. He is the divine Will that builds up in man the citadel of the Truth and effectuates the development of the gods for his attainment of Immortality. His home is the highest Truth, the supreme Truth-Consciousness above the triple world of *Bhūḥ*, *Bhuvaḥ* and *Svar*. In the physical, Agni is the law of the substance of things, in the vital he is the dynamic *prāṇa*, and in the mental it is the flaming aspiration that purifies and perfects. At the psychic level it is the pure flaming love and devotion, confident knowledge and mounting *tapasyā*. Agni therefore is the joy of self-giving and the true love and worship of the Truth. When increased and intensified in volume and intensity, Agni takes charge of the whole being of man and leads him upward to the home of the eternal Truth. The help of Agni becomes effective only when the animal nature in man is totally overcome and sacrificed, *paśumedha*. To accomplish this man needs the help and felicity of the gods, and they are brought to the altar of the sacrificer through the intervention of Agni. Agni, by virtue of his divine origin, manifests within himself the *devas* for helping out the seeker in his inner endeavour. It is in this sense that the *devas* are born in the seeker, and the seeker is reborn into their consciousness and power.

In 'Apri Hymns' the gods are invoked and implored to descend and take possession of the sacrificer. The help and presence of the gods is made possible by Agni himself. Moreover as the seeker advances in Yoga, Agni himself predicates the powers of the other gods while retaining his own unique feature of the divine Will. Agni is thus endowed with a multiple personality. In his Varuna nature he is wide and all-encompassing; in his Mitra disposition he radiates love and joy and friendliness.

Agni when awakened and made effective in the seeker not only assumes the powers of different gods but manifests out of himself his own higher powers for the effectuation of the seeker's objective. The 'Apri Hymns' refer to the many manifestations of Agni himself as well as other things and articles that are indispensable for the conduct of Yajna and for arriving at the summit goal of supramental Truth-Consciousness. In the said hymns Agni is invoked to effect progressively the advent of his own higher manifestations and those of the gods for the benefit of the ardent seeker.

Agni is the divine Will as well as the divine Voice. Awakening to the presence of the divine Will within is the new birth of man. The Flame then has to be fostered with care and consecration, devotion and knowledge enabling it to rise high and induce or facilitate the descent of the gods into the sacrificer. He is the great baptiser as well as the Purifier, *pāvaka*. He is the *hotāra* and the *purohita*, the summoner and the high priest who gives form to the sacrifice. He is the child born of the body of the worshipper and gives shape to his intense aspiration. He is the seer, and knows the way to arrive at the gods with the oblations of the worshipper and effect their advent in him. The worshipper effectuates the wine of divine delight, Soma, by his utter devotion and self-giving. This is for the acceptance and enjoyment by the descending gods. Agni calls the gods on behalf of the worshipper to come to the sacrifice and relish the *rasa*.

It is Agni again who not only initiates the sacrifice and induces the gods to manifest at the sacrifice but also carries the sacrifice to perfection as the direct representative of the supreme Godhead. The command comes from the supreme Ineffable, and the Flame is installed in the seeker to carry out the task of initiating, developing and perfecting the sacrifice.

The seat of Agni, in fact, is within the inner being of the seeker which needs to be kept pure and clean and shining. It is in the pure inner being that the immortal Godhead reveals himself totally whose guidance is clearly felt by the aspirant.

As the Yajna and Yoga proceed, there are opened for the sacrificer the divine doors revealing to him the secret splendour of the Immortal and the Eternal. The Rishi devoutly desires the presence of both Day and Night at the sacrifice, for both Knowledge and Ignorance have to be known together for crossing beyond death and to enjoy Immortality. The Rishi then invokes the twin godheads of Light and Life residing in the mid-region, *bhuvarloka*, to descend into humanity helping men on their upward journey. He also invokes the three goddesses-powers from the Sun of Truth, *ṛtam jyotir bṛhat* — Ila, Saraswati and Bharati. In the Vedic context, Ila is the Shakti of the vision of knowledge, Saraswati that of Inspiration, and Bharati of the vastness of the Truth. If Bharati removes limitation and narrowness, Ila and Saraswati provide the seeker with the vision of Knowledge and the Inspiration that expresses the truth-vision and truth-knowledge. This threefold help is necessary for the assured journey. These three goddesses as well as Twashtri are invoked by the Rishi for help and for fashioning a new life of higher consciousness for him. Twashtri is the great builder and resuscitator of new forms of beings in creation necessary for the manifestation of the divine powers in man. Then is Soma supplicated who is the Lord of the earth's growths and the tangible knowledge. Soma is the god of divine delight in all things and in all beings. His presence at the sacrifice is necessary, for any worship without delight or *rasa* cannot make a dent in the higher worlds, nor can it ever reach the gods. Moreover, the substantial knowledge that Soma brings is assured and contactual, *saṁjñāna*. Then the Rishi offers the sacrificial oblations to Indra, god of the divine Mind, with an appeal to the other gods to attend upon him, and accompany him in his sublime solicitude of men's inner adventure.

Agni, thus, is in actuality and finally all the other godheads. Where he is awakened and set to work, all his powers start manifesting, and his magnificence revealed. The Rishi invokes his powers, step by step, to fulfil their functions on the earth-plane, in the mid-region and in the inner consciousness of the seeker leading him heavenward progressively. During this journey, it is Agni who assumes the full responsibility and charge of the seeker's soul. It is in this heavenward journey that the higher powers — the various godheads, are invoked for uplifting the aspiring soul through the real and steadfast sacrifice.

1. *Susamiddho na ā vaha devā agne haviṣmate,*
hotaḥ pāvaka yakṣi ca.

2. *Madhumantaṁ tanūnapād yajñaṁ deveṣu naḥ kave,*
adyā kṛṇuhi vītaye.

3. *Narāśaṅsamiha priyamasmin yajña upa hvaye,*
madhujihvaṁ haviṣkṛitam.

4. *Agne sukhatame rathe devāñ īḷita ā vaha,*
asi hotā manurhitaḥ.

5. *Stṛnīta barhirānuṣag ghṛtapṛṣṭhaṁ manīṣiṇaḥ,*
yatrāmṛtasya cakṣaṇam.

6. *Vi śrayantāmṛtāvṛdho dvāro devīrasaśćataḥ,*
adyā nūnaṁ ca yaṣṭave.

7. *Naktoṣāsā supeśasāsmin yajña upa hvaye,*
idaṁ no barhirāsade.

8. *Ta sujihvā upa hvaye hotārā daivyā kavī,*
yajñaṁ no yakṣatāmimam.

9. *Iḷā sarasvatī mahī tisro devirmayobhuvaḥ,*
barhiḥ sīdantvasridhaḥ.

10. *Iha tvaṣṭāramagriyaṁ viśvarupamupa hvaye,*
asmākamastu kevalaḥ.

11. *Ava śrijā vanaspate deva devebhyo haviḥ,*
pra dāturastu cetanam.

12. *Svāhā yajñaṁ kṛṇotanendrāya yajvano gṛhe,*
tatra devāñ upa hvaye.[146]

1. O radiant Fire-divine, well-kindled and all purifying, may you bring to us the sacred bounties. Pray perform the sacrifice.

2. O adorable Seer-Will, brought up by the body may you perform this our sacrifice to the gods, laden with the Soma-wine, for the purpose of their participation.

3. I invoke Narasamsa, the most adorable, sweet-tongued Lord who prepares the sacred oblation, in this sacrifice.

4. O adorable Agni, most aspired for by us, come to our sacrifice, O Summoner, on your radiant chariot along with the gods.

5. O wise worshippers, may you spread the seat of sacred grass in perfect order where the Immortal One is observed.

6. May the splendorous doors of divine knowledge, truth-increasing, swing open for us this very moment, so that we can perform the sacrifice unrestrained.

7. May we invoke Night and Dawn of propitious form to arrive at this our solemn sacrifice, and take their seat on the sacred grass spread for them.

8. I invoke the presence and participation of the twin Divine Priests of the Call, sweet-tongued and eloquent; may they conduct the worship at the sacrifice.

9. May the ever-glorious three goddesses — Ila, Saraswati, Mahi, givers of supreme felicity — be seated unpummelled on the seat of sacred grass.

10. I invoke Twashtṛ, the foremost architect of all forms, and manifester of excellence. May he be our sole guide and god.

11. O adorable God, you are the great promoter of the Earth's growths. May you bear our oblations to the gods, may we be bestowed by divine knowledge.

12. May we offer our prayers to Indra, the resplendent Lord with the utterance *Svāhā*. We call him and the many gods here to our sacrifice.

The 'Apri Hymns' of the Rig-veda not only focus on the form of the sacrificer but also on the nature of activity of Agni and the other gods. The self within, the Purusha, is the true sacrificer. When the aspirant becomes mature in wisdom, he is reborn into a spiritual life. His heart aflame with the love of Truth and his soul-quest sharpened by askesis, Agni himself reveals the path to the seeker-sacrificer. Agni is the seeker, Agni is the search, Agni is the helper and increaser of the seeking. Agni himself takes over the task of the seeker, his onus and his charge, and effects the work. Agni, therefore, has to be kindled and meditated upon, nourished and increased until he establishes himself securely in one's being. He has to be praised and pleased, invoked and extolled until he expands and heightens and fills the sacrificer with his power and light and felicity. Sincere sacrifice always moves upward and opens the doors of the Truthward journey. The Rishi desirous of inner growth invokes Agni to come to the sacrifice with all the gods and make them drink their apportioned wine of divine delight.

1. *Aibhiragne duvo giro viśvebhiḥ somapītaye,*
   devebhiryāhi yakṣi ca.

2. *Ā tvā kaṇvā ahūṣata gṛṇanti vipra te dhiyaḥ,*
   devebhiragna ā gahi.

3. *Indravāyū bṛhaspatiṁ mitrāgnīṁ pūṣaṇaṁ bhagam,*
   ādityān mārutaṃ gaṇam.

4. *Pra vo bhriyanta indavo matsarā mādayiṣṇavaḥ,*
   drapsā madhvaścamuṣadaḥ.

5. *Īḷate tvāmavasyavaḥ kaṇvāso vṛktabarhiṣaḥ,*
   haviṣmanto araṁkṛtaḥ.

6. *Ghṛtapriṣṭhā manoyujo ye tvā vahanti vahnayaḥ,*
   ā devāntsomapītaye.

7. *Tan yajatrāñ ṛtāvṛdho'gne patnīvataskṛdhi,*
   madhvaḥ sujihva pāyaya.

8. *Ye yajatrā ya īḍyāste te pibantu jihvayā,*
   madhoragne vaṣatkṛti.

9. *Ākīṁ sūryasya rocanād viśvāñ devān uṣarbudhaḥ*
vīpro hoteha vakṣati.

10. *Viśvebhiḥ somyaṁ madhvagna indreṇa vāyunā,*
pibā mitrasya dhāmabhiḥ.

11. *Tvaṁ hotā manurhito'gne yajñeṣu sīdasi,*
semaṁ no adhvaraṁ yaja.[147]

1. O mighty Flame, may you come to our sacrificial endeavour with all the gods; may you accept our sacrifice and our oblations, and drink the Soma-wine.

2. O adorable Lord, men of enlightenment extol you and praise your illumined understandings; may you come to us with all the gods.

3. We invoke you as Indra and Vayu, Brihaspati and Mitra, Varuna and Pushan, Bhaga and the Adityas as well as the host of Maruts.

4. For your sake we carry meritoriously the satisfying and intoxicating Soma-wine, delicious of taste, ensconcing in the body.

5. We the wise priests of the Kanva lineage adore you, wishing rapid progress and protection against all that impedes it. For you the seat is spread out, fully sufficient and of efficient doings.

6. The horses with luminous bodies and yoked by the mind, which carry you, by them may you bring the gods to drink the Soma-wine offered by us.

7. O Agni, join Indra and all other gods, to whom we are to offer our sacrifice and who increase the Truth with their spouses. O sweet-tongued God, make them drink the portion of the ambrosial Soma-juice.

8. O Agni, all those to whom we are to offer our sacrifice, whom we are to worship, may they drink with your speech of flame-form the portion of the sweet Soma-wine.

9. May the Wise One, the radiant Summoner, bring to us all the benevolent gods that accompany the Dawn, from the shining world of the Truth-Light.

10. May Agni along with all the gods — Indra, Vayu and Mitra, drink this spiritual elixir of the Soma-juice.

11. Authorised and assigned by Manu, O enlightened one, Summoner of the gods, dweller in our sacrifices, may you supervise this our work with diligence.

12. O resplendent God, Lord of the universe, yoke to your chariot horses of crimson hue, the Rohitas, and bring by them the gods to our sacrifice.

Again, in *Sukta* 12 of the Rig-veda, the Rishi beseeches Agni, the knower of all, to be the auspicious and effective messenger to the gods. He invokes him to carry his oblations to them and bring them to the seat of the inner sacrifice. Having kindled the flame of aspiration, Agni is repeatedly invoked to summon the gods to those who in their inner being have made themselves receptive to the Truth. He is supplicated with great submission and by illumined thought to burn up the enemies and consume all darkness. He is difficult to approach for the idle and the uninitiated; it needs total surrender, earnest and sincere seeking to enkindle the flame within. Agni is the Seer-Vision and the Seer-Will; he is the power that destroys all afflictions. He is the prime increaser and the perfect purifier who makes for the happiness of the sacrificer.

1. *Agniṁ dūtaṁ vṛṇīmahe hotāraṁ viśvavedasam,*
   asya yajñasya sukratum.

2. *Agnimagniṁ havīmabhiḥ sadā havanta viśpatim,*
   havyavāhaṁ purupriyam.

3. *Agne devāñ ihā vaha jajñāno vṛktabarhiṣe,*
   asi hotā na īḍyaḥ.

4. *Tāñ uśato vi bodhaya yadagne yāsi dūtyam,*
   devairā satsi barhiṣi.

5. *Ghṛtāhavana dīdivaḥ prati ṣma riṣato daha,*
agne tvaṁ rakṣasvinaḥ.

6. *Agnināgniḥ samidhyate kavirgṛhapatiryuvā,*
havyavāḍ juhvāsyaḥ.

7. *Kavimagnimupa stuhi satyadharmāṇamadhvare,*
devamamīvacātanam.

8. *Yastvāmagne haviṣpatirdūtaṁ deva saparyati,*
tasya sma prāvitā bhava.

9. *Yo agniṁ devavītaye haviṣmāñ āvivāsati,*
tasmai pāvaka mṛḷaya.

10. *Sa naḥ pāvaka dīdivo'gne devāñ ihā vaha,*
upa yajñaṁ haviśca naḥ.

11. *Sa na stavana ā bhara gāyatreṇa navīyasā,*
rayiṃ vīravatīmiṣam.

12. *Agne śukreṇa śociṣā viśvābhirdevahūtibhiḥ,*
imaṁ stomaṁ juṣasva naḥ.[148]

1. We entreat and serve Agni, the all-knower, as our adorable messenger, our caller and protector who performs this our sacrifice perfectly.

2. With much devotion and dedication, we constantly invoke Agni, the resplendent God, beloved of the wise, guardian of the seekers, who generously bears our oblations.

3. O adorable Agni, who are manifest and radiant, may you bring here the gods to those who have prepared the seat of sacred grass; verily, you are our adored Summoner.

4. O adorable Agni, since you arc our illumined messenger, may you awaken the desirous gods. We devoutly solicit your presence on the altar-seat along with all the other gods.

5. O adorable Agni, invoked by our luminous thoughts destroy the hordes of the Adversary who are vile and demon-possessed.

6. O Agni, enkindled and intensified by Agni, seer and overseer of the house, ever youthful and bearer of our oblations, guardian and protector who has the fierce flames for his mouth.

7. O adorable Agni, seer and sustainer of the Truth-law, bright in sacrifice, may you destroy all forms of Evil through your supreme resplendence.

8. O worshipful God, Agni, the flaming messenger of Truth, may you protect and increase those who offering their oblations dedicate themselves to the work.

9. O supreme purifier, may you be propitious to the sacrificer who with devout oblations waits upon you in the sacrifice where all the other gods are seated; may you extend to him the desired felicity.

10. O adorable Agni, luminous and loving purifier, may you bring here in the sacrifice all the gods, carry our offering to them and unite them for the fulfilment of our sacrifice.

11. O mighty godhead, extolled by our hymns of praise, may you bring for us supreme felicity, power of impulsion with strength and vigour.

12. O adorable Lord, Agni, God of the pure white flame, we invoke you, and glorify you and all the gods with our chants of praise; may you be pleased by our hymns of affirmation.

There is a mystic symbolism running through all the *mantras*; the sacrificial fire is only an outward figure of a deeper perception and experience. Agni, the god and guardian of the Truth, embodies not only its illumination but also its force; it is not only a Power that knows all but one that builds up the all, both *satyam* and *ṛtam*. In addition, he is *citraśravastamaḥ*, the one who has the resourcefulness and the capacity to do perfect work. As the *hotṛ* he performs the sacrifice perfectly, as the inward force of unified and consolidated Light and Power, he communicates between heaven and earth. The gods are both the cosmic powers of external Nature as well as the universal forces in her subjective dimension.

The nature of Agni is freedom from evil and sin, the condition of perfect good and pure bliss. This he creates in the seeker when he offers the sacrifice.

1. *Yadaṅga dāśuṣe tvam*
agne bhadraṁ kariṣyasi,
tavettat satyamaṅgiraḥ.[149]

Whatever good (happiness), O adorable Agni, which thou mayst create for the giver of oblations, that indeed, O Angiras, is the truth of thee.

The sacrifice becomes effective, and progresses towards its goal only when the sacrificer constantly surrenders in his thought to the adoration of Agni, to his wisdom and action. He needs to submit to him continually in the day and in the night, in all states of consciousness, for Agni being the guardian of the Truth ever shines out in his own, bright and free.

a) *Upa tvāgne divedive*
doṣāvastardhiyā vayam
namo bharanta emasi.[150]

Bearing our oblations, with humility, we come to thee day by day, O Agni, both in the night and in the light — in obscurity and in illumination.

b) *Rajantamadhvarāṇām*
gopāmṛtasya dīdivim,
vardhamānaṁ sve dame.[151]

To thee, O Lord, who shinest out from the sacrifices, the guardian of the Truth, the sustainer of the universe, and who ever increases in his own home.

The Truth, the Right, the Vast, *satyam ṛtam bṛhat*, is the own home of Agni and of the other gods. This is the goal of the sacrifice where limitation and falsehood and division are abolished. Agni, the divine Light and Force of Truth-Consciousness, living in the limitless and the timeless, increases in the seeker the felicity and the strength to move towards the goal.

Agni is the Will, the priest and the path-finder, the worker and the fighter, the illuminator and the winner of Light and Delight for man. He is the all-seer and the conscious force who builds up the worlds and manifests in man the Truth and the Immortality:

Agnimīḷe purohitaṁ yajñasya devamṛtvijam,
hotāraṁ ratnadhātamam.[151a]

Both gods and men awaken and intensify the divine flame within by enkindling the fires of the inner sacrifice. They make it progressively effective by their sincere worship and surrender to it. And they reflect and seek to express in their pure and illumined mentality the revelations of the Truth-Consciousness. This is done with a view to enable the divine Force to express the right Word. This Force purifies the mental, vital and physical and makes the intellect to progressively reveal and manifest the Truth.

a) *Prāñcaṁ yajñaṁ cakṛma vardhatāṁ gīḥ*
samidbhiragniṁ namasā duvasyan;
divaḥ śaśāsurvidathā kavīnāṁ,
gṛtsāya cittavase gātumīṣuḥ.[152]

We, the seekers, have made the sacrifice to progressively enhance; let the Word increase. With the awakening and strengthening of his Will, with the offering of oblations and submission they set Agni to his successful workings, which give expression (in the purified mind) to the realisations of the Rishis and enable the divine Will to have the right Word (for passage to the Truth).

b) *Mayo dadhe medhiraḥ pūtadakṣo*
divaḥ subandhurjanuṣā pṛthivyāḥ;
avindannu darśatamapsva ntar
devāso agnimapasi svasṛīṇām.[153]

The gods discovered Agni in the workings of the Waters and amidst the rivers for the sacred acts; Agni full of perfect understanding, purified in discernment, marvellous builder of the earth because of his heavenly origin, friend and bestower of infinite bliss.

Agni, the divine conscious force in man, to begin with, acts as the ordinary will of man, and then successfully works out his way through the five worlds, *pañca kṛṣṭiḥ*, to the supreme Truth — his own proper seat, *svaṁ damam*. The rivers in which the gods find Agni are the sevenfold Waters of the Truth that are brought down from the summits of our inner existence by Indra. While Agni is found visible in the divine Waters, it is brought out by man after undergoing great suffering through the workings of the pure mind upon the physical. From his very birth the rivers increase his form with the nourishment of joy, and the gods strengthen his force. The divine child then rapidly grows through several stages — material heat, vital dynamis and the heavenly fire, — continually purifying and uplifting the human into the divine. Rising upward and onward the rivers eventually reveal themselves as the energies of the Eternal, the superconscient Truth, as the seven luminous expressions of the divine Mind, *sapta vāṇīḥ*.

1. *Avardhayantasubhagaṁ sapta yahvīḥ*
śvetaṁ jajñānamaruṣaṁ mahitvā;
śiśuṁ na jātamabhyāruraśvā
devāso agniṁ janimanvapuṣyan.

2. *Śukrebhiraṅgai raja ātatanvān,*
kratuṁ punānaḥ kavibhiḥ pavitraiḥ;
śocirvasānaḥ payiārurapāṁ,
śriyo mimīte bṛhatīranūnāḥ.

3. *Vavrājā sīmanadatīradabdhāḥ,*
divo yahvīravasānā anagnāḥ;
sanā atra yuvatayaḥ sayonīr
ekaṁ garbhaṁ dadhire sapta vāṇīḥ.[154]

1. The seven mighty rivers augmented him (in strength and splendour) who utterly enjoys felicity, who is pure and radiant in his birth, and takes a ruddy and rubicund complexion when grown up. They nourish the Fire in his vital dynamis and increase his conscious life-force, and the gods cherish the body in his birth.

2 Extending his shining arms he gives shape to the middle world and purifies the will-to-action by the help of the pure Powers of the Truth. Wearing his vast white glories like a robe all about the life of the

Waters he forges within himself splendours vast and without any insufficiency.

3. Agni, the fire-divine, repairs everywhere about the mighty celestial ones who are undevouring and undevoured, they who are neither clothed nor naked. These, the eternal and ever young seven channels of radiant speech who spring from the same source, hold the one Child in them as their one common embryo.

Agni then proceeds to the birth place of pure mentality where the seven rivers flow as streams of divine felicity. There he takes on universal forms of the infinite consciousness and consequently the foster mothers in the phenomenal world — the rivers of the physical and mental consciousness — nourished by the sweetness and light flowing from above become perfectly equal and harmonised. They are transformed by the all-effecting force and blaze of Agni, and bear the abundant bliss and splendour and glory and purity of his universal forms.

1. *Stīrṇā asya saṁhato viśvarūpā*
ghṛtasya yonau sravathe madhūnām;
asthuratra dhenavaḥ pinvamānā
mahī dasmasya mātarā samīcī.

2. *Babhrāṇaḥ sūno sahaso vyadyaud*
dadhānaḥ śukrā rabhasā vapūṁṣi;
ścotanti dhārā madhuno ghṛtasya,
vṛṣā yatra vāvṛdhe kāvyena.[155]

1. Outspread everywhere and extended abroad were masses of Agni in universal forms in the womb of pure mentality, in the flowings of ambrosial waters; here the seven fostering rivers stand nourishing themselves; the two Mothers of the all-effecting god become equal to the universal and harmonised.

2. Sustained by them, O thou son and source of Strength, thou shinest bright possessing thy refulgent and rapturous raiments; streams of sweetness and purity and clarity flow forth where the Lord of the abundance grows strong by the Wisdom (of the superconscient Truth).

The Lord and Master of the all is hidden in the superconscient Truth. Agni, together with the other gods, enters the world of Truth undiminished and unmitigated in his strength and splendour, and mercifully pours them out on the earth for the growth of our soul. He finds the manifold opulence of the glorious Father, the source of all-felicity, and by himself becoming the divine Child, the aspiring soul in us, reveals the universality of our existence. Agni, the lord and lover of us all, though one, ever enjoys and upholds the onward movement of us all and of the multiple cosmic energies.

Entering the Vast, he becomes enriched and increased by the many uplifting streams of consciousness; it is the natural seat of his infinitude where the rivers work harmoniously as inseparable companions blended into a single truth of the Spirit. There Agni finds himself in all things and nourishing and uplifting all things, no longer affected by any limitation or falsity. Agni thus awakens them all to the imperative need of growing into the supreme Truth — the immortal consciousness.

The Rishi implores Agni to create in him the truth of himself for happy pilgrimage. He ever aspires for Agni's increasing presence bearing the oblations. Agni, the luminous guardian of the Truth is invoked and implored by the sacrificer to intensify his seeking, and strengthen his will to reach the home of the Truth, *satyam ṛtam bṛhat.*

a) *Agniḥ pūrvebhirṛṣibhirīḍyo nūtanairuta,*
sa devāñ eha vakṣati.[156]

Agni, the Seer-Will, was adored by the ancient seers, and will be adored too by the new, for he is the shining one who brings here all the gods.

b) *Agne yaṁ yajñamadhvaraṁ viśvataḥ paribhūrasi,*
sa iddeveṣu gacchati.[157]

O adorable Lord, you protect the cosmic sacrifice surrounding it from all sides; may it reach the gods well-guarded by you.

c) *Agnirhotā kavikratuḥ satyaścitraśravastamaḥ,*
devā devebhirā gamat.[158]

Agni, the Seer-Will, the assured summoner, true in seeing and full of varied hearing, may he, himself a god, come with the rest of the gods.

d) *Sa naḥ piteva sūnave'gne sūpāyano bhava,*
sacasvā naḥ svastaye.[159]

O Lord, be therefore easy of access to us, as a father to his son. May you be ever with us for our good.

Agni, the fire-god, is closely associated in the Veda with Indra. They are, as it were, like twin brothers and paired in several hymns. While Indra is credited with bestowing on men illumination, Agni is deified as the very vital spark in them. He is the principle of evolutionary urge in animate and inanimate Nature. He is in plants and trees, in fish, fowl and man; the gods too partake of his fiery nature. He is identified with cosmic and supra-cosmic Truth as he existed even before gods and men came into existence. He is found in lightning, in the flaming sun and in the sacred sacrificial fire and in the household.

Agni and Indra are the two gods stationed on earth and in the heaven respectively. Their association with the sacrifice is bound to increase it. When they come together satisfied with Soma, the elixir of divine delight, it attracts Mitra who shares with the seeker his exhilarating companionship on his pilgrimage. These valiant ones successfully destroy the enemies. The flaming Will of Agni and the luminous consciousness of Indra then become the secure refuge of the seeker.

1. *Ihendrāgnī upa hvaye tayoritstomamuśmasi,*
tā somaṁ somapātamā.

2. *Tā yajñéṣu pra śaṅsatendrāgnī sumbhatā naraḥ,*
tā gāyatreṣu gāyata.

3. *Tā mitrasya praśastaya indrāgnī tā havāmahe,*
somapā somapītaye.

4. *Ugrā santā havāmaha upedaṁ savanaṁ sutam,*
indrāgnī eha gacchatam.

5. *Tā mahāntā sadaspatī indrāgnī rakṣa ubjatam,*
aprajāḥ santvatriṇaḥ.

6. *Tena satyena jāgṛtamadhi pracetune pade,*
indrāgnī śarma yacchatam.[160]

1. I invoke here Indra and Agni to whom we exclusively offer our oblations; may they the splendid drinkers of the Soma-wine, receive our offering.

2. O ye seekers, adore the gods Indra and Agni in the sacrifice, worship and glorify them, and sing unto them hymns in Gayatri verses.

3. We invoke both Indra and Agni together, for the sake of extolling Mitra who brings about equal delight in all; may Indra and Agni drink the Soma offered by us.

4. We invoke the valiant ones, Indra and Agni, to this our sacrifice (for they are the destroyers of the enemies of sacrifice); may they accept our prayer and come here.

5. May the mighty gods, Indra and Agni, destroy the hordes of the Adversary; may they render them powerless and issueless.

6. O glorious gods, Indra and Agni, stationed in the supreme consciousness beyond — the heaven of Immortality, by the Truth be awake; may your highest home be our settled refuge.

The Rishi asks which auspicious name of God shall we invoke for liberation and for reuniting with Aditi, our infinite Mother, and our Father, the infinite creator of the universe. He realises that Agni being the first to be born in us is the one who has to be approached for release by the teaching or instruction of the guru. The grace of Agni leads him to Savitr, the adorable.

1. *Kasya nūnaṁ katamasyāmṛtānāṁ*
manāmahe cāru devasya nāma,
ko no mahyā aditye punar dāt pitaraṁ ca
dṛśeyaṁ mātaraṁ ca.

2. *Agnervayaṁ prathamasyāmṛtānāṁ*
manāmahe cāru devasya nāma,
Sa no mahyā aditaye punardātpitaraṁ
ca dṛśeyaṁ mātaraṁ ca.

3. *Abhi tvā deva savitarīśānaṁ vāryāṇām,*
sadāvanbhāgamīmahe.[161]

1. Tell me, which auspicious Name of God among the immortal divinities shall we meditate upon for release; who can deliver us again to the mighty Aditi that we may see at once both the Father and the Mother?

2. We meditate upon the supreme god, the adorable Agni, the first among the immortal divinities who shall deliver us to the mighty Aditi that we may see at once both the Father and the Mother.

3. O divine creator, Savitṛ, you are the lord of felicities many, ever-guarded; may we be granted the desirable span of life and health and opulence all round.

Agni is the one god most worthy of sacrificial offering, for he wears the robes of light, and manages well the sacrifice. He is described by the Rishi as being ever youthful, enthusiastic, trustworthy and dependable. Urged and inspired by him the other gods Mitra, Varuna, Aryaman arrive at the inner altar. All oblations are made to Agni alone who in turn shares them equitably with the rest of the gods. Agni, the Son of strength and the most auspicious one, is invoked again and again, for he brings us happiness and enlightenment.

1. *Vasiṣvā hi miyedhya vastrāṇyūrjāṁ pate,*
semaṁ no adhvaraṁ yaja.

2. *Ni no hotā vareṇyaḥ sadā yaviṣṭha manmabhiḥ,*
agne divitmatā vacaḥ.

3. *Ā hi ṣmā sūnave pitāpiryajatyāpaye,*
sakhā sakhye vareṇyaḥ.

4. *Ā no barhī riśādaso varuṇo mitro aryamā,*
sīdantu manuṣo yathā.

5. *Pūrvya hotarasya no mandasva sakhyasya ca,*
imā u ṣu śrudhī giraḥ.

6. *Yacciddhi śaśvatā tanā devandevaṁ yajāmahe,*
tve iddhūyate haviḥ.

7. *Priyo no astu viśpatirhotā mandro vareṇyaḥ,*
priyāḥ svagnayo vayam.

8. *Svagnayo hi vāryaṁ devāso dadhire ca naḥ,*
svagnayo manāmahe.

9. *Athā na ubhayeṣāmamṛta martyānām,*
mithaḥ santu praśastayaḥ.

10. *Viśvebhiragne agnibhirimaṁ yajñamidaṁ vacaḥ,*
cano dhāḥ sahaso yaho.[162]

1. O worthy of oblations, protector of powers, put on the vestment of lustres and conduct this our sacrifice.

2. O ever youthful God, ever-fresh and wise, with all your might and light be our priest of call and be seated at the sacrifice endeared by our devout chantings.

3. O adorable God, be like a father who sacrifices for his son, like a good relative who helps his relative, and a best friend who assists his friend. This is my prayer.

4. O praise-worthy Lord, may the swallowers of our enemies, Mitra, Varuna and Aryaman, come and be seated upon our altar-seat of sacrifice, and become familiar and friendly like men.

5. O Agni, ancientmost priest of call, may you be pleased by our sacrifice and by our friendship. Pray, be gracious enough to listen patiently our chantings.

6. O Agni, O adorable Lord, whatever we continually offer by sacrifice to the host of gods, we offer that in you alone and through your flaming mediation.

7. O adorable Agni, guardian of the peoples, delighted, worthy of choice, may you be always dear to us; O auspicious God, may we too be dear to you by our earnest devotion.

8. The gods along with Agni graciously bring for us choicest gifts of enjoyment, and with auspicious Agni for our eternal companion we are able to laud and think and discern.

9. O immortal Agni, endowed with the wealth of contemplation, may the most secret and sacred words be common and communal to both, to you the immortal one and us the mortals.

10. O kind-hearted one, O Son of Strength, with your manifold flames, may you accept this our sacrifice and our hymns of praise, and bearing happiness yourself securely establish it in us.

Agni with his flaming tail decimates the destroyers of sacrifice and brings felicitous happiness to the seekers. He protects them always from all forms of sin, and wards off all dangers, wins for them famed and long-cherished opulence and the plenitude of light. He impels all to right understanding and extends to all the highest good.

1. *Aśvaṁ na tvā vāravantaṁ*
vandadhyā agniṁ namobhiḥ,
samrājantamadhvarāṇām.

2. *Sa ghā naḥ sūnuḥ śavasā*
pṛthupragāmā suśevaḥ,
mīḍhvāñ asmākaṁ babhūvāt.

3. *Sa no dūrāccāsācca ni*
martyādaghāyoḥ,
pāhi sadamidviśvāyuḥ.

4. *Imamū ṣu tvamasmākaṁ saniṁ*
gāyatraṁ navyāṁsam,
agne deveṣu pra vocaḥ.

5. *Ā no bhaja parameṣvā vājeṣu madhyameṣu,*
śikṣā vasvo antamasya.

6. *Vibhaktāsi citrabhāno sindhorūrmā upāka ā,*
sadyo dāśuṣe kṣarasi.

7. *Yamagne pṛtsu martyamavā vājeṣu yaṁjunāḥ,*
sa yantā śaśvatīriṣah.

8. *Nakirasya sahantya paryetā kayasya cit,*
vājo asti śravāyyaḥ.

9. *Sa vājaṁ viśvacarṣaṇirarvadbhirastu tarutā,*
viprebhirastu sanitā.

10. *Jarābhoda tadviviḍḍhi viśeviśe yajñiyāya,*
stomaṁ rudrāya dṛśīkam.

11. *Sa no mahāñ animāno dhūmaketuḥ puruścandraḥ,*
dhiye vājāya hinvatu.

12. *Sa revāñ iva viśpatirdaivyaḥ ketuḥ śṛṇotu naḥ,*
ukthairagnirbṛhadbhānuḥ.

13. *Namo mahadbhyo namo arbhakebhyo namo*
yuvabhyo nama āśinebhyaḥ;
yajāma devānyadi śaknavāma mā jyāyasaḥ
śaṁsamā vṛkṣi devāḥ.[163]

1. With salutations we bow down to you, O sovereign God of our sacrifices; may you with your flaming divine powers remove the enemies of sacrifice and make the journey safe for the seekers.

2. May Agni, the source of our strength, being born and growing up in us, with sublime and majestic pace and luminous power, be the showerer for us of gifts supreme.

3. May you, O mighty Flame, omnipresent and omniscient, protect us always from the sinful, afar or near, wanting to do us harm.

4. O adorable Agni, may you accept our oblations and our hymns of praise, and equitably distribute this our giving to all the gods.

5. O worshipful God, may you procure for us the wealth of heaven, of the mid-region and of the earth; help us to participate in the triple felicity.

6. O possessor of varied radiance, the generous distributor of sublime riches, may you freely bestow on the seeker gifts of grace like the river-tide flows out to the environs.

7. O Agni, those who are protected by you both internally and externally, and prompted to the inner affluences, are able to gain control over all impulsions and attain eternal wisdom.

8. O Agni, mighty overcomer of all enemies, those who take refuge in you, no one whatsoever can ever overcome them; his is the most coveted opulence.

9. May the Seer-Will, stationed in the sacrificer, win for us the plenitude of Light and Force by the victorious enleavening of life-energies; may we be the enjoyers with the illumined discernment.

10. Awakened by earnest chantings, O Agni, may you enter there (in our inmost being) where we can communicate with you directly and obtain your munificent grace in sacrifice for the well-being of all.

11. O adorable Agni, Lord of speed and strength, and of manifold delights matchless in prowess, unlimited, resplendent and smoke-bannered, may we be helped to perfect discernment and plenitude.

12. O radiant God, guardian of the peoples, may you listen to our prayers; O messenger of the gods, may you grow generous and mighty in us by our hymns of praise.

13. We offer our salutations to the great in wisdom, to the young and energetic and to the infants equally, for the Supreme exists in all. May we be capable of worshipping all the gods, for we do not intend to cut asunder the all-pervading praise of the Supreme God.

Elsewhere, Agni is addressed as Angira, the first born of the Angiras Rishis, and the most auspicious companion of gods. It is by the greatness of his deeds that the Maruts with knowledgeable action are born. Himself born of heaven and earth, by the communion of two consciousnesses, he manifests in different modes in different men. The manifestation of Agni is important for the gods too in their dispensation of good to men. Agni, the great showerer of gifts, increaser of the seeker's nourishment, is invoked and adored by those who are endowed with illumined intelligence. By his grace the divine wealth is distributed among the devotees after annihilating their superior foes. He creates in men the thirst for a new and divine birth and work for the gain of divine wealth. Agni, the ever-wakeful among gods, seated close to the two spheres of consciousness — Earth and Heaven, gives to the seeker all felicity, bestows strength, and guards him in his Truth-ward activity. He is the intimate protector and promoter of the conscious quest for the Truth, the preserver of excellent knowledge, and caller of the gods eligible for the elixir of boundless joy. It is Agni who, with his auspicious intelligence, full of plenitudes, unites his devotees in their collective endeavour.

1. *Tvamagne prathamo aṅgirā ṛṣir*
devo devānāmabhavaḥ śivaḥ sakhā,
tava vrate kavayo vidmanāpaso'jāyanta
maruto bhrājadṛṣṭayaḥ.

2. *Tvamagne prathamo aṅgirastamaḥ kavir*
devānāṁ pari bhūṣasi vratam,
vibhurviśvasmai bhuvanāya medhiro
dvimātā śayuḥ katidhā cidāyave.

3. *Tvamagne prathamo mātariśvana āvir*
bhava sukratūyā vivasvate
arejetāṁ rodasī hotṛvūrye'saghnor
bhāramayajo maho vaso.

4. *Tvamagne manave dyāmavāśayaḥ*
purūravase sukṛte sukṛttaraḥ,
śvātreṇa yatpitrormucyase paryā tvā
pūrvamanayannāparaṁ punaḥ.

5. *Tvamagne vṛṣabhaḥ puṣṭivardhana*
udyatasruce bhavasi śravāyyaḥ,
ya āhutiṁ pari vedā vaṣaṭkṛtim
ekāyuragre viśa āvivāsasi.

6. *Tvamagne vṛjinavartaniṁ naraṁ sakman*
piparṣi vidathe vicarṣaṇe,

yaḥ śūrasātā paritakmye dhane dabhrebhiś
citsamṛtā haṁsi bhūyasaḥ.

7. *Tvaṁ tamagne amṛtatva uttame martaṁ*
dadhāsi śravase divedive,
yastātṛṣāṇa ubhayāya janmane mayaḥ
kṛṇoṣi praya ā ca sūraye.

8. *Tvaṁ no agne sanaye dhanānāṁ yaśasaṁ*
kāruṁ kṛṇuhi stavānaḥ,
idhyāma karmāpasā navena devair
dyavapṛthivī prāvataṁ naḥ.

9. *Tvaṁ no agne pitrorupastha ā devo*
deveṣvanavadya jāgṛviḥ,
tanūkṛdbodhi pramatiśca kārave tvaṁ
kalyāṇa vasu viśvamopiṣe.

10. *Tvamagne pramatistvam pitāsi nastvaṁ*
vayaskṛttava jāmayo vayam,
saṁ tvā rāyaḥ śatinaḥ saṁ sahasriṇaḥ
suvīraṁ yanti vratapāmadābhya.

11. *Tvāmagne prathamamāyumāyave devā*
akṛṇvannahuṣasya viśpatim,
iḷāmakṛṇvanmanuṣasya śāsanīṁ pitur
yatputro mamakasya jāyate.

12. *Tvaṁ no agne tava deva payubhirmaghono*
rakṣa tanvaśca vandya,
trātā tokasya tanaye gavāmasyanimeṣaṁ
rakṣamāṇastava vrate.

13. *Tvamagne yajyave pāyurantaro'niṣaṅgāya*
caturakṣa idhyase,
yo rātahavyo'vṛkāya dhāyase kīreścin
mantraṁ manasā vanoṣi tam.

14. *Tvamagna uruśaṁsāya vāghate spārhaṁ*
yadrekṇaḥ paramaṁ vanoṣi tat,

ādhrasya citpramatirnuyase pitā pra
pākaṁ śāssi pradiṣo viduṣṭaraḥ.

15. *Tvamagne prayatadakṣiṇaṁ naraṁ varmeva*
syaūtaṁ pari pāsi viśvataḥ,
svādukṣadmā yo vasatau syaonakṛjjiṣayajaṁ
yamagāma dūrāt.

16. *Imāmagne śaraṇiṁ mīmṛṣo na imam*
adhvānaṁ yamagāma dūrāt,
āpiḥ pitā pramatiḥ somyānāṁ bhṛmir
asyṛṣikṛnmartyānām.

17. *Manuṣvadagne aṅgirasvadaṅgiro*
yayātivatsadane pūrvavacchuce,
accha yāhyā vahā daivyaṁ janamā
sādaya barhiṣi yakṣi ca priyam.

18. *Etenāgne brahmaṇā vāvṛdhasva śaktī*
vā yatte cakṛmā vidā vā,
uta pra ṇeṣyabhi vasyo asmāntsaṁ
naḥ sṛja sumatyā vājavatyā.[164]

1. O adorable Agni, you are the first and foremost of the Angirasas, seer and revealer of knowledge supreme, god and giver of bliss, propitious companion of gods. By your illumined deeds the Maruts are born, of radiant weapons, who act with the knowledge of seers.

2. O adorable Agni, you are the first and foremost of the Angirasas, superb and excellent among them, the seer; you grace the rite of the gods. Manifold is your manifestation for the good of the world, offspring of two mothers, you are present everywhere and in many ways for the benefit of mankind.

3. O Agni, your manifestation is necessary for the play and glory of Vayu in the sacrificer. Therefore arrive here, O shining one, for him who is desirous of good deeds. Heaven and earth tremble at your prowess; in the selected sacrifice of the seeker you sustain the burden. O supreme Puissance, you have worshipped the venerable ones.

4. O adorable Agni, you have announced the highest heaven as the divine station to be attained for the illumined thinker, and have done immense good to those who have done good to you. When you are set free everywhere by the penitence of your parents, they bring you first in front and then make you the overlord of inner regions.

5. O Agni, you are the showerer of gifts, increaser of prosperity; you are praised by those with luminous clarity of mind. You are the sole person, who blesses and elevates the one who fully understands the invocation and makes the oblation, and then gives light and wisdom to all other men.

6. O mighty and all-compassionate Seer-Will, may you well-direct the ignorant seeker on the desired path, protect and fulfil his seeking; direct him to deeds that will lead him to illumination. For attaining the divine felicity by the valorous devotees your grace is such that even though they be inferior of strength and fewer in number, they conquer the hordes of the Enemy, superior in every way, and humiliate them.

7. O adorable Agni, you establish the mortal seeker, for sustained inspiration, in the high station of Immortality. You confer on the wise one who thirsts for divine birth, the twofold felicity, both human and divine.

8. O Agni, you are lauded by us for bestowing sublime wealth; make our inner self a greater lauder for gaining glorious and divine wealth. May we prosper by undertaking new sacrifices. May the deities Heaven and Earth along with other gods increase well our sacrifices.

9. O ever-wakeful and immaculate Flame, illumined Son of two Consciousnesses, fashion for us a new body capable of divine birth. O auspicious one, be of excellent knowledge to us, your vigilant worshippers, and sow within us all desirous wealth.

10. O adorable Agni, you are all-knowing and unsullied, mighty protector and giver of strength; we are your kinsmen. O possessor of invincible strength, unassailable, you attain with auspicious valour hundredfold and thousandfold riches. May you protect all divine deeds.

11. O Agni, the gods, the manifestations of Aditi, have made you the first man of men endowed with immeasurable *prāṇic* might, and made you their kind endowed with intense ties of friendship. When you, the flaming Child of the Divine Mother, are born in us, the gods proclaim you as the goddess of vision and of knowledge, *Ila*, the seeing word — the illumined instructress of men.

12. O adorable Lord, worthy of our laudations, protect us, and guard our wealth and our bodies. Constantly protecting and preserving us in your actions, you defend the luminous cattle and their successive progeny.

13. O illumined one, you are the devoted defender of the selfless sacrificer in all the four worlds — the triple phenomenal world and the fourth highest station. You yourself in secret entreat the laudations of the sacrificer who offers his oblations to you, for the chantings are so very dear to you.

14. O adorable Agni, you work for your illumined worshippers to gain that desirable supreme felicity; you are the well-intentioned protector of those who ever need your protection. O all-knowing and wise one you always instruct the young and the callow in all directions.

15. O mighty Agni, you protect that sacrificer fully, like a strong and well-stitched armour, who liberally offers oblations and all that is pleasing to you. The sacrificer who pleases you, our supreme guest in the body, with tasty food, and performs sacrifices throughout his life comes closest to heaven.

16. O adorable Agni, forgive us our ignorance and negligence as we have gone astray and far from the desired path. You are our dearest kinsman and protector of illumined knowledge; verily, you are the summoner of the gods to the libations of the Soma, as well as the maker of seers of mortal seekers.

17. O luminous one, foremost Angiras, may you first proceed to the sacrifice house just as you go to the house of Manu, as did Angiras, Yayati and the ancient seers. Pray bring the gods here, make them sit on the sacred grass and offer them worship.

18. O Agni, may you steadily increase by this our *mantra* which we have composed according to our understanding and ability. May you grant us abundance of spiritual wealth; endow us with auspicious intelligence and opulence, make us united in divine knowledge.

The seekers of the superconscient, supramental Truth are asked to kindle the sacrificial fire after the method initiated by their ancient forefathers. To cite a few references, Vishwamitra alludes to a precedent, *prathama dharma*, in —

Samidhyamanaḥ prathamanu dharmā
samaktubhirajyate viśvavāraḥ,
śociṣkeśo ghṛtanirṇikpāvakaḥ suyajño
agniryajathāya devān.[165]

O righteous Agni, the supreme purifier, the one whose hair is flame, when first kindled and worshipped at the altar, becomes the object of adoration by all. He is intensified by sprinkling clarified butter, so that he may convey our offerings to the gods.

And Kanva appeals to Agni not to ignore the amity and accord cultivated by the ancestors. The divine Fire is implored again and again to accept the oblations of the seekers and favour the wisdom-lovers in the manner of yore.

a) *Priyamedhavadatrivajjātavedo virūpavat,*
aṅgirasvanmahivrata praskaṇvasya śrudhī havam.[166]

O Agni, all-wise, accomplisher of auspicious acts, aware of all those who are born and free from three attachments, may you accept the invocation of Praskanwa, as you have listened to those of Priyamedha, Atri, Virupa and Angirasa.

b) *Uta tvā bhṛguvacchuce manuṣvadagna āhuta,*
aṅgirasvaddhavāmahe.[167]

O Agni, worshipped with oblations, we all invoke you and adore you, as you have been adored by Bhrigu and Manu.

Agni-worship until today has been a basically uninterrupted tradition with its source in the Rig-veda. The custom and ceremony and law have helped its long preservation. Not many have access to its psychological and esoteric significance; only the initiated are beneficiaries of the inner felicity, for Agni has his abode among men and secretly dwells in them as the shining guest. This inner relationship between the sacrificer and the heavenly fire finds expression in several hymns.

Elsewhere, Agni is said to have gone away in anger and taken refuge in the waters and plants. The gods induce him to return and promise him a share of the *havis*, 'the butter of the waters', and a pith of the herbs and continued existence. It is obvious that finding their sacrificial fire extinguished, the gods renew their efforts to reinstal it, and implore Agni to return into their fold. They beseech him to make their paths negotiable, *patho devayānān*, and carry their oblations to the Supreme.

a) *(Says Agni)*
Hotrādahaṁ varuṇa bibhyadāyaṁ nedeva
mā yunajannatra devāḥ,
tasya me tanvo bahudhā niviṣṭā
etamarthaṁ na ciketahamagniḥ.[168]

O venerable Varuna, I have escaped for fear of the *hotṛ*-duty, lest the gods may engage me again as their messenger; my bodies are therefore hidden in many places. I, Agni, would no more undertake that duty.

b) *(Varuna replies)*
Ehi manurdevayuryajñakāmo'raṁkṛtyā
tamasi kṣeṣyagne,
sugānpathaḥ kṛṇuhi devayānān
vaha havyāni sumanasyamānaḥ.[169]

O Fire-divine, come, sincere men long for performing sacrifice, being prepared for it. You live in darkness, in hiding. Pray, make the paths straight and passable which lead godward. Carry our oblations with an illumined spirit.

Agni is afraid of undertaking the *hotṛ*-duty as his elder brothers pursuing it were slain; he, as such, trembles at the very thought of it:

Agneḥ pūrve bhrātaro arthametaṁ
rathīvādhvānamanvāvarīvuḥ,
tasmādbhiyā varuṇa dūramāyaṁ
gauro na kṣepnoravije jyāyāḥ.[170]

To persuade Agni to resume his native duty, Varuna and the other gods promise him undecaying life and the essence of the waters and the plants. And finally Agni accepts to come to the sacrifice and to be the bearer of the oblations:

1. *Kurmastu āyurajaraṁ yadagne yathā*
yukto jatavedo na riṣyaḥ,
athā vahāsi sumanasyamāno bhāgaṁ
devebhyo haviṣaḥ sujāta.

2. *Prayājanme anuyājāñśca kevalānūrjasvantaṁ*
haviṣo datta bhāgam,
ghṛtaṁ cāpāṁ puruṣaṁ cauṣadhīnām
agneśca dīrghamāyurastu devāḥ.[171]

Agni inspires the gods to Immortality, and in their journey creates wide space for them. He equips Indra with the thunderbolt with which all battles are won both for men and the gods. All the gods then worship him and sprinkle him with the clarified butter of their pure and illumined intelligence and instal him as their *hotṛ*:

(Says Agni)

1. *Māṁ devā dadhire havyavāhamapamluktaṁ*
bahu kṛcchrā carantam,
agnirvidvānyajñaṁ naḥ kalpayāti
pañcayāmaṁ trivṛtaṁ saptatantum.

2. *Ā vo yakṣyamṛtatvaṁ suvīraṁ yathā*
vo devā varivaḥ karāṇi,
ā bhāhvorvajramindrasya dheyamathemā
viśvāḥ pṛtanā jayāti.

3. *Trīṇi śatā trī sahasrānyagniṁ triṅśac*
ca devā nava cāsaparyan,
aukṣanghṛtairastṛṇanbarhirasmā
ādiddhotāraṁ nyasādayanta.[172]

1. The gods have made me the bearer of oblations as I traversed through varied terrain, with the words, 'Agni shall surely prepare our sacrifice whether it be threefold or sevenfold with its five courses.'

2. O gods, I implore you for immortality and enlightened progeny, so that I can create wide space for your work. I wish to endow Indra with the thunderbolt for his victory over the hostile powers.

3. Then 3339 gods instal him and worship him; they sprinkle clarified butter over him, and spread *barhis* for him.

Finally, after having succeeded in discovering Agni, and installing him on the altar, the gods find the thrice seven secret words hidden in him that preserve immortality. These words are the names of Aditi, the divine Mother, in her wide range of activity. They compose, between them, the rainbow of all creation on the three levels of existence of the Fire of sevenfold Ecstasy and Light and Truth in the inner spaces beyond.

Born of heaven and earth, and dwelling in the secret cave of the heart, Agni makes himself easily accessible to the seeker. He is the ever-awake friend and guide of those who embark upon the inner pilgrimage. He is the divine Will in them, and carries their oblations to the gods.

a) *Imaṁ no yajñamamṛteṣu dhehīmā*
havyā jātavedo juṣasva,
stokānāmagne medaso ghṛtasya hotaḥ
prāśāna prathamo niṣadya.[173]

O omniscient Agni, may you convey our sacrificial offerings to the immortals and be pleased to accept them. O adorable Lord, ever seated on the altar, may you first partake of the oblation of our love and worship.

b) *Ayaṁ kavirakaviṣu pracetā marteṣv*
agniramṛto ni dhāyi,
sa mā no atra juhuraḥ sahasvaḥ
sadā tve sumanasaḥ syāma.[174]

This far-seeing, discerning, immortal god has been stationed among the short-sighted and ignorant mortals. May you not harm us, O mighty one, in this life that we may ever be worshipful to you.

The Rishi extols Agni as the god of supreme Intuition without which the journey cannot be undertaken.

Mahāṅ asyadhvarasya praketo na ṛte
tvadamṛtā mādayante,
ā viśvebhiḥ sarathaṁ yāhi devair
nyagne hotā prathamaḥ sadeḥ.[175]

Great are you, O Agni, embodiment of dignity, without you the immortals do not rejoice; may you come in the same chariot along with the other gods, be happily seated here at the sacrifice, O ministrant priest.

He is the one who accompanies the sacrificer-seeker throughout the journey, and is a witness to his many births — he the Immortal in the mortals.

a) *Agniṁ sūnuṁ sahaso jātavedasaṁ*
dānāya vāryāṇām,
dvitā yo bhudamṛto martyeṣv
a hotā mandratamo viśi.[176]

O adorable Agni, Son of Strength, giver of all desirable things, immortal amongst mortals and the gods, who is the supremely stimulating ministrant priest in the house.

b) *Apaśyamasya mahato mahitvam*
amartyasya martyāsu vikṣu.[177]

O adorable Agni, I mark the might of you who is immortal in the hearts of mortal men.

He is the Flame divine shining forth in the gods, and who with all his light and force enters the lives of men for awakening him to the Truth.

Agnirdeveṣu rājatyagnirmarteṣvāviśan.[178]

Agni shines alike amongst the gods and in the mortals.

Agni is described in several ways. He is referred to as a Child whose identity is kept as a secret initially. Only when he increases and grows big and vigorous that he is recognised. His home is in the highest heavens. Dawn with its shining splendours and the starry Night are Agni's sisters. His birth is concealed and is carried in the Waters which make him grow in the wide unbounded space. He is sharp-faced and effulgent, bright, brilliant and radiant, and sees through the darkness of night.

a) *Ubhe bhadre joṣayete na mene gādho*
na vāśrā upa tasthurevaiḥ,
sa dakṣāṇāṁ dakṣapatirbabhūvāñjanta
yaṁ dakṣiṇato havirbhiḥ.[179]

Both Night and Day, the auspicious ones, attend upon him like two loving parents; they seek him by the paths he has gone like fond kine follow their calves. He has been the Lord of might among the mighty whom the priests propitiate on the altar and devoutly anoint.

b) *Uru te jrayaḥ paryeti budhnaṁ*
virocamānaṁ mahiṣasya dhāma,
viśvebhiragne svayaśobhirīddho'dabdhebhiḥ
pāyubhiḥ pāhyasmān.[180]

O mighty Agni, your vast and victorious splendour pervades the skies. Kindled by us, O adorable Lord, may you preserve us with all your unmitigated radiance and power.

c) *Yo viśvataḥ supratīkaḥ sadṛūṅ ṅasi*
dūre citsantaḷidivāti rocase,
rātryāścidandho ati deva paśyasyagne
sakhye mā riṣāmā vayaṁ tava.[181]

O resplendent Lord, you are of graceful form, looking alike on every side, and though remote you shine brightly as if you are near. You penetrate the darkness of night and perceive everything. May we not suffer any harm under your protecting care.

Agni destroys the Asuras and strikes down those who are malicious and wicked.

a) *Vadhairduḥśaṅsāñ apa dūḍhyo jahi dūre*
vā ye anti vā ke cidatriṇaḥ,
athā yajñāya gṛṇate sugaṁ kṛdhyagne
sakhye mā riṣāmā vayaṁ tava.[182]

O mighty Agni, conquer all enemies wicked and vile, distant or near with your punitive powers. Pray provide an easy path for the sacrifices. May we not suffer any harm under your protecting care.

b) *Agne bādhasva vi mṛidho vi durgahāpāmīvām*
apa rakṣāṅsi sedha,
asmātsamudrād bṛhato divo no'pāṁ
bhūmānamupa naḥ sṛjeha.[183]

O adorable Agni, may you destroy our adversaries, demolish their citadels, remove any infirmity and banish the baneful and bring us the bounties from above.

Tracing the growth of Agni, the Rishi speaks of Matarisvan as the one who brings him to Bhrigu as a gift. And the Bhrigus worship among men.

Vahniṁ yaśasaṁ vidathasya ketuṁ
suprāvyaṁ sadyoartham,
dvijanmānaṁ rayimiva praśasthaṁ rātiṁ
bharadbhṛgave mātariśvā.[184]

Matarisvan brought Vahni, the sacred performer of sacrifices, to Bhrigu. May the devout protector of his worshippers, the radiant messenger of the gods, the begotten of the two parents, be friendly to the wise ones.

Agni is the divine messenger who communicates with the gods on behalf of the worshippers and conducts the gods to the sacrifice. Agni and Soma are the two gods connected with inspiring, purifying and exalting the seekers and the sacrifice. They are the two aspects of the same Power that edifies and elevates and opens up the vision of the Truth. While the latter purifies through love and joy and grants illumination, the former burns down the dross and gross, and raises the mortal to the world of

Immortality. In their effort the two together enable man to enter the superconscient Truth which is the ultimate aim.[b] Agni and Soma are coupled together in many ways for augmented action; they are complementary sorts of inspiration. They together purify and up-bear the oblations.

Agni, the high-priest of sacrifice, the divine flame, is the messenger of the *devas* to the sacrificers. He is the charioteer of the transcendent Truth, the Will hidden within, and the immortal stallion who steadily carries the seeker to the goal. If Soma grants illumination through exhilaration, Agni does it through the invincible power of his aspiring will. Soma and Agni, king and the high priest, conjointly accomplish the cherished ideal. Agni, the bright chariot of the ritual, is the elected priest of every act of worship; he is the one who shares with all the gods their might and glory, and also the shining guest of men.

Hotāraṁ citrarathamadhvarasya
yajñasyayajñasya ketuṁ ruśantam,
pratyardhiṁ devasyadevasya mahnā
śriyā tvagnimatithiṁ janānām.[185]

O adorable Agni, we worship you who is the invoker of all sacred deeds, the radiant ensign of sacrificial oblations and the surpasser of all other gods in might and light. May you be the honorable guest of men.

Agni is the leader of mighty sacrifice, the *viśva mahāyajña*, and of all oblations; the Rishi pleads that he may not accept the offerings of the Adversary.

Anti citsantamaha yajñaṁ martasya ripoḥ,
nopa veṣi jātavedaḥ.[186]

O adorable Agni, all-knowing and most radiant, may you not accept the oblations of our adversary, however close to you he may pretend to be.

He is the guardian of the all-embracing *ṛta*, its friend, inspirer and upholder.

Rājantamadhvarāṇāṁ gopāmṛtasya dīdivim [187]

O Agni, we beseech you, radiant protector and sustainer of the cosmic law.

His sacrificial action is most dynamic, he who integrates the manifest with the supreme unmanifest. As the 'head of heaven' and the 'fleet messenger of earth' as well as the 'deathless oblation-bearer', he with his flaming vision and action unites men and gods, earth and heaven. His functions as an intermediary between heaven and earth, as conveyor of oblations, as the inspired high-priest and unerring in sacrifices are constantly brought out in the Veda.

Agni accomplishes his ubiquitous task among humans as indeed in all existents in accordance with the law of the supreme Truth.

a) *Adhāyyagnirmānuṣīṣu vikṣva pāṁ*
garbho mitra ṛtena sādhan.[188]

O adorable Agni, friend of the wise, you are born amidst the waters in accordance with *ṛta*, the law of the Truth.

b) *Jāto agnī rocate cekitāno vājī*
vipraḥ kaviśastaḥ sudānuḥ,
yaṁ devāsa īḍyaṁ viśvavidam
havyavāhamadadhuradhvareṣu.[189]

O Fire-divine, mighty and swift-moving, even when born, is seen your radiant glow. Supreme bearer of oblations, adorable and all-knowing, worshipped by the wise, may you be liberal in bestowing rewards.

c) *Sīda hotaḥ sva u loke cikitvānt*
sādayā yajñaṁ sukṛtasya yonau,
devāvīrdevānhaviṣā yajāsyagne
bṛhadyajamāne vayo dhāḥ.[190]

O Agni, supreme priest, fully aware of sacrificial acts, may you be seated in your proper place and initiate the ceremony in the main place alloted for worship. O bearer of oblations to the gods, may you bestow abundant nourishment to the worshippers.

Agni's very function is to carry the seeker's sacrificial oblations to the gods;

he is the true sacrificer and the one archetypal priest after whom all priesthood is modelled and perfected. He is the all-knower, *jātavedas*, *viśvavid*, the very wise, *dhīmahi pracetasam*, and the great liberator; he brings the desired illumination, the cherished intuitive perception of the Truth and the consequent release.

a) *Ni tvā yajñasya sādhanamagne*
hotāramṛtvijam,
manuṣvaddeva dhīmahi pracetasaṁ
jīraṁ dūtamamartyam.[191]

O adorable Agni supreme effectuator of sacrifices, inspirer and invoker, the destroyer of the enemies, immortal, messenger of the gods, we acknowledge you, as Manu would do, as our radiant leader and guide.

b) *Ā devānāmabhavaḥ keturagne mandro*
viśvāni kāvyāni vidvān,
prati martāñ avāsayo damūnā anu
devānrathiro yāsi sādhan.[192]

O Agni, you are the formidable announcer of the gods, bestower of bliss and cognisant of all sacred acts. Hushed, you abide in the hearts of mortals and illumine them. And like a speedy charioteer you follow the gods and fulfil them.

c) *Tribhiḥ pavitrairapupoddhy arkaṁ*
hṛdā matiṁ jyotiranu prajānan,
varṣiṣṭhaṁ ratnamakṛta svadhābhir
ādid dyāvāpṛthivī paryapaśyat.[193]

Agni, fully comprehending the Light in the heart, then purifies himself with mind, speech and deeds. He further makes himself most excellent by these self-modifications, and thence contemplates on heaven and earth.

d) *Akro na babhriḥ samithe mahīnāṁ*
didṛkṣeyaḥ sūnave bhāṛjīkaḥ,
udusriyā janitā yo jajānāpāṁ garbho
nṛtamo yahvo agniḥ.[194]

The invincible Fire-Power, he is the Supreme mover in things and their great sustainer; he in the blending of the Great Ones, seeks the supreme vision and fulfils the need to press out the Soma-wine; he who is the begetter of all Radiances now gives them a new and higher birth, himself the child of the Waters, the most mighty Agni.

It is thus that Agni and Soma help the worshippers to perceive the secret purpose of creation and to participate in the cosmic *yajña*, and finally to live in the supreme state of enlightenment — that of Immortality.

Tvāṁ viśve amṛta jāyamānaṁ śiśuṁ
na devā abhi saṁ navante,
tava kratubhiramṛtatvamāyan
vaiśvānara yatpitroradīdeḥ.[195]

O immortal Agni, all the worshippers praise you when you are born as an infant, and when you shine in the mid-region between heaven and earth the gods gain immortality through your sacred deeds.

Agni is both the flame of aspiration of the worshippers and their final achievement. He and Soma join their essences and their efforts in the attainment of immortality.

a) *Agniḥ sanoti vīryāṇi vidvāntsanoti*
vājamamṛtāya bhūṣan.[196]

O adorable Agni, you secure for us heroic might and prosperity and enlightened progeny for attaining Immortality.

b) *Ṛṣimanā ya ṛṣikṛtsvarṣāḥ*
sahasraṇīthaḥ pādavīḥ kavīnām,
tṛtīyaṁ dhāma mahiṣaḥ siṣāsant somo
virājamanu rājati ṣṭup.[197]

The mighty one, Soma, light and life bestower, far-seeing seer, strives after attaining the highest region. A leader of the wise, he is worshipped with a thousand hymns that increases his radiance.

While Agni enhances the heroic power in the worshipper, Soma provides the necessary vision and vigour in his effort to enter another level of awareness.

> 1. *Aṣāḷho agne vṛṣabho didīhi puro*
> *viśvāḥ saubhagā saṁjigīvān,*
> *yajñasya netā prathamasya pāyor*
> *jātavedo bṛhataḥ supraṇīte.*
>
> 2. *Acchidrā śarma jaritaḥ purūṇi devāñ*
> *acchā dīdvānaḥ sumedhāḥ,*
> *ratho na sasnirabhi vakṣi vājamagne*
> *tvaṁ rodasī naḥ sumeke.*[198]

> 1. O mighty Lord, showerer of benefits, may you consume all the strongholds of the Enemy and their belongings. O adorable Agni, all-knower, may you conduct the first *mahā yajña.*
>
> 2. O resplendent Lord, endowed with great and luminous intelligence, invoker of the gods, may you bring, without impatience, our oblations to the gods (as a chariot carries the food); may you, with your radiance, illumine both earth and heaven.

Agni is the one ocean, the wide foundation of all spiritual felicity, and that pure flame which ever shines forth from the heart.

> *Ekaḥ samudro dharuṇo rayīṇāmasmad*
> *dhṛdo bhūrijanmā vi caṣṭe* [199]

> O Agni, you are like an ocean of opulence; ceaselessly born, you know us perfectly. You stay concealed in the clouds and in the dew-drops.

He is the soaring flame in the human heart which is experienced while offering oblations, indicative of man's perfect integration with the Truth.

There exists a close symbiosis between the worshippers and Agni on the one hand, and the worshippers and the gods on the other. That is, when Agni is increased, the worshippers rejoice, and when the worshippers increase, the gods rejoice and become generous. Agni and the worshippers enjoy a mutuality of augmentation, and through this symbiotic relationship the other gods enjoy a progressive growth.

Agni and Soma are the gods of sacrificial fire and the sacrificial drink.

The account of Agni's birth and of his rebirth when he leaves the gods and needs to be brought back, as well as of the descent of Soma from heaven has to be understood symbolically. They are the two sources of inspiration, vision and fulfilment in respect of the worshippers. To the mere intellect, the birth and recovery of Agni appear to be enigmatic and mystifying; they are two aspects of an esoteric process of the evolution of consciousness. The withdrawal of Agni results in a crisis, and the gods implore him to rescue the worshipper from it. His reappearance becomes synonymous with the emergence of creation. Agni himself is said to be born many times, and also responsible for many births signifying the evolution of life and consciousness. Agni is described as being androgynous, both as the bull and the cow — Parjanya. He is Light as well as Force.

> *Asacca sacca parame vyoman dakṣasya*
> *janmannaditerupasthe,*
> *agnirha naḥ prathamajā ṛtasya pūrva*
> *āyuni vṛṣabhaśca dhenuḥ.*[200]

> O Agni, you exist in the manifest and in the Unmanifest, in the birthplace of Daksha and in the bosom of infinity. You are our elder brother and the ordainer of eternal laws. In primordial time you were both the bull and the cow.

A young seeker seeks Agni's guidance in knowing more about Agni. He speaks of the cosmic Agni, the sun, that disappears at night and of him who appears among mortals as the sacrificial fire, and also of him who as the power of aspiration helps the worshipper to surpass his own father, the inspiration that transfigures the worshipper. Yet, this knowledge makes him all the more aware of the impossibility of describing Agni.

(5)

Agni in the Upanishads, Epics, and Puranas

(A)

Agni in the Veda is the sacred Fire, the divine Will, in man. It is the illumined Energy which builds up and sustains the many worlds, and which upbears man to the Truth. He is divine Knowledge-in-manifest-ation, for force essentially is the operation of consciousness. Agni is the divine Will that fulfils in man the many puissances of the gods. It is the force of fulfilment through which the gods work in the seeker, and *yajña* symbolises this manifold work. Agni works infused with the Light and Power of the Truth-Consciousness. He is therefore described as *satya*, who is in perfect possession of his own truth as well as the essential truth of all things. It is this all-knowledge that enables him to act perfectly with perfect force towards perfect perfection. We have the same conception also in the Upanishads.

Agni, in the Upanishads, is spoken of in the double aspect of force and light; psychologically Agni is the divine Will. The gods of the Upanishads differ in one respect from those of the Veda. The Vedic gods are only personalities, powers and representations of the one Godhead and are conscious of their identity with It; they always dwell in their home and origin — the superconscient Truth. But at the same time, as part of their lesser and necessary movement, they manifest themselves in the phenomenal universe and put on the cast of cosmic functionings. Whereas in the Upanishadic pantheon, the gods do not occupy this high and preeminent position; they are rather cast down, as it were, and appear only in their inferior human and universal workings. The three Upanishadic gods Agni, Vayu and Indra represent the cosmic Divine on each of Its three planes — material, vital and mental. In Sri Aurobindo's words, "Agni is the heat and flame of the conscious force in Matter which has built up the universe; it is he who has made life and mind possible and developed them in the material universe where he is the greatest deity. Especially he is the primary impeller of speech of which Vayu is the medium and Indra the lord. This heat of conscious force in Matter is Agni Jatavedas, the knower of all births; of all things born, of every cosmic phenomenon he knows the law, the process, the limit, the relation."[201] In case any mighty event impedes the onward march of the gods, it is supposed to be Agni, the all-knowing and the all-powerful, who successfully meets the challenge for he is at the basis of every birth and process in the universe. Truly, "His name is Agni Jatavedas, the Power that is at the basis of all birth and process in the material universe and embraces and knows their workings and the force in him is this that all that is thus born, he as the flame of Time and Death can devour. All things are his food which he assimilates and turns into material of new birth and formations. But this all-devourer cannot devour with all his force a fragile blade of grass so long as it has behind it the power of the Eternal. Agni is compelled to return, not having discovered. One thing only is settled that this Daemon is no Birth of the material cosmos, no transient thing that is subject to the flame and breath of Time; it is too great for Agni."[202]

Similarly, the Upanishad proceeds, the other gods Vayu and Indra fail to meet the formidable challenge of Brahman. However, Indra the illumined power of the Mind with the help and grace of the many-splendoured Uma learns of the Brahman-nature of this Daemon — the blade of grass which neither the fire-power of Agni can burn nor the life-force of Vayu blow it off. It is from this supreme Nature and supreme Consciousness that the gods truly draw their strength; verily, it is from Brahman that they all proceed and must therefore depend upon it for all their activity. The One and the Supreme can be realised and possessed by the gods only when all forms of egoism — mental, vital and physical, are eliminated. It needs on the part of the gods a conscious surrender, a perfect resignation to be able to reflect totally the Infinite and the Eternal.

The subtle and profound psychology, as is revealed in the Upanishads cannot be expected to spring out of a previous spiritual void. It should be construed as the result of an onward march from knowledge to higher knowledge, or as a renewal and restatement of an earlier attainment. In this case it presupposes great origins preceding itself. In the *Isha Upanishad* Agni is invoked as the purifier from sin and the leader of the soul on its journey to the world of divine Bliss. And Surya prayed for higher revelations to be able to reach the supreme Truth.

Agne naya supathā rāye asmān
viśvāni deva vayunāni vidvān,
yuyodhyasmajjuhurāṇameno bhūyiṣṭhāṁ
te namauktiṁ vidhema.[203]

O god Agni, thou all-knowing, lead us by the good path to the attainment of spiritual felicity. Destroy the devious attraction of sin within us. We surrender ourselves totally and offer thee completely our salutations.

Surya and Agni according to the Upanishads, represent two lines of knowledge and action which lead the aspirant to the attainment of supreme vision and spiritual felicity. Growth of consciousness is the first principle of progress from death to immortality. But consciousness is incomplete without energy. Knowledge fulfils itself by action; Surya and Agni, divine Light and divine Force, are the inseparable twin-gods which lead the seeker to the world of the Truth — the world of *satyam ṛtam bṛhat.* For, these are the inseparable conditions of immortality. Whereas in the Veda, Agni is the one who when invoked manifests in the aspirant the increasing godhead. It is because of him that the sacrificial fire burns on the altar of man's soul. He is the high priest, the divine worker, the conscious will in us, the immortal guest in our mortal being, the luminous mediator between earth and the world of truth and light. Always seated before the Lord, instinct with knowledge, he is the seven-tongued power of the Truth who brings joy and peace and freedom into our lives. In the Veda, thus, the gods are the shining ones, the lords of light and divine beings. They are "powers, outwardly of physical, inwardly of psychical nature. Thus Agni outwardly is the physical principle of fire, but inwardly the god of the psychic godward flame, force, will, Tapas; Surya outwardly the solar light, inwardly the god of the illuminating revelatory knowledge; Soma outwardly the moon and the Soma-wine or nectarous moon-plant, inwardly the god of the spiritual ecstasy, Ananda. The principal psychical conception of this inner Vedic cult was the idea of the Satyam, Ritam, Brihat, the Truth, the Law, the Vast. Earth, Air and Heaven symbolised the physical, vital and mental being, but this Truth was situated in the greater Heaven, base of a triple Infinity actually and explicitly mentioned in the Vedic Riks, and it is meant therefore a state of spiritual and supramental illumination. To get beyond earth and sky to Swar, the Sun-world, seat of this illumination, home of the gods, foundation and seat of the Truth, was the achievement of the early Fathers, *pūrve pitaraḥ*, and of the seven Angiras Rishis who founded the Vedic religion. The solar gods, children of Infinity, Adityas, were born in the Truth and the Truth was their home, but they descended into the lower planes and had in each plane their appropriate functions, their mental, vital and physical cosmic motions. They were the guardians and increasers of the Truth in man and by the Truth, *ṛtasya panthāḥ*, led him to felicity and immortality. They had to be called into the human being and increased in their functioning, formed in him, brought in or born, *devavīti*, extended, *devatāti*, united in their universality, *vaiśvadevya*."[204]

(B)

Epic mythology is more or less consistent in as much as there is no dissimilarity between the character of gods in *Mahabharata* and *Ramayana*. At least there is not any significant diversity. In both the Epics the older gods are replaced by new gods. While the former personify natural phenomena, the latter embrace spiritual characters.

In the *Mahabharata* Agni is one of the eight great *Devas* — Surya, Candramas, Vayu, Agni, Yama, Varuna, Indra and Kubera. These are the world-protectors, the epic *lokapālas*. Agni has many epithets in the Epics which carry his chief attributes. He is Anala, son of Anila the wind-god. He is Suci and Pavaka, pure and purifier, Dahana and Arka, burner and light, Plavanga and Swargadwarasprisha, leaper and gleaming to heaven's door; Krishnavartman and Dhumaketu, black-tracked and smoke-bannered, Chitrabhanu and Sarvabhuj, remover of darkness and eater of all oblations. He is the wise god, Kavi, Jatavedas and the mouth of gods, *mukham devānām*. He is the maker and lord of creatures, Bhutabhavana, Bhutadi and Bhutapati. He is the child of the Waters, Apamgarbha and the maker of gold, Hiranyaretas. He is Vaishwanara and Panchajanya the universal and cosmic; he springs from the fire-sticks, Aranisuta, and is the father of Kumara, Kumarasu. Varied are the activities of Agni; the Epics speak of distinct fires. Agni appears in different roles in several epic scenes; he is eulogised as the creator, the sustainer and the all-pervading Supreme. He is described as having two heads, a big belly, six eyes and seven arms. He holds objects like the spoon, ladle pan etc., has seven tongues, four horns and three legs. He has two consorts, Swaha and Swadha; smoke is his banner and ram his vehicle. This is an anthropomorphic representation of the sacrificial fire.

Agni is one of the most ancient and sacred gods of Hindu worship; he is one of the chief three deities of the Vedas — Agni, Surya and Indra, who respectively preside over earth, air and sky. He is the mediator between men and gods, protector of men and their homes and witness of all their actions. He is described as having seven tongues each of which has a separate name. He is called upon to destroy Kravyads, the flesh-eaters or Rakshasas. In the *Mahabharata*, Agni is represented as having exhausted his strength by devouring too many oblations turns to the Khandava forest to consume it. Indra prevents him, but after obtaining the consent of Krishna, Arjuna accomplishes his object.

Agni, in the Veda, is said to be the son of Dyaus and Prithivi, Abhimani, son of Brahma, Aditya and Angirasa. In later mythology he is pictured as a red-complexioned god with dark eyes, eyebrows and hair. He is described as wearing a poita, the sacred thread, and a garland of fresh fruit. Flames of fire issue forth from his mouth, and from his body radiate streams of glory. He is the most mighty one whose commands everyone obeys; he is the most vigilant and watchful, the great nourisher and increaser. He, the guardian and custodian of Immortality, is invoked for enlightenment and liberation, and in fact for all felicity both temporal and spiritual. He is the supreme forgiver of all sin and shortcomings, the one who holds and surrounds all as the circumference of a wheel contains the spokes. In the *Mahabharata*, Agni is known by many names — Vahni he who receives the *hom*, Vitihotra he who sanctifies the worshipper, Dhananjaya he who conquers riches, Jivalana he who burns, Dhumaketu he whose sign is smoke, Chhagaratha he who rides on a ram, and Saptajihwa he who has seven tongues. In *Vishnu Purana* he is called Abhimani. His father is Brahma and wife Swāha, and by her has three sons Pavaka, Pavamana and Suchi; these have forty-five offsprings. These forty-nine persons symbolise forty-nine fires which are described in the *Vayu Purana*. Agni is known by many names and epithets; in addition to those mentioned earlier, he is known as Abja-hasta (lotus in hand), Hutasa (the devourer of things), Rohitashwa (having red horses), Chhaga-ratha (the ram-rider), Sapta-jihwa (the seven-tongued), Tomara-dhara (the javelin-bearer). He is both the *gṛhapati*, master of the house and the *dūta*, the messenger *par excellence* commuting between gods and men. He is the earliest representative in a sense of the Hindu trinity and is called *dvijanma*, twice-born. He is the master priest, the wise and omniscient one and the shining guest seated in the hearts of the seekers. He is variously called *purohita*, *adhvarya*, *vipra ritvij*, *jātavedas* and the *atithi*.

The Sama-veda sums up the many puissances of Agni in the following celebrated hymn:

Enā vo agniṁ namasorjo napātamā huve,
priyaṁ cetiṣṭmaratihañ
svadhvaraṁ viśvasya dūtamamṛtaṁ.[205]

With this hymn I invoke thee O Agni, Son of Strength, wise and endeared envoy of us all, skilled in the sacred sacrifice, and immortal.

(C)

According to one account, the Vedic religion was only an assemblage of the worship of Nature-gods and solar-myths sanctified and hallowed by sacrificial service and ritual. It is true that in the beginning this was the natural phase common to all the ancient cultures of the world — Greek, Roman and Indian. But then, in all these, with the passage of time, these gods assumed a higher significance. As Sri Aurobindo observes, "Pallas Athene who may have been originally a Dawn-Goddess springing in flames from the head of Zeus, the Sky-God, Dyaus of the Veda, has in classical Greece a higher function and was identified by the Romans with their Minerva, the Goddess of learning and wisdom; similarly, Saraswati, a River Goddess, becomes in India the goddess of wisdom, learning and the arts and crafts: all the Greek deities have undergone a change in this direction — Apollo, the Sun-God, has become a god of poetry and prophecy, Hephaestus the Fire-God a divine smith, god of labour. In India the process was arrested half-way, and the Vedic Gods developed their psychological functions but retained more fixedly their external character and for higher purposes gave place to a new pantheon. They had to give precedence to Puranic deities who developed out of the early company but assumed larger cosmic functions, Vishnu, Rudra, Brahma, — developing from the Vedic Brihaspati, or Brahmanaspati, — Shiva, Lakshmi, Durga."[206] While in India the earlier deities became inferior gods of the *Purānas*, no such change takes over to save or preserve the original characteristic features of the Greek and Roman Gods. This is mainly because of the survival and continued authority of the Rig-veda in which the inner and outer functions of the gods usefully coexist.

This transformation was apparently due to a cultural advancement in the early peoples; they became more and more mentalised, and sought for a psychological and spiritual import in the gods they worshipped. In this the contribution of the Mystics has been enormous and significant. Being men of deeper knowledge and self-knowledge they thoughtfully employed the language of symbols and eloquent and meaningful rites largely within the parameters of the more primitive religions. Of course, this varied from one culture to another depending upon its psychological milieu.

With the widening and deepening of psychic and spiritual experience, the more important Vedic forms gradually fade out, symbols transformed, and ceremony and ritual substituted by new configurations. The Vedic gods lose their original significance and are substituted by a new pantheon and the great Puranic Trinity, Brahma-Vishnu-Shiva. These symbolise a deeper truth and larger ambit of spiritual experience; they encompass a vaster formulation and a profounder perceptibility. This resulted in the replacement of the house of sacrificial Fire, *Yajña-śālā*, by the temple, the ritual of sacrifice by the temple ritual, and the sacrifice itself by adoration and elaborate external worship. The Puranic pantheon thus assumed for the masses a psycho-religious significance, at once spiritual and satisfying. Essentially both the Vedic and Puranic gods remain the same and signify the one central eternal truth. The Trinity is just the triple form of the one Brahman, and the Shaktis the different formulations of one Energy. But the great change lay in the fact that while the insight and the appreciation of the Vedic religion was limited to the initiated few, the religious and spiritual truth of the Puranic gods was shared by the common people. For the mode of worship was simpler and the godheads easy to comprehend; also the concept of the immanent Divine and the vision and work of the *Avatāra* for humanity as well as the discoverability and realisation of the Divine in one's own being popularised the Vedic and Upanishadic experience to an exceptional degree. "The Purano-Tantric system", observes Sri Aurobindo, "was a wide, assured and many-sided endeavour, unparalleled in its power, insight, amplitude, to provide the race with a basis of generalised psycho-religious experience from which man could rise through knowledge, works or love or through any other fundamental power of his nature to some established supreme experience and highest absolute status."[207]

The Vedas do not speak of any incarnation of the gods nor of their *Vibhutis*; they speak of their cosmic presence working in men. Undoubtedly, the seers clearly felt in and around them the living presence of the *devas* governing their thoughts and actions. But all this was a common experience and not a personal one. There was nothing special or individual about the presence that would bring about a radical change in the life and consciousness of the aspirant. "This is evident", says Sri Aurobindo, "from the very language when they speak of Agni as the immortal in mortals, the immortal Light in men, the inner Warrior, the Guest in human beings. It is the same with Indra or Soma. The building of the gods in man means a creation of the divine Powers, — Indra the Power of the Light, Soma the Power of the Ananda, — in the human nature."[208]

* Indicates Sri Aurobindo's translation wherever it appears in the text.

1. *Ṛg Veda* (abbreviated as RV.) IV.3.16
2. RV. I.164.46
3. Sri Aurobindo Birth Centenary Library (abbreviated as SABCL) Vol. 11, p. 6
4. RV. X.71.15
5. SABCL. Vol. 11, p. 6
6. RV. X.71.4
7. SABCL. Vol. 11, p. 6
8. Ibid., p. 9
9. Ibid., p. 12
10. Ibid., p. 13
11. Ibid.
12. SABCL. Vol. 10, p. 54

13. RV. I.164.47
14. RV. IV.21.3
15. SABCL. Vol. 11, pp. 17-18
16. Ibid., Vol. 10, p. 61
17. RV. V.82.4,5
18. RV. I.75.5
19. SABCL. Vol. 10, p. 265
20. Ibid., p. 268
21. RV. I.77.1
22. RV. I.69.2
23. RV. I.128.3
24. RV. II.9.3
25. RV. III.54.1
26. RV. VIII.43.28
27. RV. I.95.3
28. RV. II.1.1
29. RV. III.22.2
30. SABCL. Vol. 27, p. 335
31. RV. V.1.1
32. RV. VI.6.4
33. RV. X.79.7a
34. RV. VI.6.5
35. RV. X.79.4
36. RV. VII.10.1
37. RV. 5.5
38. *Atharva Veda*, III.21.1
39. RV. VI.16.39
40. RV. VII.5.3
41. RV. X.31.10
42. RV. III.3.11
43. RV. III.6.4
44. RV. VI.16.13
45. RV. V.73.6
46. RV. II.36.4
47. RV. I.15.4
48. RV. V.11.2
49. RV. V.4.8
50. RV. VI.8.7
51. RV. VIII.39.8
52. RV. III.2.9
53. RV. X.88.10
54. RV. I.151.1
55. RV. III.1.3
56. RV. III.1.13
57. RV. III.9.2
58. *Sama Veda*, Uttarachika, XX.1824
59. RV. III.1.9-11

60. RV. III.1.13,14
61. SABCL. Vol. 11, p. 493
62. Ibid., p. 494
63. Ibid., p. 495
64. RV. V.1.3
65. RV. V.1.4
66. SABCL. Vol. 11, p. 498
67. Ibid., p. 499
68. Ibid., p. 500
69. RV. V.1.5
70. RV. V.1.6
71. SABCL. Vol. 10, p. 358
72. Ibid., p. 359
73. Ibid., p. 360
74. Ibid.
75. Ibid., p. 361
76. RV. V.1.1-12
77. RV. V.2.1-12
78. RV. V.3.1-12
79. RV. V.4.1-11
80. RV. V.5.1-11
81. RV. V.6.1-10
82. RV. V.7.1-10
83. RV. V.8.1-7
84. RV. V.9.1-7
85. RV. V.10.1-7
86. RV. V.11.1-6
87. RV. V.12.1-6
88. RV. V.13.1-6
89. RV. V.14.1-6
90. RV. V.15.1-5
91. RV. V.16.1-5
92. RV. V.17.1-5
93. RV. V.18.1-5
94. RV. V.19.1-5
95. RV. V.20.1-4
96. RV. V.21.1-4
97. RV. V.22.1-4
98. RV. V.23.1-4
99. RV. V.24.1-4
100. RV. V.25.1-9
101. RV. V.26.1-9
102. RV. V.27.1-6
103. RV. V. 28.1-6
104. SABCL. Vol. 11, pp. 21-22
105. Ibid., pp. 29-30
106. SABCL. Vol. 12, p. 130

107. Ibid., Vol. 14, p. 265
108. Ibid., Vol. 18, p. 280
109. RV. I.22.20
110. RV. I.50.10
111. RV. III.54.8b
112. RV. V.62.1
   a. Trans: T. V. Kapali Sastry
113. RV. X.114.5
114. Yaska, *Nirukta* I.25 (As quoted by T. V. Kapali Sastri, *Further Lights: The Veda & Tantra* [Pondicherry, 1951], p. 40.)
115. T. V. Kapali Sastry, *Lights on the Veda* (Pondicherry, 1947), pp. 32-33
116. SABCL. Vol. 11, p. 478
117. *Sama Veda*, Uttararchika, 5.908
118. Ibid., 1.108
119. *Yajur Veda*, III.4
120. Ibid., IV.11
121. Ibid., IV.14
122. Ibid., XXXII.1
123. Ibid., XXXII.2
124. Ibid., XXXII.3
125. Ibid., XXXII.4
126. Ibid., XV.32
127. RV. III.2.3a
128. RV. III.2.8
129. RV. III.9.9
130. RV. III.29.9
131. RV. VI.7.1
132. RV. VI.7.2
133. RV. VI.4.2
134. RV. VI.5.5
135. RV. I.65.1
136. RV. I.67.3-4
137. RV. IV.7.6
138. RV. II.3.2
139. RV. III.9.1
140. RV. I.170.1
141. RV. I.18.6
142. RV. I.142.3
143. RV. I.94.13
144. RV. VIII.43.24
145. RV. V.23.2
146. RV. I.13.1-12
147. RV. I.14.1-12
148. RV. I.12.1-12
149. RV. I.1.6
150. RV. I.1.7
151. RV. I.1.8

151a. RV. I.1.1
152. RV. III.1.2
153. RV. III.1.3
154. RV. III.1.4-6
155. RV. III.1.7-8
156. RV. I.1.2
157. RV. I.1.4
158. RV. I.1.5
159. RV. I.1.9
160. RV. I.21.1-6
161. RV. I.24.1-3
162. RV. I.26.1-10
163. RV. I.27.1-13
164. RV. I.31.1-18
165. RV. III.17.1
166. RV. I.45.3
167. RV. VIII.43.13
168. RV. X.51.4
169. RV. X.51.5
170. RV. X.51.6
171. RV. X.51.7-8
172. RV. X.52.4-6
173. RV. III.21.1
174. RV. VII.4.4
175. RV. VII.11.1
176. RV. VIII.71.11
177. RV. X.79.1a
178. RV. V.25.4a
179. RV. I.95.6
180. RV. I.95.9
181. RV. I.94.7
182. RV. I.94.9
183. RV. X.98.12
184. RV. I.60.1

b. In the words of Stella Kramrisch: "Agni, Fire, the spark and flame of life, and Soma, the elixir of life, descend from heaven to earth and ascend from earth to heaven. Their track of liquid fire extends from here to there and from the beyond down to the earth with the systole and diastole as it were of inspiration and aspiration. The place where each of these gods comes to earth and whence he ascends is the place of the sacrifice, the sacrificial altar, the navel of the world... The rites of the sacrifice confirm and celebrate the tracks of these two gods which traverse the cosmos and the inner worlds of man." ('The triple structure of creations in the Rig-Veda', *History of Religions*, Vol. 2, No.1, Summer 1962, pp.143-4.)

185. RV. X.1.5
186. RV. VIII.11.4
187. RV. I.1.8a
188. RV. III.5.3a
189. RV. III.29.7

190. RV. III.29.8
191. RV. I.44.11
192. RV. III.1.17
193. RV. III.26.8
194. RV. III.1.12
195. RV. VI.7.4
196. RV. III.25.2ab
197. RV. IX.96.18
198. RV. III.15.4-5
199. RV. X.5.1ab
200. RV. X.5.7
201. SABCL. Vol. 12, p. 217
202. Ibid., pp. 217-18
203. *Isha Upanishad*, 18
204. SABCL. Vol. 11, pp. 466-67
205. *Sama Veda*, Uttararchika, I,45
206. SABCL. Vol. 11, p. 3
207. Ibid., Vol. 14, p. 153
208. Ibid., Vol. 22, pp. 110-11

II

VAYU

The universe is the oneness and integral wholeness of all manifest existences; it has its being and movement in the Unmanifest. It is the mobile Potency of the Immobile; it is the mutable nature of the immutable Self. It is the principle and the all-pervasive power of material Nature, Vayu, that supports the formative force of all other elemental movements in the infinitely vast and immense firmness and steadiness of ether. Vayu is the visible strength of the Invisible, the formative force of the Formless.

Vayu is the principle of life-stuff, Prāna, the will and energy in the entire universe working out into settled form and action, and conscious operation of being. It is an intense and less subtle condition of causal matter that emerges out of a preceding state that is exceptionally fine called Ether. It is an elemental state of Matter which is neither perceptible nor analysable. Along with other elements, Vayu underlies all forms and substances as one of their basic principle of material formation. Evolved out of ether — the common substance and mother of all elements — it operates in ether and with its chief characteristics of motion develops, variously combines and creates the innumerable substances out of which the objects of the universe are constituted. In the words of Sri Aurobindo, "Moving in ether, acting and functioning through its energy Prana, it determines the nature, motions, powers, activities of all those infinite forms which it has created. By the combinations and operations of this aerial element the sun is built up, fire is struck forth, clouds are formed, a molten globe cools and solidifies into earth. By the energy of the aerial element the sun gives light and heat, fire burns, clouds give rain, earth revolves. Not only all animate, but all inanimate existence owes its life and various activity to Matariswan and its energy, Prana."[1]

(i)

If Indra represents Mind-Power with Swar-loka as his special realm, and Surya represents 'the illumination of the *ṛtam* rising upon the mind', then Vayu is the embodiment of Prana or Life-Energy. It is Prana which supports the nervous activities in man which in turn succour the mental energies controlled by Indra. Vital and mental energies are increased and activised by the inflow of the Soma-wine.

1. *Indravāyū ime sutā upa prayobhirā gatam,*
indavo vāmuśanti hi.

2. *Vāyavindraśca cetathaḥ sutānāṁ vājinīvasū,*
tāvā yātamupa dravat.

3. *Vāyavindraśca sunvata ā yātamupa niṣkṛtam,*
makṣvitthā dhiyā narā.[2]

1. O resplendent Lords, Indra and Vayu, verily these libations are for you and your eternal order. May you come hither with nourishment; indeed the Soma-wine awaits you both.

2. O Indra and Vayu, Lords of cosmic vitality, you are assuredly aware of our libations. May we always keep the flame of our devotion burning.

3. O Indra and Vayu, may you bless us for the oblations offered. Accept the Soma-wine and help us to attain the goal of our sacrifice.

Indra and Vayu are invoked by the Rishi to perfect the workings of these essential energies by their luminous thought-participation. This radiant thought-power is the state of consciousness prior to the attainment of the plenary Truth-Consciousness.

The growth process of the seeker covers three stages of development: proper preparation of the vital energies represented by Vayu alone, then the purification and illumination of the mental energies represented together by Indra and Vayu paving the way for the activities of the *ṛtam* or Truth, followed by the direct working of Truth-Consciousness itself on the higher mentality so as to enlarge and expand it immeasurably for the cherished fulfilment. The Rishi invokes first Vayu alone to purify and prepare the vital:

1. *Vāyavā yāhi darśateme somā araṁkṛtāḥ,*
teṣāṁ pāhi śrudhī havam.

2. *Vāya ukthebhirjarante tvāmacchā jaritāraḥ,*
sutasomā aharvidaḥ.

3. *Vāyo tava prapṛñcatī dhenā jigāti dāśuṣe,*
urūcī somapītaye.[3]

1. O Vayu, Lord of universal vitality, accept our Soma offering prepared for you; hear our invocation.

2. O Vayu, Lord of universal vitality, your devotees who ever invoke you with devout chanting have prepared the Soma-juice for your enjoyment.

3. O Vayu, Lord of universal vitality, your affirmative voice eulogising the Soma oblation comes to your devotees who invoke you to drink of it.

Then Indra and Vayu are enjoined by the Rishi to increase the thought-power of the seeker. They awaken in consciousness to the offering of the Soma-juice; working together in the mind of the seeker they become conscious of the inflowings of Ananda from above. The wine of divine delight sets up a new action in the seeker and prepares him to participate in the munificence of an immortal consciousness. The Rishis invoke Indra and Vayu to perfect this new action in the thought-power that leads to the Truth. Finally the friendly couple Mitra-Varuna is implored to establish the right working of the luminous intellect. This puts the seeker securely on the passage to the summit. The vital forces working rightly thus purify the mental energies and prepare them for the activities of the Truth-Consciousness which invariably leads to the working of the Truth on the mentality of the seeker leading him to immortality.

1. *Mitraṁ huve pūtadakṣaṁ varuṇaṁ ca riśādasam*
dhiyaṁ ghṛtācīṁ sādhantā.

2. *Ṛtena mitrāvaruṇā vṛtāvṛdhāvṛtaspṛśā,*
kratuṁ bṛhantamāśāthe.

3. *Kavī no mitrāvaruṇā tuvijātā urukṣayā*
dakṣaṁ dadhāte apasam.[4]

1. I invoke Mitra, the lord of pure strength and bliss, and Varuna, the destroyer of the adverse forces. Together may they accept our *ghṛta*-offering and bring us greater wisdom.

2. O Mitra and Varuna, you are the increasers and distributors of illumined knowledge for the seekers. May you be pleased to

satisfy them in their supreme quest; may you lead them to the goal.

3. May Indra, lord of cosmic enlightenment, and Varuna, lord of vision and wide being, who exist for the good of all, increase our strength and sacrifice. They are the loving and most nourishing refuge of all.

Vayu, the wind-god is the Master of Life, inspirer of Life-Energy represented in man by his vital and nervous energies. The *Sama Veda* gives him an equal rank with the other gods, notably with Indra and Agni. He is said to be handsome and energetic, and loves to move speedily in a chariot drawn by purple horses; sometimes, depending upon the need, the number of horses yoked to the chariot is increased even up to one thousand. According to the *Sama Veda* the Vedas were revealed in the beginning of the world by the four deities Agni, Vayu, Aditya and Angara.

Abhī no arṣadivyā vasūnyabhi viśvā
pārthivā pūyamānaḥ,
abhi yena draviṇamaśnavāmābhyārṣeyaṁ
jamadgnivannaḥ.[5]

O wise one, grant us spiritual felicity, with a pure mind teach us of all things in the world. Grant us will and vigour with which we may gain pure knowledge, wealth and nourishment. Initiate us like God into Vedic wisdom obtainable through the Rishis.

The Vedic hymns deal with the actuality of conscious mental and vital activities emerging out of the subconscient: they are realities of psychological experience and perception. All our life-activities arise out of the subconscient; it is out of the sea of the subconscient that arise all the sensational and mental activities which seek to manifest progressively the eternal Truth within them. For, all this creation has been the result of the self-involution of the Divine. The Vedic Rishis envision the Divine as a Bull with four horns, two heads, three legs and seven hands. The heads represent his dual nature of Purusha and Prakriti, the horns symbolise the divine principles of Sat, Chit, Ananda and Vijnana, the legs stand for the three phenomenal principles of Mind, Life and Matter, and the hands for activities corresponding to the seven principles of existence.

The pure and clear light of the mind reflects the immanent Truth but this light lies concealed and imprisoned in the cavern of the subconscient by the Panis — the enemies of Light; Ananda lies triply bound in the subconscient. The energies of Nature progressively purified and nourished by the streams of Light flowing down from above get to be intimate with Agni which finally delivers them from all limitations; Agni thus hews for the seeker the path to immortality. It is the illumined mind therefore that links the Truth involved and immanent in the subconscient below with the Truth eternally established in the superconscient above.

Vayu, the lord of the energies of Life, Prana, is the all-pervasive force that governs material existence and its manifold activities, as well as vital existence and its nervous exercises. The Rishis see him functioning in the universe mostly either in the company of Indra or with Agni. If Indra represents the illumined Mind, Agni symbolizes the divine action of the Life-forces in man. Divine light and divine force are the conditions of the success of the sacrifice; in fact they are the prime object of all sacrifice. "Force was the condition, Light the liberating agency; and Indra and Surya were the chief bringers of Light. Moreover the Force required was the divine Will taking possession of all the human energies and revealing itself in them; and of this Will, this force of conscious energy, taking possession of the nervous vitality and revealing itself in it, Agni more than Vayu and especially Agni Dadhikravan was the symbol. For it is Agni who is master of Tapas, the divine Consciousness formulating itself in universal energy, of which the Prana is only a representative in the lower being."[6] It is because of the combined supreme effort of Agni, Indra and Surya that conscious divinity manifests out of the subconscient. And it is the meeting of Life and Mind and the evolution of the latter with the energetic support of the former that is the significant side of Vayu. "Therefore we find Indra, Master of Mind, and Vayu, Master of Life, coupled together and the latter always somewhat dependent on the former; the Maruts, the thought-forces, although in their origin they seem to be as much powers of Vayu as of Indra, are more important to the Rishis than Vayu himself and even in their dynamic aspect are more closely associated with Agni Rudra than with the natural chief of the legions of the Air."[7]

Indra and Vayu are addressed as the two lords of radiant energy and invoked to participate in the drinking spree of the Soma-wine.

1. *Vihi hotrā avītā vipo na rāyo aryaḥ,*
vāyavā candreṇa rathena yāhi
sutasya pītaye.

2. *Niryuvāṇo aśastīrniyutvāñ indrasārathiḥ,*
vāyavā candreṇa rathena yāhi
sutasya pītaye.

3. *Anu kṛṣṇe vasudhitī yemāte viśvapeśasā,*
vāyavā candreṇa rathena yāhi
sutasya pītaye.

4. *Vahantu tvā manoyujo yuktāso navatirnava,*
vāyavā candreṇa rathena yāhi
sutasya pītaye.

5. *Vāyo śataṁ harīṇāṁ yuvasva poṣyāṇām,*
uta vā te sahasriṇo ratha ā
yātu pājasā.[8]

1. O Vayu, come like a hero-warrior, the mighty stupefier and paralyzer of the Enemy, and bestow upon your devotees wealth supreme. Come in your shining chariot to drink the Soma-wine.

2. O Vayu, quelcher of detractions, who are drawn by the *Niyuts*, the sense perceptions, and have Indra himself for your charioteer, may you arrive on your refulgent chariot to drink the Soma-wine.

3. Heaven and earth, the two universal parents and alluring sources of sustenance attend upon you. Come, O god of vital breath, with your shining car to drink the Soma-wine.

4. O adorable Lord, may the ninety-nine horses harnessed together that are as swift as mind carry you. Come, O god of wind, on your radiant chariot to drink the Soma-wine.

5. O god of vital breath, yoke a hundred horses, nay, even a thousand to your shining chariot, and arrive here with utmost speed to drink the Soma-wine.

Both Indra and Vayu are the masters of mental and vital forces respectively, and their combined action is necessary for the pilgrim's steady progress. They are, in fact, implored to come in 'one common chariot' and drink together the nectar of divine delight. Among the two, Vayu is offered the first draught, for it is the vital energies which must first be made capable of divine action. Vayu is invoked always to appear with Indra and to move together; it is the movement of illumined vital energies that are of great help to the seeker-sacrificer. Elsewhere they are jointly invoked as the lords of thought:

> *Indravāyū manojuvā viprā havanta ūtaye,*
> *sahasrākṣā dhiyaspatī.*[9]

> The wise ones invoke for their felicity both Indra and Vayu who are ever present everywhere, and have a thousand eyes to witness what all we do. Verily, they are protectors and promoters of the sacrifice.

Vayu brings into conscious manifestation the sacrificial energies out of the darkness of the subconscient. He is the most effective revealer of the felicity required on the journey. Yet in his ecstatic action he is always governed by the illumined and aspiring force of Indra. Indra, Agni and Surya are the three great labourer-gods who with their flaming, mounting aspiration and action arrive at the supreme good, *bhadram*, and the lasting, vast beatitude.

Vayu is repeatedly implored to put away all forms of refusal that may impede the emergence of the Light and the Force that are eager to be revealed through the good offices of the gods. Guided by Indra, enthused by Agni and supported by Soma, Vayu succeeds in expelling all powers of limitation, obscuration and non-manifestation of the Truth. When Vayu moves in the chariot driven by Indra the entire universe of manifestation, including earth and heaven, follows him, and yokes itself to his action. Which means that the whole of the unilluminated and murky and dark and crooked consciousness between its two frontiers of the physical and the mental begins to moil under the authority of Vayu to give up the masked forms in whom it operates and reveal the true ones. Vayu's movement results in the emergence of a manifold energy of consciousness: it is the manifestation or the fullest expression of illumined consciousness. In the final condition or state we have the fullest and perfectest emergence of the most radiant consciousness — the total potentiality totally actualised, perfectly realised. In Sri Aurobindo's words, "It is the completely varied all-ensphering, all-energising mental illumination with its full perfection of being, power, bliss, knowledge, mentality, vital force, physical activity..."[10]

that the Rishi desires for. He therefore entreats the great god Vayu to come with his hundred horses on the implicit assurance that they be afterwards nourished into their fullness of a ten hundred ones, or come directly with his thousand steeds encompassing the fullest manifestation of the Truth.

Vayu, whose Vedic epithet is Matariswan, is the god of Life-Energy. He is revealed as an 'immortal principle of existence' in the light of Surya. Of him birth, life in the body and death are only overt operations. It is he the principle of Prana who lives and moves and has his being in the mother element. He inhabits all that exists and expands infinitely; all things in the universe move and increase because of this Life-Force. It is Vayu, again, who secretly installs Agni in all existence; for him the many worlds are fashioned and physiqued, constituted or structured that he may enjoy his fullest freedom of movement and action. He has limitless sway over the world of manifestation and seize everything, as it were, in his stride for his fancy or satisfaction. Nothing is too great for Vayu except the Omnipotent.[a] The Upanishads declare him as manifest Brahman.

Ye prāṇaṁ brahmopāsate,
prāṇo hi bhūtānāmāyuḥ,
tasmātsarvāyuṣamucyata iti.[11]

They who adore Brahman as Life gain a full life, for the breath is the life of all beings. Therefore it is haloed as the life of all.

Vayu embodies the power of Prana, and is manifest in Prakriti for the works of the plane of Life to which he belongs. The upward endeavour and ascension of the seeker is perennially supported by heaven and earth — the parents of the gods. They nourish and increase the mental and physical energies of men; they are linked together by mid-air, the region of vital force, *antarikṣa*, by Vayu, the master of Prana.

(ii)

The Vedic hymns call for not only the understanding of the cosmogenic origins of the five elements but also the discovery of the transcendent meaning of surface phenomena. Vayu is said to be of unknown origin, and also described as the first born. For no one really knows where the Wind comes from and where it goes. He is heard but not seen; he is invisible but is felt and experienced.

Ātmā devānāṁ bhuvanasya garbho
yathāvaśaṁ carati deva eṣaḥ,
ghoṣā idasya śṛnvire na rūpaṁ
tasmai vātāya haviṣā vidhema.[12]

O God, you are the soul of the gods, the germ of the world, and move freely according to your pleasure; though your voice is heard, you remain invisible. May we worship you who are the presiding deity of the wind.

Vayu is the life-principle and the giver of eternal life. The Rishi implores him to impart life and energize him on the journey. Verily, he is the very seed of life.

1. *Ā tvā juvo rārahāṇā abhi prayo vāyo*
vahantviha pūrvapītaye somasya pūrvapītaye,
ūrdhvā te anu sūnṛtā manastiṣṭātu jānatī,
niyutvatā rathenā yāhi dāvane vāyo makhasya dāvane.

2. *Mandantu tvā mandino vāyavindavo'smāt*
krāṇāsaḥ sukṛtā abhidyavo gobhiḥ
krāṇā abhidyavaḥ,
yaddha krāṇā iradhyai dakṣaṁ sacanta ūtayaḥ,
sadhrīcīnā niyuto dāvane dhiya upa
bruvata īṁ dhiyaḥ.

3. *Vāyuryūṅkte rohitā vāyuraruṇā vāyū rathe ajirā*
dhuri voḷhave vahiṣṭhā dhuri voḷhave,
pra bodhayā purandhiṁ jāra ā sasatīmīva,
pra cakṣaya rodasī vāsayoṣasaḥ śravase vāsayoṣasaḥ.[13]

1. O Vayu, may your swift steeds speedily moving bring you here, so that you may be the first to drink our oblation of the Soma-wine. May our sweet and truthful laudations be accepted by you. O god of glorious vitality come with your aura of life-energies to our sacrifice; grant us the objects of our sacrificial offering.

2. May our devotional chantings being well-rendered and opportune exhilarate you, O god. May your swift-coursing horses bring you to

the sacrificial hall to accept our libations; all your devotees have assembled here to obtain your boons.

3. O God of greatest vitality, may you come here on the chariot of vital energies with two swift-moving horses, red and purple, yoked to it. O Lord of Prana, inspire and arouse the receptive and intelligent sacrificer as an amorist awakens his sleeping mistress. May you light up earth and heaven, and the dawn to receive your sacrificial offerings.

The Rishi eulogizes Vayu's power, his chariot and his splendour, and pays homage to his healing capacities and his eternal felicities. He is the merciful, wholesome healer and the loving father, friend and brother.

a) *Vātasya nu mahimānaṁ rathasya rujann*
eti stanayannasya ghoṣaḥ,
divisprigyātyaruṇāni kṛṇvannuto
eti pṛthivyā reṇumasyan.

Samprerate anu vātasya viṣṭhā ainaṁ
gacchanti samanaṁ na yoṣāḥ,
tābhiḥ sayuksarathaṁ deva īyate'sya
viśvasya bhuvanasya rājā.

Antarikṣe pathibhirīyamāno na ni viśate
katamaccanāhaḥ apāṁ sakhā
prathamajā ṛtāvā kva svijjātaḥ
kuta ā babhūva.[14]

1. I announce the supremacy of the impassioned god of *antarikṣa*, Vayu; his voice spreads like thunder, he moves along sweeping the skies; staining purple the wide horizons he moves forward, resurrecting the earth.

2. A cogent body of hosts follow the cosmic Wind after him like women. Taking them all in his war-chariot the divine Lord of the world proceeds through high terrain.

3. Proceeding on heavenly pathways, Vayu neither rests nor slumbers not even for a single day. Intimate friend of the Waters, he is the first-

born, the most righteous. Who can tell whence he came and how did he originate?

b) *Ā vāta vāhi bheṣajaṁ vi vāta*
vāhi yadrapaḥ,
tvaṁ hi viśvabheṣajo devānāṁ
dūta īyase.[15]

O Wind, breathe your healing breezes; blow away all evil, for you are indeed the universal medicine and the victorious messenger of the gods.

c) *Vāta ā vātu bheṣajaṁ śambhu mayobhu*
no hṛde, pra ṇa āyūṁṣi tāriṣat.

Uta vāta pitāsi na uta bhrātota naḥ sakhā,
sa no jīvātave kṛdhi.

Yadado vāta te gṛhe'mṛtasya nidhirhitaḥ,
tato no dehi jīvase.[16]

1. May the divine Breath fill us and prolong our life-span; may he bring us health and happiness.

2. O divine Breath, you are our loving father, our brother and also our dear friend. Pray, give us strength that we may live long.

3. O divine Breath, of the supreme treasure of the immortal elixir that you possess hidden in your celestial abode pass it on to us that we may live long.

Vayu is not tied to any specific place; he is always on the move and never comes to rest. He is the swiftest of the gods and follows all seasons:

a) *Vāyau diśaḥ pratiṣṭhitā vāyor*
evādhi punarjayante.[17]

b) *Yābhirado vāyur digbhir*
anantarhitābhir upait tā etas...[18]

c) *Pradiśaścatasro vātapatnīḥ.*[19]

d) *Katham̐ vāto nelayati.*[20]

He knows no rest; his horses do not sit down.

Ime ye te su vāyo bāhvojaso'ntar
nadī te patayantyukṣaṇo
mahivrādhanta ukṣanaḥ,
dhanvañcidye anāśavo jīrāścidagiraukasaḥ,
sūryasyeva raśmayo durniyantavo hastayor
durniyantavaḥ.[21]

O Vayu, your horses are strong of limb, youthful and full of vigour; they bear you through the wide space between heaven and earth. They have grown in mass and have become strong as oxen. They do not fade away in the firmament; vituperation or slander does not slacken their speed. Nothing can stop their movement as the rays of the sun; difficult it is to immure or obstruct their movement by force.

Verily, he is the breath of the gods:

Vāyur vai sarveśām devānām̐ ātmā;[22]

Vāyum̐ hyeva sarvāṇī bhūtānyapiyanti
vāyoḥ punarvisṛjyante.[23]

According to the Atharva-veda "the atmosphere is the cow and Vayu its calf."[24] He is said to be a great purifier; he is the cause of rain and fire as well as the subduer of the intensity of fire:

Vāyauyam̐ gomṛgam ālabheta yam
ajaghnivām̐sam abhiśam̐seyuḥ,
apūtā vā etam̐ vāg recati...
vāyur vai devānam̐ pavitram.[25]

The Rig-veda often equates Vata with Vayu; if Vata is the element, Vayu is the god. Also, if Vayu is the custodian of the Soma-wine, so is Vata that of *amṛta*.

Yattvā deva prapibanti
tata ā pyāyase punaḥ,
vāyuḥ somasya rakṣitā samānāṁ
māsa ākṛtiḥ.[26]

When, O god, they drink you, then do you swell and renew yourself again; Vayu is the guardian of Soma, the divine elixir; he is also the maker of months and years.

Again, both Vata and Vayu are described as drawn by swiftest steeds.

a) *Tvamindra naryo yāñ avo nṛn*
tiṣṭhā vātasya suyujo vahiṣṭhān...[27]

O radiant god, resplendent Indra, friend of men, mount the horses who are fast and vivacious as wind and bear their burden well.

b) *Vaha kutsamindra yasmiñcākan*
syūmanyū ṛjrā vātasyāśvā...[28]

O resplendent lord, Indra, may your obedient horses bear that earnest and dedicated aspirant Kutsa as swift as the wind to the sacrificial place where you wish to convey him.

c) *Yāsi kutsena sarathamavasyustodo*
vātasya haryorīśānaḥ...[29]

You accompany Kutsa in the same chariot determined to protect him, O mighty conquerer of the enemy, drawn by powerful horses swift-moving like wind.

(iii)

Vayu, in Hindu mythology, is the personification of wind or life-breath, Prana. He is the lord of the mid-region, *antarikṣa*, and shares his power with Indra as well as his desire for the Soma-drink. He is the substance and basis of all life, *pañcaprāṇa*. He rides a chariot drawn by varying number of swift coursers — two, ninety-nine, a hundred or even a thousand. Hindu mythology describes him as blue in complexion and having four hands, holding a fan and a flag in two hands, the other two in *abhaya* and *varadā mudrās* signifying protection and granting of gifts.

Vayu the god of the wind, often associated with Indra, is described as being most handsome and one who moves noisily in a shining car drawn by red or purple horses. Vata in the Veda is another name of Vayu.

The Epics mention him as the father of Hanuman and Bhima. In another tradition Vayu, the purifier, is depicted as a white person riding on a deer and carrying a white flag. The *Purānas* speak of him as the son of Aditi. His other names are Anila, Marut, Sparshana and Gandhavaha for he is respectively the breath, air necessary for life, the cause of touch, and the one who carries the odours. He is also called Sadāgate, the ever-moving, and Jalakantara whose garden is water. His chariot has a framework of gold which touches the skies. He is connected with the other two great gods Agni and Surya. The place of Agni is on earth, of Vayu is in the mid-region, and of Surya is in the heaven. In the *Purusha-sukta*, Vayu is said to have sprung out of the breath of Purusha.

1. SABCL. Vol. 27, p. 240
2. RV. I.2.4-6
3. RV. I.2.1-3
4. RV. I.2.7-9
5. *Sama Veda* 12, 1428
6. SABCL. Vol.10, p. 298
7. Ibid., p. 298
8. RV. IV.48.1-5
9. RV. I.23.3
10. SABCL. op.cit., p. 302.

a. As is revealed in the *Kena Upanishad.*

11. *Taittiriya Upanishad*, II.3.1
12. RV. X.168.4
13. RV. I.134.1-3
14. RV. X.168.1-3
15. RV. X.137.3
16. RV. X.186.1-3
17. *Satapatha Brahmana*, X.3.3.8
18. Ibid., VIII.3.1.11

19. *Atharva Veda*, II.10.4
20. Ibid., X.7.37
21. RV. I.135.9
22. *Satapatha Brahmana*, XIV.3.2.7
23. Ibid., XI.5.3.11
24. *Atharva Veda*, IV.39.4
25. *Taittiriya Samhita*, II.1.10.2
26. RV. X.85.5
27. RV. I.121.12
28. RV. I.174.5
29. RV. IV.16.11

III

INDRA

If Agni represents Force instinct with knowledge, Indra in the Veda represents Light instinct with force. If the former supports the ascension of human consciousness from earth to heaven, the latter helps the descension of supreme felicity from heaven to earth. In his psychological role Indra is the lord of the luminous mind; he represents Mind-Power. The Rishis address him as Indra of the manifold opulence and iridescence, *indra citrabhāno*. Indra makes himself readily available to the seer of the illumined mind who by his sincere seeking presses out the Soma-wine and expresses his sublime experiences in the inspired *mantras*, *sutāvataḥ upa brahmāṇi vāghataḥ*. Supported by the Ashwins, who vitalize the happiness accompanying the action of Ananda, Indra establishes firmly that felicity in the illumined mind. Indra is not the god of physical Light; he is the god who wins the field, *kṣetra*, for the shining comrades. It is to this field that the seeker-soul is led in its seeking and sacrifice helped by the gods.

Indra, the most popular and powerful among the *devas*, with his divinely creative action manifests the *sat* out of the *asat*; by his cosmic action he strengthens and fertilizes the upward urge of the earth, widens the mid-region and supports the heavens in its progressive spiritual effectuation in the life of humanity.

a) *Yaḥ pṛthivīṁ vyathamānāmadṛhad*
yaḥ parvatānprakupitāñ aramṇāt,
yo antarikṣaṁ vimame varīyo yo dyām
astabhnātsa janāsa indraḥ.[1]

He who has made the moving earth firmly fixed, and becalms the agitated mountains, and spreads the spacious sky, and unifies and integrates the heaven, O men, is verily, Indra. (Herein earth, mountains, sky and heaven stand for human body, the senses, the vital and the mental respectively.)

b) *Yaḥ puṣpiṇiśca prasvasca dharmaṇādhi*
dāne vy avanīradhārayaḥ,
yaścāsamā ajano didyuto diva urur
ūrvāñ abhitaḥ sāsyukthyaḥ.[2]

By enlightenment and excellence you, O resplendent god, have effected the flower and fruit-bearing plants to spread over the fields, and caused the many luminaries of heaven and created the wide-bodied mountains, verily, we owe you all praise.

c) *Avaṁśe dyāmastabhāyad bṛhantam*
ā rodasī apṛṇadantarikṣam,
sa dhārayadpṛthivim paprathacca
somasya tā mada indraś cakāra.[3]

He who has fixed the heaven in unsupported space and fills earth, heaven and mid-region with light, as well as upholds and has extended the earth, does these in the exhilaration of the Soma-drink.

He who has measured out space like a chamber, and has dug the river-beds with his thunderbolt and helped them to speed forth on the well-known paths does these in the exhilaration of the Soma-drink.

d) *Sa dhārayat pṛthivim paprathacca*
Vajreṇa hatvā nirapaḥ sasarja,
ahannahimabhinadrauhiṇaṃ vyahan
vyaṁsam maghavā śacībhiḥ.[4]

It is he who supports the earth and spreads it wide; he strikes the Enemy and releases the waters, he slays Ahi and destroys Rahuniva by his valiance. He quashes and extirpates the vices in all their hideous appearances.

e) *Jajñanaḥ somaṁ sahase papātha pra*
te mātā mahimānamuvāca,
endra paprāthorvantarikṣaṁ yudhā
devebhyo varivaścakartha.[5]

O resplendent god, when born you have drunk the Soma-wine for your invigoration. Aditi, your supreme Mother, has proclaimed your greatness. Since you have gained in battle wealth for the gods, your reputation has filled the vast firmament.

Indra embodies the organising and systematizing luminous intelligence behind the whole cosmos in its Truth-ward movement. His role is of supreme psychological importance in the evolution of consciousness; he unfolds an inner world between the heaven and the earth, the spiritual and the physical, and unites them for a divine unfoldment and fulfilment. He personifies the mind's endless endeavour and hassle for illumination and freedom from chaos and ignorance.

Jyotir vṛṇīta tamaso vijānann
āre syāma duritādabhīke.[6]

His illumined and discriminating Mind separates the light from the darkness. O Indra, may we be always protected from evil.

Indra is the expanding space-maker, the victorious light-bringer and the liberator of the waters of divine felicity. He establishes order out of chaos, brings the world of manifestation and differentiation out of the unmanifest and undifferentiated condition.

Sa ittamo'vayunaṃ tatanvat
sūryeṇa vayunavaccakāra.[7]

He transforms the wide-spreading darkness of the Night of Nescience with the rising of the Sun. He is identified with the sun, the illuminer of nights; he is the winner of the Light and the heaven and the celestial waters.

a) *Sa sūryaḥ paryurū varāṅsyendro*
vavṛtyadrathyeva cakra,
atiṣṭhantamapasyaṁ na sargaṃ kṛṣṇā
tamāṅsi tvishyā jaghāna.[8]

Heroic Indra causes rays of light to revolve fiercely as an impassioned charioteer who rotates the wheels of his chariot and destroys by his resplendence the darkness of the Night like a vigorous restless steed.

b) *Dhartā divo rajasaspṛṣṭa ūrdhvo*
ratho na vāyurvasubhirniyutvān,
kṣapaṁ vastā janitā sūryasya vibhaktā
bhāgaṁ dhiṣaṇeva vājam.[9]

O resplendent Lord, supporter of heaven and the sky and the wind; you ascend the celestial regions accompanied by the Vasus like a fast-moving chariot, and illumine the Night, the parent of the sun. May you distribute nourishment to the seekers.

c) *A tu aśatrau ā gahi ny ukthāni ca hūyase,*
upame rocane divaḥ.[10]

May you, O resplendent Lord, who knows no rival, come here invoked by our devout chantings where the sacrificial fire burns casting radiance everywhere.

d) *Indro mahna rodasī paprathacchava*
indraḥ sūryamarocayat,
indre ha viśvā bhuvanāni yemira
indre suvānāsa indavaḥ.[11]

O resplendent Lord, by virtue of your excellence and valiance you have spread out all over the earth and heaven; you have lighted up the sun. In your protective care all creatures are held; to you alone we offer our Soma-oblations.

e) *Yasyāśvāsaḥ pradiśi yasya gāvo yasya*
grāmā yasya viśve rathāsaḥ,
yaḥ sūryaṁ ya uṣasaṁ jajāna yo
apāṁ netā sa janāsa indraḥ.[12]

He, the resplendent Lord, has complete control over kine and steed, habitations and *vāhanas*; it is he who brings forth the dawn and the sun, and effectuates the release of the waters.

Indra is the most eulogized and glorified god in the Rig-veda. He is the supreme master and friend of men; he is the Lord of all the worlds, the universal sovereign and the conqueror of the Enemy.

a) *Yo viśvasya jagataḥ prāṇataspatiryo*
brahmaṇe prathamo gā avindat,
indro yo dasyūn̐radharān̐ avatiran
marutvantam sakhyāya havāmahe.[13]

We devoutly invoke the resplendent God for his friendship; he who aided by the Maruts restores the stolen cows to the seekers after destroying the Dasyus. He is the lord of all that moves and breathes.

b) *Indrasya nu vīryāṇi pra vocaṁ yāni*
cakāra prathamāni vajrī,
ahannahiman vapas tatarda pra
vakṣaṇā abhinat parvatānām.[14]

May I announce the earlier heroic deeds of Indra, the great wielder of *vajra*: he clove the cloud of Darkness and cast down the Adversary. He breaks open a way out of the mountain and releases the waters.

c) *Mahāṅ asi mahiṣa vṛṣṇyebhir dhanaspṛd*
ugra sahamāno anyān,
eko viśvasya bhuvanasya rājā sa yodhayā
ca kṣayayā ca janān.[15]

O adorable, mighty Lord, you are august and distinguished; you have vanquished the Adversary by your prowess. Verily, you alone are the ruler of the world; may you fight our enemies and provide safety for your devotees.

(1)

Indra and the Maruts

Maruts are the lesser shining gods, subsidiary powers, the thought-forces who transmit to the seekers their actuation and drive towards the greater truths which belong to Indra. They activise and impel them to the knowledge of the manifold truths of Indra; more than being gods of thought they are wide-awake, impetuous operators of energy that effectuate in the mind of the seeker. Some times, Indra himself is described by the Rishis as the first among the Maruts and their eldest brother. The Rishis treat the Word as a power and even creator of worlds. For it is the active consciousness of the Infinite that expresses, rather creates what is already existing in It. The Maruts, therefore, are creators of cosmic powers that gain entry and establish not only in the seeker-sacrificer but in the outer world. As Sri Aurobindo observes,"By expression we form, by affirmation we establish. As a power of expression the word is termed *gīḥ* or *vacas*; as a power of affirmation, *stoma*. In either aspect it is named *manma* or *mantra*, expression of thought in mind, and *brahman*, expression of the heart or the Soul..."[16]

Affirmation and submission to the thought-forces is the essence of *mantra-yoga*. Springing out from the supreme *ṛtam*, shaped by the heart and validated and authenticated by the mind, as well as accepted by the *devas*, the *mantra* becomes all effective co-creator. The Maruts are powers of progressive illumination of the human mind leading to the luminous consciousness that is Indra. This great progression is brought about in humanity by the unimpaired and unmarred consecution of the Dawns. Each Dawn brings in a new opening and a new divine illumination of man's physical-mental awareness. But it is because of the transforming power of 'continuous dawns' impelled by Indra's puissance that the seeker ascends quickly to the fullest light of the Truth. "It is that supreme Intelligence which through the Dawns, through the Maruts, has been pouring itself into the human being. Indra is the Bull of the radiant herd, the Master of the thought-energies, the Lord of the luminous dawns."[17] Indra uses Maruts, the gods of the Thought-Forces, as his channels of illumination and prepares and secures a receptive base in man for the supramental knowledge to establish. And by their indefatigable energies he increases his own energy in the seeker, and fortifies his nature with his divine firmness and makes him an unshakable receptor of still greater puissances of the Truth.

1. *Yena manāsaścitayanta usrā*
vyuṣṭiṣu śavasā śaśvatīnām,
sa no marudbhir vṛshabha śrávo dha
ugra ugrebhi sthaviraḥ sahodaḥ.

2. *Tvam pāhīndra sahīyaso nṛinbhavā*
marudbhiravayātaheḷāḥ,
supraketebhiḥ sāsabhírdadhano
vidyāmeṣaṁ vṛjanam jīradānum.[18]

1. O radiant god, it is in our mornings that you help the movements of the mind grow conscient through the succession of Dawns. May you establish in us illumined knowledge with the help of the Maruts; grant us strength and inner nourishment.

2. O lord of the inner puissance, may you protect the Powers in their growing might and be free of anger against the Maruts who support your forcefulness and have the right perception. May we gain the necessary drive to swiftly break through.

The Rishi addresses Indra as the mighty doer of many conscious actions, as the one who is adored and lauded with *mantras* by those who have directly realised the substance and truth of the *mantras* by moving from plateau to plateau of the hierarchy of consciousness. It is a difficult ascent — the journey, step by step, to the summit-peak. As the seeker-pilgrim touches one peak, he acutely becomes conscious of his imperfection and ascends to the next higher peak. This he continues, and each time he feels that there is still much more left yet to be climbed. It is in this state that Indra, the compassionate god, moves in and makes himself manifest before the seeker-pilgrim with his companion gods and leads him to his own heavenly abode, *satyam ṛtam bṛhat*. Indra, the most powerful and well-inclined towards the seekers, is invoked again and again to harness his horses of special luminosity to their rescue and to manifest in their close proximity for spiritual sustenance and strength.

Mantra is the fruit of luminous knowledge, and also the means of acquiring it. So too, sacrifice is perfected by the discipline of yoga as also the means of acquiring that discipline; both of these are bestowed on the seeker by Indra. Indra is therefore beseeched and implored to manifest and increase the Word as well as the sacrifice. Word is the increaser of Indra in the sacrificer, Indra the destroyer of the enemies and the enjoyer of the friendship of his worshippers. Indra is devoutly sought for friendship, for felicity and for favourable competence. He is the master of the mountain of Inconscience, who having eliminated the Enemy purifies the mind of the seeker and liberates the radiances imprisoned in the cave for his well-being. Indra when he rises to his fullest size cannot be encompassed by heaven and earth; he who is the winner of the waters of Swar actuates the rays of luminous knowledge towards the sacrificer. He is implored by the Rishi to hear the call, bear his praises and accept his oblations and shower upon him in plenty the gifts of varied wealth. The Rishi more often addresses the adorable deity by his own name as the latter takes birth in the person of the adorer; the deity is looked upon by the Rishi as his own form. The deity having manifested is asked to drink the Soma-wine pressed out for the purpose and increase his new life and consequently grant him the sight of the supreme beyond. The Rishi adores Indra with the laudations in all states of his progress, and implores for their acceptance with love, for it is Indra's love that is the source and cause of the seeker's love of the Truth.

1. *Gāyanti tvā gāyatriṇó'rcanty*
arkamarkiṇaḥ,
brahmāṇastvā śatakrata ud
vaṅśamiva yemire.

2. *Yatsānoḥ sānumāruhad*
bhūryaspaṣṭa kartvam,
tadindro arthaṃ cetati
yūthena vṛṣṇirejati.

3. *Yukṣvā hi keśinā harī vṛṣaṇā*
kakṣyaprā,
athā na indra somapā girām
upaśrutim cara.

4. *Ehi stomāñ abhi svarābhi gṛṇīhyā ruva,*
brahma ca no vaso sacendra yajñam ca vardhaya.

5. *Uktamindrāya śaṅsyaṁ vardhanam puruniṣidhe*
śakro yathā suteṣu ṇo rāraṇat sakhyeṣu ca.

6. *Tamit sakhitva īmahe taṃ rāye taṃ suvirye,*
sa śakra uta naḥ śakadindro vasu dayamānaḥ.

7. *Suvivṛtaṁ sunirajamindra tvādātamid yaśaḥ,*
gavāmapa vrajaṁ vṛdhi kṛṇuṣva rādho adrivaḥ.

8. *Nahi tvā rodasī ubhe ṛghāyamāṇaminvataḥ,*
jeṣaḥ svarvatīrapaḥ saṁ gā asmabhyam dhunuhi.

9. *Āśrutkarṇa śrudhī havaṁ nu ciddadhiṣva me giraḥ,*
indra stomamimam mama kṛṣvā yujaścidantaram.

10. *Vidyā hi tvā vṛṣantamaṁ*
vājeṣu havanaśrutam,
vṛṣantamasya hūmaha ūtiṁ
sahasrasātamām.

11. *Ā tū na indra kauśika*
mandasānaḥ sutam piba,
navyamāyuḥ pra sū tira
kṛdhī sahasrasām ṛṣim.

12. *Pari tvā girvaṇo gira*
imā bhavantu viśvataḥ,
vṛddhāyumanu vṛddhayo juṣṭā
bhavantu juṣṭayaḥ.[19]

1. O Indra, doer of a hundred conscious deeds, the reciters of *Sāma* adore you with hymns of praise and prayer and the priests of *Ṛg* extol you who are most worthy of invocation; the seers of the *Brāhmanas* rise like a bamboo pole and attain you.

2. When the Rishi who travels on the path of inner sacrifice, climbs from one plateau to another higher plateau and realises that much more has to be realised, it is then that Indra manifests the next step, and helps the Rishi in his ascent with his troop of Maruts.

3. O resplendent god, acceptor of our Soma-oblation, may you yoke the bay-steeds of majestic mane and well-developed and strong limbs, and come closer to the sacrificial place that you may hear our praises.

4. Come nearer, O Lord of felicity, to this our place of ritual and accord us your approval of our hymns. O Indra, Lord of illumination, be propitious to our sacrifice, increase our Mantra-power and grant us abundant inner nourishment.

5. May we sing only those hymns that increase Indra, increasing whom we increase ourselves; he is the annuller and effective dispeller of the enemies, he who increasing us takes delight in us even as he would sport among his children and friends.

6. May we seek patronage and friendship of the mighty Indra who is famous for his auspicious capacity and supreme felicity. May he grow mightier by conferring wealth on us.

7. O resplendent god, your prowess and glory are well unveiled;

your splendour shines out brilliantly, cleansed by yourself, with the slaying of the enemies. O wielder of the thunderbolt break open the gates of the den and liberate the kine, procure for us ample wealth.

8. O Indra, heaven and earth, though widely extended, cannot encompass you when you grow formidable while confronting the Enemy. O winner of the waters of Swar, may you actuate towards us the rich milk-yielding cattle.

9. O omniscient One and of wide ears may you hear my call, hold my praises within you and accept them as long-nursed and treasured utterances of a worshipper-friend.

10. O benevolent god, we know you as the Lord of opulence, the generous bestower of blessings and the ready hearer of the call. We invoke you as such for protection and for the increase that gives us manifold varied wealth.

11. May you arrive here expeditiously, O son of Kushika, and having arrived, gratifyingly accept our libation of the Soma-wine pressed out for you, increase the life that merits commendation, create the seer in us that we may enjoy the perfect and supreme felicity.

12. O adorable Lord, may our hymns of praise attain to you on all sides, and in all states and in every way; may they augment your power, who are of lengthened life, may they, accepted by you with love become perennial sources of love of the Truth.

Indra as well as the other gods always grow in him who worships them. Indra, the fast-growing all-pervasive god and the lord of all existences and of manifold opulence increases in the seeker-adorer who lauds him with love. He who is the undaunted conqueror of the Enemy is entreated to root out fear from his worshippers. His treasures are inexhaustible, his gifts unending, and the increase of the sacrifices bright and immense. Youthful and insolent, invincible and universal in action, unlimited in valour and luminous in intelligence, Indra, the thunder-armed hero-warrior is extolled by the Rishi. He who with the strength of the Truth-Consciousness destroys *Vṛtra and Vala*, breaks open the dark cave and liberates the cows is celebrated by all the seers and the gods. The seekers of light, the pilgrims of the Truth come to him full of adoration, celebrating his victory, eulogizing his glory, for he has slain the cunning Shushna with his superior cunning. The seer-chanters are full of praise for him whose boons are bounteous and splendorous.

1. *Indraṁ viśvā avīvṛdhant*
   samudravyacasaṁ giraḥ,
   rathītamaṁ rathīnāṁ vājānāṁ
   satpatim patim.

2. *Sakhye ta indra vājino mā*
   bhema śavasaspate,
   tvāmabhi pra ṇonumo
   jetāramaparājitam.

3. *Pūrvīrindrasya rātayo na,*
   vi dasyantyūtayaḥ
   yadī vājasya gomataḥ stotribhyo
   ṁahate magham.

4. *Purām bhinduryuvā kavir*
   amitaujā ajāyata,
   indro viśvasya karmaṇo
   dhartā vajrī puruṣṭutaḥ.

5. *Tvaṁ valasya gomato'pāvar*
   adrivo bilam,
   tvāṁ devā abibhyuṣas
   tujyamānāsa āviṣuḥ.

6. *Tavāhaṁ śūra rātibhiḥ praty*
   āyaṁ sindhumāvadan,
   upātiṣṭhanta girvaṇo viduṣ
   ṭe tasya kāravaḥ.

7. *Māyābhirindra māyinaṃ*
   tvaṁ śuṣṇamavātiraḥ,
   viduṣṭe tasya medhirās
   teṣāṁ śravāṅsyuttira.

8. *Indramīśānamojasābhi*
stomā anūṣata,
sahasraṁ yasya rātaya uta
vā santi bhūyasīḥ.[20]

1. All our laudations increase Indra, expansive like the sea; superbly and all the time charioted valiantly among those who move and fight travelling in chariots, the lord of riches, the protector of the virtuous and master of all existences.

2. O Lord of luminous strength, richly supported by your friendship, we have no fear of the enemies; we laud you and glorify you from all sides who are ever the great conqueror and never conquered.

3. Abundant are the gifts of the all-merciful Lord; they flow endlessly and continuously to his worshippers, and yet their growth does not diminish. They are the shining gifts of knowledge and inner nourishment.

4. The ever young and wise and of unbounded strength, Indra, is the destroyer of the citadels of the Enemy; he is the supreme sustainer of all action, the thunder-armed god, the much-extolled mighty one.

5. O wielder of the thunderbolt, verily, you broke open the cave of Vala with the help of the fearless, speeding gods, the Maruts, and released the cows for the benefit of seekers.

6. O adorable god, valorous and gracious, we have come to you celebrating your glory for obtaining your felicity, for we have always known your munificence and your puissance.

7. O resplendent god, the wise seers know it that you with your superior and varied intelligence have slain the cunning and deceitful Asura. May you increase and strengthen their divine hearings.

8. O Indra, mighty ruler of the universe, the worshippers praise you with sacred hymns; verily, your gifts are plenty and bountiful and beyond any count.

Indra, the divine champion of the seeker-sacrificers, is central to all the Vedic deities and bears many names. He is both the thunder-god and the god of battle; he is the solar-hero who again and again recovers the sun as well as the one who gives us the rain of Truth. He is the *kavi* and the *kṣatra* — the Light and the Force. He is the ever new-born god, most radiant and energetic who destroys the Adversary:

...Viśve kavitamaṁ kavīnām.[21]

Indro brahmendra ṛṣirindraḥ purū puruhūtaḥ.[22]

Indra the Lord of Swar — 'the luminous world of the Divine Mind', as well as the Master of our being is also characterised in some hymns as an Angirasa. He puts on the distinctive attributes and epithets of the Angirasa Rishis. He, the Lord of the Truth, is described as descending in man with the powers of clear perception and there increasing to his full innate splendour and activity by the perfectly expressive Word and the Soma-wine. Indra then stands revealed as the Master of the Divine Mind, the lord of all illuminations.

So aṅgirobhiraṅgirastamo bhūdvṛṣā
vṛṣabhiḥ sakhibhiḥ sakha san,
ṛgmibhirṛgmī gātubhirjyeṣṭho
marutvānno bhavatindra ūtī.[23]

"May he become most Angirasa with the Angirasas, being the Bull with bulls, the Friend with friends, the Possessor of the Rik with those who have the Rik (*ṛgmibhir ṛgmī*), with those who make the journey the greatest; may Indra become associated with the Maruts (*marutvān*) for our thriving."*

Indra is described as taking upon himself all the qualities that constitute Angirasahood:

Agachadu vipratamaḥ sakhīyann
asūdayatsukṛte garbhamadriḥ,
sasāna maryo yuvabhirmakhasyann
athābhavadaṅgirāḥ sadyo arcan.[24]

"Most illumined in knowledge, becoming a friend he went; the hill sped forth its pregnant contents for the doer of the good work; strong in manhood with the young he sought fullness of riches and won possession; so at once, chanting the hymn, he became an Angirasa."*

In the process of becoming the Angirasa, Indra also takes on the role of Marutvan. Accompanied and supported by the Maruts, the luminous and violent gods, he overcomes the dark enemies — Vritra and the Dasyus. Indra assisted by the Maruts and enraptured by the Soma-wine conquers the adversaries, intensifies the aspiration of the seekers and drives him forward to the desired goal.

Yenā daśagvamadhriguṁ vepayantaṁ svarṇaram,
yenā samudramāvithā tamīmahe.
Yena sindhum mahīrapo rathañ iva, pracodayaḥ,
panthāmṛtasya yātave tamīmahe.[25]

"That rapture of the Soma we desire by which thou, O Indra, didst make to thrive the Might of Swar, that rapture ten-rayed and making a light of knowledge or shaking the whole being with its force by which thou didst foster the ocean; that Soma-intoxication by which thou didst drive forward the great waters like chariots to their sea, — that we desire that we may travel on the path of the truth."*

The Angirasas with the Word they possess increase the Truth in the seekers. And Indra to actuate them on the path joins forces with them, and together they hasten to the supreme summit.

Tamu naḥ pūrve pitaro navagvāḥ
sapta viprāso abhi vājayantaḥ,
nakṣaddābhaṁ taturim parvateṣṭhām
adroghavācam matibhiḥ śaviṣṭham.[26]

"In him our primal fathers, the seven seers, the Navagwas, increase their plenty, him victorious on his march and breaking through (to the goal), standing on the mountain, inviolate in speech, most luminous-forceful by his thinkings..."*

It is by singing the hymn of illumination that the seekers realise the solar illuminations in the cave of their being, *arcanto gā arvindan.*[27]

Armed with the oblations of the seven Rishis and strengthened by the conquering call of the Navagwas and the battle cry of the Dashagwas that Indra tears Vala into pieces:

Sa suṣṭubhā sa stubhā sapta vipraiḥ
svareṇādriṁ svaryonavagvaiḥ,
saraṇyubhiḥ phaligamindra śakra
valaṁ raveṇa darayo daśagvaiḥ.[28]

The destruction of the Enemy successfully accomplished by the call and the cry of the Navagwas and the Dashagwas is that of the Truth itself. It is the cry of the Truth again that is heard in the thunder of Indra and the advance of the Angirasas, *pra brahmāṇo aṅgiraso nakṣanta pra krandanur nabhanyasya vetu.*[29]

(2)

With the other gods

Indra the most powerful king of the gods, the victorious warrior with the thunderbolt who slays Vṛtra is not a phenomenon of Nature as some scholars believe. He is not a fanciful being dwelling somewhere in the higher regions but the godhead of supreme illuminations, the lord of divine Intelligence.

a) *Dūre tannāma guhyam parācairyattvā*
bhīte ahvayetāṁ vayodhai...[30]

Far and secret is your Name, O Lord, by which the worlds call you.

b) *Mahattannāma guhyam puruspṛg,*
yena bhūtaṁ janayo yena bhavyam.[31]

Mighty and mysterious is that Name desired of by many by which you have caused the past and will produce the future.

c) *Avācacakṣam padamasya sasvar*
ugraṁ nidhāturanvāyamichan,
apṛcchamanyāñ uta te ma āhur
indraṁ naro bubudhānā aśema.[32]

> I have discovered his strong and secret abode; desiring him, I have arrived at the place of the Self-sustainer. Upon enquiry, the awakened ones have said of him, 'Let us attain to Indra'.

The gods are conscious beings with cosmic functionings; they are different powers of the Supreme who preside over the cosmic forces of Nature. The various colours, chariots and weapons as well as the physical descriptions of the gods are symbolical and deeply communicate their native essences and functions to the inner vision of the initiates:

> a) "Indra has two green horses, Agni's ruddy, Aditya's tawny, Ashwins have two donkeys and Pushan goats; antelopes of Maruts, rosy rays of Ushas and Savitr's dusky horses along with the vehicle of Brihaspati called Vishwarupa are mentioned and Vayu's horses are called Niyuta."[33] [a]

> b) "Soma is brown, a youth active with a golden ornament; Agni is a luminous sage among the Gods; Twashtṛ the artisan holds iron knife in his hand; Indra has his thunderbolt; Rudra a pointed weapon strong with his healing medicines; Pushan watches all the ways like a thief; Vishnu with his mighty strides makes the Gods joyous; the Ashwins set their feet along with Ushas."[34] [b]

The activities of the gods proceed from the world of the highest Truth for they all are the many powers of the supreme Godhead. The seeker-sacrificer at each stage of his upward journey needs the help of one Power or the other and is aided really by all of them in his successful ascent to the Truth. There is of course a central or frontal Personality at any given stage who leads the rest of the gods and is backed by them in guiding the seeker-pilgrim. Such a Personality is seen by the seeker as the greatest God in that significant situation. There is thus a many-sided and a multi-tiered relation betweeen the *devā* and the seeker. Also numerous are the relationships between the two: The *devā* is imaged as the loving father, benevolent guardian, heroic defender and protector, or as a trusted friend and dependable guide. These relationships help the seeker at one stage or the other on his journey to the goal. The truth is that the Divine chooses for the seeker that relationship which is best suited for him to realise the Truth.

Indra, lord of the luminous mind, is the god of Swar-loka. He is intensely omnipotent and omnipresent, yet full of compassion, and inspires impassioned devotion.

a) *Na yasya devā devatā na martā*
āpaścana śavaso antamāpuḥ,
sa prarikvā tvakṣasā kṣmo divaśca
marutvānno bhavatuindra ūtī.[35]

Neither gods, nor the wise among mortals, inspite of their skilful endeavour, can ever reach the limit of the strength of that beneficient divinity. He excels and exceeds both earth and heaven by his prowess. May Indra associated by the Maruts protect us.

b) *Parā pūrveṣāṁ sakhyā vṛṇakti*
vitarturāṇo aparebhireti,
añanubhūtīravadhūnvānaḥ pūrvīr
indraḥ śaradastartarīti.[36]

The resplendent Lord, Indra, is the prototype of every form. It is his form that is seen everywhere. Multiform by his designs, he moves to his many worshippers since the steeds yoked to his chariot are a thousand in number.

c) *Pra mātrābhī ririce rocamānaḥ pra*
devebhirviśvato apratītaḥ,
pra majmanā diva indraḥ pṛthivyāḥ
prorormaho antarikṣādṛjiṣī.[37]

The resplendent Lord, unlimited and unsurpassable in brightness outshines both heaven and earth; drinking the Soma-wine the radiant one is greater than all the gods.

d) *Anuttamā te maghavannakirnu na*
tvavāñ asti devatā vidānaḥ,
na jāyamāno naśate na jāto yāni
kariṣyā kṛṇuhi pravṛddha.[38]

Verily, O compassionate god, Maghavan, nothing done by you is ineffective; among the gods no one is as wise as you. No one who is born, or who is to be born can ever surpass you in the glorious deeds which you have achieved.

e) *Tiṣṭhā su kam maghavanmā parā gāḥ*
somasya nu tvā suṣutasya yakṣi,
piturna putraḥ sicamā rabhe ta indra
svādiṣṭhayā girā śacīvaḥ.[39]

Remain with us a while, O mighty Maghavan, at our sacrificial place; I will offer to you the Soma-libation. O powerful Lord with devout chantings I cling to the hem of your robe as a child of his father's.

The Vedic Rishis often speak of collective sacrifice. The theme and goal of their sacrifice, *yajña*, is the attainment of the liberated mind which knows no obstruction or obstacle on its way to the Truth. All resistance and impediments are removed by Indra, the lord of illumined Intelligence, when he grows ecstatic by the drinking of the Soma-wine. In the Vedic conception, Soma is the divine Ananda, the source and substratum of all existence; it is the immortal nourishment of the gods who in the strength of its ecstasy increase in the seeker-sacrificer and uprear him to his own innate summits; they widen and uplift his consciousness and make him capable of sublimest experiences.

The Rishis insist that the seeker offers the secret delight in him to the lords of illumined consciousness and action and not linger back in the world of sense-consciousness and remain satisfied with his service to the Panis, the lords of the lower life. Offering can be total and perfect and purified only when the Soma-wine is squeezed out successfully. And the mystic delight can be experienced only when the illumined consciousness springs into operation. But these rays of enlightened awareness are penned up in the cavern of the dark subconscient to an extent that even Sarama, the goddess of intuition, is unable to keep track of them. Such is the concealing power of the Panis. Panis are the stealers of the rays of illumined consciousness, whereas Vritras are those who deny the seekers their own innate full powers and deprive them of their capacities. Besides, there are many other hostile forces who limit and confine, censure and obscure the energies of further self-progress and self-expression. Indra, the fully liberated Mind-Power, released from all the limitations and obscurations of the nervous workings, shapes adequate forms of thought and action for the successful upward march. The Rishis invoke Indra to make their receptive mind richer by his constant illumined activity. They eulogise his wisdom, his prowess, his love of the Soma-wine and the mighty exploits.

1. *Yo jāta eva prathamo manasvāndevo*
devānkratunā paryabhūṣat,
yasya śuṣmādrodasī abhyasetāṁ
nṛmṇasya mahnā sa janāsa indraḥ.

2. *Yaḥ pṛthivīṁ vyathamānamadṛṁhad*
yaḥ parvatānprakupitāñ aramṇāt,
yo antarikṣaṁ vimame varīyo yo dyām
astabhnātsa janāsa indraḥ.

3. *Yo hatvāhimariṇātsapta sindhūn*
yo gā udājadapadhā valasya,
yo aśmanorantaragniṁ jajāna saṁvṛk
samatsu sa janāsa indraḥ.

4. *Yenemā viśvā cyavanā kṛtāni yo*
dāsaṁ varṇamadharaṁ guhākaḥ,
śvaghnīva yo jigīvaṅ lakṣamādad
aryaḥ puṣṭāni sa janāsa indraḥ.

5. *Yaṁ smā pṛcchanti kuha seti ghoram*
utemāhurnaiṣo astītyenam,
so aryaḥ puṣṭīrvijaivā mināti śrad
asmai dhatta sa janāsa indraḥ.

6. *Yo radhrasya coditā yaḥ kṛśasya yo*
brahmaṇo nādhamānasya kīreḥ,
yuktagrāvṇo yo'vitā suśipraḥ
sutasomasya sa janāsa indraḥ.

7. *Yasyāśvāsaḥ pradiśi yasya gāvo yasya*
grāmā yasya viśve rathāsaḥ,
yaḥ sūryaṁ ya uṣasaṁ jajāna yo
apāṁ netā sa janāsa indraḥ.

8. *Yaṁ krandasī saṁyatī vihvayete*
pare'vara ubhayā amitrāḥ,
samānaṁ cidrathamātasthivānsā
nānā havete sa janāsa indraḥ.

9. *Yasmānna ṛte vijayante janāso yaṁ*
yudhyamānā avase havante,
yo viśvasya pratimānam babhūva
yo acyūtacyutsa janāsa indraḥ.

10. *Yaḥ śaśvato mahyeno dadhānān*
amanyamānāñcharvā jaghāna,
yaḥ śardhate nānudadāti śṛdhyāṁ yo
dasyorhantā sa janāsa indraḥ.

11. *Yaḥ śambaram parvateṣu kṣiyantaṁ*
catvāriṅśyām śaradyanvavindat,
ojāyamānaṁ yo ahiṁ jaghāna dānuṁ
śayānam sa janāsa indraḥ.

12. *Yaḥ saptaraśmirvṛṣabhastuviṣmān*
avāsṛjatsartave sapta sindhūn,
yo rauhiṇamasphuradvajrabāhur
dyāmārohantaṁ sa janāsa indraḥ.

13. *Dyāvā cidasmai pṛthivī namete śuṣmāc*
cidasya parvatā bhayante,
yaḥ somapā nicito vajrabāhuryo
vajrahastaḥ sa janāsa indraḥ.

14. *Yaḥ sunvantamavati yaḥ pacantaṁ*
yaḥ śasṅtaṁ yaḥ śaśamānamūtī,
yasya brahma vardhanaṁ yasya somo
yasyedaṁ rādhaḥ sa janāsa indraḥ.

15. *Yaḥ sunvate pacate dudhra ā cid*
vājaṁ dardarṣi sa kilāsi satyaḥ,
vayaṁ ta indra viśvaha priyāsaḥ
suvīrāso vidathamā vadema.[40]

1. He who from his birth has been the king of the gods, the wise one who excels every one with his prowess, protects the other gods; before the supremacy of his strength tremble both earth and heaven, he the well-known one, verily, is Indra.

2. It is Indra who fixes firmly the fluctuating, wavering earth and sets at rest the incensed mountains; he measures out the wide mid-region, *antariksha*, and extends support to the sky.

3. It is Indra, again, who slays Ahi, the most dreaded dragon and liberates the seven rivers; he recovers the luminous cattle from the cavern of Vala, and brings forth fire hidden between the rocks, the invincible lord, victorious ever.

4. He, the resplendent one, who has created the universe and made it to revolve; he who has humbled the evil forces and driven them away into oblivion, who has victoriously seized the treasures of the malicious as a hunter strikes his prey, he, verily is Indra.

5. He is the Terrible; they ask of him "where is he?" Some even speak of him, "He is not". But he is the one who inflicting chastisement destroys the dark treasures of the Adversary. Let us have faith in him, for he is the Lord, Indra.

6. He, who inspires and energizes all, both strong and feeble alike, and emboldens and invigorates the worshipper who sings his praise, and is a humble solicitor. He, the charming one, who defends those who constantly and devoutly worship him, he, verily is the Lord, Indra.

7. He, under whose control are horses and cows, villages and all chariots, and brings forth the sun and the daybreak, and leads the Waters, he, verily, is the Lord, Indra.

8. He, who is invoked both by earth and heaven, and is beseeched by both sides in the battle and also entreated (though differently),by two persons, sitting in the self-same chariot, he, verily, is the Lord, Indra.

9. He, without whose active support and benediction no one can win in battle, whose succour is constantly craved for, and is the prototype for everyone and moves even the immovable, he, verily, is the Lord, Indra.

10. He, who slays unnumbered infidels and grants no pardon to those who are sinners and do not offer him homage, he the destroyer of

the Dasyus, verily, is the Lord, Indra.

11. He, who discovered the arrogant demon Sambara dwelling in the dark rocks for forty autumns, who slew Ahi growing in strength and the sleeping son of Danu, he, verily, is the Lord, Indra.

12. He, who is the powerful, the showerer and the seven-reined who releases the seven rivers to flow forth, the mighty god whose thunderbolt causes Rauhina to stagger and stumble as he scales the heavens, he, verily is the Lord, Indra.

13. He, before whom both earth and heaven bow down, at whose might the mountains are dumbfounded and horrified, who is the famed drinker of the Soma-wine, the strong-armed, the wielder of the flashing thunderbolt, he, verily, is the Lord, Indra.

14. He, who with his aid assists all those who press the Soma-juice for him, and constantly chant hymns in his praise and toil for him, and expand their souls by prayer and by the gifts they offer to him, he, verily, is the Lord, Indra.

15. He, who is difficult to approach, who grants rich spoil seized from the fearsome Enemy to those who offer the Soma-wine and prepare the favoured food, is, verily, the Lord, Indra. May we always enjoy his favour; may we be blessed with righteous progeny, and with gusto repeat his praises at the sacrifice.

All the gods, the shining ones, in their eternal wisdom prepare the chariot which makes the many heavenly worlds lustrous and burnished. To this chariot then are yoked the bright and deep-red steeds of Indra. After which Indra the king of the gods ascends into it making the vision of his divine knowledge available to the sacrificers. With the attainment of this rare insight, by the grace of Indra, the seeker prepares for himself an appropriate new body to be able to retain steadily the divine vision and knowledge. For long this body remains concealed and unmanifest in the inactive material consciousness of the physical. The new and subtle body perceivable only by an inner vision is manifested by Indra. It is the dawn of an illumined knowledge that gives shape to that which lay hitherto concealed in the physical body.

Indra's horses are the special ones — the shining vehicles of power and illumination. They are the divine manifestations of knowledge, rays of intuition, dwellers in the high heaven.

> *Stavā vajram bāhvoruśantam*
> *stavā harī sūryasya ketu.*[41]

> We praise the thunderbolt in your hands and praise the swift-moving steeds which are the intuitive rays — the heralds of spiritual illumination.

They are yoked to the chariot of Indra by the Word proceeding from the heart of the Rishis.

> a) *Eha harī brahmayujā śagmā vakṣataḥ sakhāyam,*
> *gīrbhiḥ śrutaṁ girvaṇasam.*[42]

> May the powerful steeds, yoked by the Word, bring here unto us our luminous friend, renowned by our laudations who is fond of laudations.

> b) *Ā tiṣṭha vritrahanratham*
> *yuktā te brahmaṇā harī.*[43]

> O resplendent Lord, destroyer of Vritra, ascend your chariot, for your horses have been yoked to it by the Word.

> c) *Brahmaṇā te brahmayujā yunajmi*
> *harī sakhāyā sadhamāda āśu,*
> *sthiraṁ rathaṁ sukhamındrādhıtıṣṭhan*
> *prajānanvidvañ upa yāhi somam.*[44]

> These friendly horses that are yoked by the Word and are allies and swift-paced in battle, I harness by the Word. O all-knowing Lord, mounting on your firm and comfortable chariot, come to our sacrificial place and accept our loving oblation.

Once Indra manifests, the Rishi seeks the help of the Maruts who assay to the speeding mental movements a divine pace and assuredly a luminous direction. When the seeker securely attains an illumined mind, it is his second birth as it were, when new powers appear in him; it marks the birth of Maruts in him. This is the rebirth or the new birth of the Rishi taking him closer to the Truth. It gives him the power of holding his own nature, of sustaining and promoting it.

Once reborn, the Rishis attain the capacity to break open the rock of Inconscience and reaching the cows. This power they achieve by praising Indra for his support in doing their divine works. The Rishis thus reborn collectively call for the help of the Maruts joined to Indra. Chanting assuredly and sanguinely with the Maruts, the seer-sacrificers pray for Indra's active presence everywhere — on earth, in the *antarikṣa* and in the heaven. For, Indra's all-pervading presence promotes the Divine's increase in the seer-seekers and brightens their speech. It is inner sacrifice and inner purification that bring the seekers closer to Indra and the Maruts.

1. *Yunjanti bradhnamaruṣaṁ*
carantaṁ pari tasthuṣaḥ,
rocante rocanā divi.

2. *Yunjantyasya kāmyā*
hari vipakṣasā rathe,
śoṇa dhṛṣṇu nṛvāhasā.

3. *Ketuṁ kṛnvannaketave*
peśo maryā apeśase,
samuṣadbhirajāyathāḥ.

4. *Adaha svadhāmanu punar*
garbhatvamerire,
dadhānā nāma yajñiyam.

5. *Vīlu cidārujatnubhirguhā*
cidindra vahnibhiḥ,
avinda usriyā anu.

6. *Devayanto yathā matimacchā*
vidadvasuṁ giraḥ,
mahāmanuṣata śrutam.

7. *Indreṇa saṁ hi dṛkṣase*
sañjagmāno abibhyuṣa,
mandu samānavarcasā.

8. *Anavadyairabhidyubhir*
makhaḥ sahasvadarcati,
gaṇairindrasya kamyaiḥ.

9. *Ataḥ parijmannā gahi*
divo vā rocanādadhi,
samāsminnṛnjate giraḥ.

10. *Ito vā sātimīmahe divo*
vā pārthivādadhi,
indraṁ maho vā rajasaḥ.[45]

1. The inhabitants of the three worlds associated with Indra yoke the broad and shining chariot, they who stand around as the chariot moves; the mighty sun, the flaming fire and the moving wind all gleam in heaven.

2. They yoke to his chariot his most desirable bright coursers placed on either side that are deep-red, energetic and fervent, carrying His Lordship.

3. We mortals, owe our daily increase and the vision of knowledge to the resplendent Lord who with his effulgence gives form to the formless, wisdom to the ignorant, and life to the lifeless.

4. Thereafter, according to *svadhā* the supreme law of their self-sustenance, the Maruts again come to embryonic birth holding the secret and sacred Name signifying Indra which is befitting and felicitous to the performance of Sacrifice.

5. Accompanied by the steadfast and resolute Maruts who can break even the rock of material Inconscience, and have the capacity to enter the most obscure and darkest places, you, O Indra, have traced and liberated the shining cattle.

6. Even as the sacrificers laud Indra with their hymns of praise, the seers also, attaining a new birth upon hearing from Indra the sacred Word, laud him, and in collectivity glorify the host of Maruts with whose help the dark mountain is destroyed.

7. O Maruts, seeing you sprightly in the company of mighty and

undaunted Indra is itself a source of special rejoicing; equally splendorous and rapturous are you both in mutual fellowship.

8. To celebrate Indra, the adorable Lord, alongwith the amiable, heavenward-moving host of Maruts this sacrificial rite is performed.

9. For this reason, O all-pervading Maruts, come here — come from heaven or from the solar world; in this sacrificial rite the sacrificer exclusively chants hymns of praise for you.

10. Verily, we seek to attain Indra for the supreme felicity, whether from the earth here, or from the mid-region, *antarikṣa*, or from the heaven above, for he is everywhere.

The seer-seekers praise Indra with the hymns; they glorify him with the Words and implead his presence armed with the thunderbolt, for only he by his luminous rays of consciousness can remove all darkness. Indra the great conqueror is also an harmoniser. He impels the well-known impeller the sun, for a constant vision of the sun is possible only when Indra removes the subtlest veil that covers the face of the sun — the embodied Truth-Light. He is the unassailable god who guards all opulence and gives protection to the seer-sacrificer. He is the most luminous one, the constant donor of felicities, the uncoverable light supreme; even so he is superbly lauded, the thunder-adored Indra.

He constantly showers divine gifts on those who ceaselessly strive to attain the Truth. He impels them onward just as the strong fertilizer-bull excites the cows on entering their herd. He is invoked most above all the other gods.

1. *Indramid gathino bṛhad*
indramarkebhirarkiṇaḥ,
indraṁ vaṇiranuṣata.

2. *Indra iddharyoḥ sacā*
sammiśla ā vacoyujā
indro vajrī hiraṇyayaḥ.

3. *Indro dīrghāya cakshasa ā*
suryam rohayad divi
vi gobhiradrim airayat.

4. *Indra vājeṣu no'va*
sahasrapradhaneṣu ca,
ugra ugrābhirutibhiḥ.

5. *Indraṁ vayaṁ mahādhana*
indramarbhe havāmahe,
yujaṁ vṛtreṣu vājriṇam.

6. *Sa no vṛṣannamuṁ caruṁ*
satradāvannapā vṛdhi,
asmabhyamapratıṣkutaḥ.

7. *Tuñjetuñje ya uttare*
stomā indrasya vajriṇaḥ,
na vindhe asya suṣṭutim.

8. *Vṛṣā yutheva vaṅsagaḥ*
kṛṣṭiriyartyojasā,
īśāno apratiṣkutaḥ.

9. *Ya ekaścarṣaṇināṁ*
vasunāmirajyati,
indraḥ pañca kṣitinam.

10. *Indraṁ vo viśvataspari*
havāmahe janebhyaḥ,
asmākamastu kevalaḥ.[46]

1. The chanters of the Sama-veda extol and glorify Indra with songs, of the Rig-veda with prayers and those of Yajur-veda with divine verses.

2. The resplendent Lord, Indra, is the integrator of all elements, is the great harmoniser; he comes with his horses harnessed by the Word, he the shining one armed with the thunderbolt.

3. The resplendent Lord, Indra, has raised the sun in the sky to render all things visible. And by his rays dissolved the obscurity and darkness of the world.

4. O invincible Lord, Indra, pray protect us in the unassailable opulences gained by us, and in the secret and sacred knowledge attained and attainable by us.

5. We invoke the resplendent Lord, Indra, for great affluence and also for limited wealth. May the wielder of the thunderbolt protect us against the enemies.

6. O resplendent Lord, benevolent bestower of knowledge, granter of all boons, reveal yourself by dissolving the clouds of ignorance. May you always comply with our prayers.

7. O resplendent Lord, with each luminous actuation we have implored you with all praises. Yet no laudations we find are adequate and befitting the great wielder of the thunderbolt.

8. The mighty Lord, ever-shining, always compliant, impels the strivers with his luminous prowess, just as a bull of charming stride excites the herd of kine on entering it.

9. Indra, the sovereign striver, is the supreme ruler over all riches and over the five worlds and their inhabitants.

10. We invoke for all the strivers the most adorable Indra above all beings, and from all the worlds yet to manifest; may he be unusual and unique to us.

Indra is invoked to bring to his devotees the extraordinary wealth of illumination and of strength to be able to resist and repel the powerful enemies of light. Endowed with his power and fully guarded by him, the seeker aspires to combat and to conquer the foes. The performers of the inner sacrifice are desirous of destroying the diehard enemies — the haters of light, the dispersers of the sacrifice, who, concealing themselves under the cover of darkness deliver upon them powerful missiles of ruination. In this task they need the vast, luminous force of the thunder-armed Indra. For continual combat with the enemies the wise aspire for heroic progeny who can manifest in them a part of the gods; in this they need the benediction of Indra whose belly swells like the sea with the drink of divine delight. So does Mahi, the kind impeller to happy truths, co-streaming with Iḷa and Saraswati, turns to Indra. The glories of Indra are constantly sung by the seer-seekers that Indra may drink the Soma-wine more and more, and increase victoriously for the sacrificers.

1. *Endra sānasim rayim*
   sajitvānam sadāsaham,
   varṣiṣṭhamutaye bhara.

2. *Ni yena muṣṭihatyayā ni*
   vṛtrā ruṇadhāmahai,
   tvotāso nyarvatā.

3. *Indra tvotāsa ā vayam*
   vajram ghanā dadīmahi,
   jayema sam yudhi spṛdhaḥ.

4. *Vayam śūrebhirastṛbhir*
   indra tvayā yujā vayam,
   sasahyāma pṛtanyataḥ.

5. *Mahāñ indraḥ paraśca nu*
   mahitvamastu vajriṇe,
   dyaurna prathinā śavaḥ.

6. *Samohe vā ya āśata*
   narastokasya sanitau,
   viprāso vā dhiyāyavaḥ.

7. *Yaḥ kukṣiḥ somapātamaḥ*
   samudraiva pinvate
   urvīrāpo na kākudaḥ.

8. *Evā hyasya sūnṛtā*
   virapśī gomatī mahī,
   pakvā śākhā na dāśuṣe.

9. *Evā hi te vibhūtaya*
   ūtaya indra māvate,
   sadyaścit santi dāśuṣe.

10. *Evā hyasya kāmyā*
stoma uktham ca śamsyā,
indrāya somapītaye.[47]

1. O Indra, may you bring us for our inner increase abundant spiritual wealth which is enjoyable and everlasting, ever-conquering and full-grown, and capable of humiliating and vanquishing our enemies.

2. Give us that wealth by which we may completely destroy the enemies with fist-blows, well-guarded and protected by you fully endowed with luminous steed.

3. Well-guarded and protected by you, O Indra, may we ourselves wield the thunderbolt heavily against the enemies, may we combat and conquer them in battle.

4. O supreme Lord, with you as our protector may we combat the missile-hurling enemies arrayed in hosts against us, may we conquer them fully and superbly.

5. Mighty and supreme is the Lord, greater than the greatest, the thunder-armed; he is boundless, his prowess measureless. May his luminous forces be as vast as the heavens themselves.

6. Whatever the seer-strivers desire for progeny for the gods and for themselves in battle that is fulfilled by the resplendent Lord.

7. The belly of the resplendent Lord superbly swells like the sea when he drinks the Soma-wine, and has a natural freshness and wideness like the wide Waters from the mountain-tops.

8. Verily, Mahi the vastness of Light and Truth, manifold and full of rays turns to Indra; she the impeller to happy truths flowing plentifully like the ripe branch loaded with fruit for the sacrificer, she the true speech of Indra.

9. Verily, O Indra, your glories always increase the dedicated seekers like me and protect them all.

10. Thus indeed the desirable chants and recited praises are to be repeatedly directed to Indra, the resplendent Lord, that he may drink the Soma-wine.

The Rishi invokes Indra to descend with all his associates and accept the offerings of enjoyable, celestial foods that he may increase in strength. He then addresses his comrades in *yajña* to press out the Soma-juice and purify it for Indra, the prime doer of all divine actions. For it is through the consecration of the kernel of their inmost spiritual experiences that they can expect to ascend to the Truth. He extols the most handsome and fair-faced Indra, the seer of all, to appear accompanied by the others that he may rejoice in his laudation of him. He feels immensely gratified that his hymns composed for Indra have risen upward and reached him dwelling in heaven, and that he the supreme protector has happily accepted them. He prays that Indra may actuate towards him his varied and rare riches for pervasive and intense divine action. He again implores and also impels him towards that pervasive and excellent and celebrated wealth that is there on the summit which is impossible to attain without accompaniment and grace of Indra. That wealth there on high is full of luminous consciousness, brimming with divine inspiration and immortal life. The Rishi implores Indra for that divine hearing, *bṛhat śravaḥ*, born of divine inspiration as well as the divine light which only the initiates are capable of enjoying. He also aspires for the fast-moving excitants that can carry him securely and swiftly to the goal. Likewise he prays to Indra with songs galore for the augmentation and extension of his wealth as well as its protection. Towards this end the Rishi promises him more of Soma-libation, for it is well-known that Indra is most fond of the Soma-wine.

1. *Indrehi matsyandhaso*
viśvebhiḥ somaparvabhiḥ,
mahāñ abhiṣṭirojasa.

2. *Emenaṁ sṛjatā sute*
mandimindraya mandine,
cakriṁ viśvāni cakraye.

3. *Matsvā suśipra mandibhiḥ*
stomebhirviśvacarṣane,
sacaiṣu savaneṣvā

4. *Asṛgramindra te giraḥ*
prati tvāmudahāsata,
ajoṣa vṛṣabhaṁ patiṁ.

5. *Sacodaya citramarvag*
rādha indra vareṇyam
asaditte vibhu prabhu.

6. *Asmāntasu tatra codayendra*
rāye rabhasvataḥ,
tuvidyumna yaśasvataḥ.

7. *Saṁ gomadindra vājavad*
asme pṛthu śravo bṛhat,
viśvāyurdhehyakṣitam.

8. *Asme dhehi sravo bṛhad*
dyumnaṁ sahasrasātamam,
Indra tā rathiniriṣaḥ.

9. *Vasorindraṁ vasupatiṁ*
gīrbhirgṛnanta ṛgmiyam,
homa gantāramutaye.

10. *Sutesute nyokase bṛhad*
bṛhata edariḥ,
indrāya śuṣamarcati.[48]

1. Come, O resplendent Lord, with all those who are soaked in the Soma-juice, come and feel delighted to accept the Soma-juice; superior in prowess, overcome the enemies.

2. When the Soma-libation is prepared, offer the exhilarating and ecstatic drink to the rejoicing Indra, the victorious accomplisher of all things.

3. O resplendent Lord, fair of face, be pleased with these devotional laudations. Join us in your fellowship, may you be present in our sacrifices along with the gods.

4. O radiant God, I have composed hymns of praise for you; they have gone up to reach you, and you the great protector and showerer of gifts have happily accepted them.

5. O Indra, bestow upon us your varied and rare riches which are verily spread out and intensely concentrated with you.

6. O opulent Lord, inspire and impel us in our inner endeavour to acquire the secret wealth, for we are rapid in movement and prominent.

7. Grant us, O Indra, the opulent wealth of far-seeing vision, the mighty hearing of divine inspiration and the inexhaustible, the undecaying life of all connected with us.

8. O Indra, grant us the most powerful hearing born of divine inspiration, give us the Light enjoyable by all, and the fast-moving impulsions prayed for earlier.

9. O Indra, we invoke you with devout songs for the preservation and increase of the priceless treasures, you who are the lord and protector of all wealth; we praise you fully who are prone to us always.

10. With the libation of Soma-juice repeatedly pressed out for Indra, the striver-sacrificer lauds the mighty Indra dwelling in the luminous home of Swar.

It is the Soma-wine that sustains and supports the activity of the pure and clear-seeing Intelligence in us. For, Soma is the lord of the delight in divine existence and divine activity. Fed and enthralled by the Soma-wine, the Mind becomes in its action an ecstasy and an inspiration, and soars towards the summits of knowledge. The activity of an illuminated Intelligence must necessarily result in the construction of right thought formations. It is this Intelligence that inspires and encourages the seeker to progress to the highest Truth; intoxicated by the Soma-wine, the elixir of immortality, it becomes ecstatic in its thrust and invincible in its decisive action. The ardent and abiding action of this luminous Intelligence on the frontiers of human mentality makes the conservative resisters and confiners to willingly withdraw consenting to the farther advance of the seekers towards the Light. In the seer-vision and words of Sri Aurobindo, "They will say, in effect, 'Yes, now you have the right which we were hitherto justified in denying. Not only in the fields won already, but in other and untrod provinces pursue then your conquering march. Repose this action wholly on the divine Intelligence, not upon your lower capacities. For it is the greater surrender which gives you the greater right.'"[49] The seeker thus fights his way forward with his comrades-in-askesis even as the restrainers agreeably abjure and get off allowing thcir ascent. The luminous action of Indra finally awards the seeker the crowning peace of consummated consciousness and the fullness of human happiness. Indra himself is supported and strengthened in his intensities by the divine Ananda pouring out in the inner sensations of the seeker-sacrificers. It is the ecstatic action of Indra in man that destroys the Adversary and its hundredfold activities of inferior will and of limited thought, and assures the acquisition of greater riches. "For this Light is, in its entire greatness free from limitation, a continent of felicity; this Power is that which befriends the human soul and carries it safe through the battle, to the end of its march, to the summit of its aspiration."[50]

Indra, the king of the gods, is associated with many of them. He is frequently mentioned in the Soma hymns, appears with Agni, and is central to the functioning of the Maruts as well as of Atri, Apala and Vrishakapi.

a) *Ābhi dyām mahinā bhuvam*
abhīmam pṛthivīm mahīm,
kuvitsomasyāpāmiti.[51]

In my greatness and vastness, I surpass the sky, and so I transcend the wide earth; for I have frequently drunk of the Soma-wine.

b) *Ahamasmi mahāmaho'bhinabhyamudīṣitaḥ,*
kuvitsomasyāpāmiti.[52]

I am the supreme, the greatest of the great, elevated to the heavens and beyond, for I have frequently drunk of the Soma-wine.

c) *Gṛho yāmyaraṁkrto*
devebhyo havyavāhanaḥ,
kuvitsomasyāpāmiti.[53]

Receiving the oblations, praised and desired by the worshippers, I bear their offerings to the gods above, for I have frequently drunk of the Soma-wine.

d) *Bhūri cakartha yujyebhirasme*
samānebhirvṛṣabha pauṅsyebhiḥ,
bhūrīṇi hi kṛṇavāmā śaviṣṭhendra
kratvā maruto yadvaśāma.[54]

O mighty Indra, verily, you have done everything for us the Maruts, but equally it has been with our concerted efforts that we achieved many things. With our determined energies we can accomplish much without fail, and we are what we desire to be.

(3)

Slaying of the Enemy and the Recovery of the Cows

A massive carouser of the Soma-wine, a trusted friend and guide of the aspirant, Indra is an exclusively powerful divine hero, the slayer of Vritra.

1. *Indrasya nu viryāṇi pra vocaṁ*
yāni cakāra prathamāni vajrī,
ahannahimanvapastatarda pra
vakṣaṇā abhinatparvatānām.

2. *Ahannahiṁ parvate śisriyāṇaṁ tvaṣṭāsmai*
vajraṁ svaryaṁ tatakṣa
vāśrā iva dhenavaḥ syandamānā anjaḥ
samudramava jagmurāpaḥ.

3. *Vṛṣāyamāṇo'vṛṇita somaṁ*
trikadrukeṣvapibatsutasya,
ā sāyakaṁ maghavādatta vajramahann
enaṁ prathamajāmahīnām.

4. *Yadindrāhanprathamajāmahīnāmān*
māyināmaminaḥ prota māyāḥ,
ātsuryam janayandyamuṣasam
tāditnā śatrum na kilā vivitse.

5. *Ahanvṛtram vṛtrataram vyaṅsam*
indro vajreṇa mahatā vadhena,
skandhāṅsīva kuliśenā vivṛkṇahiḥ
śayata upapṛkpṛthivyāḥ.

6. *Ayoddheva durmada ā hi juhve*
mahāvīram tuvibādhamṛjīṣam,
nātāridasya samṛtim vadhānām
sam rujānāḥ pipiṣa indraśatruḥ.

7. *Apadahasto apṛtanyadindramāsya*
vajramadhi sānau jaghāna,
vṛṣno vadhriḥ pratimānam bubhūṣan
purutrā vṛtro aśayadvyastaḥ.

8. *Nadam na bhinnamamuyā śayānam mano*
ruhāṇā ati yantyāpaḥ,
yāścidvṛtro mahinā paryatiṣṭhat
tāsāmahiḥ patsutaḥ śīrbabhūva.

9. *Nicāvayā abhavadvṛtraputrendro*
asyā ava vadharjabhāra,
uttarā sūradharaḥ putra āsīd
dānuḥ śaye sahavatsā na dhenuḥ.

10. *Atiṣṭhantīnamaniveśanānām kāṣṭhānām*
madhye nihitam śarīram,
vṛtrasya niṇyam vi carantyāpo
dīrgham tama āśayadindraśatruḥ.

11. *Dasapatnīrahigopā atiṣṭhanniruddhā*
āpaḥ paṇineva gāvaḥ,
apām bilamapihitam yadāsīd vṛtram
jaghanvāṅ apa tadvavāra.

12. *Aśvyo vāro abhavastadindra sṛke*
yattvā pratyahandeva ekaḥ,
ajayo gā ajayaḥ śūra somam
avāsṛjaḥ sartave sapta sindhūn.

13. *Nāsmai vidyunna tanyatuḥ siṣedha*
na yām mihamakiraddhrādunim ca,
indraśca yadyuyudhāte ahiś
cotāparībhyo maghavā vi jigye.

14. *Aheryātāram kamapaśya indra*
hṛdi yatte jaghnuṣo bhīragacchat,
nava ca yannavatim ca sravantīḥ
śyeno na bhīto ataro rajāṅsi.

15. *Indro yāto'vasitasya rājā śamasya*
ca śṛṅgiṇo vajrabāhuḥ,
sedu rājā kṣayati carṣaṇīnām
arānna nemiḥ pari tā babhūva.[55]

1. I will now declare the valorous deeds of Indra, the great wielder of the *Vajra*: he killed the dark serpent and released the Waters; he cleft the mountains for the flow of the rivers of luminous consciousness.

2. He slew the serpent-demon seeking refuge on the mountain; Twashtri conquered the Adversary with his mighty *Vajra*, and the waters thus released hastened quickly to the sea like lowing cows to their calves.

3. Ardent and restive as a bull, when Indra drank the Soma-wine at the triple sacrifice, he, the mighty Maghavan struck the serpent-demon's first born with his thunderbolt.

4. Inasmuch as Indra kills the first born of the serpent-demon, he destroys the delusions of the vile and wicked ones, and gives a new life to the Sun, the Heaven and the Dawn, he finds not a single enemy pitted against him anymore.

5. Indra, the mighty warrior, and the great hero in battle challenges the drunken devil, Vritra, and destroys him with his thunderbolt; as tree-trunks are felled by an axe, so Ahi lies crushed on the ground.

6. The badly wounded, handless and footless, but arrogant Vritra defies Indra, the scatterer of the enemies and destroyer of many and

meets with the same end, and lies low with severed limbs strewn everywhere.

7. Footless and handless, the mutilated Enemy, dismembered and emasculated, still challenges Indra, who strikes upon his mountain-like back with his *Vajra*, and fells him motionless.

8. The celestial Waters that delight the mind and soul now flow over the striver, as the water of a river burst through its broken banks. Ahi lies prostrate beneath the flood of waters which Vritra by his dark cunning had obstructed for long.

9. The mighty Lord struck Danu, the mother of Vritra with his deadly *Vajra*, when she tried to save her son by bending over him. So the mother was above and the son under, as they lay like a cow with her calf.

10. The gushing Waters sweep off the nameless corpse of Vritra rolled in the midst of never-resting, ever-rushing currents. The Enemy of Indra thus sank into lasting oblivion.

11. Guarded by the serpent-demon, Ahi, enslaved and enchained like helpless wives of the Asura, the Waters stood obstructed for long like the luminous cattle confined in the cave by Panis, but Indra by slaying Vritra sets them open and free.

12. When Indra, the resplendent Lord, returns the blow inflicted on him earlier by Vritra, by his thunderbolt, *Vajra*, he becomes furious like a horse's tail. He then rescues the cows and releases the seven rivers, he, the radiant one who wins the Soma-wine.

13. Nothing avails him, either the lightning or thunder or hailstorm that Vritra hurls at Indra, or the mist that he spreads around him when they strive in the battle and Maghavan triumphs over him fully and finally.

14 When Indra had slain the serpent-demon, fear enters his heart; who knows what other demon he was looking for to destroy that he traversed nine and ninety flowing rivers like a swift hawk?

15. Indra, the resplendent Lord, the wielder of the *Vajra*, then becomes the sovereign of all that moves and moves not, of creatures tamed and horned; as he abides, Indra, rules as a king all living beings and comprehends and includes them all as the circumference of a wheel comprehends its spokes.

The hymn is a joyous adoration and celebration of the victorious God. It is a shining example of rich and compact poetry, and with its striking and apt imagery the hymn leaves upon the reader a profound and lasting impact. Elsewhere the Rishi describes Indra as letting the sun climb up the heaven when he kills Vritra with his *Vajra*:

a) *Tvamapāmapidhānāvṛṇorapādhārayaḥ*
parvate dānumadvasu,
vṛtraṁ yadindra śavasāvadhīrahim
āditsūryaṁ divyārohayo dṛśe.[56]

O Indra, you have cleft open the clouds and destroyed the Adversary and taken possession of the luminous wealth. When you have slain Vritra, you make the sun visible in the sky.

b) *Jaghanvāñ u haribhiḥ saṁbhritakratav*
indra vṛtram manuṣe gātuyannapaḥ,
ayacchathā bahyorvajramayasamadharayo
divyā sūryaṁ dṛśe.[57]

O resplendent Lord, the inner self of all, the performer of luminous deeds, desirous of helping the worshippers, you have slain Vritra with your fast moving steeds and set free the Waters, and wielding the *Vajra* cloven the dark clouds and made the sun visible in the sky.

A very graphic and symbolic description of the killing of Vritra is given in the Rig-veda. Vritra lies across the seven rivers barring the Waters from reaching the earth. He even devours them. The gods fear him, and leave Indra alone to face him. Indra strengthened and intoxicated by the Soma-wine and accompanied by the faithful Maruts — the combatant thought-forces — and Vishnu marches forward. Even as he kills the demon-serpent with the *Vajra*, the innards of the mountain open up releasing the Waters, the sun shines forth and the heavens are unveiled.

The gods rejoice the victory and the seers burst forth in songs of praise. Indra, the manipulator of the thunderbolt thus opens the path for the seekers.

a) *Indro asmāñ aradadvajrabāhurapāhan*
vṛtraṁ paridhiṁ nadīnāṁ,
devo'nayatsavitā supaṇistasya vayaṁ
prasave yāma urviḥ.

Pravacyaṁ saśvadhā vīryamtadindrasya
karma yadahiṁ vivṛścat,
vi vajrena pariṣado jaghanāyann
āpo'yanamicchamānāḥ.[58]

Indra, the wielder of *Vajra*, defines our course (say the rivers) when he destroys the Obstructor of our flow. The resplendent Lord leads us on our path, and in conformity with his command we flow as vibrant streams.

The heroic deed of Indra is to be celebrated when he cuts asunder to pieces the Enemy who obstructs the Waters, whence they flow in the desired direction.

b) *Yāḥ sūryo raśmibhirātatāna yābhya*
indro aradad gātumurmiṁ,
te sindhavo varivo dhātanā no yuyaṁ pāta
svastibhiḥ sadā naḥ.[59]

The celestial streams whom the resplendent Lord extends by his rays, and for whom he has hewn the path, may they serve us and preserve our life. May the gods ever cherish us with their blessings.

c) *Ahaṁ bhūmimadadāmāryayāhaṁ*
vṛṣṭiṁ dāśuṣe martyāya,
ahamapo anayaṁ vāvaśānā mama
devāso anu ketamāyan.[60]

I gave the earth to the virtuous, and brought rain for the good of those who offer oblations. I have let forth the luminous Waters, and the gods do my will.

d) *Bībhatsunāṁ sayujaṁ haṁsamāhur*
āpaṁdivyānāṁ sakhye carantaṁ,
anuṣṭubhamanu carcuryamānamindraṁ
ni cikyuḥ kavayo manīṣā.[61]

The sages call him swan, the sun, the friend of those who are bewildered and confounded moving in the proximity of the celestial Waters; the wise worship him who is worthy of their praises composed after the *Anustubh* metre.

c) *Abhiṣṭane te adrivo yatsthā*
jagacca rejate,
tvaṣṭā cittava manyava indra
vevijyate bhiyārcannanu svarājyam.[62]

At your war-cry, O wielder of the *Vajra*, all things, movable and immovable, start trembling; even Twashtri shakes with fear at your wrath, when you establish your sovereignty.

f) *Parīṁ ghṛṇā carati titviṣe śavo'po*
vṛtvī rajaso budhnamāśayat,
vṛtrasya yatpravaṇe durgṛbhiśvano
nijaghantha hanvorindra tanyatum.[63]

O mighty Lord, when you had struck down the wide-extended demon Vritra with your thunderbolt who was obstructing the Waters, reposing above in the firmament, your fame spread afar and your prowess was recognised by all.

g) *Nirindra bṛhatībhyo vṛtraṁ*
dhanubhyo asphuraḥ,
nirarbudasya mṛgayasya māyino
niḥ parvatasya gā ājaḥ.

Niragnayo rurucurniru sūryo
niḥ soma indriyo rasaḥ,
nirantarikṣādadhamo mahāmahiṁ
kṛṣe tadindra pauṅsyam.[64]

O resplendent Lord, you have extirpated the most wicked Vritra with your lofty weapons; you have destroyed the deceptive Arbuda and Mrigaya and snatched the luminous cattle away from the dark cave.

O resplendent Lord, it was a most wonderful act of yours when you expelled the crooked Ahi from the mid-region. Then the fires blazed and the sun shone forth in the firmament and the nectarine Soma-wine flowed out establishing your mighty prowess.

h) *Nirindra bhūmyā adhi vṛtraṁ*
jaghantha nirdivaḥ,
sṛjā marutvatīrava jīvadhanyā imā
apo'rcann a nu svarājyam.[65]

O mighty Lord, you have expelled Vritra both from the earth and the heaven by destroying him; may you now release the life-sustaining rain and establish your own sovereignty.

The Vritra-battle bears a close resemblance with the thunder-battle in several other mythologies. The description and role of Indra is similar to Donar-Thor of the Teutons; Indra's *Vajra* is similar to Thor's hammer — his weapon of lightning as well as the thunder-wedges of Iranian Mithra and the Greek Zeus. Indra is extolled in the Veda as the one who cleaves the resisting rocks — rocks that imprison the cows, and liberates the celestial rivers.

Besides releasing the Waters, Indra is credited with the recovery of the cows. There is a legend that speaks of Trita Aptya who, animated and emboldened by Indra, fights the three-headed demon Visvarupa, son of Twashtri, and cuts off the heads and releases the cows.

Sa pitryānyāyudhāni vidvānindreṣita
āptyo abhyayudhyat,
triśīrṣaṇaṁ saptaraśmiṁ jaghanvān
tvāṣṭrasya cinniḥ sasṛje trito gāḥ.

Bhūrīdindra udinakṣantamojo'vābhinat
satpatirmanyamānam,
tvāṣṭrasya cidviśvarupasya gonām
ācakrāṇastrīṇi śīrṣā parā vark.[66]

He, the son of celestial Waters, skilled to use his mighty weapons, when incited fights the Enemy and destroys the sevenfold and three-headed demon. Then Trita free from the threefold sin, sets free the cows of the son of Twashtri.

Indra, the resplendent Lord, the protector of the virtuous, attaining vast strength crushes the three heads of the multiform Asura, the son of Twashtri and liberates the luminous cattle.

Indra claims to have brought the cows to Trita from the Enemy's possession.

Ahamindro rodho vakṣo atharvaṇas
tritāya gā ajanayamaheradhi,
ahaṁ dasyubhyaḥ pari nṛmṇamā dade
gotrā śikṣan dadhīce mātariśvane.[67]

I, Indra, the Lord of all resplendence, strike off the head of the son of Atharvan, and release the celestial waters for Trita. I carry off the wealth from the Dasyus and tame the clouds for Dadhayanch, the son of Matariswan.

A parallel myth is found in the Avesta. Thraetona kills the serpent-demon with its three mouths, three heads and six eyes, and liberates two beautiful maiden from its clutches. Another similar myth in Greek mythology alludes to the release of the cows by the killing of the three-headed monster Geryones at the hands of Herakles.

The Veda, again and again, speaks of the Panis who keep the kine hidden in a rock-cave far away from the gaze and reach of the seekers. Sarama, Indra's messenger, tracks out the rock and hearing the lowing of the cows demands their liberation. The Panis send him back with repugnance and disdain. Indra then, fire-inflamed and enraged, accompanied by the Angirasa Rishis and helped by Agni and Brihaspati bursts open the rock and releases the cows for the spiritual nourishment of the people. The sun shines forth in the firmament because of the liberation of the cows, darkness disappears and the seekers rejoice in the light.

a) *Soṣāmavindatsa svaḥ so agniṁ so*
arkeṇa vi babādhe tamāṅsi,
bṛhaspatirgovapuṣo valasya nir
majjānaṁ na parvaṇo jabhāra.[68]

Brihaspati finds the dawn, the sun and Agni; he then dissolves the darkness with light. He seizes the rock-cave concealing the kine and brings them out as one extracts marrow from a bone.

b) *Te marmṛjata dadṛvāṅso adriṁ tad*
eṣām anye abhito vi vocan,
paśvayantrāso abhi kāramarcan
vidanta jyotiścakṛpanata dhībhiḥ.[69]

Rending the rocks they further cleared out the way; other wise ones also spoke of their discoveries. Unable to extricate the cattle they invoked the resplendent Lord and found the light and were enabled to worship him with proper ceremonies.

c) *Ṛtenādriṁ vyasanbhidantaḥ*
samaṅgiraso navanta gobhiḥ,
śunaṁ naraḥ pari ṣadannuṣāsam
āviḥ svarabhavajjāte agnau.[70]

By the sacrifice, the Angirasas, the fire-priests split open the mountain-cave and return with the luminous cattle. The worshippers arrive happily at the dawn and soon after the sacrificial fire is lighted the sun manifests.

To Indra again goes the credit not only of the recovery of the cows but the winning of the sun and the bringing of the dawn. He fastens the sun to the skies, establishes the heavens in the consciousness of the seekers and extends the limitations of the earth. Indra is the strongest of the strong gods, the hero-god who conquers Vritra and vanquishes the Panis, and snatches away from them the imprisoned divine felicities for the benefit of the seekers.

In addition to the slaying of Vritra and Viswarupa, Indra conquers the inhuman and demoniac Dasyus for the inner progress of the Aryans.

a) *Manyurindro manyurevāsa devo*
manyurhotā varuṇo jātavedāḥ,
manyuṁ viśa īḷate mānuṣīryaḥ
pāhi no manyo tapasā sajoṣāḥ.[71]

He who worships you O Manyu, the divine wrath, the mighty

destroyer of the Adversary, verily, enjoys all force both inner and outer; may we overcome with your help both the Dasa and the Arya, — with you who are vigorous and invigorating.

b) *Yo no dāsa āryo vā puruṣṭutādeva*
indra yudhaye ciketati,
asmābhiṣṭe suṣahāḥ santu śatravas
tvayā vayaṁ tānvanuyāma saṁgame.[72]

O resplendent Lord, adored by all, may any one, whether he be a Dasa or Arya, who intends to assault us, be conquered by us with your active help. May all enemies be overcome by us in battle.

c) *Tvaṁ ha nu tyadadamāyo dasyuṅr*
ekaḥ kṛṣṭīravanorāryāya,
asti svinnu vīryaṁ tatta indra na
svidasti tadṛtuthā vi vocaḥ.[73]

O resplendent Lord, you are the one who has tamed the Dasyus and dominate over them, you alone have rescued the Aryans and given them felicity. If it is not true, then declare it now.

d) *Indraḥ samatsu yajamānamāryaṁ*
prāvadviśveṣu śatamutir
ājiṣu svarmīḷheṣvājiṣu,
manave śāsadavratāntvacaṁ
kṛṣṇāmarandhayat,
dakṣanna viśvaṁ tatṛṣānam
oṣati nyarśasānamoṣati.[74]

Indra, the mighty Lord, the manifold protector of his worshippers in battles, defends them in all conflicts that accord heaven; he who has a hundred helps at hand punishes the evil and lawless, consumes the malignant and burns down all those who take pleasure in inflicting cruelty on the virtuous.

By conquering Vritra and the host of other enemies Indra provides freedom to the gods that bestows the highest spiritual felicity on the seekers. He is empowered by the gods and heaven and earth to destroy all the obstructing and obstinate forces of darkness and ignorance, and with his titanic strength and creative action he achieves the goal.

a) *Śaṅsā mahāmindraṁ yasminviśvā*
ā kṛṣṭayaḥ somapāḥ kāmamavyan,
yaṁ sukratuṁ dhiṣaṅe vibhvataṣṭaṁ
ghanaṁ vṛtrāṇāṁ janayanta devāḥ.[75]

I adore Indra, the mighty Lord, in whom all the worshippers drinking the Soma-wine get their desires fulfilled, and in whom the earth and heaven and gods rejoice; he is the doer of great deeds, the slayer of Vritra who is the embodiment of Ignorance and created by Vibhu.

b) *Divo na tubhyamanvindra satrāsuryaṁ*
devebhirdhāyi viśvam,
ahiṁ yadvṛtramapo vavrivāṅsaṁ
hannṛjīṣinviṣṇunā sacānaḥ.[76]

To you O Indra, as to the sun, the gods have given all strength, so that endowed with the Soma-juice you associated with Vishnu are able to subdue the dark force Ahi that obstructs the striver's progress.

c) *Devāścitte asuryāya pūrve'nu*
kṣatrāya mamire sahāṅsi,
indro maghāni dayate viṣahyendraṁ
vājasya johuvanta sātau.[77]

O Indra, the other gods have confessed your supremacy in the power of destroying the Adversary. You have slain Vritra and other enemies by the magnitude of your prowess, and given to your worshippers the rich spoils; these devotees always invoke you for spiritual sustenance.

Indra is the irresistible warrior, the mighty hero, the master of mental luminosity and the thought-awakener; he increases by the power of prayer and the sacred Word.

a) *Indraḥ pūrbhidātiraddāsamarkair*
vidadvasurdayamāno vi śatrūn,
brahmajutastanvā vavṛdhāno
bhuridātra āpṛṇadrodasī ubhe.[78]

The mighty Indra, the destroyer of the citadels of the Adversary manifesting his greatness, mercilessly overwhelms the enemies and overspreads the earth and the sky with his radiance. Inspired by the laudations, expanding in size and armed in many ways he imparts the supreme felicity to both heaven and earth.

b) *Nū indra śūra stavamāna ūtī*
brahmajutastanvā vāvṛdhasva,
upa no vājanmimīhyupa stīnyūyam
pāta svastībhiḥ sadā naḥ.[79]

O Indra, victorious and resplendent Lord, lauded and adored by all, propitiated by praise on the present occasion, may we experience your increased glory and might for our protection. Pray, bestow upon us your nourishment and habitation, and continued benediction.

c) *Prabhañgaṁ durmatīnāmindra*
śaviṣṭhā bhara
jyeṣṭhaṁ codayanmate
rayimasmabhyaṁ yujyaṁ codayanmate.[80]

O mighty Lord, the crusher of the Adversary, grant us worthy wealth that annihilates the evil-minded enemies; O inspirer, give us the most excellent riches that increase the illumined intellect.

d) *Bhuvastvamindra brahmaṇā mahān*
bhuvo viśveṣu savaneṣu yajñiyaḥ,
bhuvo ñṛnścyautno viśvasminbhare
jyeṣṭhaśca mantro viśvacarṣaṇe.[81]

O Indra, you have grown mighty through our praise, have become adorable in all our sacrificial ceremonies. In every battle you have cast down the enemies; O beholder of the universe, you are the best and most renowned.

He is the foremost to possess mind and use it perfectly, and reaches heaven kindled by his inner fire.

Tvaṁ rayiṁ puruvīrāmu naskṛdhi
tvaṁ tapaḥ paritapyājayaḥ svaḥ.[82]

O Indra, may you bestow upon the worshippers riches with numerous progeny; you have indeed won heavens by your penance.

Indra is referred to as Valahan, the shining warrior who slays Vala the withholder of illuminations and king and promoter of darkness and division, and releases the celestial rivers and helps the sun to mount high upon our being and illumines our human mentality. He is the light and power behind the mind. As Sri Aurobindo observes, "...the three gods Indra, Vayu, Agni represent the cosmic Divine on each of its three planes, Indra on the mental, Vayu on the vital, Agni on the material. In that order, therefore, beginning from the material they approach the Brahman."[83]

Indra is the cleaver of the cave wherein Vala, the demon of Darkness, keeps the kine concealed and coralled; whereas Vritra is the coverer and the conceiter. Indra is the epitome of all energy, and the strongest amongst gods. He is always in the forefront of their battle against Vritra.

a) *Jātam yattvā pari devā abhuṣan*
mahe bharāya puruhuta viśve.[84]

You who are invoked by many, and whom all the gods equip as soon as born for the great battle with the Asuras.

b) *Evā tvāmindra vajrinnatra viśve*
devāsaḥ suhavāsa ūmāḥ,
mahāmubhe rodasī vṛddhamṛṣvaṁ
nirekamidvṛṇate vṛtrahatye.[85]

O Indra, wielder of the great thunderbolt, all the protecting gods who are devoutly worshipped and invoked as well as both heaven and earth glorify you who are unparalleled and mighty, infinite and eternal, singularly capable of destroying Vritra.

c) *Adha tvā viśve pura indra devā*
ekaṁ tavasaṁ dadhire bharāya,
adevo yadabhyauhiṣṭa devān
atsvarṣātā vṛṇata indramatra.[86]

All the gods accepting you as their mighty chief then place you in life's great battle front. When the terrible Adversary attacked the gods, the Maruts extend their support to you in the relentless struggle.

d) *Indraṁ vṛtrāya hantave devāso
dadhire puraḥ,
indraṁ vāṇīranūṣatā samojase.*[87]

All the gods have accepted Indra as their foremost leader for the destruction of Vritra; their chants of praise have been addressed to him to enhance his vigour.

All the gods aid Indra, applaud him and bestow upon him the highest honour, and call him *Maharaja*.

a) *Imāṁ te dhiyaṁ pra bhare maho mahīm
asya stotre dhiṣaṇā yatta ānaje,
tamutsave ca prasave ca sāsahim
indraṁ devāsaḥ śavasāmadannanu.*[88]

O resplendent Lord, to you I offer my most excellent hymn of praise; may I become worthy of your satisfaction by my devotional offering. The gods exhilarate the mighty and victorious Indra through the strength of their prayers to gain prosperity and wealth.

b) *Tadindra preva vīryaṁ cakartha yat
sasantaṁ vajreṇabodhayo'him,
anu tvā patnīrhṛṣitaṁ vayaśca viśve
devāso amadannanu tvā.*[89]

O Indra, you did perform a glorious deed when you awakened the sleeping dark Asura Ahi to destroy him with your mighty thunderbolt. Then the Maruts and all the gods greeted you, and the wives of the gods shared in your exultation.

c) *Anu dyāvāpṛthivī tatta ojo'martyā
jihata indra devāḥ,
kṛṣvā kṛtno akṛtaṁ yatte asty
ukthaṁ navīyo janayasva yajñaiḥ.*[90]

O resplendent Lord, the heaven and earth and all the immortal gods acknowledge your prowess. O Indra, doer of many mighty deeds, may you now accomplish that which is yet undone; may you grant us a new hymn to be sung at your sacrifices.

The devotees sometimes even desert Indra and forsake him being scared of Vritra.

a) *Uta mātā mahiṣamanvavenad*
amī tvā jahati putra devāḥ.[91]

His mother enquired of the resplendent Lord, Indra, whether the gods had deserted him (afraid of being attacked by Vritra).

b) *Vi yadabheradha tviṣo*
viśve devāso akramuḥ,
vidanmṛgasya tañ amaḥ.[92]

When in their anguish the gods fled in different directions overpowered by the raging might of Ahi, the fear of the monster gripped them.

c) *Vṛtasya tvā śvasathādīṣamānā viśve*
devā ajahurye sakhāyaḥ.[93]

All the gods who were so far your friends in fear forsook you and fled away at the snorting of the demon Vritra.

Indra is the wielder of the most powerful weapons — *Vajra*, *Asman*, *Parvata* and *Adri*.

a) *Pra vartaya divo aśmānamindra*
somaśitaṁ maghavantaṁ śiśādhi,
prāktādapāktādadharādudaktād
abhi jahi rakṣasaḥ parvatena.[94]

O resplendent Lord, hurl down from heaven your fierce thunderbolt, may you sanctify and sharpen the weapon, with the Soma-wine and further temper it with poison and strike down the hordes of the Enemy coming from the front, from behind, from above and from below.

b) *Tvamāyasaṁ prati vartayo gordivo*
aśmānamupanītamṛbhvā.[95]

When invoked, you the swift slayer of the enemies, have hurled the thunderbolt with speed brought to you by Ribhu.

c) *Sasena cidvimadāyāvaho vasv*
ājāvadriṁ vāvasānasya nartayan.[96]

You have given wealth and wisdom to Vimada; verily you wield the thunderbolt for the benefit of those engaged in sacrificial worship.

d) *Ayā ha tyaṁ māyayā vāvṛdhānaṁ*
manojuvā svatavaḥ parvatena,
acyutā cidvīḷitā svojo rujo vi
dṛḷhā dhṛṣatā virapśin.[97]

O mighty Indra, you have destroyed Vritra by your thunderbolt swift as thought, who was growing in his strength by his cunning. O radiant Lord, you have demolished the citadels of the Enemies by your irresistible weapon.

The lightning is Indra's chariot, the thunderbolt and the Soma-wine his constant companions:

a) *Apāmojmānaṁ pari gobhirāvṛtam*
indrasya vajraṁ havisha ratham yaja.[98]

It (the chariot) possesses the speed of swift current, and engirdled with flaming white light and the fierce *Vajrayudha.*

b) *Yujaṁ vajraṁ vṛṣabhaścakra indro nir*
jyotiṣā tamaso gā adukṣat.[99]

Then he (Indra) grasps his thunderbolt and with its prowess tears apart the dark veil of Evil and milks out the streams (of Truth).

c) *Abhi tvā pājo rakṣaso vi tasthe mahi*
jajñānamabhi tatsu tiṣṭha,
tava pratnena yujyena sakhyā vajreṇa
dhṛṣṇo apa tā nudasva.[100]

O mighty Lord, the strength of the Enemies is concentrated fast against you; may you buttress well against that manifest might of Evil. Destroy it O valiant one, with your thunderbolt and with your friends and associates.

d) *Śatabradhna iṣustava sahasraparṇa eka it,*
yamindra cakṛṣe yujam.[101]

O mighty Indra, that single sharp weapon of yours which you have made your constant and faithful ally is hundred-pointed and thousand-feathered.

e) *Vajraśca yadbhavatho anapacyutā*
samatsvanapacyutā.[102]

His person is armed with the mighty thunderbolt, and thus does he become invincible; verily, he is invincible in the great battle.

f) *Indre bhujaṁ śaśamānāsa āśata*
sūro dṛśīke vṛṣaṇaśca pauṅsye,
pra ye nvasyārhaṇā tatakṣire yujaṁ
vajraṁ nṛṣadaneṣu kāravaḥ.[103]

Those who adore the resplendent Lord and the gods find protection under the Lord (Indra); they are blessed with universal vision and manly vigour by him. They who offer diligently to him their devout adoration get full protection of his thunderbolt; verily, they prosper in the dwellings of men.

To defeat and destroy the Enemy, Indra employs all forms of craftiness including *maya*; by whatever means he renders innocuous the guiles of the Adversary.

Bhinatpuro navatimindra pūrave
divodāsāya mahi dāśuṣe nṛto
vajreṇa dāśuṣe nṛto.[104]

O resplendent Lord, dancing with utter delight in battle, you have destroyed ninety cities of the Adversary for Puru the giver of offerings and for Divodasa the reverential one; you have destroyed them with your thunderbolt.

Indra is the one who is invoked by both sides in the battle. There are about three hundred Riks in the Rig-veda itself which praise the power of Indra. He is the god-hero, the man-god, the saviour and the liberator, and the mighty conqueror. The seeker-strivers therefore invoke and approach him for power and guidance. He is the Lord of heavens, the organiser of the earth and creator of both sun and sunrise, he the destroyer of the dark demon Vala. A warrior by birth, Indra leads the struggle against the Enemy, destroys all evil and emerges victorious over all the hostile forces. He is a passionate drinker of the Soma-wine which intoxication makes him attack Vritra successfully. He is the most luminous and the terribly terrible. He is the mighty scatterer of the foes and sends them down to nethermost darkness.

Vi na indra mṛdho jahi nīcā
yaccha pṛtanyataḥ,
yo asmāñ abhidāsatyadharaṁ
gamayā tamaḥ.[105]

O resplendent Lord, scatter our enemies who are arrayed against us; send them down to the deepest dungeon who seek to destroy us.

The Atharva-veda extols Indra as the one who contains all the worlds; the creative fervour of life and the eternal law have their ground in him. He is described as the supreme support, Skambha, in whom all the universe finds its repose:

Indre laka indre tapa indre adhyritamahitam
indram'tva veda pratyaksam
skambhe sarvam pratisthitam.[106]

Indra is frequently invoked as the wizard and the overlord of the herds of light, *gopati*; he is both the conqueror and the giver of illuminations, — the great god who brings home for man the supreme felicity of light and force. Vritra the dark and wicked dragon is said to have concealed the cows in the cave of Inconscience. The shoulderless serpent-dragon is primarily a symbol of darkness, of resistance to the increase of light, of constriction and recalcitrance. Indra destroys him using both magic and force. Danu is the mother of Vritra and of other demons, the Danavas; the Panis belong to another group of hostile forces said to have stolen the cows. The cows symbolise rays of the illumined Mind — the radiances of Truth-Consciousness; they are identified also with sacred speech.

1. *Upa hvaye sudughāṁ dhenumetāṁ*
suhasto godhuguta dohadenām,
śreṣṭhaṁ savaṁ savitā sāviṣan
no'bhīddho gharmastadu ṣu pra vocam.

2. *Hiṅkṛnvatī vasupatnī vasūnāṁ vatsam*
icchantī manasābhyāgāt,
duhamaśvibhyāṁ payo aghnyeyaṁ
sā vardhatāṁ mahate saubhagāya.[107]

1. We invoke the milch cow that is readily milked that the seeker-milker may easily milk her; may the supreme creator Savitri joyously accept our loving libation that his creative energy may increase.

2. She arrives lowing, abounding in felicity desiring her calf in her mind; may she grant her milk to the Ashwins. May she boom for our great gain.

Indra gets their release after killing Vritra.

a) 1. *Vīḷau satīrabhi dhīrā atṛndan*
prācāhinvanmanasā sapta viprāḥ,
viśvāmavindanpathyāmṛtasya
prajānannittā namasā viveśa.

2. *Vidadyadī saramā rugṇamadrermahi*
pāthaḥ pūrvyaṁ sadhryakkaḥ,
agraṁ nayatsupadyakṣarāṇāmaccha
ravaṁ prathamā jānatī gāt.

3. *Agacchadu vipratamaḥ sakhīyann*
asūdayatsukṛte garbhamadriḥ,
sasāna maryo yuvabhirmakhasyann
athābhavadaṅgirāḥ sadyo arcan.

4. *Sataḥsataḥ pratimānaṁ purobhūrviśvā*
veda janimā hanti śuṣṇam,

pra ṇo divaḥ padavīrgavyurarcan
tsakhā sakhīuřamuncanniravadyāt.

5. *Ni gavyatā manasā sedurarkaiḥ*
kṛnvānāso amṛtatvāya gātum,
idaṁ cinnu sadanaṁ bhuryeṣāṁ
yena masāň asiṣāsannṛtena.

6. *Sampaśyamānā amadannābhi svaṁ payaḥ*
pratnasya retaso dughānāḥ,
vi rodasī atapadghoṣa eṣāṁ jāte
niḥṣṭhamadaghurgoṣu vīrān.

7. *Sa jātebhhirvṛtrahā sedu havyairud*
usriyā asṛjadindro arkaiḥ,
urucyasmai ghṛtavadbharantī madhu
svādma duduhe jenyā gauḥ.[108]

1. The seven intelligent seekers, the Angirasas, having discovered that the cows were concealed in the dark cavern propitiate Indra through mental devotion; they recover them all by the path of sacrifice. Indra having realized their sacrificial acts and satisfied by their offering of homage enters the cavern to effectuate their release.

2. When Sarama discovers the partial entrance of the mountain-cave, then Indra breaks open the cave and makes a straight and wide path for the seekers as earlier promised. Then the sure-footed intelligence recognizing the lowing of the Kine comes close to their presence.

3. When the luminous Lord prompted by the friendship of the wise seekers, the Angirasas, approached the mountain-cave, then it yielded its contents to the valiant god. Aided by the youthful Maruts, who were equally enthusiastic of destroying the Asuras, Indra recovers the cows; and the Angirasas become his true worshippers.

4. May the resplendent Lord, Indra, the finest embodiment of all that is excellent, the anticipator of the Enemies and who knows all that is existent, who destroys narrow-mindedness, is far-seeing and has wide vision, be free from all admonition. He is our true and trusted friend who descends from above to restore our seeing intelligence.

5. The wise Angirasas, intent on obtaining the cows, proceed to propitiate and adore Indra with hymns of praise leading them on the road to immortality. With great perseverance they strive for long to accomplish their objective.

6. Contemplating on their own recovered milk-giving cows and bestowing the milk of luminous knowledge to their progeny, the Angirasas are delighted; their shouts of joy spread through heaven and earth. They put their faith on the recovery of the cows, and keep constant guard on the places of their station.

7. Indra, the destroyer of Vritra, assisted by the Maruts, obtains release of the cows and receives praises and oblations due to him. The excellent milch-cattle contribute richly to the sacred offerings of the seekers; they yield the butter of libation for him and the nourishing sweet milk.

b) 1. *Patirbhava vṛtrahant sunṛtānaṁ girāṁ*
viśvāyurvṛṣabho vayodhāḥ,
ā no gahi sakhyebhiḥ śivebhirmahān
mahībhīrutibhiḥ saraṇyan.

2. *Tam aṅgirasvannamasā saparyan*
navyaṁ kṛṇomi sanyase purājām,
druho vi yāhi bahulā adevīḥ svaśca
no maghavantsātaye dhāḥ.

3. *Mihaḥ pāvakāḥ pratatā abhuvantsvasti*
naḥ pipṛhi pāramāsām,
indra tvaṁ rathiraḥ pāhi no ṛṣo
makṣumakṣukṛṇuhi gojito naḥ.

4. *Adediṣṭa vṛtrahā gopātirgā antaḥ*
kṛṣñā aruṣairdhāmābhirgāt,
pra sunṛtā diśamāna ṛtena duraśca
viśvā avṛnodapa svāḥ.

5. *Śunaṁ huvema maghavānamindram*
asminbhare nṛtamaṁ vājasātau,
śṛnvantamugramutaye samatsu
ghnantaṁ vṛtrāṇi saṁjitaṁ dhanānām.[109]

1. O resplendent Lord, slayer of Vritra, you are the showerer of benefits, the provider of nourishment, may you be the lord of our true adorations; may you O mighty one, repairing to our sacrificial deeds, come to us with affection and extend to us your auspicious protection.

2. I adore you, O Indra, with deep reverence as the wise Angirasas do. I glorify you O ancient one, with ever new compositions. May you destroy the many evil oppressors, and bestow upon us O Maghavan, your own spiritual wealth for our good.

3. O Indra, your purifying streams of Truth-Knowledge are spread on all sides; may we be worthy of their munificence. Defend us from the Adversary, and make us strong enough to conquer the luminous cattle.

4. Indra, the mighty destroyer of Vritra, has discovered the cows, and by his beaming radiance dissolved the darkness of the Asuras. Indicating to us the presence of the luminous cows, may Indra throw open the gates of true knowledge.

5. We adore and invoke the resplendent and opulent Lord for our protection; he is the purifier, the brave and most distinguished in battle. Hearing our praises, may he, the destroyer of the Enemy and the conqueror of wealth, be bounteous in his gifts.

Indra is often compared to a generous milker, and is called for a rich yield of heavenly prosperity. He is called for increase of illuminations day by day.

a) *Ā tvadya sabardughāṁ huve gāyatravepasam,*
indraṁ dhenuṁ sudughāmanyām
iṣamurudhārāmaraṅkṛtam.[110]

Today I invoke Indra, the great yielder of milk, comparable to an easily yielding milch-cow who provides unfailing nourishment in ample streams.

b) *Ā tvā gīrbhirmahāmuruṁ*
huve gamiva bhojase,
Indra somasya pītaye.[111]

O Indra, I invoke you with my praises, great and strong one, to enjoy the Soma-wine as a bull runs to relish its fodder.

c) *Dohena gāmupa śikṣā sakhāyaṁ pra*
bodhaya jaritarjāramindram,
kośaṁ na pūrṇaṁ vasunā nyṛṣṭam
ā cyāvaya maghadegrāya sūram.[112]

O worshipper, prevail upon your friend Indra, like a cow for milking; O singer, wake up the supreme benefactor for distribution of wealth who is loaded with it like a vessel with water.

d) *Surupakṛtnumūtaye sudughāmivagha goduhe*
juhūmasi dyāvidyāvi.[113]

We invoke the resplendent Lord, for our increase from day to day, as a good milch-cow by the milker for milking.

Indra is frequently invoked as the wizard and the overlord of the herds of light, *gopati*; he is both the conqueror and the giver of illuminations, the great god who brings home for man the supreme felicity of light and force. He is the milch-cow, a ready source of "perfect forms and ultimate thoughts";[114] he is also the Bull of the herds, Vrishabha.

a) *Ā gāvo agmannuta bhadramakranta*
sīdantu goṣṭhe raṇayantvasme,
prajāvatīḥ pururūpā iha syurindrāya
pūrvīruṣaso duhānāḥ.

Indro yajvane pṛṇate ca śikṣatyuped
dadāti na svaṁ muṣāyati,
bhūyobhūyo rayimidasya vardhayann
abhinne khilye ni dadhāti devayum.[115]

May the blessed cows come and bring us good fortune; let them dwell in our stalls and be pleased with us. May the many-coloured ones yield rich and fecund milk for offering to the resplendent Lord on many dawns.

Indra grants the prayers of his devout worshippers who offer him sacrificial oblations. He ever gives them more and never deprives them of what they possess; more and ever more he increases their wealth and places them in fortresses fully protected from danger.

b) *Gāvo bhago gāva indro me acchān gāvaḥ*
somasya prathamasya bhakṣaḥ,
imā yā gāvaḥ sa janāsa indra icchāmid
dhṛdā manasā cidindram.

Upedamupaparcanamāsu goṣūpa pṛcyatām,
upa ṛṣabhasya retasyupendra tava vīrye.[116]

May the luminous cows be for our increase; may the resplendent Lord grant us more cows; may they yield milk and butter for the first libation. These are as auspicious as Indra himself, the Lord whose blessings we seek for with heart and mind.

O resplendent Lord, we solicit plenty of nourishment for the cows; for your steady nutriment and virility we need milk and butter, this O Lord of virility provide us by granting sturdy bulls for their insemination.

An oft-repeated figure in the Veda is that of the stolen cows. They are stolen and held back concealed in the cavern of the Inconscient and the subconscient by the Dasyus — the Panis headed by Vala. Indra and the Angirasa Rishis as also the other gods chase Vala and force him to give up his wealth of stolen cows. Indra is described as the constant seeker of the cows, the buster of the sealed cave and the restorer of the concealed illuminations. In this act of uncovering the hole of Vala he is helped by the other gods, or rather, the gods enter Indra, with their force in his final and decisive attack on Vala.

Tvaṁ valasya gomato'pāvaradrivo bilam,
tvāṁ devā abibhyuṣastujyamānāsa āviṣuḥ.[117]

"O lord of the thunderbolt, thou didst uncover the hole of Vala of the cows; the gods, unfearing, entered speeding (or putting forth their force) into thee."*

As a result of the release and recovery of the hidden radiances the vast and luminous world of the Truth, *satyam ṛtam bṛhat*, stands revealed and unfolded. The fullness of the enlightened energies of the two divine deities, Indra and Brihaspati in the seeker, and the conscious possession of the supreme Truth are, according to the Vedas, the two conditions of perfect perfection.

(4)

The finding of Swar

Indra is the one who mediates between the earth and the heaven, and victoriously discovers the world of Immortality. With the drinking of the Soma-wine, Indra makes the sun rise in the heavens and sets free the cows held within the rock of the subconscious and the unconscious. He wins not only the sun and the waters but bestows on the seeking-mind the experience of Immortality.

a) *Pavasva soma divyeṣu dhāmasu*
sṛjāna indo kalaśe pavitra ā,
sidannindrasya jaṭhare kanikradan
nṛbhiyartaḥ sūryamārohayo divi.[118]

Flow onward, O Soma, to your heavenly abode; proceed forward to the cosmic filter and into the cosmic pitcher. May you alighting upon Indra's person with a roar and guided by the chants of the worshippers make the sun ascend the heavens.

b) *Yasya gā antaraśmano*
made dṛḷhā avāsṛjaḥ,
ayaṁ sa soma indra te sutaḥ piba.[119]

Here is the exhilarating Soma-wine, the draught of which results in the liberation of the cattle firmly concealed in the rock of darkest ignorance. This is poured out to you O Indra, for acceptance.

c) *Dūraṁ kila prathamā jagmurāsām*
indrasya yāḥ prasave sasrurāpaḥ,
kva svidagraṁ kva budhna āsāmāpo
madhyaṁ kva vo nūnamantaḥ.[120]

The first of those streams which sprang forth at the behest of Indra went very far. Where is your beginning, O streams? Where is your source and where the middle? And where indeed is your destination?

d) *Pra ta indra pūrvyāṇi pra nūnaṁ vīryā*
vocaṁ prathamā kṛtāni,
satīnamanyuraśrathāyo adriṁ suvedanām
akṛnorbrahmaṇe gām.[121]

Now will I declare, O resplendent Lord, your earlier first accomplishments: resolved to send rains you cleft the clouds, and recovered the concealed cows for the supreme Lord, the Brahman.

e) *Pra su gmantā dhiyasānasya sakṣaṇi varebhir*
varāñ abhi ṣu prasīdataḥ,
asmākamindra ubhayaṁ jujoṣati yat
somyasyāndhaso bubodhati.[122]

Indra, the shining one, sends his swift-moving steeds to the service of his worshippers who anticipate his arrival. May he also come to the devotees who propitiate him with suitable adorations. The Lord acknowledges rejoicingly both devotion and oblation of the offerer of Soma-wine.

f) *Yudhendro mahnā varivaścakāra*
devebhyaḥ satpatiścarṣaṇīprāḥ,
vivasvataḥ sadane asya tāni viprā
ukthebhiḥ kavayo gṛṇanti.[123]

O virtuous Lord, you are the supreme fulfiller of the aspiration of seekers and giver of opulent rewards to the gods in the great inner struggle. The wise sages therefore glorify you with sacred hymns in the sacrificial chamber of the devotees.

It is through fierce struggle and inner conflict that Indra shows the striver the way to the highest fulfilment.

Ahaṁ sapta sravato dhārayaṁ vṛṣā
dravitnvaḥ pṛthivyāṁ sīrā adhi,
ahamarṇāsi vi tirāmi sukraturyudhā
vidaṁ manave gātumiṣṭaye.[124]

With my prowess I, the showerer of rain, support the seven rivers flowing and meandering over the earth. As a doer of good deeds, I spread out the waters, and as a victorious warrior find by war the way for the seekers.

Those seekers who succeed in their sacrifice enter the world of Swar. The attainment of Swar is conditional to the birth of the Dawn in the seeker which is accomplished by Indra and the Angirasas. It is Indra who brings the Sun into birth out of the womb of the night, *kṣapām vastā janitā sūryasya.*[125]

a) *Tvamapo vi duro viṣūcirindra*
dṛḷhamarūjaḥ parvatasya,
rājābhavo jagataścarṣaṇīnāṁ sākaṁ
sūryaṁ janayan dyāmuṣāsam.[126]

O Indra, you have set the obstructed waters free to flow in all directions. You have split the concrete barrier of the dark cloud; verily, you are the Lord over the men of the earth for you bring to birth together the Sun and Heaven and Dawn.

b) *Haryannuṣasamarcayaḥ sūryaṁ*
haryannarocayaḥ,
vidvāṅścikitvānharyaśva vardhasa
indra viśvā abhi śriyaḥ.[127]

Desiring and regaling the Soma-wine, O Lord, you have made the Dawn glow; thirsting for the same you have brought forth the Sun. Knowing and discerning all our wishes, O Lord of the tawny steeds, you increase our prosperity.

c) *Indrasya karma sukṛtā purūṇi vratāni*
devā na minanti viśve,
dādhāra yaḥ pṛthivīṁ dyāmutemāṁ
jajāna sūryamuṣasaṁ sudaṅsāḥ.[128]

Even all the gods cannot discount the greatness of your splendid and magnificent exploits, and the pious works of the one (Indra) who upholds the Earth and the Heaven. Verily, he is the performer of marvels for he has mustered up the Sun and the Dawn.

It is he who with the energetic support of the other gods secures the Sun, wins the Waters and gains the Swar.

Dasyūñchimyuñśca purūhūta evair
hatvā pṛthivyāṁ śarvā ni barhīt,
sanatkṣetraṁ sakhibhiḥ śvitnyebhiḥ
sanatsūryaṁ sanadapaḥ suvajraḥ.[129]

Indra, who is invoked and adored by many and attended by the Maruts, attacked the Dasyus and the Shimyus with his thunderbolt and killed them. He then with his radiances worked on the fields and rescued the Sun and set free the Waters.

It is by continual sacrifice that the birth of the Sun in the life of the seeker becomes possible; it is by sacrifice that Indra brings to birth the Dawn and Swar.

Anānudo vṛṣabho dodhato vadho gambhīra
ṛṣvo asamaṣṭakāvyaḥ,
radhracodaḥ śnathano vīḷitaspṛthur
indraḥ suyajña uṣasa svarjanat.[130]

Unmatched in munificence, benevolent giver of prosperity, profound and mighty hero-warrior, endowed with impassable discernment and dispenser of benefits, Indra, firm of fame and slayer of enemies, benevolent and vast in bulk has given birth to the light of the Sun.

He wins the Sun with the help of the human seekers and the Angirasas, — *asmākebhir nṛbhiḥ sūryaṁ sanat.*[131] It is the secret light, the one which is gained by the gods for all of mankind, the wakeful light that is referred to in all the hymns which sing of the birth of the Dawn:

So andhe cittamasi jyotirvidat.[132]

It is the same light for all living beings found by Agni and Soma:

a) *Avātiratam bṛsayasya śeṣo'vindatam*
jyotirekaṁ bahubhyaḥ.[133]

After killing the progeny of Brisaya, O Indra, you have brought to birth the Sun for the good of all.

b) *Bṛhadindrāya gāyata maruto vṛtrahantamam,*
yena jyotirajanayannṛtāvṛdho
devaṁ devāya jāgṛvi.[134]

The worshippers sing to Indra the most powerful evil-destroying hymn, *Bṛhat-Saman*, by which the upholders and increasers of truth brought into birth the all-waking luminary for the god.

c) *Guḷhaṁ jyotiḥ pitaro anvavindant*
satyamantrā ajanayannuṣāsam.[135]

Those ancient seer-ancestors, reciters of true hymns, found the secret light and brought to birth the Dawn.

d) *Arcanta eke mahi sāma manvata*
tena sūryamarocayan.[136]

Some worshippers called to mind the sacred and true *mantras* of the great Saman, wherewith they made the Sun to shine.

Indra, the lord of infinite puissance, making the thunderbolt his friend, cleaves open the cavern of Darkness, and milks the rays of light out of its womb. He then makes manifest the Sun. The thunderbolt is envisioned by the Rishis as carrying in it the light of Swar.

a) *Vyu vrajasya tamaso dvārocchantīr*
avrañchucayaḥ pāvakāḥ.[137]

Radiant and purifying the Dawns manifesting open the doors of the pen and even of the enveloping darkness.

b) *Gṛṇāno aṅgirobhirdasma vi var*
ūṣasā sūryeṇa gobhirandhaḥ,
vi bhūmyā aprathaya indra sānu
divo raja uparamastabhāyaḥ.[138]

O Indra, destroyer of the adversaries, with the Angirasas you have killed Vala with the cry; and hymned by the Angirasas you have opened the Dawn with the Sun. You have straightened the unevenness of the earth and strengthened the foundations of the heaven.

c) *Tavedaṁ viśvamabhitaḥ paśavyaṁ*
yatpaśyasi cakṣasā sūryasya,
gavāmasi gopatireka indra
bhakṣimahi te prayatasya vasvaḥ.[139]

All this wealth of cattle, O Indra, that you see around you with the eye of the Sun is yours. Verily, you are the sole lord of the cattle; therefore do we enjoy whatsoever wealth of cattle that you bestow upon us.

Indra is the mighty one who effectuates the radiances out of the Night. The Rishis often identify the Dawns and the Cows, and consider the breaking of the pens as the means of manifesting the Sun.[140]

Indra is fond of the Soma-wine, and gives to the Truth-seekers illuminations which sustain them on the long and arduous journey to the highest knowledge-vision.

1. *Na pañcabhirdaśabhirvaṣṭyarabhaṁ*
nāsunvatā sacate puṣyatā cana,
jināti vedamuyā hanti vā dhunirā
devayuṁ bhajati gomati vraje.

2. *Vitvakṣaṇaḥ samṛtau cakramāsajo'sunvato*
viṣuṇaḥ sunvato vṛdhaḥ,
indro viśvasya damitā vibhīṣaṇo
yathāvaśaṁ nayati dasamāryaḥ.

3. *Samīṁ paṇerajati bhojanaṁ muṣe vi*
dāśuṣe bhajati sūnaraṁ vasu,
durge cana dhriyate viśva ā purū jano
yo asya taviṣımacukrudhat.

4. *Saṁ yajjanau sudhanau viśvaśardhasāv*
avedindro maghavā goṣu śubhriṣu,
yujaṁ hyanyamakṛta pravepanyudīṁ
gavyaṁ sṛjate satvabhirdhuniḥ.

5. *Sahasrasāmāgniveśiṁ gṛṇīṣe śatrim*
agna upamāṁ ketumaryaḥ,
tasmā āpaḥ saṁyataḥ pīpayanta tasmin
kṣatramamavatveṣamastu.[141]

1. He (Indra) does not move upward either by the five or by the ten; he does not associate himself with the one who gives not the Soma-wine though he may grow and prosper. He, the terrifier in his impetuous movement punishes him or slays him. For the true seeker he gives pen full of the cows for his enjoyment.

2. Exceedingly powerful, firm holder of the wheel, he turns away from those who do not offer him the Soma-oblation but augments and encourages the Soma-giver, he the terrible is the tamer of all and keeps the ill-disciplined Dasa under his control.

3. He proceeds to dispossess the wealth of the Pani and bestows it entirely upon the Soma-giver for his enjoyment, — riches that are prized by him. That man who provokes Indra's wrath gets himself involved in great difficulty and makes his own journey hard and arduous.

4. When Indra, the Lord of opulence, comes to know the two who are rich in wealth and power exerting themselves against each other, he growing in knowledge chooses a third as his associate and rushing headlong together with the Maruts bestows upon him multitude of the cows.

5. I, the Aryan, arriving at the summit, the Truth-vision, praise Shatri, the bestower of thousands of blessings, and beyond all comparison. May the waters in their meeting nourish him, and his housing a formidable citadel of force; may the worshippers be favoured with wealth and strength.

The Angirasas are the helpers of Indra in the release of the radiances from the stranglehold of the Panis. Armed with these the seeker thrusts forward towards the goal and attains the vision of Swar:

Svardṛśaṁ ketuṁ divo rocanasthāmuṣarbudham.[142]

"...the knowledge-vision that sees Swar, that stands in the shining worlds, that awakes in the dawn."*

Indra wins for the sacrificers the divine Waters, the possession of the Light, the steeds, the wealth of the *antarikṣa*, the enjoyment of the earth and the heaven and the phenomenon of Swar. In collaboration with Vayu, Indra conducts the wholesome activity of life which leads to the world of Swar, the realm of Pure Mind. He is also the lord of the sense-mind and the sovereign of all the senses. They both are invoked for the satisfying things, — things that are in their giving necessary for the success of the sacrifice. They are implored to become conscious of the pressing of Soma so that in rich plenitude the desired work of conquering the enemy could be undertaken.

The Rishi is desirous of Indra's favour; he needs the guidance and certitude of Pure thought for the enjoyment of the elixir of divine delight. The Soma-juices too desire him for entry into the domain of the Truth, the Right and the Vast — the abode of the immortal gods. He is then praised to manifest the soul-contemplation in Word, and prayed to make the seekers to uphold the divine delight in the Soma-wine.

Indra, the Lord of Pure Intelligence accepts the offering of the Soma-wine pressed out for him by the sacrificer and in return gifts him the rays of luminous consciousness. The Rishi pleads Indra to reveal himself to the extent his vision can reach and not beyond that, and to extend to his fellow-seekers the highest good for they fully repose their confidence in him.

1. *Upa naḥ savanā gahi somasya somapāḥ piba,*
godā idrevato madaḥ.

2. *Athā te antamānāṁ vidyāma sumatīnām,*
mā no ati khya ā gahi.

3. *Parehi vigramastṛtamindraṁ pṛccha vipaścitam,*
yaste sakhibhya ā varam.

4. *Uta bruvantu no nido niranyataścidārata,*
dadhānā indra idduvaḥ.[143]

1. O Soma drinker, come to our Soma-pressing and drink the oblation, for indeed nourished by it your rapture increases our Light.

2. O Indra, reveal to us only that which we may know, the intimate right thinkings. For anything that transcends us we will not be able to see. Do not grow invisible. Come to us.

3. Come over, and far; seek Indra's guidance for he has a clear-seeing mind. He moves fast, is unharmed and helpful; he brings the highest good to your fellow seekers.

4. And let the restrainers themselves earnestly direct us to go forth and strive on in other areas, reposing fullest trust in Indra.

The seekers not only do their sacrifices for obtaining the active benedictions of Indra but place upon him the entire burden of their sacrifices. They thus abide in the peace and consciousness of Indra himself. They press Soma into the service of Indra in order to intensify him so that he could slay the coverer and carry them forward in their endeavour. They enrich him with their precious offerings with the objective of themselves guarding and enjoying what they have already attained in their inner seeking. Indra, indeed, is the friend and supporter of those who press their libation of Soma-wine unto him, — he who is himself a continent of bliss and the friend of the Soma-givers. He carries them safely and securely through the arduous journey.

1. *Uta naḥ subhagāñ arirvoceyurdasma kṛṣṭayaḥ,*
syāmedindrasya śarmaṇi.

2. *Emāśumāśave bhara yajñaśriyaṁ nṛmādanam,*
patayanmandayat sakham.

3. *Asya pītvā śatakrato ghano vṛtrāṇāmabhavaḥ,*
prāvo vājeṣu vājinam.

4. *Taṁ tvā vājeṣu vājinaṁ vājayāmaḥ śatakrato,*
dhanānāmindra sātaye.

5. *Yo rāyo'vanirmahānt supāraḥ*
sunvataḥ sakhā,
tasmā indrāya gāyata.[144]

1. And may the doers of the work, the great strivers, congratulate us and declare that we are prosperous, O Lord. May we ever abide

in the peace and felicity granted by you.

2. May we offer to Indra, the intense god, the Soma-wine that is the essence and glory of the sacrifice, exhilarating to the gods and favourite to Indra, carrying him forward who is the friend of worshippers.

3. Having drunk of this Soma-wine, O you doer of hundred activities, Shatakratu, you became the slayer of Vritra and his hordes, and protected the devotees in the opulences.

4. Thus we offer to you O Indra, lord of hundred activities, the mighty in battle, rich sacrificial offerings to enrich you all the more for the safe and peaceful enjoyment of our havings.

5. We sing the glory of Indra, who is a continent of bliss, the mighty protector of wealth, the friend of the Soma-giver and he who carries him safely through the journey, — the great accomplisher of good deeds.

Indra wards off the obstructors of the Light, as well as removes the limitations set before the seekers by them. He bestows on the sacrificer the boon of pure and luminous knowledge, — an expanse of consciousness beyond the constrictions of false knowledge of sense-objects and sense-attachment. The perfect form of self-awareness coming from Indra is capable of inducing good deeds which increase the coveted felicity. Indra is the fashioner of perfect forms, the giver of divine illuminations that uplift the seeker beyond the murky enjoyment of sense-objects. The Rishi turns to Indra, the wise and discerning god, the strong and expeditious in action, for guidance and support. He entrusts the work entirely to the illumined god for divine felicity and peace.

Performers of inner sacrifice, seekers of the Truth, come together and jointly invoke Indra and implore for his help. Indra, the abundant giver of cherished boons, is appropriately praised and offered the Soma-wine for the attainment of varied plenitudes, for his radiances and manifold riches. His domain is beyond the reach of the enemies, they cannot cast their shadow upon it; they cannot obstruct the spread of his illuminations, they dare not stop his fast-moving steeds of illuminations. To Indra are offered the three-fold oblations of gross knowledge, subtle intellect and luminous knowledge by the seekers for his pervasion and acceptance. He accepts them all together with the Soma-drink for the seekers' inner progress and pre-eminent work. It is the drinking of Soma-wine that makes Indra powerful and happy, perfect and superb. Indra and the gods are increased in the seekers by their sacrifices and their invocative words of praise. Indra alone, enhanced and manifolded in his plenitudes by the Sama chants is capable of separating all evil from the body; he removes from the seekers' system all that harms their inner growth.

1. *Ā tvetā ni ṣīdatendramābhi pra gāyata,*
sakhāyaḥ stomavāhasaḥ.

2. *Purūtamaṁ purūṇāmīśanāṁ vāryāṇām,*
indraṁ some sacā sute.

3. *Sa ghā no yoga ā bhuvat sa*
raye sa purandhyām,
gamad vājebhirā sa naḥ.

4. *Yasya saṁsthe na vṛṇvate*
harī samatsu śatravaḥ,
tasmā indrāya gāyata.

5. *Sutapāvne sutā ime śucayo yanti vītaye,*
somāso dadhyāśiraḥ.

6. *Tvaṁ sutasya pītaye sadyo vṛddho ajāyathāḥ*
indra jyaiṣṭhyāya sukrato.

7. *Ā tvā viśantvāśavaḥ somāsa*
indra girvaṇaḥ,
śaṁ te santu pracetase.

8. *Tvāṁ stomā avīvṛdhan tvāmukthā śatakrato,*
tvāṁ vardhantu no giraḥ.

9. *Akṣitotiḥ sanedimaṁ vājamindraḥ sahasriṇam,*
yasmin viśvāni pauṁsyā.

10. *Mā no martā abhi druhan*
tanunāmindra girvaṇaḥ,
īśāno yavayā vadham.[145]

1. Hasten hither, O companions, offering praises; repeatedly chant forth hymns of praise to Indra.

2. To Indra, generous and abundant, lord of many bounties and destroyer of the Enemies, pour forth the Soma-wine.

3. May Indra be favourable to us in the attainment of the objects; may he bestow on us gifts galore, may he be with us in the attainment of luminous intelligence; may he come to us with plenitudes many.

4. Let us chant to the glory of Indra whose enemies in battle do not await his two tawny horses harnessed to his chariot.

5. These Soma-juices pressed out and purified and mixed with curds are poured out for the enjoyment of the great drinker of Soma, for the increase of our prosperity.

6. O Indra, performer of great deeds, you have at once become augmented in vigour by the drink of Soma-juices pressed out for you for greater work.

7. O adorable Indra, verily, you are the object of our laudations; may these Soma-juices entering thee be propitious for your peace and happiness, and for the attainment of supreme knowledge.

8. O supreme Lord, these Sama hymns speak of your victory, and those of the Rig glorify you; may our praises magnify you.

9. O Indra, your increase is steady and undiminishing; may you enjoy these manifold sacrificial provisions, he in whom all manliness abides.

10. O Indra, the object of our adoration, may not men harm our persons; mighty are you, protect us and keep off all violence.

The seeker-sacrificers have one objective, — reaching the world of the Truth, *satyam ṛtam bṛhat.* Towards this they strive to offer themselves totally and perfectly, and in the process seek union with the many gods who possess different elements of the one supreme Truth. In their inner sacrifice they are helped by the different exteriorizations of Indra and the many gods in accordance with a divine timing suited to their steady and appropriate progress. Indra drinks the Soma-wine flowing in from all sides according to felicitous and suitable conditions of time. Likewise the Maruts also partake of the sacred Soma-juices from Indra the supreme priest of the inner sacrifice, the Ritvik, who purifies it for presentation to the sacrificers. Thereby the Maruts also render the inner sacrifice purified and sanctified, and become auspicious givers. The Rishi implores Indra to materialize with his spouse, jealously partake of the Soma wine in suitable and apt season, and make the sacrifice worthy and helpful. He desires that he brings with him all the other gods and seat them appropriately in the three places of libation and felicitate them with the nectar of divine delight in accordance with favourable provisions of time. He pleads Indra, the trusted and consistent friend of the seekers, to drink the Soma-wine from Brahma himself who is the inexhaustible treasure-chest of all felicities. He also appeals to Mitra and Varuna, the upholders of the laws, to inhabit the sacrifice in season with their power of invulnerable discernment and perspicacity. So also Agni and the Ashwins are asked to drink the Soma-wine according to the seasons that they may bring to the sacrifice their respective riches.

a) *Indra somaṁ piba ṛtunā tvā viśantvindavaḥ,*
matsarāsastadokasaḥ.[146]

O Indra, drink the Soma-juices in season; may the juices satisfying you abide in you; may they flow into you from all directions.

b) *Abhi yajñam gṛṇīhi no gnāvo*
neṣṭaḥ piba ṛtunā,
tvaṁ hi ratnadhā asi.[147]

O brightener, come with your spouse, commend our sacrifice to the gods; drink the Soma in season. Verily, you are the bearer of ecstasies many.

c) *Brāhmaṇādindra rādhasaḥ pibā*
somamṛtūn̐ranu,
taveddhi sakhyamastṛtam.[147a]

O Indra, drink the Soma-wine in season from the fount of supreme felicity of the Brahmana for whom your friendship is indeed constant.

The speedy carriers of Indra, — the fiery steeds of life-force, are praised for bringing him the luminous-eyed to the sacrifice to drink the Soma-wine. The Rishi lauds Indra and offers him the ghee-dripping grains which are the luminous powers of the mind embodied in the physical to eat. This food is befitting the Lord of the illumined Intellect. The coursers of Indra's chariot also feed themselves on this special sustenance. Whereas the Soma-wine is not only the delight of all-existence but also the essence of all our experiences. Indra is offered this wine at all times when the sacrifice is in session. He is asked to come with his fast-moving radiances, the long-maned horses, and accept the seekers' laudation as well as drink the Soma-juice pressed out at the altar like a thirsty stag.

By a number of affirmative hymns the Rishi seeks to touch the heart of Indra and invites him to the sacrificial altar where Soma is pressed out. Indra, the mighty slayer, the hero of a hundred deeds, is well contemplated by the seekers for the fulfilment of their aspiration and to grant them illumination and strength to succeed in their spiritual endeavour.

1. *Ā tvā vahantu harayo vṛṣaṇaṁ somapītaye,*
   indra tvā sūracakṣasaḥ.

2. *Imā dhānā ghṛtasnuvo harī ihopa vakṣataḥ,*
   indraṁ sukhatame rathe.

3. *Indraṁ prātarhavāmaha indraṁ*
   prayatyadhvare,
   indraṁ somasya pītaye.

4. *Upa naḥ sutamā gahi haribhiḥ*
   indra keśibhiḥ,
   sute hi tvā havāmahe.

5. *Semaṁ naḥ stomamā gahyupedaṁ*
   savanaṁ sutam,
   gauro na tṛṣitaḥ piba.

6. *Ime somāsa indavaḥ sutāso adhi barhiṣi,*
   tāṅ indra sahase piba.

7. *Ayaṁ te stomo agriyo hṛdispṛgastu śaṅtamaḥ,*
   athā somaṁ sutaṁ piba.

8. *Viśvamitsavanaṁ sutamindraḥ*
madāya gacchati,
vṛtrahā somapītaye.

9. *Semaṁ naḥ kāmamā pṛṇa*
gobhiraśvaiḥ śatakrato
stavāma tvā svādhyaḥ.[148]

1. May your steeds bring you here, O showerer of gifts, to drink the Soma-wine; may the worshippers make you manifest, O the luminous-eyed one.

2. Here upon the altar are strewn the grains steeped in ghee; may Indra's swift-moving steeds bring him here in his happy moving chariot.

3. We invoke you O Indra, at morn, and when the sacrificial rites are on; we call him to drink the Soma-wine.

4. O Indra, come with your long-maned steeds to our sacrificial altar where Soma-wine is pressed out; we call you as the Soma is poured out.

5. O resplendent Lord, may you accept our laudation, come to this our sacrificial altar where this libation is prepared; drink it like a thirsty stag.

6. Pressed out on the sacred grass are these dripping Soma-juices: drink them O mighty Lord, for greater strength and vigour.

7. May this prime hymn of praise, superb and happy, touch your heart; in gratitude we beseech you, may you drink the Soma-wine pressed out by us.

8. O Indra, slayer of Vritra and his evil hordes, come to every sacrifice where the Soma-juice is poured out; may you readily accept it for exhilaration.

9. O Indra of hundred valiant actions, Shatakratu, may you accomplish this prayer of ours with profound illuminations and life-

strength. Full of gratitude we invoke you.

Indra and Varuna are the two great increasers of the Truth. If Indra is the king of the gods by virtue of his divine Intelligence, Varuna dwelling in the Truth, full of Light, increases It. The Rishi ardently prays that they both — the upholders of the Truth-seers — increase him in sacrifice and make him happy. He seeks their intimacy, their friendship and their wealth of right illumination, right thinking and right action. Both Indra and Varuna are the givers of plenty; if the former symbolises generous giving, the latter represents vastness and is excellently adorable. The wealth that is obtained from them is exceedingly superb and unlimited. They are invoked by the Rishi for attaining their wonderful wealth to equip himself for divine action and perfect victory. He is desirous of their participation in the sacrifice and their companionship in the journey, and lauds them for increased felicity and happiness.

1\. *Indrāvaruṇayorahaṁ samrājokha*
ā vṛṇe,
tā no mṛḷātaḥ īdṛśe.

2\. *Gantārā hi stho'vase havaṁ*
viprasya māvataḥ
dhartārā carṣaṇīnām.

3\. *Anukāmaṁ tarpayethāmindrāvaruṇa rāya ā,*
tā vāṁ nediṣṭhamīmahe.

4\. *Yuvāku hi śacīnāṁ yuvāku sumatīnām*
bhūyāma vājadāvnām

5\. *Indraḥ sahasradāvnāṁ varuṇaḥ śaṁsyānām*
kraturbhavatyukthyaḥ.

6\. *Tayoridavasā vayaṁ sanema*
ni ca dhīmahi
syāduta prarecanam.

7\. *Indrāvaruṇa vāmahaṁ huve*
citrāya rādhase,
asmāntsu jigyuṣaskṛtam.

8. *Indrāvaruṇa nū nu vāṁ siṣāsantīṣu*
dhīṣvā asmabhyaṁ śarma yacchatam.

9. *Pra vāmaśnotu suṣṭutirindrāvaruṇa*
yāṁ huve yāmṛdhāthe sadhastutim.[149]

1. I seek the increase of Indra and Varuna, the sovereign rulers; may they both make us happy and prosperous.

2. O benevolent guardians, upholders of the seekers of Truth, may you grant us protection and attend to the call of an illumined minister like me for increase.

3. O Indra and Varuna, satisfy us with your wealth for our fulfilment; we always seek your protective proximity.

4. O Indra and Varuna, may we be the beings of strength that offer plenitude; may we be possessed of the strength that belongs to the activities of illumined Intelligence. May we always offer you happy plenitudes.

5. Of the bestowers of plentiful, Indra is the Will to give, the supreme giver among the givers, and Varuna deserves highest laudation among those who are laudable.

6. By their increase and through their protection we attain and enjoy manifold riches and store them by; may it still exceed even beyond what we can lay aside.

7. O Indra and Varuna, I invoke you both for manifold wealth; may you make us perfectly victorious.

8. O benevolent bestowers, give us happiness soon and directly, for our minds are desirous of participating with you in your increasing glory.

9. O Indra and Varuna, may our earnest laudations reach you both; may our conjoint praises of you increase you.

(5)

Symbolism and Significance

Surface scholars of the Vedas who interpret the hymns literally see tacit incestuous suggestions in regard to the birth and parentage of Indra. In fact they are symbolic and psychological in their description, and need the inner eye of the initiates to probe their spiritual linkage.[150] Whereas the symbolism and significance of the killing of Vritra is much too clear even for any wilful misinterpretation. Also, the liberation of the cows from the dark cave, which is repeatedly referred to in the Veda, has to be taken in the esoteric sense. Likewise Indra's well-known triumphal rejoicing from liberal and plentiful draughts of Soma-wine is apt to be misunderstood and devalue his god-nature. Soma signifies the divine delight of all-existence emboldened by which Indra, the warrior-god, destroys the Enemy, and to the seekers releases the radiances of Truth-Consciousness.[151] Indra and Soma are close companions; they are associated with each other on several occasions. Indra becomes capable of conquering the Enemy only after drinking the Soma-wine: intoxicated with the elixir of divine *ānanda* he slays Vritra and creates the necessary conditions for the pursuit of the Truth. He is the supreme Saviour who wins the Sun for the striver-sacrificer.

1. *Indrāsomā vāsayatha uṣāsamut*
   sūryaṁ nayatho jyotiṣā saha,
   upa dyāṁ skambhathuḥ skambhanenā
   prathataṁ pṛthivīṁ mātaraṁ vi.

2. *Indrāsomāvahimapaḥ pariṣṭham hatho*
   vṛtramanu vāṁ dyauramanyata,
   prārṇāṅsyairayataṁ nadīnāmā
   samudrāṇi paprathuḥ purūṇi.

3. *Indrāsomā pakvamāmāsvantarni*
   gavāmiddadhathurvakṣaṇāsu,
   jagṛbhathuranapinaddhamāsu
   ruśaccitrāsu jagatīṣvantaḥ.

4. *Indrāsomā yuvamaṅga tarutram*
   apatyasācaṁ śrutyaṁ rarāthe,

yuvaṁ śuṣmaṁ naryaṁ carṣaṇibhyaḥ
saṁ vivyathuḥ pṛtanāṣāhamugrā.[152]

1. O Indra and Soma, lords of light and bliss, you have lent light to the Dawns; you have upraised the Sun with his splendour; you have upborne the sky with the supporting pillar and stretched wide the earth, the mother of all.

2. O Indra and Soma, lords of light and bliss, you have slain Ahi and Vritra, the obstructors of the Waters, for which the heavens adore you both. You have urged on the rivers until they have replenished the many seas.

3. O Indra and Soma, lords of light and bliss, you have filled ripe milk in the youthful udders of the cows; you have enjoined the white secretion within these many-coloured cattle.

4. O Indra and Ṣoma, lords of light and bliss, you have granted us sustaining, signal wealth accompanied by offspring; O mighty divinities, you have invested the worshippers with strength that helps them to come out victorious in battle against the Enemies.

Aditi is the mother of Indra, and the father Twashtri; she keeps the son in the womb for many many years to protect him and to help him to grow. The father is jealous of his great prowess — of his radiances and his supreme warrior-strength. Indra, still inside the womb feels compelled to be born to encounter Twashtri, and inspite of the mother's dissuation comes out through her side. After his birth Indra is still concealed by his mother from his insensate and cruel father for a long time who threatens to kill him. However, when Indra grows up and becomes sufficiently strong, refusing any further protection by his mother, he follows her to his father's house and after drinking the Soma-wine, enriched and emboldened, he kills the demon father as he had no other choice. He kills him with Vishnu's help. In a later tradition Twashtri is also Vritra's father. The whole story is narrated in the fifth Mandala of the Rig-veda.[153] With the killing of Vritra the Waters are set free.[154] Further, a son of Indra performs sacrifice and invites all the gods to participate except his own father. At the insistence of his wife he makes hasty offerings to Indra and tries to compensate for his negligence. Indra is aware of his son's pretensions to be another like him and chastises him. The son then realises his folly and praises Indra.[155] Indra is the lord of Pure Intelligence, and cannot be ignored in any sacrifice of a serious nature.

Indra is repeatedly affirmed to be the supreme god. Associated with the Maruts, linked to Rudra, Vishnu and the Angirasas and intimately connected with Parjanya besides Saraswati and Pusan, he is said to have killed all the enemies of the soul's progress, namely Vala, Vritra, Sambara and the Dasyus. He is frequently hymned as the twin-brother of Agni and also associated with Surya. The association of Agni and Soma as well as of Indra and Agni occurs frequently in the Veda. Agni is supposed to entertain Indra and press the Soma-wine for him.

a) *Yadā kadā ca sunavāma somam*
agniṣṭvā dūto dhanvātyaccha.[156]

May we prepare the Soma-wine proper to the season for you; let Agni arrive as your emissary announcing your arrival.

b) *Sakhā sakhye apacattūyamagnir*
asya kratvā mahiṣā trī śatāni,
trī sākamindro manuṣaḥ sarāṅsi
sutaṁ pibadvṛtrahatyā ya somam.[157]

To help his friend Indra in his valorous deed, Agni rapidly consumes several dark animal forces, and Indra to destroy Vritra at once sips off three vessels of Soma-wine pressed out by Manu.

Agni assures Indra of his fullest support if the latter would offer him a portion of the sacrificial oblation. They then in concert with each other destroy the Enemy. The Mantras are primarily invocations to these two foremost of the gods. They are referred to as the gods of the New Moon, just as Agni and Soma are approached as those of the Full Moon. Without individualizing either of them in particular, Indra and Agni are conceived and invoked jointly in the Veda; their inner connection is significant to the striver: if the latter symbolizes intense flaming aspiration, the former signifies the illumined knowledge of the Pure Mind. Both are necessary for the total destruction of the forces of Darkness and the successful journey to the summit Truth.

Pra nu vocā suteṣu vāṁ
vīryā yāni cakrathuḥ,

hatāso vāṁ pitaro devaśatrava
indrāgnī jīvatho yuvam.[158]

When the Soma-juice being pressed out gushes forward, O Indra and Agni, we joyously celebrate your heroic adventures. The age-old adversaries have been destroyed by you, and you survive to support us.

They are variously described as sons of the same father and different mothers, as brothers and as twins. They are two cosmogenic powers who are worshipped by all.

1. *Yadindrāgnī madathaḥ sve duroṇe*
yadbrahmāṇi rājani vā yajatrā,
ataḥ pari vṛṣaṇāvā hi yātam
athā somasya mibataṁ sutasya.[159]

2. *Yadindrāgnī avamasyāṁ pṛthivyāṁ*
madhyamasyāṁ paramasyāmuta sthaḥ,
ataḥ pari vṛṣaṇāvā hi yātam
athā somasya pibataṁ sutasya.[160]

1. O adorable Indra and Agni, if you have ever been satisfied with our libations either in your own house or in that of a wise devotee or in the palace of a prince, then, O generous givers of gifts, come here quickly from wherever you are and drink our loving libation.

2. O adorable Indra and Agni, whenever you may be in the heavens or on the earth or in the mid-region, then, O generous givers of gifts, come here quickly and drink our loving libation.

Like the Ancestors their descendants also beseech Indra for his favours and help and expect the fulfilment of their prayers, for the sacrificer and the resplendent Lord have reciprocal relationship of mutual increase.

Santi kāmāso harivo dadiṣṭvaṁ
smo vayaṁ santi no dhiyaḥ.[161]

O mighty Master, you are generous, may our prayers be granted.

We are yours and our invocations are for you.

Indra is looked upon by the sacrificers as the real and supreme lord of the sacrifice. He is the generous giver of horses also.

Akāri ta indra gotamebhirbrahmāṇy
oktā namasā haribhyām,
supeśasaṁ vājamā bharā naḥ prātar
makṣū dhiyāvasurjagamyāt.[162]

Praises have been offered to you, O Indra, by the seers of yore: they have been offered to you with great adoration. O resplendent Lord, borne hither by powerful steeds, grant us the wealth of cows and horses. May the devotee who has acquired multiple wealth at your hands come here again and again at dawn.

In addition to Agnistoma sacrifice, Indra enjoys a prominent share and place in the *Mahāvrata*, *Ṣoḍaśin* and *Atirātra* sacrifices. There are in addition many other rituals and sacrifices associated with him, each characterising him with a special epithet, each inovoking him for a specific purpose in the progress of the seeker's soul.

(6)

In the Upanishads and in Later Mythology

The *Kena Upanishad* speaks of Indra, Vayu and Agni as the greatest of the gods, and yet it is Indra alone who becomes aware of the existence of Brahman who had appeared before them as the enigmatic Daemon; this becomes possible through the oblique revelation of Uma, the daughter of Himavat. Whereas the other gods are ignorant of the presence of Brahman before them. For it is only by the elimination of the mental, vital and physical egoism that it becomes possible to come into contact with the Brahmic consciousness and not otherwise.

Tasmād vā indro'titarāmivānyān devān,
sa hy enan nediṣṭham pasparśa,
sa hy enat prathamo vidāṁcakāra brahmeti.[163]

Therefore, Indra excels the other gods as he comes close to the knowledge of Brahman; for he touches Him nearest and knew that he was Brahman.

Nara and Narayana are the two seers who are eternally linked together in Indian spiritual tradition; they do *tapasya* for the attainment of true inner knowledge. Their companionship is reflected in several figures scattered in the ancient Indian scriptures — in the heavenward journey of Indra and Kutsa in the Veda, in the symbol of two birds sitting upon one tree spoken of by the Upanishads, as well as in the cast of the great battle for Light, *Kurukshetra*, appearing in the personages of Arjuna and Krishna. The roles of these inseparable companions are reversed in the *Gita* from what they were in the Veda. In the Veda the human soul and the Divine ride in one chariot towards the goal of the attainment of the summit Consciousness. There Indra is the Divine, the master of Swar-loka, the lord of divine knowledge and immortality whose help is necessary for the human seeker in his fight against the enemies of light and spiritual illumination. The goal before the Vedic Rishis is the world of Immortality, *satyam ṛtam bṛhat*, and Indra is the master-director and the master-helper in man's endeavour to reach this highest goal. Whereas Kutsa symbolises the sattwic human soul in search of divine knowledge. They both are marching towards the Truth which is the home of Indra, and by the time they arrive there Kutsa grows into the exact likeness of Indra. It is the parable of the human soul growing into the similitude of the eternal Divine. In as much as the *Gita* presents the field of conscious action, Arjuna symbolises the fighter, the enlightened pragmatist and not the seeker of mere Knowledge. He is the Kshatriya wedded to uphold *dharma*, protect justice and punish the wicked. And Krishna is the divine Teacher who lifts him up out of ignorant and egoistic action into a higher consciousness and nature, and reveals to him a new and a higher law of life and action for the fulfilment of the secret purpose of creation.

Indra though born of earth and heaven, is described as the creator of earth and heaven, for as a cosmic deity abiding between the physical and mental worlds, he recreates their powers in man. Each god in the Vedic pantheon is a separate cosmic personality; and together all the gods form the complete cosmic whole — the Supreme. All the gods are one Existence which is called by different names. Indra undoubtedly is the chief deity of the Vedic pantheon. Armed with the thunderbolt-weapon, *Vajrayudha*, he rides in a chariot whose speed exceeds that of the mind. With his awe-inspiring valour he kills Vritra and many of his demon-associates. Fond of

Soma-wine he is depicted in a human form with four arms. His prestige gradually declines in the *Purānas*. In the Vedic period he ranks first among the gods; he is not uncreate, he is born of a vigorous and powerful father and a heroic mother. He is of a ruddy or a golden colour; his forms are numerous and can assume shape at will. The Soma-wine is his special delight. In his warfare he is always escorted by the Maruts; to him are attributed the highest divine functions.

In later mythology Indra falls into the second rank. He is inferior to the Triad and yet chief of all the other gods. He reigns over Swarga, the heaven of the gods and of beautiful and blissful spirits; it is the region of great magnificence and splendour. While many of his Vedic characteristics are retained, some are magnified. Indra's names are many; he is extolled as Mahendra, Maghavan, Sakra, Arha, Vasava Ribhuksha, Datteya. His titles too are numerous: among others he is Vajrapani, the wielder of the thunderbolt weapon; Vritrahan, the slayer of Vritra; Meghavahana, the one borne upon the clouds; Devapati and Suradhipa, the chief of the gods; Swargapati, the lord of paradise; Purandara, the destroyer of cities; Divaspati, ruler of the atmosphere; Marutvan, lord of the winds; Jishnu, leader of the heavenly hosts; Uluka and Ugradhanwan, the owl and possessor of the mighty bow. "The heaven of Indra is Swarga; its capital is Amaravati; his palace, Vaijayanta; his garden, Nandana, Kandasara or Parushya; his elephant is Airavata; his horse, Uchchaih-sravas; his chariot, Vimana; his charioteer, Matali; his bow, the rainbow, Sakradhanus; and his Sword, Paranja."[164]

Indra is variously described as an accomplished artisan of the universe, friend and benefactor of men, the giant killer, the slayer of the serpent-dragon, the thunder-deity and the god of wars against the Enemies. Indra, originally a priest became a dreaded warrior-god through the slaughter of several demons, and attains the leadership of the gods.[165] He heads the gods in battle, mentions the *Ramayana*.[166] He is always young in appearance and sits among beauties indescribable.[167] He of a hundred powers, *Śatakratuḥ*, and a thousand eyes, *Sahasrākṣa*, is the Devadhipa and Trilokanatha.[168] His chariot is called Jaitraratha, the car of victory, and Mahendravaha which moves like lightning; it is sun-like, decorated with gold and drawn by ten thousand golden and peacock-coloured steeds, and descends on earth making a thunderous noise. It is riding on this chariot that he slays Namuchi, Bali, Vairochana, Sambara, Vala, Vritra and Naraka besides the seven hosts of Diti.[169]

The post-Vedic version of the killing of Vritra retains a few features of the original symbolic myth. It is described, that in the beginning of the

Krita-yuga, armies of invincible Asuras led by the dragon-demon Vritra waged a terrible war against the Devas, whom they mercilessly disbanded and dispersed in all directions. Having realized the impossibility of regaining power without the death of Vritra, the gods approached their grandsire and creator Brahma for guidance. Brahma advised them to obtain the bones of Rishi Dadhicha and from them to fashion a dreadful weapon. So the gods reached the Rishi and beseeched him for the boon of his bones. Dadhicha readily agreed to their request and gave up his life, and from his bones the great artisan, god Twashtri, shaped the mighty thunderbolt-weapon *Vajra.* With this, Indra led the Devas against the most dreaded Demon and found him surrounded by a host of exceedingly frightful and formidable Danavas who resembled dark mountain peaks. It is stated in the *Mahabharata* that the wars between the gods and demons lasted for thirty two thousand years. The greatest and most terrible was Vritra, and once again the Devas were battered and scattered as before. Vritra is described as five hundred leagues high and three hundred leagues round in size enveloping the whole earth and arresting the heaven.[170] When Indra drew closer, the doughty dragon roared in anger whereat heaven and earth shook in fear, even the mother Earth showed her great concern for the safety of her luminous son-god. Thereupon Indra became disparaged and demoralized, but with Vishnu's protection and the breakthrough boost that he obtains from the invigorating Soma-drink together with the support of the Maruts and the other gods, he grows mightier than before, feels inspired and energized and flings across the mightiest of weapons, the *Vajrayudha.* Vritra, the fiercest foe who at one time had thought of himself invulnerable and invincible soon felt vulnerable before the thunderbolt; his body slain, the celestial waters burst forth into the world. Thereafter Indra, the exalted one ruled happily the kingdom of heaven. But the surviving Danavas, panic-stricken yet revengeful, fled to the depths of the ocean and conspired to destroy the three worlds. And to accomplish this they plotted to destroy the Rishis first as they with their divine knowledge and penance were nourishing and supporting the universe. This battle between Indra and Vritra becomes the epic theme in all later mythology. In the *Mahabharata* description of this legend [171] we find that Vedic motifs are clearly interwoven with the later ones.[172]

Indra, in later mythology, is described as a handsome and ever victorious hero seated upon the elephant Airavata which is pure white in complexion and has four tusks, and resembles the sacred mountain Kailasa. He is represented pictorially as having four arms and hands; with two he holds a lance, in the third the famous thunderbolt whereas the fourth is empty. He has eyes all over the body and is a born warrior. The very hour he was born, grasping his weapons, he is said to have cried —

> "Where, mother, dwell those warriors fierce,
> Whose haughty hearts these bolts must pierce?"[173]

1. RV. II.12.2
2. RV. II.13.7
3. RV. II.15.2,3
4. RV. I.103.2
5. RV. VII.98.3
6. RV. III.39.7a
7. RV. VI.21.3a
8. RV. X. 89.2
9. RV. III.49.4
10. RV. VIII.82.4
11. RV. VIII.3.6
12. RV. II.12.7
13. RV. I.101.5
14. RV. I.32.1
15. RV. III.46.2
16. SABCL. Vol.10, pp. 258-59
17. Ibid., p. 261
18. RV. I.171. 5,6
19. RV. I.10.1-12
20. RV. I.11.1-8
21. RV. VI.18.14
22. RV. VIII.16.7
23. RV. I.100.4
24. RV. III.31.7
25. RV. VIII.12.2-3
26. RV. VI.22.2
27. RV. I.62.2
28. RV. I.62.4
29. RV. VII.42.1
30. RV. X.55.1a
31. RV. X.55.2a
32. RV. V.30.2
33. From Yaska's, *Nirukta* 1.25
 a. Trans: T.V. Kapali Sastry
34. Ibid., VIII.29

b. Trans: T.V. Kapali Sastry
35. RV. I.100.15
36. RV. VI.47.18
37. RV. III.46.3
38. RV. I.165.9
39. RV. III.53.2
40. RV. II.12.1-15
41. RV. II.11.6
42. RV. VIII.2.27
43. RV. I.84.3
44. RV. III.35.4
45. RV. I.6.1-10
46. RV. I.7.1-10
47. RV. I.8.1-10
48. RV. I.9.1-10
49. SABCL. Vol.10, p. 252
50. Ibid., p.253
51. RV. X.119.8
52. RV. X.119.12
53. RV. X.119.13
54. RV. I.165.7
55. RV. I.32.1-15
56. RV. I.51.4
57. RV. I.52.8
58. RV. III.33.6-7
59. RV. VII.47.4
60. RV. IV.26.2
61. RV. X.124.9
62. RV. I.80.14
63. RV. I.52.6
64. RV. VIII.3.19-20
65. RV. I.80.4
66. RV. X.8.8-9
67. RV. X.48.2
68. RV. X.68.9
69. RV. IV.1.14
70. RV. IV.3.11
71. RV. X.83.1
72. RV. X.38.3
73. RV. VI.18.3
74. RV. I.130.8
75. RV. III.49.1
76. RV. VI.20.2
77. RV. VII.21.7
78. RV. III.34.1
79. RV. VII.19.11
80. RV. VIII.46.19

81. RV. X.50.4
82. RV. X.167.1cd
83. SABCL. Vol.12, p. 217
84. RV. III.51.8b
85. RV. IV.19.1
86. RV. VI.17.8
87. RV. VIII.12.22
88. RV. I.102.1
89. RV. I.103.7
90. RV. VI.18.15
91. RV. IV.18.11a
92. RV. VIII.93.14
93. RV. VIII.96.7
94. RV. VII.104.19
95. RV. I.121.9
96. RV. I.51.3b
97. RV VI.22.6
98. RV. VI.47.27
99. RV. I.33.10b
100. RV. VI.21.7
101. RV. VIII.77.7
102. RV. IX.111.3c
103. RV. X.92.7
104. RV. I.130.7a
105. RV. X.152.4
106. AV. X.7.30
107. RV. I.164.26,27
108. RV. III.31.5-11
109. RV. III.31.18-22
110. RV. VIII.1.11
111. RV. VIII.65.3
112. RV. X.42.2
113. RV. I.4.1
114. SABCL. Vol.10, p. 134
115. RV. VI.28.1-2
116. RV. VI.28.5,8
117. RV. I.11.5
118. RV. IX.86.22
119. RV. VI.43.3
120. RV. X.111.8
121. RV. X.112.8
122. RV. X.32.1
123. RV. III.34.7
124. RV. X.49.9
125. RV. III.49.4
126. RV. VI.30.5
127. RV. III.44.2

128. RV. III.32.8
129. RV. I.100.18
130. RV. II.21.4
131. RV. I.100.6
132. RV. I.100.8
133. RV. I.93.4
134. RV. VIII.89.1
135. RV. VII.76.4
136. RV. VIII.29.10
137. RV. IV.51.2b
138. RV. I.62.5
139. RV. VII.98.6
140. RV. VI.17.5
141. RV. V.34.5-9
142. RV. III.2.14
143. RV. I.4.2-5
144. RV. I.4.6-10
145. RV. I.5.1-10
146. RV. I.15.1
147. RV. I.15.3
147a. RV. I.15.5
148. RV. I.16.1-9
149. RV. I.17.1-9
150. RV. IV.18; RV. X.28
151. RV. II.12
152. RV. VI.72.2-5
153. RV. V.1-13
154. RV. I.32.1-12
155. RV. X.28.1-12
156. RV. III.53.4b
157. RV. V.29.7
158. RV. VI.59.1
159. RV. I.108.7
160. RV. I.108.9
161. RV. VIII.21.6
162. RV. I.63.9
163. *Kena Upanishad*, IV.3
164. John Dowson, *Hindu Mythology and Religion* (Rupa & Co. New Delhi,1989), p. 127
165. *The Mahabharata*, XII.22.11
166. *The Ramayana*, III.59.15
167. Ibid., III.57.24; III.5.5
168. Ibid., V.10.7; VI.15.5
169. Ibid., V.104.3; III.168.73; III.165.7; III.166.5
170. *The Mahabharata*, III.101.1; AV. XI.6.3; RV. II.31.4
171. Ibid., III.100
172. Ibid., XII.282.18; V.9.45ff
173. W. J. Wilkins, *Hindu Mythology* (Rupa & Co, 1989), p. 56

IV

SURYA

(1)

The Original Antinomy

There is an original antinomy at the heart of creation between the finite and the Infinite, the limited and the Limitless, the temporal and the Eternal. There is therefore a perpetual conflict between the forces of Darkness and Light, — the *devas* and the *dānavas*. The Devas are the forces of Light and are the protagonists of the Infinite and the Eternal. The Danavas are the instruments of darkness and divisiveness, and work for the preservation of limitation, finitude and separativeness. The battle is on between them 'for the possession of the triple world of heaven, mid-air and earth'.

The Gods battle for the liberation of mind and body from all limitation, ignorance and mortality, for the strength of will and the joy of infinite existence; whereas the Titans work for bondage, division, disharmony and for the continuance of the rule and power of Darkness and Falsehood. Aditi is both the mother and daughter of Daksha. She "is originally the pure consciousness of infinite existence, one and self-luminous."[1] It is this Supreme Mother who gives birth to Daksha, "the discriminating and distributing Thought of the divine Mind."[2] She herself thus born to Daksha is "the cosmic infinite, the mystic Cow whose udders feed all the worlds." It is this divine daughter of Daksha who is the mother of the *devas*. Also Aditi is imaged as both the mother and wife of Vishnu, the all-pervading truth of being. As the son of Aditi, Vishnu is the younger brother of Indra. This has a mystical significance; Aditi is the infinite Consciousness and the mother of the cosmos, yet it is held by and is encaved in the lower world-power. And the lower Power works through the limited mind and body. This is delivered by the force of the divine or illumined Mind, — Indra. Thus it is Indra who delivers the light of the Truth, Surya, and makes it rise in heaven and dispel the darkness and falsehood of the ordinary mind. This leads to the experience of a liberated, unified and all-pervading consciousness, — Vishnu. But Vishnu comes into the picture only after Indra does his work.

Aditi is the infinite Light which is also the body of Surya. The divine world of *satyam ṛtam bṛhat*, as well as the gods are the formations of this

Light of Aditi. The gods born of her in the infinitely dynamic *ṛtam* are charged with the function of sustaining the workings of the Truth in the universe, of strengthening and supporting man in his march towards the Truth, and rebuilding the many worlds in the image of the Truth. For this purpose they liberate and release the sevenfold solar waters from the stranglehold of Vritra, and conjointly "make the light of the Truth to arise on the darkened sky of his mentality, fill with its luminous and honey-sweet satisfactions the atmosphere of his vital existence, transform into its vastness and plenitude by the power of the Sun the earth of his physical being, create everywhere the divine Dawn."[3] The divine workings thus established in the seeker, he is guided in his action fully by the Truth. Such is his identity with the Truth that he hears the Word in his thought, sees clearly the luminous path trodden by the seers and the forefathers and ascends to the Truth by the power of the Sacrifice, the Word and the Soma-wine. And travelling on the celebrated path he transcends the limitations of mind and the physical body and the trappings of the lower being. The seeker then gains entry into the supramental existence of fearless light and infinite freedom, of endless bliss and deathless life.

Surya is the self of all that is mutable and that is immutable as well as "the wide-burning Truth that is lodged in the law which upholds heaven."[4] And it is the nature of that law to manifest the Truth in all the worlds and transform them in the nature of the highest heaven above. With such luminous and integral transformation of the earth-nature, sin and suffering and death are banished from physical existence. This is accomplished when the seers and the seekers bring back Martanda, the dark Surya or the concealed and camouflaged Truth, from the cavern of Darkness and effect his release into his original, native matchless magnificence. The cosmic Aditi, not the supracosmic Mahashakti, is said to have eight sons born from her body; seven of them help her to realise the gods, to come into close contact with them and grow into their consciousness and move into the supreme life. Martanda is the eighth and black son, and being of mortal creation is cast away by her, whence he falls into the nether world of the Inconscient; he is the lost or hidden Surya whom the Danavas keep concealed in the dark kingdom of the Inconscient. Both the Gods and the Rishis effect his liberation by the power of their *tapasyā* and is brought back to preside over mortal man's life. There is thus a fugitive Truth, a disguised sun, a concealed consciousness, a hidden god who governs our mortal life, who guides the pilgrim-soul and shapes the earth's destiny. There is a divine knowledge 'obscured by the smoke of human passion and self-will', and enveloped by the unregenerate human nature. The seers discover this hidden resplendence, Martanda, lying in the dark cavern of the Inconscient. This hidden sun is variously described by the Rishi as the 'eye of the gods' concealed in the sea of Ignorance, buried under the dark debris of Falsehood, as the lost Sun and the oppressed Truth. All the gods, Indra, Agni, Brihaspati and Soma together with the seers through their cosmic *yajñas* increasingly and progressively liberate this imprisoned splendour. The barriers of the Titans are broken, the citadel of Ignorance shattered, and the Flaming Eye is helped to open on the unhorizoned spaces beyond. Awakened and arisen, the splendorous son of Aditi mounts to the world of the supramental Truth, the Swar-loka. To quote Sri Aurobindo, " 'He goes where the gods have made a path for him cleaving like an eagle to his goal'; he ascends with his seven shining horses to the utter luminous ocean of the higher existence; he is led over it by the seers in a ship. Surya, the Sun, is himself perhaps the golden ship in which Pushan the Increaser leads men beyond evil and darkness and sin to the Truth and the Immortality."[5]

Once liberated, this eighth Surya ascends with 'his seven shining horses' to the luminous world of the supramental Truth. Going beyond sin and ignorance the seeker attains the supreme Light of Surya. And guided by this Light he mounts the summit world of the infinite.

1. *Namo mitrasya varuṇasya cakṣase*
maho devāya tadṛtaṁ saparyata,
dūredṛśe devajātāya ketave divas
putrāya sūryāya śaṁsata.

2. *Sā mā satyoktiḥ pari pātu viśvato*
dyāvā ca yatra tatanannahāni ca,
viśvamanyānni viśate yadejati
viśvāhāpo viśvahodeti sūryaḥ.

3. *Na te adevaḥ pradivo ni vāsate*
yadetaśebhiḥ patarai ratharyasi,
prācīnamanyadanu vartate raja ud
anyena jyotiṣā yāsi sūrya.

4. *Yena sūrya jyotiṣā bādhase tamo*
jagacca viśvamudiyarṣi bhānuna,
tenāsmadviśvāmanirāmanāhutim
apāmīvāmapa duḥṣvapnyaṁ suva.

5. *Viśvasya hi preṣito rakṣasi vratam*
aheḷayannuccarasi svadhā anu,
yadadya tvā sūryopabravāmahai taṁ
no devā anu maṅsirata kratum.

6. *Taṁ no dyāvāpṛthivī tanna āpa*
indraḥ śṛṇvantu maruto havaṁ vacaḥ,
mā śūne bhūma sūryasya sandṛśi
bhadraṁ jīvanto jaraṇāmaśīmahi.

7. *Viśvāhā tvā sumanasaḥ sucakṣasaḥ*
prajāvanto anamīvā anāgasaḥ,
udyantaṁ tvā mitramaho divedive
jyogjīvāḥ prati paśyema sūrya.

8. *Mahi jyotirbibhrataṁ tvā vicakṣaṇa*
bhāsvantaṁ cakṣuṣe cakṣuṣe mayaḥ,
arohantaṁ bṛhataḥ pājasaspari vayaṁ
jīvāḥ prati paśyema sūrya.

9. *Yasya te viśvā bhuvanāni ketunā pra*
cerate ni ca viśante aktubhiḥ,
anāgāstvena harikeśa sūryāhnāhnā
no vasyasāvasyasodihi.

10. *Śaṁ no bhava cakṣasā śaṁ no ahnā śaṁ*
bhānunā śaṁ himā śaṁ ghṛṇena,
yathā samadhvañchamasadduroṇe
tatsūrya draviṇaṁ dhehi citram.

11. *Asmākaṁ devā ubhayāya janmane*
śarma yacchata dvipade catuṣpade,
adatpibadūrjayamānamāśitaṁ tad
asme śaṁ yorarapo dadhātana.

12. *Yadvo devāścakṛma jihvayā guru*
manaso vā prayutī devahelanam,
arāvā yo no abhi ducchunāyate tasmin
tadeno vasavo ni dhetana.[6]

1. Our adoration to the sun divine, the eye of Mitra and Varuna, the mighty, the far seer, the god-born and the manifester of all things; we celebrate the rite enjoined by him who is the son of heavens.

2. May the Word guide me and protect me always and everywhere, in whom heaven and earth, night and day are spread, in whom rest all creation in motion, in whom the waters flow and the sun rises every day.

3. No ancient *asura* can ever obstruct you, O Sun, when you drive forward in your chariot drawn by rapid steeds. A radiance sempiternal follows you whilst you rise every morn with renewed lustre.

4. O radiant Lord, may you remove from us all destitution, all resistance and inertia, with your radiance remove all darkness, banish all nightmarish thoughts and dreams; with your purifying and inspiring light put fresh faith in us, always lead us.

5. O divine sun, you who are gentle and kind when invoked, and guard rightly the laws of creation, may the gods be propitious to us in our sacred deeds.

6. May heaven and earth, the Waters, may Indra and the Maruts be pleased with our adoration; may we never be unhappy at your sight, may we attain a long enlightened life, and enjoy a felicitous old age.

7. O radiant one, may we be constantly cheerful in spirit, ever-more acute in perception blessed with felicity, free from all forms of ailment, worship you daily, may we enjoying long life behold you, O nourisher of the seekers, rising day by day.

8. May we enjoying long and luminous life behold you day after day, O Sun, who gleam over all things and invest them with great radiance; you enliven every eye and rise above the vast and mighty seas.

9. O golden-haired Lord of Light, it is by your continual guidance that all beings move by day and repose by night; may you come to us free of sin and grant us increasingly felicitous life every day.

10. O lord of radiances, bless us with more light, be propitious to us

with greater warmth; may everything be propitious to us, grant us manifold wealth that we may progress both in our homes as well as on the great journey.

11. O adorable god, may you bestow riches on all classes of living beings so that they may increasingly grow strong and healthy in all conditions; grant us felicity that we may be happy and be free from sin and ignorance.

12. O mighty god, the wrath excited in you by whatever omissions committed by us previously in sheer ignorance, may you direct it against the Enemies who assail us and terrify us all the time.

The seeker-sacrificer attains this highest vision through a long and laborious process of self-offering and perpetual self-transcendence. Surya is the configuration of this vision.

(2)

Surya: The liberating Light

Surya represents the great liberated Light beholding and following which the pilgrim-soul ascends to the Light of all lights, the highest Light of all.

Udvayaṁ tamasaspari jyotiṣ
  paśyanta uttaram,
devaṁ devatrā sūryamaganma
  jyotiruttamam.[7]

"Beholding a higher Light beyond the darkness we have followed it and reached the highest Light of all, Surya divine in the divine Being."*

It is by this Light that the seeker realises his utter identity with the Divine — *aham brahmāsmi*. In the words of Sri Aurobindo, "The light of Surya is the form, the body of that divine vision. He is described as the pure and visioned force of the Truth which shines out in his rising like the gold of Heaven. He is the great godhead who is the vision of Mitra and Varuna; he is the large and invincible eye of that Wideness and that Harmony; the eye of Mitra and Varuna is the great ocean of vision of Surya. His is that large truth-vision which makes us give to its possessors the name of seer... It is by this eye of light that Indra, who has made him arise in heaven for far vision, distinguishes the Aryan powers from the Dasyu, separating the children of light from the children of darkness so that he may destroy these but raise those to their perfection."[8]

The seer of such station not only has the 'far-vision' but the 'far-hearing'. He is receptive to the intimations from the Infinite, — the Vision as well as the Word. He has both the far-seeing eye and the deep-hearing ear; he sees the Truth as well as 'the illumined and illuminating thought', just as the guardians of the Light, Varuna and Mitra.

Yadadya sūrya bravo'nāgā udyan
mitrāya varuṇāya satyam,
vayaṁ devatrādite syāma tava priyāso
aryaman gṛṇantaḥ.[9]

"The truth that thou rising free from sin, O Sun, speakest today to Mitra and Varuna, that may we speak and abide in the Godhead dear to thee, O Aditi, and thee, O Aryaman."*

And it is this seer-light of Surya Savitri that is invoked by Rishi Vishwamitra in his *Gayatri* to provide its 'luminous impulsion' to the thoughts of the worshippers. In this great *mantra* is achieved a perfect integration of the seer-vision and the seer-will as well as the deification of this double truth of Reality. It is when this double vision awakens in the seeker helping him to embrace the entire universe of mind, life and will that he is divinely recreated. And "this new-seeing of all, things", as Sri Aurobindo observes, "this new-moulding of thought, act, feeling, will, consciousness in the terms of the Truth, the Bliss, the Right, the Infinity is a new creation."[10] It is the function of Surya the supreme seer, liberator and divine recreator to prepare the sacrificer-seeker for this "new birth and new creation by his illumination and upward voyaging."[11]

In the Vedic perception Truth and Light are synonymous even as are Darkness and Ignorance. The Devas and the Danavas are arrayed against each other in a continual conflict. They are respectively the powers of Light and Darkness ceaselessly battling for the possession of the three worlds, which battle is linked up with the destiny of man. The gods are seeking to liberate man, and lead him from limitation, ignorance and death, whereas the Titans are struggling to keep him imprisoned for ever in the den of darkness. Rooted in an original cosmic antinomy, the struggle assumes the form of a timeless syndrome. Aditi, the Infinite, is the mother of the *devas*, and Diti that of the *asuras*; as a result the *devas* descending in man tend to lead him towards light, unity, infinity and immortality, whereas the *asuras* are bent upon misleading him and keep him tied down to sin and suffering, division and death.[a]

Surya is the Light and Power of the Truth-Consciousness that steadily rises on the firmament of human existence and initiates man into the felicities of divine existence. Surya, the all-seer and creator, creates the many worlds out of the Supreme Being, as well as manifests in the inferior existence of man the self-conscious supramental Truth. He is Savitri the Creator, Twashtri the Fashioner and Pushan the Increaser. Surya Savitri manifests himself a second time in the formation of the Truth in the seeker through the cooperation of four other gods Mitra, Varuna, Bhaga and Aryaman. These are respectively "the Lords of pure Wideness, luminous Harmony, divine Enjoyment, exalted Power."[12] Surya is the sole and sovereign light and power of Truth who transforms all human energies into the terms and conditions of the Truth when consciously offered to him. For he knows all formulations, encompasses and understands their origins, subsumes and includes their laws and processes and concusses their right consequence. Man embodies within him seven formulations of sacrificial energies — physical, vital, mental, supramental and those corresponding to the worlds of Ananda, Cit-shakti and Sat. It is the anomalous and deviant action of the obscure and ignorant mind that causes suffering and evil. Surya, the lord of right knowledge and action, puts them all in their right places in the sacrifice and thus helps the sacrificer to arrive at the affirmation of the presence and working of the divine creator Surya within him. The effect of the luminous action of Surya Savitri is that the seeker undergoes a happy and constant new-and-recreation of himself, — of the universe of his entire being. Enormous and far-flung and unfathomable is the Lord's affirmation in the functioning of the universe.

Surya is the supreme seer-revealer; his Truth-vision and Truth-action illumines the entire cosmos, — all the objects of manifestations, all the phenomenal formulations of the one Consciousness without and the countless experiences within. He unveils and makes known the manifold truth in them, reveals their workings and their right relatedness as well as the means of fulfilment of their secret purpose by arranging rightly the energies of the sacrifice. It is the discovery and utilisation of the one central and supreme Truth in all that increases in the sacrificer the felicity and the good necessary for the divine effectuation. The good that is brought about by Surya in this divine change is beneficial and propitious to all living beings — *dvipada* and *catuspada*. The process of this manifestation or new creation is multifold. The Truth-light dawns first on the summit of the pure mind and there reaches the other planes of human consciousness enabling the seeker to look up above to the world of *satyam ṛtam bṛhat*. Wherever his light falls the obscurities are removed and all is illuminated. The dissolution of mental ignorance and darkness is necessary as a prelude to the descent of the supramental principle. Surya manifests light in the physical, vital and mental and shines all-pervadingly as the seeker moves forward towards the great Dawn.

Viśvā rūpāṇi prati muñcate kaviḥ
prāsāvīdbhadraṁ dvipade catuṣpade
vi nākamakhyatsavitā vareṇyo'nu
prayāṇamuṣaso vi rājati.[13]

The wise Savitri comprehends all forms in himself and brings forth what is good for bipeds and quadrupeds: the adorable Lord illumes the high vault of heavens long after the passage of the Dawn.

It is the grand movement of illumination, nay, it is the spiritual revolution that overtakes the seeker. The force of illumination of Surya expands the working of the Truth and the Light in the sacrificer resulting in the expansion of his inner capacities and potentialities leading to the attainment of largeness and fullness of 'right becoming, right action and right knowledge'. The forward movement of the Dawn is synonymous with the widening and heightening of consciousness in man; the upward movement of the Sun is the march of consciousness in the seeker. And following this march, the gods too, reach the realm of the Truth. Surya Savitri, the divine creator, by his mastery and sway not only lays out the earthly realms of light but illuminates our physical consciousness for perfect action.

Yasya prayāṇamanvanya idyayur
devā devasya mahimānamojasā,
yaḥ pārthivāni vimame sa etaśo
rajāṅsi devaḥ savitā mahitvanā.[14]

"In the wake of his march the other gods also reach by his force to the greatness of the Divinity. He has mapped out the realms of earthly light by his mightiness, — the brilliant one, the divine Creator."*

He pervades the three domains of the pure mind and puts the seeker in contact with all the divine possibilities of intuitive reason, intellect, sensations and emotion. And liberating their spiritual potentialities from phenomenal limitations fulfils the mental Purusha. It is them that the supramental manifests in the mortal, and its liberating light envelops the Night on all sides and dissolving it assumes its beatific form. The Lord of Truth becomes the Lord of Love and Bliss.

Uta yāsi savitastrīṇi rocanota
sūryasya raśmibhiḥ samucyasi,
uta rātrīmubhayataḥ parīyasa uta
mitro bhavasi deva dharmābhiḥ.[15]

"And thou reachest, O Savitri, to the three luminous heavens; and thou art utterly expressed by the rays of the Sun; and thou encompassest the Night upon either side; and thou becomest by the law of thy actions the lord of love, O God."*

The supreme Truth of all-existence — the supramental Truth-Consciousness — finally becomes the master of our existence and increases us by a persistently advancing creation until the whole of our becoming is integrally illuminated and transformed.

Uteśiṣe prasavasya tvameka iduta
pūṣā bhavasi deva yāmabhiḥ,
utedaṁ viśvaṁ bhuvanaṁ vi rājasi
śyāvāśvaste savitaḥ stomamānaśe.[16]

"And thou art powerful for every creation; and thou becomest the Increaser, O God, by thy movings; and thou illuminest utterly all this world of becomings. Shyavashwa has attained to the affirmation of thee, O Savitri."*

Outwardly Surya is the solar light, but inwardly he symbolises the illuminating revelatory knowledge. For the initiates he is the source of divine knowledge and the creator of the luminous worlds of Truth-Consciousness. The seekers of Light look to him for strength and support. Assuming all godhead-forms he creates the supreme felicity for them and manifests the shining world. All the gods follow him and make his Light their avowed goal. Surya Savitri is at his highest and best in the three worlds of Light when he dissolves all darkness and harmoniously integrates the noumenal with the phenomenal worlds. He is the supreme author of all the worlds and their luminous transformation.

The light of Surya is shut up closely in the subconscient and its glimpses are seen only in limited centres which are receptive. The 'self-vision and all-vision' of Surya is of the nature of Vijñana. The true and total knowledge that is Surya is the truth both of individual existence and all-existence. Surya working in the individual replaces his divisive and limited consciousness by his integral vision. He is the persistent Light, the insistent unifying consciousness, which leads to the increasing manifestation of the Truth in men. He is Pushan, fosterer of the Truth; his total vision of the all enables them to arrive eventually at oneness. "That intuitive vision of the totality, of one in All and All in one", observes Sri Aurobindo, "becomes the ordainer of the right law of action in us, the law of the Truth. For Surya is Yama, the Ordainer or Controller who assures the law, the Dharma. Thus we arrive at the fullness of action of the Illuminer in us, accomplish the entirety of the Truth-Consciousness. We are then able to see that all that is contained in the being of Surya, in the Vijñana which builds up the worlds is becoming of existence in the one existence and one Lord of all becoming, the Purusha, Sachchidananda. All becoming is born in the Being who himself exceeds all becomings and is their Lord, Prajapati."[17] Right and integral knowledge of the One and the All is formed by the progressive revelation of the vision of Surya in two successive stages. The intuitions coming from Surya perceive the essences of our limited concepts and percepts and arrange them in their lasting relations to each other and ultimately are led to the realization of their integral oneness. The predicament of the divisive consciousness of mind is thus overcome in the light of the original Truth-Consciousness by a total reversal of its own characteristic action. It is the action of the superconscient Surya that helps all forms of relative and even intuitive knowledge to be transformed and integrated into the self-luminous self-vision of the One Existent.

"This is Surya's godliest form of all. For it is the supreme Light, the supreme Will, the supreme Delight of existence.... This is the Lord, the Purusha, the self-conscient Being. When we have this vision, there is the integral self-knowledge, the perfect seeing, expressed in the great cry of the Upanishad, *so'ham*. The Purusha there and there, He am I. The Lord manifests Himself in the movements and inhabits many forms, but it is One who inhabits all. This self-conscient being, this real "I" whom the mental being individualised in the form is aware of as his true self — it is He. It is the All; and it is that which transcends the All."[18]

The passage from the world of mortality to that of Immortality is consequent upon the progressive illumination of the mind. Surya, the divine Light, is the gate to such attainment of infinite consciousness and life in the Truth. The egoistic individual lives by the rays of Surya and not in his full, blazing splendour. His knowledge is narrow and limited, and his action fluctuating and false, his vision is broken and lop-sided, and his will is crooked and weak. Agni and Surya, divine Force and divine Consciousness, together help him to become total and integral, fully self-conscious and self-willed, one-visioned and whole-visioned. Surya Savitri manifests in the mortal the state of immortality and transforms human life into life divine. In the *Isha Upanishad*, Surya is invoked "as the godhead of knowledge whose supreme form of effulgence is the oneness of the Spirit and his rays dispersed here on the mental level are the shining diffusion of the thought-mind and conceal his own infinite supramental truth, the body and self of this Sun, the truth of the spirit and the Eternal."[19]

Hiraṇmayena pātreṇa satyasyāpihitaṁ mukham
tat tvaṁ pūṣannapāvṛṇu satyadharmāya dṛṣṭaye.

Pūṣannekarṣe yama sūrya prājāpatya
vyūha raśmin samuha tejo.
yat te rūpaṁ kalyāṇatamaṁ tatte
paśyami yo'sāvāsau puruṣaḥ, so'hamasmi.[20]

"The face of the Truth is covered with a golden lid: O fostering Sun, that uncover for the law of the truth, for sight. O fosterer, O sole Rishi, O controlling Yama, O Surya, O son of the Father of creatures, marshal and mass thy rays: the Lustre that is thy most blessed form of all, that I see, He who is this, this Purusha, He am I."*

This psychic and spiritual vision appears earlier in the Veda in a more concentrated imagery:

Ṛtena ṛtamapihitaṁ dhruvaṁ vāṁ
sūryasya yatra vimucantyaśvān,
daśa śatā saha tasthustadekaṁ devānāṁ
śreṣṭhaṁ vapuṣāmapaśyam.[21]

"There is a Truth covered by a Truth where they unyoke the horses of the Sun; the ten hundreds stood together, there was that One;

I saw the greatest (best, most glorious) of the embodied gods."*

Surya is thus referred to in the *Isha Upanishad* as a god of revelatory knowledge who helps the seeker to arrive at the Truth. He is the divine Illumination above mind and symbolizes the Pure self-luminous Truth of things. "His realm is described as the Truth, the Law, the Vast. He is the Fosterer or Increaser, for he enlarges and opens man's dark and limited being into a luminous and infinite consciousness. He is the sole seer, seer of Oneness and Knower of the Self, and leads him to the highest Sight. He is Yama, Controller or Ordainer for he governs man's action and manifested being by the direct Law of the Truth, *satya-dharma*, and therefore by the right principle of our nature, *yatha-tathyataḥ*, a luminous power proceeding from the Father of all existence, he reveals in himself the divine Purusha of whom all beings are the manifestations. His rays are the thought that proceed luminously from the Truth, the vast but become deflected and distorted, broken up and disordered in the reflecting and dividing principle, Mind. They form there the golden lid which covers the face of the Truth. The Seer prays to Surya to cast them into right order and relation and then draw them together into the unity of revealed truth. The result of this inner process is the perception of the oneness of all beings in the divine Soul of the Universe."[22]

The Upanishadic Rishis are aware of the great need for inner purification. And *jñāna* is the supreme purifier; it saves the seeker from sin and suffering. They take cognisance of both the individual and cosmic aspects of sin and ignorance, and redemption from them. The Upanishads suggest constant adoration of Surya for perfect purification. It is the *jñānī*, the enlightened and the knower of *ātman* and *brahman*, that goes beyond good and evil.

Jñātvā devaṁ sarvapāśvāpahāniḥ kṣīnaiḥ
kleśairjanmamṛtyuprahāṇiḥ,
tasyābhidhyānāttṛtīyaṁ dehabhede
viśvaiśvaryaṁ kevala āptakāmaḥ.[23]

When a man knows God all fetters fall off; sufferings are no more, there is cessation of birth and death. By meditating on Him, on the body's dissolution, there is attained the third state, that of perfect mastery. His desires fulfilled; he is supremely free.

Surya is invoked again and again to actuate the mental movements, to illuminate the mind and to lead the supplicants to the Truth beyond. The Vedic Rishis thought of inner life as the real one, and the outer as only its figure and living symbol. For them the aim of life is to grow out of ignorance and falsehood and mortality into the world of *satyam ṛtam bṛhat*. In this great spiritual endeavour they seek the help of the gods who are the many cosmic powers of the Supreme. To the pilgrim of the Truth Indra is the god of the luminous Mind, Agni is the flame of intense aspiration and the Will-in-action, and Surya the supreme effulgence as well as the source and centre of Knowledge and Power and Freedom. In him are embodied all the creative movements of Aditi. He is the Light that innervates, stimulates and galvanizes our thought-movements and life-movements towards the Truth.

The physical sun is the figure of a mighty spiritual Force that dissolves all darkness, dispels ignorance and energizes all creative activity of the universe. He is a concentrated physical mass of the light of the supreme Truth — the symbol of the Sun of divine Truth.

Agneranikaṁ bṛhataḥ saparyaṁ
divi śukraṁ yajataṁ sūryasya.[24]

I adore the mighty Agni whose splendour and radiance are as bright as that of the Sun.

Surya for the Vedic Rishis is the presiding deity, and is invoked and approached for spiritual nourishment and strength to reach their highest goal.

1. *Sūryo devīmuṣasaṁ rocamānāṁ mayor*
na yoṣāmabhyeti paścāt,
yatrā naro devayanto yugāni vitanvate
prati bhadrāya bhadram.

2. *Bhadrā aśvā haritaḥ sūryasya*
citrā etagvā anumādyāsaḥ,
namasyanto diva ā pṛṣṭhamasthuḥ
pari dyāvāpṛthivī yanti sadyaḥ.[25]

1. The sun pursues the divine and radiant Dawns as a young lover follows a beautiful maiden. To gain appropriate rewards the wise ones seeking to be divine perform established sacrifices and worship

the auspicious sun.

2. The auspicious, well-limbed, swift steeds traverse the path and ascend the summit of the sky; they quickly roam around the earth and heaven. Our reverence to the splendour of the rays.

Surya is the divine creator and illuminator. He is the loftiest Light that springs up above all darkness — the most powerful all-effectuating Light. Following his luminous lead the Rishis arrive at the Truth and are reunited with the Divine. His expanding effulgence that exceeds the earthly splendour of a thousand suns well-protects the traveller from sin and falsehood. His outstanding resplendence dissolves ignorance and overcomes mortality. It is through the creative support of Surya, the Lord of Light and Truth, that immortality is attained. The Rishis desire the laws of Surya Savitri, the luminous child of the Waters — the streams of cosmic conscious energies.

a) *Apāṁ napātamavase savitāramupa stuhi,*
tasya vratānyuśmasi.[26]

May we worship Savitri alone for protection; his imperishable laws help us to fulfil our sacred aspirations.

b) *Vedāhametaṁ puruṣaṁ mahāntamāditya*
varṇaṁ tamasaḥ parastāt,
tameva viditvāti mṛtyumeti nānyaḥ
panthā vidyate'yanāya.[27]

I have known this mighty God who is refulgent and radiant like the Sun, and free from Ignorance. One who knows him goes beyond death; there is no path to the desired goal other than this.

Savitri, the golden-handed, is the supreme protector and the knower of all. He is made of the substance of the Truth; he is the Purusha who has become all the gods. All the gods follow his lead in the attainment of the goal. He embodies the loving virtues of Mitra, the wideness and purity of Varuna and the immortal nature of Agni. He is the golden Purusha to whom all creation turns. Inhabitant of the world of Immortality, born of the celestial waters, Surya is the Truth itself in his plenary form; born of *ṛta* he is also the law of the Truth, and increases the Truth in the lives of the seekers. Surya is the Truth, Surya is the Truth-Sun the Creator of all, the Illuminator and Increaser.

a) *Hiraṇyapāṇimūtaye savitāramupa hvaye,*
sa cettā devatā padam.[28]

I invoke Savitri, the golden-handed divine creator, for protection. He is the All-knowing; only his adoration leads the seeker to the final destination.

b) *Citraṁ devānāmudagādanīkaṁ*
cakṣurmitrasya varuṇasyāgneḥ,
āprā dyāvāpṛthivī antarikṣaṁ sūrya
ātmā jagatastasthuṣaśca.[29]

Yonder has risen the picturesque face of the gods; he is the eye of Mitra, Varuna and Agni. He has filled heaven and earth and the mid-region with his divine splendour. He is the soul of all that is movable and immovable.

c) *Nṛṣadvarasadṛtasadvyomasad*
abjā gojā ṛtajā adrijā ṛtam.[30]

He is the dweller amongst men (as consciousness), the dweller in the most excellent orb, in the Truth, in the sky; born of the waters, of the rays of light, of the Right and of the Mountain, and the Truth itself.

d) *Etāvānasya mahimāto jyāyāṁśca pūruṣaḥ,*
pādo'sya viśvā bhūtāni tripādasyāmṛtaṁ divi.[31]

Such is his glory; Purusha is greater even than this. All of creation is but one-fourth of him; the other three-fourths of his being is immortal, abiding in heaven.

Indra joined by the Navagwa and Dasagwa Angirasas — the power of the divine Mind and the flaming powers of divine Will respectively — going through winding and agonising ways trace the cows concealed by Vritra. They find the Sun 'lying in the darkness' of Ignorance and Inconscience, *satyaṁ tadindro daśabhirdaśagvaiḥ sūryaṁ viveda tamasi kṣiyantam.*[32]

The wide-seeing, golden-haired Lord of Light, in his bright chariot harnessed by the seven bright coursers speeds forth across the firmament. These horses are the seven cosmic principles underlying the creation of the seven worlds. They are the forces of illumination that proceed from his effusive and interpenetrating, all-embracing movement.

Sapta tvā harito rathe vahanti deva sūrya,
śociṣkeśaṁ vicakṣaṇa.
Ayukta sapta śundhyuvaḥ
sūro rathasya naptyaḥ,
tābhıryatı svayuktıbhıḥ.[33]

O wide-seeing, self-effulgent Surya, your seven coursers harnessed to your chariot ever bear you. O bright-haired God with the seven bright steeds yoked to your chariot you ceaselessly go forth never failing, ever-purifying.

The energies of Surya are auspicious, felicitous and radiant; they bring in their wake mental illumination, purity of mind and carry the seeker-supplicants to the summit of their seeking. They are the carriers of the all-creator Sun who encompasses the entire universe of manifestation. The refulgent god, the all-beautiful creator of Light helps the sacrificers to cross the dark ocean of Ignorance. He removes all obstacles on the way to infinite freedom by lighting up the path. He is the source and the supreme architect of all lights, both inner and outer.

Taraṇirviśvadarśato jyotiṣkṛdasi sūrya,
viśvamā bhāsi rocanam.[34]

O self-effulgent God, all-beautiful, and the bright creator of lights, you awaken each one of us to your supreme radiances, and illumine all the worlds.

Surya is the bestower of bounteous wealth, the one who brings into being all existences and also causes their withdrawal into non-existence. The Rishi seeks his triple protection on the physical, vital and mental levels.

Bṛhatsumnaḥ prasavītā niveśano jagataḥ
sthāturubhayasya yo vaśī,

sa no devaḥ savitā śarma yacchato
asme kṣayāya trivarūthamaṁhasaḥ.[35]

May that divine Savitri who is the god of great felicity, the engenderer of good deeds, he who comprehends all and is the regulator of the movable and the immovable, grant us shelter in the triple world and protect us against all evil.

The revelation of the Sun of Truth precedes a prolonged preparation on the part of the seeker. It needs a succession of dawns to make the sacrificer fully receptive to the supreme Truth. His inability to retain the Light uninterrupted for a long time necessitates the periodic withdrawal of Light. It is this withdrawal of Light for long or short periods that helps the seeker to assimilate it, whereupon he emerges into greater Light. This continues until the Sun becomes more and more effective and dispels all darkness, — until the seeker grows ready and healthy for the supreme revelation.

a) *Tatsūryasya devatvaṁ tanmāhitvaṁ*
madhyā kartorvitataṁ saṁ jabhāra,
yadedayukta, haritaḥ sadhasthādād
rātrī vāsastanute simasmai.[36]

Such is the divinity, such the might and majesty of Surya that when he has set he withdraws into himself what is spread over the unfinished task as if unyoking the horses from his chariot; then the Night extends her enveloping darkness.

b) *Udyannadya mitramaha ārohann*
uttarāṁ divam,
hṛdrogaṁ mama sūryaṁ harimāṇaṁ ca nāśaya.[37]

Radiant with benevolent light, rising and mounting to the highest heaven, O Sun may you remove my heart's ailment and the paleness of my body.

Surya is the deity who presides over the solar body that is worshipped. He is not the physical sun, for the Rishi speaks of him as being always found at the meridian in the sky and seen only by the wise 'like an eye extended in heaven'. Elsewhere he is described as 'the loftier light', 'the God among Gods' and 'the most excellent light' that transcends the senses. Surya like Agni is 'the knower of creatures', Jataveda; he is the eye of the gods because he sees and is seen by all.

a) *Udu tyaṁ jātavedasaṁ devaṁ vahanti ketavaḥ,*
dṛśe viśvāya sūryam.[38]

His radiant horses bear on high the divine all-knowing Surya, that all may see him.

b) *Adṛśramasya ketavo vi raśmayo janāñ anu,*
bhrajanto agnayo yathā.[39]

His brilliant rays, shining like blazing fires, are beheld by all.

Surya is both the rising sun and the setting sun.

a) *Viśvasya hi śruṣṭaye deva ūrdhavaḥ*
pra bāhavā pṛthupāṇiḥ sisarti,
āpaścidasya vrata ā nimṛgrā
ayaṁ cidvāto ramate parijman.[40]

The resplendent sun having risen stretches forth his arms widely for the good of all; the purifying waters flow for the performance of his rites and the wind plays in his surrounding region.

b) *Yādrādhyaṁ varuṇo yonimapyam*
aniśitaṁ nimiṣi jarbhurāṇaḥ,
viśvo mārtāṇḍo vrajamā paśurgāt
sthaśo janmāni savitā vyākaḥ.[41]

After sunset, when the sun closes his eyes, Varuna provides desirable places of rest to all creatures; and every bird and beast repair to their lairs when Savitri disperses them in different directions.

Surya is envisioned by the Rishis as drawn by seven coursers in a one-wheeled golden chariot.

1. *Sapta yuñjanti rathamekacakram*
eko aśvo vahati saptanāmā

trinābhi cakramajaramanarvaṁ
yatremā viśvā bhuvanādhi tasthuḥ.

2. *Imaṁ rathamadhi ye sapta tasthuḥ*
saptacakraṁ sapta vahantyaśvāḥ,
sapta svasāro abhi saṁ navante yatra
gavāṁ nihitā sapta nāma.[42]

1. They yoke the seven to the one-wheeled chariot: one horse, named *sapta* bears it along. The three-axled wheel is ageless, firm in its grip, and in it abide all the regions of the universe.

2. The seven who preside over the seven-wheeled chariot are the seven horses who draw it; seven sisters together ride in the chariot, and in it are hidden the seven forms of sacrifice.

Surya is regarded as the son of Aditi, and also of Dyaus. Ushas is described variously as the mother of Surya, as well as his wife, which has to be understood symbolically. He is 'golden-eyed, golden-headed, golden-tongued' and rides in a chariot drawn by radiant, white-footed steeds. He is the luminous leader of both the gods and the seekers. All follow him and he leads them to the world of immortality.

The Rishis implore Surya, again and again, for perfect sight — which is the truth-sight and the truth-vision — as well as for the right body-capacity to be able to function in the right way. The advent of the Sun swallows up all the barriers of *tamas* that obstruct the uninterrupted flow of the higher light and the force, and opens up the being fully to the Truth. Surya steadily mounts up to the ocean of the superconscient and brings into effective action his luminous powers making the seeker emerge into the sublimest Truth. Armed and enveloped by the consciousness-energy of Surya, the heroic sacrificer navigates successfully the many planes of existences in his high and strenuous endeavour. The flaming, mounting aspiration of the seeker combined with his persistent struggle melts down all forms of resistance and recalcitrance. And the streams of conscient-energy of the Sun charging him with their radiances uplift him into the purest heavens where Truth reigns in its fullest authority. This highest or summit realisation is not the supreme secret; the epiphany lies in the descent of these sublimest and loftiest Rays into the earth-consciousness and earth-nature, and their flooding and transformation of the physical being of the seeker-sacrificer.

a) *Cakṣurno devaḥ savitā*
cakṣurna uta parvataḥ,
cakṣurdhātā dadhātu naḥ.

Cakṣurno dhehi cakṣuṣe cakṣur
vikhyai tanūbhyaḥ,
saṁ cedaṁ vi ca paśyema.[43]

May the divine Savitri grant us sight; may Parvata bestow us vision, may Dhatri give us luminous seeing. O Sun, grant sight to our eyes; grant sight to the bodies that they may see, that we may look upon the world more widely and intimately.

b) *Vi sūryo amatiṁ na śriyaṁ sād*
orvād gavāṁ mātā jānatī gāt,
dhanvarṇaso nadyaḥ khādoarṇāḥ
sthūṇeva sumitā dṛṅhata dyauḥ.[44]

The radiant Surya spreads his splendrous form as light: hither comes from the firmament far above the Mother of Light knowing his arrival. The rivers flow breaking down their banks, and heaven is firmly fixed like a pillar that is mightily established in position.

c) *Ā sūryo aruhacchukramarṇo'yukta*
yaddharito vitapṛṣṭhāḥ,
udnā na nāvamanayanta dhīrā
āśṛṇvatīrāpo arvāgatiṣṭhan.[45]

The Sun ascends above the resplendent Waters where he yokes his wide and bright-backed horses. The worshippers draw him, like a ship, across the seas; the Waters hearing his commands have slowed down.

The Rishi invokes Surya to arise high in life and fill his being on all sides. He implores him to dispel all langour and gloom and grief, to grant him the true felicity and lead him to the goal. The far-seeing Surya is the joy of every living creature — his radiance flooding all existence. He is described as a red bird that has entered the womb of the first Father. He is the consummate form of Agni, and proclaims the auspicious hour of the sacrifice. He is brilliant and far-sighted, light-giving and ever victorious over evil.

1. *Utpurastātsūrya eti viśvadṛṣṭo adṛṣṭahā,*
adṛṣṭānt sarvāñjambhayant sarvāśca yātudhānyaḥ.

2. *Udapaptadasau sūryaḥ puru viśvāni jūrvan,*
ādityaḥ parvatebhyo viśvadṛṣṭo adṛṣṭahā.

3. *Sūrye viṣamā sajāmi dṛtiṁ*
surāvato gṛhe,
so cinnu na marāti no vayaṁ
marāmāre asya yojanaṁ
hariṣṭhā madhu tvā madhulā cakāra.[46]

1. The all-seeing Sun, the destroyer of the unseen, rises in the east driving away all the invisible enemies and evil spirits.

2. The Sun rising on high absolves all poison; he the all-seeing one who destroys the invisible enemies rises atop the mountain for the well-being of all living beings.

3. I stow all poison in the Sun, like in a leather container in the house of a spirit-vendor. Verily, the adorable Lord is immortal, and with all his powerful rays will not let us die; he will overtake the poison, and transform it into the elixir of eternal life.

At his early morning appearance the whole earth is enchanted, and all living beings held spellbound. With his arrival begins the sacrifice and all activity resumed, for he imparts light and warmth to all.

i) *Cikidvi bhāti bhāsā bṛhatāsiknīm*
eti ruśatīmapājan.

ii) *Kṛṣṇāṁ yadenīmabhi varpasā bhūj*
janayanyoṣāṁ bṛhataḥ piturjām.

iii) *Supraketairdyubhiragnirvitiṣṭhan*
ruśadbhirvarṇairabhi rāmamasthāt.[47]

1. He, the all-knowing and all-seeing shines forth with great lustre; he moves forward scattering all darkness.

2. Having overcome the darkness by his radiance, he begets dawn, the divine daughter of the great Father.

3. Placing the dawn before him, he spreads out his rays everywhere and overcomes the enveloping darkness.

Surya knows all things; at his approximation the night steals away like a thief, and men become enlightened. He is the god of gods, the supreme Light, *jyotir uttamam*.

(3)

Surya-Savitri: The Creator

The Ṡun is addressed in the Veda both as Surya and Savitri; it is supposed that Savitri refers to him when invisible, and Surya when he is visible to the worshippers. Surya and Savitri are perfectly analogous in the Veda; a few parallel hymns are cited below:

a) (i) *Surya*[b] —

Tatsūryasya devatvaṁ tanmāhitvaṁ
madhyā kartorvitataṁ saṁ jabhāra.[47a]

(ii) *Savitri* —

Punaḥ samavyadvitataṁ vayantī madhyā
kartornyadhacchakma dhīraḥ.[48]

Once more the night enwraps the earth like a woman weaving a garment.

b) (i) *Anantamanyadruśadasya pājaḥ*
kṛṣṇamanyaddharitaḥ saṁ bharanti.[49]

His rays extend his brilliant rays on the one hand, and on the other bring on the blackness of the night.

(ii) *Aśubhiścidyānvi mucāti nunam*
arīramadatamānaṁ cidetoḥ,
ahyarṣuṇāṁ cinnyayāñ aviṣyām
anu vrataṁ saviturmokyāgāt.[50]

The rapidly moving Sun is liberated by his rays, and stops the pilgrim from his journey. He restrains the activity of those desirous for combat, for night follows the setting of the Sun.

c) (i) *Ud u ṣya śaraṇe divo*
jyotirayaṁsta sūryaḥ.[51]

He, Surya, spreads his radiance aloft in the region of the heaven. He is bright like Agni when kindled and invoked with oblations.

(ii) *Ud u jyotiramṛtaṁ viśvajanyaṁ*
viśvānaraḥ savitā devo aśret.[52]

The divine Savitri, the supreme leader sends upwards his immortal, all-benefitting rays.

Savitri is eulogised in several ways, — as the creator, as the generous distributor of wealth and bestower of felicities many.

(a) *Tadinnvasya saviturnakirme*
hiraṇyayīṃamatiṁ yāmaśiśret,
ā suṣṭutī rodasī viśvaminve apīva
yoṣā janimāni vavre.[53]

No one differentiates my golden radiance from that of Savitri in which the inner self has found shelter. Delighted by the oblations the soul cherishes the all-upholding mind and body as a mother cherishes her off-spring.

b) *Udu ṣya devaḥ savitā yayāma*
hiraṇyayīṃamatiṁ yāmaśiśret,
nūnaṁ bhago havyo mānuṣebhir
vi yo ratnā puruvasurdadhāti.

Udu tiṣṭha savitaḥ śrudhyasya
hiraṇyapāne prabhṛtāvṛtasya,
vyurviṁ pṛthvīmamatiṁ sṛjāna
ā nṛbhyo marta bhojanaṁ suvānaḥ.[54]

The divine Savitri spreads his golden glow on high of which he is the shelter; verily, the gracious sun is to be adored since he abounding in treasures distributes them amongst his worshippers.

O divine Savitri, may you rise up and rejoice in our celebration of you at the sacrificial altar. While spreading light upon the earth may you bestow human enjoyment upon us.

c) *Sa ghā no devaḥ savitā sahāvā*
sāviṣadvasupatirvasuni,
viśrayamāṇo amatimurucīṁ
martabhojanamadha rāsaste naḥ.[55]

May the divine Savitri, the lord of lustre, empowered with infinite energy bestow upon us wealth manifold; may he advancing high, grant us felicities that make us happy.

d) *Urdhvā yasyāmatirbhā adidyutatsavīmani,*
hiraṇyapāṇiramimīta sukratuḥ kṛpātsvaḥ.[56]

The divine Savitri, possessor of sublime splendour, whose all-pervading and all-conquering effulgence is manifest in the universe, — the most active and effective force amongst all, — makes the world luminous and energetic.

Savitri spreading his golden rays illumines the entire universe.

Sūryaraśmirharikeśaḥ purastātsavitā
jyotirudayāñ ajasram...[57]

Savitri, the golden-rayed god, the yellow-haired one, sends up continuously, without any break, his undying light from the east.

He unites himself with the sun's rays; the sun is considered the bird of Surya-Savitri.

Suparṇo aṅga saviturgarutmānpūrvo
jātaḥ sa u asyānu dharma.[58]

All the divine powers accrue from this bright-winged Garutman (the Sun) strictly following the Law.

Savitri impels the sun, and nourishes him, *ahorātravyavasthānakāraṇaṃ bhagavān raviḥ.*[59] Agni Vaishwanara and Surya are essentially the same.[60]

Savitri occupies a unique place *vis-à-vis* the gods. He confers immortality upon them.

a) *Devebhyo hi prathamaṁ yajñiyebhyo*
'mṛtatvaṁ suvasi bhagamuttamam.[61]

O Savitri, you grant the gift of immortality to the adorable gods.

b) *Indrajyeṣṭhān brihadbhyaḥ parvatebhyaḥ*
kshayām̐ ebhyaḥ suvasi pastyāvataḥ.[62]

Verily, you elevate those of whom Indra is the chief, above the vast clouds; for the worshippers you provide radiant residences.

c) *Vi hotrā dadhe vayunāvideka inmahi*
devasya savituḥ pariṣṭutiḥ.[63]

He (Savitri) alone knowing the functions of the worshippers directs them; verily, great is his glory.

d) *Nūnaṁ devebhyo vi hi dhāti ratnam*
athābhajadvītihotraṁ svastau.[64]

Verily, he (Savitri) grants manifold wealth to the worshippers; may he give prosperity to those who offer oblations.

In Savitri rejoice all the gods; all the gods follow him.

a) *Abhi yaṁ devyaditirgṛṇāti savaṁ*
devasya saviturjuṣaṇā,
abhi samrājo varuṇo gṛṇantyābhi
mitrāso aryamā sajoṣāḥ.[65]

He whom the divine Aditi glorifies at his birth, whom the great gods Varuna, Mitra and Aryaman constantly adore is Savitri.

b) *Na yasyendro varuṇo na mitro vratam*
aryamā na minanti rudraḥ

nārātayastamidaṁ svasti huve
devaṁ savitāraṁ namobhiḥ.[66]

I invoke to this sacrificial place that divine Savitri whose law neither the gods Indra, Varuna, Mitra, Rudra and Aryaman violate, nor their enemies contravene.

c) *Ye savituḥ satyasavasya viśve*
mitrasya vrate varuṇasya devāḥ.[67]

May the gods, custodians of the eternal laws of Savitri, and Mitra and Varuna bestow on us felicities many. May the supreme creator grant us enlightened progeny and cattle and the capacity for spiritual deeds.

d) *Devebhirnaḥ savitā prāvatu śrutaṁ*
ā sarvatātimaditiṁ vṛṇīmahe.[68]

May the supreme impeller along with the other gods hear us and protect us. We adore the all-pervading Aditi.

In the legend of the Ribhus, Savitri is referred to as *dāsvāṁs*; he is the great sacrificer as well as the god-impeller.

a) *Saudhanvanā ṛbhavaḥ sūracakṣasa*
saṁvatsare samapṛcyanta dhītibhiḥ.[69]

O sons of Sudhanvan, through the plenitude of your penance you have come to the sacrificial hall of the creator Savitri.

b) *Hiraṇyapāṇiḥ savitā sujihvastnirā*
divo vidathe patyamānaḥ,
deveṣu ca savitaḥ ślokamaśrer
ādasmabhyamā suva sarvatātim.[70]

The sweet-voiced, golden-hued Savitri descends from above thrice daily at the assemblies of devotees; may he accept the laudations of the worshippers and fulfil their aspirations.

c) *Ya imā viśvā jatānyāśrāvayati śḷokena,*
pra ca suvāti savitā.[71]

Savitri is the one who gives life to all and inspires them, and proclaims his glory through the sacred hymns.

d) *Asme indro varuṇo mitro aryamā*
dyumnaṁ yachantu mahi śarma saprathaḥ,
avadhraṁ jyotiraditerṛtāvṛdho
devasya ślokaṁ saviturmanāmahe.[72]

May all the gods Indra, Varuna, Mitra and Aryaman grant us wealth and luminous residency; may the light of Aditi augment our sacrifice and be helpful to us. May we always recite the praises of Savitri, the divine creator.

The Rishis, again and again, refer to the sacrificial activities of Surya-Savitri in the following hymns:

a) *Veda yastrīṇi vidathānyeṣāṁ devānaṁ*
janma sanutarā ca vipraḥ.[73]

He the sun-divine knows the three cognizable worlds; he, the sage, also knows the birth and growth of the gods abiding in those worlds.

b) *Sujyotiṣaḥ sūrya dakṣapitṛn,*
anāgastve sumaho vīhi devān...[74]

O radiant Surya, may you render the luminous gods of divine origin, born of Daksha, void of offence towards us.

c) *Tava tridhātu pṛthivī uta dyaur*
vaiśvānara vratamagne sacanta.[75]

O Vaisvanara Agni, both the earth and the heaven, join together in worshipping you.

There are several hymns dedicated to Surya, his oblations and his sacrifices:

a) *Ā na ilābhirvidathe suśasti*
viśvānaraḥ savitā deva etu,
api yathā yuvāno matsathā no viśvaṁ
jagadabhipitve manīṣā.[76]

May the divine Savitri, the benefactor of all, come graciously to our sacrifice together with the other gods; may he gladden the worshippers by his presence.

b) *Prati prayāṇamasurasya vidvān*
suktairdevaṁ savitāraṁ duvasya...[77]

Conscious of the coming of the divine creator Savitri, the dispeller of darkness, may you worship him with holy hymns.

c) *Udīraya kavitamaṁ kavīnām*
unattainamabhi madhvā ghṛtena,
sa no vasuni prayatā hitāni
candrāṇi devaḥ savitā suvāti.[78]

Celebrate him who is the sage among sages with adoration, invest him with libation; may the divine creator Savitri bestow upon the devotees all delightful treasures.

d) *Devaṁ naraḥ savitāraṁ viprā*
yajñaiḥ suvṛktibhiḥ,
namasyanti dhiyeṣitāḥ.[79]

Devout and intelligent men, urged by innate wisdom worship the divine Savitri with sacred hymns and perform sacrifices.

e) *Doṣo gāya bṛhadgāya dyumaddhehi*
ātharvaṇa stuhi devaṁ savitāram.[80]

Sing, O wise men, all the time through night and day, sing of the divine creator Savitri, realise the splendid self and praise his splendour.

Savitri not only makes the *ṛta* but also is responsible for 'the orderly recurrence of natural phenomena'. He rules the course of events as well as the sacrifices with a fixed decree.

a) *Ṛtaṁ devāya kṛṇvate savitra indrāyāh*
ighne na ramanta āpaḥ,
aharaharyātyakturapāṁ kiyaty
ā prathamaḥ sarga āsām.[81]

To the divine Savitri, the creator of the Law, and to Indra the slayer of the serpent-demon flow the waters uninterruptedly; who knows at what period of time were they first dedicated.

b) *Adābhyo bhuvanāni pracākaśad*
vratāni devaḥ savitābhi rakṣate,
prāsrāgbāhu bhuvanasya prajābhyo
dhṛtavrato maho ajmasya rājati.[82]

Savitri, the divine creator, unhampered illumines the regions and protects the righteous acts. Unrestrained he helps the people of the earth, and with fixed decree he rules the wide world.

The Atharva-veda describes Surya as the 'overlord of sight', and the Rig-veda qualifies him as the 'wide-visioned one', *urucakṣas*. The Rishi sees a close link between Surya and Soma; Soma is said to generate Surya and help him to illuminate human consciousness. He 'produces' Surya in the midst of mortals for the sustenance of *ṛta* and for attaining the supreme state of immortality.

a) *Suryaścakṣusamadhipatiḥ sa māvatu*
asminbrahmaṇyasmin
karmaṇyasyāṁ purodhāyamasyāṁ
pratiṣṭhāyāmasyām[83]

Surya, the illuminer, is the overlord of sight; may he protect me in the attainment of knowledge, in all my life's acts and sacerdotal undertakings.

b) *Śaṁ naḥ sūrya urucakṣā udetu śaṁ*
naścatasraḥ pradiśo bhavantu.[84]

May the wide-visioned Sun rise for our happiness; may the four quarters exist for our felicity and be auspicious to us.

c) *Divo rukma urucakṣā udeti*
dūrearthastaraṇirbhrājamānaḥ.[85]

The bright and splendorous sun, effulgent and lustrous, rises from the firmament and traverses across the heavens spreading light.

d) *Ajījano hi pavamāna sūryaṁ vidhāre*
śakmanā payaḥ.[86]

O Pavamana, by your might, you have generated the sun in the skies.

e) *Ajījano amṛta martyeṣvāṅ ṛtasya*
dharmannamṛtasya caruṇaḥ.[87]

O immortal Soma, you have generated the Sun amongst mortals above the region of auspicious clouds that bear water.

There are several hymns in the Rig veda which speak of Soma 'mounting on Surya's chariot', Soma journeying with Surya in the sky and ascend the heavens, as well as Soma 'donning the splendour of the Sun'.

a) *Ā sūryasya bṛhato bṛhannādhi rathaṁ*
viṣvañcamaruhadvicakṣaṇaḥ.[88]

The great Soma, beholder of all, mounts the mighty Sun's chariot which traverses everywhere.

b) *Eṣa sūryamarocayat pavamāno vicarṣāṇiḥ,*
viśvā dhāmāni viśvavit.[89]

The purified, all-contemplating and all-knowing Soma gives radiance to the Sun and to all the spheres.

c) *Adhi dyāmasthādvṛṣabho vicakṣaṇo*
'rūrucadvi divo rocanā kaviḥ.[90]

The supreme showerer and great beholder takes his station in the heavens; he, the seer, illumines the luminaries of heaven.

d) *Tvaṁ kavirabhavo devavītama*
ā sūryaṁ rohayo divi.[91]

O Soma, you are a seer most devoted to the gods; you have made the Sun mount the sky.

e) *Sa sūryasya raśmibhiḥ pari vyata*
tantuṁ tanvānastrivṛtaṁ yathā vide.[92]

Soma invests himself with the radiances of the Sun for his garment, stretching out the triple thread in the way he is familiar with.

The Sama-veda variously describes Savitri as the all-pervading god, the giver of salvation, the remover of ignorance and the enjoyer of Soma-wine.

a) *Mo ṣu tvā vāghataśca nāre*
asmanni rīraman
ārāttādvā sadhamādaṅ na ā gahīha
vā sannupa śrudhi.

Ime hi te brahmakṛtaḥ su te sacā
madhau na makṣa āsate
indre kāmaṁ jaritāro vasūyavo
rathe na pādamā dadhuḥ.[93]

O adorable God, let not the learned ones lure you away from us; rather they should sing praises to bring you closer to us. O all-pervading lord, verily, you are always near us; may you come to our sacrifices, and abiding within us hear our ardent prayers.

O radiant God, the wise ones flock to you for salvation even as the honey-bees sit on honey; they hanker after soul-realisation and focus on you just as warriors eager for wealth and conquest set their foot on their chariots.

b) *Maghonaḥ sma vṛtrahatyeṣu*
codaya ye dadati priyā vasu,
tava praṇītī haryaśva sūribhirviśvā
tarema duritā.[94]

O effulgent God, supreme dispeller of darkness, the wise ones give up their wealth for salvation according to the laws prescribed by scriptures. May we with their help overcome all limitations.

c) *Ka īṁ veda sute sacā pibantaṁ*
kadvayo dadhe
ayaṁ yaḥ puro vibhinatyojasā
mandānaḥ śiprayandhasaḥ.[95]

Who can see Savitri enjoying the Soma-wine along with the other gods; who knows how long will he continue to do? Fully satisfied with drinking the elixir, he breaks down the resistance of dark clouds.

The Yajur-veda is equally eloquent in the praise of Savitri as the noblest among the noble, the most excellent light, imperishable and immortal, and the supreme strength, mental and spiritual.

1. *Udvayaṁ tamasaspari svaḥ*
paśyanta uttaram,
devaṁ devatrā sūryamaganma
jyotiruttamam.

2. *Edho'sydhiṣīmahi samidasi*
tejo'si tejo mayi dhehi

3. *Yāvatī dyāvāpṛthivī yāvacca*
sapta sindhavo vitasthire,
tāvantamindra te grahamūrjā
gṛhṇāmyakṣitaṁ mayi gṛhṇāmyakṣitam.

4. *Mayi tyadindriyaṁ bṛhanmayi*
dakṣo mayi kratuḥ,
gharmastriśugvi rājati virājā jyotiṣā
saha brahmaṇa tejasā saha.[96]

1. May we look upon Savitri most intently who is free from darkness, highest of all and the noblest among the noble — the highest light; worshipping him likewise may we attain to the highest felicity.

2. O radiant God, you who ever shine in our souls, you who are like a bright burning flame and the great illuminator of minds, grant us your light for perfect progress.

3. O effulgent God, spread wide as heaven and earth, wide-extended like the seven seas, may we take joyously your supreme power of perseverance, may we imbibe your imperishable strength.

4. O lustrous lord, our sacrificial fire shines with your triple light and helpful felicity. May your effulgent force illumine our minds,

strengthen our souls and effectuate our activity.

Life is not an insipid, meaningless affair, nor is it a mere two-dimensional flat phenomenon. It is a living and creative symbol opening on the Infinite and the Eternal. It is a progressive actualization of consciousness and bliss, force and freedom. It is a joyous interplay between gods and men leading towards the Truth. Savitri is the great blender of the human and the divine, the supreme integrator and harmoniser of the finite and the infinite. He vouchsafes to the sacrificer the wealth of Immortality and infinite peace.

1. *Hvāyamyagniṁ prathamaṁ svastaye*
   hvayāmi mitrāvaruṇāvihāvase,
hvayāmi rātrīṁ jagato niveśanīṁ
   hvayāmi devaṁ savitāramūtaye.

2. *Ā kṛṣṇena rajasā vartamāno niveśayann*
   amṛtaṁ martyaṁ ca,
hiraṇyayena savitā rathenā devo
   yāti bhuvanāni paśyan.

3. *Yāti devaḥ pravatā yatyudvatā*
   yāti śubhrābhyaṁ yajato haribhyām,
ā devo yāti savitā parāvato 'pa
   viśvā duritā badhamānaḥ.

4. *Abhīvṛtaṁ kṛśanairviśvarūpaṁ*
   hiraṇyaśamyaṁ yajato bṛhantam,
āsthādrathaṁ savitā citrabhānuḥ kṛṣṇā
   rajāṅsi taviṣīṁ dadhānaḥ.

5. *Vi jānañchyāvāḥ śitipādo akhyan*
   rathaṁ hiraṇyapraugaṁ vahantaḥ,
śaśvadviśaḥ saviturdaivyasyopasthe
   viśvā bhuvanāni tasthuḥ.

6. *Tisro dyāvaḥ saviturdvā upasthāñ*
   ekā yamasya bhuvane viraṣāt,
āṇiṁ na rathyamamṛtādhi tasthur
   iha bravitu ya u tacciketat.

7. *Vi suparṇo antarikṣāṇyakhyad*
gabhīravepā asuraḥ sunithaḥ,
kvedānīṁ sūryaḥ kaściketa katamāṁ
dyāṁ raśmirasyā tatāna.

8. *Aṣṭau vyakhyatkakubhaḥ pṛthivyās*
trī dhanva yojanā sapta sindhun,
hiraṇyākṣaḥ savitā deva āgāddadhad
ratnā dāśuṣe varyāṇi.

9. *Hiraṇyapāṇiḥ savitā vicarṣaṇirubhe*
dyāvāpṛthivī antarīyate,
apāmīvāṁ bādhate veti sūryamabhi
kṛṣṇena rajasā dyāmṛṇoti.

10. *Hiraṇyahasto asuraḥ sunithaḥ sumṛlīkaḥ*
svavāñ yātvarvāṅ,
apasedhanrakṣaso yātudhānānasthād
devaḥ pratidoṣaṁ gṛṇānaḥ.

11. *Ye te panthāḥ savitaḥ pūrvyāso*
'reṇavaḥ sukṛtā antarikṣe,
tebhirno adya pathibhiḥ sugebhī
rakṣā ca no adhi ca bruhi deva.[97]

1. I invoke first Agni for our well-being; I then invoke Mitra and Varuna for help, and the Night that it may bring rest to the world. And I invoke Savitri for manifold prosperity.

2. The radiant lord, springing through the dark regions advances in his golden chariot, and awakening both mortals and immortals, he directs his gaze on several worlds.

3. Worthy of worship, the divine Savitri, pursues his path, first upward and then downward with two resplendent horses; he comes from the ends of the earth removing all sorrow and every sin.

4. The many-rayed effulgent Savitri with power to dispel all darkness comes mounted on his mighty chariot decorated with pearls and poles of gold.

5. Harnessed to his chariot with a golden yoke, the two white-hoofed horses of Savitri have manifested light to mankind; all beings, men and creatures abide in the close presence of the divine creator.

6. There are three heavens: two in the proximity of Savitri and the third leading to the realm of Yama. Immortality depends upon Savitri as a chariot on its axle. Let those who understand this truth declare it to others.

7. The well-winged solar bird in heavens, deep quivering, life-bestowing and the perfect guide illumines the three regions. Where now is Savitri, who knows to what sphere his rays have extended?

8. He has lighted up the earth's eight peaks, its three regions of living beings and the seven rivers. May the golden-eyed god, Savitri, come here bestowing upon his worshippers wondrous wealth.

9. The gold-handed, skilful Savitri travels between the two regions of heaven and earth. He conquers diseases, and directing the sun, finally overspreads the sky, extending from the darksome space to the luminous regions.

10. May the golden-handed, life-bestowing, well-guiding, gracious god and kind leader be present here at our sacrifice. May he chase away both demons and sorcerers — the *Rakshasas* and *the Yatudhanas*.

11. Your ancient paths, O Savitri, are prepared of old and dust-free, and well-established in the vaults of heaven. Come to us by these paths, O Lord, protect us from the Enemy and bless us.

Savitri, the resplendent Sun and the unique vivifier, is the generous dispenser of all gifts. He dwells in the ocean of golden light above and dispels all the darkness here, elsewhere and everywhere. He, the refulgent one, is the giver of life and the origin of all creation. He sustains all activity, both individual and cosmic. It is in accordance with his movement and in communion with him that the seekers worship Savitri. The value of Savitri for the lives of men, and for the attainment of life's object is immeasurable and inestimable. He is the destroyer of the adversaries, and conqueror of all affliction and infirmity.

Ā cittī yaccakṛmā daivye jane
dīnairdakṣaiḥ prabhutī puruṣatvatā,
deveṣu ca savitarmānuṣeṣu ca tvaṁ
no atra suvatādanāgasaḥ.[98]

If through ignorance, pride or any omission we have committed any offence against you, O divine Savitri, or against any god or common man, may you out of your compassion absolve us from this culpability.

Savitri is described as the golden-eyed and golden-handed god riding in a chariot of gold. The gifts that life offers to man are many; among them are the experience of beauty, the realization of happiness, the recognition of a sublime ideal and the comprehension of an all-embracing divine reality within and without. Life itself is a mysterious flow of expanding awareness in accordance with an inscrutable and numinous figure which we baptize as Time. This unnameable, yet concrete experience is simultaneous with another that bears enough dependable intuitional evidence; it is the inward intimacy of the mentally incomprehensible Timeless. The two not only are commensurate with each other but coalesce into the golden body of the superconscient Truth.

Savitri, the illuminator and increaser, divinises the human in us; he is the radiant god who not only shows the way to the Truth but also journeys with us constantly nourishing us with the light and joy of the Truth. He is the friend and father of the seeker-pilgrim; he extends his golden arms to embrace all living creatures and all of the universe.

1. *Udu shya devaḥ savitā hiraṇyayā bāhu*
ayaṅsta savanāya sukratuḥ,
ghṛtena pānī abhi pruṣṇute makho
yuvā sudakṣo rajaso vidharmaṇi.

2. *Devasya vayaṁ savituḥ savīmani*
śreṣthe syāma vasunaśca dāvane,
yo viśvasya dvipado yaścatuṣpado
niveśane prasave cāsi bhūmanaḥ.

3. *Adabdhebhiḥ savitaḥ payubhiṣtvaṁ*
śivebhiradya pari pāhi no gayaṁ,
hiraṇyajihvaḥ suvitāya navyase rakṣā
mākirno aghaśaṅsa iśata.

4. *Udu shya devaḥ savitā damunā*
hiraṇyapāṇiḥ pratidoṣamasthāt,
ayohanuryajato mandrajihva ā
dāśuṣe suvati bhūri vāmam.

5. *Udu ayañ upavakteva bāhu*
hiraṇyayā savitā supratīkā,
divo rohansyaruhatpṛthivyā arīramat
patayat kaccidabhvam.

6. *Vāmamadya savitarvāmamu śvo*
divedive vāmamasmabhyaṁ sāvīḥ,
vamasya hi kṣayasya deva bhūrer
ayā dhiyā vāmabhājaḥ syāma.[99]

1. The divine Savitri extends his golden arms in potent blessing towards the sacrificer: like a youthful, sagacious priest he stretches out his hands filled with water in the service of the world.

2. May we enjoy the vitalizing force of Savitri, the divine creator, and may he grant us worthy riches. For he is the absolute procreator and perpetuator of all living beings that move on two feet or on four.

3. May the Lord of illumination with his never-failing powers of protection provide security to our dwellings and confer enduring happiness. May the golden-tongued god be vigilant and keep us always on the right path; let no calumniator have power to harm us.

4. May the divine and munificent Savitri, golden-handed and sweet-tongued, the adorable friend of our abodes and benevolent bestower of gifts galore, impart desirable gifts to the worshippers.

5. May the divine Savitri, like a priest in meditation stretch forth his

golden arms so beautiful to behold; he has ascended the heights of both heaven and earth, and moving along delights everything that exists.

6. O Lord of radiances, grant us favours today and tomorrow, and day by day; you are the benevolent giver of wealth, enrich us daily by your ample grace, and grant us graceful living. May we by your worship become partakers of your grace.

Savitri is the great inspirer-propeller and rejuvenator, as well as a prolific progenitor. He not only illumines the physical but impels the spiritual. He awakens us to the secret truth of us all, and begets a new consciousness in us. He brings to the seeker-strivers perennial streams of light from the luminous ocean above, *ṛtasya dhārāḥ*, and leads them to the apex experience of the Truth. Savitri is always with the seeker-sacrificer; he is in his eyes, in his own inner being, helping him to enjoy the fullness of the Truth-vision which he so lavishly donates to the devotee.

Savitri is the upholder as well as the promoter of the cosmic order, *ṛtam*. He is the lord of all that moves and of all that moves not. He is the revealer, observer and realiser of all.

a) *Rāyo budhnaḥ saṅgamano vasunāṁ*
viśvā rūpābhi caṣṭe sacībhiḥ,
devaiva savitā satyadharmendro na
tasthau samare dhanānām.[100]

He is the source of all treasures, the procurer of all wealth, who illumines all forms; he, the divine Savitri, the divine impeller, whose attribute is Truth stands like the supreme lord Indra in the battle for riches.

b) *Uteśiṣe prasavasya tvameka iduta*
pūṣā bhavasi deva yāmābhiḥ,
utedaṁ viśvaṁ bhuvanaṁ vi rājasi
śyāvāśvaste savitaḥ stomamānaśe.[101]

You alone rule over the lives of all living beings, O Savitri; you are Pushan by your divine movements, you are sovereign over the whole world. The great. active devotee Shyavashwa offers you praise, O creator.

Savitri raises the truth of two-dimensional existence into the glory and splendour of the truth of multi-dimensional existence by flooding the seeker with his blessings.

Asmabhyaṁ taddivo adbhyaḥ prithivyās
tvayā dattaṁ kāmyaṁ rādha ā gāt,
śaṁ yatstotṛbhya āpaye bhāvaty
uruśaṁsāya savitarjaritre.[102]

May that desirable wealth, which is granted to us, O Savitri, by you, come to us from above, from the waters and from the earth; may that continue to be a source of celestial happiness to those who worship you and to their friends.

He is the lord of all felicities; he fills the pilgrim-soul with infinite light and force and joy to be able to embrace the universe and participate in its secret workings. The *Maitri Upanishad* speaks of Surya-Savitri as the lord of incarnate time and the begetter of the universe.

Athanyatrapy uktam: annam va asya sarvasya yonih, kalas cannasya, suryo yonih kalasya... dve vava brahmano rupe kalas cakalas catha yah prag adityat so'kalo' kalo'tha ya adityad yah sa kalah... vigrahavan esa kalah sindhu-rajah prajanam, esa tatsthahsavitakhyo yasmad eveme candra-rksa-graha-samvatsaradayah suyante...[103]

"And thus it has been said elsewhere: Food, verily is the source of this whole (world), and time of food, and the Sun is the source of time... There are verily two forms of Brahman, time and the timeless. That which is prior to the Sun is the timeless, without parts. But that which begins with (has a beginning from) the Sun is time, which has parts... This embodied (incarnate) time is the great ocean of creatures. In it abides he who is called Savitṛ (the Sun as begetter) from whom, indeed, are begotten the moon, stars, planets, the year and the rest."[c]

Savitri brings to the world both peace and joy.

Śaṁ no vāto vātu śaṁ nastapatu sūryaḥ,
ahāni śaṁ bhavantu naḥ śaṁ rātri prati
dhīyatām śamuṣā no vyu'cchatu.[104]

May the wind breathe on us joy, may the Sun warm us in a joyous way, may the days pass with joy, may the nights bear manifold joy and peace, and may the Dawn break bringing joy for us.

(4)

Swar and Surya

Swar and Surya are closely connected in the Vedic vision of Reality. The substance of Swar-loka is the light of Surya. Surya is the sun who "represents the illumination of the *ṛtam* rising upon the mind," whereas "Swar is that *plane* of mental consciousness which directly receives the illumination."[105] Surya is extolled as the most wise and the illumined, *vipra*; he enlightens the mind with the illuminations of Truth-Consciousness. He is the Light of the Truth; he is *satyam ṛtam bṛhat* — the True, the Right, the Vast, the world of Swar. This Truth is withheld from humanity in the secret cave of the subconscient. On the supramental plane existence, consciousness and bliss are infinite and free, and are not enclosed or limited by the circumscribing realms of the mental and the physical. Here, the Truth enjoys unhorizoned vastness and 'equal bliss of existence'. This fear-free wideness and luminous vastness is also the essential truth of being, *satyam*. Whereas *ṛtam* is the active truth of being. Just as *svadharma* flows out of *svabhāva*, the active truth *ṛtam* wells out of the essential truth of being, *satyam*. At the supramental level there is no division between consciousness and force, knowledge and will. *Ṛtam,* says Sri Aurobindo, "is a supreme truth of movement, action, manifestation, an infallible truth of will and heart and knowledge, a perfect truth of thought and word and emotion; it is the spontaneous Right, the free Law, the original divine order of things untouched by the falsehoods of the divided and separative consciousness."[106] And Surya symbolizes this Truth, and the Rishis aspire to enter this world of Truth which is the body of Surya. This paradise of divine Light, the world of Swar is a formation of Aditi. The gods too are the many other formations of the Mother of infinite Light manifested in the active truth of her measureless movement, *ṛtam,* who guard the paradise against chaos and corruption.

Surya, the great seer, the luminous thinker-son of Aditi, whose vision is vast and limitless helps the seekers to transcend all limitations of mind and body, and carries them across all barriers to the luminous world of beatitude and immortality. "He is the light of the Truth", observes Sri Aurobindo, "rising on the human consciousness in the wake of the divine

Dawn."[107] And Dawn herself "is the constant opening out of the divine light upon the human being",[108] and the endless pouring out of the spiritual treasures of a golden heaven into the bowels of earthly existence — the wealth of light, power and joy.

Surya is repeatedly hymned in the Veda as the supreme Creator, the great Increaser and the luminous Revealer; he is the envisioner and creator, Twashtri the Fashioner of things and Pushan the Increaser. He liberates the human mind from the limited egoistic consciousness and enlarges it by removing from its movement the imposition of individual preoccupation. He is *bṛhat,* the Large, as well as *vipaścit*, the one absolutely clear in perception. His illumination is characterised by clarity, certitude and discernment; his enlargement is neither vague nor confused, he does not lose awareness of the truth of totality, its parts and their relatedness. He dissolves all the obscurity and inaccuracy of thought by exposing it to his Light and transforms them into its relative truths. He is the one who looses forth into manifestation that which 'is hidden in infinite Existence'. "Luminous vision and luminous creation are the two functions of Surya. He is Surya the creator and he is Surya the revealing vision, the all-seer",[109] observes Sri Aurobindo. Surya is 'the burning light and truth of the infinite Being', His 'infinite self-vision', and Agni is "seer-will, the omniscient creative force and flaming omnipotence of that self-vision."[110] Agni is rather the active or dynamic aspect of the self-conscious supramental Truth, and Surya the passive aspect. The supramental Truth-consciousness which is the supreme source and spring of all-creation manifests itself in this inferior world of Darkness and Inconscience as Surya Savitri so as to increasingly dissolve and transform it, and suffuse it with the illimitable harmony and light of the divine worlds. All the worlds of manifestation are envisioned and 'loosed out' of Surya, and formed and effectuated by Agni.

The Truth-Consciousness unlike the human mind is a divine faculty. With a view to remove the deformations and limitations of the human mind and to lead it increasingly to its own divine nature the Truth-Consciousness presents itself at the phenomenal level in a diluted and modulated manner so that it could be received, understood and accepted by the limited mentality. "Therefore the rays of Surya, as they labour to form our mental existence, create three successive worlds of mentality one superimposed on the other, — the sensational, aesthetic and emotional mind, the pure intellect and the divine intelligence. The fullness and perfection of these triple worlds of mind exists only in the pure mental plane of being, where they shine above the three heavens, *tisro divaḥ*, as their three luminosities, *trīṇi rocanāni*. But their light descends upon the physical consciousness and effects the corresponding formations in its realms, the Vedic *pārthivāni rajāṅsi*, earthly realms of light. They also are triple, *tisraḥ pṛthivīḥ*, the three earths. And of all these worlds Surya Savitri is the creator."[111] Each psychological level is considered by the Vedic Rishi as a world by itself. "The human individual", observes Sri Aurobindo, "is an organised unit of existence which reflects the constitution of the universe. It repeats in itself the same arrangement of states and play of forces. Man, subjectively, contains in himself all the worlds in which, objectively, he is contained."[112] The Rishis therefore speak of the physical consciousness as the physical world, *bhūr,* and the mental consciousness as heaven, *dyau*. Whereas the vital consciousness is named *antarikṣa*, *bhuvar* — the manifold creative existences that constitute the Earth. In the Vedic context a world is essentially a formation of consciousness. "A world is a *loka,* a way in which conscious being images itself. And it is the causal Truth, represented in the person of Surya Savitri, that is the creator of all its forms. For it is the causal Idea in the infinite being, — the idea, not abstract, but real and dynamic, — that originate the law, the energies, the formations of things and the working out of their potentialities in determined forms by determined processes. Because the causal Idea is a real force of existence, it is called *satyam,* the True in being; because it is the determining truth of all activity and formation, it is called *ṛtam*, the True in movement; because it is broad and infinite in its self-view, in its scope and in its operation, it is called *bṛhat*, the Large or Vast."[113]

Surya Savitri is the creator in the sense that it loosens forth, as mentioned earlier, or rather brings out by a process of self-concentration of its own consciousness, that which is hidden in it. "The action of the causal Idea does not fabricate, but brings out by Tapas, by the pressure of consciousness on its own being, that which is concealed in it, latent in potentiality and in truth already existent in the Beyond."[114]

The happenings in the physical world or its functionings are inadequate and imperfect reflections of the truths in the supraphysical. It is these truths and processes that govern the inner life of man and its development. The Vedic Rishis were aware of these forces and truths, and evolved a concrete symbolic language that satisfied the common men as well as the initiates. "The solar energy is the physical form of Surya", Sri Aurobindo makes it clear, "Lord of Light and Truth; it is through the Truth that we arrive at Immortality, final aim of the Vedic discipline. It is therefore under the images of the Sun and its rays, of Dawn and day and night and the life of man between the two poles of light and darkness that the Aryan seers represent the progressive illumination of the human soul."[115]

Surya Savitri brings forth from the divine consciousness, *Aditi,* the many worlds in accordance with the conditions of the *ṛtam* governing the respective worlds. Standing between the Goddess of infinite being and the manifold worlds he receives into the *Vijñāna* all things that are ideated to come into existence, and puts each into its right place in the divine cadence by its all-perceptive knowledge.

It is in the acme of the unified vision of the all of Surya Savitri that both the seer and creator meet. The light of Surya is seen ascending to its own home in the Truth, which in the process confers the divine vision to the seeker. This vast vision of Surya is described by the Rishis as "the eye of the infinite Wideness and the infinite Harmony",[116] with which all things are seen as forms of the one infinite Aditi. And this new-seeing of all things and all the worlds as the innumerable bodies of the bodiless infinite Being is indeed a new creation. This is characterized as the coming into the seeker of the Truth-existence which removes from the seeker all ignorance and limitation.

Surya is the illuminative power of Truth, and Savitri is his own creative power; he brings into manifestation all the worlds out of the Unmanifest. He manifests the three luminous worlds of the higher heaven in the seeker, and builds in his human existence the formations of divine consciousness and existence. He helps man to realise the universal in the individual and become the Infinite in his finite existence. Surya thus embodies the human and the divine with a creative *nisus* that helps man's growth into the epiphany of the gods, and eventually into the world of Truth, Immortality, Beatitude. Of Surya, Sri Aurobindo observes, "He is the light of Truth rising on the human consciousness in the wake of the divine Dawn whom he pursues as a lover follows after his beloved and he treads the paths she has traced for him. For Dawn the daughter of Heaven, the face or power of Aditi, is the constant opening out of the divine light upon the human being; she is the coming of the spiritual riches, a light, a power, a new birth, the pouring out of the golden treasure of heaven into his earthly existence. Surya means the illumined or the luminous, as also the illumined thinker is called *Suri*... Luminous vision and luminous creation are the two functions of Surya. He is Surya the creator and he is Surya the revealing vision, the all-seer."[117]

The Rig-veda speaks of an eternal succession of the dawns,[118] — an unending procession of the shining sun-rises, of the repeated returns of Surya, — of the accessions of Pushan and his piloting and guidance on the upward journey. The Rishi's vision of Savitri sums up the truth of the Vedic experiences. Savitri awakens 'some one' who is immanent within us, widens our consciousness and sets us there where the earlier seekers have preceded us. He brings into conscious consonance the harmonies of the dawns that have shone before with the immeasurable felicities of those that now must succeed. It is the splendour of this divine Creator that the Rishi contemplated. It is towards this luminous consummation and denouement that Savitri impels the seeker, and it is on the divine delight of this omniscient Creator and his varied formulations that the seeker must deliberate with deep devotion as he proceeds on the great journey.

Aditi, the infinitely creative Power of the Infinite, formulates the divine Word in her unitive Consciousness; it is the Word of the superconscient Truth that stands revealed only on the peaks of the seeker's ascension. Which implies that we must arise beyond the phenomenal domain of falsehood, limitation, division and death to be able to experience the perennial light and bliss and vastness and freedom of the world of the Truth. For life immortal we have therefore to submit and surrender ourselves totally and unreservedly and perfectly to the God of the Sun-Truth, and always look for his guidance; for the Word full of infinite and consummate and purest perception we have to bring forward the Truth concealed in us and consciously and constantly offer it to the ever new Creator, Savitri. For, it is this Mighty One who has the vastest knowledge, the supreme Word and the omnipotence to create the world of immortality and lasting bliss for both the gods and the seekers. A wide receptivity to the light of Savitri is necessary to be emancipated from the lower states of life and released into the higher. Varuna liberates us from sin and evil, Mitra strengthens the bonds of friendship and love with the higher states of consciousness in his all-embracing harmony, and Savitri new-creates us and grants us the increasing wideness of divine existence. Savitri nurses and furthers our knowledge with the active collaboration of the other gods and leads us towards their cosmic formations in the unitive and undistracted consciousness of the supreme Aditi. He removes from us all limitation and sin, ignorance and division, for he is the creator of the Truth, the Right, the Vast in us.

For the creation and establishment of the Truth in us the physical, the vital and the mental have to be consciously widened in their substance and made receptive to the working of Savitri in us. Mitra and Varuna support Savitri in the creation of such a state of consciousness leading to the building up the universal form of our being — "the universal form which he creates for us when with hands of golden light, with the tongue that tastes the wine of Sweetness he moves in the triple knowledge of the highest heaven of Truth, attains in the gods to the divine rhythm which he creates for his accomplished Law and takes up his abode in that golden strength of his, the Seer robed in light who first stretched out his two arms of knowledge and power to create the world. He who as Twashtri the Fashioner of things attended always by the male godheads and their female energies, powers of Purusha and powers of Prakriti, made and makes all things, shall as Savitri create for man the thinker born in a body that Truth and Immortality."[119]

Surya is the cast and conformation of this supreme vision; he is the visioned force of the supramental Truth, the wide-seeing vision of Mitra and Varuna. He is the seer with 'the triple knowledge' of the gods and their eternal births, who with his Truth-vision and Truth-force destroys the children of Darkness and sustains the sons of Light. He is not only the far-seeing eye of the gods but also the speaker of the supreme Word and the mover and mobilizer 'of the illumined and illuminating thought'. The *Gayatri mantra* most effectively epitomizes and crystallises the supreme light and creative power of Surya Savitri.

(5)

In the Upanishads and the Epics

The seed of spiritual truth contained in the Veda is found evolved later on in the Upanishads. The Vedic quest for Truth, Light, Immortality finds its echo in its successor seers of the Vedanta. The profound mystic symbolism of the Veda stands unveiled here but the mystic experience remains undiluted; the vision is the same but without any secrecy in the sense. The following hymns illustrate the identity of their inner experience:

a) *Ṛtena ṛtamapihitaṁ dhruvaṁ vaṁ sūryasya*
yatra vimucantyaśvān,
daśa śatā saha tasthustadekaṁ deṿānāṁ
śreṣṭhaṁ vapuṣāmapaśyam.[119a]

"There is a Truth covered by a Truth where they unyoke the horses of the Sun; the ten hundreds stood together, there was that One; I saw the greatest (best, most glorious) of the embodied gods."*

b) *Hiranmayena pātreṇa satyasyāpihitaṁ*
mukhaṁ tat tvaṁ pūṣann apāvṛṇu
satyadharmāya dṛṣṭaye.
Pūṣannekarṣe yama sūrya prājāpatya
vyūha raśmīn samūha tejo
yat te rūpaṁ kalyāṇatamaṁ tatte
paśyāmi yo'sāvasau puruṣaḥ,
so'hamasmi.[119b]

"The face of the Truth is covered with a golden lid. O Pushan, that remove for the vision of the law of the Truth. O Pushan (fosterer), sole seer, O Yama, O Child of the Father of beings, marshal and gather together thy rays; I see the Light which is that fairest (most auspicious) form of Thee; he who is this Purusha, He am I."*

The Sun in both these incantations, "is the Godhead of the supreme Truth and Knowledge and his rays are the light emanating from that supreme Truth and Knowledge."[120]

Surya, often identified with Aditya, is one of the three principal Vedic deities; he produces day and night, creates all beings, dissolves all darkness and activises everything. He creates and supports all life, is generous and sheds light on all. He is described as the father of Ashwins born of a nymph Ashwini. In the *Vishnu Purana*, Surya is said to be the son of Kasyapa and Aditi, whereas the *Ramayana* refers him as a son of Brahma. By Sangna, daughter of Vishwakarma, according to the *Vishnu Purana* Surya had three children — Manu Vaivashwata, Yama and the goddess Yami. From a portion of Surya's overpowering and overbearing effulgence, Vishwakarma is said to have made the weapons of the gods — the discus of Vishnu, the trident of Shiva, the lance of Kartikeya etc. Ikshavaku is the son of Manu Vaivaswata and the father of Surya-vansa from whom the Solar-race of kings draws its origin. Elsewhere it is fabled that Surya communicated the white Yajur-veda to Rishi Yajnavalkya. Surya is represented as riding in a chariot drawn by seven horses, or a horse with seven heads surrounded with rays of blazing light. The names and epithets of Surya are numerous: "He is Savitri, the nourisher; Vivasvat, the brilliant; Bhaskara, the light-maker; Dinakara, the day-maker; Arhapati, lord of the day; Loka-chakshuh, eye of the world; Karma-sakshi, witness of the deeds of men; Graha-vaja, King of the constellations; Gabhastiman, possessed of rays; Sahasrakirana, having a thousand rays; Vikartanna, shorn of his beams (by Viswakarma);

Martanda, descended from Mritanda etc."[121] Surya's wives are many; among them are Savarna, Swati and Mahavirya.

In the Puranas he is described as dark-red in complexion, has three eyes and four arms; he sits upon a red lotus and has two lotuses each in one hand, — with one he is bestowing good and with the other inspiring his worshippers. The *Bhavisya Purana* speaks of Surya as the greatest among the gods, the most effulgent and adorable, — the one who successfully leads the seekers to the goal. The *Brahma Purana* enumerates his innumerable names.

Although not many hymns are addressed to Surya, he is worshipped most through the ages. The *Gayatri mantra* in the Veda is addressed to him; the *Skanda Purana* speaks of *Gayatri* as being superior to all the *mantras* in the Veda. It is considered as the Mother of the Vedas; it is Vishnu, Brahma and Siva says the *Purana*. By repeating it Vishwamitra became a Brahmarishi; it effectuates wonders and can transform the seekers into luminous beings.

The *Surya-stotra* in the *Mahabharata* glorifies Surya as the universal principle. He is eulogized as the thousand-rayed day-maker, he is the *gavampati*, the great Illuminator who destroys the *asuras* of darkness.[122] Other synonyms of Surya as mentioned in the *Mahabharata* are Vivaswat, Ravi, Tapana, Arka, Bhaskara and Savitri.[123] Siva, Indra and the Sun all bear a common title Deveshwara, 'lord of the gods':

Bhasi divi deveśvaro yathā.[124]

The usual function of Surya is to drive away darkness and demons both from heaven and on earth.[125] According to the Epics, Light is good, and Surya is the supreme good, whereas all sinners are children and promoters of darkness.

Ādityaḥ sattvaṁ udṛktaṁ
kucaras tu tathā tamaḥ.[126]

In the *Ramayana*, Rama calls on Surya to know the whereabouts of Sita, as he is the witness of the world with his heavenly eye, and knows what is done and not done. He addresses Surya,

Āditya bho lokakṛtakṛtajña.[127]

In one of the later traditions, Surya is identified with all the gods including the Trimurtis; he is the celestial bird, lord of seven horses, *saptasapti*; he is the twelve-souled, the golden gem and the creator and destroyer of all the worlds.

1. SABCL. Vol. 10, p. 421
2. Ibid., p. 421
3. Ibid., p. 423-24
4. Ibid., p. 426
5. Ibid., pp. 426-27
6. RV. X.37.1-12
7. RV. I.50.10
8. SABCL. Vol. 10, pp. 427-28
9. RV. VII.60.1
10. Ibid., p. 428.
11. Ibid., p. 429.

a. "Aditi is originally the pure Consciousness of infinite existence one and self-luminous; She is the Light that is Mother of all things. As the Infinite she gives birth to Daksha, the discriminating and distributing Thought of the divine Mind, and is herself born to Daksha as the cosmic Infinite, the mystic Cow whose udders feed all the worlds.

"It is this divine daughter of Daksha who is the mother of the gods. In the cosmos Aditi is the undivided infinite unity of things, free from the duality, *advaya* and has Diti the separative dualising Consciousness for the obverse side of her cosmic creation, — her sister and a rival wife in the later myth. Here in the lower being where she is manifested as the earth-principle, her husband is the lower or inauspicious Father who is slain by their child Indra, the power of the divine Mind manifested in the lower creation. Indra, says the hymn, slays his father, dragging him by the feet, and makes his mother a widow. In another image forcible and expressive though repugnant to the decorousness of our modern taste, Surya is said to be the lover of his sister Dawn and the second husband of his mother Aditi, and by a variation of the same image Aditi is hymned as the wife of the all-pervading Vishnu who is in the cosmic creation one of the sons of Aditi and the younger brother of Indra. These images which seem gross and confused when we lack the key to their mystic significance, become clear enough the moment that is recovered. Aditi is the infinite consciousness in the cosmos espoused and held by the lower creative power which works through the limited mind and body, but delivered from this subjection by the force of the divine or illumined Mind born of her in the mentality of man. It is this Indra who makes Surya the light of the Truth rise in heaven and dispel the darknesses and falsehoods and limited vision of the separative mentality. Vishnu is the vaster all-pervading existence which then takes possession of our liberated and unified consciousness, but he is born in us only after Indra has made his puissant and luminous appearance."(SABCL.Vol. 10, pp. 421-22)

12. SABCL. Vol. 10, p. 425
13. RV. V.81.2
14. RV. V.81.3
15. RV. V.81.4
16. RV. V.81.5
17. SABCL. Vol. 12, pp. 125-26
18. Ibid., p. 127
19. SABCL. Vol. 14, p. 275
20. *Isha Upanishad*, 15-16
21. RV. V.62.1
22. SABCL. Vol. 12, p. 67fn.
23. *Svetasvatara Upanishad*, I.11
24. RV. X.7.3b
25. RV. I.115.2,3
26. RV. I.22.6
27. *Yajur Veda*, 31.18
28. RV. I.22.5
29. RV. I.115.1
30. RV. IV.40.5b
31. RV. X.90.3
32. RV. III.39.5
33. RV. I.50.8-9
34. RV. I.50.4
35. RV. IV.53.6
36. RV. I.115.4
37. RV. I.50.11
38. RV. I.50.1
39. RV. I.50.3
40. RV. II.38.2
41. RV. II.38.8
42. RV. I.164.2-3
43. RV. X.158.3-4
44. RV. V.45.2
45. RV. V.45.10
46. RV. I.191.8-10
47. RV. X.3.1-3

b. Translation appears earlier in the same chapter.

47a. RV. I.115.4(a)
48. RV. II.38.4a
49. ṚV. I.115.5b
50. RV. II.38.3
51. RV. VIII.25.19a
52. RV. VII.76.1
53. RV. III.38.8
54. RV. VII.38.1,2
55. RV. VII.45.3
56. *Atharva Veda*, VII.14.2

57. RV. X.139.1a
58. RV. X.149.3b
59. *Visnupurana*, II.8.12
60. *Satapatha Brahmana*, VII.5.1.8
61. RV. IV.54.2a
62. RV. IV.54.5a
63. RV. V.81.1b
64. RV. II.38.1b
65. RV. VII.38.4
66. RV. II.38.9
67. RV. X.36.13
68. RV. X.100.1b
69. RV. I.110.2b
70. RV. III.54.11
71. RV. V.82.9
72. RV. VII.82.10
73. RV. VI.51.2a
74. RV. VI.50.2a
75. RV. VII.5.4a
76. RV. I.186.1
77. RV. V.49.2a
78. RV. V.42.3
79. RV. III. 62.12
80. *Atharva Veda*, VI.1.1
81. RV. II.30.1
82. RV. IV.54.4
83. *Atharva Veda*, V.24.9a
84. RV VII.35.8a
85. RV. VII.63.4a
86. RV. IX.110.3a
87. RV. IX.110.4a
88. RV. IX.75.1a
89. RV. IX.28.5
90. RV. IX.85.9a
91. RV. IX.107.7b
92. RV. IX.86.32a
93. *Sama Veda*, XVIII.1675
94. Ibid., XVIII.1683
95. Ibid., III.297
96. *Yajur Veda*, XXXVIII.24-27
97. RV. I.35.1-11
98. RV. IV.54.3
99. RV. VI.71.1-6
100. RV. X.139.3
101. RV. V.81.5
102. RV. II.38.11
103. *Maitri Upanishad*, VI.14-16;

c. Trans: S. Radhakrishnan.
104. *Atharva Veda*, VII.69
105. SABCL. Vol. 10, p. 68
106. Ibid., Vol. 10, p. .423
107. Ibid., Vol. 10, pp. 424-25
108. Ibid., p. 425
109. Ibid., p. 110
110. Ibid.
111. Ibid., p. 275
112. Ibid.
113. Ibid., pp. 275-76
114. Ibid., p. 276
115. Ibid.
116. Ibid., p. 428
117. Ibid., pp. 424-25
118. RV. I.113.8-10
119. SABCL. Vol. 10, p. 438
119a. RV. V.62.1
119b. Isha Upanishad, 15-16
120. SABCL., Vol. 11, p. 15
121. John Dowson, *Hindu Mythology & Religion* (Rupa & Co, New Delhi, 1989), p. 311
122. *The Mahabharata*, V.108.3f
123. Ibid., I.68.13; III.18; 171.20
124. Ibid., II.50.16
125. Ibid., III.185.30
126. Ibid., VII.146.144; XIV.39.14
127. *The Ramayana*, III.63.16

V

VARUNA

Varuna is the god of all-permeating and all-pervading vastness and purity who supports and perfects the world of manifestation. He represents infinite divine existence, the all-embracing and boundless ocean of reality. He is the luminous Infinity, a limitless formless expansiveness and an immense ether of purity; he is the unbounded container of illimitable knowledge and the holder of many dawns within his vast bosom of light. He purifies and perfects the intellect by opening it to the working of the Truth-Consciousness which is the condition of Immortality that the Rishis are seeking for. The Rishis invoke Mitra of purified discrimination and clearsightedness and Varuna the annihilator of the enemies of clear understanding.

Mitraṁ huve pūtadakṣaṁ varuṇaṁ ca riśādaśam,
dhiyaṁ ghṛtācīṁ sādhantā.[1]

I invoke Mitra, god of purity and light, and Varuna the dispeller of the enemies, verily, they together accomplish the act and bestow happiness to the worshippers.

Both the gods by the power of the Truth augment and dispense it for the seekers. By doing so they enjoy and attain to a puissant calling that is of the nature of a sacrifice.

Ṛtena mitrāvaruṇāv ṛtāvṛdhāvṛtaspṛśā,
kratuṁ bṛhantamāśāthe.[2]

O Mitra and Varuna, increasers and apportioners of the waters, may you connect the sacrifices of the worshippers with appropriate rewards.

And eventually by their repeated births in the seeker on his long upward journey they, the Truth-based ones, support and upbear the power of discrimination that accomplishes the luminous task. They are the refuge of all seekers, and help them in the attainment of the goal.

Kavī no mitrāvaruṇā tuvijātā urukṣayā,
dakṣaṁ dadhāte apasam.[3]

O wise Mitra and Varuna, may we attain prosperity and grow in strength through the sacrifices. You exist for the good of all, you the sanctuary of all.

Varuna and Mitra are described by the Rishis as *riśādas* and *pūtadakṣa* respectively — as the destroyer of the hordes of hurters and the possessor of purified discernment. Together, they fight impurity of appraisal and assessment and falsification and distortion of thought-contents. Varuna as a conscious force of the Truth is the god of wideness and purity, and dissolves all that impedes or hurts in the seeker's upward journey. And Mitra as a universal power of the Light and Truth and a friend of man, represents especially Love, Joy and Harmony. He, working with Varuna, removes all forms of discord and disharmony, confusion and disorganisation in the mind, and paves the way for the effective working of the Truth-Consciousness in the human mentality. Varuna and Mitra by their effective thought-power manifest in the seeker the faculties of vision and inspiration, intuition, discernment and will-power and help him to enter progressively into the wideness and the beatitude of the Truth-Consciousness.

Indra and Vayu, the mind-power and life-power in man, operating jointly in the human mind awaken it to the inflow of the divine delight of the Soma-juice from above. This delight, so received in the human mentality, organises a new effectuation and a new process that prepares and promotes the operation of Truth-Consciousness in the seeker. This new working generates or creates in the seeker a new thought-power that is intermediate between the mind and life-power of Indra-Vayu and that of the immortal Consciousness. It is at this stage of the growth-process that Varuna and Mitra cater and support the working of the Truth-Consciousness in the seeker's mind. While Indra and Vayu perfect and energise the nervous mentality by their thought-mind, Mitra and Varuna perfect and enlarge and enrich the thought-mind and make it communicative with the Truth-Consciousness. Indra and Vayu, Varuna and Mitra thus increasingly and successfully purify and prepare, perfect and widen the human mentality towards the supreme consummation of establishing in it the supramental Truth-Consciousness. They prepare the seeker in mind and subtle body to move towards the supreme Truth as well as fulfil his life's seeking by his attainment of the Truth and the Immortality.

If Varuna represents the purity and the wideness of the infinite Truth, Mitra expresses its all-embracing, luminous harmony. Mitra is the friend of all beings and the Lord of Love. If the immortal Consciousness has to be firmly established in mortal human nature, a few conditions have to be indispensably fulfilled. It needs the operation and effectuation of four powers of the Truth; these are Varuna, Mitra, Aryaman and Bhaga. Varuna is the power of vast purity and clear wideness that destroys all sin and falsehood; Mitra is the luminous power of love and compassion that dissolves all disharmony and discord; Aryaman is the god of an immortal puissance and pure aspiration, and Bhaga of unrestrained abandon of that right enjoyment that dispels all sin and suffering, error and evil.

Varuna holds the key to the immensity and vastness of spiritual living — to the divine world of widest existence and infinite Truth. Whereas Mitra the Lord of Light and Love embracing our thought and feeling and will blends them into a divine harmony with the sublimest Truth. Impelled and uplifted by the workings of Varuna and Mitra, enters Aryaman, the illumined power, the upbearing and elevating force and the effective will of the divine Truth. And by the combined workings of all the three comes Bhaga with his enrapturing bliss, and effectuates the birth of the supreme Truth in the seeker's consciousness and being.

Varuna in a 'dualistic association' with Mitra has been the subject of diverse interpretations. As the Indian counterpart of the Greek sky-god Uranus, Varuna encounters too many odd interpretations which are mutually incompatible. According to one such approach "the highest heaven and its light are the abode of Varuna" because of the notion that "the sun represents his all-seeing eye", and that he is possessed of a shining and radiant form. Another approach interprets the following Rig-vedic hymn —

> *Tisro dyāvo nihitā antarāsmin*
> *tisro bhūmīruparāḥ ṣadvidhanāḥ.*[4]

> "Three heavens are deposited within him, below that three earths, forming a row of six..." *

to mean that Varuna is the god of the 'all-encompassing sky'. But the Veda speaks of Surya as the eye of cosmic vision of not only Varuna but also of Mitra and Agni. Elsewhere he is described as descending into the stream "like a white drop", or resembling "a hidden ocean".

Uranus of the Greek mythus is often considered by European scholars as not only identical with Vedic Varuna but as having almost the same important moral functions. But Varuna is certainly not the Indian Neptune; he is the lord of ethereal wideness and the 'upper ocean' — the purity and vastness of the Truth. It is by his vastness that he makes paths for the seekers in the pathless infinite along with other gods. Varuna by his wide being and vast vision dissolves all limits, and reveals that which Vritra obscures and withholds from the seekers. He is the spiritual image and the most illumined figure of the all-embracing infinite Truth.

On the basis of classical Sanskrit, some maintain that Varuna is the ocean-god. But this interpretation is not compatible with the many attributes that the Rig-veda endows him. Again, he is described as 'the nectar-containing moon' —

> *Sa samudro apīcyasturo dyāmiva rohati*
> *ni yadasu yajurdadhe.*[5]

> He is the hidden ocean; swiftly he mounts the heaven as the sun ascends the sky...

which epithet is not appropriate in the context of his role as the one who by destroying all resistance establishes the perfect state of rich and luminous mental activity. Varuna is the psychological power of infinite wideness.

Varuna is one of the greatest in the Vedic pantheon who symbolises the supreme majesty of the Lord; he is the overseer, the all-knower and ruler of all things, and has 'a thousand eyes' which see and survey everything.

> *Ā caṣta āsāṁ patho nadīnāṁ*
> *varuṇa ugraḥ sahasracakṣāḥ.*[6]

> Varuna, the mighty god, with a thousand eyes beholds the course of these many rivers.

He sets the cosmos in motion in conformity with certain laws and follows closely its workings; he is its friend and companion in its strenuous journey toward the Light. He governs the universe as well as in his infinite wisdom guides the doings of men to their luminous fulfilment. He rules the heavens above, and in his wide vision perceives all time; together with Mitra he protects the cosmic law as well as the moral order of men by his benign theophany. He is always intimate with the seeker-sacrificers but is feared most as he comes down heavily upon their sinful and evil nature. Nonetheless he is humane and most helpful, and frees them from all crookedness and limitation. He manifests his presence in the midst of obstructing chaos and clears the way for broad-based intelligence. Men implore this wise and merciful *deva* to be freed from the fillers of obscurantism, resistance and limitation.

a) *Uduttamaṁ varuṇa pāśamasmad*
avādhamaṁ vi madhyamaṁ śrathāya
athā vayamāditya vrate
tavānāgaso āditaye syāma.[7]

O venerable Varuna, loosen our bonds upper, middle and lower; free us from all kinds of fetters so that through faithful worship of you, O son of Aditi, we may live without any sin.

b) *Yenā pāvaka cakṣasā*
bhuranyantaṁ janāñ anu,
tvaṁ varuṇa paśyasi.[8]

With your special light you purify our souls and protect us from evil thoughts and dark deeds.

Varuna is the universal Ruler as also the god of justice and the all-encompassing one from the root *vṛ,* to cover, to encompass.

Tena viśvasya bhuvanasya rājā yavaṁ
na vṛṣṭirvyunātti bhūma.[9]

He is thence the supreme monarch of all the worlds who waters the earth even as rain bedews the barley.

He is extolled as the king, *rājan*, and the *rājasūya yajña* is offered specifically to him.

Rājā rāṣṭrānāṁ peśo nadīnam
anuttamasmai kṣatraṁ viśvāyu.[10]

He is the king of kings and the glory of the streams of thoughts; verily, his all-pervading strength and sway over the lives is irresistible.

He is the king of the universe and king of men and gods alike. He is the most prominent of the Rig-vedic gods, the undisputed ruler of the cosmos, the upholder of the cosmic law and the benevolent surveyor and director of the activities of men.

a) *Tvaṁ viśveṣāṁ varuṇāsi rājā ye ca*
devā asura ye ca martāḥ.[11]

O Varuna, mighty son of Aditi, destroyer of the adversaries, verily, you are the sovereign over all, whether they be gods or the *asuras.*

b) *Asāvanyo asura suyata dyaus*
tvaṁ viśveṣāṁ varuṇāsi rājā.[12]

O Aditi, you have given birth to Mitra, the scatterer of darkness, and to Varuna the sovereign over us all.

He is the one, says the Rig-veda who "has put intelligence in hearts, fire in the waters, the sun in the sky, and the *Soma*-plant on the hills.":

Vaneṣu vyantarikṣaṁ tatāna vājam
arvatsu paya usriyāsu,
hṛtsu kratuṁ varuṇo apsvagnim
divi sūryamadadhātsomamadrau.[13]

He is frequently paired by the Rishis with Indra and Mitra and embodies several divine attributes such as justice and compassion, purity and farsightedness, vision and sovereignty, self-rule and world-rule. He is described as the 'father heaven', *dyaus pitā.*

a) *Dyaurme pitā janitā nābhiratra*
bandhurme mātā pṛthivī mahīyam.[14]

The heaven is my father and ancestor, the navel is my kinsman and the wide earth my mother.

b) *Dyaurvaḥ pitā pṛthivī mātā*
somo bhrātāditiḥ svasā.[15]

Heaven is your father, earth your mother; Soma is your brother, Aditi your sister.

c) *Dyauṣpitaḥ pṛthivī mātaradhrug*
agne bhrātarvasavo mṛlatā naḥ.[16]

O father Heaven, the perfect mother earth, brother Agni and you, O Vasu, may you all grant us perpetual happiness.

Varuna is the Lord of the Waters, of Truth, Light and Knowledge, and with Mitra is both the dispenser of rain and the guardian of *ṛta*, the cosmic order.

Ṛtena yāvṛtāvṛdhāvṛtasya jyotiṣaspatī,
tā mitrāvaruṇā huve.[17]

I invoke the lords of *ṛta* and of light, who uphold the eternal order, *ṛta*, by means of *ṛta*.

It is through *ṛta* that Varuna establishes order in the universe and saves men 'from their inequities', as the cosmic order includes automatically the ethical sphere. Varuna is the most forgiving and merciful god, the protector as well as the great liberator. He is the most powerful of all the gods; it is by his *māyā* that he establishes the earth:

Imāmu ṣvāsurasya śrutasya mahīṁ
māyāṁ varuṇasya pra vocam,
māneneva tasthivāñ antarikṣe vi yo
mame pṛthivīṁ sūryeṇa.[18]

I will declare this marvellous and mysterious deed of Varuna, the renowned and virtuous god, who abiding in the mid-region has measured out the earth, as it were, with a yardstick.

Varuna is the warp and woof of the loom of this universe. He is one of us as well as foreign, both human and divine.

a) *Yaḥ samamyo varuṇo yo vyāmyo yaḥ saṁdeśyo*
varuṇo yo videśya'ḥ,
yo daivo varuṇo yasca mānuṣaḥ.[19]

It is Varuna, the Supreme Being who is common for every one; free from sin and evil it is he who is common to all places; transcending space and time it is Varuna who is supernatural and supremely conscious and all-conscious.

b) *Uteyaṁ bhūmirvaruṅasya rājña utāsau*
dyaurbṛhatī dūreantā,
uto samudrau varuṇasya kukṣī utāsminnalpa
udake nilīnaḥ.[20]

All this earth belongs to him and even the boundless sky above. The two oceans — those of heaven and of *antarīkṣa*, are contained within him, and yet he is wholly contained within this single drop of water.

The Rig-vedic Rishi again and again beseeches Varuna, the omnipotent god, for his help and gracious intervention without which he feels desolate and forlorn. He implores divine pardon and special favour; he needs the assurance of his spiritual renewal with each dawn. He extols Varuna to protect him from all perils.

Apo su myakṣa varuṇa bhiyasaṁ mat
samralṛtāvo 'nu mā gṛbhāya,
dameva vatsādvi mumugdhyaṅho nahi
tvadāre nimiṣaścaneśe.[21]

Ward off, O Varuna, all danger from me. O supreme monarch, receive me generously, bestow your favour upon me. Cast off all sin and troubles from me like the cords from a calf; without you I am powerless even to open my eyes.

Varuna is extolled as the great wielder of thunder, *adrivaḥ*, and the supreme watcher of men's deeds; he is also the gracious god who forgives.

a) *Kratvaḥ samaha dīnatā pratīpaṁ jagamā śuce,*
mṛḷā sukṣatra maḷaya.[22]

O opulent and pure god, if ever through infirmity I have gone astray and done what is contrary to the law, pray forgive me, and bless me with happiness.

b) *Yatkiṁ cedaṁ varuṇa daivye jane*
'bhidrohaṁ manuṣyā ścarāmasi,

acittī yattava dharmā yuyopima mā
nastasmādenaso deva rīriṣaḥ.[23]

Whatever the offence which we mortals may commit against gods, O Varuna, whatever laws of yours we may violate through ignorance, do not punish us; O merciful god, may you forgive us on account of that wrong doing.

Varuna and Mitra are described as the great inspirers, and the harbingers of freedom and delight.

a) *Nū mitro varuṇo aryamā nastasmane*
tokāya varivo dadhantu,
sugā no viśvā supathāni santu yūyaṁ
pāta svastibhiḥ sadā naḥ.[24]

May Mitra, Varuna and Aryaman grant us freedom and felicity and to our posterity; may all paths of progress be easy of access to us, and may you ever nurse and foster us with blessings.

b) *Varuṇo'pāmadipatiḥ sa māvatu,*
asminbrahmaṇyasmin
karmaṇyasyāṁ purodhāyāmasyāṁ
pratiṣṭhāyāmasyāṁ,
cittyāmasyāmā kūtyāmasyāmāśiṣyasyāṁ
devahūtyāṁ svāhā.[25]

May Varuna, Lord of the Waters, protect me in this my attainment of knowledge, in this my act and in my priestly undertaking, in this my life's stability, in my thought, purpose and intention, in this my calling on the gods, and in my activities of *yajña.* All hail.

Now Light comes to the seeker, the fairest of all lights and the Night is sent away. The radiant Dawn advances to claim the dwelling relinquished by the dark Night; it shines forth 'with the eye of the Sun', flings wide open the shining doors and brings in the golden graces of Light and Delight; it heightens and widens the consciousness of all living creatures. The seeker implores Varuna to prepare him to receive the gifts of the Dawn and be worthy of them.

Yaccitramapna uṣaso vahantījānāya
śaśamānāya bhadram,
tanno mitro varuṇo māmahantāmaditiḥ
sindhuḥ pṛthivī uto dyauḥ.[26]

Whatever wondrous wealth the dawns bring is a blessing to the sacrificer who offers worship zealously. May Mitra, Varuna and Aditi grant to us this our prayer, including the sacred ocean, the earth and heaven.

The long succession of dawns and the repeated risings of Surya followed by the increasings of Pushan results in the luminous creation of Savitri. Savitri links the pace of our present with the progress that has already been made in the past by our ancients, and thus provides the necessary impetus for future advancement. The Rishi wants us to meditate on our upward journey on the splendour of this creative godhead, Savitri, and the power and puissance of the four kings — Varuna, Mitra, Aryaman and Bhaga.

Savitri has the Word of the Truth which is revealed to us at a certain stage of our inner ascension to the undivided Consciousness. He is the mighty one who creates for the seekers the immortality and the infinite beatitude. To be able to receive this divine felicity we need to be free of sin and evil, pure and wide in consciousness and full of harmony in being. Varuna and Mitra prepare and uphold this necessary condition in the seeker for Savitri to bestow and build up the supreme felicity of universal form so very essential for abiding in the highest heaven of the golden Truth.

The formation and perfection of the cosmic form depends mainly on the working of the many gods in us and especially of the four great luminous godheads — Varuna, Mitra, Aryaman and Bhaga. The birth and growth in the seeker of all the other gods *viśve devāḥ* is an essential prerequisite in the creation of the luminous condition: "Vishnu, Rudra, Brahmanaspati... preside over the indispensable conditions, — for the one paces out the vast framework of the inner worlds in which our soul-action takes place, the other in his wrath and might and violent beneficence forces onward the great evolution and smites the opponent and the recusant and the ill-doer, and the third administers always the seed of the creative word from the profundities of the soul; so too Earth and Heaven and the divine Waters and the great goddesses and Twashtri the Fashioner of things on whom they attend, either provide the field or bring and shape the material; but over the utter creation, over its perfect vast space and pure texture, over the sweet and ordered harmony of its steps, over the illumined force and power of its fulfilment, over its rich, pure and abundant enjoyment and rapture the Sun-gods Varuna, Mitra, Aryaman, Bhaga cast the glory and protection of their divine gaze."[27]

The Rishis are ecstatic in their praise of the gods; their inspired invocations are the sublimest and most beautiful among the spiritual and hallowed literature of the world. They bring with them the light of soul-confidence and the firm feeling of friendliness with the cosmic powers. They communicate as well as evoke in us the truth of collective participation with the gods in a cosmic *mahāyajña* for the transformation of human nature and earth-nature. They deliver us out of material and mental darkness into a world of light and truth. The Light and the Truth, the Mightiness and the Immortality that the Rishis always sought for are symbolised in the figure of the Sun. The journey of the Sun is therefore the pilgrimage of the awakened seeker-soul; the goal of this long journey by the sun-lit path of the Truth is the Truth itself.

Ṛtena ṛtamapihitaṁ dhruvaṁ vaṁ
sūryasya yatra vimucantyaśvān,
daśa śatā saha tasthustadekaṁ
devānāṁ śreṣṭhaṁ vapuṣāmapaśyam.[28]

"Concealed by this Truth is that Truth of you," (of Mitra and Varuna), "where they unyoke the horses of the Sun. The ten hundreds meet there together, — That One, I have seen the supreme God of the embodied gods."*

No one can know by himself, for sure, the Transcendent.

Na nunamasti no śvaḥ kastad
veda yadadbhutam,
anyasya cittamabhi sañcareṇyam
utādhītaṁ vi naśyati.[29]

"It is neither today nor tomorrow; who knoweth That which is transcendent? When it is approached, it vanishes from us."*

It therefore becomes incumbent upon the seeker to give birth to the gods within himself, and increase their felicity and efficiency. For it is by consciously building up their divine bodies in himself that the seeker grows strong and steady to walk on the arduous path, that he is increasingly awakened to the imperative need to ever exceed himself, and is joyously impelled to move towards the world of Immortality.

The gods have a two-fold birth: "They are born above in the divine Truth as creators of the worlds and guardians of the divine Law; they are born also here in the world itself and in man as Cosmic and human powers of the Divine."[30] They are essentially psychological powers that lead man successfully to 'the fearless Light'; they are the emanations of the Infinite Mother, free from limitation, pure and profound, wide and mighty who dwell in the world awaiting to be born again and again in the seeker to support and guide and lead him to the Truth.

Dhārayanta ādityāso jagatsthā devā
viśvasya bhuvanasya gopāḥ,
dīrghādhiyo rakṣamānā asūryam
ṛtāvānaścayamānā ṛṇāni.[31]

"Sons of the Infinite, they dwell in the movement of the world and uphold it; gods, they are the guardians of all that becomes as universe; far-thoughted, full of the Truth, they guard the Might."*

The gods are undivided in their consciousness, pure in being, thought and action, ever awake and most straightforward and wide-visioned seers possessed of the luminous world of the Truth. They are the conscious powers of Aditi working in the cosmos purging it of all ignorance and falsehood.

Ya isire bhuvanasya pracetaso viśvasya
sthāturjagataśca mantavaḥ,
te naḥ kṛtādakṛtādenasaspary
adyā devāsaḥ pipṛtā svastaye.[32]

"Since ye are they who rule over the world by the power of their mind of knowledge, thinkers of all that is stable and mobile, therefore, O gods, carry us beyond the sin of that which we have done and that which we have not done to the felicity."*

The Rishis speak again and again of the 'thornless path' prepared by the gods that leads to the 'fearless peace and felicity'; they are the divine leaders who support and sustain the seekers of the imperishable Light and Immortality. Varuna, Mitra and Aryaman are the blissful kings of the luminous world of the Truth, the sons of the Infinite Mother, who produce the power of beatitude even in this world of fear and death.

a) *Yebhyo hotrāṁ prathamāmāyeje manuḥ*
samiddhāgnirmanasā sapta hotṛbhiḥ,
ta ādityā abhayaṁ śarma yachata sugā
naḥ karta supathā svastaye.[33]

"O Sons of the Infinite, effect for us the fearless peace, make us good paths of an easy going to the felicity."*

b) *Sugo hi vo aryamanmitra panthā*
anṛkṣaro varuṇa sādhurasti.[34]

"Easy of going is your path, O Aryaman, O Mitra, it is thornless, O Varuna, and perfect."*

c) *Ariṣṭaḥ sa marto viśva edhate pra*
prajābhirjāyate dharmaṇaspari.[35]

"They whom the Sons of Infinity lead with good leadings pass beyond all sin and evil to the felicity."*

d) *Āre devā dveṣo asmadyuyotanorū*
ṇaḥ śarma yacchatā svastaye.[36]

"O ye gods, put far from us the hostile (dividing) force, give us wide peace for the felicity."*

Varuna, Mitra and Aryaman, the luminous children as well as the rulers of *Swar-loka* constantly hold the seeker close to the Truth-world such that in his upraised and elevated consciousness is reflected the threefold truth of 'its infinite existence, its infinite consciousness-force and its infinite bliss.'

Tisro bhūmirdhārayan triuṙuta
dyuntrīṇi vratā vidathe antareṣām,
ṛtenādityā mahi vo mahitvaṁ tad
aryamanvaruṇa mitra cāru.

Trī rocanā divyā dhārayanta
hiraṇyayāḥ śucayo dhārapūtāḥ,
aśvapnajo animiṣā adabdhā
uruśansā ṛjave martyāya.[37]

"Three earths they hold, three heavens, three workings of these gods in the Knowledge within; by the Truth, O Sons of the Infinite, great is that vastness of yours, O Aryaman, O Mitra, O Varuna, great and beautiful. Three heavenly worlds of light they hold, the gods golden-shining who are pure and purified in the streams; sleepless, unconquerable they close not their lids, they express the wideness to the mortal who is straight."*

The four gods Varuna, Mitra, Aryaman and Bhaga are of the nature of Light and have one united action — that of perfecting in us the one indivisible Truth. They jointly build up in the seeker the divine state of perfect perfection by the coordination and integration of their respective contributing individual essential elements. "The Divine is existence all-embracing, infinite and pure; Varuna brings to us the infinite oceanic space of the divine soul and its ethereal, elemental purity. The Divine is boundless consciousness, perfect in knowledge, pure and therefore luminously right in its discernment of things, perfectly harmonious and happy in its concordance of their law and nature; Mitra brings us this light and harmony, this right distinction and relation and friendly concord, the happy laws of the liberated soul concordant with itself and the Truth in all its rich thought, shining actions and thousandfold enjoyment. The Divine is in its own being pure and perfect power and in us the eternal upward tendency in things to their source and truth; Aryaman brings to us this mighty strength and perfectly-guided happy inner upsurging. The Divine is the pure, the faultless, the all-embracing, the untroubled ecstasy that enjoys its own infinite being and enjoys equally all that it creates within itself; Bhaga gives us sovereignly that ecstasy of the liberated soul, its free and unfallen possession of itself and the world."[38] This foursome truth of the four godheads essentially constitutes the triune nature of Sachchidananda: Varuna has his basis in the all-permeating and all-pervading transparent purity of Sat, Mitra in the all-combining and blending light of Chit, Aryaman in the all-perceptive power of Tapas and Bhaga in the all-enveloping and all-encompassing ecstasy of Ananda. Varuna, undoubtedly the first and foremost among the godheads for his felicity of infinite existence, is the basis of the kind of perfection that the Vedic Rishis are seeking for. It is on the firm foundation of wideness and purity that perfection can be attempted and realised on the different planes of our being. Whereas Bhaga represents the crowning movement in the long journey; he is the possessor and giver of the spiritual puissance of beatitude supreme. Mitra and Aryaman represent the working out of the inherent truth of the world of manifestation by which infinite existence and infinite consciousness realise themselves as infinite bliss. The Rishi invokes the All-Gods, *visve devas*, to bring to a felicitous fulfilment the high hopes and aspirations of the seekers.

1. *Ko vastrata vasavaḥ ko varūtā*
   dyāvābhūmī adite trāsīthāṁ naḥ,
sahīyaso varuṇa mitra martātko vo
   'dhvare varivo dhāti devāḥ.

2. *Pra ye dhāmāni pūrvyāṇyarcānvi yad*
   ucchanviyotāro amurāḥ,
vidhātāro vi te dadhurajasrā
   ṛtadhītayo rurucanta dasmāḥ.

3. *Pra pastyāmaditiṁ sindhumarkaiḥ*
   svastimīḷe sakhyāya devīm,
ubhe yathā no ahanī nipata uṣāsānaktā
   karatāmadabdhe.

4. *Vyaryamā varuṇaśceti panthāmiṣas*
   patiḥ suvitaṁ gātumagniḥ,
indrāviṣṇu nṛvadu su ṣṭavānā śarma
   no yantamamavaḍvarūtham.

5. *Ā parvatasya marutāmavaṅsi devasya*
   trāturavri bhagasva,
patpātirjanyādaṅhaso no mitro
   mitriyāduta na uruṣyet.

6. *Nu rodasī ahinā budhnyena stuvīta*
   devī apyebhiriṣṭaiḥ,
samudraṁ na saṁcaraṇe saniṣyavo
   gharmasvaraso nadyo apa vran.

7. *Devairno devyāditirni pātu devas*
trātā trāyatāmaprayucchan,
nahi mitrasya varuṇasya dhāsi'arhamasi
pramiyaṁ sānvagneḥ.

8. *Agnirīśe vasavyasyāgnimashaḥ saubhagasya,*
tānyasmabhyaṁ rāsate.

9. *Uṣo maghonyā vaha sunṛte varyā puru,*
asmabhyaṁ vajinīvati.

10. *Tatsu naḥ savitā bhago varuṇo mitro aryamā,*
indro no rādhasā gamat.[39]

"Who of you is our deliverer? who our defender? O Earth and Heaven, free from division, deliver us; rescue, O Mitra, O Varuna, from the mortality that is too strong for us! Who of you, O gods, confirms for us the supreme good in the march of the sacrifice? They who illumine our high original seats, they who limitless in knowledge dawn out putting away our darkness, it is they, imperishable all-ordainers, who order them for us; thinkers out of the Truth, they shine forth in light, achievers. I seek for my companion by the words illumining the flowing river Aditi, she who is the divine felicity. O Night and Dawn unconquerable, so do ye make it that both the Days shall utterly protect us. Aryaman and Varuna distinguish the Path, and Agni lord of the impulsion, the path of the happy goal. O Indra and Vishnu, affirmed, extend to us perfectly the peace in which are the Powers, the mighty protection. I embrace the increasings of Parvata and of the Maruts and of Bhaga, our divine deliverer. May the master of things protect us from the sin of the world and Mitra keep us far from the sin against Mitra. Now shall one affirm the goddesses Earth and Heaven with the Dragon of the foundation by all the things desired that we must obtain; as if to possess that Ocean by their wide ranging they have uncovered the (hidden) rivers that are voiceful with the burning Light. May goddess Aditi with the gods protect us, may the divine Deliverer deliver us, unremitting; let us not diminish the foundation of Mitra and Varuna and the high level of Agni. Agni is the lord of that vast substance of riches and perfected enjoyment; he lavishes on us those abundances. O Dawn, voice of the Truth, queen of plenitude, bring to us the many desirable boons, thou who hast in thee all their plenty. To that goal may Savitri, Bhaga, Varuna, Mitra, Aryaman, Indra, move aright for us with riches of our felicity."*

The Veda essentially symbolises the search for immortality and divine beatitude which are possible only by the attainment of a wide and luminous consciousness — *satyam ṛtam bṛhat*. But within the phenomenal situation the seeker finds himself placed in an ephemeral, ever-changing and highly complex but a dynamic system of five sheaths — the *annamaya*, *prāṇamaya*, *manomaya*, *vijñānamaya* and *ānandamaya*. The first three are evolved out of 'the causal primordial Prakriti', and the last two are those of the all-inclusive and transcendental understanding and bliss. The world of immortality which is the ideal of the Vedic Rishis is that of 'truth in being', 'truth in activity' and 'truth in universality'.

Varuna and Mitra are invoked to help in the purification of discernment and the perfection of bright and wide understanding which is the *sine qua non* of entry into the plane of supramental consciousness.

Most of the Vedic hymns have a two-tiered significance, the pragmatic and the spiritual, and sometimes are of a multipurpose nature. Agni, for example, may be the simple fire, also solar heat and light, as well as, at a different level a superior intelligence, or even the light of spirituality. The same may be said of Varuna, Mitra, Indra and Vayu.

In the vision of the Vedic Rishis it is the supramental consciousness which is 'the condition of the state of immortality'. This is the reason why 'the idea of *ṛtam* is always insisted upon' in hymns especially addressed to Agni, Varuna and Mitra. The second hymn of Rishi Madhuchchandas in the Rig-veda highlights the Truth-increasing action of the gods:

1. *Mitram huve putadakṣaṁ varuṇaṁ ca ṛśādasam,*
   dhiyaṁ ghṛtāciṁ sādhantā.

2. *Ṛtenā mitrāvaruṇāvṛtāvṛdhāvṛtaspṛśā*
   kratuṁ bṛhantamāsathe.

3. *Kavi no mitrāvaruṇā, tuvijātā urukṣayā,*
   dakṣam dadhāte apasam.[40]

1. "I invoke Mitra of purified strength (or, purified discernment) and Varuna destroyer of our foes perfecting (or accomplishing) a bright understanding."

2. "By Truth Mitra and Varuna, truth-increasing, truth-touching, enjoy (or, attain) a mighty work (or a vast effective power)."

3. "For us Mitra and Varuna, seers, multiple-born, wide-housed, uphold the strength (or, discernment) that does the work."*

The word *dakṣa* in verse 7 is translated by Sayana to mean physical strength or an aggressive power capable of causing injury. But in the total context of the hymn it assumes a psychological significance. When the figure of physical action or forcible separation is carried to the mental plane *dakṣa* signifies discernment, judgement, competent and skilful attention and 'discriminative thought-power'. Moreover, as Sri Aurobindo points out, "*dakṣa* is continually associated with *kratu*", because of which *dakṣaya kratve* simply means " 'capacity and effective power' or 'will and discernment' ".[41] This psychological import of *dakṣa* is clearly brought out by the role played by the goddess Dakshina. As Sri Aurobindo observes, "Dakshina like the more famous Ila, Saraswati and Sarama, is one of four goddesses, representing the four faculties of the *ṛtam* or Truth-Consciousness, — Ila representing truth-vision or revelation, Saraswati truth-audition, inspiration, the divine word, Sarama intuition, Dakshina the separative intuitional discrimination." "*Dakṣa* then", Sri Aurobindo concludes, "will mean this discrimination whether as mental judgment on the mind-plane or as intuitional discernment on the plane of the Ritam."[42]

Indra, whose realm of residence is Swar, corresponding to the third of the Vedic worlds, *vyahṛtis*, represents the illumined mental consciousness. Whereas Vayu symbolises the Life-Energy supportive of the mental activity governed by Indra and receptive to the influx of supramental consciousness through *ṛtam*. Together, these gods, awaken and prepare the human seeker to the inflow of Ananda, the immortal Delight, Soma, from above. The Ananda thus received by the purified mental and vital energies constitutes 'a new action' that prepares 'the immortal consciousness in the mortal'. The seer implores the entry of Indra and Vayu at this stage and perfect the workings of the new action by the participation of the thought-power. The state of consciousness thus attained is "intermediate between the normal mentality represented by the combination of Indra and Vayu and the *ṛtam* or Truth-Consciousness."[43]

The action of Vayu is helpful in the preparation of the vital energies, and that of Indra in that of the mental-energies. The combined action of Indra-Vayu prepares the nervous mentality for the workings of the Truth-Consciousness in the human being. Whereas the joint action of Varuna and Mitra is precisely the working of the Truth, *ṛtam*, on the nervous-mentality with a view to perfect the intellect and enlarge and widen its scope for the full and perfect influx of Truth-Consciousness. Truth, *ṛtam*, is the manifesting dynamis of the supramental consciousness.

It is by thought, *dhi*, that the nervous mentality is perfected. But thought itself is "perfected, enriched and clarified" before it becomes "capable of free communication with the Truth-Consciousness". "Therefore Varuna and Mitra, Powers of the Truth", says Sri Aurobindo, "are invoked 'accomplishing a richly luminous thought', *dhiyaṁ ghṛtācīṁ sādhantā*."[44] Although *ghṛ* outwardly means clarified butter, inwardly or psychologically it signifies 'a rich and bright activity of the brain-power'. By *dhiyaṁ ghṛtācīṁ* the Rishi therefore means an 'intellect full of a rich and bright mental activity.'

The Vedas put before them the Truth-Consciousness and the consequent 'fulfilment of the godhead' or the attainment of immortality as the ideal and the goal. This needs a corresponding preparation and perfection of the vital and mental of the seeker; they need to be purified, made plastic and receptive to the inflowing Truth. The dyad, Indra-Vayu prepares the mentality of the seeker for the workings of the Truth-Consciousness in man, and Varuna and Mitra represent its very working in the human mind. And two are the conditions of the working of Truth-Consciousness, Light and Power, which have to be fulfilled. The Light of the Truth has to seek entry into the mental consciousness, and the Power of the Truth make its home in the enlightened human will before the Supramental Consciousness can start working in the human being.

The gods in the Veda "represent universal powers descended from the Truth-Consciousness which build up the harmony of the worlds and in man his progressive perfection", and the Dasyus and Vritras are "the hostile agencies... who seek to break up, to limit, to withhold and deny."[45] Varuna and Mitra are positive powers of Truth-Consciousness, "multiple-born", *Tuvijata*, and manifested in many forms and activities for the evolution of consciousness upon earth. They are the *devas* who possessed of the supramental consciousness use its faculties of 'vision, inspiration, intuition, discrimination' and manifest in the human being the qualities of 'wideness and purity, of joy and harmony'. Varuna destroys the forces of resistance, obscurantism, impurity, limitation and discord, *riśādasa*, and helps the intellect to reflect perfectly the Light and Power of the Truth-Consciousness. Also he promotes the purity of discernment and perfect discrimination, *viveka*. He is the power of wideness and purity, and as a constant and conscious force of the Truth present in man he destroys all sin and evil.

Mitra is the god 'possessed of a purified judgment', *putadakṣa*; he is a power of Truth-Consciousness and represents "Love, Joy and Harmony, the foundations of Mayas, the Vedic beatitude. Working with the purity of Varuna and imparting that purity to the discernment, he enables it to get rid of all discords and confusions and establish the right working of the strong and luminous intellect."[46] Together they accomplish a rich and perfect state of intellect capable of coming into luminous contact with the Truth-Consciousness, receive it and possess it. It is thus that they, utilising the Truth as an effective agency, increase its action in the seeker and transform his will-power into a dynamic instrument of Truth-effectuation. "For it is the Will", says Sri Aurobindo, "that is the chief effective agent of the inner sacrifice, but Will that is in harmony with the Truth, guided therefore by a purified discernment."[46a] The Will itself becomes 'wide and vast' as it becomes associated with the wideness of the Truth-Consciousness; all limitation gets rolled back and the impeding elements thinned out. It is the effective Will as the instrument of Truth that establishes a state of beatitude within which the lasting good, *bhadram*, is worked out. The consummating gain of the harmonious and joint working of Will and Discernment, of Light and Power, is the attainment of the Truth-Consciousness and its establishment in the 'perfected mentality' of the seeker.

(1)

Varuna: The Ascent to the Infinite

The word Varuna is derived from a root which means to surround, cover or pervade. The ancient seers used it to represent concretely the Infinite, the Boundless and the Beyond. In the words of Sri Aurobindo, the Rishis "saw God as a highest covering Heaven, felt divine existence like an encompassing ocean, lived in its boundless presence as in a pure and pervading ether. Varuna is this highest heaven, this soul-surrounding ocean, this ethereal possession and infinite pervasion... His godhead is the form or spiritual image of an embracing and illuminating Infinity."[47] Varuna has a very wide and vast being because of which his physical figure is vague. He is neither the king of the skies nor the God of Night. "Varuna of the Veda is at once King, — not of the heavens as such, for that is Dyaushpita, nor of the heavens of light, for that is Indra, — but of the highest covering ether and all oceans. All expanses are Varuna's; every infinity is his property and estate."[48] In their mystic vision, the Rishis saw two firmaments — 'the earthly and the celestial', and three oceans — the physical, the ethereal and the spiritual. They also speak of 'an unfathomable night' of Inconscience below and 'a remote ocean of light and sweetness above'. They declare that they owe their existence to 'the mighty energy', the supreme Shakti, which manifested them out of the primal Darkness, and that their existence is irrevocably bound toward the All-conscient and the absolute of existence beyond. It is the realisation of the Rishis that the ocean of Darkness below and the ocean of Light above are the extension of the Transcendent One. The former is the unexplored dark infinity with infinite potentiality, and the latter is the luminous infinity with infinite manifest light, all-enveloping and all-pervading. Between these two infinities they discovered "a third sea of ever-developing conscious being, a sort of boundless wave... climbing up or flowing up beyond heaven to the supreme seas."[49] The seeker is called upon to cross it over; the journey is perilous, there are pirates cast in by the Inconscient. We rise out of one ocean and enter another; there are, in fact, not three but several seas one within the other, rather tier upon tier — one above the other, the lowest at the nether bottom is the dark ocean of Inconscience. In the words of Sri Aurobindo — "heights that are depths and a mutual involution and evolution of vastnesses that have no ending: ether below rises to ever more luminous ether above, every stratum of consciousness rests upon many inferior and aspires to many higher strata."[50]

It is from these many oceans that the Vedic rivers flow; they descend upon the earth as well as ascend the mind illuminating it. They are 'divine waters', 'the streams of the Truth'; 'they are the rain from its luminous heavens' that fertilise the aspiring earth-nature for the harvest of Light. Varuna is the king of these oceans and these rivers; seated in their middle, he purifies them, and upholds the working of Truth in all the planes.

Pra sīmādityo asṛjadvidhartāñ
ṛtaṁ sindhavo varuṇasya yanti,
na śrāmyanti na vi mucantyete
vayo na paptu raghuyā parijman.[51]

"The Son of Infinity, the wide upholder, has loosed them forth everywhere; the rivers journey to the truth of Varuna."*

Varuna is the Dawn as well as the march of dawns, and implants the sacrificial *mantra* in them, thus spurring them on from height to greater height.

> "That is the truth of King Varuna. Thither the Dawns shining arise, the rivers travel and the Sun unyokes there the horses of his chariot."*[52]

The Rishis envision him

> "...as the oceanic surge of the hidden Divine as he rises, progressively manifested, to his own infinite wideness and ecstasy in the soul of the god-liberated seer."[53]

He is the 'King-Sage, the Hero-Thinker', the 'self-ruler and emperor', master of both thought and action, wisdom and will, consciousness and force. In him "we see revealed a divine and eternal majesty, the plenitude of consciousness and the plenitude of Force, Wisdom omnipotent, Power omniscient, Law justified, Truth fulfilled."[54]

There is a knowledge that uplifts us to the beatitude beyond, there is a Wisdom that opens the doors to this knowledge, and there is a Path that shapes in us this Wisdom. Varuna is the Path, the Wisdom, the Knowledge and the Beatitude. The Rishis see him as the destroyer of all sin and ignorance, the purifier and liberator, healer of 'our mental and moral infirmities and the Captain of the ship of the forces of Light'. He is the luminous force of cosmic existence, and "the continent and nodus of the world's uplifted puissances."[55] It is Varuna who builds the ascending edifices to the kingdom of Immortality, the harbinger and the path-maker for the Truth to follow in the manifest universe. He is the father of all the heights to which man must climb; he is the mother of all the worlds which the voyager must conquer. The final destination is the highest and most perfect triple world of Varuna.

1. *Yasya śvetā vicakṣaṇā tisro*
   bhūmiradhikṣitaḥ,
   triruttarāṇi papraturvaruṇasya dhruvaṁ
   sadaḥ sa saptānāmirajyati nabhantām
   anyake same.

2. *Yaḥ śvetāñ adhinirṇijaścakre*
   kṛṣṇāñ anu vrata

> *sa dhāma pūrvyaṁ mame yaḥ skambhena*
> *vi rodasī ajo na dyāmadhārayan*
> *nabhantāmanyake same.*[56]

> "Three delightful Dawns increase according to the law of his workings. He of the all-seeing wisdom dwells in three white-shining earths; three are the higher worlds of Varuna whence he rules over the harmonies of seven and seven. He is the builder of the original seat, 'That Truth' of Varuna; and he is the guardian and the mover."*

Varuna provides the Truth with the widest and purest framework for its operation in the universe and also its evolving substance. He is like a mighty sleepless guardian, ever awake and ever watchful, the indefatigable upholder of an ever-expanding universe of Truth. He is the eternal traveller to the supreme abode of the Sun who supports the law of an ever-perfecting action. He is the omniscient creator of a fertile climate of growth for the soul from 'the falsehood of the lower being' into the eternal sunshine of the Truth. He is 'the Lord of infinite purity and wisdom' who opens our physical-vital-mental being to the radiance and puissance of the Sun of immortal knowledge. Our salutations to Varuna the mighty master and guide of men.

Verily, Varuna is the prince 'of the puissance and the thousandfold vision' whose "oceanic movement envelops all the kingdoms of being and ascends to the Paradise of the heaven of heavens."

> *Sa samudro apīcyasturo dyāmiva*
> *rohati ni yadasu yajurdadhe,*
> *sa māyā arcinā padāstṛṇānnākam*
> *aruhannabhantāmanyake same.*[57]

> He is the hidden ocean, and swiftly he mounts the heavens beyond as the sun climbs the sky; when he places the sacrificial Word in these dawns, then he demolishes with his radiances the illusions of the Asuras and ascends to Paradise: may all our enemies be destroyed.

Varuna is the great movement, the mighty flow of the concealed Truth — the upward streaming strength that effectuates its own progressive manifestation in its ascent to the infinite immensity and ecstasy of itself in the integrally emancipated soul of the seeker. He is the king of the divine canon that demolishes all deceptive designs of Evil; he is the sea of pure existence who dissolves all sin. The Rishis again and again implore him to absolve them of all sin and liberate them from their ignorance and consequent bondage to Evil.

Yat kiṁ cedaṁ varuṇa daivye jane
'bhidrohaṁ manuṣyāścaramasi,
acitti yattava dharma yuyopima
mā nastasmādenaso deva rīriṣaḥ.[58]

Whatever be the offence, O Varuna, which we human beings may commit against the divine beings, whenever we may through ignorance violate your laws, punish us not for that sin; forgive us always, O God.

The significance and the necessity of liberation from the triple bondage of mind, life and body are suitably and succinctly brought out in the parable of Shunahshepa. Ignorance is the source and nursery of sin; it delimits and obscures the mind, ineffectuates the life, and incapacitates the physicality of the seeker. It is this threefold subjection and thraldom that is imaged and symbolised in Shunahshepa's hapless tie up to the sacrificial post. According to Sri Aurobindo '*Shunahshepa*' symbolises a certain type of spiritual realisation that is bound to be continuously repeated in the life of the human race; the term signifies 'a Ray of Bliss'. Rishi Shunahshepa finds himself bound by the triple bonds of the lower life, and implores to be released so that he could rejoin the Infinite Mother. He intensely aspires to return to the luminous source of all creation, Aditi, the Infinite Consciousness in Manifestation. To effectuate this liberation the Rishi invokes Agni, Prajapati and Savitri, and finally the godhead Varuna. Agni signifies the flaming force of Aspiration that burns down all earthly resistance and leads the seeker on the path to the Truth. He also induces and institutes a process of purification, and prepares the seeker to receive the gods within his being. Whereas Savitri is invoked for the increase of inner riches — the supreme felicity and plenitude. Then Varuna of pure comprehension and discrimination, skill and strength is requested to redeem Shunahshepa from his evil impasse. Varuna is the great purifier and liberator; he abolishes all ignorance and heals our mental and moral debilities with his wideness and righteousness. All the gods are implored in order to be restored to Aditi, the Supreme Mother.

The Ray of Delight descending from Aditi, the Infinite Consciousness is the embodied soul of man which when awakened aspires and hungers to return to her fold. In this he solicits the help of the gods, the builders of the Truth in the seeker-soul. But Shunahshepa, the embodied *Jiva*, finds himself entrenched in falsehood, and tied and bound to the tree of limited phenomenal existence. He finds himself in a dangerous predicament and implores the gods for their intervention and help. He knows that the flaming force of Agni and the white grace of Varuna alone can effectuate the release that he so devoutly desires for. It is the knowledge of the infinite Truth that has the power to emancipate him from the shackles of the ignorant mind, the imbecile life and the ineffective and inconscient physical. The vast and abundant Varuna, the puissant and most mighty god, is extolled and invoked to come to the rescue.

1. *Nahi te kṣatraṁ na saho na manyuṁ*
   vayaścanāmī patayanta āpuḥ,
   nemā apo animiṣaṁ carantīrna ye
   vātasya praminantyabhvam.

2. *Abudhne rājā varuṇo vanasyordhvaṁ*
   stupaṁ dadate pūtadakṣaḥ,
   nīcīnāḥ sthurupari budhna eṣāmasme
   antarnihitāḥ ketavaḥ syuḥ.

3. *Uruṁ hi rājā varuṇáscakāra sūryaya*
   panthāmanvetavā u,
   apade padā pratidhātave 'karutāpavaktā
   hṛdayāvidhaścit.

4. *Śataṁ te rājanbhiṣajaḥ sahasramurvī*
   gabhīrā sumatiṣṭe astu,
   bādhasva dūre nirṛtiṁ parācaiḥ kṛtaṁ
   cidenaḥ pra mumugdhyasmat.

5. *Amī ya ṛkṣā nihitāsa uccā naktaṁ*
   dadṛśre kuha ciddiveyuḥ,
   adabdhāni varuṇasya vratāni vicākaśac
   candramā naktam eti.

6. *Tattvā yāmi brahmaṇā vandamānastad*
   ā śāste yajamāno havirbhiḥ,

aheḷamāno varuṇeha bodhyuruśansa mā
na āyuḥ pra moṣīḥ.

7. *Tadinnaktaṁ taddivā mahyamāhustad*
ayaṁ keto hṛd ā vi caṣṭe,
śunaḥ śepo yamahvadgṛbhītaḥ so asmān
rājā varuṇo mumoktu.

8. *Śunaś hepo hyahvadgṛbhītastriṣv*
ādityaṁ drupadeṣu baddhaḥ,
avainaṁ rājā varuṇaḥ sasṛjyādvidvāṁ
adabdho vi mumoktu paśān.

9. *Ava te heḷo varuṇa namobhirava*
yajñebhirīmahe havirbhiḥ,
kṣayannasmabhyasura praceta rājann
enāṅsi śiśrathaḥ kṛtāni.

10. *Uduttamam varuṇa pāśamasmadavādhamaṁ*
vi madhyamaṁ śrathāya,
athā vayamāditya vrate tavānāgaso
aditaye syāma.[59]

1. These soaring birds, O Varuna, cannot attain your force and strength, nor do they have the prowess to endure your fury; neither these Waters that flow ceaselessly nor the winds that blow speedily can surpass your might.

2. The sovereign Varuna of sacred discernment, skill and strength, shining in the baseless firmament sustains a mass of radiance the rays of which stream downwards with their base above. May these rays become concentrated in us as the source of existence.

3. The imperial Varuna of abiding prowess prepares the spacial pathway for the Sun to follow; in the baseless firmament above he provides a base for the tread of his feet. May he repel whatever afflicts the heart and afflicts the course.

4. Innumerable are your medicaments, O King, a hundred balms, a thousand healers; may your gracious thought and right-mindedness

flow wide and deep towards us. May you keep afar from us Nirritti, the Daemon of Sin and Death, drive off all destructive forces, and liberate us from all sins that we may have committed.

5. These constellations set on high above, that are seen by night and go elsewhere by day, are the steady and unswerving workings of Varuna; it is by his command again that the Moon moves resplendent by night.

6. O much-lauded Varuna, I implore you for that Supreme whom the worshipper devoutly craves for with his oblations. O Lord, undisdainful, bestow a thought upon us; let not our life-span be robbed before it is fulfilled.

7. This, your praise, the wise ones repeat to me by night and by day, and it is this knowledge that my heart seeks to know. May he whom the fettered Shunahshepa has invoked, the sovereign Varuna, help us in our liberation from evil, and verily set us free.

8. Seized and bound to the threefold tree of life Shunahshepa invokes the Son of Aditi: may the sovereign Varuna, all-knowing and irresistible, deliver him from the triple bondage and liberate him.

9. O Varuna, we deflect the danger of your wrath with sacrifices and oblations, homages and prayers. Dwelling in us always, O supreme Knower and illustrious One, mitigate all evils and sins committed by us.

10. O Varuna, loosen from us all bonds — upper, lower and middle; for only then O supreme Son of Aditi, can we wholly live for Aditi, faultless in your worship.

Varuna is the mighty world-ruler and self-ruler, *samrāṭ* and *swarāṭ*; he is the master of the force of universal existence. He has the seer's expression and the hero's dynamis, and ever supports the sacrificer with the fullness of his will and wisdom. The Rishis speak of him as the supreme knower of the all and the great upholder of the many existences. In Sri Aurobindo's words, "Great Varuna is the continent and nodus of the world's uplifted puissances no less than of its arising thoughts". He is the 'vast thinker and guardian of the Truth', and "knows the things that are done and those that remain to be done."[60] The Rishis always seek his stewardship for he is the path-finder who discloses the sacred thought by the heart, and forges the divine Word deep in the foundry of the seeker's sacrificial being.

Varuna is the godhead of vastness and immensity, of oneness and multiplicity. He is the universality of knowledge and the cosmicity of force. He is intolerant of sin and all infirmity; he violently delivers men from sin and its dark earnings. He is the Pure and the puissant One, and acts swiftly and even revengefully against Ignorance and Evil.

Sin, for the Rishis, is the result of recalcitrant Ignorance which again is due to non-cognition and non-receptivity of the Truth by the mind, life and body. It is this inherent threefold weakness that necessitates Ignorance which calls for Varuna's retributive action. The Rishi cries for redemption of sin without much violence; he beseeches Varuna to act, but act with grace and consideration. He implores Varuna that he be treated for his moral and mental ailments by means other than violent destruction for he has under his dispensation several physicians to secure the purpose. In him who is almighty and omniscient the seeker is cured of all infirmities, and is lifted up to the supreme felicity and the Truth.

Varuna is the supreme promoter of human aspiration; he abides helpfully in the uprising of the Waters, and marches along to the Paradise of pure Light dissolving all falsehood.

a) *Nābhākasya praśastibhiryaḥ sindhunām*
upodaye saptasvasā sa madhyamo
nabhantāmanyake same.[61]

In the uprising of the rivers Varuna is the brother of the seven sisters (streams) in their midst. May he destroy all our adversaries.

b) *Yāsāṁ rājā varuṇo yāti madhye*
satyānṛte avapaśyañjanānām,
madhuścutaḥ śucayo yāḥ pāvakāstā
āpo devīriha māmavantu.[62]

Amidst the pure and purifying Waters marches the sovereign Lord, Varuna, honey-pouring, looking down on the truth and falsehood in men. May those waters protect us here always.

The son of the Infinite Mother, Varuna, enveloped by the Supreme

Light and accompanied by an army as it were of reconnaisancers leads forward the aspirants by the sun-lit path. These surveyors check out the hidden enemies of the Light who obstruct the discovery of the Truth-thought by psychic means. Shunahshepa cries,

Sa no viśvāhā sukraturadityaḥ
supathā karat,
pra ṇa āyuṅṣi tāriṣat.

Bibhraddrāpiṁ hiraṇyayaṁ varuṇo
vasta nirṇijam,
pari spaśo ni ṣedire.[63]

"Perfect in will, let the Son of Infinity make us by the good path and carry our life forward. Varuna puts on his golden robe of light and his scouts are all around."*

The upward march of the rivers is also the pilgrimage of the Sun, and the path itself is constantly new-made by the progressive discovery of the Truth. Varuna, the ever vigilant guide, residing in the vastness of existence ardently refuels the sacrificial fire. Eternally established in the Truth above he builds a spacious path for the Sun to pursue; he prepares the ground for the great adventure, his purity devours all resisters. The goal of the marathon journey is the infinite and omniscient Truth, it is the triple truth of the Divine — Sachchidananda. The realisation of this Truth progressively increases in the seeker according to the law of Varuna's workings in him. For Varuna is the steadfast builder of the seat of the Truth in the aspirant as well as his devout unfailing guide.

In brief, then, "Varuna is the ethereal, oceanic, infinite King of wide being, wide knowledge and wide might, a manifestation of the one God's active omniscience and omnipotence, a mighty guardian of the Truth, punisher and healer, Lord of the noose and Releaser from the cords, who leads thought and action towards the vast light and power of a remote and high-uplifted Truth. Varuna is the King of all kingdoms and of all divine and mortal beings; earth and heaven and every world are only his provinces."[64]

Varuna is the godhead of infinite wisdom and purity who steadily opens our mental, vital and physical to the Sun of the Supreme Truth and pours down into them the honeyed streams of shining knowledge. By the power of his intense and immense purity he removes all evil and imperfection, ignorance and falsehood and creates the necessary wideness for receiving the shining harvest of heaven in the mind, the flaming will in the heart and the power of supreme effectuation in the vital.

(2)

The All-knowing and All-seeing Mighty Master

The hymns of the Rig-veda have a 'sustained double sense', and are capable of both exoteric and esoteric interpretation. Hymn V.85 is an example under citation which renders itself in more than one significance. In the exoteric sense it describes Varuna as "the omniscient and omnipotent lord and creator, the godhead in his creative wisdom and might forming the world and maintaining the law of things in the earth and mid-air and heavens."[65] And in the esoteric sense he is hymned as "the infinite Godhead... in his all-pervading wisdom and purity opening the three worlds of our being to the Sun of knowledge, pouring down the streams of the Truth, purifying the soul from the falsehood of the lower being and its sin."[66]

These are the two aspects of the great *deva*, all-power and all-knowledge, omnipotence and infinite wisdom. Even as he creates the universe of manifestation and upholds the three worlds, he opens them to the Light of the transforming Truth and purifies and puts the pilgrim-soul on its evolutionary journey.

a) *The Exoteric Approach to Hymn V.85.1-8*

The Rishi hymns Varuna as the omnipotent All-ruler and renowned King who having cleft away darkness spreads out the earth under the sun. He establishes the mid-world, and puts strength in the war-steeds, milk in the cows, will in the hearts, fire in the waters, 'the sun in heaven and the Soma-plant on the mountain'. He floods the triple world with waters from above, and whenever he desires pours forth the milk of heaven, and employs his heroes of storm, the Maruts, to cast off the clouds that cover the mountains. The mighty Varuna, standing in mid-air, measures out the earth, as it were, with the sun of his infinite wisdom. Into the ocean of his omniscience flow all the rivers, and pouring themselves into it cannot alter its nature. The Rishi having become aware of the immeasurable might and mercy of Varuna implores that he may be cleansed of all sin done in ignorance against the truth.

1. *Pra samrāje bṛhadarcā gabhīraṁ brahma*
priyaṁ varuṇāya śrutāya,
vi yo jaghāna śamiteva carmopastire
pṛthivīṁ sūryāya.

2. *Vaneṣu vyantarikṣaṁ tatāna vājam*
arvatsu paya usriyāsu,
hṛtsu kratuṁ varuṇo apsvagniṁ divi
sūryamadadhātsomamadrau.

3. *Nīcīnabāraṁ varuṇaḥ kavandhaṁ pra*
sasarja rodasī antarikṣam,
tena viśvasya bhuvanasya rājā yavaṁ na
vṛṣṭirvyunatti bhūma.

4. *Unatti bhūmiṁ prithivīmuta dyāṁ yadā*
dugdhaṁ varuṇo vaṣṭyadit,
samabhreṇa vasata parvatāsastāviṣīyantaḥ
śrayayanta vīrāḥ.

5. *Imāmu ṣvāsurasya śrutasya mahīṁ māyāṁ*
varuṇasya pra vocam,
māneneva tasthivāñ antarikṣe vi yo mame
pṛthivīṁ sūryeṇa.

6. *Imamu nu kavitamasya māyāṁ mahīṁ*
devasya nakirā dadharṣa
ekaṁ yadudnā na pṛnantyenīr
āsiñcantīravanayaḥ samudram.

7. *Aryamyaṁ varuṇa mitryaṁ vā sakhāyaṁ*
vā sadamid bhrātaraṁ vā,
veśaṁ vā nityaṁ varuṇāraṇaṁ vā yatsīm
āgaścakṛmā śiśrathastat.

8. *Kitavāso yadriripurna dīvi yadvā ghā*
satyamuta yanna vidma,
sarvā tā vi ṣya śithireva devādhā te
syāma varuṇa priyāsaḥ.[67]

b) *The Esoteric Insight*

The Rishi hymns Varuna 'as the Lord of infinite purity and wisdom', the fount of 'far-heard inspirations', the source, seat and creator of wideness who cleaves wide away the veil of Darkness laminated to our being 'as one that cleaves away a skin' from a beast of prey, and enables the earth 'to receive the revelations and inspirations of the light' of the supramental gnosis. He also 'spreads out in its full wideness' the vital world to receive the immortal Ananda, pours heavenly milk into the luminous vials of thought, implants the sacrificial will in human hearts, enkindles the divine fire, Agni, in the ocean of our being, enthrones the Sun of Supreme Light in our heavens and discovers the Soma-plant of divine Delight on the mountain of our inner being. He makes the supramental gnosis operative in creation — to make the Truth-dynamis to open its doors downward and flood the lower being, the physical, vital and mental, with the light and power of the Infinite. He dissolves the clouds of ignorance that cover the mountains with the help of his valiant supporters and makes the earth widely receptive to the descending consciousness of Aditi. He brings the transforming light of the gnosis into the lives of humans, and casts and maps out their earth-existence in the measures of the Truth manifest in their minds. He is also the helpful link between the illumined mental and the physical and stationed in the vital receives the Light and creative Force from above, and passes it on to the earth. Vast and widest is the wisdom of Varuna, oceanic is his seer-knowledge and none can either measure it, or obstruct it in its operation; the seven rivers of Truth ceaselessly emptying their waters into it cannot fill it. Verily, nothing can either increase the infinitude of Varuna nor diminish it.

"He plans out", says Sri Aurobindo, "all our physical existence by his wisdom according to the truth-light of the sun of knowledge and creates in us the unity of his own infinite existence and consciousness with all the seven rivers of the Truth-plane pouring their streams of knowledge into it without filling its infinity."[68] The Rishi implores and prays that he may be forgiven of all sin done against Varuna in his power of Aryaman or Mitra or the eternal indweller and warrior against the Dasyus, and that the sin done in ignorance against the truth be cast away from him so that he may grow intimate with him.

Varuna is the all-encompassing and all-seeing deity accompanied always by his divinely discerning assistants.

a) *Kadā kṣatraśriyaṁ naramā varuṇaṁ*
karāmahe, mṛḷīkāyorucakṣasam.[69]

When shall we for our own benefit O venerable Varuna, bring ourselves completely to you who are eminent in strength, and the dependable guide of men.

b) *Viśve yadvāṁ maṅhanā mandamānāḥ*
kṣatraṁ devāso adadhuḥ sajoṣāḥ,
ri yadbhutho rodasī cidurvī
santi spaśo adabdhāso amūrāḥ.[70]

All the gods equally pleased, and rejoicing in your greatness have accepted your supremacy and conferred strength upon you; and since you are pre-eminent over the wide earth and heaven, your courses are ever unobstructed and always unimpeded.

c) *Tvaṁ dātā prathamo rādhasāmasy*
āsi satya īśānakṛt,
tuvidyumnasya yujyā vṛṇīmahe
putrasya śavaso maha.[71]

Verily, you are the principal giver of bounteous gifts; you are truthful and sovereign in your deeds. We solicit blessings most worthy of you, O lord of vast riches, and mighty source of strength.

d) *Uta yo dyāmatisarpātparastānna sa*
mucyātai varuṇasya rājñaḥ,
diva spaśaḥ pra carantīdamasya
sahasrākṣā ati paśyanti bhūmim.[72]

Even if one manages to run away from heaven, one cannot go out of the vigilance of sovereign Varuna, for his thousand-eyed chary powers are ever watchful over this earth.

e) *Sarvaṁ tadrājā varuṇo vi caṣṭe*
yadantarā rodasī yatparastāt,
saṁkhyātā asya nimiṣo janānāmakṣāniva
śvaghnī ni minoti tāni.[73]

The Supreme Being, Varuna, sees whatever exists in heaven and earth and beyond. He counts the blinks of every eye and enumerates like a skillful gambler his every move in the cosmic game.

He is the omniscient overseer and lord of the three earths and the three heavens — monarch of men, of the universe and of the gods. He holds sway over all the worlds, the waters and the heavens.

> *Astabhnād dyāmasuro viśvavedā*
> *amimīta varimāṇaṁ pṛthivyāḥ,*
> *asīdadviśvā bhuvanāni samrādviśvet*
> *tāni varuṇasya vratāni.*[74]

> The possessor of all riches, the powerful Varuna, has determined the heavens and has measured out the wide earth; he presides over all the worlds as a supreme monarch. Such are the functions of the regal lord.

He is the water-god, king of the seas and the dispenser of rain.

> a) *Mitrāvarunau vṛṣṭyādhipatī tau*
> *māvatam, asminbrahmaṇyasmin*
> *karmaṇyasyāṁ purodhāyāmasyāṁ*
> *pratiṣṭhāyamasyāṁ*
> *cittyāmasyāmākūtyāmasyāmāśiṣyasyāṁ*
> *devahutyāṁ svāhā.*[75]

> Mitra and Varuna are the master-powers of rain. Let these protect me and help me in the attainment of Knowledge, in my sacrificial undertaking and all other activities that promote life's stability, secure prosperity, and give me knowledge of the external world.

> b) *Samrājā ugrā vṛṣabhā divaspati*
> *pṛthivyā mitrāvaruṇā vicarṣanī,*
> *citrebhirabhrairūpa tiṣṭhatho ravaṁ*
> *dyaṁ varṣayatho asurasya māyayā.*[76]

> O Lords of heaven and earth, imperial and mighty showerers of rain, overseers of the universe, you approach with multiformed clouds to listen to our prayers and cause the sky to bring down rains by your supremely magical powers.

> c) *Māyā vaṁ mitrāvaruṇā divi śritā sūryo*
> *jyotiścarati citramāyudham,*

tamabhreṇa vṛṣṭyā gūhatho divi
parjanya drapsā madhumanta īrate.[77]

O Mitra and Varuna, your stratagem works above when the sun, your wonderful weapon, moves in the firmament; you invest him in the sky with cloud and rain, and then the rain falls at your behest.

d) *Ā rājānā maha ṛtasya gopā sindhupatī*
kṣatriyā yātamarvāk,
iḷaṁ no mitrāvarunota vṛṣṭim
ava diva invataṁ jīradānu.[78]

O Mitra and Varuna, mighty preservers of the waters, powerful lords of rivers, come to bless us; send down to us from above abundant rain and sustenance.

Varuna is the purifying power of the waters that cleanses men from every sin. He with his inscrutable power, *māyā* establishes the earth and keeps vigil on its workings. And through his dynamic law, *ṛta*, he eternally promotes order in the universe and also governs the lives of men.

Dharmanā mitrāvaruṇā vipaścitā vratā
rakṣethe asurasya māyayā,
ṛtena viśvaṁ bhuvanaṁ vi rājathaḥ
sūryamā dhattho divi citryaṁ ratham.[79]

O Mitra and Varuna, by the law you protect and promote your pious determinations, and by the inscrutable power of your rain-producing devices you illumine the whole universe as well as sustain the sun, the refulgent chariot in the sky.

In addition, Varuna is the most merciful and forgiving god, for he is as personal in his dealings with men as he is impersonal in matters universal. He is both the redeemer of sin and the bestower of felicity. He is the protector of the Law, *dharma*, and the promulgator of the decree, *dhāma*; he is the wielder of power, *dakṣa*, and the sustainer of will, *kratu*.

a) *Prati vāṁ sūra udite suktairmitraṁ*
huve varuṇaṁ pūtadakṣam,

yayorasuryamakṣitaṁ jyeṣṭhaṁ
viśvasya yāmannācitā jigatnu.[80]

With the coming of each dawn I invoke you, O Varuna and Mitra, lords of pure vigour, whose superior and imperishable prowess is ever triumphant in the crowded conflict over all the enemies.

b) *Pratāñ agnirbabhasattigmajambhas*
tapiṣṭhena śociṣā yaḥ surādhāḥ,
pra ye minanti varuṇasya dhāma priyā
mitrasya cetato dhruvāṇi.[81]

May the many-tongued Agni, possessed of manifold prowess, consume with his fierce radiance all those who disregard and harm the firm and steadfast laws of the most judicious Varuna and Mitra.

c) *Mama dvita rāṣṭram kṣatriyasya viśvāyor*
viśve amṛtā yathā naḥ,
kratuṁ sacante varuṇasya devā
rājāmi kṛṣterupamasya vavreḥ.[82]

Twofold is my kingdom, that of the whole Kshatriya race and of all the immortals. The gods abide by my Law, and I rule over man and those akin to him.

Varuna is described as the one who is absolutely intolerant of sin and full of anger for falsehood, *anṛta*. His helpers keep a close scrutiny of men's lives and punish them for their moral and spiritual infirmities; the seekers are mortally afraid of him and seek his forgiveness of their shortcomings, and pray for their deliverance from all sin.

a) *Prorormitrāvaruṇā pṛthivyāḥ pra diva*
ṛṣvād bṛhataḥ sudanu,
spaśo dadhāthe oṣadhīṣu vikṣv
ṛdhagyato a nimiṣaṁ rakṣamānā.[83]

O Mitra and Varuna, you are vaster than the wide earth and the expansive heaven; you sustain the beauty of the plant-kingdom and vigilantly protect the people who follow diligently the path of truth.

b) *Iyaṁ deva purohitiryuvabhyāṁ*
yajñeṣu mitrāvaruṇāvakari
viśvāṇi durgā pipṛtaṁ tiro no yūyaṁ
pāta svastibhiḥ sadā naḥ.[84]

O Mitra and Varuna, to you we offer our adoration at the sacrifices; may you remove all obstacles from our path and ever sustain us with your blessings.

Varuna not only castigates the seekers for their sin but also furnishes them with the necessary riches for their inner progress.

Mā no vadhairvaruṇa ye ta iṣṭāv
enaḥ kṛṇvantamasura bhriṇanti,
mā jyotiṣaḥ pravasathāni gamma vi
ṣu mṛdhaḥ śiśvatho jīvase naḥ.[85]

Do not harm us, O Varuna, mighty destroyer of the enemies, with weapons that demolish those who commit sin at your sacrifices. May we not depart before our appointed time from the region of Light. Destroy the malevolent that we may live.

Falsehood is an unpardonable infringement of spiritual growth; it is a violation of Varuna's law.

Yacciddhi te viśo yathā pra
deva varuṇa vratam,
minīmasi dyavi dyavi.
Mā no vadhāya hatnave jihīḷānasya
rīradhaḥ, mā hṛṇānasya manyave.[86]

In as much as all others unwisely perpetuate untruth, O compassionate one, do we everytime disfigure your worship by defaults. Punish us not by the penalty of death through your fatal wrath and displeasure.

In fact, Varuna's sovereignty lies in his enforcement of truth and righteousness.

Ayaṁ devānāmasuro vi rājati vaśā hi
satyā varuṇasya rājñaḥ,

tataspari brahmaṇā śāśadāna ugrasya
manyorudimaṁ nayāmi.[87]

Varuna, the supreme ruler, is also the all-impelling and all-enforcing power among all the forces; the law of this Lord is true and inviolable.

Varuna is omnipresent and omniscient; he is all-pervading and all-seeing. He knows everything in the cosmos and of the human heart. His sense of retribution is strong and is dreaded by men; nonetheless he is merciful and loving.

a) *Bṛhanneṣāmadhiṣṭhātā antikādiva paśyati,*
ya stāyanmanyate carantsarvaṁ
devā idaṁ viduḥ.[88]

b) *Yastiṣṭhati carati yaśca vañcati*
yo nitayaṁ carati yaḥ pratañkam,
dyau saṁniṣadva yanmantrayete
rājā tadved varuṇastṛtīyaḥ.

1. Varuna, the mighty ordainer and overseer on high, sees all our deeds, as if from near at hand. Sustaining the worlds he knows them all; the gods know everything that men do through him, though they contrive to do things unnoticingly.

2. Whether men walk or stand or run or hide themselves, or think secretly, or whisper sitting together, the Lord knows all being present everywhere as the third one.

a) *Ye te pāśā varuna saptasapta tredhā*
tiṣṭhanti viṣitā ruśantaḥ
chinantu sarve anṛtaṁ vadantaṁ yaḥ
satyavādyati taṁ sṛjantu.

b) *Śatena pāśairabhi dhehi varuṇainaṁ mā*
te mocyanṛtavāṅ nṛcakṣaḥ,
āstāṁ jālma udaraṁ śraṁsayitvā
kośa ivābandhaḥ parikṛtyamānaḥ.[89]

1. May the seven times seven snares of yours, O Varuna — a fatal trap

indeed to catch the unguarded — ensnare those who speak untruth, but protect him and pass safely by who speaks the truth.

2. O the supreme watcher of men, entrap and bind those with a hundred nooses who speak lies. May the miscreant be detained with his belly inflated like a bursting barrel whose strips are torn asunder and contents overflowing.

The Rishi implores Varuna for forgiveness and favour; he prays for redemption from all sin and deliverance from all fear. He extols him for perpetual renewal and peace and harmony on all planes of existence.

a) *Tava syāma purūvīrasya sarmann*
uruśaṁsasya varuṇa praṇetaḥ,
yūyaṁ naḥ putrā adite radabdhā
abhi kṣamadhvaṁ yujyāya devāḥ.[90]

O adorable one, great guide of men, whose words reach far, may we ever abide in your protective felicity. O invincible sons of Aditi, forgive us our sins; may you have compassion and grant us your companionship.

b) *Vi macchrathāya raśanāmivāga*
ṛdhyāma te varuṇa khāmṛtasya,
mā tantuśchedi vayato dhiyaṁ me mā
mātrā śāryapasaḥ pura ṛtoḥ.[91]

Cast away sin from me, O Lord, as if it were a rope that binds me. May my life be enriched by your streams of Truth, let not the thread of my life be cut abruptly when it is still engaged in weaving pious deeds; let not my work be cut short before its fulfilment.

c) *Para ṛṇā sāvīradha matkṛtāni māhaṁ*
rajannanyakṛtena bhojam,
avyuṣṭā innu bhūyasīruṣāsa
ā no jīvānvaruṇa tāsu śādhi.[92]

O venerable Lord, discharge me from the sins I have committed; let me not suffer for the sins committed by others. Many are the mornings that have yet to dawn; may we be alive to partake of them.

Rishi Vasistha while accepting his shortcomings surrenders himself humbly before the great godhead and seeks his forgiveness. This act of the seer has an almost universal application.

1. *Dhīrā tvasya mahinā janūṁṣi vi yas*
   tastambha rodasī cidurvī,
pra nākamṛṣvaṁ nunude bṛhantaṁ dvitā
   nakṣatraṁ paprathacca bhūma.

2. *Uta svayā tanvā saṁ vade tatkadānv*
   antarvaruṇe bhuvāni,
kiṁ me havyamahṛṇāno juṣeta kada
   mṛḷīkaṁ sumanā abhi khyam.

3. *Pṛcche tadeno varuṇa didṛkṣūpo emi*
   cikituṣo vipṛccham,
samānaminme kavayaścidāhurayaṁ ha
   tubhyaṁ varuṇo hṛṇīte.

4. *Kimāga āsa varuṇa jyeṣṭhaṁ yat*
   stotāraṁ jighāṁsasi sakhāyam,
pra tanme voco duḷabha svadhāvo'va
   tvānenā namasā tura iyām.

5. *Ava drugdhāni pitryā sṛjā no'va*
   yā vayaṁ cakṛmā tanūbhiḥ,
ava rajanpaśutṛpaṁ na tāyuṁ sṛjā
   vatsaṁ na dāmno vasiṣṭam.

6. *Na sa svo dakṣo varuṇa dhrutiḥ sā sura*
   manyurvibhīdako acittiḥ,
asti jyāyānkanīyasa upāre svapnaścaned
   anṛtasya prayotā.

7. *Araṁ dāso na miḷhuṣe karāṇyahaṁ*
   devāya bhūrṇaye'nāgāḥ,
acetayadacito devo aryo gṛtsaṁ rāye
   kavitaro junāti.

8. *Ayaṁ su tubhyaṁ varuṇa svadhāvo hṛdi*
   stoma upaśṛtāścidastu,

śaṁ naḥ kṣeme śamu yoge no astu
yūyaṁ pāta svastibhiḥ sadā naḥ.[93]

1. Men grow wise through the greatness of him who has fixed in their stations the vast heaven and earth, who has put on high both the sun and the beautiful constellations, and spread out the earth.

2. And I muse silently in my heart and ask: when will I be one with Varuna? When will my oblations be accepted by him without rancour? And when shall I reassured and rejoicing in mind behold the presence of that giver of bounteous felicity?

3. Desirous of seeing you, O Varuna, I inquire what is my offence; I seek out the wise to know the answer: and they all say the same thing, "The great God is angry with you."

4. What then, O venerable Lord, has been my great sin for which you would seek to destroy your friend and worshipper? Tell me soon, O God, who knows all, so that freed from sin, I may quickly approach you with deep and profound veneration.

5. Release us from the yoke of the sins of our forefathers, and also of those we ourselves have committed in our persons. Liberate us, O regal God, like a calf from its cord, like a thief set free from his crime.

6. The evil, O Varuna, was not committed on our own choice; it was wine, wrath, gambling and ignorance that led us astray. And again, it is the handicap of misleading the younger by the elder; sometimes even a dream is provocative to sin.

7. Liberated and set free from sin, I am eager to serve you diligently as a slave. May the showerer of divine benefits, the supreme sustainer of the universe, give intelligence to the simple who are devoid of understanding; may the most wise Lord guide the worshipper on the path of supreme felicity.

8. O god of self-subsisting power, may these laudations now reach you and heartily appreciated. May we succeed in retaining what we have, and acquire more through your grace. May you ever protect us and cherish us with your blessings.

Varuna is repeatedly described as at once the dispenser of severest punishment and the bestower of peace. He avenges the evil-monger as well as pardons him and blesses him with prosperity and happiness. The human predicament is as much essential as it is existential; it is both pressing and elusive. The Rishi turns to Varuna for solution: it is the Lord's mercy that brings about the final liberation.

1. *Mo ṣu varuṇa mṛṇmayaṁ gṛhaṁ*
rajannahaṁ gamam,
mṛḷā sukṣatra mṛḷaya.

2. *Yademi prasphuranniva*
dṛtirna dhmāto adrivaḥ,
mṛḷā sukṣatra mṛḷaya.[94]

1. May I never pass, O sovereign Lord, to the house of clay. Forgive me for all my omissions and commissions, bless me, O supreme Saviour, have mercy.

2. If I become tremulous and totter along, O wielder of thunder, like an inflated wine-skin, forgive me for all my omissions and commissions; bless me, O supreme Saviour, have mercy.

(3)

Varuna and the Cosmic Order

The Adityas have a collective character, and act constantly for the well-being of the earth and men according to a supreme Law which is itself laid down by them. There is a celestial kingdom of 'luminous magnificence', that of the supreme Truth, that rules over our world-order. It is on behalf of this most radiant and sacred domain that the Adityas rule the earth and preserve, protect and promote the order of the cosmos. Among them Varuna and Mitra, looking at the world from their heavenly abode, mount their chariot at the rising of the sun and seeing and knowing everything, open the paths for men.

Of the highest god living in us all, the Atharva-veda says: "In the evening he is Varuna, Agni; in the morning he is Mitra rising".[95] Again it says, "what is pressed together by Varuna is opened up by Mitra in the morning."[96] These repeat the idea that Mitra is associated with the day and

Varuna with the night. European scholars make an unconvincing attempt to equate Varuna and Mitra with the Avestic pair Ahura and Mithra — both great gods, though there are some features common to them.

The idea of *ṛta* bears a close resemblance, or rather has an intimate bearing on the ordinances, *dhaman*, and the injunctions, *vrata*, of Varuna and Mitra. The pair Varuna-Mitra causes celestial rain; Varuna the sovereign who puts men on the right path moves amidst the purifying waters of the Truth. The two are the strengtheners of the Truth, they cling to the Truth; they develop the intellect and are wedded to doing good. They are vast in dimension and are entreated to bestow on men strength, activity and righteousness.

Ṛtena· mitrāvaruṇāvṛtāvṛdhāvṛtaspṛśā,
kratuṁ bṛhantamāśāthe.
Kavī no mitrāvaruṇā tuvijātā urukṣayā,
dakṣaṁ dadhāte apasam.[97]

Varuna is the source and support of the cosmic order as well as its supreme dispenser and regulator; he is also that wherein the universe of manifestation disappears and reappears — the point of dissolution and recreation. He is also the ocean of wisdom and the source of the streams of the Truth. Varuna wraps himself with the waters as a robe.

a) *Abhi tripṛṣṭhaṁ vṛṣaṇaṁ vayodham*
āṅguṣaṇāṁavāvaśanta vaṇīḥ,
vanā vasāno varuno na sindhunvi
ratnadhā dayate vāryāṇi.[98]

The praises of the devotees resound about him the triple-backed, who is the showerer of benefits and the giver of food. Varuna is arrayed in the rivers even as the elixir is mixed with water.

b) *Apādindro apādagnirviśve devā amatsata,*
varuṇa ıdiha kṣayattamāpo
abhyanūṣata vatsaṁ saṁśiśvarīriva.

Sudevo asi varuṇa yasya te sapta sindhavaḥ,
anukṣaranti kakudaṁ sūrmyaṁ
suṣirāmiva.[99]

Agni and Indra drink the Soma-juice; all the gods drink it with great delight. Let Varuna taste it with joy and fix his dwelling place therein; may the devout worshippers appreciate it as the mother cows low on meeting their calves.

O blissful Lord, Varuna, verily, you are full of divine delight; the seven streams keep pouring into you always as a fair-flowing stream into an abyss.

Residing in the waters of undifferentiated material existence Varuna, one of the earlier godheads, shapes the universe and shapes it out in a threefold order.

Ahamapo apinvamukṣamānā dhārayaṁ
divaṁ sadana ṛtasya,
ṛtena putro aditerṛtāvota
tridhātu prathayadvi bhūma.[100]

I distribute the cosmic waters, and uphold the sky as the abode of the waters and the Law. Being the preserver of the cosmic order, the son of Aditi, I create the universe according to the eternal laws, and spread wide the world in space in three-fold order.

Out of his unique power, *māyā*, Varuna sets the sun in perpetual motion, the fire of aspiration in the Waters and the milk of nourishment in the udders. He envelops and contains the nights and secures and institutes the mornings. He is all-pervasive and all-prevailing and supports both heaven, earth and the mid-region.

Tisro dyāvo nihitā antarasmintisro
bhūmīruparāḥ ṣadvidhānāḥ,
gṛtso rājā varuṇaścakra etaṁ divi
preṅkhaṁ hiraṇyayaṁ śubhe kam.[101]

In him rest the three regions, and in him are confided the three earths with their six seasons sown in him; the adorable sovereign Lord has made this golden sun undulating in the sky, and made it to diffuse golden light.

Varuna is the creator of the Law, *satyadharman*, its overseer and its custodian, for his eye is the sun itself. Each godhead is governed and sustained by a law unique to himself, *dharman*, and in his own singular way upholds its action. *Dharman* in his cosmic and divine essence that defines and determines his own mode of functioning that is in conformity and in complete harmony with the rest of the gods. The deep-visioned Varuna is the embodiment of *dharman* that supports the universe as well as upholds the good of human society. The Veda repeatedly brings home to us the terrifying regality of Varuna and the decisive role he plays in tearing apart the roots of sin and evil from the lives of men, and bringing them back to the felicitous path.

a) *Ātmā te vāto raja ā navīnotpaśur*
na bhūrniryavase sasavān,
antarmahī bṛhatī rodasīme viśvā
te dhāma varuṇa priyāṇi.[102]

The wind is your breath which gives out sounds through the region like a wild beast that seeks his food in pastures. O venerable Varuna, between the vast heaven and earth are manifested all the glorious forms that you love.

b) *Viśveṣāṁ vaḥ satāṁ jyeṣṭhatamā*
gīrbhirmitrāvaruṇā vavṛdhadhyai,
saṁ yā raśmeva yamaturyamiṣṭhā
dvā janāñ asamā bāhubhiḥ svaiḥ.[103]

I advance by offering my praises to exalt you O Varuna and Mitra, the foremost of all existing ones. You two, though apparently not the same, are the firmest controllers with your arms, and hold men back from evil as best riders check their horses with their command of reins.

Varuna is the wide and strong support of all the worlds; in his supreme wisdom he encompasses them and controls them as well as all the gods in accordance with an eternal order.

a) *Yo dhartā bhuvanānāṁ ya usrāṇām*
apicyā veda nāmāni guhya,
sa kaviḥ kāvyā puru rūpaṁ dyaur
iva puṣyati nabhantāmanyake same.[104]

He who is the supreme sustainer of the worlds, knows the hidden names of the Rays. He is the great sage who cherishes the deeds of sages as the heaven fosters innumerable forms. May all our enemies perish.

b) *Ya āśvatka āśaye viśvā jātānyeṣām,*
pari dhāmāni marmṛśadvaruṇasya
puro gaye viśve devā anu vrataṁ
nabhantāmanyake same.[105]

He who wraps the three regions as a robe gives refuge to all their creatures. All the gods herald the chariot of Varuna when manifesting his glories at the time of worship. May all the enemies perish.

Varuna determines men's supreme destiny and guides and leads them to it tearing apart their inertia and animal nature. His noose of retribution for going astray from the desired path is difficult to avoid for the sinful transgressor.

Tā bhūripāśāvanṛtasya setū
duratyetū ripave martyāya.[106]

You hold many fetters and raise barriers against the evil and irreligious mortals who find it difficult to overcome them.

His noose like a determined terrific missile follows the offender until falsehood gets uprooted from his life. The trident of the great Aditya destroys the threefold ignorance of the mental, vital and physical. The Rishi implores that he may be released from his triple bondage and the native purity restored.

Uduttamaṁ mumugdhi no vi
pāśaṁ madhyamaṁ cṛta,
avādhamāni jītvase.[107]

May you release us from the upper bonds, untie the bonds of the mid-region and liberate us from those of the lower, that we may live (in true peace and freedom).

It is the transgression of Varuna's laws of purity and perfection, truth and righteousness, that calls for his avengeful action which is not only dreadful but painful. The Rishis pray to Rudra and Soma to be released from the threefold noose of Varuna.

Tigmāyudhau tigmahetī suśevau
somarudrāviha su mṛlataṁ naḥ,
pra no muñcataṁ varunasya pāśād
gopāyataṁ naḥ sumanasyamānā.[108]

O sharp-weaponed, sharp-arrowed and greatly worshipped Soma and Rudra, grant us happiness in this world; propitiated by our offerings, preserve us, be merciful to us. Release us from the noose of Varuna the supreme ordainer. Let your grace protect us.

But, indeed, it is hard to escape the wrathful eye of Varuna that is as wide as the sky itself, says the Atharva-veda.[109] No one can circumvent him for he is ever too vigilant and watchful; he is time and again implored not to strike the sinner and inflict wounds on him for his infraction and misbehaviour. The seekers cannot face his anger and are mortally afraid of his severe and harsh and cruel punishment. He is as such entreated not to entail death or curtail their life-span, but forgive them and protect them.

Varuna is the lord of unsurpassing strength and the slayer of the enemy; he is the subduer and the mighty victor who vouchsafes potency to the participant in battle.

1. *Abhīhi manyo tavasastavīyan*
tapasā yujā vi jahi śatrūn,
amitrahā vṛtrahā dasyuhā ca viśvā
vasunyā bharā tvaṁ naḥ.

2. *Tvaṁ hi manyo abhibhūtyojāḥ*
svayambhūrbhāmo abhimātiṣāhaḥ,
viśvacarṣāṇiḥ sahuriḥ sahāvān
asmāsvojaḥ pṛtanāsu dhehi.[110]

1. O divine wrath incarnate Manyu, come to us, who are of unsurpassing strength; with Tapas as your ally you are the fierce queller of the foe and the slayer of all adversaries. Pray provide us with all the riches.

2. O divine wrath incarnate Manyu, come to us, who are of the victory-winning strength, irate and self-existent, victorious in battle and supreme subduer, you are the beholder of everything. Pray grant us superior strength in battles.

It is human imbecility and indulgence in all forms of vice, thoughtlessness and impurity that warrant his violent intervention. It is quite often that Agni protects the seeker from the fury of Varuna.

Sa nastrāsate varuṇasya dhūrter
maho devasya dhūrteḥ.[111]

He (Agni) protects and preserves us from the malignant anger of Varuna, from the fury of the mighty god for our sin.

He is also the merciful god who pardons the trespasser when appeased through service and righteousness; he releases the sinner from his evil that he may conduct himself in accordance with the supreme *ṛta*.

Aryamyaṁ varuṇa mitryaṁ vā sakhāyāṁ
vā sadamid bhrātaraṁ vā,
veśaṁ vā nityaṁ varuṇāraṇaṁ vā yat
sīmāgaścakṛmā śiśrathastat.[112]

O virtuous Varuna, if ever we have committed an offence against a friend, well-wisher, a companion, a brother or near neighbour or a stranger, pray remove the sin from us.

Varuna is generous and compassionate and forgiving when men follow their unique divine essence, *dharman*, the Law as manifesting in the individual.

a) *Yo mṛḷayāti cakruṣe cidago vayaṁ*
syāma varuṇe anāgāḥ,
anu vratānyaditerṛdhanto yūyaṁ
pāta svastibhiḥ sadā naḥ.[113]

May we be found faultless against Varuna who is merciful even to him who commits sin. May we accomplish the laws of Aditi, and may we ever cherish his blessings.

b) *Ebhirna indrābabhirdaśasya durmitrāso*
hi kṣitayaḥ pavante,
prati yaccaṣṭe anṛtamanenā ava
dvitā varuṇo māyī naḥ sāt.[114]

O Indra, bless us so that unfriendly men may make reconciliation; may the falsehood that wise Varuna perceives in us, may that through your favour doubly disappear.

Generous disposition and gracious commiseration constitute Varuna's nature. Verily, he has a thousand ways of healing the repentant and the wounded. His merciful temperament holds the possibility of the elimination of evil.

(4)

Varuna in later Mythology

In the earliest period Varuna was conceived as the god of the sky; at a later date he is described as the ocean-god. He is portrayed as a godhead with incompatible traits; the Vedas and the Brahmanas differ from each other not inconsiderably in their perception of Varuna. At a time when the sky was envisioned as the naturalistic basis of creation Varuna was the Lord of the skies. With the emergence of the dual formation of Mitrāvaruṇan the earlier hypothesis undergoes a substantial change; the perception becomes psychological rather than naturalistic.

Mythology has him as the all-encompasser and the all-embracer, as an embodiment of the all-suffusing heavens and the creator and king of the universe. He is the supreme godhead of infinite knowledge, pure and perfect in action and the chief among the Adityas with sublimest cosmic functions. He dwells in all the worlds and upholds them; he makes the sun shine in the skies and the waters flow into the ocean below. He is the author of earth-nourishing statutes and witness and vindicator of human behaviour leading to the Truth. Together with Mitra he is a barricade against sin and falsehood as well as the gracious guide to Immortality.

According to the *Mahabharata* he is said to be the son of Kardama and the father of Pushkara. His wife Varunani, born out of the churning of the ocean, is the goddess of wine. Varuna is hymned frequently together with Mitra. He is said to reside in a mansion having a thousand doors. He has a deep and clear insight into the nature of men and is ever accessible to them. He is puissant and powerful, formidable and frightful; none can defy his authority. "It is he who makes the sun to shine in heaven; the winds that blow are but his breath; he has hollowed out the channels of the rivers which flow at his command, and he has made the depths of the sea. His ordinances are fixed and unassailable; through their operation the moon walks in brightness, and the stars, which appear in the nightly sky, vanish in daylight. The birds flying in the air, rivers in their sleepless flow, cannot attain a knowledge of his power and wrath. But he knows the flight of the birds in the sky, the course of the far-travelling wind, the paths of ships on the ocean, and beholds all the secret things that have been or shall be done. He witnesses men's truth and falsehood."[115]

Both Varuna and Mitra are personifications of purity and righteousness; they both promote the Truth in men and avenge sin and falsehood. They enable the streams of the Truth to flow for they are purifying. Varuna is pictured in the Hindu pantheon as a godhead with a white body and seated upon *makara*, a legendary sea-fiend, whose head and legs are of an antelope and the body and tail of a fish. He is described as always carrying in his right hand a terrific noose with which he catches sin and evil.

Varuna is known by several of his epithets: he is Prachetas the wise, Jalapati the lord of the waters, Uddama the surrounder or the encompasser, Pasabhrit the noose-carrier, Amburaja the king of the waters and Yadahpati the king of aquatic animals. His favourite resort is said to be Pushpagiri the flower-mountain, and his city the legendary Vasudhanagara. He holds on his head an umbrella formed of the hood of a cobra named Abhoga.

In Indian myth and legend, Varuna symbolises 'the investing sky'; he is the all-enveloping godhead who sustains the universe. He is the supreme monarch of all the worlds and lives in the highest heaven. In mythological literature he is pictured as holding in two of his four arms a serpent and a noose and riding on a crocodile. He is also described as riding in a chariot drawn by seven swans and holding a lotus, a noose, a conch and a vessel of wealth in his four hands.

1. RV. I.2.7
2. RV. I.2.8
3. RV. I.2.9
4. RV. VII.87.5a
5. RV. VIII.41.8
6. RV. VII.34.10

7. RV. I.24.15
8. RV. I.50.6
9. RV. V.85.3b
10. RV. VII.34.11
11. RV. II.27.10a
12. RV. X.132.4a
13. RV. V.85.2
14. RV. I.164.33a
15. RV. I.191.6a
16. RV. VI.51.5a
17. RV. I.23.5
18. RV. V.85.5
19. *Atharva Veda* IV.16.8
20. Ibid. IV.16.3
21. RV. II.28.6
22. RV. VII.89.3
23. RV. VII.89.5
24. RV. VII.63.6
25. *Atharva Veda* V.24.4
26. RV. II.113.20
27. SABCL. Vol.10, pp. 438-39
28. RV. V.62.1 *Sri Aurobindo's Trans.
29. RV. I.170.1 *Sri Aurobindo's Trans.
30. SABCL. Vol. 10, p. 440
31. RV. II.27.4 *Sri Aurobindo's Trans.
32. RV. X.63.8
33. RV. X.63.7 *Sri Aurobindo's Trans.
34. RV. II.27.6a *Sri Aurobindo's Trans.
35. RV. X.63.13a
36. RV. X.63.12b
37. RV. II.27.8-9 *Sri Aurobindo's Trans.
38. SABCL. Vol. 10, pp. 444-45
39. RV. IV.55.1-10 *Sri Aurobindo's Trans.
40. RV. I.2.7-9 *Sri Aurobindo's Trans.
41. SABCL. Vol. 10, p. 68
42. Ibid.
43. Ibid., p. 69
44. Ibid., p. 70
45. Ibid., p. 71
46. Ibid.
46a Ibid., p. 72
47. Ibid., p. 448
48. Ibid.
49. Ibid., p. 449
50. Ibid., p. 450
51. RV II.28.4 *Sri Aurobindo Trans.
52. SABCL. Vol. 10, p. 450

53. Ibid., p. 451
54. Ibid., p. 454
55. Ibid.
56. RV. VIII.41.9,10
57. RV. VIII.41.8
58. RV. VII. 89.5
59. RV. I.24.6-15
60. SABCL. Vol. 10, p. 454 (RV I.25.11)
61. RV. VIII.41.2b
62. RV. VII. 49.3
63. RV. I.25.12-13 *Sri Aurobindo's Trans.
64. SABCL. Vol. 10, p. 455
65. Ibid., p. 531
66. Ibid.
67. RV. V.85.1-8
68. SABCL. Vol. 10, p. 533
69. RV. I.25.5
70. RV. VI.67.5
71. RV. VIII.90.2
72. *Atharva Veda*, IV.16.4
73. Ibid., IV.16.5
74. RV. VIII.42.1
75. *Atharva Veda*, V.24.5
76. RV. V.63.3
77. RV. V.63.4
78. RV. VII.64.2
79. RV. V.63.7
80. RV. VII.65.1
81. RV. IV.5.4
82. RV. IV.42.1
83. RV. VII.61.3
84. RV. VII.61.7
85. RV. II.28.7
86. RV. I.25.1-2
87. *Atharva Veda*, I.10.1
88. Ibid., IV.16.1,2
89. Ibid., IV.16.6,7
90. RV. II.28.3
91. RV. II.28.5
92. RV. II.28.9
93. RV. VII.86.1-8
94. RV. VII.89.1-2
95. *Atharva Veda*, XIII.3.13
96. Ibid., IX.3.18
97. *Sama Veda*, IV.848-9
98. RV. IX.90.2
99. RV. VIII.69.11,12

100. RV. IV.42.4
101. RV. VII.87.5
102. RV. VII.87.2
103. RV. VI.67.1
104. RV. VIII.41.5
105. RV. VIII.41.7
106. RV. VII.65.3a
107. RV. I.25.21
108. RV. VI.74.4
109. *Atharva Veda*, IV.16.4
110. RV. X.83.3,4
111. RV. I.128.7b
112. RV. V.85.7
113. RV. VII.87.7
114. RV. VII.28.4
115. Dr. Muir, *Original Sanskrit Texts*, V, 58ff.

VI

MITRA

According to a well-known German indologist Mitra like Varuna was inherited by the Vedic Indians from Indo-Iranian prehistory. It is true that his name is found in Iran and Armenia, but the conclusion that he was borrowed by ancient Indian Rishis from outside of India is erroneous. Again, the finding that Mitra plays an insignificant role and that whatever position he occupies is solely through his association with Varuna is inadmissible. It is also not true that there is an identity of objectives between Varuna and Mitra although they seem to converge on helping the seeker to be receptive to Truth. Mitra is not a mere name and an attributive designation of Varuna as is misconceived by some; he is an independent deity though only one hymn is dedicated to him in the Rig-veda, and is often seen in the company of Varuna.

The word *mitra*, according to Dayananda, is derived from the root *nimida*[a]; for him Mitra stands for friendliness, love and harmony, whereas Varuna embodies majesty and purity. In Sri Aurobindo's view "the name Mitra comes from a root which meant originally to contain with compression and so to embrace and has given us the ordinary Sanskrit word for friend, *mitra*, as well as the archaic Vedic word for bliss, *mayas*."[1] If the word *varuna* signifies infinity and purity, the word *mitra* symbolises light and harmony. If Varuna provides the pure and vast framework of divinity, Mitra fills it with the content of 'beauty and perfection'.

As Sri Aurobindo observes, "...the Vedic ideal is not satisfied simply with a large, unfulfilled plan of the divine image. There must be noble and rich contents in this vast continent; the many-roomed tenement of our being contained in Varuna has to be ordered by Mitra in the right harmony of its utility and its equipment."[2] The manifesting godhead is not a void, or an empty plenum; he is "a plenitude as well as infinity."[3] If Varuna is like the infinite sea surging toward the Supreme Godhead of All-consciousness and All-force, Mitra is the strength of love and joy that helps to touch the Transcendent; if Varuna is like the tidal-tower of active wisdom, up-gathered and supportive of the transparent workings of the original *daivic* energies, Mitra is the supreme helper and harmoniser of the cosmic workings engaged in accomplishing the secret purpose of creation; if Varuna is the great guide, the effective force and 'the guardian of the Truth', Mitra is its luminous content that gives stability and meaning to the endless movement for immortality. In Sri Aurobindo's words, Varuna "keeps, drives even the shining herds, but does not assemble them in the pastures, an upholder of our powers and remover of obstacles and enemies much more than a builder of our parts."[4] The one, who, indeed, links, interrelates and integrates the divine workings is Mitra. "Mitra is the harmoniser, Mitra the builder, Mitra the constituent Light, Mitra the god who effects the right unity of which Varuna is the substance and the infinitely self-enlarging periphery. These two Kings are complementary to each other in their nature and their divine works."[5] Between them they establish harmony in the vastness of will and blend love with wisdom; together they constitute 'the great duo of the self-fulfilling godhead', they are "the inseparable builders of an increasing Truth."[6] Of their 'united divinity', Rishi Madhuchchhandas sings most enthusiastically; he describes them as the dwellers in the infinite wideness, the great Truth-increasers and the upholders of the judgement at its works.[7]

Mitra is the friendly personality of the godhead, that of divine Love; the word *mitra* itself reveals the function of the Deva. For the Vedic symbolists "Mitra was essentially the Lord of Love, a divine friend, a kindly helper of men and immortals... the most beloved of the gods."[8] According to the Upanishads, Love is the home of infinite bliss, *ānanda*; it is the source of inner delight of things. If Ananda is "the principle of inner felicity independent of all objects" for the Vedic Rishis, Love is "its outflowing as the delight and pleasure of the soul in objects and beings."[9] Love is the outflowing of Ananda in terms of creation and its divinisation. It is Ananda that helps the human sacrificer to experience the pure and transparent happiness in all things. And this happiness itself is established by the Truth-Consciousness in the expansive freedom worked out by Varuna.

Mitra is marked for his all-embracing universality, loving reconciliation and blissful harmony. He secures for the seeker the 'happy freedom of all-possession', and harmonises the many workings of the Truth. He embraces and contains within his blissful wideness the diverse parts of the cosmic whole, and by his friendly vigilance and luminous ordinances makes the universe an abode of security, grace and felicity.

Anamīvāsa iḷayā madanto mitajñavo
varimannā pṛthivyāḥ,
ādityasya vratamūpakṣiyanto vayaṁ
mitrasya sumatau syāma.[10]

"Free from all undelightfulness rejoicing with rapture in the goddess of the Word, bowing the knee in the wideness of earth, may we attain to our abiding-place in the law of working of Mitra, son of Infinity, and dwell in his grace."*

Mitra's workings are founded in the harmony and happiness, consciousness and force of the Truth. It is the *Maya* of Mitra — 'the comprehending, measuring, forming knowledge' — that blends in its 'supreme and faultless creative wisdom' the numberless planes of our being. Mitra being "a Lord of the Light, a Son of Infinity and a Guardian of the Truth"[11] effectuates the aspirations of Aryaman. He is not only the upholder of the Law that holds things together but also places the Law "in a founded harmony which creates for us our plane of living and the character of our consciousness, action and thought."[12]

If Varuna signifies wideness and purity, Mitra makes for love, friendliness and harmony. In Varuna we find pillared the tireless traveller of the Infinite, the great godhead of strength and discernment; in Mitra is secured the trusted friend in the long journey, the giver of divine felicity, the great harmoniser and integrator. If Varuna is the force and the will and the guide, Mitra is the friend, the bringer of felicity and the helper. If Varuna makes for immortal light and might, Mitra makes for infinite love and delight.

Sri Aurobindo in his exposition of the Vedic psychology brings out the subtle and yet significant distinction between the words *mayas* and *prayas* constantly used by the Rishis. While *mayas* is "the principle of inner felicity independent of all objects, *prayas* (is) its outflowing as the delight and pleasure of the soul in objects and beings".[13] The Vedic happiness constitutes the rich and luminous and profound experience of this divine felicity which qualifies the human sacrificer to possess and to enjoy all things in their sublime essence. Such 'sinless pleasure' is made possible because of the universal presence and working of *satyam ṛtam bṛhat* — the Truth, the Right and the Vast. The one who learns and abides by Mitra's sacred law, the law of this self-radiant Lord of illumination, of this Son of Infinity, says the Rishi, "is possessed of *prayas*, the soul's satisfaction in its objects":[14]

1. *Mitro jānanyātayati bruvāno mitro*
   dadhāra prithivīmuta dyām,
mitraḥ kṛṣṭīrānīmiṣābhi caṣṭe
   mitrāya havyaṁ ghṛtavajjuhota.

2. *Pra sa mitra marto astu prayasvān*
   yasta āditya śikṣati vratena,
na hanyate na jīyate tvoto nainaṁ
   ariho aśnotyantito na dūrāt.

3. *Anamīvāsa iḷayā madanto mitajñavo*
   varimannā pṛthivyāḥ,
ādityasya vratamupakṣiyanto vayaṁ
   mitrasya sumatau syāma.

4. *Ayaṁ mitro namasyaḥ suśevo rājā*
   sukṣatro ajaniṣṭa vedhaḥ,
tasya vayaṁ sumatau yajñi
   yasyāpi bhadre saumanase syama.

5. *Mahāṅ ādityo namasopasadyo yātayajjano*
   gṛṇate suśevaḥ,
tasmā etatpanyatamāya juṣṭam
   agnau mitrāya havirā juhota.

6. *Mitrasya carṣaṇīdhṛto'vo devasya sānasi,*
   dyumnaṁ citraśravastamam.

7. *Abhi yo mahinā divaṁ mitro*
   babhuva saprathāḥ,
abhi śravobhiḥ prithivīm.

8. *Mitrāya pañca yemire janā abhiṣṭiśavase,*
   sa devānviśvanbibhurti.

9. *Mitro deveṣvayuṣu janāya vṛktabarhiṣe,*
   iṣa iṣṭavratā akaḥ.[15]

A free rendering of the hymn would be —

May we offer to Him our extreme devotion who is the self-radiant Lord of illumination and sustainer of both the terrestrial and celestial kingdoms, the ever-vigilant protector of men and the one who strengthens the seekers in their sacrifice. That mortal who abides by his immutable law neither dies nor decays, nor can any evil take possession of him. It is he who fulfils all the soul's seekings.

> May we be exempt from disease and decay, and be made capable of realising the rich food of widest freedom; may we, ever dwelling in the all-governing law of the infinite, grow intimate with our gracious God.
>
> The most adorable Lord of illumination, the kindly and merciful creator of the universe has come to us extending his hand of friendliness and protection. May we enjoy his solicitude and grace, and take refuge in his propitious kindliness.

He who is the eternal and the infinite has to be approached with devotion and reverence, for he is the great inspirer of men to action, and the giver of divine felicity to those who offer and honour him with their homage of love and admiration. Glory and splendour and wealth and wisdom are among the many gifts of this great sustainer of the human race. He is the all-pervasive and all-embracing Lord of both heaven and earth, and surpasses them by his gifts of felicitous food. He is full of 'a varied inspiration' and the 'hewings of its knowledge' to which the five classes of Aryan peoples are drawn for illumination and sustenance. He is the radiant and blissful Lord who bears in his wideness every one, and with his boons of luminous force and nourishment leads all those upon the path who are desirous of divine life.

The purity and vastness of Varuna welded with the love and harmony of Mitra together increase the receptivity of the seeker to the influx of the Truth. Varuna and Mitra, as Sri Aurobindo observes, represent two supreme statuses or planes of the soul. They are the two mighty and omniscient powers of the Aditi of the Truth and Light who ceaselessly work for our attainment of immortality.

Mitra is the godhead of love, joy and harmony even as Varuna is the lord of all-encompassing and all-transfusing purity and immensity that sustains and consummates the world. They represent the working of the Truth in the world and in the mind of men. Mitra is described as *pūtadakṣa*, the one who has and enjoys a clarified ratiocination and persuasion. The two impediments which hamper the effective operation of Truth-Consciousness in the intellect, namely pollution of perception and falsification of the thoughts that formulate it are destroyed by the twin godheads, Mitra and Varuna. Together they secure for the seeker "the Light of the Truth working in the knowledge, *dhiyaṁ ghṛtācīm*, the Power of the Truth working in the effective and enlightened Will, *kratuṁ bṛhantam*."[16] Bearing the Truth-Consciousness within them and using its powers of 'vision, inspiration, intuition, discrimination' they manifest themselves in many modes and movements; consequently the puissances of 'wideness and purity, of joy and harmony' are increasingly effectuated in the seeker. The burden of the Vedic Rishis has thus constantly been, in the words of Sri Aurobindo, "the preparation of the human being in mind and body and the fulfilment of the godhead or immortality in him by his attainment and development of the Truth and the Beatitude."[17] And Varuna and Mitra have their significant share in this fulfilment.

Mitra is one of the four effective Puissances who increase the Truth in the world brought forth by Surya Savitri from Aditi, the Divine consciousness. He is the godhead of Love that sustains the law of eternal harmony and fulfils itself in the soundness and rightness of all things, *mitrasya dhāmabhīḥ*. He is the friend of all and befriends all the other gods to man; he is therefore the friend of gods and men. Being the Lord of Love and Harmony he blends the varied workings of the Truth in us as well as the many threads of our sacrifice. He unites and integrates all the lines of our inner progress, and constantly promotes it until it attains its consummation in Sachchidananda.

The four great gods Varuna, Mitra, Aryaman and Bhaga with their complementary puissances in their common action consummate the aspiration of the seeker. Jointly they perfect in him the one Truth, and build up the whole divine condition in his 'consenting universality'. Mitra almost always hymned with the other gods is a cosmic co-worker of Agni; he is concretely revealed in them as their loving friend only when they arrive in their action to the harmony and the light which they persistently seek for. If Varuna provides 'the infinite wideness and purity' for the release and effective operation of the Truth-Consciousness in man, Mitra effectuates the lambent integration of the workings of the many gods at all levels; it is by their joint operation that Sat and Chit realise themselves as Ananda. "If purity, infinity, strong royalty of Varuna are the grand framework and majestic substance of the divine being", observes Sri Aurobindo, "Mitra is its beauty and perfection".[18] Together they not only compose the grand design of the cherished Vedic ideal but also constitute its divine contents. If Varuna is both the ocean and the heaven rolled into one pure infinite extension surging into effectuation, Mitra the harmoniser and builder brings about the right unity of action. These two "are a great duo of the self-fulfilling godhead and the Vedic word calls them together to a vaster and vaster sacrifice to which they arrive as the inseparable builders of an increasing Truth."[19]

Mitra is the dependable friend who brings in bliss and love to the sacrificer; the Rishis verily speak of him as 'the most beloved of the gods'. In him there is no limitation or sin; he secures for the seeker immortal light and fearless joy, and fulfils his life's ageless seekings. His universality and all-embracing harmony are the source of infinite freedom that men seek for. He is the sweetest Son of Infinity whose loving disposition grants the seeker immortal satisfaction; the drives and actuations that he creates and promotes in gods and men lead to the enjoyment of immortal delight, *payas* supreme. Mighty Mitra creates in the seekers a perfect and joyous frame of mind and feeling; he is ever vigilant and happily conducts the affairs of the world. The Rishi implores again and again to secure an abiding place in the working of his rapturous laws. It is only in the luminous integration of divine Will and divine Love that lies the supreme fulfilment of the sacrificer. "The well-accorded happiness of the truth is Mitra's law of working; for it is upon Truth and divine Knowledge that this harmony and perfect temperament are founded; they are formed, secured and guarded by the Maya of Mitra and Varuna."[20]

Mitra is full of a diversified inspiration, and by it he embraces all of the earth and heaven, gods and men, and guides them all on the path of the Truth. Mitra and Varuna represent two supreme planes of consciousness, and are supportive of our spiritual action. Perfect in will and possessed of a vast luminous puissance, they are the great keepers of Truth. In their unbroken vision of the all they know the Goal and the Path and uphold us in our quest, and nourish us with the streams of Truth-thoughts to be able to reach the Truth. "By Truth they come to the Truth, nourishing in their lordship of things our thoughts, and in their purified judgment they open the eye of consciousness to all wisdom by the perception in men. Thus all-seeing and all-knowing they by the law, by the Maya of the mighty Lord, guard our actions, even as they govern the whole world in the power of the Truth."[21] They are the mighty Truth-seers and Truth-hearers, masters of Truth-existence and the increasers of Truth-content in the aspirants by releasing the celestial rivers — the secret wealth of spiritual felicity — the freedom and bliss and peace and Immortality.

Varuna and Mitra by their clear vision and knowledge of the Path as well as by their power of discernment lead us to the world of Immortality. They are seers of Swar, and possessed of Truth and seated in it, they increase its empire in us. Armed with their supreme Sun-power, *Māyā*, they the far-hearers of the secret Knowledge, 'masters of true being', increase the Truth in us, strengthen the forces of Truth-manifestation, nourish the earth with the shining ambrosia of heaven, and bring down the streams of Truth-Consciousness which the seers aspire for.

"They are the two Sons perfect in their birth from of old who support the law of our action; children are they of a vast luminous power, offspring of the divine discerning thought and perfect in will. They are the guardians of Truth, possessed of its law in the supreme ether. Swar is their golden home and birth-place."[22]

(1)

Hymns to Mitra and Varuna

Behind the veil of the mutable is the immutable Truth; to discover it, to reach and realise it is the ideal of the Rishis. It is the eternal and the unchangeable, the formless and the infinite that unites all the felicities of power and knowledge, purity and harmony, being and bliss. On the journey to this goal, in the conscious endeavour to ascend to it Mitra and Varuna are among the foremost gods who impel and support the sacrifice. They pour within him 'the milk of the herds' and 'the dawns of the inner light'. They sustain and raise the harvest of earth-existence as well as support and advocate the radiances of the highest heaven. Consequently they build for themselves in the seeker a formidable fortress of light and purity, harmony and infinity, force and freedom. Luminously established in this felicitous home of the Truth they constantly foster the traveller in his ascent to the radiant summit. They are the masters of this many-splendoured home of Truth and Bliss.

1. *Ṛtena ṛtamapihitaṁ dhruvaṁ vāṁ sūryasya*
   yatra vimucantyaśvān,
   daśa śātā saha tasthustadekaṁdevānāṁ
   śreṣṭhaṁ vapuṣamapaśyam.

2. *Tatsu vāṁ mitrāvaruṇā mahitvamīrmā*
   tasthuṣīrahābhirduduhre,
   viśvāḥ pinvathaḥ svasarasya dhenā anu
   vāmekaḥ pavirā vavarta.

3. *Adhārayataṁ pṛthivīmuta dhyāṁ mitrarājānā*
   varuṇā mahobhiḥ,
   vardhayatamoshadhiḥ pinvatam gā ava
   vṛṣṭiṁ sṛjataṁ jīradānū.

4. *Ā vāmaśvāsaḥ suyujo vahantu*
yataraśmaya upa yantvarvāk,
ghṛtasya nirṇiganu vartate vām
upa sindhavaḥ pradivi kṣaranti.

5. *Anu śrutāmamatiṁ vardhadurvīṁ*
barhiriva yajuṣā rakṣamāṇā,
namasvantā dhṛtadakṣādhi garte
mitrāsāthe varuṇeḷāsvantaḥ.

6. *Akravihastā sukṛte paraspā yaṁ*
trāsāthe varuṇeḷāsvantaḥ,
rājānā kṣatramahṛṇīyamānā
sahasrasthūṇāṁ bibhrithaḥ saha dvau.

7. *Hiraṇyanirṇigayo asya sthūṇā vi*
bhrājate divya śvājanīva,
bhadre kṣetre nimitā tilvile vā
sanema madhvo adhigartyasya.

8. *Hiraṇyarupamuṣaso vyuṣṭāvayaḥ*
sthuṇamudita sūryasya,
ā rohatho varuṇa mitra gartamataś
cakṣāthe aditiṁ ditiṁ ca.

9. *Yadbaṅhiṣṭhaṁ nātividhe sudānū*
acchidraṁ śarma bhuvanasya gopā,
tena no mitrāvaruṇāviṣṭaṁ siṣasanto
jigīvāṅsaḥ syāma.[23]

1. By the active cosmic truth of the manifest universe is veiled the eternal Truth of the Unmanifest of which it is a manifestation. The eternal Truth is the goal of the upward rising divine energies that journey ceaselessly through the superconscient seas of Light; there stand converged the entire ranges of spiritual felicities in their manifold outpourings of knowledge, force and joy. That One, the supreme Deva, have I beheld, veiled by his own fairest form of the divine Sun.

2. That is the self-exceeding and ever-expanding vastness of yours,

O Mitra and Varuna; there the Lord of the movement (the Sun), through succeeding days milks the herds of his stable radiances. Together, you augment the unified movement of the world-illumining rays of the Blissful One, where its lower wheel is struck away as the inferior truth of the manifest world.

3. O Mitra and Varuna, you uphold by your greatnesses, both earth and heaven: you increase the growths of the plant kingdom, you nourish the shining herds of heaven and send down the rain, O swift in sinews.

4. May your perfectly harnessed horses bear you both here, and with well-governed veins of light come down to us. The form of lucidity and perspicuity follows in your advent and the streams of Truth flow in front of heaven.

5. Augmenting the inner strength that comes to us, increasing and guarding the wide realm of yours, just as our seats of sacrifice are protected by prayer, O Mitra and Varuna, abounding in felicities many, may you take your seat in your luminous abode within the revealings of knowledge.

6. With hands that spare not the defaulter, you are the protectors of the performers of the pious acts; for them you safeguard the beyond, and deliver him who dwells within the revealings of knowledge, you the sovereign ones, free from wrath and passion, together you uphold the mighty mansion of a thousand columns.

/. The form of their home is of golden light; its pillars are of iron, and shine in heaven as if the swift lightning; in the Bliss-World it is shaped, or in the world of the Light. May we gain the sweet honey, Soma, which is secreted in that place.

8. At the break of Dawn, in the rising of the Sun, ascend O Mitra and Varuna to that summit home whose form is of golden light, and the pillars are of iron and then behold the infinite and the finite earth.

9. O munificent Mitra and Varuna, strong guardians of the world, bless us with that bliss of yours which is most perfect and exceeding and without any gap; may we ever be possessed of that supreme

felicity and peace, and be victorious over the enemy.

Mitra and Varuna are the showerers of bounty and the bringers of widest bliss, they who are the keepers and custodians of the Truth and its supreme Law. Established in the Truth, they are the rulers of the world of manifestation and the generous givers of spiritual riches. They are the possessors of divine knowledge who destroy all ignorance. They are the powers that be who maintain the workings of the Truth in men, and by the Truth they set the pilgrim-soul on the journey to the abode of the golden Sun.

Samrājāvasya bhuvanasya rājatho
mitrāvaruṇā vidathe svardṛśā,
vṛṣṭiṁ vāṁ rādho amṛtatvamimahe
dyāvāpṛthivī vi caranti tanyavaḥ.[24]

Imperial rulers of this world of becoming, O Mitra and Varuna, in the gaining of luminous knowledge you are the great seers of the kingdom of Light; we ask of you the rain, the felicitous treasure and immortality. And lo, the Maruts — the Life-Powers and Thought-Powers traverse across earth and heaven spreading the light of Truth for the success of all our activities.

Mitra and Varuna are extolled by the Rishis as the lords of illimitable amplitude, fullness and concord who encompass in their being the supreme heaven of the Truth and Bliss, and lead and guide men to ascend to it. The Rishis entreat them to unfold their 'awakened consciousness and knowledge' for the enjoyment of their wideness and harmonies of felicity. They invoke them to bring into their being the plenitude and the happiness germane to 'the dawning of the divine light and the divine force'.

1. *Varuṇaṁ vo riśādasamṛcā mitraṁ havāmahe,*
   pari vrajeva bāhvorjaganvāṅsā svarṇaram.

2. *Tā bāhavā sucetuna pra yantamasmā arcate,*
   śevaṁ hi jāryaṁ vāṁ visvāsu kṣāsu joguve.

3. *Yannūnamaśyāṁ gatiṁ mitrasya yāyāṁ pathā,*
   asya priyasya śarmanyahinsanasya saścire.

4. *Yuvābhyāṁ mitrāvaruṇopamaṁ dheyāmṛca,*
yaddha kṣaye maghonāṁ stotṛṇām ca spūrdhase.

5. *Ā no mitra sudītibhirvaruṇasca sadhastha ā,*
sve kṣaye maghonāṁ sakhīnāṁ ca vṛdhase.

6. *Yuvaṁ no yeṣu varuṇa kṣatram*
brihacca bibhrithaḥ,
uru ṇo vājasātaye kṛtaṁ rāye svastaye.

7. *Ucchantyām me yajatā devakṣatre ruśadgavi,*
sutaṁ somaṁ na hastibhira paḍbhir
dhāvataṁ narā bibhratāvarcanānasaṁ.[25]

1. We invoke you O Varuna, the destroyer of the enemy, and Mitra by this hymn; you encompass the solar world of the Truth with your arms as if cast around the pens of the shining cattle.

2. O adorable gods, may you stretch out your arms of heightened consciousness to those who worship you with illumined hymns; your desirable felicity spreads through all the worlds.

3. May I even now walk on the path of Mitra who creates perfect harmonies of our inner existence, the trusted and loving friend of all; so every one adheres securely to the gift of happy felicity of that benignant god in whom there is no harm.

4. May we by our dedication and devotion gain that sublime puissance which is your supreme possession, so that manifesting in all those who walk on your path, it may raise them up to its own proper summit position.

5. O Mitra and Varuna, come to our assembly with your splendorous gifts for increase of the gods in their own house, the *Swar-loka*, and for the increase of your devout worshippers in their own respective abodes.

6. In response to our earnest and sincere adoration pray bring to us, O Mitra and Varuna, the divine force and the vastness. May you form in us the wide world, *bṛhat*, for the realisation of our own divine

potentialities, for the attainment of bliss, for the lasting happiness of our soul.

7. May you O Mitra and Varuna, sovereign lords of our sacrifices, come to us in the breaking of the dawn with the flashing of the first ray of light, in the power of the lords of the plenitudes, to accept the Soma-wine pressed out by us. O shining gods, hasten with your speeding steeds to the illumination created by our worshipful words.

Mitra and Varuna are not only the lords of the home of the Truth and Bliss but also of the journey to it. They steadily increase the Truth in the pilgrims and lead them out of the narrowness of Ignorance into the vastness of Knowledge.

1. *Yaściketa sa sukraturdevatrā sa bravītu naḥ,*
   varuṇo yasya darśato mitro vā vanate giraḥ.

2. *Tā hi śreṣṭhavarcasā rājānā dīrghaśruttamā,*
   tā satpatī ṛtāvṛdha ṛtāvānā janejane.

3. *Tā vāmiyāno'vase pūrvā upa bruve sacā,*
   svaśvasaḥ su cetunā vājāñ abhi pra davane.

4. *Mitro aṁhościdāduru kṣayāya gātuṁ vanate,*
   mitrasya hi pratūrvataḥ sumatirasti vidhataḥ.

5. *Vayaṁ mitrasyāvasi syāma saprathastame,*
   anehasastvotayaḥ satrā varuṇaśeṣasaḥ.

6. *Yuvaṁ mitremaṁ janaṁ yatathaḥ saṁ ca nayathaḥ,*
   mā maghonaḥ pari khyataṁ mo asmākamṛṣīṇāṁ
   gopīthe na uruṣyatam.[26]

1. He who knows Him perfectly, verily becomes perfect in will and performs good works; let such a one speak for us all in the assembly of the gods: Mitra and Varuna take delight in his laudation.

2. These two kings have the divine sight and the divine hearing; they are the lords of our true being and increase the Truth in us for they are the possessors of the Truth.

3. O lords of Light and Bliss, travelling on the felicitous journey, I call you together for protection; possessed of luminous and dynamic energies we invoke them; the perfect in knowledge, for the gaining of many plenitudes.

4. Mitra, the compassionate Lord, leads us out of our limited and narrow and ignorant existence into the wideness of perfect mentality; it is He who conquers the path for us to the home of the Truth, for He is of the perfect mind, and conquering all resistance harmonises everything and helps us to move forward rapidly to the goal of the Truth.

5. May we always live and enjoy the guardianship of Mitra, for himself increasing he increasingly gives us our wide and enlightened existence, and fostering us constantly liberates us from all forms of sin and harm, we the children of Varuna, the Lord of infinite vastness.

6. O Mitra and Varuna, may you together set me on the right path and wholly guide me to the desired goal. Do not immure us from our greater plenitudes, pray deny us not the sublime felicities who are the seers of the truth. Always protect us in our prayers and in the drinking of the milk of Light.

Mitra and Varuna successfully subdue the forces of crookedness and resistance and gain for us the large bliss of wide and true existence. They change our defective, ignorant nature into one of perfection and luminosity, and thus help the Truth to manifest within us. It is the progressive expression of the solar Heaven in us that makes us to arrive at perfect self-rule, it not only purifies our discernment and helps us to be recipients of sublimest inspirations but also makes the earth itself as the vast field of manifest Truth.

1. *A cikitāna sukratū devau marta riśādasā,*
varuṇāya ṛtapeśase dadhīta prayase mahe.

2. *Tā hi kṣatramavihrutaṁ samyagasurya māśāte,*
adha vrateva mānuṣaṁ svarṇa dhāyi darśatam.

3. *Tā vāmeṣe rathānāmurviṁ gavyutimeṣām,*
rātahavyasya suṣṭutiṁ dadhṛkstomairmanāmahe.

4. *Adhā hi kāvyā yuvaṁ dakṣasya pūrbhiradbhutā,*
ni ketunā janānāṁ cikethe pūtadakṣasā.

5. *Tadṛtaṁ pṛthivī bṛhacchravȧ eṣa ṛṣiṇām,*
jrayasānāvaraṁ pṛthvati kṣaranti yāmabhiḥ.

6. *Ā yadvāmiyacakṣasā mitra vayaṁ ca sūrayaḥ,*
vyaciṣṭhe bahupāyye yatemahi svarājye.[27]

1. O awakened seeker, take refuge in the two godheads who are perfect in will and the performers of good deeds and destroyers of your enemies. Offer your oblation to Varuna whose form is that of the Truth and Light, direct your adoration to Mitra for his delight.

2. For it is these two gods who are possessed of pure and irresistible force and the mighty strength to subdue the adversary; only then will your being and nature become a perfect field for their effective workings, and the world of the Truth and Light be well established in you.

3. Therefore we glorify you both that your chariots may rush forward in the wide pastures of the Light. When the Lord accepts our devout oblations, our minds powerfully appropriate his perfect affirmation.

4. Then indeed, O adorable gods, do you conquer the seer-knowledge by the full overflowings of enlightened discrimination. May you who are possessed of purified judgement and clear perception approve and accept the adoration of these worshippers of yours.

5. O wide Earth, most vast field for the workings of the Truth, and for the movements of the knowledge of the seer-seekers, the twin godheads Mitra and Varuna move fully and freely within and without; our chariots too move beyond the domain of limited mortal mentality to the planes of luminous supramental Truth.

6. O Mitra and Varuna, when you have your far-reaching vision, may we in our striving arrive at the perfect and luminous self-empire extending widely open and controlling the lives of many seekers.

Mitra and Varuna possess in abundance the Truth-Knowledge and the Truth-Force, and armed with these they lead the seeker of light to the world of immortality, and bestow upon them its peace and happiness. They protect the pilgrims on the path against the hostile forces, and create in them the wideness necessary for the manifestation of the superconscient, for such is the object of the continual sacrifice.

1. *Baḷitthā deva niṣkṛtam*
ādityā yajataṁ bṛhat,
varuṇa mitrāryamanvarṣiṣṭhaṁ
kṣatramāśāthe.

2. *Ā yadyoniṁ hiraṇyayaṁ varuṇa*
mitra sadathaḥ,
dhartārā carṣaṇīnāṁ yantaṁ
sumnaṁ riśādasā.

3. *Viśve hi viśvavedaso varuṇo mitro aryamā,*
vratā padeva saścire pānti martyaṁ riṣaḥ.

4. *Te hi satyā ṛtaspriśa ṛtāvāno janejane,*
sunīthāsaḥ sudānavo'ṅhościdurucakrayaḥ.

5. *Ko nu vāṁ mitrāstuto varuṇo vā tanūnām,*
tatsu vāmeṣate matiratribhya eṣate matiḥ.[28]

1. O you two sons of Aditi, we perform sacrifices for attaining the Vastness that is rightly perfected by you. Verily, you two and Aryaman possess its supreme and abundant strength.

2. O Mitra and Varuna, supporters of strivers and destroyers of the enemies, when you enter the home of the golden Light and the Truth, you bring to your devotees the felicity of supreme bliss.

3. Mitra, Varuna and Aryaman, who are omniscient and firmly maintain the Law, are also steadfastly stationed in the seats to which they reach; they protect the seekers from their enemies.

4. Verily, they are observers of the Truth and true in their being; it is because of this that they touch and hold the Truth in each and every

being. Because they are perfect leaders in the journey, and perfect in heroic strength, they deliver the seeker from all distress and narrowness and create in him the necessary wideness of being.

5. Which of you, O Mitra and Varuna, has not been rightly and richly celebrated by us (on all the planes of our existence). Fully and always our thoughts seek that from you; all the seeker-travellers desire that for their delight.

Mitra and Varuna are the holders of the great and victorious war-force of the superconscient that leads men to the infinitude of the Truth. It is by this sovereign strength that they manifest their puissances in the rest of the godheads as well as in the seeker-strivers. "They reach the Truth by the Truth", as Sri Aurobindo puts it; they have a conscious equation with the Truth-Consciousness, and a luminous impulsion which brings down the bounty from above that securely establishes the seekers in the home of the Truth.

1. *Pra vo mitrāya gāyata varuṇāya vipā girā,*
   mahikṣatrāvṛtaṁ bṛhat.

2. *Samrājā yā ghṛtayonī mitraścobhā varuṇaśca,*
   devā deveṣu praśastā.

3. *Tā naḥ śaktaṁ pārthivasya maho rāyo divyasya,*
   mahi vāṁ kṣatraṁ deveṣu.

4. *Ṛtamṛtena sapanteṣiraṁ dakṣamāśāte,*
   adruhā devau vardhete.

5. *Vṛṣṭidyāvā rītyāpeṣaspatī dānumatyāḥ,*
   bṛhantaṁ gartamāśāte.[29]

1. May you sing loud with inspired incantations that enlighten; they are the mighty godheads for they have the supreme Truth, the vastest and the most excellent.

2. Both Mitra and Varuna are the sovereign rulers; they are the sources of clarity, most eminent among the gods and manifest in them by the Word.

3. They alone are able to put forth strength that secure for us the happy wealth of the wide Truth in our higher consciousness and in our earthly being. Great is your might among the gods.

4. By consciously tending to Truth you attain to the knowledge of the Truth; verily, you possess the straight and right impulsion that leads you to greater Truth; O gods, may you constantly grow and not suffer any setback.

5. O mighty godheads, senders of rain from heaven, winners of the luminous march, and masters of that felicitous impulsion, may you take possession of your home of the Truth.

Mitra and Varuna are the upbearers of the triple truth of Sachchidananda in which the mental, vital and physical find the light and the law of their individual essence. From the threefold luminous heaven descend the waters of the truth and found and establish in the sacrificer the infinite consciousness and force which in turn effectuate the divine workings. Ordinarily the workings of the vital and the physical are confused and chaotic, dark and recalcitrant, but Varuna and Mitra by upholding the three refulgent superconscient worlds suffuse the phenomenal with the light and purity of the noumenal and make its operations transparent and truthful.

1. *Trī rocanā varuṇa trīṁruta dyūntrīṇi*
mitra dhārayatho rajāṁsi,
vāvṛdhānāvamatiṁ kṣatriyasyānu vrataṁ
rakṣamāṇāvajuryam.

2. *Irāvatirvaruṇa dhenavo vāṁ madhumadvāṁ*
sindhavo mitra duhre,
trayastasthurvṛṣabhāsastisṛṇāṁ
dhiṣaṇānāṁ retodhā vi dyumantaḥ.

3. *Prātardevīmaditiṁ johavīmi madhyandina*
uditā sūryasya,
rāye mitrāvaruṇā sarvatāteḷe tokāya
tanayāya śaṁ yoḥ.

4. *Yā dhartārā rajaso rocanasyotādityā*
divyā pārthivasya,

na vāṁ devā amṛtā ā minanti vratāni
mitrāvaruṇā dhruvāṇi.[30]

1. O Mitra and Varuna, together you uphold the three realms of Light, the three heavens and the three mid-regions; verily, you increase the prowess of the seeker-soldier and protect him in the imperishable law of your operation.

2. O Mitra and Varuna, your luminous cows are full of milk at your behest, and the rivers yield their honeyed milk. And through you stand wide the three luminous Bulls that fertilise the triple consciousness making the Truth active and creative in the seeker-sacrificer.

3. I invoke the infinite Mother, Aditi, at dawn, in the mid-day and at sunrise; I implore Mitra and Varuna for the peace and the luminous impulsion in the extension of the universal being and of the divine being for the supreme felicity and for the creation of the shining godhead within the seekers.

4. I devoutly worship you, O Mitra and Varuna, who are the upholders of the mid-world and of the earth. O radiant sons of Aditi, the immortal gods do not impair your luminous workings which are firm and wide and full of harmony for ever. You uphold in us always the Truth by your wideness and friendliness.

The two godheads nurse and nourish our beings with their respective felicities and with their true and perfect impulsions lay the foundation in us of the divine order. The Rishi implores them to protect the seeker-sacrificers from their enemies and deliver them from their dark control as well as increase the Truth in their various modes of existence.

1. *Purūruṇā ciddhyastyavo nūnaṁ vāṁ varuṇa,*
mitra vaṅsi vāṁ sumatim.

2. *Tā vāṁ samyagadruhvāṇeṣamaśyāma dhāyase,*
vayaṁ te rudrā syāma.

3. *Pātaṁ no rudrā payubhiruta trāyethāṁ sutrātrā,*
turyāma dasyūntanūbhiḥ.

4. *Mā kasyādbhuta kratu yakṣaṁ bhujemā tanūbhiḥ,*
mā śeṣasā mā tanasā.[31]

1. Indeed, O Mitra and Varuna, you foster our being in many ways by the wideness of the Truth; I fully enjoy the perfection of your luminous thought-mind.

2. Verily, you are benignant and do not harm us in our divine progress; may we ever enjoy your perfect force of impulsion for our luminous growth-process; may we steadfastly move towards the supreme felicity, O ye vigorous gods.

3. Protect us, O gods of benevolent violence, from the enemies of our progress; deliver us (by destroying the Sons of Darkness). Help us in our upward endeavour; break through the resistance of the enemies for our good.

4. Supremely exceeding in will-power and in the performance of wondrous deeds, let us not suffer in our embodyings the control of any of the enemies, nor our progeny, nor our creative endeavour.

Mitra and Varuna are again and again entreated by the Rishi to arrive at the Soma-offering and annihilate the Adversary, and help the participants in the sacrifice by increasing the purity and power of their thoughts with their wise counsel and action.

Ā no gantaṁ riśādasā varuṇa
mitra barhaṇā,
upemaṁ cārumadhvaram.[32]

O Varuna and Mitra, scatterers of the enemies come to increase in us the largenesses (proper to arrive at the Truth), come to this our delightful sacrifices.

Upa naḥ sutamā gataṁ varuṇa
mitra dāśuṣaḥ,
asya somasya pītaye.[33]

Come, O Mitra and Varuna, to our Soma-offering, to the sacrificial place that you may drink of this wine of the offerer.

(2)

More Hymns

Mitra occupies a lofty position in the Vedic pantheon in association with Varuna; he is the god of intimate and loving friendship. He is the godhead of an immortal puissance, the luminous power of love and pure comprehension that harmonises all our thoughts, acts and impulses. While he brings to the seeker the harmony of life, Varuna brings with him the wideness of existence and Aryaman carries the power of *tapasya*, whereas Bhaga bears the all-capturing and all-possessing bliss of Truth-Consciousness. Speaking of the seekers' fourfold inner progress, Sri Aurobindo observes, "by Yoga Varuna is born in us, a vast sky of spiritual living, the Divine in his wide existence and infinite truth; into that wideness Mitra rises up, Lord of Light and Love who takes all our activities of thought and feeling and will, links them into a Divine harmony, charioteers our movement and dictates our works; called by this wideness and this harmony Aryaman appears in us, the Divine in its illumined power, uplifted force of being and all-judging effective Will; and by the three comes the indwelling Bhaga, the Divine in its pure bliss and all-seizing joy who dispels the evil dream of our jarring and divided existence and possesses all things in the light and glory of Aryaman's power, Mitra's love and light, Varuna's unity."[34]

Mitra is variously described as the source of light and bliss, as the honourer of the Law.

Yajā no mitrāvaruṇā yajā devāñ ṛtaṁ bṛhat,
agne yakṣi svaṁ damam.[35]

O adorable Agni, may we offer our sacrifice to Mitra and Varuna in our name; verily, they are the source of light and bliss. Let us honour them according to the Law in your own house.

Mitra and Varuna together upbear and rule the earth and the sky, guard and protect the world, promote *Dharma* and punish its violators. The Rishi seeks their counsel and protection; he pleads for their forgiveness.

Purūruṇā cid hayastyavo nūnaṁ vāṁ varuṇa,
mitra vagvañsi vagvañsumatim.[36]

O Mitra and Varuna, verily, great is your protection; may you both give me good counsel.

The Sama-veda refers to Mitra and Varuna as *prana* and *apana* respectively:

Rasaṁ te mitro aryamā pibantu varuṇaḥ kave
pavamānasya marutaḥ.[37]

O sage, may Mitra, Varuna, Aryaman and other life-forces in the body, enjoy your perennial strength.

They are the generous givers of bounty, and are also referred to as *iḍā*, *pingalā* and *suṣumṇā.*

a) *Tvaṁ varuṇa uta mitro agne tvāṁ*
vardhanti matibhirvasiṣṭhāḥ,
tve vasu suṣaṇanāni santu yūyaṁ pāta
svastibhiḥ sadā naḥ.[38]

O Mitra and Varuna, both seers and seekers adore you with their hymns of praise. Through you may knowledge and wealth bring them lasting happiness. Pray, protect us with your blessings.

b) *Pibanti mitro aryamā tanā pūtasya varuṇaḥ,*
triṣadhasthasya jāvataḥ.[39]

Mitra, Varuna and Aryaman verily, realise divine joy in *iḍā*, *pingalā* and *suṣumṇā* respectively, which in turn gives highest knowledge when purified through the mind.

(3)

Other References

The Rig-veda mentions the names of six Adityas; they are Mitra, Varuna, Aryaman, Bhaga, Daksha and Amsa. Mitra is one of them. In addition to these, some more are mentioned as the offsprings of Aditi — Surya, Savitri and Indra. The *Taittiriya Upanishad* mentions Mitra, Varuna, Aryaman, Amsa, Bhaga, Indra and Vivasvat (Surya) as the Adityas. The *Satapatha*

Brahmana speaks of the superiority of Agni, Indra and Surya over the others.

According to a naturalistic interpretation Varuna is identified with the Night and Mitra with the Day,[40] whereas Aryaman and Bhaga are distinguished as the Sun, and the Ribhus made out of the former's rays. Also, Mitra is sometimes identified with Agni. Agni, the divine Conscious Force encompasses and embodies all the other godheads — the Powers and Puissances of light and knowledge, strength and action, glory and greatness. When the world is rescued from its tortuous ways and liberated out of its ignorant nature, then Agni, the deity of Will and Energy is revealed as Mitra, the godhead of Love and Harmony.

a. The *Nirukta* (X.21) explains the word differently because Mitra saves from destruction *(pramites trayate)*, and is the one who impregnates whilst moving. He is the one 'who measures out the entire universe', and also the 'one who awards the fruits of action'. The Rig-Veda is perceptive of his powers of invigoration and sustenance when praised by his devotees:

Mitro janānyātayati bruvāṇo mitro
dādhāra pṛthivīmuta dyam
mitraḥ kṛṣṭiranimiṣābhi caṣṭe
mitrāya havyaṁ ghṛtavajjuhota
(RV.III.59.1)

1. SABCL. Vol. 10, p. 457
2. Ibid., p. 456
3. Ibid.
4. Ibid.
5. Ibid.
6. Ibid., p. 457
7. RV. I.2.7-9
8. SABCL. Vol. 10, p. 457
9. Ibid.
10. RV. III.59.3
11. SABCL. Vol. 10, p. 459
12. Ibid.
13. Ibid., p. 457
14. Ibid., p. 458
15. RV. III.59.1-9
16. SABCL. Vol. 10, p. 72
17. Ibid., p. 74

18. SABCL. Vol. 10, p. 456
19. Ibid., pp. 456-57
20. Ibid., p. 459
21. Ibid., p. 460
22. Ibid., p. 460
23. RV. V.62.1-9
24. RV. V.63.2
25. RV. V.64.1-7
26. RV. V.65.1-6
27. RV. V.66.1-6
28. RV. V.67.1-5
29. RV. V.68.1-5
30. RV. V.69.1-4
31. RV. V.70.1-4
32. RV. V.71.1
33. RV. V.71.3
34. SABCL. Vol. 16, p. 297
35. RV. I.75.5
36. *Sama Veda*, VI.985
37. Ibid., VII.1078
38. Ibid., X.1306
39. Ibid., XX.1786
40. *Atharva Veda*, IX.3.18

VII

ARYAMAN

The four godheads Varuna, Mitra, Aryaman and Bhaga persistently appear in the Veda as intimately linked in their disposition and operation. Oftentimes Varuna and Mitra are conjoined and addressed together; sometimes a triad shows up composed of Varuna, Mitra and Aryaman or Bhaga. These are the solar-powers that issue forth from Surya-Savitri, the creative and illuminative form of divine consciousness. Of these four effective Puissances, "Varuna represents the principle of pure and wide being, Sat in Sachchidananda; Aryaman represents the light of the divine consciousness working as Force; Mitra representing light and knowledge, using the principle of Ananda for creation, is Love maintaining the law of harmony; Bhaga represents Ananda as the creative enjoyment; he takes the delight of the creation, takes the delight of all that is created."[1]

These four deities portray the same essentials of the human psyche, and develop in man the truths of different planes of his being with a view to recast them into collaborative conditions and coeval forces and footings of the one supreme Truth. In this luminous task if Varuna represents the vastness and the purity of infinite Truth-existence, Mitra embodies Its love and friendliness and all-integrating harmony of virtue. Whereas Aryaman takes up the puissances of the great duo and fulfils their happy impulsions. He is the force that fulfils Varuna and Mitra, and does not have a distinct personality of his own independent of the former. However, he is the aspiring force of effectuation of the Truth in the seeker. And, Bhaga, of course, has a well-defined function; he is the godhead of divine beatitude and brings into the cosmos and into human life this supreme felicity. He is an outstanding Power through which Savitri increases the Truth in man and manifests himself. He figures in the hymns to the All-Gods, *visvedevas*, largely with the other great Adityas, Varuna, Mitra and Bhaga. The four deities together in their felicitous action strengthen the aspiration of the Rishis for the realisation of the substance as well as the summit of the infinite Truth. All the four have a united nature of light and truth and a common achievement inspite of the fact that they have their own unique individual nature and operation. And it is by their unified action within the assenting and receptive wideness of our nature that the edifice of the Truth is progressively built in us. In this foursome felicity Aryaman's contribution is the stream of massive strength and perfectly shepherded happy aspiration, for he has his foundation in the all-perceptive force of mighty

Tapas. Yet his power is rarely regarded or acknowledged as an independent principium, — "just as force in the world is only a manifestation, movement or dynamic value of existence, is only a working out, a liberation of consciousness, of knowledge, of the inherent Truth of things into stuff of energy and form of effect, or is only the effective term of the self-discovering and self-seizing movement by which Being and Consciousness realize themselves as Bliss. Therefore Aryaman is invoked always in conjunction with Aditi or Varuna or Mitra or in the great Triad or in the realised quaternary or in the general invocation of the All-Gods and the Adityas."[2]

Aryaman represents and embodies the steadfast strength of aspiration, and fulfils himself in the infinite universality of Varuna, even as Mitra and Bhaga make respectively for harmony and its divine enjoyment. Although there are no hymns, except one, that speak exclusively of him he is often mentioned along with one of three other sons of Aditi. It is from these half or quarter *ṛks* that he emerges as embodying and expressing the characteristic puissances of the Truth namely, Knowledge and Power, Vastness and Happiness. He is looked upon as the 'God of the Path' and also the head of the *pitṛs*, the ancient ones who following the Path attained to the supreme heaven of Immortality.

Aryaman is the third of the four kings of cosmos — the great solar godheads — who govern the progression of the earth-consciousness. The name Aryaman etymologically is derived from the word *ārya*, by which is distinguished the one who follows the special path of the Vedic experience. In the words of Sri Aurobindo,

> "The Aryan is the traveller on the Path, the aspirant to immortality by divine sacrifice, one of the shining children of Light, a worshipper of the Masters of the Truth, a fighter in the battle against the powers of darkness who obstruct the human journey. Aryaman is the godhead in whose divine power this Aryahood is rooted; he is this Force of sacrifice, aspiration, battle, journey towards perfection and light and celestial bliss by which the path is created, travelled, pursued beyond all resistance and obscuration to its luminous and happy goal."[3]

As a leader on the Aryan Path, Aryaman joins the ranks of Varuna and Mitra in their luminous help of men on their arduous journey to the Truth. He is full of the perfect felicity of Mitra, his pure happiness and harmony even as he walks beside Varuna in hewing the highway for the human sacrificers. Endowed with manifold births, like Varuna, he impoverishes the impeders of spiritual progress, and renders the hurters harmless. The seeker-sacrificer who abides by the sacred law of Varuna and Mitra and is guided by their wisdom and will 'is guarded in his progress' by Aryaman.

In the Rig-veda we find only scattered references and not any cohesive group of hymns suggestive of Aryaman's functions. Most often he is mentioned alongside Varuna and Mitra, and is invoked invariably in association with kindred Adityas. There are no hymns, except one, that speak exclusively of him. The few hymns that partially refer to him bring out the nature of his unique role in collaboration with other deities as well as are expressive of his epithets. It is from these half or quarter-*ṛks* that he emerges as embodying and expressing the characteristic puissances of the Truth namely, Knowledge and Power, Vastness and Happiness. He is looked upon as the 'God of the Path' and also the head of the *pitṛs* — the ancient ones, who following the Path attained to the supreme heaven of Immortality. The one hymn that differentiates and well defines the activity appropriate to him is in the Tenth Mandala of the Rig-veda. It describes Aryaman as —

Atūrtapanthāḥ pururatho aryamā
saptahota viṣurūpeṣu janmasu.[4]

"Aryaman of the unbroken path, of the many chariots, who dwells as the sevenfold offerer of sacrifice in births of diverse forms."*

He is the force and the presiding Deity of the long journey that protects the pilgrim and ensures his constant progress. Many are his chariots that help the seeker through the 'manifold movement' of his evolution. "It is the journey of the human sacrifice which has a sevenfold energy of its action because there is a sevenfold principle in our being which has to be fulfilled in its integral perfection; Aryaman is the master of the sacrificial action who offers this sevenfold working to the godheads of the Divine Birth."[5]

By the strength of their pure and sincere aspiration the ancient forefathers were led on a unique path that helped them to the summit of Reality through innumerable ascending planes of existence. It must be the aspiration of every genuine seeker to discover this path and enter the solar world of Immortality. It is in such a quest and endeavour that the Aryaman secretly established within us helps us to evolve through successive births. "Thus", says Sri Aurobindo, "Aryaman sums up in himself the whole aspiration and movement of man in a continual self-enlargement and self-transcendence to his divine perfection. By his continuous movement on the unbroken path Mitra and Varuna and the sons of Aditi fulfil themselves in the human birth."[6]

Thus Aryaman, in the Vedic tradition, is the foremost among the ancient illumined Fathers "who discovered the Knowledge, created and followed the Path, reached the Truth, conquered Immortality"; he is therefore hymned as 'the God of the Path'.

In the Puranic tradition the memorial rites of the departed souls as well as the *piṇḍa* are suitably and acceptably offered to Aryaman. In the Gita, Krishna enumerating to Arjuna a few of his prominent divine forms, declares —

1. *Ādityānāmahaṃ viṣnur*

Of the Adityas I am Vishnu,

2. *Rudrāṇāṁ śaṅkaraścā 'smi*

Of the Rudras I am Sankara,

3. *Maharśīṇāṁ bhṛgurahaṁ*

Of the great sages I am Bhrgu,

4. *devarṣīṇāṁ ca nāradaḥ*

Of the divine seers I am Narada,

5. *Anantaścā'smi nāgānāṁ*
varuṇo yādasāmaham,
pitṛṇāmaryamā cā'smi
yamaḥ saṁyamatāmaham.[7]

Of the Nagas I am Ananta,
Of the dwellers in Water I am Varuna,
Of the ancient fathers, I am Aryaman,
Of those who maintain law and order, I am Yama.

Aryaman, the godhead of the journey and its consummation, takes up the happy impulsions of both Varuna and Mitra and fulfils them. He is full of the flawless felicity of Mitra, complete in the longing and the calling of sacrifice, and like Varuna manifold in his upbearing and destructive of the enemies of inner progress. He is the one who epitomises both the path and the supernal goal; he is the deathless power of perceptive aspiration and the enduring energy of its fulfilment.

(1)

As the companion of other Godheads

Aryaman is a companion god of other Adityas; he is the god of formal hospitality. He is seen as a god intermediary between Varuna and Mitra — the god of twilight, *ubhayor madhyavarti*. The path is the essential trait of Aryaman just as the killing of Vritra is that of Indra. The Rig-veda speaks of his path in two hymns:

a) *Atūrtapanthāḥ pururatho aryamā*
saptahota viṣurūpeṣu janmasu.[8]

The ordainer whose path is not transgressed, unchecked and unapproachable, and who makes everyone happy, and who comes with seven chariots and seven rays to perform his many deeds.

b) *Kadva ṛtasya dharṇasi kadvaruṇasya cakṣaṇam,*
kadaryamṇo mahaspathāti krāmema dūḍhayo.[9]

Where, O ye gods, is your adherence to the Law, where is the benignant regard of Varuna and where the path of the mighty Aryaman so that we may overcome the enemies? May I become conscious, O heaven and earth, of the cause of my affliction.

The most prominent characteristic of Aditya Aryaman is 'the Path'; the path is described as *anāptaḥ.*[10] Among the many epithets of Aryaman are *sahasrākṣa*, *gotrabhid*, *vajrabāhu* and *saptahotṛ*. To these may be added *purujāta,*[11] *mandra* and *sṛprabhojas*[12] and *viṣitastupaḥ.*[13]

In one of the legends,[14] the *Taittiriya Brahmana* speaks of Aryaman as playing the role of *gṛhapati* for the seven *hotṛs* to achieve success and attain heaven. He has several things in common with Agni; both are designated as *saptahotṛ*, and also ride a chariot. Again, Agni is directly identified with Aryaman in the matter of matrimonial ceremonies; the latter is the patron deity of matrimony according to one tradition. But this has to be understood in its figurative sense, for the union is that of the seeker-striver with the Truth. He is the match-maker as well as the suitor; in the Veda, the Maruts are compared to *aryamanaḥ*, 'suitors'.[15] This allusion to the celestial marriage between the seeker and the summit Truth is unmistakable and clear through all the hymns addressed to Aryaman in this context. The hierogamy of Surya and Soma is the divine prototype for human marriages. Many of the hymns which are supposed to be of a magical nature are recited at the time of wedding.

a) *Anṛkṣurā ṛjavaḥ santu panthā yebhiḥ*
sakhāyo yanti no vareyam,
samaryamā saṁ bhago no ninīyātsaṁ
jāspatyaṁ suyamamastu devāḥ.[16]

O benevolent gods, may the paths on which our friends go courting be smooth and straight; may Aryaman and Bhaga together conduct us, and may the union of the lovers be easily accomplished.

b) *Gṛbhṇāmi te saubhagatvāya hastaṁ,*
mayā patyā jaradaṣṭiryathāsaḥ,
bhago aryamā savitā purandhirmahyaṁ
tvādurgārhapatyaya devāḥ.[17]

I accept your hand for greater felicity, that you may attain old age (illumination) with me as your spouse (guide). The gods Bhaga, Aryaman, Savitri and Purandhi have given you to me, that I may be the master of your household (destination).

c) *Ā naḥ prajāṁ janayatu prajāpati*
rājarasāya samanaktvaryamā,
adurmaṅgalīḥ patilokamā viśa śaṁ no
bhava dvipade śaṁ catuṣpade.[18]

Let Prajapati grant us progeny, may Aryaman anoint us into enlightened maturity; free from all evil may you, O bride (seeker), enter the world of your husband (domain of the Truth); may you bring supreme prosperity to all beings.

Aryaman is the chief of the *pitṛs*; if Varuna represents the vast purity and transparent wideness that destroys sin and falsehood, Mitra embodies the luminous puissance of love and understanding, then Aryaman is the enduring energy and the deathless power of perceptive aspiration.

1. SABCL. Vol. 10, pp. 289-90
2. Ibid., p. 446
3. Ibid., p. 462
4. RV. X.64.5b
5. SABCL. Vol. 10, pp. 462-63
6. Ibid., p. 463
7. *The Gita*, X.29
8. RV. X.64.5b
9. RV. I.105.6
10. RV. I.100.2
11. RV. VII.35.21; *Atharva Veda*, XIX.10.2
12. RV. VI.48.14
13. *Atharva Veda*, VI.60.1
14. *Taittiriya Brahmana*, II.3.5.3
15. RV. V.54.8
16. RV. X.85.23
17. RV. X.85.36
18. RV. X.85.43

VIII

BHAGA

The infinite delight of the solar world of Truth is the goal of the long journey of our being. There is a joy which is the secret truth of everything; joy is the essence of every being, and 'illimitable joy' is at the heart of the Infinite and the Eternal. It is the enjoyment of this divine bliss that is the goal of life, rather it is the divine enjoyment of existence that is being unfolded in everything. Men seek for it consciously or unconsciously, "with knowledge or with ignorance, with the divine strength or the weakness" of their unregenerate nature. Bhaga is the godhead of this secret joy. It is he "who brings this joy and supreme felicity into the human consciousness; he is the divine enjoyer in man."[1]

> *Anu tanno jāspatirmaṁsīṣṭa*
> *ratnaṁ devasya savituriyānaḥ,*
> *bhagamugro 'vase johavīti bhagam*
> *anugro adha yāti ratnam.*[2]

> The strong and ardent seeker invokes Bhaga for the constant increasing of inner joy, whereas the weak and ignorant one asks for external possessions. May he, the great protector, ever bestow upon us the delight of the shining wealth.

The Rishi calls in the Dawn on Bhaga, 'the strong and victorious' son of Aditi, the wide and great upholder, and invokes him to grant limitless enjoyment both human and divine as well as abundant wealth celestial and terrestrial. He invokes the divine and supreme enjoyer to accept his prayers and possess him so that he in turn could be the possessor of Bhaga's infinite riches. He pleads with him to take up the leadership of the long and arduous journey which would enable him to overcome every obstacle. The goal of the pilgrim-soul being infinite beatitude, the Rishi seeks Bhaga's blessings for an 'increasing felicity' of his soul as well as the 'unending growth' of its divine possessions. It is only through the birth of Bhaga in the seeker that the latter can progress towards divine perfection.

Bhaga is the Lord of enjoyment just as Surya is of illumination, Mitra is of love and harmony and Varuna of vastness and purity. He shares a common psychological nature with Mitra and is continually coupled together with him. His operations are more clearly pronounced than the others and are the same in man and in the universe. He is often linked up with Savitri, the creative Lord of Truth; it is Bhaga who stands for enjoyment in all created things 'of the immortal and immortalising Ananda'. It is this divine beatitude that Surya Savitri best enjoys; truth is the path which leads to Ananda, and Ananda is the one which leads to the Truth. It is Surya Savitri who through the agency of Bhaga leads men to the right enjoyment of all things in the world. It is only when the physical, vital and mental of the seeker receive the divine munificence of Bhaga that Ananda manifests itself in him and in the world. Bhaga is the dispenser of divine delight; nothing can resist him nor diminish his felicitous disposition; he is in perfect possession of himself in the infinite vastness of the Truth. And because of this absolute and flawless self-possession he makes available to the pilgrim the seven delights, *sapta ratnā*. The supreme ecstasy is immanent in the world and in all created things and beings as in the Divine; it has only to be released and made operative in the outer existence and consciousness. And this is accomplished by Bhaga, for he himself is this sevenfold delight: "The rich and varied amplitude of this sevenfold delight," observes Sri Aurobindo, "perfect on all the planes of our being, is the *bhāga*, enjoyment or portion of Bhaga Savitri in the completed sacrifice, and it is that varied wealth which the Rishi seeks for himself and his fellows in the sacrifice by the acceptance of the divine Enjoyer."[3]

It is Bhaga who 'creates a wide and vast force' in the being of the sacrificer that creates the widest and most integral enjoyment, both mortal and eternal. The Vedic ideal is not one of world-and-life negation or ascetic renunciation of earthly joys. In Sri Aurobindo's words it is "the inclusion of all life and all joy, divine and human, the wideness and plenty of earth and the vastness and abundance of heaven, the treasures of the mental, vital, physical existence uplifted, purified, perfected in the form of the infinite and divine Truth. It is this all-including felicity which is the gift of Bhaga."[4] The Vedic paradigm being integral and all-inclusive, Bhaga is called on by the Rishis to ordain equitably and wholly the many felicities of both the heaven and the earth — the thrice-seven delights of Aditi. As Sri Aurobindo puts it, "it is when the Divine as Bhaga, Pushan, Aditi, the infinite, the undivided puts on the radiances of the infinite consciousness like a robe and distributes without division all desirable boons that divine felicity comes to us in its fullness."[5] The Vedic vision is clear: it is only when Aditi is invoked as Bhaga that the many radiances and splendrous gifts are granted to the seeker-sacrificer; it is Bhaga again who helps him to fully enjoy the divine delight of infinite consciousness *ānanda*, by creating in him the widest and vastest force. Rishi Vasistha implores for the luminous growth and pure intensity of Truth-thought in him by which alone eternal bliss is attained.

> *Bhaga praṇetarbhaga satyarādho bhagemāṁ*
> *dhiyamudavā dadannaḥ,*
> *bhaga pra ṇo janaya gobhiraśvairbhaga*
> *nṛbhirnṛvantaḥ syāma.*[6]

> O Bhaga, our great and gracious guide, and possessor of the wealth of the Truth, may you by granting it unto us raise up and increase the Truth-thought in us. By which may we attain the highest felicity.

Aditi, then, fulfils herself in man by the repeated birth and growth and full manifestation of her four sons in him.

The Rishi implores Bhaga to grant men a blessing that promises rich soul-growth and the amplitude of creative Ananda. He entreats him to release upon them luminous streams of the Truth and dispel from their lives evil and ignorance, falsehood and limitation, *viśvāni duritāni*. Bhaga is the Lord of all that is auspicious and right and happygoing; he dismisses the evil dream produced by the Adversary. Bhaga Savitri is the creator of the happy path to the Truth and promoter of perfect and flawless sacrifice that liberates the seeker and leads him to the world of 'undivided consciousness'. The bliss that Bhaga brings to the seeker is capable of unveiling and delivering a consciousness that is universal; which in turn initiates a right perception of the divine intention in all manifestation, and accomplishes the freedom that unites and embraces them all.

The One Supreme, *tad ekam*, creates the universe in accordance with the stipulations of the Truth. It is to this universal Divine, Bhaga Savitri, that the sacrificers open themselves by means of the *mantras*. And Bhaga Savitri, the divine creator, pours out his immeasurable delight into the seeker's soul; whereas in the person of Surya Savitri the Divine transcends and directs both the manifest and the unmanifest, the subconscient and the superconscient in him to interact and to integrate, and bring out the divine Light and Truth out of the night of Inconscience and Falsehood. For, in the Master of the Truth there is no evil and no error. Bhaga as Surya Savitri by his gnostic consciousness, *vijñāna*, receives the creative Word from above and releases it into the movement of things for their right conduct, *bhadram*, leading to infinite beatitude. Bhaga provides the luminous linkage between the infinite and the many worlds within us and without. By the Word, he activises the secret Delight in all things and brings out of them their right rhythm and recasts them into things of that Delight. Such is the splendour of Bhaga, the glorious accomplishment in the cosmic *mahāyajña*.

1. *Tatsaviturvṛṇīmahe*
vayaṁ devasya bhojanam,
śreṣṭhaṁ sarvadhātamaṁ turaṁ
bhagasya dhīmahi.

2. *Asya hi svayaśastaraṁ savituḥ kaccana priyam,*
na minanti svarājyam.

3. *Sa hi ratnāni dāśuṣe suvāti savitā bhagaḥ,*
taṁ bhāgaṁ citramīmahe.[7]

1. "Of Savitri divine we embrace that enjoying, that which is the best, rightly disposes all, reaches the goal, even Bhaga's, we hold by the thought."

2. "For of him no pleasure in things can they diminish, for too self-victorious is it, nor the self-empire of this Enjoyer."

3. " 'Tis he that sends forth the delights on the giver, the god who is the bringer forth of things; that varied richness of his enjoyment we seek."*

The puissances of the four more important Adityas Varuna, Mitra, Aryaman and Bhaga are respectively infinite and all-embracing purity of being, boundless and perfect knowledge concordant with the supreme Truth, mighty strength and happy inner upsurging and the sovereign ecstasy of the liberated soul. These powers constitute the triune truth of Sachchidananda wherein each contains the felicity of the other two. "Yet as all these things form one in the realised godhead, as each element of the trinity contains the others in itself and none of them can exist separately from the rest, therefore each of the Four also possesses by force of his own essential quality every general attribute of his brothers. For this reason if we do not read the Veda as carefully as it was written, we shall miss its distinctions and see only the indistinguishable common functions of these luminous Kings, — as indeed throughout the hymns the unity in difference of all the gods makes it difficult for the mind not accustomed to the subtleties of psychological truth to find in the Vedic divinities anything but a confused mass of common or interchangeable attributes. But the distinctions are there and have as great a force and importance as in the Greek and Egyptian symbolism. Each god contains in himself all the others, but remains still himself in his peculiar function."[7a] Together they all support the upward movement of the pilgrim-soul. Bhaga is the crest of this luminous operation to realise and to possess the supreme truth of all existence that is Beatitude. Bhaga is the all-enjoyer who fulfils himself in the divine purpose of his creation. He is therefore both the path and the goal of our endeavour, the possessor and giver of our numinous completeness — our spiritual fulfilment. With a high-aspiring hope the Rishis invoke the gods to bring to successful culmination their long and arduous undertaking. Varuna makes for the necessary strength with his wideness and purity, Mitra for the all-reconciling and all-embracing harmony, Aryaman for the amplitude of right aspiration and Bhaga for divine bliss.

The goal of the journey is Beatitude and Immortality — the boundless joy of the Truth and the infinitude of Being. Bhaga is the godhead who brings this dual felicity to the seeker-soul. The Rishis again and again invoke Bhaga to bring them this divine enjoyment.

a) *Prātarjitaṁ bhagamugraṁ huvema*
vayaṁ putramaditeryo vidhartā,
ādhraścidh yaṁ manyamānasturaścid
rājā cidh yaṁ bhagaṁ bhakṣītyāha.[8]

Let us invoke at dawn the strong and victorious Bhaga, the son of Aditi, who is the wide-upholder and sustainer of the universe on whom both the king and the commoner meditate and ask of him, "Give us the supreme enjoyment."

b) *Bhaga eva bhagavāñ astu devāstena*
vayaṁ bhagavantaḥ syāma,
taṁ tvā bhaga sarva ijjohavīti sa
no bhaga puraeta bhaveha.[9]

O gracious God, possessor of the Enjoyment, through your grace, may we too possess the enjoyment. Verily, every one calls you and devoutly invokes you O Bhaga, may you become the guide and leader of our journey.

The repeated birth and growth of Bhaga in the consciousness of the seeker sustains him on the long journey and helps him to overcome all resistance. Verily, it is joy that dissolves all impurity and limitation and creates the necessary force for the completion of the journey.

Life on earth is a nightmare of inconscience, a chaotic abyss of falsehood, and a dark stranglehold of light and truth. It is Bhaga, 'the youngest and the greatest' of Adityas "who brings forth from the unmanifest Divine the truth of a divine universe."[10] Of Bhaga Savitri, Sri Aurobindo observes, "An infinite being delivered out of imprisoning limits, an infinite knowledge and strength receiving in thought and working out in will a divine Truth, an infinite beatitude possessing and enjoying all without division, fault or sin, this is the creation of Bhaga Savitri, this that greatest Delight."[11]

The four Adityas ever supported by their infinite Mother are responsible to bring into light a divine creation. "This is the divine creation", says Sri Aurobindo, "of the fourfold Savitri founded on Varuna, combined and guided by Mitra, achieved by Aryaman, enjoyed in Bhaga. Aditi the infinite Mother realises herself in the human being by the birth and works of her glorious children."

(1)

With Other Gods

Bhaga has a distinct personality of his own who grants happiness, and is said to preside over marriages. He is connected with the names of other individual gods:

a) *Indro bhago vājadā asya gāvaḥ pra*
jāyante dakṣiṇa asya pūrvīḥ.[12]

The gods (Indra and Bhaga) provide prosperity; verily their contributions are generous and manifold.

b) *Yadindra rādho asti te māghonaṁ maghavattama,*
tena no bodhi sadhamādhyo vṛdhe
bhago dānāya vṛtrahan.[13]

O Indra, the mighty destroyer of the enemies, sovereign among the gods, may you come hither with Bhaga for good and drink our oblation.

Indra is said to bring Bhaga to the sacrifice *vasuttaye*:

a) *Tvaṁ hyehi cerave vidā bhagaṁ vasuttaye.*[14]

O bounteous Lord, Indra, come here with Bhaga and get wealth for distribution.

b) *Apnasvatī mama dhīrastu śakra vasuvidaṁ*
bhagamindrā bharā naḥ.[15]

O resplendent god, Indra, may my understanding be productive of good works; may you bring Bhaga with you, the giver of bounty.

Bhaga is also mentioned alongwith Agni, Vayu, Brihaspati, Mitra, Pushan, Aryaman, and Savitri:

a) *Indravāyū bṛhaspatiṁ mitrāgniṁ*
pūṣaṇaṁ bhagam,
ādityān mārutaṁ gaṅam.[16]

We invoke you, O Indra, Vayu, Brihaspati, Mitra, Agni, Pushan, Aryaman and Bhaga — the Adityas, and the host of Maruts.

b) *Vi naḥ pathaḥ suvitāya ciyanv*
indro marutaḥ,
pūṣā bhago vandhyāsaḥ.[17]

O Indra, the Maruts, Pushan and Bhaga, may you so direct our paths, that they may lead to the supreme felicity.

c) *Vāmaṁ-vāmaṁ ta ādure devo*
dadātvaryamā,
vāmaṁ pūṣa vamaṁ bhago vāmaṁ
devaḥ karūḷatī.[18]

O destroyer of the enemies, may the divine Aryaman grant us more and more of the precious wealth, may Pushan and Bhaga and the gracious God and lover of craftsmen bestow upon us the desired wealth.

d) *Adatrayā dayate vāryyāṇi pūṣā*
bhago aditirvasta usraḥ,
indro viṣṇurvāruṇo mitro agnirahāni
bhadrā janayanta dasmāḥ.[19]

Each of the godheads Pushan, Bhaga, Aditi bestow nourishing food; the radiant sun and the friendly and adorable deities Indra, Vishnu, Varuna, Mitra, Agni provide for us happy days.

More often Bhaga is mentioned along with Aryaman, roughly eleven times in the Rig-veda and five times in the Atharva-veda. He is frequently described side by side with Savitri or as being in possession of Savitri.

a) *Trirā divaḥ savitārvāryāṇi divediva*
ā suva trirno ahnaḥ,
tridhātu rāya ā suvā vasūni bhaga trātar
dhiṣaṇe sātaye dhāḥ.[20]

O luminous Savitri, descended from heaven, may you thrice bless us every day; may the gracious Bhaga grant his happy wealth of the three regions thrice a day. May Dhishana help us to acquire the wholesome felicity.

b) *Devasya saviturvayaṁ vājayantaḥ purandhyā,*
bhagasya rātimīmahe.[21]

Desirous of wealth and wisdom we invoke you with earnest and devout praises, O Bhaga Savitri, may you grant us the gift of affluence.

c) *Tatsu naḥ savitā bhago varuṇo*
mitro aryamā,
indro no rādhasā gamat.[22]

May the supreme creator Savitri and Bhaga, Varuna, Mitra, Aryaman, Indra come to us to bestow rich felicity.

d) *Devo bhagaḥ savitā rāyo aṅśa indro*
vṛtrasya sañjito dhanānām,
ṛbhukṣā vāja uta vā purandhiravantu
no amṛtāsasturāsaḥ.[23]

May the divine Bhaga Savitri, the Lord of opulence, Ansha, and Indra the destroyer of Vritra as well as all the conquerors of wealth, Ribhukshin, Vaja and Purandhi, distinguished deities, hasten to our sacrifice and protect us.

e) *Uta sya devaḥ savitā bhago no'pāṁ*
napādavatu danu papriḥ.[24]

May the divine creator Savitri and Bhaga and the Lord of lightning Agni preserve us by pouring down gifts on us.

f) *Tvamagne vīravadh yaśo devaś*
ca savitā bhagaḥ,
ditiśca dāti vāryam.[25]

May you, O adorable Agni, give us illustrious progeny; may Savitri, Bhaga and Diti give us riches.

g) *Yadadhya sūra udite'nāgā mitro aryamā,*
suvāti savitā bhagaḥ.[26]

May Mitra, the destroyer of Evil, Aryaman, Savitri, Bhaga grant us this day at dawn what we devoutly pray for.

h) *Indro mitro varuṇaḥ saṁ cikitrire 'tho*
bhagaḥ savitā pūtadakṣasaḥ.[27]

Indra, Mitra, Varuna, Bhaga and Savitri all unite and recognise his (Agni's) merit with one accord.

i) *Abhikṣadāmaryamaṇaṁ suśevaṁ trātṝn*
devānt savitāraṁ bhagaṁ ca.[28]

I invoke with devotion Aryaman, the vanquisher of enemies, and Savitri and Bhaga for protection and happiness.

j) *Yaściddhi ta itthā bhagaḥ
śaśamānaḥ purānidaḥ,
adveṣo hastayordadhe.*

*Bhagabhaktasya te vayamudaśema tavāvasā,
mūrdhānaṁ rāya ārabhe.*[29]

We invoke you, O Bhaga, for that happy felicity which you possess and is exempt from envy or hatred. O Lord, we diligently strive to attain your summit affluence under your guidance and protection.

In some passages Bhaga denotes the Sun-god:

*Adarśi gātururave varīyasī panthā
ṛtasya samayaṅsta raśmibhiś
cakṣurbhagasya raśmibhiḥ,
dhyukśaṁ mitrasya sādanamaryamṇo
varuṇasya ca,
athā dadhāte bṛhadukthyaṁ vaya
upastutyaṁ bṛhadvayaḥ.*[30]

The most marvellous Dawn has been proceeding to participate in the cosmic *yajña*. The path of the sun has been lighted up by its rays, and the eyes of men on earth opened up by Bhaga; the lambent home of Mitra, Varuna and Aryaman has been illuminated. And therefore may you accept our abundant adoration.

The Rishi, sometimes, depicts Bhaga as the god of wealth.

a) *Tvaṁ bhago nṛpate vasva irśiṣe tvaṁ
pāyurdame yaste'vidhat.*[31]

O protector of men, Bhaga, you are the ruler of all riches; you are the cherisher of him who ever serves you with devotion.

b) *Arvācīnaṁ vasuvidaṁ bhagaṁ no ratham
ivāśvā vājina ā vahantu.*[32]

May the Dawns bring to us Bhaga, the graceful god and bestower of prosperity.

c) *Madhvaḥ sūdaṁ pavasva vasva utsaṁ*
vīraṁ ca na ā pavasva bhagaṁ ca.[33]

Pour forth, O Bhaga, a spring of riches, grant us brave progeny and happy fortune.

d) *Ayaṁ pūṣā rayirbhagaḥ somaḥ punāno arṣati.*[34]

This divine elixir, being purified hastens to the container; it is fostering and wealth-giving to be enjoyed by every one.

Bhaga is supposed to accompany the sacrificial horse on the great journey:

Anu tvā ratho anu maryo arvannanu
gāvo 'nu bhagaḥ kanīnām.[35]

O god, you move like a chariot with shining horses attached to it; men and luminous kine follow you, and fair maidens wait upon you.

Bhaga is extolled as the bringer of success in love, and the hope of maidens. He conducts the bride or the bridegroom into the house.[36]

Bhaga is one of the four powers of the Truth of Surya — the power of the right enjoyment of all things. He removes the division and limitation of our existence and opens in us the greater and limitless existence — that of our native nature, the supernature. As regards individual personal characteristics ascribed to each god, *vīrya* is ascribed to Indra, *payas* to Soma, *rūpa* to Twashtri, *tapas* to Vishnu, *kalyāna*, *maṅgala* and *bhagavat* are ascribed to Bhaga.

1. SABCL. Vol. 10, p. 463
2. RV. VII.38.6
3. Op.cit., pp. 291-92
4. Ibid., p. 464
5. Ibid.
6. RV. VII.41.3
7. RV. V.82.1-3
7a. SABCL. Vol. 10, p. 445
8. RV. VII.41.2
9. RV. VII.42.5

10. SABCL. Vol. 10, p. 464
11. Ibid.
12. RV. III.36.5b
13. RV. VIII.54.5
14. RV. VIII.61.7b
15. RV. X.42.3b
16. RV. I.14.3
17. RV. I.90.4
18. RV. IV.30.24
19. RV. V.49.3
20. RV. III.56.6
21. RV. III.62.11
22. RV. IV.55.10
23. RV. V.42.5
24. RV. V.50.13a
25. RV. VII.15.12
26. RV. VII.66.4
27. RV. X. 92.4b
28. RV. VI.50.1b
29. RV. I.24.4,5
30. RV. I.136.2
31. RV. II.1.7b
32. RV. VII.41.6b
33. RV. IX. 97.44a
34. RV. IX. 101.7a
35. RV. I. 163.8a
36. *Atharva Veda*, I.51 & 59

IX

THE VEDIC TRIAD

(1)

Brahmanaspati

Brahman, the Supreme Being, endlessly manifests its infinite contents in Itself. It is both the Superconscient and the Inconscient; as Atman It is the former, and as holder of Its contents equivocally and darkly in Itself, It is the latter. It is the descent of the Superconscient into the subconscient and the Inconscient that brings about the increasing emergence of the soul into the light of the Truth.

> "*Brahman* in the Veda signifies ordinarily the Vedic Word or Mantra in its profoundest aspect as the expression of the intuition arising out of the depths of the soul or being. It is a voice of the rhythm which has created the worlds and creates perpetually. All world is expression or manifestation, creation by the Word. Conscious Being luminously manifesting its contents in itself, of itself, *ātman*, is the superconscient; holding its contents obscurely in itself it is the subconscient. The higher, the self-luminous descends into the obscure, into the night, into darkness concealed in darkness, *tamaḥ tamasā gūḷham*, where all is hidden in formless being owing to fragmentation of consciousness, *tucchyenābhvapihitam*. It arises again out of the Night by the Word to reconstitute in the conscient its vast unity, *tan mahināj́āyataikam*. This vast Being, this all-containing and all-formulating consciousness is Brahman. It is the Soul that emerges out of the subconscient in Man and rises towards the superconscient. And the word of creative Power welling upward out of the soul is also *brahman*."[1]

In the beginning there was only the sea of the Inconscient:

Tama āsīttamasā gūḷhamagre 'praketaṁ
salilaṁ sarvamā idam,
tucchayenābhvapihitaṁ yadāsīttapasas
tanmahināj́āyataikam.[2]

In the beginning was darkness hidden by darkness,
And all was an ocean of Inconscience. When
That lay concealed by endless fragmentation, the One came
To be by the power of his infinite austerity.

The Supreme Being manifesting Itself as the conscious creative soul-power, creates the numberless worlds out of the vast Waters by the Word that is Brahma. That is to say, the Divine becomes Brahma, the creative soul-power, which in turn creates the worlds by the supreme Word. And Brihaspati is the master of this Word that is given to the gods led by Indra who work in unison with each other in the seeker and help him to attain to the superconscient supramental Truth. Brahmanaspati combines the two roles of Brahma and Brahmanaspati; he is the Creator as well as the great Teacher In the words of Sri Aurobindo his is the "link-name between the general and the special aspects of the same deity."[3]

Existence, to begin with, is an indefinite movement, an undeterminable flux. Brihaspati creates out of this chaotic drift a stable and steady composition and establishes the basis for all conscient life; he sets up as it were the very limits of material consciousness and consequently determines with precision the boundaries of earth-existence. This he accomplishes by overcoming the resistance of the Inconscient and the subconscient.

Yastastambha sahasā vi jmo antān
bṛhaspatistriṣadhaṣtho raveṇa,
taṁ pratnāsa ṛṣayo dīdhyānāḥ puro
viprā dadhire mandrajihvam.[4]

The wise one of yore, illustrious and intelligent, have placed before them the sweet-tongued Brihaspati, who sustains the universe by his might, and who abides with supremacy in the three regions.

"This great creation he effects", says Sri Aurobindo, "by establishing the triple principle of mind, life and body, always present together and involved in each other or evolved out of each other in the world of the cosmic labour and fulfilment. The three together form the triple seat of Agni and there he works out the gradual work of accomplishment or perfection which is the object of the sacrifice."[5] Brahmanaspati is the lord of the inner impulsion manifesting in man as mantric inspiration. Often he is described as welding the worlds into effective form.

> *Brahmaṇaspatiretā saṁ karmāraivādhamat,*
> *devānaṁ pūrvye yuge 'sataḥ sadajāyata.*[6]

> Brahmanaspati fills the many gods with his soul-breath as a black-smith his bellows; In the beginning, the manifest comes out of the Unmanifest.

He is the formless Fire, *tapas* — the creative and contemplative action — the primordial power of supreme consciousness that burgeons the universe into shape. He embodies the divine Word — the basic constituting substance of the gods — by virtue of which Indra himself increases in strength and splendour. As the vibrant Word divine he is in the heart of the gods and the Rishis; he is a luminous blend of both cosmic sound-initiation and infinite creative action. The Rishis by meditating on him become illumined in consciousness and extol him as 'the god of the ecstatic tongue'. As a result they succeed in activating the soul-thoughts and become able to taste the secret joy of existence. Thus they move out from the subconscient to the superconscient — out of *apraketam* to *supraketam*. They again and again invoke Brihaspati and pray that their supreme felicity of Truth-Consciousness be guarded against the Adversary who is ever trying to obscure and deny it.

Brihaspati is the first one who manifests out of the vastness of the supreme superconscient with his sevenfold conscious being and drives away all possible darkness with his multiple soul-forces. Brahma is the creative power of the Word, and the Word has many powers; as such there are many Brahmas transfused by the Word — the creators charged as it were by a divine cadence. It is by the cry of these forces that Brihaspati destroys Vala, the cause and reason of all darkness. The seekers intuitively respond to the radiant call of Brihaspati and perform sacrifices that carry them onward to the goal of the Truth.

> "This self-expressive Soul, Brihaspati, is the Purusha, the Father of all things;... it is the Bull of the herds, the Master and fertilizer of all these luminous energies evolved or involved, active in the day or obscurely working in the night of things, which constitute the becoming or world-existence, *bhuvanam*. To the Purusha under the name of Brihaspati the Rishi would have us dispose in the order of a sacrifice all the materials of our being by sacrificial action in which they are given up to the All-Soul as acceptable oblations offered with adoration and surrender. By the sacrifice we shall become through the

> grace of this godhead full of heroic energy for the battle of life, rich in the offspring of the soul, masters of the felicities which are attained by divine enlightenment and right action."[7]

It is by consciously upbearing this conscious Soul-Power and holding it within themselves as the foremost instrumentation that the seekers arrive rapidly at the goal. It is because of Brihaspati that they become capable of mastering all that comes to them in their births as well as the many planes of consciousness that open upon their intellection of the path. They all joyously submit themselves to the Truth in him for he is the creator and realiser of all — the complete teacher and the consummate counsellor. "Indra and Brihaspati", observes Sri Aurobindo, "are thus the two divine powers whose fullness in us and conscious possession of the Truth are the conditions of our perfection."[8] Rishi Vamadeva rightly invokes them to increase in the seekers by increasing in them the state of right mentality and perfect felicity — the mental-force and the soul-force — necessary for the much-coveted consummation. He calls on them "to drink in this great sacrifice the wine of immortal Ananda, rejoicing in the intoxication of its ecstasies, pouring out abundantly the substance and riches of the spirit. Those outpourings of the superconscient beatitude must enter into the soul-force and there take being perfectly."[9]

1. *Dhunetayaḥ supraketaṁ madanto bṛhaspate*
   abhi ye nastatasre,
   pṛṣantaṁ sṛpramadabdhamūrvaṁ
   bṛhaspate rakṣatādasya yoniṁ.

2. *Bṛhaspate yā paramā parāvadata ā*
   ta ṛtaspriśo ni ṣeduḥ,
   tubhyaṁ khātā avatā adridugdhā madhvaḥ
   ścotantyabhito virapśam.

3. *Bṛhaspatiḥ prathamaṁ jāyamāno maho*
   jyotiṣaḥ parame vyoman,
   saptāsyastuvijāto raveṇa vi saptaraśmira
   dhamattamāṅsi.

4. *Sa suṣṭubhā sa ṛkvatā gaṇena valaṁ*
   ruroja phaligaṁ raveṇa,
   bṛhaspatirusriyā havyasūdaḥ kanikradad
   vāvaśatirudājat.

5. *Evā pitre viśvadevāya vṛṣṇe yajñair*
vidhema namasā havirbhiḥ,
bṛhaspate suprajā viravanto vayaṁ
syāma patayo rayīṇāṁ.

6. *Sa idrājā pratijanyani viśvā śuṣmeṇa*
tasthāvabhi vīryeṇa,
bṛhaspatiṁ yaḥ subhṛtaṁ bibharti
valgūyati vandate pūrvabhājam.

7. *Sa itkṣeti sudhita okasi sve tasma*
iḷa pinvate viśvadānīm,
tasmai viśaḥ svayamevā namante
yasminbrahmā rājani pūrva eti.

8. *Apratīto jayati saṁ dhanāni pratijanyā*
nyuta yā sajanyā,
avasyave yo varivaḥ kṛnoti brahmaṇe
rājā tamavanti devāḥ.

9. *Indraśca somaṁ pibataṁ bṛhaspate'smin*
yajñe mandasānā vṛṣaṇvasū,
ā vāṁ viśantvindavaḥ svābhuvo'sme
rayiṁ sarvavīraṁ ni yacchatam.

10. *Bṛhaspata indra vardhataṁ naḥ sacā*
sā vaṁ sumatirbhūtvasme,
avistaṁ dhiyo jigṛtaṁ purandhīrjajastam
aryo vanuṣamarātīḥ.[10]

1. They, your devout worshippers, O Brihaspati, vibrating with the impulse of their sacred movement, rejoicing in illumined consciousness, have woven for us this invincible, wide world from which this being was born. May you protect them from their enemies.

2. O Brihaspati, they mounting up from this world have attained their seat in the highest and supreme Kingdom of the Truth. For you they dig the wells of honey which deplete the hill, and their sweetnesses flow out in streams running in all directions.

3. O Brihaspati, born first from the highest heaven of supernal light, with your seven mouths (fronts) and seven rays, and with many births, you drive away all darkness with your fierce cry.

4. O Brihaspati, you with the support of your associates, the Angirasas, adherents of the secret rhythm that affirms, have destroyed the crooked Vala with your cry; you have set free the luminous cattle for our felicitous progress. You shout loudly as you lead them upward and they respond quite gratefully.

5. Thus may we offer our worship, our sacrifices and our oblations most devoutly to the Father, to the universal Godhead, the Bull of the herds (the showerer of benefits); grant, O Brihaspati, that we may become possessed of energy and riches and excellent progeny and felicities many.

6. Verily, he is the King who conquers by his heroic strength and prowess all that opposes him, who bears Brihaspati in him always and glorifies and honours him, and offers him the first fruits of oblations.

7. Truly, he abides in peace and prosperity in his own home and for him the earth bears fruit at all times. To him all creatures willingly pay homage; indeed he is the King in whom the Soul-Power, duly worshipped, goes in front.

8. Unassailed by any, he conquers the riches of the hostile worlds and possesses the wealth of his own world; he who for the Soul-Power that constantly seeks to manifest itself creates that highest good in himself, is always cherished and protected by the gods.

9. O Brihaspati, may you and Indra both exulting at our sacrifice and showering bounty, drink the Soma-wine; may you be fully and truly satisfied and take the desirable perfect form, and bestow upon us felicities that bear every luminous energy.

10. O Brihaspati and Indra, may you both increase in us, and create in us the felicity of your perfect mind; may you together foster our thoughts and bring out the mind's luminous potencies. May you abolish all limitations and weaknesses that the adversaries of the Aryan seekers bring with them.

Brihaspati, as mentioned earlier, is the father and priest of the creative and inspired Word and also the chief of all the high priests of the world. He is the Guru of the gods and possessor of supreme wisdom. He is associated with the other gods in the liberation of the streams of the supreme Light. He is also described as an Angirasa; he being the master of the vibrant Word, his stentorian full-mouthed cry creates the gods, splits Vala to pieces and helps the release of the concealed cows and lifts up the world out of the enveloping darkness.

a) *Tava śriye vyajihīta parvato gavāṁ gotram*
udasṛjo yadaṅgiraḥ,
indreṇa yujā tamasā parīvṛtaṁ bṛhaspate
nirapāmaubjo arṇavam.[11]

For your triumphant delight when the hill goes asunder you did set free the concealed cattle, and with Indra as your associate you force down the flood of the waters which was enveloped by the darkness.

The Veda brings out very powerfully and lucidly the importance and the role of Brihaspati in the release of the herds. Indra, Soma, Agni and Brihaspati are seen as joining hands to get the cows back.

Brihaspati is the *Purohita*, the priest of both gods and men, the inspirer of priests who presides over prayer — the lord of the sacred speech — the *Kavi* of all *Kavis*, the creator of all systems of thought, the suppliant and the sacrificer, the priest and the protector against the impious.

a) *Tvaṁ taṁ brahmanaspate soma indraśca martyam,*
dakṣiṇā pātv aṁhasaḥ.[12]

O Brahmanaspati, may you and Indra and Soma and Dakshina protect us, and keep us away from sin.

b) *Endro barhiḥ sīdatu pinvatāmiḷā*
bṛhaspatiḥ sāmabhirṛkvo arcatu,
supraketaṁ jīvase manma dhīmahi tad
devānāmavo adhyā vṛṇīmahe.[13]

May Indra be seated on the sacred grass, may Ila be propitious with her wisdom, may Brihaspati hymned with devotional praises bless us:

may we have the right approach to life. We seek today the protection of the gods.

c) *Vi ṣā hotrā viśvamaśnoti varyaṁ bṛhaspatira ramatiḥ panīyasī,*
grāvā yatra madhuṣuḍhucyate bṛhada vīvaśanta matibhirmanīṣiṇaḥ.[14]

That divine voice of wisdom, never ceasing, the panegyrist of the gods, the protectress of the mighty, procures for us all desirable riches. At its behest the sweet Soma-juice is pressed out by the grinding stones, and the devout seekers by their incantations inspire everyone to participate in the sacrifice.

d) *Indra ukthena śavasā parurdadhe bṛhaspate pratarītāsyāyushaḥ,*
yajño manuḥ pramatirnaḥ pitā hi kamā sarvatātimaditiṁ vṛṇīmahe.[15]

By his mighty strength Indra sustains my body, and you, O Brihaspati prolong my life. May the great sage Manu and the sacrifice grant us wisdom and happiness. We adore and pray Aditi for everything.

In the words of Sri Aurobindo:

> "Brihaspati is the Master of the creative Word. If Agni is the supreme Angirasa, the flame from whom the Angirasas are born, Brihaspati is the one Angirasa with the seven mouths, the seven rays of the illuminative thought and the seven words which express it, of whom these seers are the powers of utterance. It is the complete thought of the Truth, the seven-headed, which wins the fourth or divine world for man by winning for him the complete spiritual wealth, object of the sacrifice. Therefore Agni, Indra, Brihaspati, Soma are all described as winners of the herds of the Sun and destroyers of the Dasyus who conceal and withhold them from man. Saraswati, who is the stream of the Word or inspiration of the Truth, is also a Dasyu-slayer and winner of the shining herds; and they are discovered by Sarama, forerunner of Indra, who is a solar or dawn goddess and seems to symbolise the intuitive power of the Truth. Usha, the Dawn, is at once herself a worker in the great victory and in her full advent its luminous result."[16]

Born of Agni, Brihaspati is worshipped as Agni himself; the Rishi speaks of his *tapas pavitram*[a]. Like Agni, he is *hiraṇya varṇa*; he is the god of light who subdues darkness.

a) *Ā vedhasaṁ nīlapṛṣṭhaṁ bṛhantaṁ*
bṛhaspatiṁ sadane sādayadhvam,
sādadhyoniṁ dama ā dīdivāṅsaṁ hiraṇyavarṇama
ruṣaṁ sapema.[17]

The devotees enshrine in their hearts the mighty Brihaspati, the creator, whose back is dark blue. May we worship him in the chamber of sacrifice, who shines everywhere, and is golden-hued, and most radiant.

b) *Ā vibādhyā parirāpastamausi ca jyotiṣmantaṁ*
rathamṛtasya tiṣṭhasi,
bṛhaspate bhīmamāmitradambhanaṁ
rakṣohaṇaṁ gotrabhidaṁ svarvidam.[18]

Having vanquished the enemies and dispersed the darkness, O Brihaspati, you mount upon the chariot of the truth which is formidable and is the destroyer of evil-doers, the clearer of the clouds and attainer of heaven.

c) *Udga ājadābhinadbrahmaṇā valama*
gūhattamo vyacakṣayat svaḥ.[19]

He (Brihaspati) by the power of the Word destroys Vala, disperses the darkness and causes the light.

d) *Usraiva sūryo jyotiṣā maho viśveshām*
ijjānitā brahmaṇāmasi.[20]

As the adorable sun generates rays with his radiance, so do you, O Brihaspati, generate our knowledge (and disperse the darkness of Ignorance).

e) *Uttiṣṭha brahmaṇaspate devan*
yajñena bodhaya,
āyuḥ prāṇaṁ prajāṁ paśūnkīrtiṁ
yajamānaṁ ca vardhaya.[21]

> O Brihaspati, master of the Vedic Word, we implore that you may rise to excellence and increase in those wise ones who seek Truth through performance of sacrifices.

Brihaspati is not only connected with wisdom and sacrifice but is also described as a mighty fighter, and as associated with the Manes.

> *Abhi śyavaṁ na kṛśanebhiraśvaṁ*
> *nakṣatrebhiḥ pitaro dhyāmapiṅśan,*
> *rātryāṁ tamo adadhurjyotirahan*
> *bṛhaspatirbhinadadriṁ vidadgāḥ.*[22]

> The protecting gods decorate the heavens with stars and constellations like a brown horse with pearls and golden trappings; these Manes establish darkness in night and light in the day. Brihaspati cleaves the rock and recovers the shining cattle.

Vishnu, Rudra and Brahmanaspati preside over the birth and growth of the gods in the seekers so very necessary for integral human perfection on all levels and to reach successfully the desired supreme summit.

> "Brahmanaspati is the Creator; by the word, by his cry he creates, — that is to say, he expresses, he brings out all existence and conscious knowledge and movement of life and eventual forms from the darkness of the Inconscient. Rudra, the Violent and Merciful, the Mighty one, presides over the struggle of life to affirm itself; he is the armed, wrathful and beneficient Power of God who lifts forcibly the creation upward, smites all that opposes, scourges all that errs and resists, heals all that is wounded and suffers and complains and submits. Vishnu of the vast pervading motion holds in his triple stride all these worlds; it is he that makes a wide room for the action of Indra in our limited mortality; it is by him and with him that we rise into his highest seats where we find waiting for us the Friend, the Beloved, the Beatific Godhead."[23]

The three together support and promote total and perfect inner development. While Brahmanaspati manifests all existence by his creative cry, and gives birth to knowledge and formulates life out of the formless chaos of Inconscience, Rudra the mighty one ordains the affirmation of life's cosmic struggle pushing forward the great ascent. Whereas Vishnu, the all-pervading puissance paces out the infinite spaces of inner life in which the soul-effectuation takes place.

Brahmanaspati is often identified with Brahman; he is Brahman himself, says the *Satapata Brahmana*:

a) *Brahma vai bṛhaspatiḥ*;[24]

b) *Brahmāṇāṁ ca bṛhaspatim.*[25]

He is Brahma, he is Siva, Indra and Vishnu, says the *Kaivalya Upanishad*:

Sa brahmā sa śivaḥ sendraḥ
so'kṣaraḥ paramaḥ svarād,
sa eva viṣṇuḥ sa prānaḥ
sa kālo'gniḥ sa candramāḥ.[26]

Sometimes Brihaspati and the Sun appear as mythological synonyms, *asya (bṛhaspateh) śloko divīyate pṛthivyām*:[27] 'his glory spreads through heaven and earth like the Sun'. He is also referred to as *mandrajihva*[28] and *sucikranda*.[29]

In the post-Vedic period he came to be the regent of the planet Jupiter. A person born under this planet is believed to be bestowed with an affable disposition, is kindly and courteous and possesses all forms of riches.

(2)

Rudra

Brahmanaspati, Vishnu and Rudra represent respectively the creative, conservative and destructive processes in the cosmos. They are the Vedic precursors of the later Puranic triumvirate, Brahma-Vishnu-Shiva, and provide the essential prerequisites of effective and continual Vedic action. While Brahmanaspati is the creative prime Word that summons the ordered universe out of the formless, chaotic abyss of the Inconscient and accelerates the evolutionary process, Rudra the omnipotent provides perennially the necessary force for the upward movement of the soul.

> "For the upward movement of Brahmanaspati's formations Rudra supplies the force. He is named in the Veda the Mighty One of

Heaven, but he begins his work upon the earth and gives effect to the sacrifice on the five planes of our ascent. He is the Violent One who leads the upward evolution of the conscious being; his force battles against all evil, smites the sinner and the enemy; intolerant of defect and stumbling he is the most terrible of the gods, the one of whom alone the Vedic Rishis have any real fear. Agni, the Kumara, prototype of the Puranic Skanda, is on earth the child of this force of Rudra. The Maruts, vital powers which make light for themselves by violence, are Rudra's children...."[30]

The Mighty One has also another aspect — that of gracious and kindly countenance; he is both the terrible destroyer and the supremely wholesome healer. He is "the Master of the force that acts in the worlds and the Yogin who enjoys the supreme liberty and peace."[31]

Varuna and Mitra as well as Maruts and the other gods oftentimes assume the role of Rudra and break through the barriers of the Adversary, and deliver the seekers.

Pātaṁ no rudra pāyubhir
uta trāyethāṁ sutrātrā,
turyāma dasyūntanūbhiḥ.[32]

O mighty Lord, protect us with your protectings and deliver us with your perfect deliverances. May we with our strength in our embodyings overcome the wicked Dasyus.

Rudra is the supreme destroyer and the great thunderer, the Terrible One and the most Merciful One. The Rishi approaches him with a prayer for puissance and for protection.

1. *Ā te pitarmarutāṁ sumnametu mā naḥ*
sūryasya sandriśo yuyothāḥ,
abhi no vīro arvati kṣameta pra jā
yemahi rudra prajābhiḥ.

2. *Tvādattebhī rudra santamebhiḥ śataṁ*
himā aśīya bheṣajebhiḥ,
vya'smaddveṣo vitaraṁ vyaṁho vy
amīvāścātayasvā viṣūcīḥ.

3. *Śreṣṭho jātasya rudra śriyāsi*
tavastamastavasāṁ vajrabāho,
parṣiṇaḥ pāramaṅhasaḥ svasti visvā
abhītī rapaso yuyodhi.

4. *Mā tvā rudra cukrudhāmā namobhirma*
duṣṭutī vṛṣabha mā sahūtī,
unno vīrāñ arpaya bheṣajebhir
bhiṣaktamaṁ tvā bhiṣajāṁ śṛṇomi.

5. *Havīmabhirhavate yo havirbhirava*
stomebhī rudraṁ diṣīya,
ṛdūdaraḥ suhavo mā no asyai babhruḥ
suśipro rīradhanmanāyai.

6. *Unmā mamanda vṛṣabho marutvān*
tvakṣīyasā vayasā nādhamānam,
ghṛṇīva cchāyāmarapā aśīyā vivāseyaṁ
rudrasya sumnam.

7. *Kva sya te rudra mṛḷayākurhasto yo*
asti bheṣajo jalāṣaḥ,
apabhartā rapaso daivyasyābhī nu mā
vṛṣabha cakṣamīthāḥ.

8. *Pra babhrave vṛṣabhāya śvitīce maho*
mahīṁ suṣṭutimīrayāmi,
namasyā kalmalīkinaṁ namobhirgriṇīmasi
tveṣaṁ rudrasya nāma.

9. *Sthirebhirangaiḥ pururūpa ugro babhruḥ*
śukrebhiḥ pipiśe hiraṇyaiḥ,
īśānādasya bhuvanasya bhūrerna vā u
yoṣadrudrādasuryam.

10. *Arhanbibharṣi sāyakāni dhanvārhan*
niṣkaṁ yajataṁ viśvarūpam,
arhannidaṁ dayase viśvamabhvaṁ na vā
ojīyo rudra tvadasti.

11. *Stuhi śrutaṁ gartasadaṁ yuvānaṁ mṛgaṁ
na bhīmamupahatnumugram,
mṛḷā jaritre rudra stavāno'nyaṁ te
asmanni vapantu senaḥ.*

12. *Kumāraścitpitaraṁ vandamānaṁ prati
nānāma rudropayantam,
bhurerdātāraṁ satpatiṁ gṛṇīṣe stutas
tvaṁ bheṣajā rāsyasme.*

13. *Yā vo bheṣajā marutaḥ śucīni yā śantamā
vṛṣaṇo yā mayobhu,
yāni manuravṛṇītā pita nastā śaṁ ca
yośca rudrasya vaśmi.*

14. *Pari ṇo hetī rudrasya vṛjyāḥ
tveṣasya durmatirmahī gāt,
ava sthirā maghavadbhyastanuṣva mīḍhvas
tokāya tanayāya mṛḷa.*

15. *Evā babhro vṛṣabha cekitāna yathā
deva na hṛṇīṣe na haṅsi,
havanaśrunno rudreha bodhi bṛhad
vadema vidathe suvīrāḥ.*[33]

1. O Father of the Maruts, may your felicity extend to us. Do not deprive us of the sight of the sun. Grant that our children may overcome the enemies; O Rudra, may we live forth in our progeny.

2. Nourished by your remedial edibles may I live a span of hundred winters. Extirpate all hatred from us, and scatter away sin and our infirmities many.

3. O Rudra, mightiest of the mighty and most renowned, wielder of the thunderbolt, may you carry us safely across the ocean of sin and frustrate all assaults of evil.

4. O Lord, may we not ever provoke you by our imperfect adorations and unworthy praises. Restore our hero-warriors and invigorate them by your medicaments, for we know, you are the mightiest and best of healers.

5. With invocations and adorations I seek to please and pacify him; may the supreme lord of mercy, of beautiful form and pleasing disposition, and easy of entreaty, never subject us to his anger.

6. May the showerer of felicities many, escorted by the Maruts, bring me strong comfort and invigorating nourishment; may I free from sun find shelter in him as from distressing heat one finds relief in the shade.

7. O supreme healer, how I aspire for your healing touch which heals and brings profound solace, which softens the punishments of all the gods; O compassionate One, be gracious unto me.

8. To the great lord, the supreme Bull, I address a big hymn of earnest praise; I adore his infinite splendour with sincere prostrations; we glorify the mighty and illustrious name of Rudra.

9. The mighty One of many forms fierce and brown-coloured has adorned himself with brilliant golden ornaments. The power divine is inseparable from him, the supreme ruler and lord of the universe.

10. O Lord, worthy are you of the bow and arrows you bear, worthy of the adorable insignia; you are capable of overcoming all adverse forces, for none, O Rudra, is more mighty than you.

11. Adorable is the Lord, who is youthful and far-famed like a high-throned king and formidable and fierce like a wild beast. O Rudra, praised and propitiated by us, grant happiness to us; may your hosts spare us and destroy our adversaries.

12. As a son bows down with reverence before his father, so I bow down to you, O God, where you approach us at our sacrifice; I glorify you, mighty Lord, bestower of treasures, protector of the righteous, grant us your remedial herbs when we extol and adore you.

13. O powerful Maruts, your medicaments are pure and effective and bring us joy and felicity; they were chosen by our ancestor Manu. Those that alleviate suffering, O Lord, bestow upon me for my well-being.

14. May the Lord's missile avoid us; may his wrath not hit us. O showerer of gifts, turn away your bow of destruction from those who devoutly worship you, have mercy on our progeny and bestow happiness upon them.

15. O mighty Rudra, the showerer of gifts many, omniscient and divine, bearer of our supplications, listen to our prayer; do not be angry or destroy us. May we sing of your splendour and glory at the sacrifice, bless us with worthy progeny.

The Rishi extols Rudra as the supreme forgiver and the benevolent healer.

Somārudrā yuvametānyasme viśvā
tanūṣu bheṣajāni dhattam,
ava syataṁ muñcataṁ yanno asti
tanūṣu baddhaṁ kṛtameno asmat.[34]

O Soma and Rudra, lords of bliss and power, may you grant us all needful medicaments for the ailments of our body and being; set us free from our omissions and commissions the ills of which cling to us from within.

Rudra is not a liminal figure but quite a central deity with the Vedic Rishis. He is extolled as the most compassionate, and yet fierce and wild and frightful of all the gods.

1. *Imā rudrāya tavase kapardine kṣayadvīrāya*
pra bharāmahe matīḥ,
yathā śamapaddvipade catuṣpade viśvaṁ
puṣṭaṁ grāme asminnanāturam.

2. *Mṛḷā no rudrota no mayaskṛdhi kṣayad*
vīrāya namasā vidhema te,
yacchaṁ ca yośca manurāyeja pitā tada
śyāma tava rudra praṇītiṣu.

3. *Aśyāma te sumatiṁ devayajyayā kṣyad*
vīrasya tava rudra mīḍhvaḥ,
sumnāyannidviśo asmākamā carāriṣṭavīrā
juhavāma te haviḥ.

4. *Tveṣam vayaṁ rudraṁ yajñasādhaṁ vaṅkuṁ*
 kavimavase ni hvayāmahe,
āre asmaddaivyaṁ heḷo asyatu sumatimid
 vayamasyā vṛṇīmahe.

5. *Divo varāhamaruṣaṁ kapardinaṁ tveṣaṁ*
 rūpaṁ namasā ni hvayāmahe,
haste bibhradbheṣajā varyaṇi śarma
 varma chardirasmabhyaṁ yaṅsat.

6. *Idaṁ pitre marutāmucyate vacaḥ svādoḥ svādīyo*
 rudrāya vardhanam,
rāsvā ca no amṛta martabhojanaṁ tmane
 tokāya tanayāya mṛḷa.

7. *Mā no mahāntamuta mā no arbhakaṁ mā na*
 ukṣantamuta mā na ukṣitam,
mā no vadhīḥ pitaraṁ mota mātaraṁ mā naḥ
 priyāstanvo rudra rīriṣaḥ.

8. *Mā nastoke tanaye mā na āyau mā no goṣu*
 mā no aśveṣu rīriṣaḥ,
vīrānma no rudra bhāmito vadhīhāviṣmantaḥ
 sadamittvā havāmahe.

9. *Upa te stomānpaśupā ivākaraṁ rāsvā pitar*
 marutāṁ sumnamasme,
bhadrā hi te sumatirmṛḷayattamāthā vayam
 ava itte vṛṇīmahe.

10. *Āre te goghnamuta puruṣaghnaṁ kṣa*
 yadvīra sumnamasme te astu,
mṛḷā ca no adhi ca brūhi devādhā ca
 naḥ śarma yaccha dvibarhāḥ.

11. *Avocāma namo asmā avasyavaḥ śṛṇotu*
 no havaṁ rudro marutvān,
tanno mitro varuṇo māmahantāmaditiḥ
 sindhuḥ pṛthivī uta dhyauḥ.[35]

1. We offer these prayers to the mighty Rudra, the god with braided splendours, the divine healer who is the ruler and protector of our hero-warriors, so that it may be well with all living beings, two-footed and four-footed, around us and they prosper well unharmed.

2. O divine healer, have mercy on us, may you grant us the life-force that brings us happiness and freedom from all ailments. O ruler and protector of our hero-warriors, we offer you our oblations. Whatever our great ancestor Manu obtained by sacrifice, may you grant us that for our progress and well-being.

3. O Rudra, bestower of bliss, protector and ruler of our hero-warriors, may we through your devout worship obtain your favour. May you come to our families, the tireless strivers, may we offer our oblations to you for their safety, happiness and prosperity.

4. We invoke the mighty Lord, Rudra, for protection, for successful completion of our sacrifice. May the impassioned and perfect healer repel from us the anger of the gods; verily we earnestly seek his favour.

5. We ardently and reverently invoke him who is the divine healer, who is stout and strong, radiant and peerless, and a dreaded form with braided splendours, holding in his hand the healing medicaments. May the Lord grant us health, protection and a secure shelter.

6. These hymns of praise are addressed to Rudra, the father of the Maruts, hymns which in turn increase us from within. May he, the immortal, grant us food, good and beneficial to mortals, and bestow happiness on us and on our earnest progeny.

7. O Rudra, do not harm us who are young or old, those who are growing or fully-grown; may you not afflict our bodies which are so very dear to us.

8. O Rudra, do not harm us in our children, or grandchildren, nor in our life-span, nor in our cattle or in our horses. Inflamed with anger slay not our hero-warriors, for we ever invoke you and offer you our homage of oblations.

9. O Supreme healer, we direct our praises to you as the herdsmen drive their cattle. O father of the Maruts, may you grant us happiness and health. Your benevolence and blessings have always brought us rich felicity; so do we always seek your help and protection.

10. O mighty Rudra, lord and ruler of the hero-warriors, keep far away from us your powerful weapons of mass-destruction. Have mercy and be gracious to us, grant us the supreme felicity — the double prosperity of both realms, mundane and spiritual.

11. Seeking help and protection, we devoutly invoke him, the divine healer; may Rudra with his host of Maruts accept our invocations. May Mitra, Varuna and Aditi grant us our prayers.

(3)

Vishnu

The Veda speaks of two oceans, the lower and the upper, 'the dark sleep of the subconscient' below and 'the luminous secrecy of the Superconscient' above. This is clearly brought out in the famous Puranic Symbol of Maha Vishnu sleeping on the folds of the hundred hooded snake Ananta upon the ocean of milk. It is the ocean of infinite and eternal existence, the absolute sweetness and bliss, upon which the all-pervading god rests during the times of non-creation.

Vishnu is the all-pervading, all-enveloping deity, the supreme blissful godhead constantly descending to help and support the ascent of the earth. He is the unity and totality of all positive forces, the Maruts, engaged in the endless battle for light. In fact, the Rishi hymns him as Evayamarut, the source of all Maruts.

1. *Pra vo mahe matayo yantu viṣṇave marutvate*
girijā evayāmarut,
pra śardhāya prayajyave sukhādaye tavase
bhandadiṣṭaye dhunivrataya śavase.

2. *Pra ye jātā mahinā ye ca nu svayaṁ pra*
vidmanā bruvata evayāmarut,
kratva tadvo maruto nādhṛṣe śavo dānā
mahnā tadeṣāmadhṛṣṭāso nādrayaḥ.

3. *Pra ye divo bṛhataḥ śṛṇvire gira suśukvānah*
subhva evayāmarut,
na yeṣāmirī sadhastha īṣṭa āṅ agnayo na
svavidhyutaḥ pra syandrāso dhunīnām.

4. *Sa cakrame mahato nirurukramaḥ samānasmāt*
sadasa evayāmarut,
yadāyukta tmana svādadhi ṣṇubhirviṣpardhaso
vimahaso jigāti śevṛdho nṛbhiḥ.

5. *Svano na vo'mavānrejayadvṛṣā tveṣo*
yayistaviṣa evayāmarut,
yenā sahanta ṛñjata svarociṣaḥ stha
raśmāno hiraṇyayāḥ svāyudhāsa iṣmiṇaḥ.

6. *Apāro vo mahimā vṛddhaśavasastveṣam*
śavo'vatvevayāmarut,
sthātāro hi prasitau sandṛśi sthana te na
uruṣyatā nidaḥ śuśukvāṅso nāgnayaḥ.

7. *Te rudrāsaḥ sumakhā agnayo yathā tuvidhyumna*
avantvevayāmarut,
dīrghaṁ pṛthu paprathe sadma pārthivaṁ
yeṣāmajmeṣvā mahaḥ śardhaṅsyadbhutainasām.

8. *Adveṣo no maruto gātumetana śrotā havaṁ*
jariturevayāmarut,
viṣṇormahaḥ samanyavo yuyotana smadrathyo
na daṅsanāpa dveṣānsi sanutaḥ.

9. *Gantā no yajñaṁ yajñiyāḥ suśami śrotā havam*
arakṣa evayāmarut,
jyeṣṭhāso na parvatāso vyomani yūyaṁ tasya
pracetasaḥ syāta durdhartavo nidaḥ.[36]

1. May our laudations to Evayamarut reach you, O all-pervading Lord Vishnu, attended by the Maruts; may they reach the one who is strong, adorable, brilliantly adorned, vigorous, and fast-moving, the one who charges forth with joy to crush the dark forces of evil.

2. Evayamarut lauds those who manifest with Indra spontaneously and speedily with the knowledge. O Maruts, your strength in action marked by your generous munificence is incomprehensible. Verily, you are immovable as mountains.

3. Evayamarut lauds those who descending from the vast heaven look brilliant and happy, and hear his invocation; in whose dwelling place no one can disturb them, and who, like self-radiant fires are the actuators of the streams.

4. When Evayamarut harnesses his chariot with swift-moving steeds at his spacious dwelling-place, the Maruts, emulous and vigorous, conferring rich felicity sally forth from their common home.

5. Let not the mighty roar of your approach, O Maruts, which announces the rain, which is irradiating and loud, frighten Evayamarut. May that sound of yours, who are ever victorious, self-luminous, decked with gold-ornaments, providers of nourishment and fully armed with weapons many, always accomplish your functions.

6. O Evayamarut, possessor of enormous prowess, may your unbounded greatness and brilliant vigour protect us, for, verily, you in your omniscience know everything, and in times of trouble help us and save us from shame; preserve us from the maligners, you who are resplendent like the glowing fire.

7. May those Rudras, worthy of worship, who are like resplendent fires, protect Evayamarut: they have extended and made spacious and luminous this celestial abode. They are free from blame, and manifest mighty energies at the time of encountering the adversaries.

8. O Maruts, who are free of enmity, and pure, come to our place of worship where praises are offered profusely, hear the invocations of devout Evayamarut. May you, the associates of Vishnu, drive away as brave warriors our hidden adversaries.

9. O adorable Maruts, come to the place of our worship with grace, and undeterred by the enemies hear the invocation of Evayamarut. Living in mid-heaven like lofty mountains O profoundly wise ones, may you strike down without mercy the wicked and the evil.

Rudra is also described as the fierce Father of the Maruts, who along with other gods, functions and fulfils the supreme need of the seeker in his great ascent. The three prime divinities Vishnu, Rudra and Brahmanaspati furnish the requisites of Vedic action and nourish from behind the many godheads engaged on the front. Among themselves Rudra supplies the necessary impetus for the upward movement of the formations of Brahmanaspati, and both for the formations of Brahmanaspati's Word and for the functioning of Rudra's force, it is Vishnu who provides the indispensable steady elements of space, the many planes of existences, the regulated operativeness of the worlds and the desired summit objective. With his three long and purposeful strides, Vishnu creates and covers widest space within which he sets up and secures the innumerable worlds. Again, it is in these worlds that he eternally abides and provides the necessary leeway for the action of the respective gods.

Indra invokes Vishnu, his supreme friend and guide, to ambulate for him enough room to grapple with Vritra and destroy him.

Viṣṇoḥ karmāṇi paśyata
yato vratāni paspaśe,
indrasya yujyaḥ sakhā.[37]

Behold the wondrous deeds of Vishnu through which the seekers have accomplished their sacred vows; verily, he is the true friend of Indra.

Vishnu is the prime partner of all the gods and the seeker-sacrificers in their marathon struggle to reach the goal. His ultimate step, *paramam padam*, is the summit seat of Light and Truth and Bliss that the Vedic Rishis aspire and seek for. They ecstatically acclaim it as 'the shining eye of vision' extended in heaven.[38] The Vedic Rishi further eulogizes the three strides of Vishnu; they are earth, heaven and the triune foundation, *tridhatu*, the source of all existences and the supreme seat of the all-enveloping Lord — *nākasya pṛṣthe.*

Nākasya pṛṣṭhe adhi tiṣṭhati śrito
yaḥ pṛṇāti sa ha deveṣu gacchati.[39]

He who pacifies and conciliates the gods, and provides food generously to the gods, sits on the summit of heaven.

These three strides are entirely different from the Puranic account of Vamana's strides which secured earth, heaven and *patala*, the sub-earthly domain. Unlike the *Puranas*, the Vedic pantheon does not recognise any hierarchy among the gods; all of them are the aspects of one sole existent supreme God, *ekam tad*.

> "In the Veda indeed its fundamental conception forbids the Puranic arrangement of the supreme Trinity and the lesser gods. To the Vedic Rishis there was only one universal Deva of whom Vishnu, Rudra, Brahmanaspati, Agni, Indra, Vayu, Mitra, Varuna are all alike forms and cosmic aspects. Each of them is in himself the whole Deva and contains all the other gods. It was the full emergence in the Upanishads of the idea of this supreme and only Deva, left in the Riks vague and undefined and sometimes even spoken of in the neuter as That or the one sole existence, the ritualitic limitation of the other gods and the progressive precision of their human or personal aspects under the stress of a growing mythology that led to their degradation and the enthronement of the less used and more general names and forms, Brahman, Vishnu and Rudra, in the final Puranic formulation of the Hindu theogony."[40]

Vishnu, in the Vedas, is the all-conscient deity wide-awake and wide-moving, all-pervading and all-extending, *sa paryagāt*. He is the ultimate augur, supreme ideator and absolute and final configurator. He supports the earth, the mid-world and the mental world as well as the triple heavens of the Superconscient beyond.

> "Vishnu is the wide-moving one. He is that which has gone abroad, — as it is put in the language of the Isha Upanishad, *sa paryagat*, — triply extending himself as Seer, Thinker and Former, in the superconscient Bliss, in the heaven of mind, in the earth of the physical consciousness, *tredhā vicakramāṇaḥ*. In those three strides he has measured out, he has formed in all their extension the earthly worlds; for in the Vedic idea the material world which we inhabit is only one of several steps leading to and supporting the vital and mental worlds beyond. In those strides he supports upon the earth and mid-world, — the earth the material, the mid-world the vital realms of Vayu, Lord of the dynamic Life-principle, — the triple heaven and its three luminous summits, *trīṇi rocanā*. These heavens the Rishi describes as the higher seat of the fulfilling. Earth, the mid-world and heaven are

> the triple place of the conscious being's progressive self-fulfilling, *triṣadhastha*, earth the lower seat, the vital world the middle, heaven the higher. All these are contained in the threefold movement of Vishnu."[41]

Vishnu, the supreme and absolute author of the formations of all the worlds is also spoken of in the Veda as "That" in which status he becomes identified with Rudra, Master of the lower worlds, who moving through difficult terrain removes all obstacles and promotes earth-evolution. Vishnu is also the Master of *Maharloka*, the world of the superconscient supramental Truth towards which both Brahmanaspati and Rudra move and support world-existence in its upward movement. He is thus not only the summit-god, the Delight of Existence, but also the energising power and self-fulfilling truth of all existence. He forms the five worlds as well as fills them with the bliss of his being, sustains them constantly and conserves them indestructibly. "He is the One, he alone is, the sole-existing Godhead," observes Sri Aurobindo, "and he holds in his being the triple divine principle to which we attain in the world of bliss, earth where we have our foundation and heaven also which we touch by the mental person within us. All the five worlds he upholds."[42]

It is in the supreme stride of Vishnu that Ananda dwells; it is towards this fulfilling divine ecstasy that Vishnu, the lord of all existences and absolute bliss, the all-pervading godhead, takes us in his upward march.

1. *Viṣṇornu kaṁ vīryāṇi pra vocaṁ yaḥ*
   pārthivāni vimame rajāṅsi,
   yo askabhāyaduttaraṁ sadhasthaṁ vicakra
   māṇastredhorugāyaḥ.

2. *Pra tadviṣṇuḥ stavate vīryeṇa mṛgo na*
   bhīmaḥ kucaro giriṣṭhāḥ,
   yasyoruṣu triṣu vikramaṇeshva
   dhikṣiyanti bhuvanāni viśvā.

3. *Pra viṣṇave śūṣametu manma girikṣita*
   urugāyāya vṛṣṇe,
   ya idaṁ dīrghaṁ prayataṁ sadhasthameko
   vimame tribhiritpadebhiḥ.

4. *Yasya trī pūrṇā madhunā padānyakṣīyamāṇā*
   svadhayā madanti,

ya u tridhātu prithivīmuta dyāmeko
dādhāra bhuvanāni viśvā.

5. *Tadasya priyamabhi pātho aśyāṁ naro*
yatra devayavo madanti,
urukramasya sa hi bandhurittha viṣṇoḥ
pade parame madhva utsaḥ.

6. *Tā vāṁ vāstūnyuśmasi gamadhyai yatra*
gāvo bhūriśṛngā ayāsaḥ,
atrāha tadurugāyasya vṛṣṇaḥ paramaṁ
padamava bhāti bhūri.[43]

1. Of Vishnu I now proclaim the mighty deeds who has measured out the earthly regions and supports the celestial seat above; he traverses wide spaces in the three strides of his universal movement.

2. Vishnu is avouched on high by his supreme prowess; he is like a ravenous lion that wanders at will in difficult terrain and inhabits the mountains. In his wide-covering three paces all the worlds abide.

3. Now may our strength and our prayer ascend to the all-pervading, far-striding Vishnu, the mighty Bull whose dwelling place is upon the mountain-tops. Unaided and alone he has measured out with his three strides this far-extending seat of our self-accomplishing.

4. His three paces are filled with the immortal honey-wine; they are imperishable and ecstatic by nature. Alone and by himself he supports the three regions — earth and sky and even all the worlds.

5. May I attain to that abode of Vishnu, the goal of his movement and enjoy it — the seat and source of infinite delight where the seeker-souls rejoice; there within that highest step of the supreme strider is the perpetual fount of purest honey.

6. Those are your realms which we aspire to attain as the summit of our seeking, where the tireless many-horned herds of Light go journeying; it is from here, the highest step of widely-striding Vishnu, that his multiple magnificence shines down on us.

It is the highest stride, *pade parame*, the summit goal which the seekers aspire to attain. Vishnu is the sun-home of seeker-souls. The wise ones always see it as an eye extended in the heavens.

> *Tadviṣṇoḥ paramaṁ padaṁ sadā paśyanti sūrayaḥ.*[44]

The Rishi goes still further —

> *Tadviprāso vipanyavo jāgṛvāṅsaḥ samindhate,*
> *viṣṇoryatparamaṁ padam.*[45]
>
> The wise, ever vigilant and persevering in praise realize the all-pervading Vishnu within their inmost being which is his supreme abode (of Light and Joy).

Vishnu is mentioned in the Rig-veda in all the *Mandalas*, except I, IX and X, mostly in the context of the three strides he takes to win back the worlds from the Asuric hold.

> *Indras ca ha vai visnus casurair yuyudhate*
> *tan ha sma jivocatuh kalpamaha iti,*
> *te ha tathety asura ucuh,*
> *so 'bravid indro yavad evayam visnus trir*
> *vikramate tavad asmakam atha yusmakam itarad iti,*
> *sa imanl lokan vicakrame 'tho vedan atho vacam...*[46]

> a) *Viṣṇuṁ stomāsaḥ purudasmamarkā*
> *bhagasyeva kāriṇo yāmani gman,*
> *urukramaḥ kakuho yasya pūrvīrna*
> *mardhanti yuvatayo janitrīḥ.*[47]
>
> May our praises and prayers, that have caused felicities many, attain for us at this sacrifice the all-pervading Lord Vishnu, he the wide-moving one who traverses all regions with his three strides. The many blending regions and the twin mothers of all beings never disobey his commands.

> b) *Śaṁ no viṣṇuḥ śaṁu pūṣa no astu*
> *śaṁ no bhavitraṁ śamvastu vāyuḥ.*[48]

May the all-pervading Lord, Vishnu, may Pushan promote our happiness, may the firmament be propitious to us; may Vayu blow for us happiness.

The Yajur-veda extols him as the friend and all-pervading lord of the worshippers:

Pṛcchāmi tvā citaye devasakha
yadi tvamatra manasā jagantha,
yeṣu viṣnustriṣu padeṣveṣṭasteṣu
viśvaṁ bhuvanama viveśa.[49]

O Lord, supreme friend of the wise ones I need to know if you in spirit indeed pervade the entire universe? Are all the created worlds contained in the three strides in which you are worshipped?

In the Puranas

The *Puranic* Vishnu is the lord of the waters of existence and sustains it in seed form within himself even during the periods of *pralaya*. It is the seed of his cosmic consciousness out of which Brahma creates the universe anew. He is described as resting or, rather reclining on the body of the many hooded serpant *ananta* which symbolises his infinite power of self-manifestation in space and time. Ananta itself is described as floating on the motionless causal sea that springs into creative action at the instance of Brahma. It is Vishnu again who progressively incarnates in a physical body — the successive steps in the manifestation of consciousness upon earth leading to the desired divine denouement. The *Puranas* in general and the Gita in particular speak of such a psychological and spiritual evolution. "In some such spirit", observes Sri Aurobindo, "some would interpret the ten incarnations of Vishnu, first in animal forms, then in the animal man, then in the dwarf man-soul, Vamana, the violent Asuric man, Rama of the axe, the divinely natured man, a greater Rama, the awakened spiritual man, Buddha, and, preceding him in time, but final in place, the complete divine manhood, Krishna, — for the last Avatar, Kalki, only accomplishes the work Krishna began, — he fulfils in power the great struggle which the previous Avatars prepared in all its potentialities."[50]

The goal of Nature's evolutionary endeavour is not only to create the spiritual man and perfect him, but to transform integrally and divinize him. It is to help man to substitute his ego — the ignorant, limited and divisive individuality — by the Self, his true individuality, which is at once universal and transcendental, and to help him into its innate perfection. Vishnu through his incarnations manifests and integrates the many powers and puissances necessary for such an integral perfection and transformation. Through the succession of the *Yugas*, he comes as the *Avatar* and the *Vibhuti*, the seer and the King, the legislator and the warrior, and finally as the supreme *Yogin* and the *Yajña* to support the evolutionary action of the cosmos and establish firmly and perfectly the Kingdom of God both within and without.

The *Puranas* call Vishnu by many names; he is called Madhusudana and Kaitabhajit, as he destroys the two demons Madhu and Kaitabha who issue forth from his ears as he lay resting on Ananta. Among the more popular names are Kesava, Madhava, Swayambhu, Hari, Mukunda, Yajneswara and Purushottama.

1. SABCL. Vol. 10, p. 306
2. RV. X.129.3
3. SABCL. Vol. 10, p. 307
4. RV. IV.50.1
5. SABCL. Vol. 10, p. 307
6. RV. X.72.2
7. SABCL. Vol. 10, p. 311
8. Ibid., p. 313
9. Ibid.
10. RV. IV.50.2-11
11. RV. II.23.18
12. RV. I.18.5
13. RV. X.36.5
14. RV. X.64.15
15. RV. X. 100.5
16. SABCL. Vol. 10, p. 235; RV. IX.83.2
a. RV. IX.83.2
17. RV. V.43.12
18. RV. II.23.3
19. RV. II.24.3b
20. RV. II.23.2b
21. *Atharva Veda*, XIX.63.1a
22. RV. X.68.11
23. SABCL. Vol. 11, p. 33

24. *Satapata Brahmana*, IV.6.6-7
25. RV. X.141.3
26. *Kaivalya Upanishad*, 8
27. RV. I.190.4a
28. RV. IV.50.1
29. RV. VII.97.5
30. SABCL. Vol. 10, p. 334
31. Ibid., p. 335
32. RV. V.70.3
33. RV. II.33.1-15
34. RV. VI.74.3
35. RV. I.114.1-11
36. RV. V.87.1-9
37. RV. I.22.19
38. RV. I.22.20
39. RV. I.125.5a
40. SABCL. Vol. 10, p. 335
41. Ibid., p. 336
42. Ibid., p. 337
43. RV. I.154.1-6
44. RV. I.22.20
45. RV. I.22.21
46. *Aitareya Brahmana*, VI.15.11
47. RV. III.54.14
48. Ibid., VII.35.9b
49. *Yajur Veda*, XXIII.49
50. SABCL. Vol. 13, p. 157

X

THE FIVE VEDIC GODDESSES: THE CONSORTS OF TRUTH-CONSCIOUSNESS

(1)

Mahi or Bharati

Bharati and Saraswati are different puissances in the Vedic context, whereas in the Puranic exegesis they are two names of the same goddess. In the Vedic pantheon the three deities Ila, Saraswati and Bharati are invariably associated, for their functions are closely connected with each other. They are companions in the sacrifice, sisters in the spiritual illumination of seekers and figures of truth-vision, truth-audition and vastness of Truth respectively. They together bring to the seeker-sacrificer fullness of the truth of being, knowledge and action. Bharati or Mahi carries in her the luminous vastness of the Truth, *satyam ṛtam bṛhat*; she represents the wideness and the largeness of Truth-Consciousness and bears in her bosom the Word and the Power of a blissful Truth. Mahi carries in her the supreme bliss, *māyās*, with which she absolves division, pain and suffering and bestows upon men a happy and right state of existence. "The Deva is both Male and Female and the gods... are either activising souls or passively executive and methodising energies. Aditi, infinite Mother of the gods, comes first; and there are besides five powers of the Truth-Consciousness, — Mahi or Bharati, the vast Word that brings us all things out of the divine source; Ila, the strong primal word of the Truth who gives us its active vision; Saraswati, its streaming current and the word of its inspiration; Sarama, the Intuition, hound of heaven who descends into the cavern of the subconscient and finds there the concealed illuminations; Dakshina, whose function is to discern rightly, dispose the action and the offering and distribute in the sacrifice to each godhead its portion. Each god, too, has his female energy."[1]

(2)

Ila

According to Sri Aurobindo, Ila, Saraswati and Sarama respectively represent individually and independently three different yet related faculties or expressive functions of the 'intuitive reason', *ṛtam* namely revelation, inspiration and intuition. They symbolise three female energies corresponding to certain psychological experiences in the path of Yoga. The fourth faculty of the Truth-Consciousness is Dakshina, 'the separative intuitional discrimination'. These four goddesses are clearly and unmistakably psychological symbols associated together in the ascent of consciousness of the Rishi. Whereas the fifth one symbolises largeness, vastness and greatness.

Ā no yajñaṁ bhāratī tūyamety
iḷā manuṣvadiha cetayantī,
tisro devīrbarhiredaṁ syonaṁ
saraswatī svapasaḥ sadantu.[2]

"May Bharati come speeding to our sacrifice and Ila hither awakening our consciousness (or, knowledge or perceptions) in human wise, and Saraswati, — three goddesses sit on this blissful seat, doing well the Work."*

Ila is also the word of the Truth awakening the consciousness of the seeker-sacrificer to knowledge supreme, *cetayantī*; the word gives him the active vision of the Truth. Ila is the plenary word of the supreme revelation, the great teacher of men. Ila is the highest Word, "the premier energy of the Truth-Consciousness, she who is the direct revealing vision in knowledge and becomes in that knowledge the spontaneous self-attainment of the Truth of things in action, result and experience, — Ila grows perpetually in body and richness."[3] Ila is "full of energy, *suvīrā*, and brings knowledge. She is also connected with Surya, the Sun, as when Agni, the Will, is invoked to labour by the rays of the Sun, Lord of the true Light, being of one mind with Ila, *iḷayā sajoṣa yatamāno raśmibhiḥ sūryasya*. She is the mother of the Rays, the herds of the Sun. Her name means she who seeks and attains and it contains the same association of ideas as the words *ṛtam* and Rishi. Ila may therefore well be the vision of the seer which attains the truth."[4]

In the Vedic Yoga, Ila is closely connected with Saraswati, as they represent respectively *dṛṣṭi* and *śruti*, whereas Mahi is the infinite vastness of the Truth-Consciousness which in its advent brings in the former two related powers. And these three puissances conjointly yield for the seeker the divine delight *māyās*. The relation between the Truth-Consciousness and Truth-Joy or *ānanda* is one of intimate companionship; if Truth is the passage, Bliss is the goal, or else, if the former is the foundation, the latter is the felicitous result.

(3)

Saraswati

Saraswati is the power of the intuitive intellect, a faculty of the Truth-Consciousness, a function of *ṛtam*. She is one of the four Vedic goddesses representing the divine inspiration, the truth-audition, the power of the truth-word; she is the goddess of the Word. The other three Ila, Sarama and Dakshina respectively represent truth-vision, pure intuition and intuitional perspicacity and discernment.

Saraswati is the divine Word, *śruti*, who signifies streams of revelation and inspiration that flow from the supreme and radiant planes of the Superconscient.

Pāvakā naḥ sarasvatī vājebhirvājinīvatī;
yajñaṁ vaṣṭu dhiyāvasuḥ.
Codayitrī sūnṛtānāṁ, cetantī sumatīnām;
yajñaṁ dadhe sarasvatī.
Maho arṇaḥ sarasvatī, pra cetayati ketunā;
dhiyo viśvā vi rājati.[5]

"May purifying Saraswati with all the plenitude of her forms of plenty, rich in substance by the thought, desire our sacrifice.
"She, the impeller to happy truths, the awakener in consciousness to right mentalisings, Saraswati, upholds the sacrifice.
"Saraswati by the perception awakens in consciousness the great flood (the vast movement of the *ṛtam*) and illumines entirely all the thoughts."*

The Vedic sacrifice is intimately connected to a certain state of consciousness that unmistakably leads to the attainment of the Truth. For, the object of sacrifice and the purpose of the Soma-offering itself is the achievement of the Truth-Consciousness. It is the crowning fulfilment and glory of the efforts of Indra and the Ashwins and all the gods in the vital and mental planes of earth-existence and human existence. It needs a rarefied and qualified consciousness — a purified and clarified mental, a richness of aspiration and soul-content and the right impulsion to the

Light — to link the seeker with the Truth. Saraswati is the goddess of inspiration and revelation that comes from the Truth-Consciousness to lead the seeker to the luminous world of Swar — the world of Immortality and Beatitude. "Saraswati awakes to consciousness or makes us conscious of the 'Great Ocean and illumines all our Thoughts'. It is surely not the River Goddess whom he[a] is thus hymning but the Power, the River if you will, of inspiration, the word of the Truth, bringing its light into our thoughts, building up in us that Truth, an inner knowledge."[6] She is intimately and effectively connected with the inner operations of the seeker-sacrificer's life and mind and soul, and therefore with the upward movement of his life, his nervous energy and his consciousness. She is the stream of inspiration and as such associated with a particular river bearing a psychological significance; she is constantly connected with the other goddesses Ila and Bharati or Mahi.

Iḷā saraswatī mahī tisro devīrmayobhuvaḥ,
barhiḥ sīdantvasridhaḥ.[7]

May the three ever-glorious goddesses, givers of joy, Ila, Saraswati and Mahi, occupy their places at our sacrifice, they who do not hurt.

She is the actuator of joyous and felicitous truths, *codayitrī sunṛtānām*; she is also the vibrant Word of wideness that carries with it the dynamic action of the Truth, *ṛtam bṛhat*, as well as the all-embracing power of Thought, *varūtri diṣaṇā*:

Ā gnā agna ihāvase hotraṁ yaviṣṭa bhāratīm,
varūtrīṁ dhiṣaṇāṁ vaha.[8]

O youthful, adorable Agni, may you bring here for our protection the goddesses Hotra, Bharati, Varutri and Dhishana.

In the words of Sri Aurobindo, Saraswati is "an awakener of the consciousness to right thinkings or right states of mind, *cetantī sumatīnām*,"[9] even as Ila is *cetayantī* — the one who brings to the sacrifice the awakened consciousness.

"As Saraswati represents the truth-audition, *sruti*, which gives the inspired word, so Ila represents *dṛṣṭi*, the truth-vision. If so, since *dṛṣṭi* and *śruti* are the two powers of the Rishi, the Kavi, the seer of the Truth, we can understand the close connection of Ila and Saraswati.

> Bharati or Mahi is the largeness of the Truth-Consciousness which, dawning on man's limited mind, brings with it the two sister Puissances. We can also understand how these fine and living distinctions came afterwards to be neglected as the Vedic knowledge declined and Bharati, Saraswati, Ila melted into one."[10]

The three goddesses Ila, Saraswati and Mahi in their conjoint action bring to birth for the seeker the supreme joy, *ānanda*. Between the Truth and the Bliss there is a constant relation of invariable concomitance; infinite consciousness is bound to bring in infinite bliss. "For the Vedic Rishi Truth is the passage and the antechamber, the Bliss of the divine existence is the goal, or else Truth is the foundation, Bliss the supreme result."[11]

Saraswati is then a power of the Truth, the unfailing current of inspiration that constantly flows from the Truth-ocean, *mahān arṇavaḥ*. The power of the Truth comes to the seeker as inspiration that purifies him of all erroneousness and sham, perfidy and apostasy. "Saraswati, the inspiration," observes Sri Aurobindo, "is full of her luminous plenitudes, rich in substance of thought. She upholds the Sacrifice, the offering of the mortal being's activities to the divine by awakening his consciousness so that it assumes right states of emotion and right movements of thought in accordance with the Truth from which she pours her illuminations and by impelling in it the rise of those truths which, according to the Vedic Rishis, liberate the life and being from falsehood, weakness and limitation and open to it the doors of the supreme felicity. By this constant awakening and impulsion, summed up in the word, perception, *ketu*, often called the divine perception, *daivya ketu*, to distinguish it from the false mortal vision of things, — Saraswati brings into active consciousness in the human being the great flood or great movement, the Truth-Consciousness itself, and illumines with it all our thoughts."[12] And this Truth-Consciousness is the superconscient supramental that is beyond our waking being. It comes to us as a light and a voice that create in us a new discernment and a changed perception; it creates truth of vision which in turn organises and establishes truth of being. Saraswati by constantly acting in us awakens us to the transformative light and power of the supreme Truth. The Rishis refer to her as 'the secret self of Indra', for both inspiration and the illumined mind have their common source in the Truth-Consciousness. As a power of the Word descending from the Truth she is also the slayer of the Enemy and liberator of the shining cows. She then possesses the Truth, is the river of the Truth, *maho arṇaḥ* and awakens and illumines the thoughts, *viśvā dhiyo vi rājati.*

Saraswati later, in the *Puranas*, becomes the wisdom goddess, the mother of the Vedas, and the Muse and divine protector of learning and fine arts. She is the power and consort of Brahma connected with felicity and purity. She is celebrated under the names Sarada, Satarupa, Savitri, Gayatri, Vagishwari, Mahavidya and Brahmi. She is the 'flowing one', the Mother of all graces and the embodiment of all fine arts, sciences and skills. She is pictured as clad in spotless white and seated on a lotus holding in her hands *vīnā*, *akṣamālā* and *pustaka*, lute, rosary and book, respectively symbolising harmony and creativity, askesis and meditation, knowledge and perception. She represents the supreme creative intelligence of Brahma with which he brings into existence a perfectly organised creation. She is accompanied by a peacock and a swan signifying knowledge of multiplicity and discrimination.

Sri Aurobindo gives a most profound and esoteric significance of Mahasaraswati as one of the four major aspects of Aditi, the Divine Mother:

> "Mahasaraswati is the Mother's Power of Work and her spirit of perfection and order. The youngest of the Four, she is the most skilful in executive faculty and the nearest to physical Nature. Maheshwari lays down the large lines of the world-forces, Mahakali drives their energy and impetus, Mahalakshmi discovers their rhythms and measures, but Mahasaraswati presides over their detail of organisation and execution, relation of parts and effective combination of forces and unfailing exactitude of result and fulfilment. The science and craft and technique of things are Mahasaraswati's province. Always she holds in her nature and can give to those whom she has chosen the intimate and precise knowledge, the subtlety and patience, the accuracy of intuitive mind and conscious hand and discerning eye of the perfect worker. This Power is the strong, the tireless, the careful and efficient builder, organiser, administrator, technician, artisan and classifier of the worlds. When she takes up the transformation and new-building of the nature, her action is laborious and minute and often seems to our impatience slow and interminable, but it is persistent, integral and flawless. For the will in her works is scrupulous, unsleeping, indefatigable; leaning over us she notes and touches every little detail, finds out every minute defect, gap, twist or incompleteness, considers and weighs accurately all that has been done and all that remains still to be done hereafter. Nothing is too

small or apparently trivial for her attention; nothing however impalpable or disguised or latent can escape her. Moulding and remoulding she labours each part till it has attained its true form, is put in its exact place in the whole and fulfils its precise purpose. In her constant and diligent arrangement and rearrangement of things her eye is on all needs at once and the way to meet them and her intuition knows what is to be chosen and what rejected and successfully determines the right instrument, the right time, the right conditions and the right process. Carelessness and negligence and indolence she abhors; all scamped and hasty and shuffling work, all clumsiness and *à peu près* and misfire, all false adaptation and misuse of instruments and faculties and leaving of things undone or half done is offensive and foreign to her temper. When her work is finished, nothing has been forgotten, no part has been misplaced or omitted or left in a faulty condition; all is solid, accurate, complete, admirable. Nothing short of a perfect perfection satisfies her and she is ready to face an eternity of toil if that is needed for the fullness of her creation. Therefore of all the Mother's powers she is the most long-suffering with man and his thousand imperfections. Kind, smiling, close and helpful, not easily turned away or discouraged, insistent even after repeated failure, her hand sustains our every step on condition that we are single in our will and straightforward and sincere; for a double mind she will not tolerate and her revealing irony is merciless to drama and histrionics and self-deceit and pretence. A mother to our wants, a friend in our difficulties, a persistent and tranquil counsellor and mentor, chasing away with her radiant smile the clouds of gloom and fretfulness and depression, reminding always of the ever-present help, pointing to the eternal sunshine, she is firm, quiet and persevering in the deep and continuous urge that drives us towards the integrality of the higher nature. All the work of the other Powers leans on her for its completeness; for she assures the material foundation, elaborates the stuff of detail and erects and rivets the armour of the structure."[13]

(4)

Sarama

Of the four Vedic goddesses who together in their action manifest the Truth-Consciousness, Sarama is the one who discovers the cows concealed in the cave by the Panis. It is only then that Indra under the effect of the Soma-wine and accompanied by the Angirasas follows the trail and enters the cave and rescues the herds after defeating the Panis.

Sarama is almost a form of the Dawn symbolic of the path of the Truth. The journey of Indra and the Angirasas proceeds on the path shown by Sarama; Sarama forewarns the Panis of their coming to conquer them. She is the power of the Light and the Truth who pilots in the search for the hidden cows, and in the process exposes the path as well as the secret cave where the herds are hidden. As such she is certainly the precursor of the advent of the Truth in the human consciousness. She is the discoverer of the light of the Truth in the darkness of human existence but not its owner or holder. In the words of Sri Aurobindo, "Sarama is the traveller and seeker on its path who does not herself possess but rather finds that which is lost. Neither is she the plenary word of the revelation, the Teacher of man like the goddess Ila; for even when what she seeks is found, she does not take possession but only gives the message to the seers and their divine helpers who have still to fight for the possession of the light that has been discovered."[14] And the Veda speaks of her as the visible guide to the home of the Dasyus:

> *Prati yatsya nīthādarśi dasyoroko*
> *nācchā sadanaṁ jānatī gāt.*
> *adha smā no maghavañcakṛtādinmā no*
> *magheva niṣpapī parā dāḥ.*[15]

> As the path which leads to the hiding place of the Dasyus has now been seen and discovered by you, like the cow knows the way to her shed, may you O Lord, protect us against the enemies. Do not throw us away or neglect us as an incontinent one wastes away his wealth.

The knowledge of the whereabouts of the herds comes to her intuitively, naturally and spontaneously as it were, and with that knowledge, *jānatī gāt*, Sarama leads Indra and the Angirasas as well as the rest of the powers to the seat of the Adversary. Sarama has the instinctive fore-vision and the fore-knowledge of the place of concealment of the cows, and with that she guides the rest of the host of deities that seek them. "And she leads to that seat, *sadanam*, the home of the Destroyers, which is at the other pole of existence to the seat of the Truth, *sadanam ṛtasya*, in the cave or secret place of darkness, *guhāyām*, just as the home of the gods is in the cave or secrecy of light. In other words, she is a power descended from the superconscient Truth which leads us to the light that is hidden in ourselves, in the subconscient."[16]

The Rishi sings in praise of Sarama and calls upon all the seekers to repeat her attainments.

a) *Vidadyadī saramā rugṇamadrermahi*
pāthaḥ pūrvyaṁ sadhryakkaḥ,
agraṁ nayatsupadyakṣarāṇāmacchā
ravaṁ prathamā jānatī gāt.[17]

When Sarama discovers the entrance to the mountain-cave, Indra makes a broad and straight path to it. Then the quick mind recognizing the concealed shining cattle by their lowing proceeds and comes close to the hidden illuminations.

b) *Eto nvadya sudhyo bhavāma pra ducchunā*
minavāmā varīyaḥ,
āre dveṣāṅsi sanutardadhāmāyāma
prāñco yajamānamaccha.

Etā dhiyaṁ kṛṇavāmā sakhāyo'pa
yā mātāñ ṛṇuta vrajaṁ goḥ,
yayā manurviśiśipraṁ jigāya yayā
vaṇigvaṅkurāpā purīṣam.[18]

"Come now, today let us become perfected in thought, let us destroy suffering and unease, let us embrace the higher good... far from us let us put always all hostile things (all the things that attack and divide, *dveṣāṁsi*); let us go forward towards the Master of the sacrifice. Come, let us create the Thought, O friends, (obviously, the seven-headed Angirasa-thought), which is the Mother (Aditi or the Dawn) and removes the screening pen of the Cow.*

Following Sarama, the seven seers and Brihaspati reach the concealed cows, and strengthened and enforced by their illuminations they get united and integrated in the 'level wideness', *samāna ūrve*, from where the supreme Truth descends upon the mental consciousness. It is here in the infinite Truth-Consciousness that all the seven seers get unified into a single Angirasa — the seven-headed and seven-mouthed Ayasya — who corrects all falsehood and ignorance and turns all life and thought and works into transparent figures of the Truth, *sangatāsaḥ saṁ jānate na yatante mithas te.*[19] And this is made possible by Sarama's intuitive discovery and action that leads straight to the Truth by the direct highway to the Truth and not through the circuitous track of error and ignorance.

The Angirasas unitedly ascend to the world of the Superconscient following upon Sarama's intuitive disclosure of the imprisoned herds. It is Sarama, the power of Intuition, that leads and guides and succeeds in finding the hidden illuminations, and thereby paves the path royal for both the gods and the seekers to enter the higher places above. Sarama precedes and prepares the way for the advent of the Divine Mind; she brings in her wake the streams of the Truth confined in the bosom of the rock.

Apo yadadriṁ puruhūta dardarāvir
bhuvatsaramā pūrvyaṁ te,
sa no netā vājamā darṣi bhūriṁ
gotrā rujannaṅgirobhirgṛṇānaḥ.[20]

Invoked by many, when you (O Indra) clove open the obstructing clouds, for releasing the rains, Sarama appeared before you and showed the path. And you the bringer of felicity, supported by the Angirasas, have brought us illuminations by clearing the clouds.

The great conquests of Indra and the Angirasas are entirely because of Sarama's gaining knowledge of the secret place where the cows remained incarcerated. With the release of the immured illuminations the Angirasas enter their seats in the Truth and prepare the path towards Immortality, and Indra by his irresistible and invincible energies brings into being, together, the Sun and the Dawn, the Path and the Flame.

a) *Pitre ciccakruḥ sadanaṁ samasmai*
mahi tviṣīmatsukṛto vi hi khyan,
viṣkabhnantaḥ skambhanenā janitrī āsīnā
ūrdhvaṁ rabhasaṁ vi minvan.[21]

The Angirasas performing sacrifices made for their protector a spacious and splendid home which they celebrated; seated at the sacrifice they support heaven and earth with the pillar of the firmament, and uphold on high the great Indra.

b) *Mahi kṣetraṁ puru ścandraṁ vividvān*
aditsakhibhyaścarathaṁ samairat,
indro nṛbhirajanaddīdyānaḥ sākaṁ
sūryamuṣasaṁ gātumagnim.[22]

The resplendent Lord, Indra, bestows upon his devotees vast treasure and wide pastures, and generates life and luminous energies. The radiant god in association with the Maruts brings in the Sun and the Dawn, the earth and the fire.

And by the Truth, Indra shows the truths to all the seekers thus opening their entry into the world of *Swar*:

Pra sūnṛta diśamāna ṛtena duraś
ca viśvā avṛṇodapa svāḥ.[23]

May he (Indra) opening all the portals of knowledge for us bring us the supreme felicity (of Swar).

It is Sarama who first finds the citadel and the adytum of the hidden illuminations, their amplitude and their scope which the seekers now dote upon. She is the dispenser of the grotto bonanza, a very special faculty of the Truth, the mistress and the felicity of the divine Dawn.

Vidadgavyaṁ saramā dṛḷhamūrvaṁ
yenā nu kaṁ mānuṣī bhojate viṭ.[24]

For you Sarama discovers the milk of higher consciousness with which the progeny of Manu is ever nourished.

In the words of Sri Aurobindo,

"Sarama leads to the wideness of the cows... Sarama brings us to the truth, to the sun-vision which is the way to the bliss; these dogs[b] bring the weal to man in this world of suffering so that he shall have the vision of the Sun. Whether Sarama figures as the fair-footed goddess speeding on the path or the heavenly hound, mother of these wide-ranging guardians of the path, the idea is the same, a power of the Truth that seeks and discovers, that finds by a divine faculty of insight the hidden Light and the denied Immortality."[25]

Sarama, *parākāt*, descends from the world of the Superconscient, the kingdom of the Truth — of pure Light without the shadow of darkness — and crossing the ocean of the Night arrives at the citadel of the Dasyus, the sons of Inconscience — the powers that be of falsehood and ignorance. This inspires Indra to break open the secret cave and release the illuminations for the benefit of the seekers. Sarama, the precursor and initiator of Indra, is the dawn goddess and symbolises the intuitive power of the Truth; she is "the discovering intuition, who penetrates into the cave of the subconscient where the niggard lords of sense-action have hidden the radiant herds of the Sun and gives information to Indra."[26]

(5)

Dakshina

Ila, Sarama, Saraswati and Dakshina are the four consorts of the Truth, the four faculties of Truth-Consciousness — the four goddesses who constantly accompany the supramental superconscient in its effective manifestation upon earth. Dakshina is the female counterpart of Daksha, or, rather his own female form. She is associated with the manifestation of intuitional knowledge, the intuitional discrimination and discernment. She is the goddess who upholds the power of luminous percipience that effects the sacrifice. She is the nodus of clear judgement and obliquely a delineation of the Dawn. She is invested with the strength of effectuating illuminations — a power that is inherent in her name itself — and dispelling the darkness of ignorance and falsehood; Indra, having Dakshina with him separates the light from the darkness, *jyotir vṛṇīta tamaso vijānan*.

She is the 'discerning knowledge', the sun-eyed strength or the right hand power of Indra, with which he presides over the sacrifice and distributes the offerings of the sacrificers equitably to the various gods. Dakshina is extolled in the Veda as the goddess of 'pure intuitive discernment' who enables Agni to grow in the seeker from strength to greater strength and finally to empower and commission Indra to break open the cave where the shining cows lie concealed. Whereas Sarama is the quick and unmistakable discovering intuition who ingresses into the citadel of the subconscient where the Panis have hidden the herds of light. It is only then that Indra, the lord of the luminous intelligence, invades the hideous hideout of the Adversary, liberates the cows and drives them towards the supreme Truth-Consciousness which is the foundation of

Immortality, *yatrāmṛtāsa āsate.*[27] She is "the goddess of the discriminating and distributing Thought of the divine Mind."[28] She helps the seeker to discern rightly and dispose the sacrificial action perfectly and to enable him to distribute his benefactions properly among the many gods.

There is an intimate and fundamental relationship between force and consciousness; wherever there is knowledge there is power. The purified and liberated intellect with its right discernment takes up its station in right action. Dakshina and Surya are thus interrelated and well-connected in their upward endeavour to reach as well as manifest the Truth. As Sri Aurobindo observes,

> "Dakshina, the discriminative intellect is the energy of *dakṣa*, master of the works or unerring right discernment but unerring in the ideality, in *mahas* or *vijñāna*, his and her own home, not unerring in the intellect, but only straining towards hidden truth and right out of the mental dualities of right and wrong, truth and falsehood. This deputy and messenger of the Ritam Brihat seated in *manas* as reason, discernment, intellect, can only attain its end and fulfill its mission when Agni, the divine Force, manifests in the Prana and Manas and uplifts her to the ideal plane of consciousness. Therefore in this new activity she is described as straining and extending herself upwards, *uttānām* to follow and reach Agni where are his topmost planes, *ūrdhva*, in the ideal being. From there he leans down and feeds on her, *adhayat*, through the flames of the divine activity, *juhūbhiḥ*, burning in the purified and upward aspiring activities of the intellectual mind."[29]

Daksha later came to represent the male principle of creation and also is identified with Prajapati.[30] He is the creator-god who realises in space-time what is envisioned or ideated elsewhere. Although he is mentioned as one of the Adityas, Daksha is deemed to be preceding them; this seeming paradox also occurs in the Hymn of Creation.

> *Bhūrjajña uttānapado bhuva āśā ajāyanta,*
> *aditerdakṣo ajāyata dakṣādvaditiḥ pari;*
>
> *Aditirhyajaniṣṭa dakṣa yā duhitā tava,*
> *tāṁ devā anvajāyanta bhadrā amṛtabandhavaḥ.*[31]
>
> The earth was born from the onward-moving creation and the quarters were born from the earth; Daksha was born from Aditi and later Aditi from Daksha.

O Daksha, Aditi who was your daughter, has now brought forth you and the gods adorable, freed from the fetters of death.

The Vedas describe Daksha as an eminent and towering godhead, as that divine primary stimulus — the subtle and supreme creative power — which manifests the universe of space and time from the Unmanifest. He represents the divine Intelligence that expresses itself in all of creation and through all its creatures. He is referred to as the father of the gods as well as of the Adityas, and the mighty power and discerning knowledge inherent in them.

a) *Yā dhārayanta devaḥ sudakṣā dakṣāpitarā,*
asuryāya pramahasā.[32]

You are the one, O Lord, whom the gods support and vindicate for their own strengthening, those who are themselves great and wise and of diffusive radiance.

b) *Napātā śavaso mahaḥ sūnū dakṣasya sukratū,*
sṛpradanū iṣo vāstvadhi kṣitaḥ.[33]

They are the offsprings of Daksha, sons of mighty strength, doers of good deeds and great benefactors; they preside over the production of food.

Daksha is mentioned in the Veda both as an epithet and a personification of discerning intelligence, dexterity and abstract potency. He is the divine ideation of which the cosmic consonance is the grand design.

1. SABCL. Vol. 11, p. 32
2. RV. X.110.8
3. SABCL. Vol. 10, p. 312
4. Ibid., p. 91
5. RV. I.3.10-12
6. SABCL. Vol. 11, p. 10
a. The Rishi

7. RV. I.13.9
8. RV. I.22.10
9. SABCL. Vol. 10, p. 91
10. Ibid.
11. Ibid., p. 92
12. Ibid., pp. 95-6
13. SABCL. Vol. 25, pp. 33-5
14. SABCL., p. 203
15. RV. I.104.5
16. Op. cit., p. 204
17. RV. III.31.6
18. RV. V.45.5-6
19. RV. VII.76.5
20. RV. IV.16.8
21. RV. III.31.12
22. RV. III.31.15
23. RV. III.31.21b
24. RV. I.72.8b

b. The Sarameya dogs which have the same essential characteristics of Sarama.

25. SABCL. Vol. 10, p. 214
26. Ibid., p. 319
27. RV. IX.15.2
28. SABCL. Vol. 10, p. 421
29. SABCL. Vol. 11, pp. 496-97
30. *Satapatha Brahmana*, II.4.4.2
31. RV.X.72.4-5
32. RV. VII.66.2
33. RV. VIII.25.5

XI

MARUTS

Maruts are the Life-Powers, the luminous and vital energies in action that working in the seeker, support his mortal consciousness to grow into the immortality of the supreme Truth. They are the violent gods of the storm and lightning that combine in themselves the impassioned intensity of Vayu the Lord of the Life-plane and the refulgent power of Agni. They are therefore both seers and battling forces that knock down all barriers of obscurity and worn-out establishment in which the hosts of Darkness breed darkly. They share the characteristic features of the Angirasas, and rightly moving on the desired path, *adhi sānu pṛśneḥ*,[1] bring to the seekers the felicity of light and joy. They possess the power of the Angirasa action and the virgin energies of Agni; they have the Word that opens on the world of the Truth and know the right path which leads to the Immortality and the Beatitude.

The Maruts are the 'thought-attaining powers' of Life who by the sheer strength of their motion break down all that which is static and stagnant and established, and help to realize new formations and movements. To the uninitiated and untrained the Maruts are mere powers of fierce wind and storm and rain. Undoubtedly they are brilliant and impassioned, lustrous and glorious, and share with the other gods their helpfulness to humanity. They are authors of Light and promoters of the Truth.

Yūyaṃ tatsatyaśavasa āviṣkarta mahitvanā,
vidhyatā vidyutā rakṣaḥ;
gūhatā guhyaṁ tamo vi yāta viśvamatriṇam,
jyotiṣkartā yadhuśmasi.[2]

"O ye who have the flashing strength of the Truth, manifest that by your might; pierce with your lightning the Rakshasa. Conceal the concealing darkness, repel every devourer, create the Light for which we long."*

They represent, nay, embody the mind's quick movement for Truth, its fiery and fervent search as well as its manifold play of action. Also they bring with them the light of knowledge and the nectar of bliss.

Nityaṁ na sūnuṁ madhu bibhrata upa
krīḷanti krīḷā vidatheṣu dhṛṣvayaḥ.[3]

"They carry with them the sweetness (of the Ananda) as their eternal offspring and play out their play, brilliant in the activities of knowledge."*

Maruts are Indra's brothers and helpers in the struggle for perfect perfection as planned and firmly willed, directed and settled by the divine Intelligence. Whenever they go astray and help individual rabid and wild ambitions as in the case of Agastya, Indra would firmly put his foot down and oppose and stop their activity. In their integral movement towards the Truth, the seekers do need the splendid energies of Maruts. In the luminous orchestration of the inner and outer action the role of Maruts is supremely effective; in the absence of any discord and disorder they become most efficient and beneficient instruments of yogic perfection and victory.

"The Maruts represent the progressive illumination of human mentality, until from the first obscure movements of mind which only just emerge out of the darkness of the subconscient, they are transformed into an image of the luminous consciousness of which Indra is the Purusha, the representative Being. Obscure, they become conscient; twilit, half-lit or turned into misleading reflections, they surmount these deficiencies and put on the divine brilliance. This great evolution is effected in Time gradually, in the mornings of the human spirit, by the unbroken succession of the Dawns."[4]

Indra with the help of the Maruts brings about increasing illumination, and finally establishes the supramental knowledge of the seeker; it is by their energies that he progressively provides him with his divine firmness and force. The Maruts get their illumined guidance from Indra and find in him their requisite amplitude and concord, right perception and right impulsion.

1. *Prati va enā namasāhamomi sūktena bhikṣe*
sumatiṁ turāṇām,
rarāṇatā maruto vedyābhirni heḷo dhatta vi
mucadhvamaśvān.

2. *Eṣa vaḥ stomo maruto namasvānhṛdā taṣṭo
manasā dhāyi devāḥ,
upemā yāta manasā juṣāṇā yūyaṁ hi ṣṭhā
namasa idvṛdhāsaḥ.*

3. *Stutāso no maruto mṛḷayantūta stuto
maghavā śambhaviṣṭhaḥ,
ūrdhvā naḥ santu komyā vanānyahāni viśvā
maruto jigīṣā.*

4. *Asmādahaṁ taviṣādīshamāṇa indrādbhiyā
maruto rejamānaḥ,
yuṣmabhyaṁ havyā niśitānyāsantānyāre
cakṛmā mṛḷatā naḥ.*[5]

1. I approach you, O Maruts, with deep reverence, and with this hymn I seek right mentality from those who are fast in movement against me. Pacified by our praises, O Maruts, may you lay aside your anger and unyoke your horses.

2. This hymn of praise, O Maruts, is for you and sings of your affirmation; it is filled with my reverence for you and is offered from the heart and comes from our conscious mind. Receive these laudations, accept them with favour, for, verily, you are the augmenters of the sacrificial quest for Truth.

3. May the Maruts now affirmed by us be gracious and kind to us, may Maghavan the lord of plenitude become propitious and creative of felicity to us. May our pleasant growths be ever uplifted, O Maruts, may we always move upward victoriously by the will towards the supreme epiphany.

4. O Maruts, through fear of Indra, and overpowered by his prowess, I have put far away the oblations intensely prepared for you. Nevertheless, may your grace be with us.

The Maruts are the energies of the Mind that possess, transform and drive our animal propensities towards the luminous truths of Indra and the world of Swar. Although they very much resemble the powers of Vayu, in their dynamism and impassioned action they are intimately associated with Agni; they are Rudra's children in the measure they relentlessly break down all barriers of obscurity and defective formation. They are the leaders of the protracted and grim and savage struggle against the powers of Darkness. As such Rudra is named by his preeminent position as their invincible parent, whereas Vishnu is hymned as their very source and innate strength in their ascent to the Truth. The Maruts unite in themselves the violent powers of Vayu and the force and seer-will of Agni; they are seers who work by the knowledge, as well as the soldiers who fight by the Force. They are the Life-Powers and the Thought-Powers that support the seeker in his journey to the Truth and the Beatitude. They are described by the Rishis as working like the Angirasas both in illumination and action, and move justly and correctly on the trial, *itthā nakṣanto aṅgirasvat.*[6] They are even construed as the Angirasas taking different forms, *viśvarūpā aṅgiraso na sāmabhiḥ.*[7]

The Maruts are also spoken of as being associated with the breaking of the hill and conquering the treasures of supreme felicity.[8] They are the actuators of illumined thought and right speech, and battle towards the Truth and Bliss. Enforced and enriched by Agni, the Maruts prepare the action of Indra, the finder of the Truth, the Right and the Vast, *satyam ṛtam bṛhat.* The clear and limpid imagery employed by the Rishis to describe the Maruts as also the other godheads brings out unequivocally their nature and function. The Maruts are the children of Rudra and Prishni the dappled Cow — the great Mother of the mid-region.

a) *Etāni dhīro niṇyā ciketa pṛśnir*
yadūdho mahī jabhāra.[9]

The wise one knows the white-complexioned gods as the Maruts born of the vast mother Prishni at her udders.

b) *Rudrasya ye mīḷhuṣaḥ santi putrā*
yāṅśco nu dādhṛvirbharadhyai,
vide hi mātā maho mahī ṣā set
pṛśniḥsubhve garbhamādhāt.[9a]

They (the Maruts) who are the sons of the mighty Rudra whom the nursing mother Prishni is able to sustain, and of whom the wide mid-region received the life-germ for the benefit of mankind.

They move constantly and swiftly in large groups with their shining weapons. The impetuous ones move in glorious jalopies, and send down torrents of rain whacking and inundating everything well-established that resists change. These fierce ones are also 'friends of Truth and creators of Light'; they protect the seekers from demerit and degeneracy, *aghāt rakṣata*,[10] and are described as the restorators of perfect health, *mārutasya bheṣajasya avahat*.[11]

The Maruts are active both in the cosmos as well as in the individual, and play an effective role in the life of the seeker-sacrificers in their endeavour to attain to Immortality. They unite in themselves, as Sri Aurobindo observes, the powers of Vayu the Wind-God and Agni the Seer-Will and "are therefore seers who do the work by the knowledge, *kavayo vidmanā-apasaḥ*, as well as battling forces who by the power of the heavenly Breath and the heavenly lightning overthrow the established things, the artificial obstructions, *kṛtrimāṇi rodhāmsi*, in which the sons of Darkness have entrenched themselves, and aid Indra to overcome vritra and the Dasyus. They seem to be in the esoteric Veda the Life-Powers that support by their nervous or vital energies the action of the thought in the attempt of the mortal consciousness to grow or expand itself into the immortality of the Truth and Bliss."[12] These heroic helpers of humanity, borne by many-hued horses, are brilliant messengers of light. Living together in the mid-region, *antarikṣa*, they open up the upward way and powerfully support the pilgrims' progress.

Ka īṁ vyaktā naraḥ sanīḷā rudrasya
maryā adhā svaśvāḥ.[13]

Who are these brave leaders, resplendent and radiant, dwellers in one abode, the heroic offsprings of Rudra, mounted on graceful horses?

No one really knows of their origin and the purpose of their birth; only they truly know of each other and of all the rest.

Nakirhyeṣāṁ janūṁṣi veda te
aṅga vidre mitho janitram.[14]

Verily, no one knows whence they came; they and they only know of each other's birth.

They are the shining hosts who perennially nourish the striver; only the gifted ones can have a glimpse of their movement; only the blessed ones receive the waters of the higher consciousness that they bring with them.

Aitānratheṣu tasthuṣaḥ kaḥ śuśrāva
kathā yayuḥ,
kasmai sasruḥ sudāse anvāpaya iḷābhir
vṛṣṭayaḥ saha.[15]

Who has heard them, when mounting their chariots whither they went forth? Who is the munificent man for whom their cognate waters stream down together with manifold knowledge?

The Maruts are cosmic workers constantly engaged in liberating men from the stranglehold of ignorance, inertia and inaction. Refulgent in form and expeditious in action, the Maruts increase Indra in the being of their worshippers and firmly establish in them the knowledge of the Truth. They are the movers and mobilisers and the luminous inspirers who help to express all that springs from the soul.

The Maruts are also described as sons of the radiant Cow, *gomātaraḥ*, and as offsprings of the sea of supreme Consciousness, *sindhumātaraḥ*. They inherit the healing power of Rudra and the vitality of Aditi, the Mother of manifold creation. They come into manifestation to help the striver in his great and difficult inner journey to attain the light of the Truth in his thought.

Yadyūyaṁ pṛśnimātaro martāsaḥ syātana,
stotā vo amṛtaḥ syāt.[16]

O Maruts, we know that you are the sons of Prishni born in us mortals; now surely your worshippers would grow immortal.

Maruts, the gods of the *antariksha*, are mighty powers of the Life-Plane; they embody the force and dynamism of the vital world with which is carried out the perfect purification of thought, and the mind enabled to reach its luminous heights. These are the powers of thought, liberated energies, soaring upward towards the Truth. They are mankind's friends of unfailing strength who effectuate light and power in the lives of men against the enemies. They give themselves generously and fully to the seeker and play out their part in a hundred brilliant ways. As powers of pure thought and constant movement they bring the sweetness of Ananda to the worshipper. They are irresistible energies with the Truth as their source — mighty warriors free from fear or falsehood,[17] surging forward freely towards the Truth. They scrupulously and spontaneously follow the Law, and with their manifold opulence enliven the inner being of the sacrificer.

> *Haye naro maruto mṛlatā nastuvīmaghāso*
> *amṛtā ṛtajñāḥ,*
> *satyaśrutaḥ kavayo yuvāno bṛhad girayo*
> *bṛhadukṣamāṇāḥ.*[18]

> O Maruts, hero-warriors of the Truth, be gracious and favourable to us; may you who are infinitely opulent, immortal, renowned for the knowledge of the Law, seers, youthful and greatly glorified, of august speech, and grown increasingly puissant.

They possess the secret of Immortality which they share with their worshippers; they are the seers and the hearers of the Truth, and have the illumined Word that fulfils the sacrifice.

> *Vandasva mārutaṁ gaṇaṁ tveṣaṁ*
> *panasyumarkiṇam,*
> *asme vṛddhā asanniha.*[19]

> Sing to the glory of Maruts who are brilliant and worthy of our praises, they of the flaming Word; may they be exalted by this our worship.

The Maruts are friends and followers of Indra who initiate and effectuate the flow of celestial waters that fertilise the fields of the inner life of the worshippers; they illumine their being and rejuvenate it. These puissant powers are awakened and acquitted into action with the advent of Agni the flaming Seer-Will. Their forms and their attire, their armour and their chariots are all self-luminous and efficacious.

> *Ye pṛṣatībhirṛṣṭibhiḥ*
> *sākaṁ vaśībhirañjibhiḥ,*
> *ajāyanta svabhānavaḥ.*[20]

> Those who are borne by spotted deer, with weapons, and war-cries penetrating like spears, and glittering ornaments are self-luminous.

The Maruts are benevolent and self-giving to the adherents of the *Ṛta*, the Law of Truth. They are opponents of passivity; they initiate and support the movement of the Waters. They conquer all resistance, *tamas*, and awaken and effectuate the dormant energies in the worshippers with their unique weapons. To the seekers they are kindly and helpful, for them are their varied gifts of progress and delight. With their puissant Life-Force they not only purify the Thought-powers but also awaken the Consciousness in the physical. They perpetually endeavour to arrive at the levels of the Pure Mind; they activise the vital and the thought-being of the worshippers, and orient them to focus and to converge on the higher reaches of the Mind. When Agni, the divine Flame, manifests in the earth-nature and urges men to move forward, the way is already well-laid for the aspiring soul to reach the summit. He is the first one to taste the concealed Truth and with it vitalizes and innervates the thought-forces. The Maruts are born out of this great churning; firmly rooted in the vital they leap forward to reach the illumined mental. They are the harbingers of light who continuously strive to attain the highest knowledge.

The Maruts are almost a part of Rudra's being — his troops, *rudrāya senābhyaḥ*. They are mentioned many a time with Indra for they help him in his battle against Vritra; Indra is called *marūtvat*.[21]

a) *Ta innvasya madhumadvivipra*
indrasya śardho maruto ya āsan,
yebhirvṛtrasyeṣito vivedāmarmaṇo
manyamānasya marma.[22]

Those are the Martus who worshipping his prowess augment the might of Indra; animated by them Indra pierces the vital part of Vritra who imagines himself invincible and impregnable.

b) *Sajoṣā indra sagaṇo marudbhiḥ somaṁ*
piba vṛtrahā śūra vidvān.[23]

O hero-warrior, Indra, rejoicing with and accompanied by the Maruts, drink the Soma-wine, for verily, you are the slayer of Vritra.

c) *Aptūrye maruta āpireṣo'mandann*
indramanu dātivārāḥ.[24]

O Maruts, this resplendent lord, Indra, is your friend for sending the streams. You, the givers of great strength and support, have given him full cooperation and gratification.

d) *Yañ ābhajo maruta indra some ye tvām*
avardhannabhavanganaste,
tebhiretaṁ sajoṣā vāvaśāno'gneḥ
piba jihvayā somamindra.[25]

O Indra, associated with the Maruts who have supported you, you have shared in this our libation. May you along with them relish this drink most enthusiastically with the tongue of Agni.

The Maruts are associated also with Agni, *maruto'dbhir agnim atamayan.*[26]

1. *Prati tyaṁ cārumadhvaraṁ gopīthāya pra hūyase,*
marudbhiragna ā gahi.

2. *Nahi devo na martyo mahastava kratuṁ paraḥ,*
marudbhiragna ā gahi.

3. *Ye maho rajaso vidurviśve devāso adruhaḥ,*
marudbhiragna ā gahi.

4. *Ya ugra arkamānṛcuranādhṛṣṭāsa ojasā,*
marudbhiragna ā gahi.

5. *Ye śubhrā ghoravarpasaḥ sukṣatrāso riśādasaḥ,*
marudbhiragna ā gahi.

6. *Ye nākasyādhi rocane divi devāsa āsate,*
marudbhiragna ā gahi.

7. *Ya iṅkhayanti parvatān tiraḥ samudramarṇavam,*
marudbhiragna ā gahi.

8. *Ā ye tanvanti raśmibhistirah samudramojasā,*
marudbhiragna ā gahi.

9. *Abhi tvā pūrvapītaye sṛjāmi somyaṁ madhu,*
marudbhiragna ā gahi.[27]

1. We assiduously invoke you to this our perfect sacrifice to accept our loving oblation of the Soma-wine. Come, O Agni, with the Maruts.

2. None of the gods nor any man deserves our dedication; to you alone O mighty one is our sacrifice. Come, O Agni, with the Maruts.

3. You are truly divine and without malice; you are the one who knows how to cause the descent of the waters. Come, O Agni, with the Maruts.

4. O adorable god, you are truly unsurpassed in strength, fierce and unconquerable, you are the one who sends down the rain. Come, O Agni, with the Maruts.

5. O adorable god, you who are brilliant, and of terrific forms and possess manifold felicity, come, O Agni, with the Maruts.

6. O adorable lord, Agni, may you come with the Maruts working behind the divinities abiding in celestial regions beyond the sun.

7. O adorable lord, Agni, may you come with the Maruts who scatter the clouds and agitate the seas with their vigour.

8. O adorable lord, Agni, may you come with the Maruts who spread through the heavens along with the rays of the sun and with their strength convulse the ocean.

9. O adorable lord, Agni, may you come with the Maruts; we offer you our devout praises like the Soma-wine for your acceptance and delight.

The association of the Maruts with Agni is eulogized by the *Taittiriya Samhita*:

Agnir va ito vrstim ud brayati marutah
srstam nayanti yada khalu va asav adityo
nyan rasmibhih paryavartate 'tha varsati
dhamacchad iva khalu vai bhutva varsati.[28]

The Maruts are described by the Rishis as wind and storm gods who live and move and work as a group; they adorn themselves richly, and swiftly moving together accomplish marvels. Singing their songs in gusto they strengthen Indra in driving away the attackers; with shining anklets on their feet, golden ornaments on their bodies and fiery weapons in their hands they are described as darting thunderbolts on the Enemy. Drawn by dappled gazelles their chariots speed forward as thought and make for themselves a broad seat in the skies. Alongside Indra, they fight the common Enemy with admirable fortitude.

a) *Pra ye śumbhantc janayo na saptayo*
yāmanrudrasya sūnavaḥ sudaṁsasaḥ,
rodasī hi marutaścakrire vṛdhe
madanti vīrā vidatheṣu ghṛṣvayaḥ.[29]

The Maruts, performers of great deeds, who swiftly move forward go forth fully decorated like damsels; they glide through the air, the sons of Rudra, and promote the welfare of both heaven and earth; the brave ones take delight in the sacrifices.

b) *Ta ukṣitāso mahimānamāśata divi*
rudrāso adhi cakrire sadaḥ,
arcanto arkaṁ janayanta indriyamadhi
śriyo dadhire pṛśnimātaraḥ.[30]

Initiated by the gods, the Maruts have attained majesty; these sons of Rudra through dedication establish their dwelling above the sky. Inspiring and supporting Indra, these sons of Prishni have attained their eminent and illustrious position.

The episode of Agastya, Indra and the Maruts in the Veda has an important bearing on the nature of relation between the seeker-sacrificer and the summit-goal of his endeavour. Agastya is said to have dedicated a hundred dappled cows to the Maruts but they were all taken away by Indra. This angers the Maruts in the beginning, but are reconciled when they realise the purpose of the sacrifice. Agastya who is initially in a dilemma apologises to both Indra and the Maruts, and offers prayers to all of them.[31]

The Rishis again and again entreat the Maruts to lift the seekers out of the obscurity of the physical, and with their luminous power destroy the antagonists of their inner progress; they pray to be given a decisive victory over the powers of Darkness and set them securely in the domain of Light so that they could grow steadily from knowledge to greater knowledge. Finally, they implore them to be cured of all the illnesses of the physical, vital and the mental, as well as the sickness of the soul, and grant them perfect peace.

1. RV. VI.6.4
2. RV. I.86.9-10
3. RV. I.166.2
4. SABCL. Vol. 10, p. 261
5. RV. I.171.1-4
6. RV. VI.49.11
7. RV. X.78.5
8. RV. VI.66.8
9. RV.VII.56.4

9a. RV.VI.66.3

10. RV. I.166.8
11. RV. VIII.20.23
12. SABCL. Vol. 10, p. 163
13. RV. VII.56.1
14. RV. VII.56.2
15. RV. V.53.2
16. RV. I.38.4
17. RV. V.61.14
18. RV. V.58.8
19. RV. I.38.15
20. RV. I.37.2
21. RV. IV.21.3
22. RV. III.32.4
23. RV. III.47.2a
24. RV. III.51.9a
25. RV. III.35.9
26. *Taittiriya Brahmana*, I.1.3.12
27. RV. I.19.1-9
28. *Taittiriya Samhita*, II.4.10.2
29. RV. I.85.1
30. RV. I.85.2
31. RV. I.165.1-15; I. 170.1-5

XII

THE RIBHUS

The gods in the external sense are 'universal powers of physical Nature personified', and in the inner sense are her subjective force of Life, Mind etc. The Veda makes a clear distinction between the ordinary human action of these powers and their divine intention. The human seeker by his conscious and judicious use of the mental functioning of the gods on his inner sacrifice can transform them into their divine nature and himself become immortal.

The Ribhus, likewise, to begin with are human and imaged as human faculties, but by their total dedication to perfection in their works become divine powers; and this becomes possible because of their constant sacrifice and self-offering. As Sri Aurobindo observes, "It is a continual self-offering of the human to the divine and a continual descent of the divine into the human which seems to be symbolised in the sacrifice."[1] The Ribhus thus become immortal and help the seekers to attain the state of perfect felicity, *satyam ṛtam bṛhat*. They initially shape things by the mind but build up a state of divinity and immortality through conscious consecration and perfection in work; verily, they are the artisans of Immortality.

The Ribhus are solar powers who through their *māyā*[a] help Indra in raising man towards the same divine status which they themselves have attained by their perfection in works. They are born out of the radiant Energy — the innate luminous strength of Matter, Sudhanwan, that motivates the journey to Immortality. In fact they are powers of Light and the Truth born as human propensities urging to grow divine.

> *Indrasya sūno śavaso napāto'nu*
> *vaścetyagriyaṁ madāya.*[2]
>
> O Powerful sons of Indra, grandsons of never failing luminous strength, this great sacrifice is for your celebration and exhilaration.

The Ribhus are also called Vibhus and Vajas suggesting their unique nature. If the Ribhus are skilful knowers, the Vibhus are all-pervading and self-diffusing energies whereas the Vajas are the generous bestowers of plenitudes many.

"Ribhu, the eldest is the first in man who begins to shape by his thoughts and works the forms of immortality; Vibhwa gives pervasiveness to this working; Vaja, the youngest, supplies the plenitude of the divine light and substance by which the complete work can be done."[2a]

Besides being a collective name, Ribhu thus designates one of the three 'brothers'; the name is used not only as a proper noun but also as a denomination.

a) *Taṁ nemimṛbhavo yathā namasva sahūtibhiḥ.*[3]

O Angiras, with the Ribhus associated in the invocation, direct the sacrifice towards yourself.

b) *Ṛbhurna rathyaṁ navaṁ*
dadhātā ketamādiśe.[4]

As a wise one sets before him a worthy chariot so may you grant to our lord.

c) *Ṛbhū rathasyevāṅgāni saṁ dadhat*
paruṣā paruḥ.[5]

Let Ribhu, the proficient physician join his limb with limb as an expert mechanic joins the parts of a car.

d) *Yaste parumṣi saṁdadhau*
rathasyevaṛbhurdhiyā.[6]

Let this artifice consider as novices and return back to Ribhu, the proficient one who by his expertise has made the parts of it like a skilled artisan.

The Rishis affirm the divine mission and action of the Ribhus: the Ribhus are born to bring to man the beatitude and the immortality and the ecstasies of divine life which they have gained by dedication. The Ribhus by their own example and inner realisation help man to accomplish in his station what they have attained, and assist the gods in his divinisation.

They actively support and supplement him in his struggle to ascend to the Truth and the Beatitude. In pursuit of this objective the Ribhus accomplish several things. They provide Indra with two shining horses harnessed by the flaming Word to their luminous operations. For it is only the divine Mind that opens up to the works their immortalising potential. Secondly, they design the chariot of the Ashwins which signifies the shaping of "the happy movement of the Ananda in man which pervades with its action all his worlds or planes of being, bringing health, youth, strength, wholeness to the physical man, capacity of enjoyment and action to be vital, glad energy of the light to the mental being, — in a word, the force of the pure delight of being in all his members."[7] They also fashion the perennially obliging Cow of Radiances; they deliver her out of her 'covering skin' — the skin representing Nature's outward blind movement and ignorant action. Aditi is the Cow, "the infinite Conscious Being which is the mother of the worlds."[8] The Ribhus bring out this Consciousness imbedded in the bowels of physical Nature and fashion in the seeker a dynamic figure of her. It is this creative reunion of the soul in the phenomenal world with its infinite mother that assures the ascent of the pilgrim to the Truth and the attainment of Immortality. Also, the Ribhus with the discerning light of Indra, the movement of the blissful Ashwins and the nourishment of the fostering Cow rejuvenate the aging Heaven and Earth. They give a new lease of ingenious and innovative life to the physical and mental levels of existence. They water them with streams of Truth and nourish them and restore to them their original youth and vigour.

a) *Yadāramakrannṛbhavaḥ pitṛbhyāṁ*
pariviṣṭī veṣaṇā daṅsanābhiḥ,
ādiddevanamupa sakhyamāyan
dhīrāsaḥ puṣṭimavahanmanāyai.[9]

When the Ribhus, by serving their parents with restoration of their youth and vigour and by performing other good deeds achieve enough, thereupon they turn to the community of the gods and bring felicity to the devout worshippers.

b) *Punarye cakruḥ pitarā yuvānā sanā*
yūpeva jaraṇā śayānā,
te vājo vibhvaṅ ribhurindravanto
madhupsaraso no'vantu yajñam.[10]

> May the Ribhus who again rejuvenate their haggard and wasted parents and render them youthful and energetic — Vaja, Vibhwan and Ribhu associated with Indra, drinkers of the Soma-wine — always protect our sacrifices.

In the words of Sri Aurobindo, "They pervade heaven with their workings, they bring divine increase to the mentality, they give to it and the physical being a fresh and young and immortal movement. For from the home of the Truth they bring with them the perfection of that which is the condition of their work, the movement in the straight path of the Truth and the Truth itself with its absolute effectivity in all the thoughts and words of the mentality. Carrying this power with them in their pervading entry into the lower world, they pour into it the immortal essence."[11]

a) i. *Anaśvo jāto anabhīśurukthyo rathās*
tricakaḥ pari vartate rajaḥ,
mahattadvo devyasya pravācanaṁ dyām
ṛbhavaḥ pṛthivīṁ yacca puṣyatha.

ii. *Rathaṁ ye cakruḥ suvṛtaṁ sucetaso*
'vihvarantaṁ manasaspari dhyayā,
tañ ū nvasya savanasya pītaya ā vo
vājā ṛbhavo vedayāmasi.

iii. *Tadvo vājā ṛbhavaḥ supravācanaṁ*
deveṣu vibhvo abhavan va mahitvanam,
jivrī yatsantā pitarā sanājurā
punaryuvānā carathāya takṣatha.[12]

1. O Ribhus, the splendid three-wheeled chariot fashioned by you for the Ashwins traverses across the firmament without horses, without any reins; it is sufficient evidence of your great prowess by which you cherish heaven and earth.

2. We invoke you most devoutly, O Vajas and Ribhus, artisans of Immortality, to drink of this libation of ours, for you are the wise and skillful ones who have made the most dependable and unerring and undeviating high-rolling chariot of the Ashwins.

3. Therefore, O Vaja, Ribhu and Vibhwan, was your greatness proudly declared amongst the gods that you made your haggard and wasted parents once again young and energetic.

b) *Niścarmaṇo gamarinīta dhītibhir*
yā jarantā yuvaśā tākṛṇotana,
saudhanvanā aśvādaśvamatakṣata
yuktvā rathamupa devāñ ayātana.[13]

O sons of Sudhanwan you have fashioned a living cow out of a hideless one; by your marvellous acts you rejuvenated your aged parents, and from one horse you have fabricated another; may you now harness your chariot and repair to the sacrificial altar to enjoy the oblations.

The Ribhus bring for the seeker 'the wine of the immortal essence', and sit at his sacrifice with Indra and the Maruts, and Varuna, Mitra, Aryaman and Bhaga thus assuring him of the supreme felicity of infinite Love and Light and Harmony and Bliss.

Taking Twashtri's gift of the physical as their foundation, the Ribhus fashion a threefold body — vital, mental and the causal, — thus enabling the seeker to offer to the gods the nectar of his illumined consciousness in a 'fourfold bowl'.

Ekaṁ vi cakra camasaṁ caturvayaṁ niś
carmaṇo gāmariṇīta dhītibhiḥ,
athā deveṣvamṛtatvamānaśa śruṣṭī
vājā ṛbhavastadva ukthyam.[14]

You have fashioned the single bowl fourfold; by your craftsmanship you have transformed the cow into a new and living one. Verily, therefore you have attained immortality amongst the gods. Such acts, O Vajas and Ribhus, have to be extolled and glorified.

It is this special and unique capability of the Ribhus that helps the seeker sacrificer to live and have his being always in the Truth-Consciousness, and enjoy 'the thrice seven ecstasies of the supreme existence', which he finds poured into his mind, life and body. The Ribhus ever sustain and support these ecstasies in the sacrificer which he spares equitably and effectively and perfectly with the gods. It is for this reason that the Ribhus are invoked by the Rishis to the sacrifice.

1. *Ayaṁ devāya janmane stomo viprebhirāsayā,*
akāri ratnadhātamaḥ.

2. *Ya indrāya vacoyujā tatakṣurmanasā harī,*
śamībhiryajñamāśata.

3. *Takṣannāsatyābhyāṁ parijmānaṁ sukhaṁ ratham,*
takṣandhenuṁ sabardughām.

4. *Yuvānā pitarā punaḥ satyamantrā ṛjūyavaḥ,*
ṛbhavo viṣṭyakrata.

5. *Saṁ vo madāso agmatendreṇa ca marutvatā,*
ādityebhiśca rājabhiḥ.

6. *Uta tyaṁ camasaṁ navaṁ tvaṣṭurdevasya niṣkṛtam,*
akarta caturaḥ punaḥ.

7. *Te no ratnāni dhattana trirā sāptāni sunvate,*
ekamekaṁ suśastibhiḥ.

8. *Adhārayanta vahnayo'bhajanta sukṛtyayā,*
bhāgaṁ deveṣu yajñiyam.[15]

1. This hymn of affirmation has been addressed by the illumined ones for the divine Birth with the breath of their own mouth that gives perfectly the supreme happiness.

2. Even those who fashioned for Indra his two horses that are harnessed by words have enjoyed the sacrifice by the performance of sacred deeds.

3. They fashioned for the twin Nasatyas their universally-moving happy chariot, and fashioned the fostering cow that yields nectarine milk.

4. The Ribhus, who always seek the straight path, in their pervasion, uttering unfailing prayers, who make young again their aging Parents, have the Truth in their mentalisings.

5. Together, the Ribhus, Indra and the Maruts as well as the Adityas receive and enjoy the raptures of the exhilarating Soma-juices.

6. The Ribhus, these enlightened and skilled sages make again into four the new laddle, the work of the divine Twashtri.

7. May the Ribhus, inspired and impressed by our praises, give to us the thrice seven ecstasies, each separately by flawless manifestations of them.

8. As offerers of sacrifices the Ribhus held in them a mortal existence; by their sacred deeds and by perfection in their works, they obtained the sacrificial share of the enjoyment with the gods.

The Ribhus thus elevate themselves and enrich man with the manifold plenitude and the strength for performing sacrificial works; they help him to fight the hostile forces heroically, and to hold within him the entire range of ecstasies and the fertilising forces that successfully take him beyond ordinary human existence into the divine existence.

1. *Sa vājyarvā sa ṛṣirvacasyayā sa śūro*
   astā pṛtanāsu duṣṭaraḥ,
sa rāyaspoṣaṁ sa suvīryaṁ dadhe yaṁ vājo
   vibhvāñ ṛbhavo yamāviṣuḥ.

2. *Śreṣṭhaṁ vaḥ peśo adhi dhāyi darśataṁ stomo*
   vājā ṛbhavastaṁ jujuṣṭana,
dhīrāso hi ṣṭhā kavayo vipaścitastānva enā
   brahmaṇā vedayāmasi.

3. *Yūyamasmabhyaṁ dhiṣaṇābhyaspari vidvāṅso*
   viśvā naryāṇi bhojanā,
dyumantaṁ vājaṁ vṛṣaśuṣmamuttamamā no rayim
   ṛbhavastakṣatā vayaḥ.

4. *Iha prajāmiha rayiṁ rarāṇā iha śravo*
   vīravattakṣatā naḥ,
yena vayaṁ citayemātyanyāntaṁ vājaṁ
   citramṛbhavo dadā naḥ.[16]

1. He becomes vigorous and full of plenitude for the task, he becomes a Rishi worthy of homage by power of eloquent self-expression, he becomes a hero, invincible in battles, and a fierce striker hard to hold in combat, and keeps within himself ample wealth of bliss and strength whom Vaja and Vibhwan and the Ribhus foster.

2. May you who are seers and thinkers with clear discernment be gratified with our praises; you have assumed a most happy form O Vajas and Ribhus. As such with this prayer of our soul we make known to you our knowledge.

3. May you, O Ribhus, who are wise bestow upon us, in your knowledge moving about our sacrifices, all human enjoyments, and fabricate for us wealth and nourishment, resplendent, invigorating and supreme felicity.

4. Gratified fully by our adorations give to us, O Ribhus, on this occasion rich felicity, great energy of inspiration and that multiple plenitude by which we shall increase in our consciousness of things which greatly excels all the others.

1. SABCL. Vol.10, p.62
a. *Maya* is the power of vision, thought and speech.
2. RV. IV. 37.4
2a. SABCL. Vol. 10, pp. 326-27
3. RV. VIII.75.5a
4. RV. IX.21.6a
5. *Atharva Veda*, IV.12.7
6. Ibid., X.1.8a
7. SABCL. Vol. 10, pp. 327-28
8. Ibid., p. 328
9. RV. IV.33.2
10. RV. IV.33.3
11. SABCL. Vol. 10, pp. 328-29
12. RV. IV.36.1-3
13. RV.I.161.7
14. RV. IV.36.4
15. RV. I.20.1-8
16. RV. IV. 36.6-9

XIII

THE ASHWINS

The Ashwins are 'the swift-footed lords of bliss, much-enjoying', these twin-gods are multi-operational divine souls who are thought-containing and heedful, and approve and greatly and vigorously rejoice the Word. They are fierce and swift-moving powers on the shining path and efficacious in action. They are the great riders on the horse, full of the life-force. "Their common character is that they are gods of enjoyment, seekers of honey; they are physicians, they bring back youth to the old, health to the sick, wholeness to the maimed."[1]

They move rapidly and wildly and irresistibly in an invincible and impregnable chariot, and bring happiness and satisfaction to men. In their swiftness they are like the mind, the wind and the birds.

a) *Hiraṇyatvaṅ madhuvarṇo ghṛtasnuḥ pṛkṣo*
vahannā ratho vartate vām,
manojavā aśvinā vātaraṅhā yenātiyātho
duritāni viśvā.[2]

O Ashwins, your chariot, approaches, gold-plated, honey-tinted, water-dripping, laden with ambrosia, swift as mind and as quick as the wind with which you pass over all hurdles and impediments.

b) *Aśvināveha gachataṁ nāsatyā mā vi venatam,*
haṅsaviva patatamā sutaṅ upa.[3]

O Ashwins, come hither to us, O Nasatyas be not ill-inclined to us; descend like a pair of swans to enjoy our oblations.

The Ashwins give the necessary luminous energy for the celebrated work that takes the seeker beyond all darkness. It is the work that has the Truth for its substance as well as its goal. They take Surya, the daughter of the Lord of the Truth for their bride, and carry the pilgrim to the other shore — to the shore of supramental consciousness. They carry with them many felicities and powerful and puissant energies and bring the Truth and the Bliss and the Light. They are passionate lords of the luminous Word and create ever new formations in the consciousness of the sacrificer, and fruitfully retain them in his intellect for the decisive divine action. They come to the sacrifice to effect the action of the sacrifice; they fulfil the sacrifice by conquering all antagonism and contrariety,

> "They come as powers of the Aryan journey, lords of the great human movement, *nāsatyā*. We see throughout that it is energy which these Riders on the Horse are to give; they are to take delight in the sacrificial energies, to take up the word into an energetic thought, to bring to the sacrifice their own violent movement on the path. And it is effectiveness of action and swiftness in the great journey that is the object of this demand for energy."[4]

The Vedic Ashwins, the twin horsemen, riders in the shining chariot, are ferrymen over the turbulent waters and are invested with special powers; they save the seekers from all dangers and deliver them safely in the domain of the Truth. The Rishi implores them to arrive at the sacrifice and accept his libations.

1. *Aśvinā yajvarīriṣo dravatpāṇī śubhaspatī,*
   purubhujā canasyatam.

2. *Aśvinā purudaṁsasā narā śavīrayā dhiyā,*
   dhiṣṇayā vanataṁ giraḥ.

3. *Dasrā yuvākavaḥ sutā nāsatyā vṛktabarhiṣaḥ,*
   ā yātaṁ rudravartanī.[5]

1. O Ashwins, fosterers of sacred deeds that benefit every one, may you accept joyously with outstretched hands the sacrificial food.

2. O Ashwins, replete with righteous acts, helpers of the devotees, endowed with courage and character, may you accept without reserve our adorations.

3. O Ashwins, vanquishers of the enemies, free from falsehood, leaders among the heroes, may you come to partake of the libations at our sacrifice.

The shining Twins are described as the seekers of honey and the carriers of the wealth of boundless joy. The Rishi praises their chariots and their all-pervading operativeness. They are twin divine powers "whose special function is to perfect the nervous or vital being in man in the sense of action and enjoyment. But they are also powers of Truth, of intelligent action, of right enjoyment, they are powers that appear with the Dawn, effective powers of action born out of the ocean of being who, because they are divine, are able to mentalise securely the felicities of the higher existence by a thought-faculty which finds or comes to know that true substance and true wealth."[6]

Yā dasrā sindhumātarā, manotarā rayīṇām;
dhiyā devā vasuvida.[7]

O Ashwins, who are divine and of pleasing dispensation, sons of the sea and generous distributors of wealth, and providers of suitable dwellings to the seeker-sacrificer.

The Ashwins descend from the Truth-Consciousness; their action effects the worlds of body, life and mind. As they are associated with the Sun and his daughter Surya they bring to men the light of the Truth and the honey of divine delight. In Sri Aurobindo's words:

"They are lords of bliss, *śubhaspatī*; their car or movement is loaded with the satisfactions of the delight of being in all its planes, they bear the skin full of the over flowing honey; they seek the honey, the sweetness, and fill all things with it. They are therefore effective powers of the Ananda which proceeds out of the Truth-Consciousness and which manifesting itself variously in all the three worlds maintains man in his journey. Hence their action is in all the worlds. They are especially riders or drivers of the Horse, Ashwins, as their name indicates — they use the vitality of the human being as the motive-force of the journey: but also they work in the thought and lead it to the Truth. They give health, beauty, wholeness to the body; they are the divine physicians. Of all the gods they are the most ready to come to man and to create for him ease and joy, *āgamiṣṭhā*, *śubhaspatī*. For this is their peculiar and perfect function. They are essentially lords of weal, of bliss, *śubhaspatī*."[8]

Every moment and always the springs of the superconscient supramental Truth rise up to reach and to create the illumined Mind. It is rising of the Sun in the seeker that effectuates and hastens the all-pervading action of the Ashwins in him. Whence is realised the heavenly beatitude —

the fullness of the profoundest satisfactions on all planes of his existences, physical, vital and mental; their chariot holds these threefold satisfactions. Drenched and fully impregnated by the sweetness of these satisfactions the whole of the lower existence begins to soar upward towards the Truth and the Bliss.

> *Eṣa purū dhiyāyate bṛhate devatātaye,*
> *yatrāmṛtāsa āsate.*[9]
>
> This supreme elixir engages in many sacrifices for the attainment of that where are found the seats of Immortality.

This upward march of the Ashwins dissolves the darkness and opens the pilgrim to the Light; it shapes all the powers and faculties of the lower world into the illuminations of the intuitive Mind, which is capable of receiving the most intimate intimations of the divine Truth.

The perfect and perfecting movement of the golden-winged Twins transforms the pilgrimage into a voyage of love and light and sweetness and ecstasy. Their chariot is the beloved of all pilgrims, for it carries for them the ecstasies of superconscient beatitude. In its ascent towards the heavens above, the horses that pull the honeyed chariot change into celestial swans signifying the upsoaring of liberated energies. These Swans are described as bearing golden plumes of luminous knowledge, for they are birds that awake and arise with the golden Dawn. These winged, radiant energies are instinct with rapture, replete with rhapsody; they are fully intoxicated with the immortal wine and are in constant contact with the superconscient, supramental being. The Ashwins, the lords of divine delight, come to the sacrifice to share the honeyed joys as well as seek whatever honey they can gather that can serve them for greater delight. Their upward movement is always strengthened by Agni:

> "For the flames of the Will, the divine Force burning up in the soul, are also drenched with the overflowing sweetness and therefore they perform perfectly from day to day their great office of leading the sacrifice progressively to its goal. For that progress they woo with their flaming tongues the daily visitation of the brilliant Ashwins who are bright with the light of the intuitive illuminations and uphold them with their thought of flashing energy."[10]

The integral needs of the individual are fully served by the triple satisfactions effected by the twin harbingers of Light and Bliss, and by the fourth that streams down from *Svar*. This happens only when he attains to the condition of having a purified physical, a fulfilled vital and an illumined mental. This supreme victory is won by a double divine energy — the flames of the Seer-Will stroking from below and the Sun of Truth sustaining from above. In Sri Aurobindo's words:

> "...not only the fires of the Will are at work to transform the lower consciousness. The Sun of Truth yokes also his lustrous coursers and is in movement; *sūraścid aśvān yuyujāna īyate*. The Ashwins too take knowledge for the human consciousness of all the paths of its progress so that it may effect a complete, harmonious and many-sided movement. This movement advancing in many paths is combined in the light of the divine knowledge by the spontaneous self-arranging action of Nature which she assumes when the will and the knowledge are wedded in the perfect harmony of a fully self-conscious, intuitively guided action. *Viśvān anu svadhayā cetathas pathaḥ*."[11]

This movement of the blissful Ashwins is ceaseless and perennial, for it is the movement of Bliss itself that does not diminish or deplete. It puissantly carries the individual through all opposition and darkness to the luminous summit.

1. *Eṣa sya bhānurudiyarti yujyate rathaḥ*
   parijmā divo asya sānavi,
   pṛkṣaso asminmithuna adhi trayo dṛtis
   turīyo madhuno vi rapśate.

2. *Udvāṁ pṛikṣāso madhumanta īrate rathā*
   aśvāsa uṣaso vyuṣṭiṣu,
   aporṇuvantastama ā parīvṛtaṁ svarṇa
   śukraṁ tanvanta ā rajaḥ.

3. *Madhvaḥ pibataṁ madhupebhirasabhir*
   uta priyaṁ madhune yuñjāthāṁ ratham,
   ā vartaniṁ madhunā jinvathaspatho dṛtiṁ
   vahethe madhumantamaśvina.

4. *Haṁsāso ye vaṁ madhumanto asridho hiraṇyaparṇā*
   uhuva uṣarbudhaḥ,

udapruto mandino mandinispriśo madhvo na ma kṣaḥ savanāni gacchathaḥ.

5. *Svadhvarāso madhumanto agnaya usrā jarante prati vastoraśvinā,*
yanniktahastastaraṇirvicakṣaṇaḥ somaṁ suṣāva madhumantamadribhiḥ.

6. *Ākenipāso ahabhirdavidhvataḥ svarṇa śukraṁ tanvanta ā rajaḥ,*
sūraścidaśvānyuyujāna īyate viśvāñ anu svadhayā cetathaspathaḥ.

7. *Pra vāmavocamaśvina dhiyandhā rathaḥ svaśvo ajaro yo asti,*
yena sadyaḥ pari rajāṅsi yātho haviṣmantaṁ taraṇiṁ bhojamaccha.[12]

1. Yonder the sun rises up and your shining chariot, O Ashwins, traversing the regions is being associated with the Heaven on high. Within it are placed the satisfying delights in their triple pairs and the fourth leather-like vessel overflows with honey.

2. Your honey-laden, food-bearing, well-horsed chariots rise upwards in the wide-shinings of the opening Dawn dispersing like the sun the surrounding darkness and extend their bright radiances to the lower world like that of the luminous firmament.

3. O lords of bliss, may you drink of the honey with your honey-drinking mouths: harness your beloved chariot for the honey (Soma-juice). With the honey come to the dwelling of the sacrificer ever gladdening his movements on the path; may you bring the leather-vessel, O Ashwins, filled with the heavenly elixir.

4. Fully intoxicated are these swans with the Soma-juice that bear you; golden-winged, flying with the Dawn, persistent in action are they the dispensers of the waters and the bearers of burdens; they are full of rapture and touch that which holds the supreme ecstasies. Like honey-bees to the pourings of honey may you come to the Soma-offerings.

5. Full of the honey the sacred fires, the instruments of the sacred sacrifice, woo your increasing brightness, O Ashwins, day after day, when the observant with purified hands and with a perfect vision and the power to go through to the desired goal, presses out the Soma juice with the grinding-stones.

6. Drinking the Soma-juice available to them, the fires ride and run in all directions and extend their shining radiances to the lower world enveloping it with light and transforming it into a shining form like that of the luminous firmament. The Sun also goes harnessing his horses; and by the force of Nature's self-arranging ways do you move consciously along all the paths.

7. Celebrating the sacrifice and holding the sacred thought I glorify you, O Ashwins: well-horsed and undecaying is your chariot — your chariot by which you quickly traverse all the worlds and come to our sacrifice abounding in oblations for enjoyment that helps you to reach the desired goal.

The Ashwins primarily help the individual to develop a healthy and happy and enlightened condition of mind, life and body so very necessary for the reception of the Light. They are perfect healers of disease, disorder and disability, and effective supporters of the joyous ascent. They are known as *mayavins* as their chariot carries wonder-working felicities for the seeker; they foster for the seeker; they foster for him wealth, victory and happiness.

The radiant Twins are ever young and handsome, swift and golden-brilliant, and are the harbingers of the Dawn. Their chariot possessed of puissances many hastens onwards before the Dawn and prepares the path for her; they are as such called her parents. As heavenly physicians they are called Dasras and Nasatyas. They are named as Abdhijan, 'ocean-born', and Pushkarasrajan, 'wreathed in lotuses'. They are the physicians of the gods and guardians and rescuers of men; in them both cosmical and human elements are beautifully blended. They are the earliest of Light and hold a distinct position in the entire range of the Vedic deities of Light. Originally the Ashwins said to be renowned mortals who later were admitted to the fellowship of the gods.

The Rishis eulogise the many beneficient deeds of the Ashwins and implore them for lasting happiness and greater spiritual energy.

a) i) *Aśvina vartirasmadā gomaddasrā hiraṇyavat,*
arvāgrathaṁ samanasā ni yacchatam.

ii) *Yāvitthā ślokamā divo jyotirjanāya chakrathuḥ,*
ā na urjaṁ vahatamaśvina yuvam.

iii) *Eha devā mayobhuvā dasrā hiraṇyavartanī,*
uṣarbudho vahantu somapītaye.[13]

i) O Ashwins, destroyers of the enemies, who work wonders, turn your chariot that brings cattle and gold towards our abode. Return to us with one mind.

ii) O Ashwins, who have brought down from heaven adorable light for mankind, may you bring us spiritual strength.

iii) May the radiant steeds who wake at dawn bring here the benevolent Ashwins the destroyers of the enemies, the givers of happiness to drink our Soma-oblations, they who walking on paths of gold work wonders.

b) *Anārambhaṇe tadavīrayethām*
anāsthāne agrabhaṇe samudre,
yad aśvinā ūhathurbhujyumastaṁ
śatāritrāṁ nāvamātasthivāṅsam.[14]

O Ashwins, by your valour you have done the deeds of heroes in that ocean which has no beginning and has nothing to support, no handhold and nothing to cling to, whence you carried home Bhujyu after he had climbed on board your hundred-oared ship, to his father.

c) i) *Yuvaṁ narā stuvate pajriyāya kakṣīvate*
aradataṁ purandhim,
kārotarācchaphādaśvasya vṛṣṇaḥ śataṁ
kuṁbhāñ asiñcataṁ surāyāḥ.

ii) *Himenāgniṁ ghraṅsamavārayethāṁ pitumatīm*
ūrjamasmā adhattam,
ṛbīse atrimaśvināvanītamunninyathuḥ
sarvagaṇaṁ svasti.

iii) *Parāvataṁ nāsatyānudethāmuccābudhnaṁ*
cakrathurjihmavāram,
kṣarannāpo na pāyanāya rāye sahasrāya
tṛṣyate gotamasya.

iv) *Jujuruṣo nāsatyota vavriṁ prāmuñcataṁ*
drāpimiva cyavānāt,
prātirataṁ jahitasyāyurdasrāditpatim
akṛṇutaṁ kanīnām.[15]

1. O leaders of sacrifice, you granted Pajriya Kaksivat varied knowledge when he devoutly offered you praises. You poured forth from the hoof of your vigorous stallion a hundred jars of the Soma-wine as if from a cask.

2. With cold water you quenched the blazing flames that encircled Atri and supplied him sustaining nourishment; you extricated him and all his followers from the dark cavern into which they were thrown, and restored them to every kind of welfare.

3. O Nasatyas, you overturned the well, and made the base on the top and the rim slanting downward so that the streams flowed as nourishment for the thousand thirsty people of Gotama.

4. O Nasatyas, slayers of the enemies, you have removed the entire skin from the aged Chyavana as if it were a coat of mail and gave him a new and fresh lease of youthful life. You reversed the life of the sage when he was abandoned, and made him the husband of a hundred maidens.

d) i) *Rayiṁ sukṣatraṁ svapatyamāyuḥ suvīryaṁ*
nāsatyā vahantā,
ā jahnāvīṁ samanasopa vājaistrirahno
bhāgaṁ dadhatīmayātam.

ii) *Pariviṣṭaṁ jāhuṣaṁ viśvataḥ sīṁ sugebhir*
naktamūhathū rajobhiḥ,
vibhinduna nāsatyā rathena vi parvatāñ
ajarayū ayātam.

iii) *Ekasyā vastorāvataṁ raṇāya vaśamaśvinā
sanaye sahasrā,
nirahataṁ ducchunā indravantā pṛthuśravaso
vṛṣaṇāvarātiḥ.*

iv) *Śarasya cidārcatkasyāvatādā nīcāduccā
cakrathuḥ pātave vāḥ,
śayave cinnāsatyā śacībhirjasuraye
staryaṁ pipyathurgām.*[16]

1. O Nasatyas, bearing strength and wealth with good kingship, long life, with posterity and vigour-sustaining food, you came with one mind to the family of Jahnavi who offered you a sacrificial portion three times a day.

2. O unaging Nasatyas, you carried Jahusna by night on good paths in your enemy-conquering chariot that breaks through all barriers, and went to inaccessible mountains for victory.

3. O Ashwins, you helped Vasha, to obtain in a single day a thousand acceptable gifts; O showerer of benefits, associated with Indra, you destroyed the malignant foes of Prithushravas.

4. O Ashwins, you raised the water from the bottom to the top of the well for the drinking Shara, the son of Richatka; and by using your powers, O Nasatyas you made the barren cow swell with milk for the sake of the weary Shayu.

e) *Pra vāṁ daṁsāṁsyaśvināvavocamasya
patiḥ syāṁ sugavaḥ suvīraḥ,
uta paśyannaśnuvandīrghamāyurastam
ivejjarimāṇaṁ jagamyām.*[17]

I have proclaimed your wondrous exploits, O Ashwins; may I become the master of this place having abundant cattle and good progeny, let me retain good vision and enjoy a long life-span, and may I enter old age as a master enters his own house.

1. SABCL. Vol. 10, pp. 77-8
2. RV. V.77.3

3. RV. V.78.1
4. SABCL. Vol. 10, p. 79
5. RV. I.3.1-3
6. SABCL. Vol. 10, p. 78
7. RV. I.46.2
8. SABCL. Vol. 10, pp. 316-17
9. RV. IX.15.2
10. SABCL. Vol. 10, p. 321
11. Ibid., pp. 322-23
12. RV. IV.45.1-7
13. RV. I.92.16-18
14. RV. I.116.5
15. RV. I.116.7-10
16. RV. I.116.19-22
17. RV. I.116.25

XIV

PUSHAN, THE LUMINOUS FOSTERER

If Savitri is the creator of the supreme illuminations, Pushan is their increaser and Surya the infinite self-vision and luminous action of the Supreme. Pushan, in fact, is a manifestation of the Surya-power who nourishes the 'striver'; he enriches the seeker's sacrifice and advances his endeavour. "Pushan is described" by the Rishis, "as himself a stream of the divine riches and a lavish heap of its substance. He is lord of the vast treasure of its joy and companion of our felicity."[1] He assures the constant spiritual progress of the pilgrim through the succession of the dawns. Between the successive dawns when the Night intervenes he fights the forces of ignorance and inertia, and conquers for the seeker the many sustaining plenitudes. He brings back for him the lost kine which illumine his path and the hidden sun. He is the chief catalyst who provides the necessary stimulus and the right impulse that urges the hero-warrior to victorious action. He has the total vision of all the worlds of manifestation and the supreme knowledge, and therefore he is the trusted fosterer of right felicity and giver of happiness. He absolves the individual of his sin and evil and augments and heightens the godhead in him.

a) *Pūṣā gā anvetu naḥ pūṣā*
rakṣatvarvataḥ,
pūṣā vājaṁ sanotu naḥ.

Pūṣannanu pra gā ihi
yajamānasya sunvataḥ,
asmākaṁ stuvatāmuta.[2]

May Pushan the nourisher come to look after our luminous cattle, may he guard our war-horses; may he conquer for us the desired food.

Come, O Pushan, to protect the cattle of the preceptor of the worship and presenter of the libations; guard the cows of those who worship you.

b) *Pari pūṣā parastāddhastaṁ*
dadhātu dakṣiṇam,
punarno naṣṭamājatu.[3]

May Pushan hold forth his right hand over us in front to restrain our cows from going astray; may he bring back to us that which we have lost.

c) *Ā pūṣañcitrabarhiṣam*
āghṛṇe dharuṇaṁ divaḥ,
ājā naṣṭaṁ yathā paśum.

Pūṣā rājānamāghṛṇir
apagūḷhaṁ guhā hitam
avindaccitrabarhiṣam.[4]

O resplendent and swift-moving Pushan, bring to us the radiant God of the multiple amplitude of light, who upholds the firmament as if a cowherd our lost cattle.

The resplendent Pushan, the fosterer of all, discovers the shining King who was hidden from us and dwelling in the cave.

Pushan is 'the knower and thinker and guardian' of the shining herd; he is the keeper and protector of the illumined minds and impels them to attain perfection of their thoughts.

> "It is this Increaser", observes Sri Aurobindo, "who stirs and impels the minds of the illumined and is the means of accomplishement and perfection of their thoughts; he is the seer set in man the thinker, the comrade of his illumined mind who moves him upon the path. He manifests in us the thought which wins the Cow and the Horse and all the plenitude of the wealth. He is the friend of every thinker; he cherishes the thought in its increase as a lover cherishes his bride. The thoughts that seek the supreme felicity are the forces that the Increaser yokes to his car..."[5]

Pushan is the one who inspires and sustains and promotes the growth process towards the Truth. Verily, he is himself both the chariot and the charioteer who carries us to the Truth. He is the vision as well as the seer of the Truth who has equal knowledge of the physical, the supraphysical and spiritual worlds. He lends us and takes us all beyond all impediments; he slays the enemies of our soul and smites down the oppressors of our pilgrimage, and leads us beyond all the obstacles to the Light and the

Truth and the Beatitude. He, who knows, is again and again invoked to lead the seeker to pastures green.

a) 1. *Saṁ pūṣannadhvanastira vyaṅho*
vimuco napāt,
sakṣvā deva pra ṇaspuraḥ.

2. *Yo naḥ pūṣannagho vṛko duḥśeva ādideśati,*
apa sma taṁ patho jahi.

3. *Apa tyaṁ paripanthinaṁ muṣīvāṇaṁ huraścitam,*
dūramadhi sruteraja.

4. *Tvaṁ tasya dvayāvino'ghaśaṅsasya kasya cit,*
padābhi tiṣṭha tapuṣim.

5. *Ā tatte dasra mantumaḥ pūṣannavo vṛṇīmahe,*
yena pitṛnacodayaḥ.

6. *Adhā no viśvasaubhaga hiraṇyavāśīmattama,*
dhanāni suṣaṇā kṛdhi.

7. *Ati naḥ saścato naya sugā naḥ supathā kṛṇu,*
pūṣanniha kratuṁ vidaḥ.

8. *Abhi sūyavasaṁ naya na navajvāro adhvane,*
pūṣanniha kratuṁ vidaḥ.

9. *Śagdhi pūrdhi pra yaṅsi ca śiśīhi prāsyudaram,*
pūṣanniha kratuṁ vidaḥ.

10. *Na pūṣaṇaṁ methāmasi sūktairabhi gṛṇīmasi,*
vasūni dasmamīmahe.[6]

1. O Pushan, great liberator, remove all obstructions from the path, take us across all the impediments, and be with us to guide.

2. O God, drive away the wicked from our path, and the ill-intentioned one who wants to harm us — the cruel and the deceitful.

3. Keep away from our path those who cunningly hinder our journey, chase them away, the cheats and the exploiters.

4. Trample underneath your feet, O god, who are mischievous and wicked and double-tongued and dubious, whoever they be.

5. O wise and wonder-working Pushan, we solicit today that self-same protection which you provided to our forefathers.

6. So, O mighty God, giver of favours, you who possess shining riches and wield the golden weapons, bestow upon us wealth that may be liberally distributed.

7. Help us to avoid all opponents; lead us by the safe path. O fosterer, you know how best to protect us on the journey.

8. O benevolent God, lead us to pastures green; protect us from extreme difficulties; you know how to protect us on the journey.

9. O loving fosterer, be gracious to us, give us abundantly; give us vigour and nourishment, you know how best to protect us on the journey.

10. We have nothing adverse against our god; we always glorify him with praises. We seek shining riches from the mighty and good-looking God.

b) 1. *Āyurviśvāyuḥ pari pāsati tvā*
pūṣā tvā pātu prapathe purastāt,
yatrāsate sukṛto yatra te yayus
tatra tvā devaḥ savitā dadhātu.

2. *Pūṣemā āśā anu veda sarvāḥ*
so asmāñ abhayatamena neṣat,
svastidā āghṛnih sarvavīro'prayucchan
pura etu prajānan.

3. *Prapathe pathāmajaniṣṭa pūṣā prapathe*
divaḥ prapathe pṛthivyāḥ,
ubhe abhi priyatame sadhasthe
ā ca parā ca carati prajānan.[7]

1. May the all-pervading Vayu, lord of all the living creatures, guard you; may Pushan the fosterer protect you in your forward path to heaven. May the divine Savitri, the luminous impeller, set you where the virtuous ones, the doers of good works, have already gone.

2. Pushan knows all the regions; let him lead us by the path which is free from peril. Let the giver of prosperity, the radiant one who possesses all the energies and ever vigilant conduct us all steadily in our front by his luminous knowledge.

3. Pushan, the great fosterer, has been born in our upward journeying on the best of paths leading through the earth and through the heaven; he knows best for he moves in both the worlds which are full of felicity for us; it is here that he extends in his knowledge and goes beyond.

c) 1. *Prapathe pathāmajaniṣṭa pūṣā*
prapathe divaḥ prapathe pṛthivyāḥ,
ubhe abhi priyatame sadhasthe
ā ca parā ca carati prajānan.

2. *Pūṣemā āśā anu veda sarvāḥ so asmañ*
abhayatamena neṣat,
svastidā āghṛṇiḥ sarvavīro'prayucchan
pura etu prajānan.

3. *Pūṣantava vrate vayaṁ na*
riṣyema kadā cana,
stotārasta iha smasi.

4. *Pari pūṣā parastāddhastam*
dadhātu dakṣiṇam
punārno naṣṭamājatu saṁ
naṣṭena gamemahi.[8]

1. Pushan, the supreme guardian of all, is manifest on distant pathways remote from heaven and earth. He comes to the two regions that are more dear to him, then departs knowing everything of them.

2. Pushan, the supreme guardian of all, knows and traverses all heavenly realms. May he lead us on paths wholly secure and totally free from all fears and dangers; may he the guarantor of our welfare, the illuminator of all and the most valiant amongst all, lead us on the path with vigilance and without any failure.

3. O Lord, supreme guardian, we are your worshippers who seek your protection; may we never incur any harm who take refuge under your law.

4. May Pushan the supreme guardian of the universe stretch out his right hand, *dakshinamhastam*, to protect us from all sides. May he recover for us that which we have lost, may we be united with all that which is lost.

Pushan is the Surya who fosters and fulfils, he is the seer who removes division and limitation. His unifying and integral vision of the Truth removes falsity and limitation, and helps the seeker to realise the oneness of existence. He is a form of Sun-god who is invoked for the retrieval of the stolen cows, and is seen as associated with Soma.

d) 1. *Somāpūṣaṇā jananā rayīṇāṁ jananā divo*
jananā pṛthivyāḥ,
jatau viśvasya bhuvanasya gopau devā
akṛṇavannamṛtasya nābhim.

2. *Imau devau jayāmānau juṣantemau tamāṅsi*
gūhatāmajuṣṭā,
ābhyāmindraḥ pakvamāmāsvantaḥ somāpūṣabhyāṁ
janadusriyāsu.

3. *Somāpūṣaṇā rajaso vimānaṁ saptacakraṁ*
rathamaviśvaminvam,
viṣūvṛtaṁ manasā yujyamānaṁ taṁ jinvatho
vṛṣaṇā pañcaraśmim.

4. *divya nyaḥ sadanaṁ cakra uccā pṛthivyām*
anyo adhyantarikṣe,
tāvasmabhyaṁ puruvāraṁ purukṣuṁ rāyas
poṣaṁ vi ṣyatāṁ nābhimasme.

5. *Viśvānyanyo bhuvanā jajāna viśvamanyo*
abhicakṣāṇa eti,
somāpūṣaṇāvavatam dhiyaṁ me yuvābhyāṁ
viśvāḥ pṛtanā jayema.

6. *Dhiyaṁ pūṣā jinvatu viśvaminvo rayiṁ*
somo rayipatirdadhātu,
avatu devyaditiranarvā bṛhadvadema
vidathe suvīrāḥ.[9]

1. O Soma and Pushan, generators of all wealth, creators of heaven and earth, you are born as the guardians of the whole world; the gods have made you the source of *amṛta* — the nectar of immortality.

2. The gods rejoiced at the birth of these two godheads, for they dispelled at once the disagreeable darkness. With Soma and Pushan, Indra produced the ripeness in the raw and young cows.

3. O Soma and Pushan, givers of plenty, direct towards us the heaven-measuring seven-wheeled chariot which does not tow everybody but turns to everywhere, your master-chariot that is harnessed by the mere thought, the five-reined one.

4. One of them, Pushan, has made his abode above in heaven; the other, Soma, in the mid-region, *antarikṣa*. May they together grant us much-coveted and much-commended precious cattle-wealth the source of perennial happiness.

5. One of them, Soma, has created all beings, the other, Pushan moves beholding all. Soma and Pushan together protect my sacrifice. With you both may we conquer the enemies.

6. May Pushan, the benefactor and the all-impelling one, be propitious to us; may Soma, the lord of riches, grant us affluence; may Aditi the one without an adversary protect us so that blessed with worthy progeny we can glorify you.

Hymns of praise are sung in connection with Pushan's association with Indra and the other gods; at times, he is styled as Indra's brother.

a) *Bhrātendrasya sakhā mama.*[10]

May (Pushan) the brother of Indra be our friend.

b) *Yadindro anayadrito mahīr*
apo vṛṣantamaḥ,
tatra pūshabhavatsacā.[11]

Pushan is the compassionate kinsman of earth and heaven; he is the lord of nourishment, the possessor of wealth and of gracious form. The gods give him to Indra, mighty and well-moving, and satisfied by the offerings of the worshippers.

Pushan shares his solar nature with Agni and Surya.

a) *Ā mā pūṣannupa drava śaṁsiṣaṁ*
nu te apikarṇa āghṛṇe,
aghā aryo arātayaḥ.[12]

Hasten to me, O Pushan; O radiant god, may you repel all the deadly assailing enemies. I celebrate your might with my praises close to your ears.

b) *Aditsantaṁ cidāghṛṇe pūṣan*
dānāya codaya,
paṇescidvi mradā manaḥ.[13]

O Pushan, resplendent nourisher, exhort even the worst miser to give us liberally and soften the heart of the niggard.

He is among the gods of Light like Surya, Savitri and Mitra. Elsewhere the Rishi mentions Pushan and Saraswati together.

Tvaṁ devi sarasvatyavā vājeṣu vājini,
radā pūṣeva naḥ sanim.[14]

O Saraswati, rich in wisdom, protect us in our struggle and like the divine fosterer Pushan, give us opulence.

Pushan is said to know the entire universe at a time, and is addressed as the guide of the seekers and the protector of cattle. He is the supreme increaser and the knower of the path by which one can reach the goal. He is again and again invoked to conduct the traveller on the desired path, to remove distress and destroy the wicked waylayers with his golden spear. He is extolled as the wonder-working wise god who delivers the pilgrim from all difficulties.

1. SABCL. Vol. 10, p. 434
2. RV. VI.54.5-6
3. RV. VI.54.10
4. RV. I.23.13-14
5. SABCL. Vol. 10, p. 435
6. RV. I.42.1-10
7. RV. X.17.4-6
8. *Atharva Veda*, VII.9.1-4
9. RV. II.40.1-6
10. RV. VI.55.5b
11. RV. VI.57.4
12. RV. VI.48.16
13. RV. VI.53.3
14. RV. VI.61.6

XV

SOMA

Soma at some point of time was considered to be a plant which produced the mystic-juice for performing the Vedic Yajna. Later, it became the moon-god, and came to appear as mind in man. Its psychological significance is powerfully brought out by Sri Aurobindo. It is "the intoxication of the Ananda, the divine delight of being, inflowing upon the mind from the supramental consciousness through the *ṛtam* or Truth."[1]

The Soma-wine represents the replacement of sense-pleasure by the divine delight. This is brought about by the sublimation and divinisation of Thought-action. The potent and energetic Soma-wine swiftly carries the seeker-sacrificers to the summit of many enjoyments — to the luminous ecstasy of the Truth.

Eṣa dhiyā yātyaṇvyā
śūro rathebhiraśubhiḥ,
gacchannindrasya niṣkṛtam.

Eṣa purū dhiyāyate, bṛhate devatātaye,
yatrāmṛtāsa āsate.[2]

This Soma, heroically forges forward with his swift-moving chariots, impelled by the strength of his subtle thought to the field of consummate activity of resplendent Indra. And takes many forms of consciousness to arrive at that vast luminous stretch out of the supreme godhead where the immortals abide.

The Veda speaks of 'a honeyed wave' that mounts up from the ocean below to that which is above taking the seeker to the domain of deathlessness and beatitude supreme; that wave is Soma, the nodus of immortality.

Samudrādūrmirmadhumāñ udārad
upaṁśunā samamṛtatvamānaṭ;
ghṛtasya nāma guhyaṁ yadasti,
jihvā devānāmamṛtasya nābhiḥ.[3]

> The honeyed wave swells up from the ocean by which the seeker is carried to the celestial regions above and attains immortality. That wave (Soma) is the secret name of clarified butter, the tongue of the gods, the navel of nectar divine.

The Soma-wine, the upsurging stream of divine delight symbolises the action of evolving consciousness, *ghṛtasya*, that liberates life and being from the weaknesses and limitations of the lower existence. It is the honeyed wave of the delight of existence, *ānanda*, which yields immortality to the persistent seeker. Soma is behind all our enlightened mental activity striving to express the secret truth of our being. Soma is therefore referred to as 'the tongue of the gods' that gives us the taste of the delight of existence — of the truth of the immortal state of infinite existence. The Rishi seeks to give expression to this master office of Soma, the great liberator.

Vayaṁ nāma pra bravāmā ghṛtasya
āsminyajñe dhārayāmā namobhiḥ,
upa brahmā śṛṇavacchasyamānaṃ
catuḥśṛṅgo'vamidgaura etat.[4]

> Let us celebrate this secret name of *Ghṛta* and hold it in the world-sacrifice by our surrenderings to the divine Will, Agni. May the four-horned Bull of the worlds be glorified, for when he listens to the soul-thought of the seeker, he throws out Soma from its place of concealment.

(1)

Soma: The leading figure and fountain of Ananda

Soma-wine is one of the leading figures of the Vedic exegesis; it is the capital resource of strength, struggle and subjugation. It is a means of victory and attainment of Immortality. Soma-drink is the greatest love of the gods; Indra and Ashwins are the great drinkers, the Angirasas come out victorious under its spell, and the Panis are overcome by Sarama in the heightened conditions of its rapture.

Eha gamannṛṣayaḥ somaśitā
ayāsyo aṅgiraso navagvāḥ.[5]

Animated and emboldened by the Soma-wine the Navagwa Angirasas headed by Ayasya will come here.

The force and resourcefulness of the Soma-wine empower and sustain men to successfully undertake the journey to the Truth. It is intoxicated and enthused with Soma that Indra breaks open the cave and overcomes the enemies of Light. Soma, for the Rishis, is the elixir of life-eternal which streams down from heaven and 'immortalises the mortal'.

Soma the honeyed *ghṛta madhumad ghṛtam*, and clarified butter the yield of the shining cow are always closely connected in the Vedic figuring and bring about the final and supreme illumination. The Veda speaks of three worlds of the mind, rather three levels of mental consciousness are taken care of and presided over by Surya, Indra and Soma respectively. Taking cognisance of the nature of the three godheads "We may hazard the conjecture", observes Sri Aurobindo, "that Soma releases the divine light from the sense mentality, Indra from the dynamic mentality, Surya from the pure reflective mentality."[6]

Soma, verily, is the infinite delight of immortal existence secret in all things that is pressed out for the enjoyment of gods and men. It exists in the ocean below, in the waters upon earth and flows up to rhapsodise the gods to accomplish their supreme task. It is by drinking the Soma-wine that all obstructions are dissolved in the mind, and men obtain clarity of vision and enlightenment. Ghrita and Soma, divine light and divine delight, are both concealed and confined in forms of lower consciousness and have to be released and restored for the gain of the travellers. They have to be extracted from the sense-objects and purified, increased and accentuated until they grow luminous and radiant, and exalt them to the experience of the supreme Truth.

The gods grow in their strength and delight by drinking the Soma-wine, and thereupon help men in the illumination and liberation of their mind. Soma is the divine ambrosia, the elixir of immortality — the principle of Ananda, the source and substance of all existence; also, it is the truth and support of the mental being.

The Upanishads speak of Soma as the divine delight that expresses itself in physical consciousness as sensation, in vital consciousness as *rasa*, and in the mental consciousness as the joy of purity, clarity and illumination. In the material universe this supreme *ānanda* is concealed and imprisoned, as it were, and has to be extracted and released, distilled and purified, increased and intensified and offered to the gods as their principal food. The gods thus fed on the Soma-juice exalt the seeker-sacrificer to the realisation of his infinite potential. Those who do not voluntarily and consciously and joyously offer their delights of physical, vital and mental consciousness to the gods necessarily deny themselves the ecstasies of the supreme experiences of the Truth and Immortality. For such persons are not worshippers of the gods but lovers of the Panis who keep their devotees tied down to the life of lower existence. It is these powers of limited existence who conceal the herds of Light and Truth in "The cavern of the sub-conscient, in the dense hill of matter, corrupting even Sarama, the hound of heaven, the luminous intuition, when she comes on their track to the cave of the Panis."[7]

Verily, the obstructors are galore and the Adversary diehard; alongside the Panis who are the stealers of the Rays travel Vritras, the Coverers and Concealers who keep the seekers away and separated from their own immense possibilities. And Vala is the subtlest enemy who withholds the Light, and when all these are overcome there are still the vilest among them all, the Confiners or Censures, as Sri Aurobindo names them, who conspire and contrive to set the progress already made by the seeker as an impediment on his road to further progress. Indra is the mighty god of Mind-Power who successfully strikes down the multiform Enemy and puts the seeker on the steady path of increasing illumination. And Indra is fond of the Soma-wine; the Rishis therefore desire that the sacrificers offer this elixir of immortal life to Indra and help him to liberate them fully from the vile and wicked Enemy. In Sri Aurobindo's words, "The activity of the pure illuminated Intelligence is sustained and increased by the conscious expression in us of the delight in divine existence and divine activity typified by the Soma-wine. As the Intelligence feeds upon it, its action becomes an intoxicated ecstasy of inspiration by which the rays come pouring abundantly and joyously in."[7a]

Upa naḥ savanā gahi somasya somapāḥ piba,
godā idrevato madaḥ.[8]

"Come to our Soma-offerings. O Soma-drinker drink of the Soma-wine; the intoxication of thy rapture gives indeed the Light."*

Soma, as such, cannot be taken as a mere mountain plant. He is a very important Vedic deity and is extolled as the all-seeing one whose illumining rays encompass the universe.

Viśvā dhāmāni viśvacakṣa ṛbhvasaḥ prabhos
te sataḥ pari yanti ketavaḥ,

vyānaśiḥ pavase soma dharmabhiḥ
patirviśvasya bhuvanasya rājasi.[9]

O all-seeing one, your mighty rays surround all the worlds; permeating all things you flow, O Soma, through your functionings. You rule everyone as the sovereign lord of the whole world.

Soma is also mentioned as the 'all-purifying' sacred drink used at the time of all sacrifices. The Soma-juice is luminous and golden-yellow in colour, is invigorating and inspiring which promotes sunshine and life.

a) *Eṣa sūryamarocayat pavamāno vicarṣaṇiḥ,*
viśvā dhāmāni viśvavit.[10]

This purified, all-contemplating, all-knowing sovereign Soma lends radiance to the sun and all the orbs of light.

b) *Sa tritasyādhi sānavi pavamāno arocayat,*
jāmibhih sūryaṁ saha.[11]

This pure Soma-juice, during the sacrifice set on high by the triply-operating priest (Trita) lights up the sun and the other luminous celebrities.

Soma is invoked by the Rishis as the possessor of the universe and the father of heaven and earth.

a) *Tubhyaṁ vātā abhipriyastubhyamarṣanti sindhavaḥ,*
soma vardhanti te mahaḥ.[12]

O Soma, for you the winds are gracious, for you flow the rivers; they all celebrate your greatness.

b) *Pra hinvāno janitā rodasyo ratho na*
vājaṁ sanisyannayāsīt,
indraṁ gacchannāyudhā saṁśiśāno
viśvā vasu hastayorādadhānaḥ.[13]

Invoked and impelled by the worshippers, Soma the generator of heaven and earth advances like a chariot, keen to distribute food.

Whetting his weapons, holding all the wealth in his hands he goes to Indra.

Soma is a mighty warrior, purifier and destroyer of all enemies.

a) i) *Mahāñ asi soma jyeṣṭha*
ugrāṇaminda ojiṣṭhaḥ,
yudhvā sañchaśvajjigetha.

ii) *Ya ugrebhyaścidojīyāñ*
chūrebhyaściccHuratarah,
bhūridābhyaścinmaṁhīyān.[14]

i) O Soma, you are great and most worthy of all praise; you are the most spirited and strenuous among the mighty. Engaged in battle you are ever victorious.

ii) You are mightier than the mighty, bravest of the brave and most magnanimous and benevolent among the generous.

b) *Iṣamūrjamabhyarṣāśvaṁ gām*
uru jyotiḥ kṛṇuhi matsi devān,
viśvāni hi suṣahā tāni tubhyaṁ
pavamāna bādhase soma śatrūn.[15]

O Soma Pavamana, bring us food and drink, horses and cattle and ample light. May you exhilarate the gods, for all the enemies get easily destroyed by you.

Many hymns are dedicated to Soma as in the Soma-sacrifice both gods and men are found participating. All the 114 hymns of the Ninth *Mandala* of the Rig-veda as well as several other hymns in other *Mandalas* are sung in his honour eulogising his many heroic deeds.

a) 1. *Tvaṁ soma kratubhiḥ sukraturbhustvaṁ*
dakṣaiḥ sudakṣo viśvavedāḥ,
tvaṁ vṛṣā vṛṣatvebhirmahitvā
dyumnebhirdyumnyabhavo nṛcakṣāḥ.

2. *Rājño nu te varuṇasya vratāni bṛhad*
gabhīraṁ tava soma dhāma,
śuciṣṭvamasi priyo na mitro
dakṣāyyo aryamevāsi soma.

3. *Yā te dhāmāni divi yā prithivyā*
yā parvateṣvoṣadhīṣvapsu,
tebhirno viśvaiḥ sumanā aheḷan
rājant soma prati havyā gṛbhāya.[16]

1. O Soma, you are the accomplisher of excellence and perfection through righteous deeds. You are mighty and powerful by your energetic resources, you are most wise and all-knowing, and are glorious by your greatnesses. You who are the guide of men are well-fed by sacrifices.

2. In your deeds you are like the sovereign Varuna, in glory great and profound. You are the purifier like the benevolent benefactor Mitra, and the increaser and nourisher of all like Aryaman.

3. Gifted with all the glories of heaven and earth, of those in the mountains and in the plants and in waters, O celebrated Soma, may you be well-disposed towards us and without any rancour accept our oblations.

b) 1. *Yaḥ soma sakhye tava rāraṇaddeva martyaḥ,*
taṁ dakṣaḥ sacate kaviḥ.

2. *Uruṣyā ṇo abhiśasteḥ soma ni pāhyaṅhasaḥ,*
sakhā suśeva edhi naḥ.

3. *Ā pyāyasva sametu te viśvataḥ soma vṛṣṇyam,*
bhavā vājasya saṅgathe.[17]

1. The skilled and seasoned sage commends that mortal man, O Soma, who takes delight in worshipping you.

2. O Soma, protect us from detraction and slander, protect us from sin and distress; pleased with our worship may you be our gracious friend.

3. O Soma, may you steadily increase in us, may our vigour turn towards you always; may our knowledge too be concentrated in you.

c) 1. *Aṣāḷhaṁ yutsu pṛtanāsu papriṁ svarṣām*
atsāṁ vṛjanasya gopām,
bhareṣujam sukṣitim suśravasam jayantam
tvam anu madema soma.

2. *Tvamimā oṣadhīḥ soma viśvāstvam*
apo ajanayastvaṁ gāḥ,
tvamā tatanthorvantarikṣaṁ tvaṁ
jyotiṣā vi tamo vavartha.

3. *Devena no manasā deva soma rāyo*
bhāgaṁ sahasāvannabhi yudhya,
mā tvā tanadīśiṣe vīryasyobhayebhyaḥ
pra cikitsā gaviṣṭau.[18]

1. We glorify and celebrate you, O Soma; you are unconquerable and inviolable in battle, victorious against the enemies, the giver of rain and sunshine. Born from sacrifices you occupy a radiant dwelling, renowned and commanding.

2. O Soma, you have developed the herbs, caused the waters and brought about the cows; you have spread out the vast mid-regions and dispelled darkness with light.

3. O divine and celebrated Soma, bestow upon us something of your wisdom, a part of your felicity; may no adversary touch us; supreme in valour, may you defend us in battle against the enemies.

d) 1. *Svādorabhakṣi vayasaḥ sumedhāḥ*
svādhyo varivovittarasya,
viśve yaṁ devā uta martyāso madhu
bruvanto abhi saṅcaranti.

2. *Antaśca prāgā aditirbhavāsy*
avayātā haraso daivyasya,
indavindrasya sakhyaṁ juṣāṇaḥ
śrauṣṭīva dhuramanu rāya ṛdhyaḥ.[19]

1. May I with knowledge and devotion enjoy the most tasteful and greatly exalted health-promoting ambrosia which all the gods and men proclaiming it to be delicious and sweet seek to obtain.

2. O divine drink, you are supremely pure, and when you enter within unimpaired, you obviate the umbrage of the gods. May you enjoy the friendship of Indra, and bring us riches as a swift horse carries its burden.

e) 1. *Agniṁ na mā mathitaṁ saṁ didīpaḥ*
pra cakṣaya kṛṇuhi vasyaso naḥ,
athā hi te mada ā soma manye revāṅ
iva pra carā puṣṭimaccha.

2. *Iṣireṇa te manasā sutasya*
bhakṣīmahi pitryasyeva rāyaḥ,
soma rājan pra ṇa āyūṅṣi tarīr
ahānīva sūryo vāsarāṇi.[20]

1. O Soma, kindle me like the fire produced by attrition; give us a clear insight and richly enlighten us. I worship you for the invigoration; may you now nourish us with abundant wealth and wisdom.

2. May we enjoy the luminous effusion you give us as men enjoy their ancestral wealth. O Soma, prolong our lives as the sun makes the days grow longer.

f) 1. *Tvaṁ hi nastanvaḥ soma gopā*
gātregātre niṣasatthā nṛcakṣāḥ,
yatte vayaṁ pramināma vratāni sa no
mṛla suṣakhā deva vasyaḥ.

2. *Ṛdūdareṇa sakhyā saceya yo mā na*
riṣyeddharyaśva pītaḥ,
ayaṁ yaḥ somo nyadhāyyasme,
tasmā indraṁ pratiramemyayuḥ.[21]

1. O Soma, you are the guardian of our bodies, you dwell in each limb as the observer of all men. Though you trespass and impair your sacrificial rites, O divine lord, may you, possessed of good nourishment, be gracious to us.

2. O Soma, lord of bay horses, may we have a friend who even when drunk will not harm us. I ask of Indra, may this elixir be permanently established within us.

g) 1. *Tvaṁ soma pitṛbhiḥ saṁvidāno'nu*
dyavāpṛthivī ā tatantha,
tasmai ta indo haviṣā vidhema
vayaṁ syāma patayo rayīṇām.

2. *Trātāro devā adhi vocatā no mā no*
nidrā īśata mota jalpiḥ,
vayaṁ somasya viśvaha priyāsaḥ
suvīrāso vidathamā vadema.

3. *Tvaṁ naḥ soma viśvato vayodhāstvaṁ*
svarvidā viśā nṛcakṣaḥ,
tvaṁ na inda ūtibhiḥ sajoṣāḥ pāhi
paścātāduta vā purastāt.[22]

1. In association with our ancestors, O Soma, you spread out extensively heaven and earth. So, may we, worshipping you with oblations become possessors of great wealth.

2. O guardian gods, great protectors, may you be kind to us. Let not wild dreams or vain gossip overpower us. May we be ever dear to Soma, and possessed of valiant progeny may we always offer hymns of praise in his honour.

3. O Soma, happily you give us food everywhere; verily you are the bestower of heaven. O Lord, perfect beholder of all, enter us with your powers of protection, guard us from all directions.

h) 1. *Vidadyatpūrvyaṁ naṣṭam*
udimṛtāyumīrayat,
premāyustārīdatīrṇam.

2. *Suśevo no mṛḷayākuradṛptakraturavātaḥ,*
bhavā naḥ soma śaṁ hṛde.

3. *Mā naḥ soma saṁ vīvijo*
mā vi bībhiṣathā rājan,
mā no hārdi tviṣā vadhīḥ.

4. *Ava yatsve sadhasthe devānāṁ durmatīrīkṣe,*
rājannapa dviṣaḥ sedha
mīḍhvo apa sridhaḥ sedha.[23]

1. Soma urges on the sacrificer when he regains his lost felicity, and inspiring him to move forward he lengthens out his life.

2. O most gracious Soma, may you be tender to us void of pride, and always dwell in our hearts most auspiciously.

3. O Soma, do not frighten us, cause us not to tremble; do not harm us by your dazzling radiance.

4. Dwelling in my house when I keep watch against the enemies of the gods, O Soma, drive away those who hate us, and shower your blessings upon us.

It is under the purifying and elevating influence of Soma-juice that the seekers feel closer to Light and Truth. Its energy and its radiance scatter all darkness and stimulate and inspire the seeker-sacrificer to greater tasks. It is consciously and carefully pressed out of the triple world of mind, life and matter and offered to the gods as part of the sacrificial oblations. The whole of the universe is thus engaged in the supreme *yajña* of straining the Soma-juice for offering it to the *devas* so that in turn they may strengthen and enthuse men in their ascent to the Truth.

Soma has its source and station on the summits of all-existence.

a) *Somasyeva maujavatasya bhakṣo*
vibhīdako jāgṛvirmahyamacchān.[24]

The exciting dice (says the gambler) animates me as the taste of exhilarating Soma of Maujavat delights the gods.

b) *Yajjāyathāstadaharasya kāmeṅ*
'śoḥ pīyūṣamapibo giriṣṭhām.[25]

On the day on which you were born, you drank the Soma-juice abiding on the mountain-tops.

c) *Madhvo rasaṁ sugabhastirgiriṣṭhām*
caniścadad duduhe śukramaṅśuḥ.[26]

The rejoicing adept-fingered priest strains to press out the mountain-born sweet Soma-juice, and that Soma yields its pure ambrosia.

d) *Pari suvāno giriṣṭhāḥ pavitre somo akṣāḥ,*
madeṣu sarvadhā asi.[27]

O elixir of divine delight, with your dwelling on mountain-tops, when effused you flow upon the straining cloth. O Soma, you are the supreme sustainer among those who give us ecstatic delight.

Soma is the offspring and milk of the supreme heaven of Truth.

a) *Abhi brahmīranūṣata yahvīrṛtasya mātaraḥ,*
marmṛjayante divaḥ śiśum.[28]

When they purify and decorate the offspring of heaven, the priests offer hymns of praise from scriptures pertaining to sacrifice.

b) *Divaḥ pīyūṣamuttamaṁ somamindrāya vajriṇe,*
sunotā madhumattamam.[29]

May you profusely outpour the most sweet-flavoured Soma, the best elixir of heaven for Indra, the wielder of the mighty thunderbolt.

According to a legend Soma-juice was brought to earth by an eagle from a secret place in the world of Gandharvas; figuratively, it is the receptive luminous mind that funnels the nectar and makes it available to the phenomenal world below.

The litany and liturgy of the Soma-sacrifice so elaborately delineated in the Veda formed an essential feature of the popular Vedic religion. But they have an esoteric significance and a deeper truth. The outer sacrificial ritual in all its details was symbolic of a concrete inner experience in the life of the ancient mystics. The Soma extraction, its purification and offering to the gods is such an instance in hand; each of them conceals a deeper truth or relevance in the seeker's inner progress; in the course of his self-offering the seeker-sacrificer finally gives his finest and best — the essence of his precious gains in life, the Soma. Soma is the essential delight of existence obtained at the summit of one's long askesis; it is in the higher altitudes of one's being and consciousness that streams of Soma-wine rush forth enriching and enrapturing the soul. It is only when all illumined life-force intensifies the flame of aspiration in the seeker accompanied by a strenuous striving that the Soma-wine flows down the slope into the soul.

Avindaddivo nihitaṁ guhā nidhiṁ verna garbhaṁ
parivītamaśmanyanante antaraśmani,
vrajaṁ vajrī gavāmiva siṣāsannaṅgirastamaḥ
apāvṛṇodiṣa indraḥ parīvṛtā dvāra iṣaḥ parīvṛtaḥ.[30]

He (Indra) discovered the secret treasure (Soma) brought from heaven and hidden like the nestling of a bird in the vast Rock of Existence. Desiring to partake of the nourishing ambrosia, Indra armed with the thunderbolt, most Angiras-like strove to reach the hiding place of the Cows and laid bare the impulsions that were shut up within; he broke open the Rock and spread over the impulsions upon earth.

Soma and Indra are the two gods who are most intimately associated with each other.

Indrāsomā yuvamaṅga tarutram
apatyasācaṁ śrutyaṁ rarāthe,
yuvaṁ śuṣmaṁ naryaṁ carṣaṇibhyaḥ
saṁ vivyathuḥ pṛtanāṣuhamugrā.[31]

O Indra and Soma, verily, do you bestow upon us renowned riches that can absolve pain and penury, and also grant us progeny. O mighty ones, you have invested your worshippers with strength that helps them to come out victorious against all adversaries.

It is indeed under the spell of the Soma-drink that Indra becomes capable of carrying out his valorous callings. Indra slays the most dreadful dragon Vritra in companionship with Soma and releases the imprisoned Rays and brings sunshine and happiness to the earth. Together they drive away all darkness and evil. In the victory over the enemies of Light, Soma is associated again and again with Indra and Agni. It is repeatedly mentioned in the Veda that Indra sunders the impediments of the Enemy in the exaltation of the Soma-wine.

Bhinadvalamaṅgirobhirgṛṇāno vi
parvatasya dṛṁhitanyairat,
riṇagrodhaṅsi kṛtrimaṇyeṣāṁ
somasya tā mada indraścakāra.[32]

Praised by the Angirasas, he (Indra) destroyed Vala; he broke open the strong shut doors of the mountain. He cast down the artificial defences of Evil; these things Indra did in the exhilaration of Soma.

Soma, the elixir of immortal delight lies secreted within the material nature of man. It is because of the physical body that man stands firm and dauntless like a rock amidst the myriad hostile forces. It is only when the physical man evolves into an enlightened mental man that the Soma-wine emerges and is discovered by Indra. And partaking of this divine drink he destroys the mighty Enemy and releases the Rays of illumination from the confines of Ignorance. When Soma is strained out, sieved and cleansed, it flows swiftly into the physical through the subtler planes and dynamises it.

Pra te dhārā atyaṇvāni meṣyaḥ
punānasya saṁyato yanti raṅhayaḥ,
yad gobhirindo camvoḥ samajyasa
ā suvānaḥ soma kalaśeṣu sīdasi.[33]

O Soma, when you are purified, the rapid streams of ecstatic delight that flow being collected together move swiftly over the subtle powers of the unwinking Eye. O celestial drink, when you are well blended with the yield of the luminous Rays within the physical body you come down, when pressed out, into the Jars.

Pure and illumined mental consciousness is the strainer spread high and vast in the heaven of the being. Passing through it Soma becomes mobile and many-sided and courses freely in the being of the sacrificer and illumines his nature. In its purifying operation Soma embraces both earth and heaven — the lower physical consciousness as well as the higher mental.

Evā deva devatāte pavasva mahe
soma psarase devapānaḥ,
mahaściddhi ṣmasi hitāḥ samarye
kṛdhi suṣṭāne rodasī punānaḥ.[34]

O divine elixir Soma, verily you are the beverage of the gods; you flow at the cosmic sacrifice for our abundant food. Urged on by you, may we be victorious against all adversaries. Purified and cleansed perfectly you render both heaven and earth happy dwellings for us.

(2)

Soma: the God of beatitude and immortality

Soma-wine is both the beverage of inviolable strength and the source of infinite enjoyment — "Soma, the food of divine beings, the supreme distilling highest production of the great Producer",[35] Surya Savitri. It is the path of the Truth and led by the Truth that leads to this supreme felicity, the divine beatitude, *ānanda*, secret in all things. If the Truth and the Right lead to *ānanda*, it is also equally true that *ānanda* leads to the Truth and the Light in all things. Soma brings in *ānanda* that gives birth to the gods and increases them in the seeker-sacrificers.

The streams of this celestial drink course down from the *ānanda*-plane of Sachchidananda like rapturous rain in the wide spaces of Existences; they come from the supreme heights for the enjoyment of Indra.

Eṣā yayau paramādantaradreḥ kūcit
satīrūrve gā videva,
divo na vidyutstanayantyabraiḥ
somasya te pavata indra dhārā.[36]

This stream of Soma-juice has come down from the loftiest heights and detected the kine hidden somewhere within the mountain. This stream flows for you, O Indra, like lightning from heaven, thundering through the clouds.

The aspirant too enjoys them when he climbs up those high altitudes of the superconscient. These streams can be enjoyed both on the highest heights and in the deepest depths of one's being as well as in the purified and rarefied regions of the subtle physical, *śaryanavat*. It is the privilege of the pure and the true participants to partake of the peerless drink. It is the reward of a life-time of consecration and striving to reorganise and focus all the inner and outer movements of oneself onto the one unified Truth of all existences. And the home of the Truth is also the purified, glorified body of the seeker.

Imamindra sutaṁ piba jye
ṣṭhamamartyaṁ madam,
śukrasya tvābhyaskṣaran
dhārā ṛtasya sādane.[37]

Drink, O Indra, this immortal effusion, excellent, exalted and most exhilarating. The streams of this transparent Soma-juice flow towards you in the chamber of sacrifice — the place of your sacred worship.

Soma, the elixir of delight, is the basis of all life; it is offered to the gods by the seeker of the Truth. It is his soul's highest and best offering. The body and being of the seeker yield this celestial juice because of the kindly and gracious pounding by Vajra, the omnipotent weapon of Indra himself and the effective Word of Power and Light issuing forth from the superconscient above. The onslaughts of Vajra and the Vak mercilessly crush the oppressors and the resisters, confiners and the coverers. They slay Vritra and release the river of Light; they constantly herald a happier and a greater dawn. The Soma-juices thus released by the Powers that be and by the purified subtle bodies of the seeker-souls desire Indra; they yearn to reach him, and the pilgrim-sacrificers offer them to Indra and the attending godheads.

To those men who offer themselves and the Soma-wine the gods bring all felicities. The gifts that flow from above are those of Light and strength and manifold puissance that make for an immortal existence. Carried on the crest of the rapturous Soma-wine the traveller swings to the world of the Truth, *satyam ṛtam bṛhat.* Soma wins for the Yajamana, the seeker-sacrificer both beatitude and immortality as well as all the wealth of the Spirit.

a) *Abhi tvā yoṣaṇo daśa jāraṁ na kanyānuṣata,*
mṛjyase soma sātaye.[38]

O Soma, the ten fingers greet you, as a maiden greets her lover; you are purified and refined to bestow wealth on us.

b) *Tamīmevīḥ samarya ā*
gṛbhṇanti yoṣaṇo daśa.
svasāraḥ pārye divi.[39]

The ten self-moving subtle powers (fingers) seize him (Soma) firmly in the sacrifice and hold him aloft on the final and most auspicious day of the oblation.

The Soma-wine flowing from above is quaffed either mixed with milk, the luminous yield of the sacred cow, *gavāśira soma*, or with curds, *dadhyāśira soma*, or with corn, *yavāśira soma*. These are respectively the blending of the streams of divine delight with the light of Knowledge — of the Pure Mind, with the fixation of the light of the intellectual mind, and with the rudiment of light ingrained in the physical mind. The streams of the Soma-wine imbibed and absorbed in the light of Knowledge manifested in the three levels of existence are then poured into proven jars — the purified and perfected physical bodies of the sacrificers. The jars are of four orders — physical, vital, mental and causal; these are the four principal planes of the being which offer the truth and the delight of themselves to the gods. The delight thus offered as food to the gods in turn increases the gods within them and strengthens them in the journey. The juices are constantly distilled and made increasingly universal before they are offered to the cosmic godheads, Agni or Indra. In the process, the seeker himself comes out of the confines of the physical, vital and the gross mental and enlarges himself so as to encompass the inner ocean of *ānanda*. Soma itself is this all-embracing, all-engulfing flood of Ananda.

The many godheads in the Veda indeed represent one Godhead; they express variously and individually the manifold truth of one Supreme Truth. They are cosmic manifestations of one Divine Existence, aspects and personalities of one *Deva*. Each of the godheads contains all the other godheads, and is a different yet complete personality of the one Supreme Godhead. Agni, Mitra, Varuna, Indra, Soma and all the gods and goddesses are hymned by the Rishis as being the many powers of the one Supreme, *tad ekam*.

The Rishis intuited Soma as a living entity, a godhead presiding over the workings of the universe and helping humanity to grow out of the involving, enticing animality, and progressively grow into the vicissitudes of Truth. He is the lord of infinite beatitude ever ready to help the mortal in his ascent to immortality. An inner sacrifice, *yajña* is the principal truth of Vedic worship and the assured means of spiritual progress. It is by *yajña* that men call upon the gods to accept their oblations, and by their boons grow in strength and felicity to reach the goal. The performers and participants of this *yajña* seek the inner riches of luminous cows and swift horses as well as the Soma-wine so that they can expeditiously arrive at the summit.

Soma is the godhead of *ānanda*, the divine delight of all true existences found in all creation; he owns the soul out of which he brings out a new and divine creation. He helps the seeker to progressively purify his mind and heart and sensations and makes them true channels of infinite *ānanda*. The Soma-wine thus pouring into the being first emerges concentrated at some unique point and then from there it permeates the whole being and soaks it in *ānanda*. Not all men can hold or bear and enjoy this flaming ecstasy. In the language of the Rishis only those whose being is 'baked in the flame of Truth', whose *ādhāra* is prepared by the necessary *tapasyā*, and becomes sufficiently strong can taste it and enjoy it, for the wine itself is concentrated, terrible and inundating. "The wine of the divine life poured into the system", observes Sri Aurobindo, "is a strong, overflooding and violent ecstasy; it cannot be held in the system unprepared for it by strong endurance of the utmost fires of life and suffering and experience. The raw earthen vessel not baked to consistency in the fire of the kiln cannot hold the Soma-wine; it breaks and spills the precious liquid."[40] The flooding of this fierce nectar has to be mellowed down before it is brought to the seeker, and this can be done only by the purified mental and emotional consciousness — The wine of immortality is spread out in all existence and can be funnelled into the being of the pilgrim-soul only by a purified mind through conscious suffering, enlightened endurance and hard askesis, for "it is *divaspade*, in the seat of Heaven", Sri Aurobindo makes it clear, "that the Soma-strainer is spread out to receive the Soma".[41] It is the streams of the Soma-wine that progressively purify the mental, emotional and sensational, and rising through the heart uplift the seeker to the world of Swar and truly liberate him.

The cosmic godhead Soma is the one who shoulders the universe seeking inner abundance and makes the dawnings possible both in the lives of men and in the many worlds. He is described as 'the dappled Bull', the multi-formed and many-hued godhead who brings into existence the universe of manifestation from the Ananda-Consciousness of the Divine. He is the fertilising force of infinite consciousness who fashions the worlds as well as carries them to the summit heaven of Truth. In the words of Sri Aurobindo, "He makes the Dawns shine out — the dawns of illumination, mothers of the radiant herds of the Sun; and he seeks the plenitude, that is to say the fullness of being, force, consciousness, the plenty of the godhead which is the condition of the divine delight. In other words it is the Lord of the Ananda who gives us the splendours of the Truth and the plenitudes of the Vast by which we attain to Immortality."[42] Soma is extolled as the Gandharva, the promoter of delight and the guardian of the gods of the Truth, *gandharva itthā padam asya rakṣati.*[43] He is the supreme One who presides over 'the birth of the gods', the manifestation of the many puissances of the Mother Aditi in the universe and in the seeker. It is Soma who increases the manifold godhead of Ananda in man as well as protects him against the onslaught of the enemies of Light and Delight and their dark and misleading formations. For he provides man with a profounder framework of world-experience and Truth-experience other than that given by the ignorant sense-mind and the obscure surface-mind. It is in the light of this inner consciousness generated by Soma that man is able to accord his thoughts and his actions with the perfect laws of the inner Truth and Light which ultimately leads to the enjoyment of infinite beatitude.

In the Veda, Soma is invoked both as the divine food as well as the supreme offerer of that food. He is the miracle ambrosia and also its generous dispenser, the wine of divine delight and the lord of the superconscient delight. Impersonally, he flows into the worlds and makes the upward journey possible and personally, as the godhead of transforming bliss, he takes charge of all our activities, enlightens our mind, energises our nature and divinises our entire being. And "Like a Sun or a fire, as Surya, as Agni, engirt with a thousand blazing energies he conquers the vast regions of the inspired truth, the superconscient knowledge; *rājā pavitraratho vājam āruhaḥ sahasrabhṛṣṭir jayasi śravo bṛhat.* The image is that of a victorious king, sunlike in force and glory, conquering a wide territory. It is the immortality that he wins for man in the vast Truth-Consciousness, *śravas*, upon which is founded the immortal state. In his own true seat, *itthā padam asya*, that the God concealed in man conquers ascending out of the darkness and the twilight through the glories of the Dawn into the solar plenitudes."[44]

1. *Pavitraṁ te vitataṁ brahmaṇaspate prabhur*
   gātrāṇi paryeṣi viśvataḥ,
   ataptatanūrna tadāmo aśnute śṛtāsa id
   vahantastatsamāśata.

2. *Tapoṣpavitraṁ vitataṁ divaspade śocanto*
   asya tantavo vyasthiran,

avantyasya pavītāramāśavo divaspṛṣṭham
adhi tiṣṭhanti cetasā.

3. *Arūrucaduṣasaḥ pṛsniragriya ukṣā bibharti*
bhuvanāni vājayuḥ,
māyāvino mamire asya māyayā nṛcakṣasaḥ
pitaro garbhamā dadhuḥ.

4. *Gandharva itthā padamasya rakṣati pāti*
devānāṁ janimānyadbhutaḥ,
gṛbhṇāti ripuṁ nidhayā nidhāpatiḥ sukṛttamā
madhuno bhakṣamāśata.

5. *Havirhaviṣmo mahi sadma daivyaṁ nabho*
vasānaḥ pari yāsyadhvaram,
rājā pavitraratho vājamāruhaḥ sahasrabhṛṣṭir
jayasi śravo bṛhat.[45]

1. Wide stretched out for you is the sieve of your purifying process, O Lord of divine enlightenment; you who are the sovereign entering the creature pervade his members from all sides. He who is unripe and whose body is not baked properly in the heat of the fire does not know the taste of that delight; only the mature ones who are prepared by the flame can bear that and enjoy it.

2. The filter through which his foe-scorching heat is purified is spread out on the summit of heaven; the lustrous filaments of this filter shine out and lie extended. His brilliant swift-flowing ecstasies foster the soul that purifies the seeker; he with his conscious heart attains the highest summit of Heaven.

3. This is the divine dappled Bull that makes the Dawns to shine forth, the supreme supporter that bears the worlds and nourishes them and seeks the plenitude; the ancient fathers fashioned for him a form by the intelligence which is his; being strong in vision, with their supreme insight they set him within as a divine Child to be born.

4. As the Gandharva verily, he protects his true station; as the marvellous One he preserves and promotes the births of the gods; Lord of the inner condition, he seizes the enemy by his spiritual skill.

They who are virtuous and perfected in actions enjoy the sweetness of the elixir of life.

5. O Lord, you are possessed of the good; verily, you are the divine food, you are the vast divine home; wearing the very heavens as a robe you surround and envelope the entire march of the sacrifice. Mounted on the chariot of your purifying sieve, O King, you ascend to the plenitude and with a thousand brilliant weapons you conquer the nourishment of vast and luminous knowledge for us.

If Surya is the godhead of the supreme Truth — the truth of being, of knowledge and of the growth-process leading to the highest Beatitude, then Soma is the godhead of that beatitude. Impersonally he is concealed in all existence and in the growth-process of all. We are called upon by the Rishis to press out this Soma-juice and offer them to the gods that they may increase in us and enable us to fight all obscurity and resistance on the journey. Soma, the wine-god of the Rig-veda, is the godhead of spiritual ecstasy, *ānanda*, the supreme felicity of *satyam ṛtam bṛhat.* Soma-wine is the physical symbol of the immortalising delight that is so assiduously and consciously sought after by continual sacrifices. This divine ecstasy so gained is offered to the gods — the universal powers which represent the highest Self in man, in all things and in the entire universe. The offering of the Soma-wine symbolises the sincere and total consecration by the seeker of his physical, vital and mental energies to the gods.

Each plane of consciousness needs a corresponding substance as its habitat; the ascent of man from the physical consciousness through the mental to the Supramental must open out the possibility of a corresponding escalade in the quality of substance proper to the domiciliation of that grade of consciousness. The power of a higher quality of substance liberates the lower substance from its limitations and transforms it. As such the supramental substance is bound to liberate and transform the physical and render it possible for a supramental life on earth — a life of earthly immortality. It is then that the Lord of Immortality, Soma, pours into 'the mentalised living matter' the wine of divine *ānanda* and divinises it.

The *Taittiriya Upanishad* speaks of *ānanda* as the source and substance of all creation, as its sustenance and its cessation.

Ānando brahmeti vyajānāt,
anandāddhyeva khalvimāni

bhūtāni jāyante,
ānandena jātāni jīvanti,
ānandaṁ prayantyabhisaṁviśantīti.[46]

He realised that Brahman is bliss; for verily, from bliss all things are born; and when born do they live by bliss, and into bliss, at the time of departure, do they merge.

Ananda is the self-existent delight of Brahman that is constantly sought and worshipped. Man is divorced from the truth of his own existence by Ignorance, but this knowledge is progressively recovered by a seeking that is supported by Ananda itself. A conscious force working imperceptibly in the universe dissolves the darkness, a flame of Truth steadily burns down the roots of Ignorance, and an underlying everlasting ecstasy replaces mortality by Immortality. It is this sap of secret delight that is named Soma by the Vedic Rishis. Soma presides over the secret *rasa* of all-existence and supports its growth and its fulfilment in the lives of men. It is also the most favourite food of the *devas* and most cherished and treasured by them; it is 'the immortal and immortalising' divine drought, *amṛta*, that both gods and men seek for.

Soma is indeed the preserver of our being and the guardian of our body. He abolishes all debility and disease, and enables the body to respond successfully and satisfyingly to the challenges and needs of the unique and ubiquitous journey.

Apa tyā asthuranirā amīvā nir
atrasantamiśīcīrabhaiṣuḥ
ā somo asmāñ aruhadvihāyā
aganma yatra pratiranta āyuḥ.[47]

May these irremovable sicknesses and debilities depart; let the terrible pains which have made us awfully afraid go away. May the mighty Soma be effective in us now that we have obtained that elixir by which men prolong life.

This truly needs a long and strong preparation of both the being and the body; it needs a fit human system, *ādhāra*. For he who is unready and unripe and immature cannot bear the burden of supreme ecstasy, nor can he enjoy it fully and truly. The body and being have to be sufficiently baked in the kiln of askesis, *tapasyā*, and fully liberated from *tamas* and rendered pliant, for only a resilent system can yield the necessary *rasa* for offering to the gods. This secret sap is extracted from every movement and experience of the striver by an enlightened life-force in him and set to flow towards the gods who eagerly and anxiously await its arrival for enjoyment. This *rasa* has to be poured into the higher vital-mental nature of the seeker where it is purified of its dross before it is ready for the offering. Satisfied and strengthened by the offered *rasa*, the nectar of divine delight, the gods led by Indra help the offerer-seeker in his difficult ascent and eventual victory. The gods are thus fulfilled in the fulfilment of the pilgrim's quest.

Soma is the drink of immortal delight aflow in all-existence, the blissful essence of all things of which gods are thirsty and covetous. By his continuing, enduring sacrifice the Rishi prepares the banquet of Bliss on the inner altar for the gods to partake; he offers them this sweetest *rasa* of his life for their enjoyment and feels fulfilled. For it is by self-offering verily that he becomes immortal; it is the most coveted possession of the seeker-sacrificer that could be offered to the gods for his supreme fulfilment.

Soma the instrument of immortality is itself the elixir of immortality — the sea and the seer of all things, *tad yat tad amṛtam somaḥ sa.*[48] It helps both gods and men to attain immortality.

Yo na induḥ pitaro hṛtsu pito
'martyo martyāñ āviveśa,
tasmai somāya haviṣā vidhema
mṛḷike asya sumatau syāma.[49]

That Soma which drunk into our hearts has entered, immortal into us mortals. Let us therefore, O Fathers, worship him with devotion; may we always abide in his grace and bliss.

Soma is a cleansing drink purifying in its effects, transforming and elevating in its power, integrating and harmonising in its action. It humanises gods even as it divinises men and creates conditions for the manifestation of a higher dimension of the Divine.

1. *Sanā ca soma jeṣi ca pavamāna mahi śravaḥ,*
   athā no vasyasaskṛdhi.

2. *Sanā jyotiḥ sanā svar'viśvā ca soma saubhagā,*
   athā no vasyasaskṛdhi.

3. *Sana dakṣamuta kratumapa soma mṛdho jahi,*
athā no vasyasaskṛdhi.

4. *Pavītāraḥ punītana somamindrāya pātave,*
athā no vasyasaskṛdhi.

5. *Tvaṁ sūrye na ā bhaja tava kratvā tavotibhiḥ,*
athā no vasyasaskṛdhi.

6. *Tava kratvā tavotibhirjyokpaśyema sūryam,*
athā no vasyasaskṛdhi.

7. *Abhyarṣa svāyudha soma dvibarhasaṁ rayim,*
athā no vasyasaskṛdhi.

8. *Abhyarṣanapacyuto rayiṁ samatsu sāsahiḥ,*
athā no vasyasaskṛdhi.

9. *Tvāṁ yajñairavīvṛdhan pavamāna vidharmaṇi,*
athā no vasyasaskṛdhi.

10. *Rayiṁ naścitramaśvinamindo viśvāyumā bhara,*
athā no vasyasaskṛdhi.[50]

1. O Soma, most cleansing and nourishing drink, welcome the gods to our sacrifice; mighty conqueror of the adversaries, make us happy and perfect.

2. O Soma, give us light, give us the light celestial and all the joys; make us happy and prosperous and perfect.

3. O Soma, increase our skills, give us wisdom; drive away our adversaries and make us happy and prosperous and perfect.

4. O Supreme purifier, press out this divine drink for Indra to enjoy; make us happy and prosperous and perfect.

5. O Soma, by your prowess, wisdom and protection give us a place in the Sun; make us happy and prosperous and perfect.

6. O sovereign and almighty god, by your wisdom, prowess and protection may we long behold the Sun; make us happy and prosperous and perfect.

7. O blissful, almighty lord, grant us abundant wealth of both the worlds; make us happy and prosperous and perfect.

8. O ever-victorious King, invincible in battle, shower upon us your shining wealth; make us happy and prosperous and perfect.

9. O purifying Soma, emboldened by our worship you grant us gifts galore; make us happy and prosperous and perfect.

10. O blissful god, grant us varied wealth — abundant in cattle and a full life; make us happy and prosperous and perfect.

The Rishis desire the friendship of Soma the beneficient godhead of bliss and the mighty defender of the Truth.

a) *Divaspṛthivyā adhi bhavendo dyumnavardhanaḥ,*
bhavā vājānāṁ patiḥ.[51]

O Soma, increase our luminous riches of heaven and earth; may you be the lord of food.

b) *Ā pyāyasva sametu te*
viśvataḥ soma vṛṣṇyam,
bhavā vājasya saṅgathe.[52]

O Soma, elixir of divine delight, may all the powers unite in you from all sides; may you give us strength in the battle of life.

He is invoked to inspire and enthuse them in their journey to the desired goal.

1. *Asarji rathyo yathā pavitre camvoḥ sutaḥ*
karṣmanvājī nyakramīt.

2. *Sa vahniḥ soma jāgṛviḥ pavasva devavīrati*
abhi kośaṁ madhuścutam.

3. *Sa no jyotiṅṣi pūrvya pavamāna vi rocaya,*
   kratve dakṣāya no hinu.

4. *Śumbhamāna ṛtāyubhirmṛjyamāno gabhastyoḥ,*
   pavate vāre avyaye.

5. *Sa viśvā dāśuṣe vasu somo divyāni pārthivā,*
   pavatāmāntarikṣya.

6. *Ā divaspriṣṭhamaśvayurgavyayuḥ soma rohasi,*
   vīrayuḥ śavasaspate.[53]

1. Pressed between the two boards Soma speeds through the strainer like a chariot-horse and spurts into the jar — yea, the courser steps out on the battle field.

2. O elixir of divine delight, bearer of oblations, devoted to the gods, become purified as you flow with due care through the strainer to the honey-dripping jars.

3. O foremost purifier, let your lights shine on us now, animate and inspire us to greater skill of mind and hand for performing the sacrificial rites.

4. Adorned and enhanced in lustre by the hands of devout and wise worshippers you are purified as you flow through the strainer.

5. May the blissful lord bestow on the worshipper all treasures of both heaven and earth and those that pertain to *antarikṣa.*

6. O Soma, lord of divine delight, you ascend to the heights of heaven in search of cows and horses and brave progeny.

Soma is the lord of the heavenly light and delight, most sacred and surpassing all. Glory to him, sings the Rishi, who nourishes the seekers with the wine of bliss, and repels all their enemies.

Pavamāna svarvido jāyamāno'bhavo mahān,
   indo viśvāñ abhīdasi.[54]

O purifying Soma, O heavenly light, grant us all boons; as soon as born you wax great, O blissful lord, and overcome all adversaries.

He is the supreme master of ecstasies, destroyer of the demon and the bestower of prosperity and power.

1. *Sa no madānāṁ pata indo devapsarā asi,*
sakheva sakhye gatuvittamo bhava.

2. *Sanemi kṛdhyasmadārakṣasaṁ kaṁ cidatriṇam,*
apādevaṁ dvayumaṁho yuyodhi naḥ.[55]

1. O Soma, master of ecstasies, you are the much adored drink of the immortal gods, may you be our true guide and show us the path.

2. O ancient friend, reveal to us your cherished friendship; drive away from us the wicked and the voracious, the evil and the impious, the evil-mongers and double-dealers; also keep away from all sin and evil.

1. SABCL. Vol. 10, p. 69
2. RV. IX.15.1-2
3. RV. IV.58.1
4. RV. IV.58.2
5. RV. X.108.8a
6. SABCL. Vol. 10, p. 185
7. Ibid., p. 250
7a. Ibid., p. 251
8. RV. I.4.2
9. RV. IX.86.5
10. RV. IX.28.5
11. RV. IX.37.4
12. RV. IX.31.3
13. RV. IX.90.1
14. RV. IX.66.16,17
15. RV. IX.94.5
16. RV. I.91.2-4

17. RV. I.91.14-16
18. RV. I.91.21-23
19. RV. VIII.48.1,2
20. RV. VIII.48.6,7
21. RV. VIII.48.9,10
22. RV. VIII.48.13-15
23. RV. VIII.79.6-9
24. RV. X.34.1b
25. RV. III.48.2a
26. RV. V.43.4b
27. RV. IX.18.1
28. RV. IX.33.5
29. RV. IX.52.2
30. RV. I.130.3
31. RV. VI.72.5
32. RV. II.15.8
33. RV. IX.86.47
34. RV. IX.97.27
35. SABCL. Vol. 10, p. 291
36. RV. IX.87.8
37. RV. I.84.4
38. RV. IX.56.3
39. RV. IX.1.7
40. SABCL. Vol. 10, p. 344
41. Ibid., p. 345
42. Ibid., p. 346
43. RV. IX.83.4a
44. SABCL. Vol. 10, p. 348
45. RV. IX.83.1-5
46. *Taittiriya Upanishad*, III.6.1
47. RV. VIII.48.11
48. *Satapatha Brahmana*, IX.5.1.8
49. RV. VIII.48.12
50. RV. IX.4.1-10
51. RV. IX.31.2
52. RV. IX.31.4
53. RV. IX.36.1-6
54. RV. IX.59.4
55. RV. IX.104.5,6

XVI

USHA

Usha, the daughter of heaven, is the goddess of the divine Dawn; she is the lady of light and spouse of Surya Savitri. She unites in herself a vision of new creation, a hope of man's golden destiny and the establishment on earth of the Kingdom of the Sun of Truth. She is the earliest to shine forth in the firmament and on the earth.

Eṣo uṣa apūrvyā vy
ucchati priyā divaḥ.[1]

She opens out the pen of darkness and releases the cows of radiances:

Jyotirviśvasmai bhuvanāya kṛṇvatī
gāvo na vrajaṁ vyuṣā āvartamaḥ.[2]

She is described as *gomati aśvavati*, the creator of light for all the world; she is drawn in her chariot by 'ruddy cows',

Yuṅkte gavāmaruṇanāmanīkam.[3]

She is the mother of radiances who creates the vision:

Gavāṁ janitryakṛta pra ketum.[4]

It is she who removes the darkness and guides the days:

a) *Saṁ te gavastama ā vartayanti*
jyotiryacchanti saviteva bāhū.[5]

O Dawn, your radiances dispel darkness; they spread their light when the Sun stretches out his arms.

b) *Gavāṁ mātā netriahnāmaroci,*[6]

As the luminous guide of the days she shines forth.

She is also the giver of the herds of Light to the seeker sacrificer, and the establisher of a state of supreme felicity; she also brings for him 'luminous impulsions' of the Sun that carry him across the engulfing darkness. Usha plays her own unique role in the liberation of cows from the stranglehold of the Adversary.

a) *Satyā satyebhirmahatī mahadbhirdevī*
devebhiryajatā yajatraiḥ,
rujad dṛḷhāni dadadusriyāṇāṁ
prati gāva uṣasaṁ vāvaśanta.[7]

"True with the gods who are true, great with the gods who are great, she breaks open the strong places and gives of the shining herds; the cows low towards the dawn."*

b) *Gomatīriṣa ā vahā duhitardivaḥ,*
sākaṁ sūryasya raśmibhiḥ.[8]

"Bring to us, O daughter of Heaven, luminous impulsions along with the rays of the Sun."*

Usha symbolises the bursting forth of infinite light from the Unknown upon the world of manifestation; the emergence of Dawn is the most joyous experience, complete and perfect and *sui generis*. She bears in her luminous bosom the message as well as the promise of Truth, Goodness and Beauty — *satyam ṣivam sundaram*. The shining goddess Usha is closely associated with her fond lover, the Sun, who follows her.

Sūryo devīmuṣasaṁ rocamānāṁ
maryo na yoṣamabhyeti paścāt.[9]

The sun follows the radiant dawn in the same manner as a young lover follows a maiden.

Dawn, resplendent with light, drives away all darkness; her radiance dissolves all shadows of malignity and gloom.

Eṣā śubhrā na tanvo vidanordhveva
snātī dṛśaye no asthāt,
apa dveṣo bādhamānā tamāṅsyuṣā
divo duhitā jyotiṣāgāt.[10]

Exposing her body and being like a well-dressed damsel, she stands before our gaze, gracefully leaning like a young lady just out of her bath. Usha, the daughter of heaven, dispersing the encircling dark gloom comes with all radiances.

Like a war-goddess and a radiant archer she repulses the darkness of ignorance and beats back the enemies of Light and Truth. With her ruddy and all-embracing radiance she drives away all gloom, and illumines the path for the ardent seekers.

a) *Vahanti śimaruṇāso ruśanto gavaḥ*
subhagāmurviyā prathānām,
apejate śūro asteva śatrūn bādhate
tamo ajiro na voḷhā.[11]

Ruddy and resplendent are the rays that bear the expanding, radiant Dawn; like a valiant warrior and a swift archer she scatters the adversaries and drives away the gloom.

b) *Vyuṣā āvo divijā ṛtenāviṣkṛṇvānā*
mahimānamāgāt,
apa druhastama āvarajuṣṭam
aṅgirastamā pathyā ajīgaḥ.[12]

Usha, the daughter of Heaven, has rolled out; she comes manifesting her glory in accordance with the law. She scatters the enemy and dispels all darkness; she illumines the paths of all living beings.

The Dawn is ever faithful to the eternal law of the universe and emerges punctiliously day by day, fair and bright, out of the gloomy darkness. She arouses from deep slumber all living creatures both four-footed and two — birds, beasts and men — to pursue their well-assigned work.

a) *Jānatyahnaḥ prathamasya nāma śukrā*
kṛṣṇādajaniṣṭa śvitīcī,
ṛtasya yoṣā na mināti dhāmāhar
aharniṣkṛtamācaranti.[13]

The radiant Dawn, announcing the beginning of the day, ascends white-shining out of the enveloping darkness. Cleansed by the radiance of the sun, she does not undermine his splendour nor transgress the law, but comes at the appointed hour and increases his lustre.

b) *Yūyaṁ hi devirṛtayugbhiraśvaiḥ*
pariprayātha bhuvanāni sadyaḥ,
prabodhayantīruṣasaḥ sasantaṁ dvipāc
catuṣpaccarathāya jīvam.[14]

O divine Dawn, with swift-moving horses harnessed by the eternal order you quickly travel through space; may you awaken the sleeping ones, both two-footed and four-footed, to pursue their assigned works.

c) *Vayaścitte patatriṇo dvipac*
catuṣpadarjuni,
uṣaḥ prārannṛtūṅranu
divo antebhyaspari.[15]

O radiant Usha, on your advent all bipeds and quadrupeds are awakened, and birds from all directions flock around to welcome you.

Usha with her radiance illumines all the horizons. The seers sing her glory, and implore for eternal wealth and wisdom.

Vyuechantī hi raśmibhirviśvam
ābhāsi rocanam,
tāṁ tvāmuṣarvasūyavo gīrbhiḥ
kanvā ahūṣata.[16]

O Usha, you come illumining the universe with your rays and dispersing the darkness. The enlightened seekers, desirous of felicity, sing your glory with their sacred hymns.

She brings with her the most resplendent of all lights; night yields up to the morning and the Dawn flings open her shining doors to all. She brings the divine wealth of life and light to all creation, raising to waking consciousness all sentient beings. Some rise to increase their consciousness through worship, some their wealth and others to acquire skill in their profession.

Bhāsvatī netrī sūnṛtānāmaceti
citrā vi duro na āvaḥ,
prārpyā jagadvyu no rāyo akhyad
uṣā ajīgarbhuvanāni viśvā.[17]

Usha, the luminous guide of the seekers of truth, the many-splendoured one is recognised by us; having illuminated the world she opens our doors and manifests the wealth we need. She restores all the regions swallowed up by Darkness.

1. *Jihmaśyecaritave maghonyabhogaya*
iṣṭaye rāya u tvaṁ,
dabhraṁ paśyadbhya urviyā vicakṣa uṣā
ajīgarbhuvanāni viśvā.

2. *Kṣatrāya tvaṁ śravase tvaṁ mahīyā*
iṣṭaye tvamarthamiva tvamityai,
visadriśā jīvitābhipracakṣa uṣā
ajīgarbhuvanāni viśvā.[18]

The exuberant, lush Dawn awakens, all the sleeping ones — some to enjoyment, others to the acquisition of wealth and some others to pure devotion. She enables the near blind to see clearly, and restores all the regions swallowed up by Darkness.

She awakens some to acquire riches, others to earn their livelihood and yet others to achieve greatness; while she induces some to perform sacrifices, she makes others to pursue their own activity and helps all to their varied means of maintaining life. She restores all the regions swallowed up by Darkness.

Usha, auspicious daughter of Heaven, fairest lady of Light clothed in the most shining garments and wielder of all the wealth of the worlds beyond, is invoked again and again to illumine the seeker-sacrificer.

Eṣā divo duhitā pratyadarśi vyucchantī
yuvatiḥ śukravāsāḥ,
viśvasyeśānā pārthivasya vasva uṣo
adyeha subhage vyuccha.[19]

The young one, the white-robed daughter of heaven, the mistress of all felicities is seen emerging forward dissipating all darkness. May the auspicious Usha shine upon us all in the sacrificial hall.

Usha is the power of Aditi, the supreme Consciousness-Force:

Mātā devānāmaditeranīkaṁ,[20]

"Mother of the gods, form (or, power) of Aditi."*

She is as such associated in the Veda with the *ṛtam* and is seen as always pursuing the path of the Truth:

Ṛtasya panthāmanveti sādhu,[21]

"Following effectively the path of the Truth."*

She knows the Truth and therefore does not confine the infinity of *bṛhat, prajānatīva na diśo mināti.*[22] Usha is described elsewhere as essentially and imperatively associated with the Truth and bringing with her the most luminous wealth of Light:

Dyutadyāmānaṁ bṛhatīm
ṛtena ṛtāvarīmaruṇapsuṁ vibhātīm.[23]

"(*She is*) of a luminous movement, vast with the Truth, supreme in (or possessed of) the Truth, bringing with her Swar."*

By the light inherent in her she reveals all things, and by the power of the Truth manifests infinite vastness:

a) *Vyuṣā āvo divijā ṛtenā*
viṣkṛṇvānā mahimānamāgāt,[24]

"Dawn born in heaven opens out things by the Truth, she comes manifesting the greatness."*

b) *Satyā satyebhirmahatī mahadbhir*
devī devebhiḥ.[25]

"Dawn true in her being with the gods who are true, vast with the Gods who are vast."*

She awakens all life for upward operation and by its vast vision releases mind into its fullest wideness. Usha is the source of perceptive knowledge, *pracetaḥ*, and begets to the mind its luminous discernment:

Gavāṁ janityakṛta pra ketum.[26]

The Mother of the early radiances has revealed herself and created this 'perceptive vision of the mind.'

She is herself the 'perceptive vision' and the 'perceptive power' possessed of the 'happy truths', *cikitvit sunṛtavari.*[27]

Vi nūnamucchādasati pra ketur
gṛhaṅgṛhamupa tiṣṭhāte agniḥ.[28]

Assuredly a new perceptive vision bursts forth and dispels darkness; let her effulgence increasingly manifest and the sacred fire be kindled in each and every dwelling.

It is the vision and perception of the state of Immortality, *amṛtasya ketuh.*[29] She repels darkness and evil and awakens and leads the seekers to the right and the light.

Prati ṣīmagnirjarate samiddhaḥ
prati viprāso matibhirgṛṇantaḥ,
uṣā yāti jyotiṣā bādhamānā viśvā
tamāṅsi duritāpa devī.[30]

The Dawn divine increases steadily everywhere and the priests glorify her with their hymns. She rises up repelling all darkness with her lustre.

She is *gomati aśvavati vīravatī*, full of perfect light and sight, force and felicity, amplitude of vision and perfect consciousness, divine knowledge and spiritual opulence.

(1)

Dawn: the Mother of the Herds

The term Usha refers to a deeper psychological plane; concurrently it also means the physical dawn. Most of the Vedic expressions have an esoteric significance and are capable of transporting us to higher realms. The words *go* (cow), *aśva* (horse), *ghṛta* (clarified butter), *vīra* (son or hero), *apaḥ* (the waters), *hiraṇya* (gold), *vaja* (plenty), *apatya or prajā* (offspring) have to be understood in a deeper and symbolic sense. The Vedic *gau* is a symbol of light, whereas *aśva* signifies 'conquering energy' and 'force of vitality'. Similarly, the other words too assume a symbolic significance.

In the Vedic experience, the image of *gau* is invariably associated with *Usha* and *Surya Savitri* — the Dawn and the Sun. The hymns constantly refer to the 'herds of the Dawn' and those of the Sun, the herds symbolising the innumerable rays of Light. In the words of Sri Aurobindo 'cow' is "the concrete image and verbal figure" of 'light'. There is yet another expression *sapta gāvaḥ*, which signifies the 'seven Lights' or 'seven Radiances' of Aditi, the Divine Mother — the Mother of infinite existence and infinite consciousness. "The sevenfold principle of existence", observes Sri Aurobindo, "is therefore imaged from the one point of view in the figure of the Rivers that arise from the ocean, *sapta dhenavaḥ*, from the other in the figure of the Rays of the all-creating Father, Surya Savitri, *sapta gāvaḥ*."[31]

The cows (herds of the Dawn) are stolen by the Panis and concealed by Vala; Vala is the withholder of Light from the seekers. It is Indra who after battling with Vala restores the stolen cows to the sacrificers. In the Vedic hymns Dawn is delineated every time as *gomatī* which certainly would not mean "cowful" but in a symbolic sense suggest being "luminous or radiant"; it is not only *gomatī*, but is also *aśvāvatī*. Usha is both radiant and dynamic, full of light and life-energy. Like a cow yielding her udder, she bears her secret body of Truth to the sacrificer and "creates light for all the world and opens out the darkness as the pen of the Cow:"[32]

Adhi peśaṅsi vapate nṛtūrivāporṇute
vakṣa usreva barjaham,
jyotirviśvasmai bhuvanāya kṛṇvati
gāvo na vrajaṁ vyuṣā āvartamaḥ [33]

In Riks of the Rig-veda I.4 there is a reference to Indra "the maker of perfect forms who is a good milker in the milking of the cows, that his ecstasy of the Soma-wine is verily 'cow-giving', *godā id revato madaḥ.*"[34]

Surūpakṛtnumūtaye sudughāmivagha goduhe,
juhūmasi dyavidyavi.
Upa naḥ savanā gahi somasya somapāḥ piba,
godā idrevato madaḥ.[35]

Day after day we invoke the resplendent Lord, the doer of good works for our appropriation just as a milch-cow is called by the milker for milking. O drinker of the Soma-wine, may you come to our daily sacrifices and accept our libation; your satisfaction, O bestower of felicity supreme, is verily the giving us of luminous kine.

Day after day Indra, the resplendent God, is thus invoked by the sacrificer for increasing Light. He is described as an efficient and benevolent milker, the gatherer of light and generous 'cow-giver' as well as the bestower of luminous plenitude when he is in a state of Soma-ecstasy. The hymn cannot be understood in any sense other than in this psychological sense. "It is the height of absurdity and irrationality", observes Sri Aurobindo, "to understand by this phrase (*godā id revato madaḥ*) that Indra is a very wealthy god and, when he gets drunk, exceedingly liberal in the matter of cow-giving."[36]

Usha too, like Indra, is a giver of the Light to the seeker-sacrificers. She participates, alongwith the other gods, in the restoration of the stolen 'herds' and making them available to men.

1. *Prati dyutānāmaruṣāso aśvāścitrā*
adṛśrannuṣasaṁ vahantaḥ,
yāti śubhrā viśvapiśā rathena dadhāti
ratnaṁ vidhate janāya.

2. *Satyā satyebhirmahatī mahadbhirdevī*
devebhiryajatā yajatraiḥ,
rujad dṛḷhāni dadadusriyāṇāṁ prati
gāva uṣasaṁ vāvaśanta.

3. *Nū no gomadvīravaddhehi ratnamuṣo*
aśvāvatpurubhojo asme,
mā no barhiḥ puruṣatā nide kar
yūyaṁ pāta svastibhiḥ sadā naḥ.[37]

A free rendering of these would be —

> Usha advances in a chariot of manifold movements drawn by radiant and energetic steeds of varied colours. She brings to her people shining treasures. True with the truthful gods, great and divine with the great gods, holy with those who are holy, she breaks open the citadels of Darkness and restores the shining herds. The true seekers long for the Dawn to emerge. The Rishi implores that she may bestow upon him divine wealth, luminous vigour, abundant food for inner progress and progeny to help in the ascent of the sacrifice. He needs her constant protection against the enemies of Light, and her loving benediction.

The Rishis pray for luminous force and divine delight. They are not satisfied with enlightenment alone; they need sublime strength to pursue their goal.

> *Uta no gomatīriṣa ā vahā duhitardivaḥ,*
> *sākaṁ sūryasya raśmibhiḥ śukraiḥ*
> *śocadbhirarcibhiḥ sujāte aśvasūnṛte.*[38]

> Bring to us, O daughter of Heaven, bright-born and rightly praised for the gift of horses, abundant food and cattle together with luminous impulsions, along with the pure rays of the Sun.

Certainly it is not the radiant food of cow's flesh that is sought for by the Rishi, but the pure force and effulgence of the Sun. The daughter of Heaven is invoked for the gift of enlightenment and vigour "that carry the seeker across to the other shore of this darkness", *jyotiṣmatī tamas tiraḥ.*[39]

Our great ancestors, the ancient Rishis, who were observants of truth, discovered the hidden Truth. And adhering to the law of their secret journey and keeping close to the guidance of their seeking itself they brought to birth the Dawn.

> *Ta iddevānāṁ sadhamāda āsann*
> *ṛtāvānaḥ kavayaḥ pūrvyāsaḥ,*
> *gūḷhaṁ jyotiḥ pitaro anvavindan*
> *tsatyamantrā ajanayannuṣāsam.*[40]

> Those seers of yore, our ancient fore-fathers, regardful of truth, rejoicing together with the gods, discover the light concealed in

the womb of Darkness and with right impulsions generate the Dawn.

The sun of Truth is lost in obscurity — the Superconscient lies concealed in the bottom of Inconscience, or rather, the Light is enveloped by the Night. The emergence of Dawn out of the bosom of Darkness is the familiar Vedic figure. The Rishis pray to the gods for effecting 'the great change from inner obscuration to illumination'. They invoke the Ashwins and pray that they be led by 'a joyous upward action of the mind and the vital powers' suffused and supported by the ecstasy of the immortal Soma-wine. It is the delight of Soma-drink that 'dissolves all mental constructions', and takes the seeker "through the heaven of the pure mind... to the other side of... the great human journey." [41]

Dawn is 'the Mother of the Herds', 'the guide of the days', 'the bringer of the Truth' and is herself the golden glow of *satyam ṛtam bṛhat.* "She is the divine Dawn", says Sri Aurobindo, "and the physical dawning is only her shadow and symbol in the material universe."[42]

Usha is repeatedly described by the Rishis as *gomatī, aśvavati, vīravati* which does not mean "cowful and horseful and man-accompanied", indeed an irrelevant and absurd literal translation. The words can only mean full of radiances, sublime and swift life-forces accompanied by conquering energies.

Yā gomatiruṣasaḥ sarvavīrā
vyucchanti dāśuṣe martyāya.[43]

May the offerer of oblations obtain from Usha the gift of luminous cattle, swift horses and brave progeny.

"The Dawn", according to Sri Aurobindo, "is the inner dawn which brings to man all the varied fullnesses of his widest being, force, consciousness, joy; it is radiant with its illuminations, it is accompanied by all possible powers and energies, it gives man the full force of vitality so that he can enjoy the infinite delight of that vaster existence."[44]

Most of the words used in the hymns cannot be taken in a physical and literal sense; they must be understood in a spiritual sense. They are luminous figures that hold the key to the secret of the Vedas — the heart of a higher and liberating knowledge. The Rishis speak of a 'divine hearing' and a 'divine vision' of the Truth, of a spiritual felicity and luminous knowledge. It is the vision of the Infinite and the receptivity of yonder vibrations from the Infinite that the seers refer to in the hymns. They invoke Usha for divine prosperity and for fostering helpful progeny.

Mahe no adya suvitāya bodhyuṣo
mahe saubhagāya pra yandhi,
citraṁ rayiṁ yaśasaṁ dhehyasme,
devi marteṣu mānuṣi śravasyum.[45]

O Usha, awaken us to the need for supreme felicity, promote inner prosperity and grant us splendid wealth for fostering effective and beneficial progeny.

The prayer is repeated again and again in the Veda:

Taccitraṁ rādha ā bharoṣo
yaddīrghaśruttamam.[46]

O mighty Goddess, bring us such wondrous wealth that would be long lasting and luminously enjoyable.

(2)

Usha and the Vision of Truth

The Vedic Dawn represents the awakening of the Rishis to the vision of Truth as well as their right movement toward the solar world of Truth — that of Immortality.

Viśvāni devī bhuvanābhicakṣyā pratīcī
cakṣururviyā vi bhāti,
viśvaṁ jīvaṁ carase bodhayantī viśvasya
vācamavidanmanāyoḥ.[47]

"The goddess fronts and looks upon all the worlds, the eye of vision shines with an utter wideness; awakening all life for movement she discovers speech for all that thinks."*

Dawn, opens up a perceptive vision in the mind of the Rishi, and gives him a unique inner knowledge. She is in fact this special faculty of this sensitive and discerning knowledge, the mother of Radiances. She spreads herself in all directions and fills heaven and earth with her loving radiance and bestows the delight of an inner entellection. She embraces every one and transcends all; she smiles and unmasks her shining wealth to those who seek for it. Having vacated her place for her sister, the Dawn, the Night departs. Shining forth with the luminous wealth of Surya like beautiful and well-adorned women trooping to a joyous meeting, Usha reaches the seekers of Light and the Truth.

Dawn after dawn, the Rishi has been blessed with the divine wealth of Light; even so he prays for the coming dawns to bless him with increasing enlightenment. Usha has been quite liberal in the distribution of her bountics; the Rishi prays that she may be generous and munificent especially with the spiritually wise and creative. The Rishi is overjoyed that the maiden of Radiances has beamed forth where there was nought before; she breaks out into a celestial vision of Truth that dispels all darkness. It is his ardent prayer that every one be helped with this perceptive vision.

1. *Evedeṣā purutamā dṛśe kaṁ nājāmiṁ na pari*
vṛṇakti jāmim,
arepasā tanvā śāśadānā nārbhādīṣate na
maho vibhātī.

2. *Abhrāteva puṅsa eti pratīcī gartārugiva*
sanaye dhanānām,
jāyeva patya uśatī suvāsā uśā hasreva
ni riṇīte apsaḥ.

3. *Svasā svasre jyāyasyai yonimaraig*
apaityasyāḥ praticakṣyeva,
vyucchantī raśmibhiḥ sūryasyañjy
aṅkte samanagā iva vrāḥ.

4. *Āsāṁ pūrvāsāmahasu svasṛṇāmaparā pūrvām*
abhyeti paścāt,
tāḥ pratnavannavyasīrnūnamasme revad
ucchantu sudinā uṣāsaḥ.

5. *Pra bodhayoṣaḥ pṛṇato maghonyabudhyamānāḥ*
paṇayaḥ sasantu,
revaduccha maghavadbhyo maghoni revatstotre
sūnṛte jārayantī.[48]

1. Verily, Usha shines for all and bestows them the ecstasy of vision; she does not ignore the stranger nor those of her own. She manifests her faultless personage for all, passing beyond everything, big and small.

2. Usha goes westward like a woman who has no brother repairs to her kinsmen, or like one ascending the court-steps for the recovery of his property she ascends in the sky to vindicate her luminosity. And as a fond wife yearning to please her husband puts on an attractive attire she unmasks her radiant charms.

3. Night, the younger sister, makes way for the Day, her elder one, and having made her aware of this, she withdraws. Dawn then bedecks herself with the shining rays of the sun like eager women ambulating to a festive gathering.

4. Of all those dawns who have gone before, a later one has always succeeded every day. So may the future dawns, like their predecessors, shine brightly for us and bring us bounteous wealth for our progress.

5. O munificent Dawn, may you awaken those who rejoice in making devout offerings; let the faithless niggards reluctant to wake continue to sleep. O Dawn, bestow your opulence to those who worship the Truth; O luminous radiator of Truth and the waster away of one's age, may you enrich those who worship you.

The Dawn is said to have a clear perception of Immortality,

Uṣaḥ pratīcī bhuvanāni viśvordhvā
tiṣṭhasyamṛtasya ketuḥ.[49]

O Usha, you who spread your rays over all the regions and stay on high are the radiant banner of the immortal Sun.

Diffusing her lustre from the bounds of earth and heaven Usha ever promotes the sacred acts of all worshippers.

Ūrdhvaṁ madhudhā divi pājo aśretpra
rocanā ruruce raṇvasandrik.[50]

Carrying celestial sweetness, Usha manifests her radiances in the skies above and illuminates all the regions.

Usha is essentially the divine Dawn, the one that brings divine illuminations and the world of divine Truth and Bliss to the seekers for she brings in her wake the Sun of the superconscient Truth. Truly she dispels all darkness and reveals the light of the Truth. In Sri Aurobindo's words, "Usha herself is the Truth, *sunṛta*, and the mother of Truths".[51] Rich in store of her substance of Light she opens the doors of divine illumination on the seekers' consciousness, *vājena vājini*, *maghoni*; on the upward journey many are her boons of light and bliss, of divine action and divine existence, *ānanda* and *amṛta*. She symbolises the constant opening out of the divine illuminations upon the human mentality; she is the continuous descent of divine felicity into the bowels of earth-nature. She represents the perennial downpour of the golden Light of the divine Truth into the Night of human ignorance. She is invoked again and again by the Rishis to shine out on men and grant them the perceptive knowledge and the perfect truth and all the desirable boons, and lead them to the world of Immortality, *satyam ṛtam bṛhat*.

Uṣo devyamartyā vi bhāhi
candrarathā sūnṛtā īrayantī,
ā tvā vahantu suyamāso aśvā
hiraṇyavarṇāṁ pṛthupājaso ye.[52]

"O Dawn divine shine out on us immortal, in thy chariot of bliss, uttering the words of Truth; let horses bring thee that are well-governed, golden of hue, wide in their strength".*

They rejoice in the supreme epiphany and cry out —

Udīrdhvaṁ jīvo asurna āgādapa
prāgāttama ā jyotireti,
āraikpanthāṁ yātave sūryāyāganma
yatra pratiranta āyuḥ.[52a]

"Arise, life and force have come to us, the darkness has departed, the Light arrives; she has made empty the path for the journey of the Sun; thither let us go where the gods shall carry forward our being beyond these limits."*

In the dark life and ignorant consciousness of men Usha comes to awaken them to the need for the Light and the Truth, and with it the practice of sacrifices. And sacrifices in their turn dilute the Night and take them closer to the Truth; constant and conscious sacrifice rescues the herds of Light concealed by the Panis in the caves of the Inconscient and the subconscient. By the sacrifice descend upon earth the sevenfold waters of heaven helping men towards higher existence; it brings in streams upon streams of the Soma-wine that uplifts the seeker-sacrificers to the summit Truth.

Usha is described in the Rig-veda as the Angirasa-power as well as the Indra-power, *aṅgirastame indratamā*, opulent in the wealth of Light and Power of the Truth, full of the illumined intelligence and flaming radiance of the Truth.

Abhūduṣā indratamā maghony
ajījanat suvitāya śravāṅsi
vi divo devī duhitā dadhāty
aṅgirastamā sukṛte vasūni.[53]

The supremely resplendent and opulent Usha has risen; she brings celestial felicity that increases our inner enlightenment. The daughter of heaven, most vigilant and benevolent, most full of Angirasahood gives her wealth to devout doers of good works.

She manifests the infinite vastness of the Truth and dissolves the immense obscurity of darkness. Her lustres bring to birth the workings of the Truth in men, and fill them with luminous strength on the arduous journey. She is the living goddess installed in the mortals ever leading them towards immortality, *devi marteṣu manasi* — 'the goddess human in mortals'.

1. *Mahe no adya suvitāya bodhyuṣo mahe*
saubhagāya pra yandhi,
citraṁ rayiṁ yaśasaṁ dhehyasme devi
marteṣu mānuṣi śravasyum.

2. *Ete tye bhānavo darśatāyāścitrā*
uṣaso amṛtāsa āguḥ,
janayanto daivyāni vratānyāpṛṇanto
antarikṣā vyasthuḥ.[54]

1."Today, O Dawn, awake for us for the journey to the vast bliss (*mahe suvitāya*) extend (thy riches) for a vast state of enjoyment, confirm in us a wealth of varied brightness (*citraṁ*) full of inspired knowledge (*śravasyum*), in us mortals,

2."O human and divine. These are the lustres of the visible Dawn which have come varied-bright (*citrā*) and immortal; bringing to birth the divine workings they diffuse themselves, filling those of the mid-region".*

(3)

More hymns to the Dawn

1) In the Vedic parlance while Night is the symbol of the darkness of Ignorance, sin and suffering, Day is that of the light of Knowledge, Truth and Happiness. When the Dawn rises up, she drives away all darkness, evil and gloom. They are celestial sisters who always move along the same path. They are the twin-daughters of heaven and the twin-mothers of the order, one dark in complexion and the other of bright colour. If the former decorates herself with stars, the latter enrobes with the splendour of the sun; they are described respectively as the mother-cow and daughter-cow.

Mātā ca yatra duhitā ca dhenū
sabardughe dhāpayete samīcī.[55]

Where two fecund milch-cows, mother and daughter, unite,
they nurse and cherish each other.

2) Most graceful of all goddesses who adorn the Vedic pantheon — the most beautiful of all flowers that blossomed in the springtime of Sanskrit literature, Usha is the dearest and blissful daughter of Heaven, and the beautiful bride and beloved of the Sun. The Dawn is described as the fairest of all lights shining bright, the glorious bringer of golden graces awakening to action all of creation. Auspicious Dawn, she is the luminous sister of Night who inspires and summons forth the worshippers to kindle the immortal fires and offer sacrifices to the gods. Throwing off the robes of Darkness she heralds the coming of the Kingdom of Light and works consciously for more bright mornings to follow. She is the luminous link in

the series of ascending Dawns, and prepares the pathway for the Sun of the Truth to arrive. She, the shining daughter of Aditi, is ever desired by all for wealth and wisdom, benediction and bliss.

1. *Śaśvatpuroṣā vyuvāsa devyatho*
adyedaṁ vyāvo maghonī,
atho vyucchāduttarāñ anu dyūn
ajarāmṛtā carati svadhābhiḥ.

2. *Vyañjibhirdiva ātāsvadyaudapa*
kṛṣṇāṁ nirṇijaṁ devyāvaḥ,
prabodhayantyaruṇebhiraśvairoṣā
yāti suyujā rathena.

3. *Āvahantī poṣyā vāryāṇi citraṁ ketuṁ*
kṛṇute cekitānā,
īyuṣīṇāmupamā śaśvatīnāṁ vibhātīnāṁ
prathamoṣā vyaśvait.[56]

1. The divine Usha, source of celestial riches, has been dawning continually since times sempiternal. And she still continues to shine today, so will she give her splendorous light tomorrow and hereafter through the future, for immune from any defilement or enfeeblement she goes on as ever in her shining glory.

2. The divine Usha lights up the heavens with her refulgent rays; she throws off her veil of darkness, and awaking those who are asleep comes in her radiant chariot drawn by purple steeds.

3. Bringing with her life-supporting valediction and divine felicity, she gives life and lustre to the famished, and imparts awareness to the ignorant and the unconscious; she adorns the earth with her wonderful radiance. She is the luminous link between those innumerable dawns that have gone by and the countless dawns that are to come.

3) Usha is seen everywhere approaching and ushering in the light; she dispels all gloom and makes the goal visible to the mind's eye. The Sun, her fond lover, who even follows her sends forth his rays and makes visible many planes of existence. The Dawn and the Sun are invoked by the Rishis

to grant them their apportioned divine sustenance — health, wealth and happiness and their steady spiritual progress towards Immortality.

Śravaḥ sūribhyo amṛtaṁ vasutvanaṁ
vājāñ asmabhyaṁ gomataḥ,
codayitrī maghonaḥ sūnṛtāvaty
uṣā ucchadapa sridhaḥ.[57]

O Usha, grant the seekers spiritual opulence and immortality; grant us divine nourishment and luminous cattle. May you who are the supporter and promoter of the sincere sacrificers and seekers of the Truth, drive away our adversaries.

4) Dawn shines radiant in the loving arms of the Sun, like a youthful lady of light, stirring to activity the whole of creation. She kindles the divine Fire for the spiritual well-being of men, and scatters the obstructing forces of Darkness. Clothed in pure and brilliant vesture of Truth she rises upon the world, and with her golden lustre illumines it. The most auspicious Dawn mounting on her white and beautiful horse shines forth bestowing on all her store of wondrous wealth. The beautiful One is implored to disperse the enemies, render the cow-pastures free from peril and reward the worshippers with treasures of luminous cattle, valorous horses and enduring chariots — light and power and means of effective upward movement. She is invoked for continuous inspiration, constant protection and blessings.

a) *Upo ruruce yuvatirna yoṣā viśvaṁ*
jīvaṁ prasuvantī carāyai,
abhūdagniḥ samidhe manuṣaṇam
akarjyotirbādhamānā tamāṅsi.[58]

O Usha, you shine brightest in the proximity of the Sun like a youthful maiden and invigorate all existence to activity. Agni, the divine fire, has to be kindled for the good of all men. Verily, your light disperses the obstructing darkness.

b) 1. *Devānāṁ cakṣuḥ subhagā vahantī śvetaṁ nayantī*
sudṛśīkamaśvam,
uṣā adarśi raśmibhirvyaktā citrāmaghā viśvam
anu prabhūtā.

2. *Antivāmā dūre amitramucchorvīṁ gavyūtim*
abhayaṁ kṛdhī naḥ,
yāvaya dveṣa ā bharā vasūni codaya rādho
gṛṇate maghoni.

3. *Asme śreṣṭhebhirbhānubhirvi bhāhy*
uṣo devi pratirantī na āyuḥ,
iṣaṁ ca no dadhatī viśvavāre gomad
aśvāvadrathavacca rādhaḥ.

4. *Yāṁ tvā divo duhitarvardhayantyuṣaḥ*
sujāte matibhirvasiṣṭhāḥ,
sāsmāsu dhā rayimṛṣvaṁ bṛhantaṁ
yūyaṁ pāta svastibhiḥ sadā naḥ.[59]

1. The auspicious Usha, the shining eye of the gods, mounts on her white and beautiful courser; she is seen by her radiances, the one who comes with her bounties for all.

2. O Usha, you are the bearer of desirable wealth; pray keep our adversaries far from us. May you render the cattle-pastures free from peril, and drive away those who hate us. Grant us spiritual riches, and bestow your graces upon those who worship you.

3. O divine Usha, illumine us with your most refulgent rays; may you prolong our life-span. Grant us suitable nourishment, O adorable goddess, who possesses in abundance the wealth of cattle, horses and chariots.

4. O daughter of heaven incarnate, whom the seekers devoutly worship with choicest praises, may you bestow upon us shining and abundant wealth, and may you cherish us with your benedictions supreme.

5) The *Brihadaranyaka Upanishad* speaks of Dawn as the head of the sacrificial Horse; it signifies the opening out of the phenomenal existence to the forward movement and action of the Supreme Being. It images the impulse of the world towards manifest divine existence. It is this luminous emergence which the earlier Rishis worshipped as the Dawn; they all hail its advent.

Idaṁ śreṣṭhaṁ jyotiṣāṁ jyotirāgāc
citraḥ praketo ajaniṣṭa vibhvā,
yathā prasūtā savituḥ savāyañ
evā ratryuṣase yonimāraik.[60]

This most excellent and radiant luminary of all luminaries has arrived; the most wonderful and far-extending revealer of all things has been born. Even as Night exists for the uprising of the Sun, so she becomes the birthplace for the Dawn.

6) The Atharva-veda describes the Dawn as the 'image of the year' and is invoked to unite for the worshippers long-living progeny with riches.

Prathamā ha vyu'vāsa sā
dhenurabhavadyame,
sā naḥ payasvatī duhāmuttarā
muttarāṁ samām.[61]

7) The *Maitrayani Samhita* addresses Usha as —

Ṛtunam patni, ahnam netri [62]

8) Usha is frequently referred to as the mother of the cows.

Etā u tyā uṣasaḥ ketumakrata purve
ardhe rajaso bhānumañjate,
niṣkṛṇvānā āyudhānīva dhṛṣṇavaḥ
prati gāvo'ruṣīryanti mātaraḥ.[63]

The Dawns have now spread their light manifesting their splendour in the eastern firmament brightening all things. Like hero-warriors burnishing their weapons these radiant mothers arise daily every morning.

9) The quiet resplendence of the Dawn inspired the Vedic Rishis to sing some of the most memorable hymns in Sanskrit literature.

a) *Īyuṣṭe ye pūrvatarāmapaśyan*
vyucchantimuṣasaṁ martyāsaḥ,
asmābhirū nu praticakṣyābhūdo te
yanti ye aparīṣu paśyān.[64]

Gone are those men who in the days before us gazed intently at the rising of the pristine Usha. It is we the living who now behold her golden splendour, and they are coming who will enjoy her glory in aftertimes.

b) *Syūmanā vāca udiyarti vahniḥ stavāno*
rebha uṣaso vibhātīḥ,
adyā taduccha gṛṇate maghony
asme āyurni didīhi prajāvat.[65]

The ardent priest, reciting hymns of praise celebrates the divine Usha in the well-ordained words of the sacred love. As such, O generous Dawn, shine today, for your worshipper. May you confer on us the gifts of life and worthy progeny.

Proudly, the Dawn sets up her banner of radiances in the eastern sky; her red-gold lights flowing up freely in the firmament bring the nourishment of higher consciousness to the worshippers. Usha creates light for the entire universe and dispels the encircling abyss of darkness. The shining goddess awakens into action everything that lives and brings them the wealth of light and strength.

10) Usha is the beloved of Surya, 'the eye of the gods'; she leads him and creates a path for him, *devānām cakṣuḥ subhāgā vahantī.*[66]

a) *Vājinīvatī, sūryasya yoṣā citrāmaghā*
rāya īśe vasūnām,
ṛṣiṣṭutā jarayantī maghonyuṣā
ucchati vahnibhirgṛṇānā.[67]

She is the bride of Surya, giver of food, possessor of miraculous wealth; she reigns supreme over riches of every kind. She is extolled by the Rishis, she the reckoner of our life and the mistress of opulence. When she rises, she is amply glorified by the worshippers.

The sun follows the divine Usha even as a lover follows his beloved.

b) *Sūryo devīmuṣasaṁ rocamānāṁ maryo*
na yoṣāmabhyeti paścāt.[68]

The sun follows the radiant Usha even as a young lover pursues a charming and elegant maiden.

In the Ashwin hymns, Usha is described as the daughter of Surya, *sūryasya duhitṛ, divo duhitṛ*. The Sun is also said to dissolve the Dawn.

c) *Vyucchā duhitardivo mā ciraṁ*
tanuthā apaḥ,
nettvā stenaṁ yathā ripuṁ tapāti
sūro arciṣā sujāte aśvasūnṛte.[69]

O daughter of the heavens, nobly born, shine forth; may you be praised for the gift of strength. Pray, do not delay our sacrifice lest the sun should burn you with his scorching heat as one punishes a hostile thief, or subjugates an adversary.

Usha is the favourite goddess of celebration with the Rishis; she is the undying maiden, the immortal being born everyday who jades down the lives of successive generations. Beautifully dressed and bedecked with the most ornate jewellery she travels in a shining chariot drawn by healthy, rubicund cows. And with irresistible charm she unfolds her enchanting and bewitching bosom to the gaze of her loving beholders. She renders great service to the gods by awakening the worshippers to the Truth and the need for Light.

1. RV. I.46.1
2. RV. I.92.4b
3. RV. I.124.11a
4. RV. I.124.5a
5. RV. VII.79.2b
6. RV. VII.77.2b
7. RV. VII.75.7
8. RV. V.79.8
9. RV. I.115.2a
10. RV. V.80.5

11. RV. VI.64.3
12. RV. VII.75.1
13. RV. I.123.9
14. RV. IV.51.5
15. RV. I.49.3
16. RV. I.49.4
17. RV. I.113.4
18. RV. I.113.5-6
19. RV. I.113.7
20. RV. I.113.19
21. RV. I.124.3b
22. Ibid.
23. RV. V.80.1a
24. RV. VII.75.1a
25. RV. VII.75.7a
26. RV. I.124.5a
27. RV. IV.52.4
28. RV.I. 125.11b
29. RV. III.61.3
30. RV. VII.78.2
31. SABCL. Vol. 10, p. 118
32. Ibid., p. 120
33. RV. I.92.4
34. SABCL. Vol. 10, p. 120
35. RV. I.4.1-2
36. SABCL., Vol. 10, p. 120
37. RV. VII.75.6-8
38. RV. V.79.8
39. RV. I.46.6
40. RV. VII.76.4
41. SABCL. Vol. 10, p. 125
42. Ibid.
43. RV. I.113.18
44. SABCL. Vol. 10, p. 131
45. RV. VII.75.2
46. RV. VII.81.5a
47. RV. I.92.9
48. RV. I.124.6-10
49. RV. III.61.3a
50. RV. III.61.5
51. SABCL. Vol. 10, p. 236
52. RV. III.61.2
52a. RV. I.113.16
53. RV. VII.79.3
54. RV. VII.75.2 3
55. RV. III.55.12a
56. RV. I.113.13-15

57. RV. VII.81.6
58. RV. VII.77.1
59. RV. VII.77.3-6
60. RV. I.113.1
61. *Atharva Veda*, III.10.1
62. *Maitrayani Samhita*, II.13.10
63. RV. I.92.1
64. RV. I.113.11
65. RV. I.113.17
66. RV. VII.77.3a
67. RV. VII.75.5
68. RV. I.115.2a
69. RV. V.79.9

XVII

VISHWADEVAS

Vishwadevas or 'the All-gods' is 'the gods in their generality'; the term means the extensive and all-inclusive assemblage of the cosmic powers. They come to the sacrifice collectively, when invoked, and share among themselves the Soma-offering equitably for their successful and joyous working. Each partakes of the divine drink necessary for his effective participation in the sacrifice. They all are generally called for a common action which fulfils the functions of the Ashwins. The Rishi repeats his plea to them to arrive at the Soma-sacrifice expeditiously. They need to wade through the wide waters — the many planes of consciousness dividing the physical. They are required to show up like cattle speeding to their stalls at sunset. When they thus arrive at the sacrifice, they support it and strengthen the seeker in his struggle to reach the world of the Truth.

All the gods share a common character; their functions are almost the same, They have the same collective responsibility. They together increase and intensify the aspiration of the seeker and uphold his upward endeavour; they foster him jointly, and jointly bring him the abundance of heaven and the puissance of Swar. They pour into his being the fullness of the upper waters. They collectively fight the common enemy and attain their true goal — the Truth and The Bliss. In the words of Sri Aurobindo, "The all-gods increase man, they uphold him in the great work, they bring him the abundance of the waters of Swar, the streams of the Truth, they communicate the unassailably integral and pervading action of the Truth-Consciousness with its wide formations of knowledge, *māyāḥ*."[1] The supreme consummation and 'the perfected fullness' of being depends on the birth and growth of the All-gods, *viśvedevāḥ*, in the seeker.

1. *Omāsaścarṣaṇīdhṛto viśve devāsa ā gata,*
   dāśvāṁso dāśuṣaḥ sutam.

2. *Viśve devāso apturaḥ sutamā ganta tūrṇayaḥ,*
   usrā iva svasarāṇi.

3. *Viśve devāso asridha ehimāyāso adruhaḥ,*
   medhaṁ juṣanta vahnayaḥ.[2]

1. "O fosterers who uphold the doer in his work, O all-gods, come and divide the Soma-wine that I distribute.

2. "O all-gods who bring over to us the Waters, come passing through to my Soma-offerings as illumined powers to your places of bliss.

3. "O all-gods, you are not assailed nor come to hurt, fire-moving in your forms of knowledge, cleave to my sacrifice as its upbearers."*

Between the noumenal and the phenomenal there is an intermediary level of manifestation wherein the gods appear who shape and support the universe and its destiny. The roles of these many gods at first seem to be diverse and bewildering, but at a deeper level they all have a single focus. It is the steady evolution of consciousness of the race and the ascent of humanity to the Truth. They are trusted regents of the earth and the celestial cosmic powers expressing themselves through receptive individuals. They are both personal and impersonal, individual and yet collective in action. They are all interlinked and interdependent, essentially benevolent and helpful. Functionally they fuse into each other, and in several areas are identified with each other. Their solidarity of purpose, as well as their luminous thrust are brought out throughout in the Veda. There is an undying oneness among them, one life breath as it were, and one lofty animus, a single goal — the attainment of the Truth and Immortality.

Viśve devāḥ samanasaḥ saketā ekaṁ
kratumabhi vi yanti sādhu.[3]

All-gods, one minded and of one intention proceed unerringly and unobstructed to the accomplishment of one purpose.

All the gods are powers and personalities of the One, *tad ekam*, and are invoked and worshipped as his representatives. They are the many manifestations and varied expressions of the supreme nameless Essence; each is a deputy of the Divine, each a delegate of the All-god, *viśve devāḥ*.

Ā viśvadevaṁ satpatiṁ sūktairadyā vṛṇīmahe,
satyasavaṁ savitāram.[4]

We glorify Savitri this day with suitable hymns, the protector of the good and the illuminator of all, the embodiment of Truth and one with All-gods.

So too, are Agni, Vayu, and Chandrama.

> *Tadevāgnistadādityastadvāyustadu chandramaḥ*
> *Tadeva sukram tadbrahm tā āpah sa prajāpatiḥ.*[5]

> The Divine is Agni being self-refulgent; he is Aditya as he submerges all at the time of the dissolution of the universe; he is Vayu as he is omnipotent; he is Chandrama as he is full of happiness and the giver of happiness; he is Shukra as he is absolutely pure and perfect and quick in action; he is Brahma as he is great and almighty; he is the all-pervading Apa and Prajapati being the guardian of all creatures.

He is the lord of heaven, says the Sama-veda, *patim divo ya ekta*. He is the One who looses forth as the all,

> *Ekaṁ vā idaṁ vi babhūva sarvam.*[6]

The gods are the sons of the Infinite, the Supreme Craftsman.

1. *Devānāṁ nu vayaṁ jānā pra vocāma vipanyayā,*
   uktheṣu śasyamāneṣu yaḥ paśyāduttare yuge.

2. *Brahmaṇaspatiretā saṁ karmāraivādhamat,*
   devānāṁ pūrvye yuge'sataḥ sadajāyata.

3. *Devānāṁ yuge prathame'sataḥ sadajāyata*
   tadāśā anvajāyanta taduttānapadaspari.

4. *Bhurjajña uttānapado bhuva āśā ajāyanta*
   aditerdakṣo ajāyata dakṣadvaditiḥ pari.

5. *Aditirhyajaniṣṭa dakṣa yā duhitā tava*
   tāṁ devā anvajāyanta bhadrā amṛtabandhavaḥ.

6. *Yaddevā adaḥ salile susaṁrabdhā atiṣṭhata*
   atrā vo nṛtyatāmiva tīvro reṇurapāyata.

7. *Yaddevā yatayo yathā bhuvanānyapinvata*
   atrā samudra ā gūḷhamā sūryamajabhartana.

8. *Aṣṭau putrāso aditerye jatastanva'spari*
devāñ upa praitsaptabhiḥ parā mārtaṇḍamāsyat.

9. *Saptabhiḥ putrairaditirupa praitpūrvyaṁ yugam*
prajāyai mṛtyave tvatpunarmārtāṇḍamābharat.[7]

1. With a clear and pleasing voice let us annunciate and celebrate the many generations of gods, that men to come may know the truth of the rewards of our praises.

2. Brahmanaspati, the lord of universe, filled generations of gods with breath like a smith his bellows. In the beginning, the existence came out of the non-existent.

3. In the beginning, the manifest came out of the Unmanifest. There came into existence the cardinal quarters, and after that evolved the upward-moving creation.

4. And from the upward-moving creation sprang up earth, and from earth the cardinal quarters. Daksha was born from Aditi, and later Aditi from Daksha.

5. Then did Aditi come into being, she who was Daksha's daughter. After her were born the blessed gods, the sharers of immortal life, the adorable ones.

6. At the time you were abiding in the Waters, O gods, pressed together, close-clasping one another, there arose a piquant dust from you as from the stumping feet of dancers.

7. Where, O gods, you filled the worlds with your radiances as clouds fill the earth with rain, then you brought forth the sun who was lying hidden beneath the ocean.

8. Eight are the sons of Aditi born from her body; with seven she joined the galaxy of gods, the eighth one, known as Martanda, the sun, she planted on high.

9. With her seven sons, therefore, Aditi goes to meet an earlier age;

she brings Martanda alone to earth that he might bring all creatures to life and then pass them on to death.

The children of the infinite, *viśve devāḥ*, hew out the path for the Truth-striver; they are the lords of Love and Strength and Purity. They bring to the seeker the right impulses of a right vision, and lead him beyond darkness and evil. They take him to the other shore of suffering and bestow upon him the felicity and the happiness. They remove the hurters on the path, erase all division and discord and bring illumination and immortality.

a) 1. *Udvāṁ prikṣāso madhumanto asthura sūryo*
aruhacchukramarṇaḥ,
yasmā ādityā adhvano radanti mitro aryamā
varunṇaḥ sajoṣāḥ.

2. *Ime cetāro anṛtasya bhūrermitro aryamā*
varuṇo hi santi,
ima ṛtasya vāvṛdhurduroṇe śagmāsaḥ
putrā aditeradabdhāḥ.

3. *Ime mitro varuṇo dūḷabhāso'cetasaṁ cic*
citayanti dakṣaiḥ,
api kratuṁ sucetasaṁ vatantastiraścid
aṁhaḥ supathā nayanti.

4. *Ime divo animiṣā pṛthivyāścikitvāṅso*
acetasaṁ nayanti,
pravrāje cinnadyo gādhamasti pāraṁ no
asya viṣpitasya parṣan.[8]

1. For you, O Mitra and Varuna, the nectar-flavoured edibles have been prepared; the sun is ascending the firmament, for whom all the Adityas and the gods make ready the pathways with perfect agreement and harmony.

2. O Mitra, Varuna, Aryaman, adorable discoverers of hidden untruth, verily, you are the invincible sons of Aditi; may you bestow happiness to the sacrificers, may you be glorified at the sacrificial place by them.

3. The unconquerable gods — Mitra, Varuna and Aryaman awaken the ignorant, unconscious sleepers to light and wisdom. Also, they lead them by safe and easy paths to the goal by removing all obstacles and evil.

4. With ever vigilant eyes, and cognizant of all the things in the universe, these gods conduct the ignorant men to duty, for there is a bottom to every deep-flowing river, and they help the seeker to discover the Truth. May they lead us all to the other shore of the vast expanse.

b) 1. *Sasvasciddhi samṛtistveṣy*
eṣāmapīcyena sahasā sahante,
yuṣmadbhiya vṛṣaṇo rejamānā
dakṣasya cinmahina mṛḷatā naḥ.

2. *Yo brahmaṇe sumatimāyajāte*
vājasya sātau paramasya rāyaḥ,
sīkṣanta manyuṁ maghavāno arya
uru kṣayāya cakrire sudhātu.[9]

1. The conjunction of these gods is of mysterious import; by their tie-up they overcome all enemies. O generous givers of gifts, through fear of you the opponents tremble. May you in the mightiness of strength have mercy upon your devout worshippers.

2. These bounteous gods together and jointly accept the praises of the worshippers and bestow upon them a spacious dwelling; the worshippers for the sake of divine felicity and food devote themselves to their glorification.

Viśve devāḥ, the all-gods, are addressed as the saviours of men and the givers of gifts. In later times their accounts are rather obscure; they are said to be twelve in number. They are Vasu, Satya, Kratu, Daksha, Kala, Kama, Dhuti, Kuru, Pururama, Madravas, Rochaka and Dhuri. The Atharva-veda[10] adds *Viśve devāḥ* to the other gods. the Rig-veda[11] includes Ashwins and Agni among the all-gods.

1. SABCL. Vol. 10, p. 84
2. RV. I.3.7-9

3. RV. VI.9.5b
4. RV. V.82.7
5. *Yajur Veda*, XXXII, 1
6. RV. VIII.59.2b
7. RV. X.72.1-9
8. RV. VII.60.4-7
9. RV. VII.60.10-11
10. *Atharva Veda*, VI.47
11. a) RV. VI.49.5 b) RV. IX.97.20

XVIII

ADITI

Aditi, in the Vedic pantheon, is a preeminent and principal godhead, magnificent and dominant among the entire range of gods and goddesses. In fact, she is the mother and sustainer of them all. She personifies absolute freedom, expresses infinitude and signifies boundlessness and luminosity. She creates all the gods as well as contains and supports them.

a) *Bhago vibhaktā śavasāvasā gamad*
uruvyaca aditiḥ śrotu me havam.[1]

May gracious Bhaga, the wise allocator of wealth come with abundance and protection; may the all-pervading Aditi accept my adoration.

b) *Jyotiṣmatīmaditiṁ dhārayatkṣitiṁ...*[2]

The Infinite and the Illimitable, full of luminosity and divinity, is the upholder of all.

She is the earth, heaven and the mid-region, *antarikṣa*, the mother of all the graded levels of creation.

Aditirdyauraditirantarikṣamaditir
mātā sa pitā sa putraḥ
viśve devā aditiḥ pañca janā aditir
jātamaditirjanitvam.[3]

Aditi is heaven and the mid-region; Aditi is the mother, the father and the son; Aditi is all the gods and the five classes of men. Aditi is all that has been and that which shall be born.

She is the material cause as well as the effective cause of creation; she is the boundless One Beyond who puts on numberless forms, indentured and finite. The Rishis sing of the magnificence of her impersonality and the munificence of her personality. She is both accessible to the devout seeker and also far beyond his comprehension. She is the loving mother and the great builder helping men and the gods in their work of sacrifice and world-evolution respectively. And as the infinite power of *ṛtam*, Aditi symbolises the eternal process of self-effectuation of the Supreme. Her strength is manifold, her guidance to the goal is faultless and her protection impregnable. She is possessed of the Right, she is inseparable and inalienable from the Right, she is the Right, *ṛtam* itself. The gods, too, are possessed of *ṛtam*.

Tā vāṁ viśvasya gopā devā deveṣu yajñiyā,
ṛtavānā yajase pūtadakṣasā.[4]

O Mitra and Varuna, you who are most adorable among the gods, protectors of the universe, are true to the eternal law and endowed with infinite power.

Her play is manifold, her role multi-sided; she is the all-powerful queen of all creation. She is the immeasurable, incomprehensible and inconceivable Vastness in whose vacuity the many universes wallow and vanish into nothingness.

Aditi leads all her children from the night of Falsehood and Ignorance to the dawn of the Truth and Beatitude, from the cruel and rough seas of suffering to the luminous shores of Consciousness and Felicity, *bhadram*, from the pits of penury to the summit-planes of plenitude.

a) *Sunāvamā ruheyamasravantīmanāgasam,*
śatāritrāgvañ svastaye.[5]

May I ascend for felicity the most auspicious ship free from any defect, without fault, and equipped with manifold actuators and securers.

b) *Vājasya nu prasave mātaraṁ mahī*
maditiṁ nāma vacasā karāmahe,
yasyā upastha urva'nta rikṣaṁ sā naḥ
śarma trivarūthaṁ ni yacchāt.[6]

To secure wealth and knowledge, we invoke with adoration the great Mother Aditi, in whose subsisting power is the vast mid-world. May the Mother Divine grant us happiness of the three abodes.

She extends her wings of protection to cover the three concurrent statuses of existence — physical, vital and mental, and upholds the good of the peoples.

Aditi is the luminous link between *parārdha* and *aparārdha*, between the worlds of Sat, Chit and Ananda and those of matter, life and mind. *Mahas* or *Swar* is therefore the seat of Aditi. She is the Mother of Maruts, daughter of Vasus, sister of Aditya and the beaming hub of Immortality.[7]

Aditi is described by the Rishis as the Cow of Light, of Truth and the Right; she is envisioned as the godhead of infinite existence and consciousness who brings with her the uplifting, transforming Word. The Rishi exhorts the seeker to arrange the seat for her wide in his inner being, and to enlarge his consciousness to be able to embrace all existence, and be prepared to receive her supreme felicity.

Aditi, the infinite Mother, is referred to by the Vedic Rishis as the Cow unassailable and unslayable. She is the radiant godhead of the seven Thoughts, and the omnipotent goddess of sevenfold action on the seven planes of existence. She is the source and strength of all things that take form in the seven worlds and the inseparable consort of *ṛtam* — the Lord of the Supreme Truth-in-manifestation; she is the fountainhead of the Truth-principle and the vast and absolute continent of the Great Waters, *maho arṇaḥ*. She is envisioned in the Vedas as the primal Cow, the prime Light manifest in the form of Seven Radiances, *sapta gāvaḥ*. She is conceived as Infinite Existence from whom all the gods and goddesses are born; she is infinite Consciousness by whom all the forms are shaped.

She is the Cow of Light connected with the Vedic Dawn symbolic of the attainment of Immortality and the supreme Beatitude. It is the progressive formation and activity of Aditi, the infinite divine Consciousness, in the seeker that ensures his growth into the being of the Mother which is termed Immortality. She brings forth the worlds from her indivisible infinite being according to the truth of these worlds: "...she is the first Radiance, Aditi, the infinite Consciousness of the infinite Conscious Being which is the mother of the worlds".[8]

While Aditi is the undivided Infinite and Mother of the gods, Diti is the divided separative consciousness and Mother of the Titans; therefore, the gods strive in the seeker for unity and infinity, whereas the Titans promote division and darkness and limitation.

Mātā devānāmaditeranīkaṁ yajñasya
keturbṛhatī vibhāhi,
praśastikṛdbrahmaṇe no vyucchā
no jane janaya viśvavāre.[9]

O Mother of the Gods, form of Aditi, the life-force of the earth,

> illuminator of the sacrifice, may you shine forth dignified and ennobled bestowing rewards upon the sacrificers. O adorable Mother, make us eminent among the people.

Aditi, the pure Consciousness of the Infinite gives birth to Daksha the eclective and allocating Thought of the divine Mind, and is herself born to him as the Cosmic Infinite that sustains the worlds: The many gods are also born of her in the *ṛtam*; they are rather manifested in the active truth of her eternal movement. Man then embodies the double movement of both Aditi and Diti, and seeks to realise the Infinite in the finite cast of his being.

The impeding stopper-powers of the seeker-striver's progress are the Vritras; they are Danus, Danavas, Daityas who are children of Diti or Danu and dwellers of the nether darkness. Aditi is the infinite power of self-effectuation of the Truth-Consciousness; she is the Consciousness, the Force and the Law, the Wisdom and Love and Delight of the Supreme-in-manifestation; she contains in herself the Supreme, and also upholds all the universe in her bosom. Besides, there are five other powers: they are Mahi, Ila, Saraswati, Sarama and Dakshina, the executive energies of the Mother.

We are called upon to possess and to grow into the godheads, *ādityasaḥ*; we have to become wide-visioned sons of the Truth, sons of the Infinite, the children of Immortality, *amṛtasya putrāḥ*. It is Aditi of the Truth, the undivided supreme Being who prepares us all in the measure of our receptivity and self-giving to attain to the luminous forcefulness of the world of Light and Truth and Ananda.

Aditi was prior to all creation; indeed it is she who commences the creative operations. Incomparable and beyond all comprehension she commands reverence in all the worlds and preserves the unity and integrity of all the universes which she creates. She is the Mother of the gods and the inner and outer support of all things and beings. She is the mother of the Supreme for she reveals and manifests Him.

The One, *tad ekam*, contains both *asat* and *sat*; these are abeyant and immanent in the highest heaven which is the springboard of Daksha and the womb of Aditi, *aditer-upasthe* —

> *Asacca sacca parame vyoman dakṣasya*
> *janmannaditerupasthe,*
> *agnirha naḥ prathamajā ṛtasya pūrva*
> *āyuni vṛṣabhaśca dhenuḥ.*[10]

> Aditi is the generative energy, the prime matrix and the primeval mother of the worlds. She brings forth the gods and contains within her all that is and would be born; she is the mother and magazine of the manifest and the unmanifest.

> *Aditirdyauraditirantarikṣamaditirmātā*
> *sa pitā sa putraḥ,*
> *viśve devā aditiḥ pañca janā aditirjātam*
> *aditirjanitvam.*[11]

> Aditi is heaven, Aditi is the mid-region, *antarikṣa*; she is the mother, father and son; Aditi is all the gods and the five classes of men. Aditi is what was born and what is to be born.

Aditi represents the Supreme in its transcendentality as well as the infinitude of possibilities through and in which Daksha plays the creative intelligence. This action of Daksha's creative ideation gives birth to the more tangible form of Aditi that contains and nourishes all creatures.

> *Aditerdakṣo ajāyata dakṣādvaditiḥ pari.*[12]

> From Aditi was born Daksha, the infinite creative Intelligence, and again from Daksha was born Aditi the Infinite Mother.

Aditi is the infinite womb, says the Yajur-veda, within which all the universes move and have their being; she is the supreme eternal ruler, gracious guide and loving guard of all.

> *Sutrāmāṇaṁ pṛthivīṁ dyāmanehasagvañ*
> *suśarmāṇamaditigvañ supraṇītiṁ,*
> *daivīm nāvagvañ svaritrāmanāgasamasravantīmā*
> *ruhemā svastaye.*[13]

> We pray to thee, O Aditi, Mother of those who strictly follow the Law, for protection. Builder and rearer of Truth, untouched by decay, equipped with excellence and replete with felicity supreme, O thou great ruler of the all; guide us safely on the path.

She is the mighty mother in whom the entire universe of manifestation is established. She is envisioned by the Rishis as the bottomless rondure, *abudhne*, kept straight and steady by the cosmic pillar, *skambha*.

Aditi appears to the seeker as the splendorous Dawn, for Light is her innermost essence.

Mātā devānāmaditeranīkaṁ yajñasya
keturbṛhatī vibhāhi.[14]

O mighty Usha, co-mother along with Aditi, great illuminator of the sacrifice, shine forth; accepting our prayers dawn upon us.

a) *Yasmai putrāso aditeḥ*
pra jīvase martyāya,
jyotiryacchantyajasram.[15]

No one can hurt that mortal upon whom the sons of Aditi bestow the eternal light of life and extend all form of protection.

b) *Avadhraṁ jyotiraditerṛtāvṛdho*
devasya ślokaṁ saviturmanāmahe.[16]

May the divine light of Aditi be propitious and pleasant to us and to our worship. May we ever be full of praise for the supreme creator.

Aditi is free and unbounded, luminous and all-pervading, and mother and succour of all beings. Adityas are the 'lords of light and omniscience' born from the body of Aditi, the infinite Mother. Originally they are eight, the last being Martanda whom she rejects and casts him away for the state of existence in space and time, and approaches the gods with the first seven. These seven are the sun-gods which later increased to twelve; they are inviolable and imperishable and the eternal sustainers of life and light upon earth. These Adityas are mentioned in the Veda as also the sons of Daksha.

Huve vo devīmaditiṁ namobhir
mṛḷīkāya varuṇaṁ mitramagnim.[17]

O radiant Surya, render the luminous ones (Adityas) who have Daksha for their progenitor, kind and benevolent towards us.

Elsewhere Aditi is described as the thousand-syllabled Word stationed in the highest heaven, through which emerges the universe. The omniscient and omnipotent eternal Vak was born in the abode of the Cow, says the Rishi, with the shining forth of the first Dawn.

Sri Aurobindo on Aditi, the Divine Mother

"There are three ways of being of the Mother of which you can become aware when you enter into touch of oneness with the Conscious Force that upholds us and the universe. Transcendent, the original supreme Shakti, she stands above the worlds and links the creation to the ever unmanifest mystery of the Supreme. Universal, the cosmic Mahashakti, she creates all these beings and contains and enters, supports and conducts all these million processes and forces. Individual, she embodies the power of these two vaster ways of her existence, makes them living and near to us and mediates between the human personality and the divine Nature.

"The one original transcendent Shakti, the Mother stands above all the worlds and bears in her eternal consciousness the Supreme Divine. Alone, she harbours the absolute Power and the ineffable Presence; containing or calling the Truths that have to be manifested, she brings them down from the Mystery in which they were hidden into the light of her infinite consciousness and gives them a form of force in her omnipotent power and her boundless life and a body in the universe. The Supreme is manifest in her for ever as the everlasting Sachchidananda, manifested through her in the worlds as the one and dual consciousness of Ishwara-Shakti and the dual principle of Purusha-Prakriti, embodied by her in the Worlds and the Planes and the Gods and their Energies and figured because of her as all that is in the known worlds and in unknown others. All is her play with the Supreme; all is her manifestation of the mysteries of the Eternal, the miracles of the Infinite. All is she, for all are parcel and portion of the divine Conscious-Force. Nothing can be here or elsewhere but what she decides and the Supreme sanctions; nothing can take shape except what she moved by the Supreme perceives and forms after casting it into seed in her creating Ananda.

"The Mahashakti, the universal Mother, works out whatever is transmitted by her transcendent consciousness from the Supreme and enters into the worlds that she has made; her presence fills and supports them with the divine spirit and the divine all-sustaining force and delight without which they could not exist. That which we call Nature or Prakriti is only her most outward executive aspect; she marshals and arranges the harmony of her forces and processes, impels the operations of Nature and moves among them secret or manifest in all that can be seen or experienced or put into motion of life. Each of the worlds is nothing but one play of the Mahashakti of that system of worlds or universe, who is there as the cosmic Soul and Personality of the transcendent Mother. Each is something that she has seen in her vision, gathered into her heart of beauty and power and created in her Ananda.

"But there are many planes of her creation, many steps of the Divine Shakti. At the summit of this manifestation of which we are a part there are worlds of infinite existence, consciousness, force and bliss over which the Mother stands as the unveiled eternal Power. All beings there live and move in an ineffable completeness and unalterable oneness, because she carries them safe in her arms for ever. Nearer to us are the worlds of a perfect supramental creation in which the Mother is the supramental Mahashakti, a Power of divine omniscient Will and omnipotent Knowledge always apparent in its unfailing works and spontaneously perfect in every process. There all movements are the steps of the Truth; there all beings are souls and powers and bodies of the divine Light; there all experiences are seas and floods and waves of an intense and absolute Ananda. But here where we dwell are the worlds of the Ignorance, worlds of mind and life and body separated in consciousness from their source, of which this earth is a significant centre and its evolution a crucial process. This too with all its obscurity and struggle and imperfection is upheld by the Universal Mother; this too is impelled and guided to its secret aim by the Mahashakti.

"The Mother as the Mahashakti of this triple world of the Ignorance stands in an intermediate plane between the supramental Light, the Truth life, the Truth creation which has to be brought down here and this mounting and descending hierarchy of planes of consciousness that like a double ladder lapse into the nescience of Matter and climb back again through the flowering of life and soul and mind into the infinity of the Spirit. Determining all that shall be in this universe and in the terrestrial evolution by what she sees and feels and pours from her, she stands there above the Gods and all her Powers and Personalities are put out in front of her for the action and she sends down emanations of them into these lower worlds to intervene, to govern, to battle and conquer, to lead and turn their cycles, to direct the total and the individual lines of their forces. These Emanations are the many divine forms and personalities in which men have worshipped her under different names throughout the ages. But also she prepares and shapes through these Powers and their emanations the minds and bodies of her Vibhutis, even as she prepares and shapes minds and bodies for the Vibhutis of the Ishwara, that she may manifest in the physical world and in the disguise of the human consciousness some ray of her power and quality and presence. All the scenes of the earthplay have been like a drama arranged and planned and staged by her with the cosmic Gods for her assistants and herself as a veiled actor.

"The Mother not only governs all from above but she descends into this lesser triple universe. Impersonally, all things here, even the movements of the Ignorance, are herself in veiled power and her creations in diminished substance, her Nature-body and Nature-force, and they exist because, moved by the mysterious fiat of the Supreme to work out something that was there in the possibilities of the Infinite, she has consented to the great sacrifice and has put on like a mask the soul and forms of the Ignorance. But personally too she has stooped to descend here into the Darkness that she may lead it to the Light, into the Falsehood and Error that she may convert it to the Truth, into this Death that she may turn it to godlike Life, into this world-pain and its obstinate sorrow and suffering that she may end it in the transforming ecstasy of her sublime Ananda. In her deep and great love for her children she has consented to put on herself the cloak of this obscurity, condescended to bear the attacks and torturing influences of the powers of the Darkness and the Falsehood, borne to pass through the portals of the birth that is a death, taken upon herself the pangs and sorrows and sufferings of the creation, since it seemed that thus alone could it be lifted to the Light and Joy and Truth and eternal Life. This is the great sacrifice called sometimes the sacrifice of the Purusha, but much more deeply the holocaust of Prakriti, the sacrifice of the Divine Mother.

"Four great Aspects of the Mother, four of her leading Powers and Personalities have stood in front in her guidance of this Universe and in her dealings with the terrestrial play. One is her personality of calm wideness and comprehending wisdom and tranquil benignity and inexhaustible compassion and sovereign and surpassing majesty and all-ruling greatness. Another embodies her power of splendid strength and irresistible passion, her warrior mood, her overwhelming will, her impetuous swiftness and world-shaking force. A third is vivid and sweet and wonderful with her deep secret of beauty and harmony and fine rhythm, her intricate and subtle opulence, her compelling attraction and captivating grace. The fourth is equipped with her close and profound capacity of intimate knowledge and careful flawless work and quiet and exact perfection in all things. Wisdom, Strength, Harmony, Perfection are their several attributes and it is these powers that they bring with them into the world, manifest in a human disguise in their Vibhutis and shall found in the divine degree of their ascension in those who can open their earthly nature to the direct and living influence of the Mother. To the four we give the four great names, Maheshwari, Mahakali, Mahalakshmi, Mahasaraswati."[18]

1. RV. V.46.6b
2. RV. I.136.3a
3. RV. I.89.10
4. RV. VIII.25.1
5. *Yajur Veda*, XXI.7
6. *Atharva Veda*, VII.6.4
7. RV. VIII.101.15
8. SABCL. Vol. 10, p. 328
9. RV. I.113.19
10. RV. X.5.7a
11. RV. I.89.10
12. RV. X. 72.4d
13. *Yajur Veda*, XXI.5
14. RV. I.113.19a
15. RV. X.185.3
16. RV. VII.82.10b
17. RV. VI.50.1a
18. SABCL. Vol. 25, pp. 20-26

Part Two

THE VEDIC DEMONS

XIX

PANIS AND DASYUS

The great Rishis discover the passage from the darkness of Falsehood to the light of the Truth, from the domain of Death to the kingdom of Immortality, from the world of pain, suffering and division to that of supreme felicity and bliss. In their heroic struggle they are helped by the gods who are the sons of Aditi and the increasers of the Light and the Truth. Whereas they are opposed in their efforts by the demons who are the sons of Diti, the coverers and devourers of Light, the crooked confiners and obstructors of the Truth. These are the enemies of unity and integrity, powers that oppose freedom and peace; these are variously described in the Veda as Vritras and Valas, Rakshasas and Sambaras, Pisachas and Namuchis. They are the hurters and haters of aspiring humanity who impede all possibility of spiritual life and action.

> "Vritra, the Serpent", observes Sri Aurobindo, "is the grand Adversary; for he obstructs with his coils of darkness all possibility of divine existence and divine action. And even when Vritra is slain by the light, fiercer enemies arise out of him. Shushna afflicts us with his impure and ineffective force, Namuchi fights man by his weaknesses, and others too assail, each with his proper evil. Then there are Vala and the Panis, miser traffickers in the sense-life, stealers and concealers of the higher Light and its illuminations which they can only darken and misuse, — an impious host who are jealous of their store and will not offer sacrifice to the Gods. These and other personalities, — they are much more than personifications, — of our ignorance, evil, weakness and many limitations make constant war upon man; they encircle him from near or they shoot their arrows at him from afar or even dwell in his gated house in the place of the Gods and with their shapeless stammering mouths and their insufficient breath of force mar his self-expression."[1]

Many are the Vedic demons: if Shushna is the deceptive demon who distorts all knowledge and action with impure and abortive energy, knowledge and action, then Namuchi is the one who opposes and assails the seeker with his own shortcomings and failings. However all the demons assault and pummel him with the evil proper to them. But all these have to be fought and cast out,completely eliminated from the earth-scene, and substituted by the children of Light, allies of the Infinite. The latter augment and amplify the seeker's consciousness by themselves amplifying in him so as to possess his being with their manifold puissance; they materialize the universe and materialize in it. These are the *devas* who support the striver in his struggle to reach the summit goal against the *danavas* — the sons of Darkness who are invariably spoken of as Dasyus. The Dasyus do not share their wealth of cows and horses either with the seers or with the gods. The Panis and the Vritras represent two major sections of Dasyus; while the Panis are known to intercept the cows, the Vritras are associated with the withholding of the streams of the Truth. Both refuse and retard the attainment of luminous felicity by the seekers; they debar from them the vision of Swar and oppose their journey to the world of *satyam ṛtam bṛhat*.

The Panis are the robbers of Light, the plunderers of the divine plenitude and the devourers. The Rishi implores that they be slain and he be protected.

Apa tyaṁ vṛjinaṁ ripuṁ stenam
agne durādhyam,
daviṣṭhamasya satpate kṛdhī sugam.

Grāvāṇaḥ soma no hi kaṁ
sakhitvanāya vāvaśuḥ,
jahī nyatriṇaṁ paṇiṁ vṛko hi ṣaḥ.[2]

"Cast away utterly far from us the enemy, the thief, the crooked one who places falsely the thought; O master of existence, make our path easy to travel. Slay the Pani for he is the wolf, that devours."*

Agni, Saraswati and Soma as well as Indra are invoked to help the seeker against the onslaught of the Panis. The seers seek the enslavement of the lords of Ignorance to the pilgrims of the Truth.

a) *Ayaṁ devaḥ sahasā jāyamāna*
indreṇa yujā paṇimastabhāyat.[3]

This divine Soma, when born with Indra, holds back the Panis by force.

b) *Sarasvati devanido nibarhaya*
prajāṁ viśvasya bṛsayasya māyinaḥ.[4]

O Saraswati, celestial stream of pure awareness, totally destroy those who impede the progress of the gods.

c) *Agnīṣomā ceti tadvīryaṁ vāṁ yad*
amuṣṇītamavasaṁ paṇiṁ gāḥ,
avātiratam̐ bṛsayasya śeṣo'vindataṁ
jyotirekaṁ bahubhyaḥ.[5]

"O Agni and Soma, then was your strength awakened when you robbed the Pani of the cows and found the one Light for many."*

The Panis are the spiritual enemies of the sacrificers; they are powers of Darkness which conceal the cows in the cave. To recover this vast wealth the seekers perform sacrifices helped by the gods. Sarama finds out the cave and the Angirasas chant the right mantra, whereas Indra enthused with the Soma-wine breaks open the cave, vanquishes the Panis and liberates the cows.

a) *Sa goraśvasya vi vrajaṁ*
mandānaḥ somyebhyaḥ,
puraṁ na śūra darṣasi.[6]

Exhilarated by the Soma-drink, O Indra, you break open the cave like a hostile city and effect the release of the cows and the horses.

b) *Ā no gavyānyaśvyā sahasrā śūra dardṛhi,*
divo amuṣya śāsato divaṁ
yaya divāvaso.[7]

Break open for us, O thou hero, thousands of both cattle and horses. Ruling yonder heaven, O radiant one return thither for our good.

The Panis have to perish for uncovering the confined treasure; they have to be defeated for releasing the divine puissance. They represent the worst impairment that the sacrificers suffer at the hands of the Adversary; Darkness itself is their home, and their profession is the stoppage of Light from reaching the pilgrim-seekers. The journey is long and arduous and hazardous; only the wealth of Light and Power and Knowledge can nourish the heroic pilgrim in his pursuit of the Truth and Bliss. The workings of the mid-world are too very intricate and need the lustres of a greater Light to negotiate. They need to be infused by the refulgence of the greater Truth. Which means that the captive herds of Light and Truth have to be recovered and released, and the divine Dawn brought into human existence. The Panis impede this process; they prevent the Truth from arising out of the subconscient situation as well as steal its radiances from the seeker. They constantly strive to nip the sacrificer in the Night. The Panis obstruct the flow of the sevenfold waters of the Truth from above and also foil and frustrate the impulsions of the Truth from within. It is because of the intervention of Agni and his divine doings that the seeker-sacrificer is well set on the path, and is led securely towards the summit. The summit is his own home as well as the abode of all the other gods. It is the state of infinite plenitude and eternal beatitude. The Panis are of course the Dasyus of whom the Veda constantly mentions. They are eventually slain by Indra with the help of Agni, Soma and the Angirasas, and the wealth of the radiant herds is regained from the cave of the subconscient. The terrible war is waged on the frontiers of the mid-region, *antarikṣa*, and the Dasyus are driven out of both heaven and earth.

The Veda speaks also of a volitional giving up of the wealth by the Panis at the behest of Pushan, the shining one, the luminous seer.

1. *Vayamu tvā pathaspate rathaṁ na vājasātaye*
   dhiye pūṣannayujmahi.

2. *Abhi no naryaṁ vasu vīraṁ prayatadakṣiṇam*
   vāmaṁ gṛhapatiṁ naya.

3. *Aditsantaṁ cidāghṛṇe puṣandānāya codaya*
   paṇeścidvi mrada manaḥ.

4. *Vi patho vājasātaye cinuhi vi mṛdho jahi*
   sādhantāmugra no dhiyaḥ.

5. *Pari tṛndhi paṇīnāmārayā hṛdayā kave*
   athemasmabhyaṁ randhaya.

6. *Vi puṣannarayā tuda paṇericcha hṛdi priyam*
   athemasmabhyaṁ randhaya.

7. *Ā rikha kikirā kṛṇu paṇīnāṁ hṛdayā kave*
   athemasmabhyaṁ randhaya.

8. *Yāṁ puṣanbrahmacodanīmārāṁ bibharṣyaghṛṇe*
tayā samasya hṛdayamā rikha kikirā kṛṇu.

9. *Yā te aṣṭrā gūpaśāghṛṇe paśusādhanī*
tasyāste sumnamīmahe.

10. *Uta no goṣaṇiṁ dhiyamaśvasāṁ vājasāmuta*
nṛvatkṛṇuhi vītaye.[8]

"O Pushan, Lord of the Path, we yoke thee like a chariot for the winning of the plenitude, for the Thought. ...O shining Pushan, impel to giving the Pani, even him who giveth not; soften the mind even of the Pani. Distinguish the paths that lead to the winning of the plenitude, slay the aggressors, let our thoughts be perfected. Smite the hearts of the Panis with thy goad, O seer; so make them subject to us. Smite them, O Pushan, with thy goad and desire in the heart of the Pani our delight; so make him subject to us. ...Thy goad thou bearest that impels the word to rise, O shining seer, with that write thy line on the hearts of all and sever them, (so make them subject to us). Thy goad of which thy ray is the point and which perfects the herds (of thought-vision, *paśusādhanī*, cf. *sādhantāṁ dhiyaḥ* in verse 4), the delight of that we desire. Create for us the thought that wins the cow, that wins the horse, that wins the plenitude of the wealth."*

However, for the steady and assured ascent to the Truth the Panis have to be slain. Elsewhere the Rishi implores and pleads with the goddess of Dawn not to awaken the Panis who are deep asleep in their ignorance.

Pra bodhayoṣaḥ pṛṇato maghony
abudhyamānāḥ paṇayaḥ sasantu.[9]

O Usha, may you awaken only those who delight in holy offerings; let the dark and faithless traders sleep on.

The Dawn creates the path for the genuine seekers and fills their being with the supreme Light full of the Truth.

Agni reaches the nether depths of Darkness and liberates the Dawns imprisoned in it allowing them to rise to the summit heights.

1. *Nyakratūn grathino mṛdhravācaḥ*
   paṇīnraśraddhāñ avṛdhāñ ayajñān,
prapra tāndasyūñragnirvivāya
   pūrvaścakārāparāñ ayajyūn.

2. *Yo apācīne tamasi madantīḥ prācīś*
   cakāra nṛtamaḥ śacībhiḥ,
tamīśānaṁ vasvo agniṁ gṛṇīṣe'nānataṁ
   damayantaṁ pṛtanyūn.

3. *Yo dehyo anamayadvadhasnair*
   yo aryapatnīruśasaścakāra,
sa nirudhyā nahuṣo yahvo agnirviśaś
   cakre balihṛtaḥ sahobhiḥ.[10]

"Panis who make the knot of the crookedness, who have not the will to works, spoilers of speech, who have not faith, who increase not, who do not sacrifice, them has Agni driven farther and farther; supreme, he has made them nethermost who will not sacrifice. And (the Cows, the Dawns) who rejoiced in the nether darkness, by his power he has made to move to the highest... He has broken down by his blows the walls that limit, he has given the Dawns to be possessed by the Aryan", *arya-patnīr uṣasaś cakāra.**

Agni thus gives the Dawns to the Aryan-strivers for their spiritual fulfilment; it is by this abundant wealth of Light that the seekers ascend Truthward, and it is by this opulence that Immortality is born in the sacrificers. The Aryan-striver is the warrior of the Light who ceaselessly struggles to reach and realise the Truth. He fights the Panis — powers of sense-consciousness — who are vile traders in the narrow and static and stinking tunnels of Ignorance. The Panis conceal, rather seal up the Light and the Bliss immanent in the physical from the reach of the seeker; the streams of Consciousness rising from the heart of things are stopped from his experience, and are confined in the caverns of the subconscient; the herds are shut up in a hundred pens of the Darkness. Only when the wine of the gods is blended with the luminous milk of the shining Cow that the Aryan-striver can succeed in establishing himself in Ananda. It is the Dawn divine that dissolves all darkness and drives away the Panis. The Rishi therefore invokes —

Uṣo devyamartyā vi bhāhi candrarathā
sūnṛta īrayantī,
ā tvā vahantu suyamāso aśvā
hiraṇyavarṇaṁ pṛthupājaso ye.[11]

O Usha, Dawn divine and immortal, shine out on us mounted in thy chariot of bliss; shine with golden radiance uttering the words of Truth. May thy well-trained and vigorous steeds, golden of hue, ample in their power carry thee hither.

Panis are miserly barterers, niggardly traders; they are unbelievers who want to confine themselves to the domain of Darkness. They are malicious monsters who withhold and shield the celestial treasures. They are not only non-believers and do not perform any sacrifice but scoffers who speak the language of the enemy — uncivil and barbarian.

The Veda speaks of a protracted struggle between the forces of Light and Darkness, Knowledge and Ignorance in the quest for Immortality. The Dasyus are powers of Falsehood, Darkness and Ignorance who possess the coveted wealth of Light and Truth. They have stolen them and concealed them from the seekers; they disdain the sacred Word, and stand in the way of the great ascent. They refuse the seekers the vision of the Sun and Swar and obstruct the streams of the Truth reaching them.

Indra is described as slaying the Dasyus and winning the cows and horses from them for the benefit of the seekers. He is said to conquer the wicked hordes of the crooked ones and make the vision of the Truth available to man. He overcomes the forces of Falsehood with his many forms of Knowledge and ushers in the Dawn.

1. *Ayā rucā hariṇyā punāno viśvā dveṣaṁsi*
tarati svayugvabhiḥ sūro na svayugvabhiḥ,
dhārā sutasya rocate punāno aruṣo hariḥ
viśvā yadrūpa pariyātyṛkvabhiḥ saptāsyebhirṛkvabhiḥ.

2. *Tvaṁ tyatpaṇīnāṁ vido vasu saṁ mātṛbhir*
marjayasi sva ā dama ṛtasya dhītibhirdame,
parāvato na sāma tadyatrā raṇanti dhītayaḥ
tridhātubhiraruṣībhirvayo dadhe rocamāno vayo dadhe.

3. *Pūrvāmanu pradiśaṁ yāti cekitatsaṁ raśmibhir*
yatate darśato ratho daivyo darśato rathaḥ,

agmannukthāni paunsyendraṁ jaitrāya harṣayan
vajraśca yadbhavatho anapacyutā samatsyanapacyutā.[12]

"By this brilliant light he, purifying himself, breaks through all hostile powers by his self-yoked horses, as if by the self-yoked horses of the Sun. He shines, a stream of the outpressed Soma, purifying himself, luminous, the brilliant One, when he encompasses all forms (of things) with the speakers of the Rik, with the seven-mouthed speakers of the Rik (the Angirasa powers). Thou, O Soma findest that wealth of the Panis; thou by the Mothers (the cows of the Panis, frequently so designed in other hymns) makest thyself bright in thy own home (Swar) by the thoughts of the Truth in thy home *saṁ mātṛbhiḥ marjayasi sva ā dame ṛtasya dhītibhir dame.* As if the Sama (equal fulfiment, *samāne ūrve*, in the level wideness) of the higher world *paravatah*), is that (Swar) where the thoughts (of the Truth) take their delight. By those shining ones of the triple world (or triple elemental nature) he holds the wide manifestation (of knowledge), shining he holds the wide manifestation."*

The *devas* and the *dānavas* are accosting each other across the triune world of earth, heaven and mid-region, *antarikṣa*. The seeker battles against the powers of darkness and strives to ascend to the Truth beyond the three worlds. He is helped in his struggle by the *devas* who uphold the Word — that which he finds in his continual sacrifice. Whereas the Dasyus are the destroyers of the Word; They cannot comprehend its truth, and as such are haters of the Truth-seekers. They are the devourers, the plunderers, the tearers whom the sacrificers seek to be slain:

Jahī nyatriṇaṁ paṇiṁ vṛko hi ṣaḥ.[13]

May you destroy the devourer, the Pani, for verily, he is the greedy wolf, the wicked tearer.

The Dasyus are undivine beings or, rather anti-divine traffickers in darkness who steal and conceal the felicity of Light and the Truth from the sacrificers; they are the powers of Ignorance who oppose the seers and give not the sacred offering to them, they are the confiners of the Infinite and Coverers of illumined Consciousness.

Diti, as opposed to Aditi, is the matrix of nether darkness and divided consciousness, and the source of Ignorance and Falsehood, deviation and fraud. It is therefore that the gods — the sons of Aditi and children of the Infinite — move towards infinity and unity, and in the process fight the Dasyus who are the supporters and promoters of separative Consciousness.

1. SABCL. Vol. 11, p. 29
2. RV. VI.51.13-14
3. RV. VI.44.22a
4. RV. VI.61.3a
5. RV. I.93.4
6. RV. VIII.32.5
7. RV. VIII.34.14
8. RV. VI.53.1-10
9. RV. I.124.10a
10. RV. VII.6.3-5
11. RV. III.61.2
12. RV. IX.111.1-3
13. RV. VI.51.14b

XX

VRITRA

Vritra embodies the Vedic perception of a major negative power that limits man's mind only to sense-action; it is the internal enemy who confines the Infinite to finite effectuation. Only when the lightning action of the all-knowing Intelligence of Indra releases the streams of Truth-Consciousness from the stranglehold of Vritra that the seeker-sacrificer breaks these limits and proceeds towards the desired goal. If Vala is the arch miser and immurer, Vritra is the chief obstructor and concealer. If the former prevents the emergence of the Truth from the subconscient and unremittingly moils to appropriate its illuminations from the seeker, the latter occludes and impedes the free flow of the impulsions of the Truth from reaching him. Both Vala and Vritra represent the enemies of Light, and their fight with the *devas* and the seekers of the Truth symbolises a deeper, inner struggle between the powers of Darkness and of Light; they are the sworn adversaries of the seekers of Light and of the Truth, the natural enemies of the sacrificers.

If Vritra is the personification of the Inconscient that withholds the waters of the Superconscient entering human existence, Vala is the embodiment of the subconscient who denies the manifestation of Light in the seeker. Vritra in particular is the grand adversary, for he with his coils of Darkness entangles the Truth and prevents all possibility of Truth-vision and Truth-action. He is the thick dark shadow that covers the Truth and hides it away in the Night of Inconscience. He is undivine, nay, anti-divine for he denies man the freedom and the joy of the vast existence. He obscures and withholds from him his divine right of infinite existence. It is Varuna who by his vastness and all-embracing amplitude removes this clouding menace of the wicked interceptor and illuminates the seeker.

Vritra is the dragon of chaos and falsehood who encloses the waters; he is the dragon of inconscient matter out of which the universe is shaped by the gods.

The slaying of Vritra by Indra is symbolic of initiating the cosmos into creative action; it signifies the rendering the forces of inertia powerless and making the forces of evolution active. It is symbolic of the struggle between the forces of Darkness and those of Light. The withholding of the celestial Waters, *apo vavrivansam vṛtram*, is repeatedly mentioned in the Veda.

a) *Guhā hitaṁ guhyaṁ gūḷhamapsv*
apīvṛtaṁ māyinaṁ kṣiyantam,
uto apo dyaṁ tastabhvāṅsam
ahannahiṁ śūra vīryeṇa.[1]

By thy mighty prowess, O Indra, thou hast destroyed the serpent demon hidden in the cave, lurking in the Inconscient, blocking the flow of the Waters and arresting the rains in the sky.

b) *Adhvaryavo yo apo vavrivāṅsaṁ*
vṛtraṁ jaghānāśasanyeva vṛkṣam
tasmā etaṁ bharata tadvasayañ eṣa
indro arhati pītimasya.[2]

O seeker-worshippers, offer your libation to the resplendent Lord who has destroyed Vritra, the demon of Ignorance. He has struck him down with his thunderbolt who obstructs the flow of the Waters. Verily, he is worthy of your laudations.

c) *Apo vṛtraṁ vavrivāṅsaṁ parāhanprāvat*
te vajraṁ pṛthivī sacetāḥ,
prarṇāṅsi samudriyānyainoḥ patir
bhavañchavasā śūra dhṛṣṇo.[3]

Your protecting thunderbolt, O Indra, has destroyed the demon Vritra who has been obstructing the flow of the Waters. The conscious earth, O valiant one, cooperates with you; may you by your prowess send down the Waters from the firmament.

d) *Ahiṁ yadvṛtramapo vavrivāṅsaṁ*
hannṛjīṣinviṣṇunā sacānaḥ.[4]

Associated with Vishnu, O glorious one, you have annihilated the mighty Adversary that obstructed the Waters.

e) *Sa pavasva ya āvithendraṁ*
vṛtrāya hantave,
vavrivāṅsaṁ mahīrapaḥ.[5]

Flow onward, as is your wont, to help Indra to destroy the vilest demon Vritra who obstructs the progression of the great streams.

The two demons Vritra and Vala create various impediments to the realisation of Truth; they obstruct and arrest the streams all around.

a) *Tvamapo yaddha vṛtraṁ jaghanvāñ*
atyāñiva prāsṛjaḥ sartavājau
śayānamindra caratā vadhena
vavrivāṅsaṁ pari devīradevam.[6]

Inasmuch as you destroy the sluggish, eyeless Asura, O Indra, you let forth the streams like horses rushing into battle.

b) *Atarpayo visṛta ubja ūrmīn*
tvaṁ vṛtāñ ariṇā indra sindhūn.[7]

(O Indra) you have shattered the dark demon Vritra and set free the obstructed streams.

c) *Tvaṁ vṛtrāṇi śṛṇviṣe jaghanvān*
tvaṁ vṛtāñ ariṇā indra sindhūn.[8]

O resplendent Indra, you are renowned as the slayer of Vritra; you have, verily, set the plugged streams free to flow.

Indra opens up the *vajra* after killing Vritra.

Vadhīṁ vṛtraṁ vajreṇa mandasāno
'pa vrajaṁ mahinā dāśuṣe vam.[9]

Greatly rejoicing have I slain Vritra with the thunderbolt and by my prowess have released the rivers for the offerers of oblations.

Indra unbars the ambit of the great dark mountain and releases the waters.

Adardarutsamasṛjo vi khāni tvam
arṇavānbadbadhānāñ aramṇāḥ,
mahāntamindra parvataṁ vi yadvaḥ
srjo vi dhārā ava dānavaṁ han.[10]

O Indra, you have rent asunder the wicked cloud and set free the streams; you have ripped open the dark mountain and gave vent to the showers having slain the Asura.

The Vedic *vṛ* essentially means to cover, hinder, obstruct, imprison etc; the root *vṛ* primarily conveys the meaning of covering, restraining or constricting. From this '*Vṛtra*' symbolizes evil, — that which imprisons the Waters. He lays stretched across the Waters, — against the course of the rivers:

a) *Tvamutsāñ ṛtubhirbadbadhānāñ aṁraha*
ūdhaḥ parvatasya vajrin,
ahiṁ cidugra prayutaṁ śayānaṁ
jaghanvāñ indra taviṣīmadhatthāḥ.[11]

You, O mighty Lord, have set free the obstructed clouds in their seasons; you have let flow the streams by destroying the serpent demon that lay slumbering deep in the Waters and have thus proved your prowess.

b) *Tvamadha prathamaṁ jāyamāno'me*
viśvā adhithā indra kṛṣṭiḥ,
tvaṁ prati pravata āśayānamahiṁ
vajreṇa maghavanvi vriścaḥ.[12]

O resplendent Lord, verily, you are the destroyer of demons many; O wielder of the mighty thunderbolt, you slay the sinful Asura who obstructs the flow of the rivers.

Having tightly locked up the great Waters, Vritra, the most vicious and vile one, lay at the bottom of space [a]; he is described as the most crooked encompasser of the rivers, the withholder of the rains, *svavṛṣṭi*:

a) *Yasta indra mahīrapaḥ*
stabhūyamāna āśayat,
ni taṁ padyāsu śiśtathaḥ.[13]

O Indra, you have cast him down under the rushing streams who lay obstructing their free flow.

b) *Indro asmāñ aradadvajrabāhur*
apāhanvṛtraṁ paridhiṁ nadīnām.[14]

Indra, wielder of the mighty thunderbolt, helps the flow of the rivers when he slayṣ Vritra, their chief obstructor.

c) *Abhi svavṛṣṭiṁ made asya*
yudhyato raghvīriva pravaṇe
sasrurūtayaḥ.[15]

His intimate allies buoyed up by libations preceded him warring against the restrainer of the rains as they rushed down the declines of the mountain.

d) *Nota svavṛṣṭiṁ made asya yudhyata*
eko anyaccakṛṣe viśvamānuṣak.[16]

O Indra, your prowess is unequalled when with excited animation you wage war against the withholder of the rains.

Vritra is the father *asura*; he is the shoulderless serpent whose arms and legs have been cut off by Indra in the fierce encounter in which both use magic. Elsewhere, he is described as a cloud pierced in his loins who has swallowed the universe.[b] He has several lesser demons as his associates. They are Arbuda, Susna, Ahishuva, Pipru, Sribinda, Anarshani, Sambara and Kuyava etc. Indra successfully destroys them all.

a) *Yaḥ sṛbindamanarśaniṁ pipruṁ*
dāsamahīśuvam,
vadhīdugro riṇannapaḥ.[17]

The fierce and almighty Lord has slain the wicked and crooked ones — Sribinda, Anarshani, Pipru and Ahishuva.

b) *Yadasya manyuradhvanīdvi*
vṛtraṁ parvaśo rujan,
apaḥ samudramairayat.[18]

Replete with anger he thundered cutting Vritra bit by bit and set free the Waters to the ocean.

c) *Devakaṁ cinmānyamānaṁ jaghanthāva*
tmanā bṛhataḥ śambaraṁ bhet.[19]

(O mighty one) you have slain Devaka the son of Manyamana, and on your own accord cast down Shambara from the lofty mountain-top.

After destroying Vritra and the host of his allies Indra places the sun in the sky.

Vṛtraṁ yadindra śavasāvadhīr
ahimāditsūryaṁ divy
ārohayo dṛśe.[20]

When, O Indra, you had destroyed the malignant
Vritra, you made the sun visible in the sky.

1. RV. II.11.5
2. RV. II.14.2
3. RV. IV.16.7
4. RV. VI.20.2b
5. RV. IX.61.22
6. RV. III.32.6
7. RV. IV.19.5b
8. RV. IV.42.7b
9. RV. X.28.7b
10. RV. V.32.1
11. RV. V.32.2
12. RV. IV.17.7
a. RV. I.52.6; RV.II.11.5
13. RV. VIII.6.16
14. RV. III.33.6a
15. RV. I.52.5a
16. RV. I.52.14b
b. RV. I.32
17. RV. VIII.32.2
18. RV. VIII.6.13
19. RV. VII.18.20b
20. RV. I.51.4b

XXI

VALA

If Vritra is the great resister who restrains and denies the flow of the waters of conscient existence — the Truth-consciousness — Vala holds back in his lair the herds of the Light. Though Vala is not himself the embodiment of Inconscience as Vritra is, he is still the cause and producer of darkness. He is made of the substance of Light, and yet disallows its conscious manifestation in the seeker. He is the vile trafficker, the darkest miser and stealer and concealer of the herds of Light who refuses to offer them to the gods; he is jealous of his stolen wealth and hates to share it with them. He is described in the Veda as *alātṛṇa*, 'not giving' or 'not sharing'.

Vala is primarily the imprisoner of Cows; living in a burrow in the mountains he keeps vigil on the much coveted wealth of Light. To restore these stolen cows the seeker has to perform the sacrifice. It is Sarama who first surmises the whereabouts of the cows; she finds them out in the cave and shows the way. Indra, then, strengthened and emboldened by the Soma-wine and supported by the Angirasas breaks open the cave, defeats the adversaries and delivers the cows.

Vala is the vilest, crookedest camouflager of Light. And it is this concealed, imprisoned Light that Indra wins back for the seeker-sacrificer.

Indro dīrghāya cakṣasa
ā sūryaṁ rohayad divi.[1]

Indra, the resplendent Lord, to render all things visible elevates the sun in the sky.

He enables the sun to ascend in heaven, and hastens him all over the hill by his rays —

Vi gobhiradrimairayat.[2]

The rays are referred to as the luminous cows who have been stolen by Vala, the captain of the Panis. The redemption of these lost cows is the recurring theme of the Rig-vedic hymns. This wealth of Light has to be discovered and recovered for the evolution of the human race by the help of the gods; it has been withheld by Vala, the meanest demon — the leader of the Dasyus. "The Dasyus who withhold or steal the cows" says Sri

Aurobindo, "are called the Panis, a word which seems originally to have meant doers, dealers or traffickers; but this significance is sometimes coloured by its further sense of 'misers'. Their chief is Vala, a demon whose name signifies probably the circumscriber or 'encloser', as Vritra means the opponent, obstructer or enfolding coverer."[3]

Vala is called in the Veda as *svavṛṣṭim*, the one who confiscates and usurps the wealth for himself. He is rich in cows, *gomataḥ*, and has a hidden cowshed, *vrajo goḥ*.[4] His nature is fully revealed by the Rishis in the following hymn:

> *Eṣo apaśrito valo gomatīm*
> *ava tiṣṭhati.*[5]
>
> ...He dwells hidden in the land rich in cattle.

Rich in cows, *gomatī*, he dwells in a hole, *bila* —

> *Tvaṁ valasya gomato'pāvaradrivo bilam.*[6]

His dwelling is variously described as a prison, *jāsu* [7], as a cave, *guha* [8], and as a fence, *parīdhin*.[9] He is seen as immovable, invincible, *acyuta*, and as *tamas* incarnate.[10]

In several places in the Rig-veda, Vala is described by the term *phaligā* — as a receptacle of the Waters.

> a) *Saraṇyubhiḥ phaligamindra śakra*
> *valaṁ raveṇa darayo daśagveḥ.*[11]
>
> Desirous of providing protection you have struck fear by your voice in the dissonant, fructifying dark cloud.
>
> b) *Sa suṣṭubhā sa ṛkvatā gaṇena*
> *valaṁ ruroja phaligaṁ raveṇa.*[12]
>
> Supported by the devout Angirasas he destroys with his terrifying voice the crooked Vala.

Indra thus removes the barring, and liberates the firmly imprisoned Waters; rather, he breaks open the never-raptured ridge, *ārugna* of Vala and releases the Waters. Vala is the one who pens up the cows in a mountain; he is the one who hides and hoards the wealth of Light which Indra liberates after destroying him.

> *Ayamuśānaḥ paryadrimusrā*
> *ṛtadhītibhirṛtayugyujānaḥ,*
> *rujadarugṇaṁ vi valasya sānuṁ,*
> *paṇīṅrvacobhirabhi yodhadindraḥ.*[13]

> Intent on liberating the cows imprisoned in the mountain-cave, the mighty Indra associated with the wise Angirasas and invigorated by their incantations breaks open the infrangible rock of Vala and overwhelms the horde of Panis.

1. RV. I.7.3a
2. Ibid.
3. SABCL. Vol. 10, p. 134
4. RV. III.30.10
5. RV. VIII.24.30b
6. RV. I.11.5
7. RV. X.68.6
8. RV. VIII.14.8
9. RV. I.52.5
10. RV. II.24.3
11. RV. I.62.4b
12. RV. IV.50.5
13. RV. VI.39.2